P9-CFZ-479

Concise
English–Chinese
Romanized
Dictionary

Containing over 10,000
English words and expressions
with equivalent Chinese characters
and their romanized readings

James C. Quo

TUTTLE PUBLISHING
Tokyo • Rutland, Vermont • Singapore

Published by Tuttle Publishing, an imprint of Periplus Editions
(HK) Ltd., with editorial offices at 364 Innovation Drive, North
Clarendon, Vermont 05759 U.S.A. and 130 Joo Seng Road #06-01,
Singapore 368357.

LCC Card No. 55-11585
ISBN-13: 978-0-8048-0117-1
ISBN-10: 0-8048-0117-7

Printed in Singapore

First edition, 1956

Distributed by:

North America, Latin America & Europe
Tuttle Publishing,
364 Innovation Drive, North Clarendon, VT 05759-9436 U.S.A.
Tel: 1 (802) 773-8930 Fax: 1 (802) 773-6993
info@tuttlepublishing.com
www.tuttlepublishing.com

Japan
Tuttle Publishing,
Yaekari Building, 3rd Floor, 5-4-12 Osaki, Shinagawa-ku
Tokyo 141-0032
Tel: (81) 03 5437-0171 Fax: (81) 03 5437-0755
tuttle-sales@gol.com

Asia Pacific
Berkeley Books Pte. Ltd.,
Berkeley Books Pte. Ltd., 130 Joo Seng Road #06-01, Singapore 368357
Tel: (65) 6280-1330 Fax: (65) 6280-6290
inquiries@periplus.com.sg
www.periplus.com

09 08 07 06   44 43 42 41 40

CONTENTS

ABBREVIATIONS

a.	adjective
adv.	adverb
art.	article
conj.	conjunction
int.	interjection
n.	noun
prep.	preposition
v. aux.	auxiliary verb
US	United States
**	indicates terms used or created exclusively by the Chinese Communists
*	indicates terms used exclusively by the Government of the Republic of China

[軍] 軍語 (Military Terminology)
[空] 空軍 (Air Force)
[步] 步兵 (Infantry)
[騎] 騎兵 (Cavalry)
[砲] 砲兵 (Artillery)
[兵] 兵器 (Weapon)
[汽] 汽車 (Automobile)
[化] 化學 (Chemistry)
[海] 航海 (Navigation)
[航] 航空 (Aviation)
[機] 機械 (Mechanics)

[電] 電學 (Electricity)
[建] 建築 (Architecture)
[攝] 攝影 (Photography)
[礦] 礦物 (Mineralogy)
[植] 植物 (Botany)
[魚] 魚類 (Ichthyology)
[生] 生理 (Physiology)
[樂] 音楽 (Music)
[律] 法律 (Law)
[美] 美國 (United States)

A

a *art., a.* (*any*) mei³ i¹ 每一, (*one*) i¹ 一.
abandon *v.* fang⁴ ch'i⁴ 放棄.
abandoned *a.* pei⁴ ch'i⁴ te¹ 被棄的.
abase *v.* chiang⁴ ti⁴ 降低.
abash *v.* hsiu¹ ts'an² 羞慚.
abate *v.* chien³ ch'ing¹ 減輕.
abbess *n.* ni² yüan⁴ chang³ 尼院長.
abbey *n.* (*monks*) ssu⁴ 寺, (*nuns*) an¹ 庵, (*Western*)
　　hsiu¹ tao⁴ yüan⁴ 修道院.
abbot *n.* (*Orientals*) fang¹ chang⁴ 方丈, (*Western*)
　　hsiu¹ tao⁴ yüan⁴ chang³ 修道院長.
abbreviate *v.* so¹ hsieh³ 縮寫.
abbreviation *n.* so¹ hsieh³ 縮寫.
abdicate *v.* (*throne*) sun⁴ wei² 遜位, (*office*) tz'u²
　　chih² 辭職, (*power*) ch'i⁴ ch'üan² 棄權.
abdomen *n.* fu⁴ 腹.
abduct *v.* yu⁴ kuai³ 誘拐.
abet *v.* chiao⁴ so¹ 教唆.
abhor *v.* tseng¹ e⁴ 憎惡.
abide *v.* (*stay*) liu² 留, (*dwell*) chü¹ chu⁴ 居住,
　　(*wait*) teng³ hou⁴ 等候.
ability *n.* neng² li⁴ 能力.
able *a.* neng² kan⁴ te¹ 能幹的.
abnormal *a.* i⁴ ch'ang² te¹ 異常的.
aboard *adv.* (*ship*) tsai⁴ ch'uan² shang⁴ 在船上.
abolish *v.* fei⁴ ch'u² 廢除.
abolition *n.* fei⁴ ch'u² 廢除.
abortion *n.* (*miscarriage*) liu² ch'an³ 流產.
abound *v.* to¹ 多.
about *prep.* (*concerning*) kuan¹ yü² 關於, (*approx-
　　imately*) ta⁴ yüeh¹ 大約; "~ face!" hsiang⁴
　　hou⁴ chuan³ 向後轉(軍).
above *prep.* tsai⁴ kao¹ ch'u⁴ 在高處; *a.* tsai⁴ shang⁴
　　te¹ 在上的.
abreast *adv., a.* ping⁴ lieh⁴ 並列.
abridge *v.* so¹ tuan³ 縮短, (*deprive of*) po¹ to² 剝
　　奪
abroad *adv.* kuo² wai⁴ 國外.

1

abrogate v. fei⁴ ch'u² 廢除.

abrupt a. (sudden) t'u² jan² te¹ 突然的, (steep) hsien³ chün⁴ te¹ 險峻的.

abscess n. nung² chung³ 膿腫.

absence n. ch'üeh¹ hsi² 缺席; ~ without leave, pu² chia⁴ wai⁴ ch'u¹ 不假外出.

absent a. ch'üeh¹ hsi² te¹ 缺席的; ~ without leave, pu² chia⁴ wai⁴ ch'u¹ 不假外出.

absolute a. chüeh² tui⁴ te¹ 絕對的; ~ ceiling, chüeh² tui⁴ ting² tien³ 絕對頂點; ~ quarantine, chüeh² tui⁴ ko² li² 絕對隔離; ~ temperature, chüeh² tui⁴ wen¹ tu⁴ 絕對溫度; ~ zero, chüeh² tui⁴ ling² tu⁴ 絕對零度.

absolutely adv. chüeh² tui⁴ ti⁴ 絕對地.

absolution n. she⁴ mien³ 赦免.

absolve v. she⁴ mien³ 赦免.

absorb v. hsi¹ shou¹ 吸收.

absorbing a. chuan¹ hsin¹ i² chih⁴ te¹ 專心一致的.

absorption n. hsi¹ shou¹ 吸收, (interest) chuan¹ hsin¹ 專心.

abstain v. (refrain) chin⁴ 禁. ⌞

abstemious a. chieh² chih⁴ te¹ 節制的.

abstinence n. chieh² chih⁴ 節制.

abstract a. ch'ou¹ hsiang⁴ te¹ 抽象的.

abstruse a. shen¹ ao⁴ te¹ 深奧的.

absurd a. pei⁴ li³ te¹ 背理的.

abundance n. feng¹ to¹ 豐多.

abundant a. feng¹ fu⁴ te¹ 豐富的.

abuse v. (misuse) wang⁴ yung⁴ 妄用, (mistreat) nüeh⁴ tai⁴ 虐待, (revile) ju⁴ ma⁴ 辱罵; n. (mistreatment) nüeh⁴ tai⁴ 虐待, (of authority) lan⁴ yung⁴ 濫用, (verbal) ju⁴ ma⁴ 辱罵.

abut v. chieh¹ chieh⁴ 接界.

abysmal a. shen¹ yüan¹ te¹ 深淵的.

academy n. (school of art or science) chuan¹ men² hsüeh² hsiao⁴ 專門學校.

accede v. (consent) chun² hsü³ 准許.

accelerate v. ts'u⁴ chin⁴ 促進.

accent n. chung⁴ yin¹ 重音; v. chia¹ chung⁴ yin¹ fu² hao⁴ 加重音符號.

accentuate v. (emphasize) chu⁴ chung⁴ 注重, (accent) tu² chung⁴ yin¹ 讀重音.

accept v. (receive) ling³ shou¹ 領收, (consent) ch'eng² no⁴ 承諾.

access n. (approach) chieh¹ chin⁴ 接近, (way of approach) t'ung¹ lu⁴ 通路.

accessible a. i⁴ chieh¹ chin⁴ te¹ 易接近的.

accession n. (consent) yün³ no⁴ 允諾, (increase) tseng¹ chia¹ 增加.

accident n. huo⁴ huan⁴ 禍患, i⁴ wai⁴ shih⁴ 意外事.

accidental a. ou³ jan² te¹ 偶然的, i⁴ wai⁴ te¹ 意外的.

acclaim v. ho⁴ ts'ai³ 喝采, kao¹ hu¹ 高呼.

acclamation n. ho⁴ ts'ai³ 喝采, huan¹ hu¹ 歡呼.

acclimate v. fu² shui² t'u³ 服水土.

acclimatize v. fu² shui² t'u³ 服水土.

accommodate v. (fit) shih³ shih⁴ ying⁴ 使適應, (reconcile) t'iao² t'ing² 調停.

accompany v. p'ei² pan⁴ 陪伴, (music) pan⁴ tsou⁴ 伴奏.

accomplice n. kung⁴ fan⁴ 共犯, t'ung² mou² 同謀.

accomplish v. wan² ch'eng² 完成, ch'eng² chiu⁴ 成就.

accomplished a. (completed) wan² ch'eng² te¹ 完成的, (skilled) shou³ lien⁴ te¹ 熟練的.

accord n. ho² i⁴ 合意, ho² hsieh² 和諧; v. hsiang¹ ho² 相合.

accordingly adv. i¹ chao⁴ 依照, yü² shih⁴ 於是.

accordion n. shou³ feng¹ ch'in² 手風琴.

accost v. chao¹ hu¹ 招呼.

accouchement n. sheng¹ ch'an³ 生產, fen¹ mien³ 分娩.

account v. (explain) shuo¹ ming² 說明, (consider) jen⁴ wei² 認為; n. chang⁴ mu⁴ 賬目, (reason) li³ yu² 理由.

accountant n. k'uai⁴ chi⁴ yüan² 會計員.

accounting n. k'uai⁴ chi⁴ hsüeh² 會計學.

accouter, accoutre v. (equip) she⁴ pei⁴ 設備, (array) chuang¹ shih⁴ 裝飾.

accredit v. (authorize) shou⁴ ch'üan² 授權, (trust) hsin⁴ jen⁴ 信任.

accretion n. (growth) sheng¹ chang³ 生長, (increase) tseng¹ chia¹ 增加.

accrue v. (increase) chia¹ tseng¹ 加增, (grow) sheng¹ chang³ 生長.

accumulate v. tui¹ chi¹ 堆積, chi¹ chü⁴ 積聚.

accurate a. cheng⁴ ch'üeh⁴ te¹ 正確的.

accursed a. pei⁴ chü³ chou⁴ te¹ 被咀咒的.

accusation *n.* k'ung⁴ su⁴ 控訴.

accuse *v.* k'ung⁴ su⁴ 控訴, ch'ien³ tse² 譴責.

accustom *v.* kuan⁴ yü² 慣於.

ace *n.* (*dice*) yao¹ tien³ 么點, (*pilot*) fei¹ hsing² ying¹ hsiung² 飛行英雄.

acetate *n.* ts'u⁴ suan¹ yen² 醋酸鹽.

acetic *a.* ts'u⁴ suan¹ te¹ 醋酸的.

acetylene *n.* erh⁴ t'an⁴ chüeh⁴ 二炭炔.

ache *n.* t'ung⁴ 痛; *v.* shou⁴ t'ung⁴ 受痛.

achieve *v.* wan² ch'eng² 完成.

aching *a.* shou⁴ t'ung⁴ te¹ 受痛的.

achromatic *a.* wu² se⁴ te¹ 無色的.

acid *a.* suan¹ te¹ 酸的; *n.* suan¹ chih² 酸質.

acidulous *a.* wei¹ suan¹ te¹ 微酸的.

acknowledge *v.* ch'eng² jen⁴ 承認.

acme *n.* tsui⁴ kao¹ tien³ 最高點.

acorn *n.* hsiang⁴ kuo³ 橡果.

acoustic *a.* t'ing¹ chüeh⁴ te¹ 聽覺的.

acquaint *v.* (*familiarize*) shou² hsi¹ 熟習, (*inform*) t'ung¹ chih¹ 通知.

acquiesce *v.* mo⁴ hsü³ 默許.

acquire *v.* huo⁴ te² 獲得, chan⁴ yu³ 佔有.

acquisitive *a.* t'an¹ te² te¹ 貪得的.　　　　「還清.

acquit *v.* shih⁴ fang⁴ 釋放, (*pay off*) huan² ch'ing¹

acre *n.* ying¹ mu³ 英畝.　　　　　　　　「te¹ 性急的.

acrid *a.* hsin¹ la⁴ te¹ 辛辣的, (*temper*) hsing⁴ chi²

acrimonious *a.* tz'u⁴ chi¹ te¹ 刺激的.

acrobat *n.* mai⁴ i⁴ che³ 賣藝者.　　　　　　「橫過.

across *adv.* heng² ch'ieh¹ 橫切; *prep.* heng² kuo⁴

act *v.* tso⁴ wei² 作爲, (*play*) pan⁴ yen³ 扮演; *n.* (*deed*) hsing² wei² 行爲, (*play*) hsi⁴ chih¹ i² mu⁴ 戲之一幕.

action *n.* (*conduct*) hsing² wei² 行爲, (*combat*) tso⁴ chan⁴ 作戰, (*movement*) tung⁴ tso⁴ 動作, (*lawsuit*) su⁴ sung⁴ 訴訟; "～ **front!**" hsiang⁴ ch'ien² fang⁴ lieh⁴ hsia⁴ chia⁴ 向前放列下架(軍); "～ **left!**" hsiang⁴ tso³ fang⁴ lieh⁴ hsia⁴ chia⁴ 向左放列下架(軍); "～ **rear!**" hsiang⁴ hou⁴ fang⁴ lieh⁴ hsia⁴ chia⁴ 向後放列下架(軍); "～ **right!**" hsiang⁴ yu⁴ fang⁴ lieh⁴ hsia⁴ chia⁴ 向右放列下架 (軍).

4

active *a.* huo² p'o¹ te¹ 活潑的, chu³ tung⁴ te¹ 主勁

actor *n.* ling² jen² 伶人. ⌈的.

actual *a.* chen¹ te¹ 眞的, shih² tsai¹ te¹ 實在的.

actuary *n.* k'uai² chi⁴ yüan² 會計員.

actuate *v.* shih³ tung⁴ tso⁴ 使動作, chi¹ tung⁴ 激勁.

acumen *n.* ts'ung¹ ming² 聰明, ching¹ jui⁴ 精銳.

acute *a.* jui⁴ li⁴ te¹ 銳利的, min³ jui⁴ te¹ 敏銳的.

adage *n.* chen¹ yen² 箴言, yen⁴ yü³ 諺語, ko² yen² ⌈格言.

adagio *a., adv.* hsü² man⁴ 徐慢.

adamant *n.* chien¹ wu⁴ 堅物.

adapt *v.* shih³ shih⁴ ying⁴ 使適應.

add *v.* chia¹ 加.

adder *n.* tu² she² 毒蛇.

addict *v.* kuan⁴ yü² 慣於, tan¹ ni⁴ 耽溺.

addition *n.* chia¹ 加, chia¹ t'ien¹ wu⁴ 加添物.

addled *a.* hun¹ luan⁴ te¹ 昏亂的.

address *v.* (*speak to*) yen³ shuo¹ 演說; *n.* (*speech*) chiang² yen³ 講演, (*mail*) ti⁴ chih³ 地址.

addressee *n.* shou¹ hsin⁴ jen² 收信人.

adduce *v.* chü³ shih⁴ 舉示, yin³ cheng³ 引證.

adept *n.* shou² shou³ 熟手, chuan¹ chia¹ 專家.

adequacy *n.* tsu² kou⁴ 足够. ⌈恰好的.

adequate *a.* tsu² kou⁴ te¹ 足句多的, ch'ia⁴ hao³ te¹

adhere *v.* chan¹ chu⁴ 黏住, i¹ fu⁴ 依附. ⌈贊助者.

adherent *a.* i¹ fu⁴ te¹ 依附的; *n.* tsan⁴ chu⁴ che³

adieu *int.*, *n.* tsai⁴ hui⁴ 再會.

adipose *a.* chih¹ fang¹ te¹ 脂肪的.

adjacent *a.* lin² chin⁴ te¹ 鄰近的.

adjoin *v.* chieh¹ chin⁴ 接近. ⌈散會.

adjourn *v.* chan⁴ t'ing² 暫停, (*meeting*) san⁴ hui⁴

adjudge *v.* p'an⁴ chüeh² 判決, (*award*) shou⁴ yü³

adjudicate *v.* ts'ai² p'an⁴ 裁判. ⌈授與.

adjunctive *a.* fu⁴ shu³ te¹ 附屬的.

adjure *v.* ch'i³ shih⁴ 起誓.

adjust *v.* shih³ shih⁴ ho² 使適合, an¹ p'ai² 安排.

adjutant *n.* fu⁴ kuan¹ 副官, chu⁴ shou³ 助手.

administer *v.* kuan³ li³ 管理.

admirable *a.* k'o³ ch'in¹ yang³ te¹ 可欽仰的.

admiral *n.* (*navy*) shang⁴ chiang¹ 上將(海).

admire *v.* t'an⁴ shang³ 嘆賞.

admission *n.* chin⁴ ju⁴ 進入, hsü³ chin⁴ 許進.

5

admit *v.* chin⁴ ju⁴ 進入, chun² hsü³ 准許.

admix *v.* hun⁴ ho² 混合.

admonish *v.* (*warn*) ching³ kao⁴ 警告.

adolescent *a.* ch'ing¹ nien² te¹ 青年的.

adopt *v.* hsüan² na³ 選納, ming² ling² 螟蛉.

adoptee *n.* ming² ling² tzu³ 螟蛉子.

adorable *a.* ch'ung² pai⁴ te¹ 崇拜的.

adoration *n.* tsun¹ ch'ung² 尊崇.

adore *v.* ch'ung² pai⁴ 崇拜.

adorn *v.* chuang¹ shih⁴ 裝飾.

adrift *adv.*, *a.* p'iao¹ liu² 漂流.

adroit *a.* shou² lien¹ te¹ 熟練的.

adulation *n.* kuo⁴ yü⁴ 過譽, ch'an³ mei² 諂媚.

adult *n.* ch'eng² jen² 成人 ; *a.* ch'eng² shou² te¹ ⌐成熟的.

adulterant *n.* ts'an¹ tsa³ wu⁴ 參雜物. ⌐成熟的.

adulterate *v.* ch'an¹ chia¹ 攙假.

adultery *n.* t'ung¹ chien¹ 通姦.

advance *v.* chin⁴ hsing² 進行, (*lend*) yü⁴ fu⁴ 預付.

advantage *n.* li⁴ i⁴ 利益.

advent *n.* lai² lin² 來臨.

adventitious *a.* wai⁴ lai² te¹ 外來的.

adventure *n.* mao⁴ hsien³ 冒險 ; *v.* mao⁴ hsien³ 冒險, kan³ wei² 敢爲.

adversary *n.* ti² shou³ 敵手, ch'ou² jen² 仇人.

adverse *a.* ch'ou² ti² te¹ 仇敵的, (*harmful*) pu² li te¹ 不利的.

adversity *n.* pu² hsing¹ 不幸, tsai¹ huo⁴ 災禍.

advert *v.* (*refer*) lun⁴ chi² 論及, kuan¹ hsin¹ 關心.

advertise *v.* kuang³ kao⁴ 廣告.

advertisement *n.* kuang³ kao⁴ 廣告.

advice *n.* chung¹ kao⁴ 忠告.

advisable *a.* ho² li³ te¹ 合理的.

advise *v.* chung¹ kao⁴ 忠告.

adviser *n.* ku⁴ wen⁴ 顧問. ⌐辯護.

advocate *n.* pien⁴ hu⁴ jen² 辯護人 ; *v.* pien⁴ hu⁴

adz, adze *n.* shou³ fu³ 手斧.

aeon, eon *n.* yung³ shih⁴ 永世. ⌐ch'i⁴ 通氣.

aerate *v.* chu⁴ ju⁴ k'ung¹ ch'i⁴ 注入空氣, t'ung¹

aerial *a.* k'ung¹ chung¹ te¹ 空中的.

aerolite *n.* yün³ shih² 隕石.

aeronautics *n.* hang² k'ung¹ hsüeh² 航空學.

aerostatics *n.* ch'i⁴ t'i³ ching⁴ li⁴ hsüeh² 氣體靜力學.

aesthetic *a.* mei³ hsüeh² te¹ 美學的, (*sensitive to beauty*) shen² mei³ te¹ 審美的. 「審美論.

aesthetics *n.* mei³ hsüeh² 美學, shen² mei³ lun⁴

afar *adv.* tsai⁴ yüan² ch'u⁴ 在遠處.

affable *a.* ho² ai³ te¹ 和藹的.

affair *n.* shih⁴ wu⁴ 事務.

affect *v.* (*influence*) ying³ hsiang³ 影響.

affectation *n.* hsü¹ shih⁴ 虛飾.

affected *a.* shou⁴ ying² hsiang³ te¹ 受影響的, (*unnatural*) chia³ chuang¹ te¹ 假裝的. 「動情的.

affecting *a.* kan³ jen² te¹ 感人的, tung⁴ ch'ing² te¹

affection *n.* (*feeling*) kan³ tung⁴ 感動, (*love*) ai⁴ ch'ing² 愛情, (*disease*) chi² ping⁴ 疾病. 「婚約.

affiance *v.* shih³ ting⁴ hun¹ 使訂婚, n. hun¹ yüeh¹

affidavit *n.* hsüan¹ shih⁴ shu¹ 宣誓書. 「蛤.

affiliate *v.* lien² hsi¹ 聯繫, (*adopt*) ming² ling² 螟

affinity *n.* (*relation*) yin¹ ch'in¹ 姻親, (*resemblance*) chin⁴ ssu⁴ 近似.

affirm *v.* ch'üeh⁴ shuo¹ 確說.

affirmation *n.* ch'üeh⁴ shuo¹ 確說, yen² chung⁴ hsüan¹ yen² 嚴重宣言. 「許可.

affirmative *a.* k'en³ ting⁴ te¹ 肯定的; *n.* hsü³ k'o³

affix *v.* lien² chieh¹ 連接; *n.* t'ien¹ fu⁴ yü³ 添附語.

afflatus *n.* ling² kan³ 靈感.

afflict *v.* shih³ t'ung⁴ k'u³ 使痛苦.

affluence *n.* feng¹ fu⁴ 豐富.

afford *v.* ch'an³ sheng¹ 產生, kung¹ chi³ 供給.

affray *n.* ch'ao³ nao⁴ 吵鬧, hsüan¹ hua² 喧嘩.

affright *v.* shih³ k'ung³ pu⁴ 使恐怖.

affront *v.* wu³ ju³ 侮辱; *n.* wu³ ju⁴ 侮辱, (*confront*) fan³ k'ang⁴ 反抗.

afire *adv., a.* chao² huo³ 著火.

afloat *adv., a.* p'iao¹ fu² te¹ 漂浮的.

afoot *adv.* pu⁴ hsing² 步行, (*going on*) chin⁴ hsing² chung¹ 進行中.

aforesaid *a.* ch'ien² shu⁴ te¹ 前述的.

afraid *a.* p'a⁴ te¹ 怕的.

afresh *adv.* ch'ung² hsin¹ 重新, tsai⁴ 再.

aft *adv., a.* chin⁴ ch'uan² wei³ 近船尾.

after prep. (time) tsai⁴ hou⁴ 在後, (following) chui¹ sui² 追隨, (concerning) kuan¹ yü² 關於, (imitating) mo² fang³ 摹仿, (according to) i¹ ts'ung² 依從; adv. tsai⁴ hou⁴ ti⁴ 在後地, (time) tsai⁴ hou⁴ 在後; a. hou⁴ lai¹ te¹ 後來的; conj. hou⁴ yü² 後於.

afternoon n. hsia⁴ wu³ 下午, wu³ hou⁴ 午后.

afterward, ~s adv. hou⁴ lai² 後來, i³ hou⁴ 以後.

again adv. tsai⁴ 再. 「反對.

against prep. tui⁴ 對, hsiang¹ fan³ 相反, fan³ tui⁴

agape adv., a. chang¹ k'ou³ te¹ 張口的.

agate n. ma² nao³ 瑪瑙. 「歲.

age n. (period) shih² tai⁴ 時代, (life) nien² sui⁴ 年

aged a. nien² lao³ te¹ 年老的.

agent n. tai⁴ li³ che⁴ 代理者.

agglomerate v. t'uan² chü³ 團聚.

agglutinate v. chan¹ ho² 黏合, chiao¹ ho² 膠合.

aggrandize v. tseng¹ ta⁴ 增大.

aggravate v. chia¹ chü⁴ 加劇, chi¹ nu⁴ 激怒.

aggregate v. chü² chi² 聚集; n. chi² ho² t'i³ 集合

aggression n. ch'in¹ lüeh⁴ 侵略. 「體.

aggressive a. hao⁴ ch'in¹ lüeh⁴ te¹ 好侵略的.

aggressor n. ch'in¹ lüeh⁴ che⁴ 侵略者.

aggrieve v. ya¹ p'o⁴ 壓迫, sun³ hai⁴ 損害.

aghast a. piao³ shih⁴ k'ung³ pu⁴ te¹ 表示恐怖的

agile a. huo² p'o¹ te¹ 活潑的, ling² min³ te¹ 靈敏的.

agitate v. chi¹ tung⁴ 激動, (discuss) t'ao³ lun⁴ 討論.

ago adv., a. kuo⁴ ch'ü⁴ te¹ 過去的, i² wang³ te¹ 已

agog adv., a. k'o³ wang⁴ te¹ 渴望的. 「往的.

agonize v. shih³ shou⁴ k'u³ t'ung⁴ 使受苦痛.

agony n. chi² t'ung⁴ 極痛, k'u² ch'u³ 苦楚.

agrarian a. t'u³ ti⁴ te¹ 土地的; ~ reform, t'u³ ti⁴

agree v. t'ung² i⁴ 同意. 「kai³ ko² 土地改革.

agreeable a. yüeh⁴ i⁴ te¹ 悅意的. 「業.

agriculture n. nung² hsüeh² 農學, nung² yeh⁴ 農

aground adv., a. ch'u⁴ chiao¹ te¹ 觸礁的, ko¹

ague n. nüeh⁴ chi² 瘧疾. 「ch'ien¹ te¹ 擱淺的.

ahead adv. tsai⁴ ch'ien² 在前.

aid v. pang¹ chu⁴ 幫助, fu² chu⁴ 扶助.

aide-de-camp n. fu⁴ kuan¹ 副官. 「生病.

ail v. shih³ k'u³ nao³ 使苦惱, (be sick) sheng¹ ping⁴

aileron n. fu³ i⁴ 輔翼.

8

ailment *n.* chi² ping⁴ 疾病. 「準.

aim *n.* (*purpose*) mu⁴ ti⁴ 目的; *v.* miao² chun³ 瞄

air *n.* k'ung¹ ch'i⁴ 空氣, (*melody*) ch'ü³ tiao⁴ 曲調, (*manner*) t'ai⁴ tu⁴ 態度; *v.* lou⁴ yü² k'ung¹ ch'i⁴ chung¹ 露於空氣中.

aircraft *n.* fei¹ chi¹ 飛機, hang² k'ung¹ chi¹ 航空 機; ~ **carrier,** hang² k'ung¹ mu³ chien⁴ 航空母 艦.

airdrome *n.* fei¹ chi¹ ch'ang³ 飛機場. 「地.

airily *adv.* k'uai¹ le⁴ ti⁴ 快樂地, huo² p'o⁴ ti⁴ 活潑

airman *n.* fei¹ chi¹ shih¹ 飛機師, fei¹ hsing² yüan² 飛行員.

airplane *n.* fei¹ chi¹ 飛機. 「飛行員.

airport *n.* fei¹ chi¹ ch'ang³ 飛機場.

airship *n.* fei¹ t'ing³ 飛艇.

aisle *n.* tsou³ lang² 走廊, t'ung¹ lu⁴ 通路.

ajar *adv.* pu⁴ t'iao² ho² ti⁴ 不調和地.

akin *a.* yu³ hsüeh⁴ t'ung³ te¹ 有血統的.

alacrity *n.* huo² p'o⁴ 活潑, yung³ yüeh¹ 踴躍.

alarm *n.* ching¹ k'ung³ 驚恐, (*warning*) ching³
kao⁴ 警告.

alas! *int.* wu¹ hu¹ 嗚呼. 「kao⁴ 警告.

albatross *n.* hsin⁴ t'ien¹ weng¹ 信天翁(鳥).

albeit *conj.* sui¹ jan², chi² shih³ 即使.

albino *n.* pai² kung¹ 白公(醫).

album *n.* (*pictures*, *stamps*) t'ieh¹ (hsiang⁴, yu²) pu⁴ 貼(像, 郵)簿.

albumen *n.* tan⁴ pai² 蛋白.

alchemy *n.* lien⁴ chin¹ shu⁴ 煉金術.

alcohol *n.* chiu³ ching¹ 酒精.

alder *n.* ch'ih⁴ yang² 赤楊(植).

ale *n.* mai⁴ chiu³ 麥酒.

alee *a.*, *adv.* tsai⁴ hsia⁴ feng¹ te¹ 在下風的.

alert *a.* chin³ fang² te¹ 謹防的.

alewife *n.* shih² yü² 鰣魚.

alfalfa *n.* tzu³ mu⁴ su⁴ 紫苜蓿(植).

alga *n.* hai² tsao³ 海藻(植).

algebra *n.* tai⁴ shu⁴ hsüeh² 代數學. 「國人.

alien *a.* wai⁴ kuo² te¹ 外國的; *n.* wai⁴ kuo² jen² 外

alienate *v.* (*transfer*) jang⁴ tu⁴ 讓渡, su¹ yüan¹ 疏
遠. 「fa¹ yen² 發焰.

alight *v.* hsia⁴ lai² 下來; *a.*, *adv.* chao² huo³ 著火,

align *v.* p'ai² lieh⁴ ch'eng² hang² 排列成行.

9

alike *a.* hsiang¹ ssu⁴ te¹ 相似的; *adv.* t'ung² teng³ 同等.

aliment *n.* shih² wu⁴ 食物, tzu¹ yang³ p'in³ 滋養品.　「yang³ te¹ 營養的

alimentary *a.* tzu¹ yang³ wu⁴ te¹ 滋養物的, ying²

alimony *n.* li² hun¹ chan¹ yang³ fei⁴ 離婚瞻養費.

aliquant *a.* ch'u² pu² chin⁴ te¹ 除不盡的.

aliquot *a.* ch'u² te² chin⁴ te¹ 除得盡的, neng² fen¹ p'ing² chün¹ te¹ 能分平均的.

alive *a.* (*living*) huo² te¹ 活的, (*active*) huo² tung⁴ te¹ 活動的.

alkali *n.* chien³ chih² 鹼質(化).

alkaloid *n.* chih² wu⁴ chien³ chih² 植物鹼質.

all *a.* so² yu³ te¹ 所有的; *n.* ch'üan² pu⁴ 全部, ch'üan² t'i³ 全體.　「ch'ing¹ 減輕

allay *v.* (*quiet*) p'ing² ching⁴ 平靜, (*relieve*) chien³

allegation *n.* tuan⁴ yen² 斷言.

allegory *n.* p'i⁴ yü⁴ 譬喻, yü⁴ yen² 寓言.

allegretto *a.* wei¹ su² te¹ 微速的(樂).

allegro *a.* chi² su² te¹ 急速的(樂).

alleviate *v.* an¹ wei⁴ 安慰, chien³ ch'ing¹ 減輕.

alley *n.* hsia² lu⁴ 狹路, hsiang⁴ 巷.

alliance *n.* lien² meng² 聯盟.

alligator *n.* e⁴ yü² 鱷魚.

allot *v.* fen¹ p'ai⁴ 分派.

allow *v.* chun² hsü³ 准許.

alloy *n.* ho² chin¹ 合金.

allude *v.* an⁴ chih³ 暗指.

allure *v.* yu⁴ huo⁴ 誘惑, kou¹ yin³ 勾引.

allusion *n.* an⁴ shih⁴ 暗示.

alluvium *n.* ch'ung¹ chi¹ ti⁴ 冲積地.

ally *v.* lien² ho² 聯合, lien² meng² 聯盟; *n.* lien² meng² che³ 聯盟者.

almanac *n.* li⁴ shu¹ 歷書.

almighty *a.* wan⁴ neng² te¹ 萬能的, ch'üan² neng²

almond *n.* hsing⁴ jen² 杏仁.　「te¹ 全能的.

almost *adv.* chi¹ hu¹ 幾乎, chin⁴ hu¹ 近乎.

alms *n.* chen⁴ chi⁴ wu⁴ 賑濟物.

almshouse *n.* p'in² min² yüan⁴ 貧民院.

aloft *adv.* tsai⁴ kao¹ ch'u⁴ 在高處.　「自的.

alone *a.* ku¹ chi¹ te¹ 孤寂的, (*only*) tu² tzu⁴ te¹ 獨

along *adv.* yen² 沿, (*onward*) hsiang⁴ ch'ien² 向前;
　　prep. yen² 沿.

aloof *adv.* tsai⁴ yüan³ ch'u⁴ ti⁴ 在遠處地, yüan³
　　li² ti⁴ 遠離地.

aloud *adv.* kao¹ sheng¹ ti⁴ 高聲地.

alpaca *n.* yang² t'o² t'o², t'o² mao² pu⁴ 駝毛布.

alphabet *n.* tzu⁴ mu³ 字母.

already *adv.* i³ ching¹ 已經.

also *adv.* ch'ieh³ 且, i⁴ 亦.

altar *n.* chi⁴ t'an² 祭壇.

alter *v.* kai³ pien⁴ 改變.

alteration *n.* kai³ pien⁴ 改變.

altercation *n.* cheng¹ lin⁴ 爭論, k'ou² chiao³ 口角.

alternate *a.* lun² liu² 輪流, chiao¹ t'i⁴ 交替; *n.* t'i⁴
　　tai⁴ jen² 替代人.

alternative *a.* chiao¹ hu⁴ te¹ 交互的.

although *conj.* sui¹ jan² 雖然, tsung⁴ shih³ 縱使.

altitude *n.* kao¹ tu⁴ 高度.

alto *n.* nü³ ti¹ yin¹ 女低音(樂).　　　　　「然.

altogether *adv.* wan² ch'üan² 完全, chin⁴ jan² 盡

altruism *n.* li⁴ t'a¹ chu³ i⁴ 利他主義.

alum *n.* ming² fan² 明礬.

aluminum *n.* lü³ 鋁.　　　　　　　　　　「遠.

alumnus *n.* hsiao⁴ yu³ 校友.

always *adv.* ch'ang² ch'ang² 常常, yung² yüan³ 永

amass *v.* chü⁴ chi¹ 聚積.　　　　　　　　　「的.

amateur *n.* ch'ing¹ k'o⁴ 清客; *a.* yeh⁴ yü² te¹ 業餘

amaze *v.* ching¹ hai⁴ 驚駭.

ambassador *n.* ta⁴ shih³ 大使.

amber *n.* hu³ p'o⁴ 琥珀.

ambergris *n.* lung² yen² hsiang¹ 竜涎香.

ambiguous *a.* han² hun⁴ te¹ 含混的, shuang¹
　　kuan¹ te¹ 雙關的.

ambition *n.* yeh³ hsin¹ 野心, ta⁴ chih⁴ 大志.

ambulance *n.* chiu⁴ hu⁴ ch'e¹ 救護車.

ambuscade *n.* mai² fu² 埋伏.

ambush *n.* mai² fu² 埋伏; *v.* chü¹ chi¹ 狙擊.

amen! *int.*, *adv.* a¹ men² 阿們.

amend *v.* hsiu¹ cheng⁴ 修正.

amends *n.* p'ei² ch'ang² 賠償.

amerce *v.* k'o¹ fa² 科罰.

11

Americanism *n.* mei³ kuo² feng¹ 美國風.

amethyst *n.* tzu² shui³ ching¹ 紫水晶.

amiable *a.* k'o³ ai⁴ te¹ 可愛的.

amicable *a.* yu³ shan⁴ te¹ 友善的.

amid, amidst *prep.* tsai⁴ tang¹ chung¹ 在當中, tsai⁴ ch'i² chung¹ 在其中.

amiss *a., adv.* ts'o⁴ wu⁴ te¹ 錯誤的.

amity *n.* yu³ i² 友誼, ho² mu⁴ 和睦.

ammeter *n.* tien⁴ liu² chi¹ 電流計.

ammonia *n.* lu³ ching¹ 磠精.

ammunition *n.* chün¹ huo³ 軍火, tan⁴ yao⁴ 彈藥.

amnesty *n.* ta⁴ she⁴ 大赦.

amoeba *n.* pien⁴ hsing² ch'ung² 變形蟲.

among *prep.* tsai⁴ ch'i² chung¹ 在其中.

amorous *a.* ai⁴ te¹ 愛的, chung¹ ch'ing² te¹ 鍾情的.

amorphous *a.* wu² ting⁴ hsing² te¹ 無定形的.

amortize *v.* ch'ing² chai⁴ 清償.

amount *n.* tsung³ shu⁴ 總數, tsung³ e² 總額.

ampere *n.* an¹ p'ei² liang⁴ 安培量(電).

amphibious *a.* liang³ hsi¹ te¹ 兩棲的.

amphitheater *n.* yüan² hsing² chü⁴ ch'ang³ 圓形劇場. 「te¹ 巨大的.

ample *a.* ch'ung¹ tsu² te¹ 充足的, (*large*) chü⁴ ta⁴

amplify *v.* fang¹ ta⁴ 放大, hsiang² shu⁴ 詳述.

amplitude *n.* chü⁴ ta⁴ 巨大, kuang³ k'uo⁴ 廣闊.

amputate *v.* ko¹ ch'ü⁴ 割去, ch'ieh¹ tuan⁴ 切斷.

amulet *n.* hu⁴ shen¹ fu² 護身符, fu² lu⁴ 符籙.

amuse *v.* yü² lo⁴ 娛樂.

an *a., art.* jen⁴ i¹ 任一.

anaconda *n.* ta⁴ she² 大蛇, chü⁴ mang³ 巨蟒.

anaemia *n.* p'in² hsüeh⁴ 貧血(醫).

anaesthesia *n.* shih¹ chih¹ chüeh² 失知覺(醫), ma² tsui⁴ 痲醉(醫). 「ma² yao⁴ 痲藥.

anaesthetic *n.* shih³ ma² tsui⁴ te¹ 使痲醉的; *n.*

anagram *n.* tzu⁴ mi² 字謎.

analogy *n.* hsiang¹ ssu⁴ 相似.

analysis *n.* fen¹ hsi¹ 分析, fen¹ chieh³ 分解. 「的.

anarchic *a.* wu² cheng⁴ fu³ chu³ i⁴ te¹ 無政府主義

anarchism *n.* wu² cheng⁴ fu³ chu³ i⁴ 無政府主義.

anarchy *n.* wu² cheng⁴ fu³ 無政府.

anathema *n.* chou⁴ tsu³ 咒詛.

anatomy *n.* chieh² p'ou³ hsüeh² 解剖學.

ancestor *n.* tsu³ tsung¹ 祖宗.

ancestry *n.* chia¹ hsi⁴ 家系.

anchor *n.* mao² 錨.

ancient *a.* ku³ tai⁴ te¹ 古代的. 「是.

and *conj.* chi² 及, ping⁴ ch'ieh³ 並且, k'o³ shih⁴ 可

anecdote *n.* ch'i² wen² 奇聞, i⁴ shih⁴ 軼事, i⁴ shih⁴

anew *adv.* ch'ung² hsin¹ 重新, tsai⁴ 再. 「逸事.

angel *n.* t'ien¹ shih³ 天使.

angelic *a.* ju² t'ien¹ shih³ te¹ 如天使的.

anger *n.* nu⁴ 怒.

angle *n.* chiao³ 角.

angler *n.* tiao⁴ yü² che³ 釣魚者.

angry *a.* nu⁴ te¹ 怒的.

anguish *n.* t'ung⁴ k'u³ 痛苦, k'u³ men⁴ 苦悶.

angular *a.* yu³ chiao³ te¹ 有角的, chien¹ chiao³ te¹

animal *n.* tung⁴ wu⁴ 動物. 「尖的的.

animate *v.* shih² yu³ sheng¹ ming⁴ 使有生命.

animation *n.* shih³ yu³ sheng¹ ming⁴ 使有生命.

animosity *n.* ch'ou² hen⁴ 仇恨, ti² i⁴ 敵意.

ankle *n.* hua⁴ 踝.

annals *n.* nien² shih³ 年史.

annex *v.* ho² ping⁴ 合併.

annihilate *v.* hsiao¹ mieh⁴ 消滅.

annihilation *n.* hsiao¹ mieh⁴ 消滅. 「念日.

anniversary *n.* chou¹ nien² chi⁴ nien⁴ jih⁴ 周年紀

announce *v.* hsüan¹ kao⁴ 宣告. 「告.

announcement *n.* hsüan¹ pu⁴ 宣佈, pu⁴ kao⁴ 佈

annoy *v.* fan² nao³ 煩惱, k'un⁴ jao³ 困擾.

annoyance *n.* fan² nao³ 煩惱, sao¹ jao³ 騷擾.

annual *a.* mei³ nien² te¹ 每年的.

annuity *n.* nien² chin¹ 年金, nien² hsin¹ 年薪.

annul *v.* tso⁴ fei⁴ 作廢, ch'ü³ hsiao¹ 取消.

anoint *v.* fu¹ yu² 敷油.

anomalous *a.* fan³ ch'ang² te¹ 反常的. 「則.

anomaly *n.* fan³ ch'ang² 反常, pu⁴ kuei¹ tse² 不規

another *a.* pieh² 別.

answer *n.* hui² ta² 回答.

ant *n.* i³ 蟻.

antagonist *n.* tui⁴ k'ang⁴ che³ 對抗者. 「在前的.

anterior *a.* i³ ch'ien² te¹ 以前的, tsai⁴ ch'ien² te¹

13

anthem *n.* tsan⁴ mei³ shih¹ 讚美詩, tsan⁴ mei³ ko¹ 讚美歌.

anti-aircraft *n.* fang² k'ung¹ 防空, kao¹ she⁴ 高射; ～ **gun,** kao¹ she⁴ p'ao⁴ 高射砲; ～ **machine gun,** kao¹ she⁴ chi¹ kuan¹ ch'iang¹ 高射機關鎗.

anticipate *v.* ch'i¹ wang⁴ 期望, (*foresee*) yü⁴ liao⁴ 預料.

anticipation *n.* hsien¹ wei² 先爲, yü⁴ liao⁴ 預料.

anti-freeze *a.* fang² tung⁴ te¹ 防凍的. 「相容.

antipathy *n.* yen⁴ wu⁴ 厭惡, pu⁴ hsiang¹ jung² 不

antiquarian *a.* k'ao² ku³ te¹ 考古的, ku³ wu⁴ te¹

antiquary *n.* k'ao² ku³ chia¹ 考古家. 「古物的.

antique *a.* ku³ te¹ 古的, ku³ tai⁴ te¹ 古代的.

anvil *n.* t'ieh³ chen¹ 鐵砧.

anxiety *n.* chiao¹ chi² 焦急, yu¹ lü⁴ 憂慮. 「念的.

anxious *a.* yu¹ lü⁴ te¹ 憂慮的, hsüan² nien¹ te¹ 懸

any *a.* jen⁴ i¹ 任一, mei³ 每, mou³ 某.

apart *adv.* fen¹ k'ai¹ 分開, ko² yüan³ 隔遠, tsai⁴ p'ang² 在旁.

apartment *n.* fang² chien¹ 房間, i² t'ao⁴ fang² chien¹ 一套房間; ～ **house,** kung¹ yü⁴ 公寓.

ape *n.* yüan² 猿, mo² fang³ che³ 墓仿者.

aperient *a.* ch'ing¹ hsieh⁴ te¹ 輕瀉的; *n.* ch'ing¹ hsieh⁴ yao⁴ 輕瀉藥.

aperture *n.* k'ung³ 孔, (*camera*) k'uai⁴ men² 快門 (攝), (*rifle*) chao⁴ men² 照門(兵).

apologize *v.* tao⁴ ch'ien⁴ 歉道, (*defend*) pien⁴ pai² 辯白. 「辯白.

apology *n.* tao⁴ ch'ien⁴ 道歉, (*defense*) pien⁴ pai²

apoplexy *n.* chung⁴ feng¹ 中風(醫), nao³ ch'ung¹ hsüeh⁴ 腦充血(醫).

apothecary *n.* yao⁴ chi¹ shih¹ 藥劑師.

appal *v.* shih³ ching¹ hai⁴ 使驚駭, k'ung³ ho⁴ 恐嚇.

apparatus *n.* i² ch'i⁴ 儀器.

apparel *n.* i¹ fu² 衣服, fu² chuang¹ 服裝.

apparent *a.* hsien³ jan² te¹ 顯然的.

appeal *n.* (*law*) shang⁴ su⁴ 上訴, (*request*) k'en³ ch'iu² 懇求; *v.* k'en³ ch'iu² 懇求. 「ssu⁴ 形似.

appear *v.* (*be seen*) ch'u¹ hsien⁴ 出現, (*seem*) hsing²

appearance *n.* ch'u¹ hsien⁴ 出現, (*aspect*) wai⁴ mao⁴ 外貌, (*apparition*) hsing² hsiang⁴ 形象.

14

appease *v.* (*satisfy*) man³ tsu² 滿足, (*quiet*) p'ing²
ching⁴ 平靜.

appendicitis *n.* mang² ch'ang² yen² 盲腸炎.

appertain *v.* shu³ yü² 屬於, kuan¹ yü² 關於.

appetite *n.* shih² yü² 食慾, yü⁴ wang⁴ 慾望.

applaud *v.* ho⁴ ts'ai³ 喝采, ch'eng¹ tsan⁴ 稱讚.

applause *n.* ho⁴ ts'ai³ 喝采, ch'eng¹ tsan⁴ 稱讚.

apple *n.* p'in² kuo³ 蘋菓.

applicant *n.* shen¹ ch'ing² che³ 申請者.

application *n.* (*use*) ying⁴ yung⁴ 應用, (*request*)
shen¹ ch'ing³ 申請.

applied *a.* ying⁴ yung⁴ te¹ 應用的；～ **tactics**,
ying⁴ yung⁴ chan⁴ shu⁴ 應用戰術.

apply *v.* (*put*) fu¹ 敷, (*request*) ch'ing³ ch'iu² 請求.
～ **for leave**, ch'ing³ chia⁴ 請假.

appoint *v.* (*choose*) jen² ming⁴ 任命, (*set*) ting⁴ 定,
(*equip*) she⁴ pei⁴ 設備.

appointment *n.* (*commission*) jen⁴ ming⁴ 任命,
(*position*) chih² wei⁴ 職位, (*engagement*) yüeh¹
ting⁴ 約定.

appreciate *v.* (*think highly of*) chien⁴ shih⁴ 鑑識,
(*be thankful for*) kan³ p'ei⁴ 感佩, (*be sensitive to*)
pien⁴ pieh² 辨別, (*raise*) t'ai² kao¹ 擡高.

appreciation *n.* (*a valuing*) tsun¹ chung⁴ 尊重,
(*understanding*) t'i³ hui⁴ 體會.

apprehend *v.* (*dread*) k'ung³ chü⁴ 恐懼, (*arrest*)
cho¹ 捉, (*understand*) liao² chieh³ 了解.

apprehension *n.* (*dread*) k'ung³ chü⁴ 恐懼, (*arrest*) pu³ huo⁴ 捕獲, (*understanding*) liao² chieh³
了解.

apprehensive *a.* (*able to learn*) neng² liao² chieh³
te¹ 能了解的, (*afraid*) k'ung³ chü⁴ te¹ 恐懼的.

apprentice *n.* hsüeh² t'u² 學徒；*v.* shih³ wei²
hsüeh² t'u² 使爲學徒.

approach *n.* chieh¹ chin⁴ 接近, (*access*) chin⁴ lu⁴
進路, (*likeness*) hsiang⁴ 像；*v.* chieh¹ chin⁴ 接近.

approbation *n.* chia¹ na⁴ 嘉納, jen⁴ k'o³ 認可.

appropriate *a.* shih⁴ i² te¹ 適宜的；*v.* po¹ ch'ung¹
撥充, (*take for oneself*) shan⁴ ch'ü³ 擅取.

appropriation *n.* kuei¹ tso⁴ mou³ yung⁴ 歸作某用.

approval *n.* (*consent*) p'i¹ chun³ 批准.

15

approve *v.* (*consent to*) p'i¹ chun³ 批准.

approximate *a.* ta⁴ yüeh¹ te¹ 大約的.

apricot *n.* hsing⁴ tzu¹ 杏子.

April *n.* ssu⁴ yüeh⁴ 四月.

apron *n.* wei² ch'ün² 圍裙.

apt *a.* (*suitable*) ho² i² te¹ 合宜的, (*likely*) kuan⁴ ch'ang² te¹ 慣常的, (*quick*) min³ chieh² te¹ 敏捷的.

aptitude *n.* (*ability*) ts'ai² neng² 才能, (*fitness*) ho² i² 合宜, (*quickness*) min³ chieh² 敏捷.

aquarium *n.* shui³ tsu² kuan³ 水族館.

arable *a.* shih⁴ yü² keng¹ chung⁴ te¹ 適於耕種的.

arbitrary *a.* wu³ tuan⁴ te¹ 武斷的, (*capricious*) wu² heng² hsin¹ te¹ 無恒心的.

arbitration *n.* kung¹ tuan⁴ 公斷.

arbitrator *n.* kung¹ tuan⁴ jen² 公斷人.

arbor *n.* chi¹ chou² 機軸.　　　　　　　　「lang² 拱廊.

arcade *n.* lien² huan² kung³ lang² 連環拱廊, kung³

arch *a.* (*chief*) chu³ yao⁴ te¹ 主要的, (*mischievous*) chiao³ hua² te¹ 狡猾的; *v.* shih³ ch'eng² kung¹ chuang⁴ 使成弓狀; *n.* kung³ 拱.

archbishop *n.* ta⁴ chu³ chiao⁴ 大主教.　　　「弓形的.

arched *a.* hu² hsing² te¹ 弧形的, kung¹ hsing² te¹

archipelago *n.* ch'ün² tao³ 群島, to¹ tao² hai³ 多島

architect *n.* chien⁴ chu² chia¹ 建築家.　　　　「海.

architecture *n.* chien⁴ chu² shu⁴ 建築術.

archway *n.* kung³ tao⁴ 拱道, kung³ men² 拱門.

arctic *a.* pei³ chi² te¹ 北極的, chi² han² te¹ 極寒的.

ardent *a.* (*eager*) je⁴ hsin¹ te¹ 熱心的, (*glowing*) fa¹ kuang¹ je⁴ te¹ 發光熱的.

ardor *n.* je⁴ ch'ing² 熱情, je⁴ hsin¹ 熱心.

arduous *a.* (*steep*) hsien³ chün¹ te¹ 險峻的, (*difficult*) fan² nan² te¹ 煩難的.

argue *v.* pien⁴ lun⁴ 辯論.

argument *n.* pien⁴ lun⁴ 辯論, (*reason*) li³ yu² 理由.

arise *v.* sheng¹ ch'i³ 升起.　　　　　「chi¹ 特殊階級.

aristocracy *n.* kuei⁴ tsu² 貴族, t'e⁴ shu¹ chieh¹

arithmetic *n.* suan⁴ shu⁴ 算術, shu⁴ hsüeh² 數學.

arm *n.* pei⁴ 臂, (*weapon*) wu³ ch'i⁴ 武器; *v.* wu³ chuang¹ 武裝; ~ **band**, pei⁴ chang¹ 臂章.

armament *n.* chün¹ tui⁴ 軍隊, (*equipment*) chün¹

armchair *n.* an¹ le⁴ i³ 安樂椅.　　　　「pei⁴ 軍備.

armistice *n.* hsiu¹ chan⁴ 休戰.

armor *n.* chia³ chou⁴ 甲冑.

armored *a.* chuang¹ chia³ te¹ 裝甲的; ~ **car,** chuang¹ chia³ ch'e¹ 裝甲車; ~ **division,** chuang¹ chia³ shih¹ 裝甲師; ~ **force,** chuang¹ chia³ pu⁴ tui⁴ 裝甲部隊.

armory *n.* ping¹ kung¹ ch'ang³ 兵工廠, chün¹ hsieh⁴ k'u⁴ 軍械庫.　　　「chang¹ 紋章.

arms *n.* (*weapons*) wu³ ch'i⁴ 武器, (*designs*) wen²

army *n.* chün¹ 軍 (*Army*) lu⁴ chün¹ 陸軍.

aroma *n.* fen¹ fang¹ 芬芳.

aromatic *a.* fang¹ hsiang¹ te¹ 芳香的.　　　「周.

around *adv.* chou¹ wei² 周圍; *prep.* ssu⁴ chou¹ 四

arouse *v.* (*excite*) chi¹ ch'i³ 激起, (*awaken*) huan⁴ hsing³ 喚醒.　　　「t'iao² t'ing² 調停.

arrange *v.* cheng² li³ 整理, pu⁴ chih⁴ 佈置, (*settle*)

arrangement *n.* cheng² li³ 整理, pu⁴ chih⁴ 佈置, (*settle*) t'iao² t'ing² 調停.

array *v.* (*adorn*) chuang¹ shih⁴ 裝飾, (*arrange in order*) cheng³ lieh⁴ 整列; *n.* (*clothes*) i¹ fu⁴ 衣服, (*order*) cheng³ lieh⁴ 整列.

arrears *n.* ch'ien⁴ k'uan³ 欠款.

arrest *v.* cho¹ na² 捉拿, (*stop*) t'ing² chih³ 停止; *n.* tai⁴ pu³ 逮捕, (*stop*) tsu³ chih³ 阻止.

arrival *n.* lai² tao⁴ 來到.

arrive *v.* tao⁴ ta² 到達.

arrogance *n.* ao⁴ man⁴ 傲慢, tzu⁴ ta⁴ 自大.

arrogant *a.* ao⁴ man⁴ te¹ 傲慢的.

arrow *n.* shih³ 矢.

arrowhead *n.* chien⁴ t'ou² 箭頭.

arsenal *n.* ping¹ kung¹ ch'ang³ 兵工廠.

arsenic *n.* p'i¹ shuang¹ 砒霜.

art *n.* i⁴ shu⁴ 藝術, (*skill*) chi⁴ ch'iao³ 技巧, (*human skill*) jen² kung¹ 人工, (*trick*) kan¹ chi⁴ 奸計; ~ **gallery,** mei³ shu⁴ kuan³ 美術館.

artery *n.* tung⁴ mo⁴ 動脈.

artful *a.* (*deceitful*) chiao³ hua² te¹ 狡猾的, (*skillful*) chiao³ miao⁴ te¹ 巧妙的.

arthritis *n.* kuan¹ chieh² yen² 關節炎 (醫).

artichoke *n.* chü² ts'ao³ 菊草 (植), ch'ao² hsien¹ chi⁴ 朝鮮薊 (植).

17

article *n.* (*item*) wu⁴ chien⁴ 物件, (*clause*) t'iao²
k'uan³ 條款, (*essay*) lun⁴ wen² 論文, (*grammar*)
kuan¹ tz'u² 冠詞.

articulate *a.* yu³ kuan¹ chieh² te¹ 有關節的; *v.* fa¹
yin¹ ch'ing¹ hsi¹ 發音清晰.

articulation *n.* (*joint*) ku³ chieh² 骨節, (*enuncia-
tion*) fa¹ sheng¹ ch'ing¹ hsi¹ 發聲清晰.

artifice *n.* (*trick*) ch'iao³ chi⁴ 巧計.

artificial *a.* jen² tsao⁴ te¹ 人造的, chia³ te¹ 假的.

artillery *n.* (*cannon*) ta⁴ p'ao⁴ 大礮, (*branch*) p'ao⁴
ping¹ 砲兵; **~ action**, p'ao⁴ chan⁴ 砲戰(軍); **~
fire**, p'ao⁴ huo³ 砲火(軍); **~ officer**, p'ao⁴ ping¹
chün¹ kuan¹ 砲兵軍官(軍); **~ position**, p'ao⁴
ping¹ chen⁴ ti⁴ 砲兵陣地(軍); **~ range**, p'ao⁴
ping¹ she⁴ chi¹ ch'ang³ 砲兵射擊場(軍).

artisan *n.* chi¹ hsieh⁴ shih¹ 機械師, kung¹ chiang⁴
工匠.

artist *n.* i⁴ shu⁴ chia¹ 藝術家.

artistic *a.* i⁴ shu⁴ te¹ 藝術的.

as *conj.* (*same degree*) t'ung⁴ teng³ 同等, t'ung⁴
yang⁴ 同樣, (*while*) cheng⁴ chih² 正值, (*because*)
yin¹ wei⁴ 因爲, (*though*) sui¹ 雖; **~ a rule**, an⁴
t'ung¹ li⁴ 按通例; **~ far as**, chiu⁴ 就; **~ follows**, ju² hsia⁴ 如下; **~ for** (*or to*), chih⁴ yü²
至於; **~ if** (*or though*), hao³ hsiang⁴ 好像; **~
it is**, tsai⁴ shih² chi⁴ shang⁴ 在實際上; **~ it
were**, wan³ ju² 宛如; **~ regards**, kuan¹ yü² 關
於; **~ soon as**, i² ssu⁴ 一俟; **~ usual**, ju²
ch'ang² 如常; **~ well as**, t'ung² 同; **~ yet**,
ch'i³ chin¹ 迄今.

asbestos *n.* shih² mien² 石棉.

ascend *v.* (*rise*) shang⁴ sheng¹ 上升, (*climb*) p'an¹
teng¹ 攀登.

ascendant *a.* (*rising*) kao¹ sheng¹ te¹ 高升的, (*superior*) yu¹ yüeh⁴ te¹ 優越的.

ascension *n.* shang⁴ sheng¹ 上升.

ascent *n.* (*rising*) shang⁴ sheng¹ 上升, (*climbing*)
teng¹ kao¹ 登高, (*slope*) hsieh² p'o¹ 斜坡.

ascertain *v.* ch'üeh⁴ chih¹ 確知.

ascribe *v.* kuei⁴ yü² 歸於.

ash *n.* (*timber*) huai² shu⁴ 槐樹(植), hui¹ chin¹ 爐.

ashes *n.* hui¹ 灰.

ashore *adv.* tsai⁴ an⁴ shang⁴ 在岸上, hsiang⁴ an⁴ 向岸

aside *adv.* tsai⁴ i⁴ pien¹ 在一邊, tsai⁴ p'ang² 在旁.

ask *v.* (*inquire*) wen⁴ 問, (*request*) ch'ing³ ch'iu² 請求, (*invite*) yao¹ ch'ing³ 邀請.

asleep *a.* shui⁴ chao² te¹ 睡着的.

asparagus *n.* lu² sun³ 蘆筍(植).

aspect *n.* (*look*) yang⁴ tzu¹ 樣子, (*countenance*) jung² mao⁴ 容貌, (*direction*) fang¹ wei⁴ 方位.

asphalt *n.* pai² yu² 柏油, t'u³ li⁴ ch'ing¹ 土瀝青.

aspire *v.* je⁴ wang⁴ 熱望, (*rise*) sheng¹ kao¹ 升高.

aspirin *n.* a¹ ssu¹ pi⁴ ling² 阿司必靈.

ass *n.* (*donkey*) lü² 驢, (*silly person*) tai¹ jen² 呆人.

assail *v.* meng³ kung¹ 猛攻, t'ung⁴ chi¹ 痛擊.

assailant *n.* meng³ kung¹ che³ 猛攻者.

assassin *n.* tz'u⁴ k'o⁴ 刺客, an⁴ sha¹ che³ 暗殺者.

assassinate *v.* an⁴ sha¹ 暗殺.

assassination *n.* an⁴ sha¹ 暗殺.

assault *n.* meng³ kung¹ 猛攻; *v.* kung¹ chi¹ 攻擊.

assemble *v.* (*personnel*) chao⁴ chi² 召集, hui⁴ chi² 會集, chi² ho² 集合(軍), (*put together*) chieh² ho² 結合(兵), chuang¹ p'ei⁴ 裝配.

assembly *n.* hui⁴ 會, (*law making group*) i⁴ hui⁴ 議會. ～ **area,** chi² ho² ti⁴ 集合地.

assent *n.* t'ung² i⁴ 同意; *v.* t'ung² i⁴ 同意.

assert *v.* tuan⁴ yen² 斷言, ch'üeh⁴ shuo¹ 確說.

assertion *n.* tuan⁴ yen² 斷言, chu³ chang¹ 主張.

assess *v.* (*tax*) k'o⁴ shui⁴ 課稅, (*estimate*) ku¹ chia⁴ 估價.

assets *n.* tzu¹ ch'an³ 資產. 「估價.

assiduous *a.* ch'in² mien³ te¹ 勤勉的. 「tu⁴ 讓渡.

assign *v.* (*appoint*) chih³ p'ai⁴ 指派, (*transfer*) jang⁴

assignee *n.* shou⁴ jang⁴ jen² 受讓人.

assignment *n.* (*appointment*) chih³ ting⁴ 指定, (*transfer*) jang⁴ tu⁴ 讓渡.

assimilate *v.* (*liken*) shih³ hsiang¹ ssu⁴ 使相似, (*absorb*) hsi¹ shou¹ 吸收.

assist *v.* pang¹ chu⁴ 幫助, fu² chu⁴ 扶助.

assistance *n.* yüan² chu⁴ 援助.

assistant *n.* chu⁴ shou³ 助手.

associate *a.* pan⁴ lü³ 伴侶, p'eng² yu³ 朋友; *v.* chieh² chiao¹ 結交, lien² ho² 聯合.

association *n.* (*society*) hsieh² hui⁴ 協會.

assort *v.* p'ai² lieh⁴ 排列, pu⁴ chih⁴ 佈置.

19

assume v. shan⁴ ch'ü³ 攬取, (*pretend*) mao⁴ ch'eng¹ 冒稱, (*suppose*) chia³ ting¹ 假定.

assumption n. shan⁴ ch'ü³ 攬取, (*thing assumed*) mao⁴ ch'eng¹ 冒稱, (*presumption*) chia³ ting⁴ 假定.

assurance n. pao³ cheng⁴ 保證, pao² hsien³ 保險.

assure v. pao³ cheng⁴ 保證.

asthma n. ch'uan³ hsi² cheng¹ 喘息症(醫).

astonish v. ching¹ e⁴ 驚愕, ya⁴ i⁴ 訝異.

astonishment n. ching¹ e⁴ 驚愕, ya⁴ i⁴ 訝異.

astringent a. shou¹ chin³ te⁴ 收緊的, shou¹ lien⁴ te⁴ 收斂的.

astronomer n. t'ien¹ wen² hsüeh² chia¹ 天文學家.

astronomy n. t'ien¹ wen² hsüeh² 天文學.

asunder adv. fen¹ k'ai¹ 分開, fen¹ li² 分離.

asylum n. (*for criminals*) pi⁴ nan⁴ so³ 避難所, (*for unfortunate persons*) yang³ yü⁴ yüan⁴ 養育院.

at prep. (*near*) chin⁴ 近, (*in*) tsai⁴ 在, (*by*) tsai⁴ p'ang² 在旁, (*on*) tsai⁴ shang⁴ 在上; "~ ease!" shao¹ hsi¹ 稍息(軍); "~ ease, march!" pien⁴ pu⁴ tsou³ 便步走(軍); "~ my command!" tai⁴ ming⁴ 待命(軍).

athlete n. yün⁴ tung⁴ chia¹ 運動家.

athletic a. yün⁴ tung⁴ te¹ 運動的, (*strong*) ch'iang² chuang⁴ te¹ 强壯的.

atmosphere n. k'ung¹ ch'i⁴ 空氣, ta⁴ ch'i⁴ 大氣.

atom n. yüan² tzu³ 原子, wei¹ li² 微粒.

atomic a. yüan² tzu³ te¹ 原子的, (*small*) chi² wei¹ te¹ 極微的, yüan² tzu³ shih² tai⁴ 原子時代; ~ **bomb**, yüan² tzu³ tan⁴ 原子彈(軍); ~ **cannon**, yüan² tzu³ p'ao⁴ 原子礮(軍); ~ **energy**, yüan² tzu³ neng² 原子能; ~ **Energy Commission** (US), yüan² tzu³ neng² wei³ yüan² hui⁴ 原子能委員會(美); ~ **number**, yüan² tzu³ shu⁴ 原子數; ~ **warfare**, yüan² tzu³ chan⁴ cheng¹ 原子戰爭(軍); ~ **weight**, yüan² tzu³ liang⁴ 原子量.

atrocious a. ts'an² k'u⁴ te¹ 殘酷的, hsiung⁴ pao⁴ te¹ 兇暴的.

attach v. (*join*) chieh² ho² 結合, (*fasten*) hsi⁴ lao² 繫牢, (*attribute*) kuei¹ yü² 歸於, (*units or weapons*) p'ei⁴ shu³ 配屬(軍), (*personnel*) fu⁴ shu³ 附屬(軍).

attack v. kung¹ chi¹ 攻擊.

attain *v.* (*arrive*) tao⁴ 到, (*gain*) te² 得.

attempt *n.* ch'ang² shih⁴ 嘗試, nu³ li⁴ 努力; *v.*

attend *v.* fu² shih⁴ 服侍. ⌊ch'ang² shih⁴ 嘗試.

attendant *n.* (*servant*) shih⁴ che³ 侍者, (*person attending*) ch'u¹ hsi² che³ 出席者; *a.* fu² shih⁴ te¹ 服侍的.

attention *n.* (*care*) chu⁴ i⁴ 注意, (*courtesy*) li³ mao⁴ 禮貌, (*in drill*) li⁴ cheng⁴ 立正(軍).

attentive *a.* liu² hsin¹ te¹ 留心的, (*polite*) yu³ li³ mao⁴ te¹ 有禮貌的.

attire *n.* i¹ fu² 衣服, fu² chuang¹ 服裝; *v.* ch'uan¹ i¹ 穿衣, ta³ pan⁴ 打扮.

attitude *n.* tzu¹ shih⁴ 姿勢, t'ai⁴ tu⁴ 態度.

attorney *n.* tai⁴ li³ jen² 代理人, (*lawyer*) lü⁴ shih¹ 律師; ～ **General** (**US**), chien³ ch'a² chang³ 檢

attract *v.* hsi¹ yin³ 吸引, yin³ yu⁴ 引誘. ⌊察長.

attraction *n.* hsi¹ yin³ li⁴ 吸引力, yin³ yu⁴ 引誘物. ⌈te¹ 有吸引力的.

attractive *a.* tung⁴ jen² te¹ 動人的, yu³ hsi¹ yin³ li⁴

attribute *n.* pen³ hsing⁴ 本性, t'e⁴ hsing⁴ 特性; *v.* kuei¹ yü³ 歸與, kuei¹ wei³ 歸諉.

auction *n.* p'ai⁴ mai⁴ 拍賣.

auctioneer *n.* p'ai⁴ mai⁴ che³ 拍賣者. ⌈li³ 無禮.

audacity *n.* (*boldness*) ta⁴ tan³ 大膽, (*rudeness*) wu²

audible *a.* k'o³ t'ing¹ chien⁴ te¹ 可聽見的.

ɔuditor *n.* (*hearer*) t'ing¹ che³ 聽者, ch'a² chang⁴

augment *v.* tseng¹ chia¹ 增加. ⌊yüan² 查賑員.

augmentation *n.* tseng¹ chia¹ 增加.

August *n.* pa² yüeh¹ 八月. ⌈te¹ 生命的.

auriferous *a.* ch'an³ chin¹ te¹ 產金的, sheng¹ chin¹

authentic *a.* chen¹ cheng⁴ te¹ 眞正的, ch'üeh⁴ shih² te¹ 確實的. ⌈確實.

authenticity *n.* chen¹ cheng⁴ 眞正, ch'üeh⁴ shih²

author *n.* chu¹ tso⁴ che³ 著作者.

authority *n.* (*power*) chih³ ch'üan² 職權, (*individual or office*) tang¹ chü² 當局, (*expert*) ch'üan² wei¹ 權威.

authorize *v.* shou⁴ ch'üan² 授權, hsü² k'o³ 許可.

autobiography *n.* tzu⁴ ch'uan² 自傳.

automobile *n.* ch'i⁴ ch'e¹ 汽車, tzu⁴ tung⁴ ch'e¹

autumn *n.* ch'iu¹ chi¹ 秋季. ⌊自動車.

21

auxiliary *a.* pang¹ chu⁴ te¹ 幫助的；*n.* (*helper*) chu⁴ shou³ 助手；～ **aiming point,** pu³ chu⁴ miao² chun¹ tien³ 補助瞄準點(軍)；～ **target,** pu³ chu⁴ mu⁴ piao¹ 補助目標(軍)；～**verb,** chu⁴ tung⁴ tz'u² 助動詞.

avail *v.* (*help*) chu⁴ 助, (*take advantage of*) yu³ yung⁴ 有用；*n.* li⁴ i⁴ 利益.　「hsiao⁴ te¹ 有効的.

available *a.* k'o³ yung⁴ te¹ 可用的, (*valid*) yu³

avenge *v.* pao⁴ fu⁴ 報復, fu⁴ ch'ou² 復仇.

average *a.* p'ing² chün¹ te¹ 平均的, (*usual*) p'u³ t'ung¹ te¹ 普通的；*n.* p'ing² chün¹ 平均.　「的.

averse *a.* hsien² wu⁴ te¹ 嫌惡的, fan³ tui⁴ te¹ 反對

aversion *n.* hsien² wu⁴ 嫌惡.　「i² 轉移.

avert *v.* (*avoid*) p.⁴ mien³ 避免, (*turn aside*) chuan

aviation *n.* hang² k'ung¹ shu⁴ 航空術.

aviator *n.* hang² k'ung¹ yüan² 航空員.

avocation *n.* fu⁴ yeh⁴ 副業.

avoid *v.* pi⁴ mien³ 避免, (*annul*) ch'ü³ hsiao¹ 取消.

avow *v.* ming² yen² 明言, chih² shuo¹ 直說.

avowal *n.* ming² yen² 明言, chih² shuo¹ 直說.

await *v.* teng³ hou⁴ 等候；～ **orders,** tai⁴ ming⁴ 待命(軍).　「hsing³ 醒.

awake *a.* hsing³ te¹ 醒的；*v.* huan¹ hsing³ 喚醒

award *n.* (*decision*) p'an⁴ chüeh² 判決, (*prize*) chiang² shang³ 獎賞；*v.* (*adjudge*) p'an⁴ chi³ 判給, (*grant*) chiang² chi³ 獎給.　「悉的.

aware *a.* chih¹ chüeh² te¹ 知覺的, chih¹ hsi² te¹ 知

away *adv.* tsai⁴ yüan³ ch'u⁴ 在遠處, li² k'ai¹ 離開.

awe *n.* ching⁴ wei⁴ 敬畏；*v.* wei⁴ chü⁴ 畏懼.

awful *a.* k'o³ wei⁴ te¹ 可畏的.

awkward *a.* pen⁴ cho¹ te¹ 笨拙的.

axe *n.* fu³ 斧.

axiom *n.* yüan² li³ 原理, kung¹ li³ 公理.

axis *n.* chou² 軸, ti⁴ chou² 地軸.

axle *n.* lun² chou² 輪軸, ch'e¹ chou² 車軸.

azimuth *n.* fang¹ wei⁴ 方位.　「te¹ 天青的.

azure *n.* wei⁴ lan² se⁴ te¹ 蔚藍色的, t'ien¹ ch'ing¹

B

baboon *n.* fei⁴ fei⁴ 狒狒.

baby *n.* ying¹ erh² 嬰兒.

bachelor *n.* wei⁴ hun¹ nan² tzu¹ 未婚男子, (*degree*) ta⁴ hsüeh² hsüeh² shih⁴ 大學學士.

back *n.* (*of body*) pei⁴ pu⁴ 背部; *a.* tsai⁴ hou⁴ mien⁴ te¹ 在後面的; *adv.* hsiang⁴ hou⁴ ti¹ 向後地.

backbone *n.* chi² ku³ 脊骨.

background *n.* pei⁴ ching³ 背景.

backward(s) *adv.* hsiang⁴ hou⁴ fang¹ ti¹ 向後方地; *a.* (*wrong way*) ni⁴ hsing² te¹ 逆行的.

bacon *n.* hsien² jou⁴ 鹹肉.

bacteria *n.* hsi⁴ chün¹ 細菌.

bad *a.* pu⁴ shan⁴ te¹ 不善的, yu³ hai⁴ te¹ 有害的.

badge *n.* piao¹ chi⁴ 標記.

badger *n.* huan¹ 獾.

badly *adv.* e⁴ lieh⁴ ti⁴ 惡劣地.

baffle *v.* (*struggle without success*) ts'o⁴ che² 挫折.

bag *n.* tai⁴ 袋.

baggage *n.* hsing² li³ 行李.　　　　　　「傘.

bail *n.*, *v.* pao³ shih⁴ 保釋; ～ **out**, t'iao⁴ san³ 跳

bait *n.* erh³ 餌.

bake *v.* hung¹ kan¹ 烘乾.

bakelite *n.* tien⁴ mu⁴ 電木, chiao¹ mu⁴ 膠木.

baker *n.* mien⁴ pao¹ shih¹ 麵包師.

bakery *n.* mien⁴ pao¹ tien⁴ 麵包店.

balance *n.* (*equality*) p'ing² heng² 平衡, (*difference*) ch'a¹ e² 差額; *v.* shih³ p'ing² heng² 使平衡.

balcony *n.* yang² t'ai² 陽臺, (*theater*) pao¹ hsiang¹

bald *a.* t'u¹ t'ou² te¹ 禿頭的.　　　　　　「包廂.

ball *n.* ch'iu² 球, (*dance*) t'iao⁴ wu³ hui⁴ 跳舞會; ～ **firing**, shih² tan⁴ she⁴ chi¹ 實彈射擊(軍).

ballast *n.* ya¹ ts'ang¹ wu⁴ 壓艙物, (*road*) tao⁴ ch'uang² 道牀.

ballistics *n.* tan⁴ tao⁴ hsüeh² 彈道學.

balloon *n.* ch'ing¹ ch'i⁴ ch'iu² 輕氣球.

ballot *n.* hsüan² chü³ p'iao⁴ 選舉票.

balmy *a.* chen⁴ t'ung⁴ te¹ 鎮痛的, (*fragrant*) yu³

fang¹ hsiang¹ te¹ 有芳香的.

bamboo n. chu² 竹.

ban n. chin⁴ ling⁴ 禁令; v. chin⁴ chih³ 禁止.

banana n. hsiang¹ chiao¹ 香蕉.

band n. (group) tui⁴ 隊, (music) yüeh⁴ tui⁴ 樂隊, (military music) chün¹ yüeh⁴ tui⁴ 軍樂隊, (strap) tai⁴ 帶; v. (together) chieh² tui⁴ 結隊, (a box) yung¹ tai⁴ chieh² 用帶結.

bandage n. peng¹ tai⁴ 繃帶.

bandit n. t'u² fei³ 土匪. 「覆額髮.

bang n. meng³ chi¹ sheng¹ 猛擊聲, (hair) fu⁴ e² fa³

banish v. fang⁴ chu² 放逐, liu² hsing² 流刑.

banishment n. fang⁴ chu² 放逐, liu² hsing² 流刑.

bank n. yin² hang² 銀行, (of river) an⁴ 岸; ~ **bill**, hui⁴ p'iao⁴ 匯票; ~ **discount**, t'ieh¹ hsien⁴ 貼現.

banker n. yin² hang² chia¹ 銀行家, (gambling) chuang¹ chia¹ 莊家.

banknote n. ch'ao⁴ p'iao⁴ 鈔票.

bankruptcy n. p'o⁴ ch'an³ 破產.

banner n. ch'i² 旗.

baptism n. hsi² li³ 洗禮.

baptist n. shih¹ hsi² li³ che³ 施洗禮者.

baptize v. hsing² hsi² li³ 行洗禮.

bar n. (stick) chang⁴ 杖, (drinks) chiu³ pa¹ chien¹ 酒吧間, (law) fa³ t'ing² 法庭; v. so³ 鎖.

barb n. tao³ kou¹ 倒鈎. 「jen² 化外人.

barbarian n. yeh³ man² jen² 野蠻人, hua⁴ wai⁴

barbarous a. yeh³ man² te¹ 野蠻的, ts'u¹ lu³ te¹ 粗

barber n. li² fa³ shih¹ 理髮師. 「魯的.

bare a. ch'ih⁴ lo³ te¹ 赤裸的.

barefoot a. ch'ih⁴ tsu² te¹ 赤足的.

barely adv. ch'ia⁴ hao³ ti⁴ 恰好地.

bargain n. chiao¹ i⁴ 交易; v. t'an² p'an⁴ 談判.

barge n. yu² t'ing³ 遊艇, hua⁴ fang³ 畫舫.

baritone, barytone n. nan² chung¹ yin¹ 男中音.

bark n. (wood) shu⁴ p'i² 樹皮, (dog) fei⁴ sheng¹ 吠聲, (ship) hsiao³ fan¹ ch'uan² 小帆船; v. ts'a¹ lao⁴ 擦落, (dog) kou⁴ fei⁴ 狗吠.

barley n. ta⁴ mai⁴ 大麥.

barn n. ma³ fang² 馬房.

barnacle n. lo² ssu¹ 螺螄.

baron *n.* nan² chüeh² 男爵.

barometer *n.* ch'ing² yü³ chi¹ 晴雨計.

barracks *n.* ping¹ ying² 兵營. 「鎗身.

barrel *n.* ta⁴ t'ung³ 大桶, (*of gun*) ch'iang¹ shen¹

barren *a.* pu⁴ mao² te¹ 不毛的.

barrier *n.* tsu³ ai¹ 阻礙.

barrister *n.* lü⁴ shih¹ 律師, pien⁴ hu⁴ shıh⁴ 辯護士.

barter *v.* chiao¹ i⁴ 交易.

base *n.* (*music*) ti¹ yin¹ 低音, (*foot*) chu⁴ chiao³ 柱脚, (*foundation*) chi¹ ch'u³ 基礎, (*of operations*) chi¹ ti⁴ 基地, (*chemical*) yen² chi¹ 鹽基, (*baseball*) lei³ 壘; *a.* (*mean*) hsia⁴ chien⁴ te¹ 下賤的.

baseball *n.* (*game*) pang⁴ ch'iu² hsi⁴ 棒球戲.

baseless *a.* wu² ken¹ chü¹ te¹ 無根據的.

basement *n.* ti⁴ hsia⁴ ts'eng² 地下層.

bashful *a.* p'a⁴ hsiu¹ te¹ 怕羞的.

bashfully *adv.* hsiu¹ ch'üeh¹ ti¹ 羞怯地.

basic *a.* chi¹ ch'u³ te¹ 基礎的.

basin *n.* (*for washing*) shui³ p'en² 水盆.

bask *v.* ch'ü² nuan³ 取暖.

basket *n.* lan² 籃, tiao⁴ k'uang¹ 吊筐.

basketball *n.* (*game*) lan² ch'iu² hsi⁴ 籃球戲.

bass *n.* nan² ti¹ yin¹ 男低音, (*music*) ti¹ yin¹ pu⁴ 低 「音部.

bastard *n.* ssu¹ sheng¹ tzu³ 私生子.

baste *v.* (*meat*) t'u² yu² 塗油, (*clothes*) ch'ang² chen¹ feng² jen⁴ 長針縫紉.

bastion *n.* leng² pao³ 稜堡.

bat *n.* pang⁴ 棒, (*animal*) pien¹ fu² 蝙蝠.

bath *n.* mu⁴ yü⁴ 沐浴.

bathe *v.* mu⁴ yü⁴ 沐浴.

bathrobe *n.* yü⁴ i¹ 浴衣.

bathroom *n.* yü⁴ fang² 浴房.

battalion *n.* ying² 營, (*in certain special units*) ta⁴ tui⁴ 大隊; ~ **commander**, ying² chang³ 營長; ~ **headquarters**, ying² pu⁴ 營部.

batter *v.* lien² chi¹ 連擊.

battery *n.* (*artillery*) p'ao⁴ ping¹ lien² 砲兵連, (*electric*) tien⁴ ch'ih² 電池; ~ **commander**, lien² chang³ 連長(砲); ~ **commander's telescope**, chien³ hsing² ching⁴ 剪形鏡(砲); ~ **headquarters**, lien² pu⁴ 連部(砲).

battle *n.* chan⁴ cheng¹ 戰爭.

battlefield *n.* chan⁴ ch'ang³ 戰場.

battlement *n.* chih⁴ tieh⁴ 雉堞.

battleship *n.* chan⁴ chien⁴ 戰艦.

bawdy *a.* yin² tang⁴ te¹ 淫蕩的

bawl *v.* k'uang² chiao⁴ 狂叫.

bay *n.* hai³ wan¹ 海灣. 「劈柯(軍).

bayonet *n.* tz'u¹ tao¹ 刺刀; ～ **fighting,** p'i¹ tz'u⁴

bazaar, bazar; *n.* shih⁴ ch'ang³ 市場.

be *v.* hsi⁴ 係, shih⁴ 是, wei¹ 為.

beach *n.* sha¹ t'an¹ 沙灘.

beachhead *n.* t'an¹ t'ou² pao³ 灘頭堡.

beacon *n.* teng¹ t'a³ 燈塔.

bead *n.* hsiao³ chu¹ 小珠.

beak *n.* niao³ hui⁴ 鳥喙. 「hui¹ 光輝.

beam *n.* (*wood*) heng² liang² 橫梁, (*of light*) kuang¹

bean *n.* tou⁴ 豆.

bear *n.* hu² hsiung² 熊; *v.* (*carry*) hsieh² tai⁴ 攜帶, (*endure*) jen³ shou⁴ 忍受, (*yield*) ch'an³ sheng¹ 產生 (*a child*) sheng¹ yü⁴ 生育.

beard *n.* hu² hsü¹ 翻翻. 「jen² 持票人.

bearer *n.* t'iao¹ fu¹ 挑夫, (*of check*) ch'ih² p'iao⁴

bearing *n.* fu⁴ ho⁴ 負荷, (*direction*) fang¹ wei⁴ 方

beast *n.* shou⁴ 獸. 「位.

beat *v.* (*hit*) chi¹ 擊, (*defeat*) ta³ sheng⁴ 打勝.

beautiful *a.* mei³ li⁴ te¹ 美麗的.

beautify *v.* shih² mei³ li⁴ 使美麗.

beauty *n.* mei³ li⁴ 美麗; ～ **parlor,** mei³ jung²

beaver *n.* hai³ li² 海狸. 「yüan⁴ 美容院.

because *conj.* yin¹ wei² 因為.

beckon *v.* shih⁴ i⁴ 示意.

become *v.* ch'eng² wei² 成為.

bed *n.* ch'uang² 床, wo⁴ t'a⁴ 臥榻.

bedbug *n.* ch'ou⁴ ch'ung² 臭蟲.

bedclothes *n.* ch'in³ i¹ 寢衣.

bedding *n.* pei⁴ ju⁴ 被褥.

bedroom *n.* ch'in³ shih⁴ 寢室.

bedspread *n.* pei⁴ tan¹ 被單.

bedstead *n.* ch'uang² chia⁴ 牀架.

bee *n.* mi⁴ feng¹ 蜜蜂.

beech *n.* shan¹ mao² chü³ 山毛櫸(植).

beef *n.* niu² jou⁴ 牛肉.

beefsteak *n.* niu² p'ai² 牛排.

beehive *n.* feng¹ fang² 蜂房, feng¹ wo¹ 蜂窩.

beer *n.* p'i² chiu³ 啤酒.

beeswax *n.* mi⁴ la⁴ 蜜蠟; *v.* t'u² mi⁴ la⁴ 塗蜜蠟.

beet *n.* t'ien² ts'ai⁴ 甜菜.

beetle *n.* chia³ ch'ung² 甲蟲.

before *prep.* (*time*) tsao³ yü² 早於, (*place*) tsai⁴...te¹ ch'ien² fang¹ 在...的前方; *adv.* tsai⁴ ch'ien² ti⁴ 在前地; *conj.* i³ ch'ien² 以前. 「ch'ien² 在前.

beforehand *a.* i³ ch'ien² te¹ 以前的; *adv.* tsai⁴

befriend *v.* tai⁴ i² yu³ tao⁴ 待以友道.

beg *v.* ch'i³ ch'iu² 乞求.

beget *v.* (*produce*) ch'an³ sheng¹ 產生.

beggar *n.* ch'i³ kai⁴ 乞丐.

begin *v.* k'ai¹ shih³ 開始.

beginner *n.* ch'u¹ hsüeh² che³ 初學者.

beginning *n.* k'ai¹ shih³ 開始.

behave *v.* ch'u³ shen¹ 處身.

behavior *n.* hsing² wei² 行為, p'in³ hsing² 品行.

behead *v.* chan³ shou³ 斬首.

behind *adv., prep.* tsai⁴ hou⁴ 在後, lao⁴ hou⁴ 落後.

behold *v.* chien⁴ 見.

beholder *n.* p'ang² kuan¹ che³ 旁觀者.

being *n.* shih² tsai⁴ 實在. 「信奉.

belch *v.* t'u⁴ ch'u¹ 吐出.

belief *n.* (*trust*) hsin⁴ jen⁴ 信任, (*faith*) hsin⁴ feng⁴

believe *v.* hsin⁴ jen⁴ 信任.

bell *n.* (*large*) chung¹ 鐘, (*small*) ling² 鈴.

bellow *v.* niu² hou³ 牛吼.

bellows *n.* feng¹ hsiang¹ 風箱.

belly *n.* fu⁴ pu⁴ 腹部.

belong *v.* shu³ yü² 屬於.

belongings *n.* ts'ai² wu⁴ 財物.

beloved *a.* hsin¹ ai⁴ te¹ 心愛的.

below *adv., prep.* tsai⁴ hsia⁴ 在下, hsia⁴ 下.

belt *n.* tai⁴ 帶.

bench *n.* ch'ang² teng⁴ 長凳, ch'ang² i³ 長椅.

bend *v.* (*submit*) ch'ü¹ fu² 屈服, (*twist*) shih³ wan¹ ch'ü¹ 使彎曲. 「下.

beneath *adv., prep.* hsia⁴ yü² 下於, tsai⁴ hsia⁴ 在

27

benediction *n.* chu⁴ fu² 祝福.

benefactor *n.* en¹ jen² 恩人.

beneficial *a.* yu³ i⁴ te¹ 有益的.

benefit *n.* li⁴ i⁴ 利益.

benevolence *n.* shan⁴ hsing² 善行.

bent *a.* wai¹ ch'ü¹ te¹ 歪曲的, (*inclined*) ch'ing¹

bequeath *v.* i² tseng⁴ 遺贈.　　　　［hsin¹ te¹ 傾心的.

bequest *n.* i² tseng⁴ 遺贈.

bereave *v.* shih³ sang⁴ shih¹ 使喪失.

beriberi *n.* chiao³ ch'i⁴ ping⁴ 脚氣病.

berry *n.* chiang¹ kuo³ 漿果.

berth *n.* wo⁴ p'u¹ 臥鋪.

beseech *v.* k'en³ ch'iu² 懇求.　　　　　　　　　　「圍.

beset *v.* wei² kung¹ 圍攻, (*surround*) pao¹ wei² 包

beside *prep.* tsai⁴...te¹ p'ang² pien¹ 在...的旁邊.

besides *prep.* ch'u²...i³ wai⁴ 除...以外.

besiege *v.* wei² kung¹ 圍攻.

besieger *n.* wei² kung¹ che³ 圍攻者.

best *a.* tsui⁴ hao³ te¹ 最好的; ~ **man**, nan² pin⁴
　　hsiang⁴ 男儐相; ~ **seller**, ch'ang⁴ hsiao¹ shu¹ 暢

bestow *v.* tz'u⁴ yü³ 賜與.　　　　　　　　「銷書.

bet *v.* tu³ po² 賭博; *n.* tu³ wu⁴ 賭物.

betray *v.* pei⁴ p'an⁴ 背叛.

betroth *v.* hsü³ hun¹ 許婚.　　　　　　「ti¹ 更好地.

better *a.* chiao⁴ hao³ te¹ 較好的; *adv.* keng⁴ hao³

between *prep.* tsai⁴ ch'i² chung¹ 在其中.

beverage *n.* yin³ liao⁴ 飲料.

bewail *v.* ai¹ tao⁴ 哀悼.

beware *v.* liu² hsin¹ 留心, chin³ fang² 謹防.

bewilderment *n.* k'un⁴ huo⁴ 困惑.

beyond *prep.* yüan³ ko² 遠隔; *adv.* tsai⁴ yüan³
　　fang¹ ti⁴ 在遠方地.

bias *n.* (*prejudice*) p'ien¹ ch'a¹ 偏差.

bib *n.* wei² tsui³ 圍嘴.

Bible *n.* sheng⁴ ching¹ 聖經.

biceps *n.* erh⁴ t'ou² chin¹ 二頭筋.

bicycle *n.* tzu⁴ hsing² ch'e¹ 自行車, chiao³ t'a⁴
　　ch'e¹ 脚踏車.

bid *v.* (*command*) ming⁴ ling⁴ 命令, (*offer a price*)
　　ch'u¹ chia¹ 出價.　　　　　　　　「chia⁴ 屍架.

bier *n.* (*coffin*) kuan¹ chia⁴ 棺架, (*dead body*) shih¹

28

big *a.* ta⁴ te¹ 大的.

bile *n.* tan³ chih¹ 膽汁.

bill *n.* chang⁴ tan¹ 賬單; ～ **of fare**, ts'ai⁴ tan¹ 菜單; ～ **of lading**, t'i²⁴ huo⁴ tan¹ 提貨單.

billet *n.* ying² she⁴ 營舍.

billiards *n.* tan⁴ tzu¹ hsi⁴ 彈子戲.

billion *n., a.* (*US & France*) shih² i⁴ 十億, (*Britain & Germany*) wan⁴ i⁴ 萬億, chao⁴ 兆.

billow *n.* chü⁴ lang⁴ 巨浪.

bind *v.* fu² 縛, (*books*) chuang¹ ting¹ 裝釘.

binoculars *n.* shuang¹ yen³ ching⁴ 雙眼鏡.

biography *n.* ch'uan² chi⁴ 傳記.

biology *n.* sheng¹ wu⁴ hsüeh² 生物學.　　　　「學

biophysics *n.* sheng¹ wu⁴ wu⁴ li³ hsüeh² 生物物理

birch *n.* hua⁴ mu⁴ 樺木.

bird *n.* niao³ 鳥.

bird's-eye *a.* niao³ k'an⁴ te¹ 鳥瞰的.

birth *n.* tan⁴ sheng¹ 誕生, (*descent*) chia¹ hsi⁴ 家系; ～ **control**, sheng¹ yü⁴ chieh² chih⁴ 生育節制; ～ **rate**, ch'u¹ sheng¹ lü⁴ 出生率.

birthday *n.* tan⁴ sheng¹ jih⁴ 誕生日.

birthplace *n.* ch'u¹ sheng¹ ti⁴ 出生地.

biscuit *n.* ping³ kan¹ 餅乾.

bishop *n.* chu³ chiao⁴ 主教.

bit *n.* (*portion*) shao² hsü³ 少許, (*horse*) hsien² 銜.

bite *v., n.* yao³ 咬.

bitter *a.* k'u³ te¹ 苦的.

bivouac *n., v.* lu⁴ ying² 露營.

black *a.* hei¹ te¹ 黑的; *v.* shih³ hei¹ 使黑.

blackboard *n.* hei¹ pan³ 黑板.　　　　「毀謗.

blacken *v.* t'u² hei¹ 塗黑, (*speak evil of*) hui³ pang⁴

blackout *n.* teng¹ huo² kuan³ chih⁴ 灯火管制.

blacksmith *n.* t'ieh³ chiang⁴ 鐵匠.

bladder *n.* p'ang² kuang¹ 膀胱.

blade *n.* (*shaving*) tao¹ p'ien⁴ 刀片.

blame *v.* ch'ien³ tse² 譴責.

blameless *a.* wu² tsui⁴ te¹ 無罪的.

blank *n.* k'ung⁴ pai²⁴ ch'u⁴ 空白處; *a.* k'ung⁴ pai²⁴　　　　「te¹ 空白的.

blanket *n.* mao² t'an³ 毛毯.

blaspheme *v.* mao² tu⁴ 冒瀆.

blast *v.* (*blow up*) cha⁴ hui³ 炸毀.

blaze *n.* huo³ yen⁴ 火焰; *v.* fa¹ huo³ yen⁴ 發火焰.

bleach *v.* p'iao³ pai² 漂白.

bleak *a.* (*chilly*) han² leng³ te¹ 寒冷的.

bleat *v.* ming² 鳴.

bleed *v.* ch'u¹ hsüeh⁴ 出血.

blend *v.* hun³ ho² 混合.

bless *v.* chu⁴ fu² 祝福.

blessing *n.* chu⁴ fu² 祝福.

blind *a.* mang² mu⁴ te¹ 盲目的; ～ **flying,** mang² mu⁴ fei¹ hsing² 盲目飛行(軍); ～ **landing,** mang² mu⁴ chiang⁴ lao⁴ 盲目降落(軍).

blindness *n.* mang² mu⁴ 盲目.

blink *v.* sha⁴ yen³ 霎眼; *n.* shan³ kuang¹ 閃光.

bliss *n.* huan¹ le⁴ 歡樂.　　　　「起泡.

blister *n.* shui³ p'ao⁴ 水泡; *v.* shih³ ch'i³ p'ao⁴ 使

blitzkrieg *n.* shan³ tien⁴ chan⁴ 閃電戰(軍).

blizzard *n.* pao⁴ feng¹ hsüeh³ 暴風雪.

block *n.* mu⁴ p'ien⁴ 木片; *v.* feng¹ so³ 封鎖.

blockade *n.* feng¹ so³ 封鎖.

blockhouse *n.* tiao¹ pao³ 碉堡.

blood *n.* hsüeh⁴ 血; ～ **bank,** hsüeh⁴ k'u⁴ 血庫; ～ **transfusion,** shu¹ hsüeh⁴ 輸血; ～ **type,** hsüeh⁴ hsing² 血型; ～ **vessel,** hsüeh⁴ kuan³ 血管.　　「管.

bloodhound *n.* lieh⁴ ch'üan³ 獵犬.

bloody *a.* hsüeh⁴ te¹ 血的.

bloom *v.* k'ai¹ hua¹ 開花.

blossom *n.* k'ai¹ hua¹ 開花.

blot *v.* t'u² wu¹ 塗污; *n.* wu¹ tien³ 污點.

blotter *n.* hsi¹ mo⁴ chih³ 吸墨紙.

blouse *n.* shang⁴ i¹ 上衣.　　　　「ou¹ ta³ 毆打.

blow *v.* ch'ui¹ 吹; *n.* (*blast*) ch'ui¹ feng¹ 吹風, (*hit*)

blue *a.* ch'ing¹ te¹ 青的.

bluebell *n.* tiao⁴ chung¹ hua¹ 吊鐘花.

blueprint *n.* lan² t'u² 藍圖.

bluff *n.* (*cliff*) ch'iao⁴ pi⁴ 峭壁; *v.* tung⁴ ho² 恫嚇.

blunder *n.* ts'o⁴ wu⁴ 錯誤, kuo⁴ shih¹ 過失; *v.* tso⁴ ts'o⁴ 做錯.　　　　　　　　　「直的.

blunt *a.* tun⁴ te¹ 鈍的, (*frank*) shuai³ chih² te¹ 率

bluntly *adv.* wu² li³ ti⁴ 無禮地.

blur *v.* shih³ pu⁴ ming² 使不明.

blush *v.* hsiu¹ ts'an² 羞慚; *n.* mien⁴ ch'ih⁴ 面赤.

boar *n.* yeh³ chu¹ 野猪.

board *n.* pan³ 板, (*committee*) wei³ yüan² hui⁴ 委員會; *v.* (*ship*) shang⁴ ch'uan² 上船, (*feed*) chi shih² 寄食; ～ **of directors**, tung³ shih⁴ hui⁴ 董事會.

boast *v.* k'ua¹ yen² 誇言; *n.* ch'ui¹ niu² 吹牛, tzu⁴

boastful *a.* tzu⁴ fu⁴ te¹ 自負的, ao⁴ man⁴ te¹ 傲慢 └的.

boat *n.* hsiao³ ch'uan² 小船.

boatman *n.* chou¹ tzu¹ 舟子.

bobbin *n.* (*sewing machine*) ssu¹ chüan⁴ 絲卷, (*weaving*) hsi⁴ sheng² 細繩.

bodily *a.* shen¹ t'i³ te¹ 身體的; *adv.* (*as a whole*) ch'üan² t'i³ 全體.

body *n.* shen¹ t'i³ 身體.

bodyguard *n.* wei⁴ tui⁴ 衛隊.

bog *n.* chao³ ti⁴ 沼地.

bogy *n.* e⁴ mo² 惡魔. └fei⁴ 煮沸.

boil *v.* (*liquid*) fei⁴ 沸, (*solids*) chu³ 煮; *n.* chu³

boiler *n.* chu³ ch'i⁴ 煮器.

boisterous *a.* k'uang² pao⁴ te¹ 狂暴的.

bold *a.* ta⁴ tan³ te¹ 大膽的.

bolt *n.* lo² ting¹ 螺釘, (*door*) shuan¹ 閂.

bomb *n.* cha⁴ tan⁴ 炸彈.

bomber *n.* hung¹ cha⁴ chi¹ 轟炸機.

bond *n.* (*government*) kung¹ chai⁴ 公債.

bondage *n.* nu² i⁴ 奴役.

bone *n.* ku³ ko² 骨骼.

bonnet *n.* wu² pien¹ mao⁴ 無邊帽.

bonus *n.* hung² li⁴ 紅利.

book *n.* shu¹ 書; *v.* chi⁴ tsai⁴ 記載.

bookcase *n.* shu¹ ch'u² 書櫥.

bookkeeper *n.* pu⁴ chi⁴ yüan² 簿記員.

bookkeeping *n.* pu⁴ chi⁴ 簿記.

booklet *n.* hsiao² pen³ shu¹ 小本書.

bookseller *n.* shou⁴ shu¹ che³ 售書者.

bookstore *n.* shu¹ tien⁴ 書店.

boot *n.* ch'ang² t'ung³ hsüeh¹ 長統靴.

bootblack *n.* ts'a¹ hsieh¹ jen² 擦靴人.

booth *n.* hsiao³ wu¹ 小屋.

booty *n.* chan⁴ li⁴ p'in³ 戰利品.

borax *n.* p'eng² sha¹ 硼砂.

31

border *n.* pien¹ 邊, (*frontier*) ching⁴ chieh⁴ 境界；
  v. p'i² lien² 毗連.   「k'ung⁴ 穿孔.

bore *v.* (*make weary*) yen⁴ fan² 厭煩, (*drill*) ch'uan¹

borrow *v.* chieh¹ ju⁴ 借入.

bosom *n.* hsiung¹ 胸.

boss *n.* (*foreman*) kung¹ t'ou² 工頭, (*leader*) ling³
  hsiu⁴ 領袖；*v.* chih³ hui¹ 指揮.

botany *n.* chih² wu⁴ hsüeh² 植物學.

both *a.* shuang¹ fang¹ te¹ 雙方的；*pron.* shuang¹

bother *v.* fan² nao³ 煩惱.   「fang¹ 雙方.

bottle *n.* p'ing² 瓶.

bottom *n.* ti³ 底.

bottomless *a.* wu² ti³ te¹ 無底的.

bough *n.* ta⁴ chih¹ 大枝.

boulder *n.* yüan² shih² 圓石.   「hsien⁴ 界線.

bound *v.* (*leap*) t'iao⁴ 跳；*n.* (*boundary*) chieh⁴

boundary *n.* ching⁴ chieh⁴ 境界.

boundless *a.* wu² chieh⁴ hsien⁴ te¹ 無界限的.

bouquet *n.* hua¹ su⁴ 花束.

bourgeois *n.* chung¹ ch'an³ chieh¹ chi² che³ 中產
  階級者；*a.* chung¹ ch'an³ te¹ 中產的.

bourgeoisie *n.* tzu¹ ch'an³ chieh¹ chi² 資產階級.

bout *n.* pi³ sai⁴ 比賽.

bow *n.* chü² kung¹ 鞠躬, (*archery*) kung¹ 弓, (*ship*)
  ch'uan² shou³ 船首；*v.* (*bend the head*) chü²

bowel *n.* ch'ang² 腸.   「kung¹ 鞠躬.

bowl *n.* po¹ 鉢, wan³ 碗.

box *n.* hsiang¹ 箱.

boxer *n.* ch'üan² shu⁴ chia¹ 拳術家.

boxing *n.* ch'üan² shu⁴ 拳術.

boy *n.* nan² hai² 男孩, (*servant*) shih⁴ che³ 侍者；
  ∼ **scout,** t'ung² tzu³ chün¹ 童子軍.

boycott *n.* (*import*) ti³ chih⁴ wai⁴ huo⁴ 抵制外貨.

boyhood *n.* t'ung² nien² shih² tai⁴ 童年時代.

brace *v.* (*support*) chih¹ ch'ih² 支持；*n.* chih¹ chu⁴

bracelet *n.* shou³ cho² 手鐲.   「支柱.

brackish *a.* yu³ yen² wei⁴ te¹ 有鹽味的.

brag *v.* k'ua¹ ta⁴ 誇大, tzu⁴ k'ua¹ 自誇.

brain *n.* nao³ 腦.

brainless *a.* yü² ch'un³ te¹ 愚蠢的, wu² ssu¹
  hsiang³ te¹ 無思想的.

brake *n.* chih⁴tung⁴ chi¹ 制動機, yang² ch'ih³ chih² wu⁴ 羊齒植物.

bramble *n.* ching¹ chi⁴ 荊棘.

bran *n.* fu¹ p'i² 麩皮, k'ang¹ 糠.

branch *n.* (*of tree*) chih¹ 枝, (*division*) pu⁴ men² 部門, (*a local office*) chih¹ tien⁴ 支店.

brand *n.* (*trademark*) shang¹ piao¹ 商標.

brandy *n.* pai⁴ lan² ti⁴ chiu³ 白蘭地酒.

brass *n.* huang² t'ung² 黃銅.　　　　　　「險.

brave *a.* yung² kan³ te⁴ 勇敢的; *v.* mao⁴ hsien³ 冒

bravely *adv.* yung² kan³ ti⁴ 勇敢地.

bravery *n.* yung² kan³ 勇敢.

bray *v.* t'i² 啼, chiao¹ 叫.

brazier *n.* huo³ po¹ 火鉢.

breach *n.* (*violation*) wei² pei⁴ 違背, (*gap*) t'u² p'o⁴ k'ou³ 突破口; ~ **of discipline**, wei² fan³ chün²　　　　　　　　　　　　　　　 「chi⁴ 違反軍紀.

bread *n.* mien⁴ pao¹ 麵包.

breadth *n.* kuang³ k'uo⁴ 廣濶.

break *v.* p'o⁴ lieh⁴ 破裂; *n.* wei² fan³ 違反.

breakdown *n.* chang⁴ ai⁴ 障礙.

breakfast *n.* tsao³ ts'an¹ 早餐.

breakwater *n.* fang² po¹ ti¹ 防波堤.

breast *n.* hsiung¹ 胸.

breastplate *n.* hu⁴ hsiung¹ chia³ 護胸甲.

breast-work *n.* hsiung¹ ch'iang² 胸牆(軍).

breath *n.* ch'i⁴ hsi² 氣息.

breathe *v.* hu¹ hsi¹ 呼吸.

breathless *a.* wu² ch'i⁴ hsi² te¹ 無氣息的.

breed *v.* fan² chih² 繁殖.

breeze *n.* wei² feng¹ 微風.

brethren *n.* ti⁴ hsiung¹ 弟兄, t'ung² pao¹ 同胞.

brevity *n.* chien³ chieh² 簡潔.

brew *v.* niang⁴ tsao⁴ 釀造.

bribe *n.* hui⁴ lu⁴ 賄賂; *v.* hsing² hui⁴ 行賄.

bribery *n.* hsing² hui⁴ 行賄.

brick *n.* chuan¹ wa³ 磚瓦.

bride *n.* hsin¹ niang² 新娘.

bridegroom *n.* hsin¹ lang² 新郎.

bridesmaid *n.* nü³ pin⁴ hsiang⁴ 女儐相.

bridesman *n.* nan² pin⁴ hsiang⁴ 男儐相.

bridge *n.* ch'iao² 橋.

bridle *n.* ma³ le¹ 馬勒.

brief *a.* tuan³ te¹ 短的.

brier, briar *n.* ching¹ chi¹ 荊棘.

brigade *n.* lü³ 旅(軍). 「將.

brigadier *n.* (*brigadier general*) chun³ chiang⁴ 准

bright *a.* kuang¹ ming¹ te¹ 光明的.

brighten *v.* shih³ kuang¹ ming¹ 使光明.

brilliance *n.* kuang¹ tse² 光澤.

brilliant *a.* kuang¹ ming¹ te¹ 光明的.

brim *n.* yüan² 緣, pien¹ 邊.

brine *n.* yen² shui³ 鹽水, hai² shui³ 海水.

bring *v.* tai² lai² 帶來.

brink *n.* ai² 崖.

brisk *a.* ch'ing¹ k'uai⁴ te¹ 輕快的.

briskly *adv.* ch'ing¹ k'uai⁴ ti¹ 輕快地.

bristle *n.* kang¹ mao² 剛毛.

brittle *a.* i⁴ sui⁴ te¹ 易碎的.

broad *a.* kuang³ te¹ 廣的.

broadcast *v.* kuang³ po⁴ 廣播, fang⁴ sung⁴ 放送;

brocade *n.* chin³ tuan⁴ 錦緞. 「n. po⁴ yin¹ 播音.

broil *v.* pei¹ je⁴ 焙熱.

broken *a.* ch'ai¹ tuan⁴ te¹ 拆斷的.

broker *n.* chi⁴ chi⁴ jen⁴ 紀紀人, ch'ien² k'o⁴ 掮客.

bronchitis *n.* ch'i⁴ kuan³ chih⁴ yen² 氣管支炎.

bronze *n.* ch'ing¹ t'ung² 青銅.

brood *n.* i⁴ fu¹ te¹ ch'u² 一孵的雛; *v.* fu¹ 孵.

brook *n.* hsiao³ ch'i¹ 小溪. 「hua¹ 金雀花.

broom *n.* sao⁴ chou³ 掃帚, (*flower*) chin¹ ch'iao³

broth *n.* jou⁴ t'ang¹ 肉湯.

brothel *n.* chi⁴ yüan⁴ 妓院, yao² tzu¹ 窰子.

brother *n.* hsiung¹ ti⁴ 兄弟.

brotherhood *n.* hsiung¹ ti⁴ kuan¹ hsi⁴ 兄弟關係.

brow *n.* (*forehead*) e² 額, (*eyebrow*) mei² mao² 眉

brown *a.* ho² se⁴ te¹ 褐色的. 「毛.

bruise *v.* ta³ shang¹ 打傷.

brush *n.* mao² shua¹ 毛刷; *v.* shua¹ 刷.

brushwood *n.* ts'ung² lin² 叢林.

brutal *a.* ts'an² pao⁴ te¹ 殘暴的.

brute *n.* shou⁴ 獸.

bubble *n.* p'ao⁴ 泡.

buck *n.* (*deer*) mu³ lu⁴ 牡鹿, (*rabbit*) mu³ t'u⁴ 牡兔,

(*goat*) mu³ yang² 牡羊.

bucket *n.* tiao⁴ t'ung³ 吊桶.

buckwheat *n.* ch'iao² mai⁴ 蕎麥.

buckle *n.* k'ou⁴ tzu¹ 扣子.

bud *n.* ya² 芽.

Buddha *n.* fo² 佛.

Buddhist *n.* fo² chiao⁴ t'u² 佛教徒.

Buddhism *n.* fo² chiao⁴ 佛教.

budget *n.* yü⁴ suan⁴ 預算.

bug *n.* ch'ou⁴ ch'ung² 臭蟲.

bugle *n.* la³ pa¹ 喇叭, (*military*) chün¹ hao⁴ 軍號.

bugler *n.* la³ pa¹ shou³ 喇叭手, (*military*) hao⁴ ping¹ 號兵(軍).

build *v.* chien⁴ chu² 建築.

building *n.* chien⁴ chu² wu⁴ 建築物.

bulb *n.* ch'iu² ching¹ 球莖, (*electric*) tien⁴ teng¹ p'ao⁴ 電燈泡.

bulk *n.* ta⁴ hsiao³ 大小.

bulky *a.* lung² ta⁴ te¹ 龐大的.

bull *n.* mu³ niu² 牡牛.

bullet *n.* tzu³ tan⁴ 子彈.

bulletin *n.* kao⁴ shih⁴ 告示.

bullfight *n.* tou⁴ niu² 鬥牛.

bullfrog *n.* i⁴ chung³ shih² yung⁴ wa¹ 一種食用蛙.

bump *v.* chuang⁴ 撞; *n.* meng³ chi¹ 猛擊.

bunch *n.* i² shu⁴ 一束.

bundle *n.* shu⁴ 束, (*parcel*) pao¹ 包.

bunk *n.* chia⁴ ch'uang² 架床.

buoy *n.* fu² piao¹ 浮標, (*life buoy*) chiu⁴ sheng¹ ch'uan¹ 救生圈.

burden *n.* fu⁴ ho⁴ 負荷, chung⁴ ho⁴ 重荷.

burdensome *a.* kuo⁴ chung⁴ te¹ 過重的.

bureau *n.* i¹ kuei⁴ 衣櫃, (*government*) pu⁴ 部, chü² 局, ch'u⁴ 處, so³ 所; ~ of the Budget (US), yü⁴ suan⁴ chü² 預算局(美).

bureaucracy *n.* kuan¹ liao² chu³ i⁴ 官僚主義, kuan¹ liao² cheng⁴ chih⁴ 官僚政治.

burglar *n.* yeh⁴ tao⁴ 夜盜.

burial *n.* mai² tsang⁴ 埋葬.

burlesque *n.* ta⁴ t'ui³ hsi⁴ 大腿戲.

burn *v.* (*by fire*) shao¹ 燒; (*to destroy by fire*) shao¹ hui³ 燒燬; *n.* huo³ shang¹ 火傷.

burrow *n.* hsüeh⁴ 穴; *v.* (*live*) hsüeh⁴ chü¹ 穴居.

burst *v., n.* pao⁴ lieh⁴ 爆裂.

35

bury v. mai² tsang¹ 埋葬.

bus n. kung¹ kung⁴ ch'i⁴ ch'e¹ 公共汽車.

bush n. hsiao³ kuan⁴ mu⁴ 小灌木.

busily adv. ts'ung¹ mang² ti⁴ 匆忙地.

business n. (occupation) chih² yeh⁴ 職業, (matter) shih⁴ wu⁴ 事務.

bust n. (art) pan⁴ shen¹ hsiang⁴ 半身像.

bustle v. hsüan¹ nao⁴ 喧閙.

busy a. mang² lu⁴ te¹ 忙碌的.

but conj. k'o³ shih⁴ 可是; prep. ch'u² 除.

butcher n. t'u² fu¹ 屠夫.

butler n. nan² kuan³ chia¹ 男管家.

butt n. ti³ pu⁴ 底部, (range) she⁴ to³ 射梁(軍); ∼ **plate**, t'o¹ ti² pan³ 托底鈑(兵); ∼ **swivel**, p'i² tai⁴ k'ou⁴ huan² 皮帶扣環(兵).

butter n. huang² yu² 黃油, nai³ yu² 奶油.

butterfly n. hu² t'ieh² 蝴蝶.

button n. niu³ k'ou⁴ 鈕釦; v. k'ou⁴ chin³ 扣緊.

buttonhole n. niu³ k'ou⁴ k'ung³ 鈕釦孔.

buttress n. fu² ch'iang² 扶牆.

buy v. kou⁴ mai³ 購買.

by adv. tsai⁴ ts'e⁴ ti⁴ 在側地; prep. (near) tsai⁴...ts'e⁴ 在...側, (through) ching¹ 經, (by means of) yu² 由, (before) tsai⁴...ch'ien² 在...前. 「往事.

bygone a. kuo⁴ ch'ü⁴ te¹ 過去的; n. wang³ shih⁴

by-path n. chien⁴ tao⁴ 間道, chih¹ lu⁴ 支路.

by-product n. fu⁴ ch'an² p'in³ 副產品.

bystander n. p'ang² kuan¹ che² 旁觀者.

C

cab n. (taxicab) ch'u¹ tsu¹ ch'i⁴ ch'e¹ 出租汽車. (carriage) ch'u¹ tsu¹ shiao² ma³ ch'e¹ 出租小馬車.

cabaret n. t'iao⁴ wu³ ch'ang³ 跳舞場.

cabbage n. chüan³ shin¹ ts'ai⁴ 卷心菜.

cabin n. hsiao³ wu¹ 小室, (ship) fang² ts'ang¹ 房艙, (airplane) chi¹ ts'ang¹ 機艙.

cabinet n. kuei¹ 櫃, (government) nei⁴ ko² 內閣.

cable n. (rope) sheng² so³ 繩索, (underwater) hai²

ti³ tien⁴ pao⁴ 海底電報.　　「fang² 商船上廚房.

caboose *n.* (*ship*) shang¹ ch'uan² shang⁴ ch'u²

cacao *n.* (*tree*) k'o² k'o³ shu⁴ 可可樹, (*seeds*) k'o²
·k'o³ tzu¹ 可可子.　　「軍官學校學生.

cadet *n.* chün¹ kuan¹ hsüeh² hsiao⁴ hsüeh² sheng¹

cadre *n.* kan⁴ pu⁴ 幹部.

cage *n.* (*bird*) lung² 籠.

caisson *n.* tan⁴ yao⁴ ch'e¹ 彈藥車.

cake *n.* ping³ 餅.

calamity *n.* tsai¹ huo⁴ 災禍.

calculate *v.* chi⁴ suan⁴ 計算.

calculation *n.* chi⁴ suan⁴ 計算.

calendar *n.* jih⁴ li⁴ 日曆, (*lunar*) yin¹ li⁴ 陰曆
(*solar*) yang² li⁴ 陽曆.

calf *n.* tu² 犢, (*leg*) hsiao² t'ui⁴ 小腿.

calico *n.* yang² pu⁴ 洋布.

call *v.* hu¹ han³ 呼喊, (*visit*) fang³ wen⁴ 訪問, (*telephone*) ta³ tien⁴ hua⁴ 打電話, (*give a name to*)
chiao⁴ 叫; "~ off!" pao⁴ shu⁴ 報數(軍); ~ **the**
roll, tien³ ming² 點名.

calm *a.* chen⁴ ching⁴ te¹ 鎮靜的.

camel *n.* lo⁴ t'o² 駱駝.

camellia *n.* shan¹ ch'a² 山茶.

camera *n.* chao¹ hsiang⁴ chi¹ 照相機.

camouflage *n.*, *v.* wei⁴ chuang¹ 僞裝; ~ **discipline,** wei⁴ chuang¹ chün¹ chi⁴ 僞裝軍紀; ~ **net,**
wei⁴ chuang¹ wang³ 僞裝網(軍).

camp *n.* ying² ti⁴ 營地; *v.* lu⁴ ying² 紮營.

campaign *n.* (*operations*) chan⁴ i⁴ 戰役, (*activi-
ties*) yün² tung⁴ 運動, (*election*) hsüan² chü³ yün⁴
tung⁴ 選舉運動.

camphor *n.* chang¹ nao³ 樟腦.

campus *n.* hsüeh² hsiao⁴ ch'ang³ ti⁴ 學校場地.

can *n.* kuan⁴ 罐; *v.* *aux.* neng² 能, k'o³ 可.

canal *n.* yün⁴ ho² 運河.

canary *n.* chin¹ ssu¹ ch'iao² 金絲雀.

cancel *v.* ch'ü³ hsiao¹ 取消.

cancellation *n.* ch'ü³ hsiao¹ 取消.

cancer *n.* yen² 癌(醫).

candidate *n.* hou⁴ pu² che⁴ 候補者.

candle *n.* la¹ chu² 蠟燭.

candlelight *n.* chu² kuang¹ 燭光.

candlestick *n.* chu² t'ai² 燭臺.

candy *n.* t'ang² kuo³ 糖果.

cane *n.* kan¹ che⁴ 甘蔗.

cannibal *n.* shih² jen² jou⁴ che³ 食人肉者.

cannon *n.* ta⁴ p'ao⁴ 大砲, chia¹ nung² p'ao⁴ 加農 ⌈砲.

cannot *v.* pu⁴ neng² 不能.

canoe *n.* tu² mu⁴ chou¹ 獨木舟.

canopy *n.* ping² 屏, mu⁴ 幕.

canteen *n.* (*container*) shui³ hu² 水壺, (*post exchange*) chün¹ chung¹ fan⁴ mai⁴ pu⁴ 軍中販賣部.

canvas *n.* fan¹ pu⁴ 帆布.

canvass *v.* k'ao³ ch'a² 考查.

cap *n.* mao⁴ 帽.

capable *a.* yu³ tzu¹ ko² te¹ 有資格的.

capacity *n.* jung² liang⁴ 容量. ⌈角.

cape *n.* p'i¹ chien¹ 披肩, (*headland*) hai³ chiao³ 海

capital *a.* chu³ yao⁴ te¹ 主要的; *n.* (*city*) shou³ tu¹ 首都, (*letter*) ta⁴ hsieh³ tzu⁴ mu³ 大寫字母, (*money*) tzu¹ pen³ 資本.

capitalism *n.* tzu¹ pen² chu³ i⁴ 資本主義.

capitol *n.* i⁴ shih⁴ so³ 議事所.

captain *n.* (*army*) shang¹ wei⁴ 上尉, (*navy*) shang⁴ hsiao⁴ 上校, (*of a team in sports*) tui⁴ chang³ 隊 長, (*of warship*) chien⁴ chang³ 艦長, (*of merchant ship*) ch'uan² chang³ 船長.

captive *n.* fu² lu³ 俘虜. ⌈獲.

capture *n.* pu³ huo⁴ wu⁴ 捕獲物; *v.* pu³ huo⁴ 捕

car *n.* ch'e¹ 車, (*auto*) ch'i⁴ ch'e¹ 汽車.

caravan *n.* lü³ hsing² tui⁴ 旅行隊. ⌈卡賓館.

carbine *n.* tuan³ ch'iang¹ 短鎗, k'a³ pin¹ ch'iang¹

carbolic *a.* shih² t'an⁴ suan¹ te¹ 石炭酸的.

carbon *n.* t'an⁴ 炭.

carburetor *n.* hua⁴ yu² ch'i⁴ 化油器(汽).

carcass *n.* shih¹ t'i³ 屍體.

card *n.* (*playing*) chih³ p'ai² 紙牌, (*calling*) ming² p'ien⁴ 名片; ～ **system,** k'a³ p'ien⁴ chih⁴ 卡片 ⌈制.

cardboard *n.* chih³ pan³ 紙板.

cardinal *n.* hung² i¹ chu³ chiao⁴ 紅衣主教.

care *n.* (*worry*) yu¹ lü⁴ 憂慮; *v.* kua⁴ lü⁴ 掛慮.

career *n.* ching¹ li⁴ 經歷.

careful *a.* hsiao³ hsin¹ te¹ 小心的, chin³ shen⁴ te¹ 謹慎的.

careless *a.* pu² chu⁴ i⁴ te¹ 不注意的, pu⁴ chin³ shen⁴ te¹ 不謹慎的. 「輕率.

carelessness *n.* pu² chu⁴ i⁴ 不注意, ch'ing¹ shuai⁴

carmine *n.* yang² hung² 洋紅.

caress *v.* ch'ung³ ai⁴ 寵愛.

cargo *n.* huo⁴ ch'uan² 貨船.

carnival *n.* k'uang² huan² chieh² 狂歡節.

carol *n.* sung⁴ ko¹ 頌歌.

carp *n.* li³ yü² 鯉魚.

carpenter *n.* mu⁴ chiang⁴ 木匠.

carpet *n.* ti⁴ chan¹ 地氈.

carrier *n.* (*aircraft*) hang² k'ung¹ mu³ chien⁴ 航空母艦; ~ **pigeon,** t'ung¹ hsin⁴ ko¹ 通信鴿.

carrot *n.* hu² lo² po⁴ 胡蘿蔔.

carry *v.* (*take*) hsieh² tai⁴ 携帶, (*transport*) 「sung⁴ 運送.

cart *n.* ch'ing¹ pien⁴ huo⁴ ch'e¹ 輕便貨車. 「汤.

cartoon *n.* feng³ tz'u⁴ hua⁴ 諷刺畫, k'a³ t'ung¹ 卡

cartridge *n.* tzu³ tan⁴ 子彈; ~ **belt,** tzu³ tan⁴ tai⁴ 子彈帶; ~ **clip,** tzu³ tan⁴ chia¹ 子彈夾.

carve *v.* (*sculpture*) tiao¹ k'o¹ 彫刻.

carver *n.* (*sculptor*) taio¹ k'o¹ chia¹ 彫刻家.

case *n.* (*condition*) ch'ang² hsing² 情形, (*disease*) ping⁴ cheng⁴ 病症, (*affair*) shih⁴ chien⁴ 事件, (*law*) an⁴ chien⁴ 案件, (*box*) hsiang¹ 箱.

casement *n.* ch'uang¹ fei¹ 窗扉.

cash *n.* hsien⁴ chin¹ 現金; *v.* tui⁴ huan⁴ hsien⁴ chin¹ 兌換現金.

cashier *n.* ch'u¹ na⁴ yüan² 出納員.

cask *n.* hsiao² t'ung³ 小桶.

casket *n.* (*coffin*) kuan¹ ts'ai² 棺材.

cast *v.* t'ou² she⁴ 投射.

caste *n.* chieh¹ chi² 階級(印度).

castle *n.* ch'eng² pao³ 城堡.

casualty *n.* shang¹ wang² 傷亡.

cat *n.* mao¹ 貓.

catalogue, catalog *n.* mu⁴ lu⁴ 目錄.

catastrophe *n.* tsai¹ huo⁴ 災禍.

catch *v.* pu³ cho¹ 捕捉.

category *n.* chung³ lei⁴ 種類.

caterpillar n. mao² ch'ung² 毛蟲.

cathedral n. ta⁴ li³ pai⁴ t'ang² 大禮拜堂.

Catholic a. t'ien¹ chu³ chiao⁴ te¹ 天主教的.

cattle n. niu² 牛.

cause v. je² ch'i³ 惹起; n. (origin) yüan² yin¹ 原因, (purpose) li³ yu² 理由, (lawsuit) su⁴ sung⁴ 訴訟. ⌈kao⁴ 忠告.

caution n. chin³ shen⁴ 謹慎, (warning) chung¹

cautious a. chin³ shen⁴ te¹ 謹慎的.

cavalry n. ch'i² ping¹ 騎兵.

cave n. tung⁴ 洞.

cavity n. tung⁴ 洞.

cease v. t'ing² chih³ 停止.

ceaseless a. pu⁴ t'ing² te¹ 不停的.

ceiling n. t'ien¹ hua¹ pan³ 天花板, (prices) hsien⁴ chia⁴ 限價.

celebrate v. chu⁴ ho⁴ 祝賀.

celebration n. ch'ing⁴ chu⁴ 慶祝.

celerity n. hsün⁴ su² 迅速.

celery n. ch'in² ts'ai⁴ 芹菜.

cell n. (hermit) yin³ she⁴ 隱舍, (prison) chien¹ fang² 監房, (of body) hsi⁴ pao¹ 細胞, (electric) tien⁴ ch'ih² 電池.

cellar n. ti⁴ hsia⁴ shih⁴ 地下室.

cemetery n. mu⁴ ti⁴ 墓地.

censer n. hsiang¹ lu² 香爐.

censure v. chih³ chai¹ 指摘.

census n. hu⁴ k'ou³ tiao⁴ ch'a² 戶口調查.

cent n. fen¹ 分.

center n. chung¹ hsin¹ 中心.

centigrade a. yu² pai³ tu⁴ te¹ 有百度的.

centipede n. wu² kung¹ 蜈蚣.

central a. chung¹ yang¹ te¹ 中央的; ~ **government**, chung¹ yang¹ cheng⁴ fu³ 中央政府; ~ **People's Government Council****, chung¹ yang¹ jen² min² cheng⁴ fu³ wei³ yüan² hui⁴ 中央人民政府委員會; ~ **Military Academy***, chung¹ yang¹ chün¹ hsiao⁴ 中央軍校.

century n. shih⁴ chi⁴ 世紀.

cerebral a. ta⁴ nao³ te¹ 大腦的; ~ **anaemia**, nao³ p'in² hsüeh⁴ 腦貧血(醫); ~ **hemorrhage**, ta⁴ nao³ ch'u¹ hsüeh⁴ 大腦出血(醫).

ceremony n. i² shih⁴ 儀式.

certain *a.* ch'üeh⁴ ting⁴ te¹ 確定的.

certificate *n.* cheng⁴ ming² shu¹ 證明書.

certify *v.* cheng⁴ ming² 證明.

cessation *n.* t'ing² chih³ 停止.

chaff *n.* k'ang¹ 糠.

chain *n.* lien⁴ t'iao² 鏈條.

chair *n.* i³ tzu¹ 椅子.

chairman *n.* hui⁴ chang³ 會長, chu³ hsi² 主席.

chalk *n.* (*for writing*) fen² pi³ 粉筆. 「戰.

challenge *n.* t'iao³ chan⁴ 挑戰; *v.* t'iao³ chan⁴ 挑

challenger *n.* t'iao³ chan⁴ che³ 挑戰者.

chamber *n.* shih⁴ 室.

champagne *n.* hsiang¹ pin¹ chiu³ 香檳酒.

champion *n.* hsüan² shou³ 選手.

chance *n.* (*opportunity*) chi¹ hui⁴ 機會.

change *n.* pien⁴ hua⁴ 變化, (*money*) hsiao³ ch'ien²
小錢; *v.* keng¹ huan⁴ 更換.

changeable *a.* i⁴ pien⁴ te¹ 易變的.

channel *n.* ho² ch'uang² 河床.

chaos *n.* hun⁴ luan⁴ 混亂.

chapel *n.* hsiao³ chiao⁴ t'ang² 小敎堂.

chapter *n.* chang¹ 章.

character *n.* hsing⁴ ko² 性格, (*person*) jen² wu⁴ 人
物, (*written*) tzu⁴ t'i³ 字體.

charcoal *n.* mu⁴ t'an⁴ 木炭.

charge *v.* (*load*) chuang¹ t'ien² 裝塡, (*electric*)
ch'ung¹ tien⁴ 充電, (*accuse*) k'ung⁴ kao⁴ 控告,
(*price*) so³ chia⁴ 索價.

charitable *a.* jen² tz'u² te¹ 仁慈的.

charity *n.* tz'u² shan⁴ 慈善. 「hsiao¹ hun² 銷魂.

charm *n.* mo² li⁴ 魔力, (*amulet*) fu² chou⁴ 符咒; *v.*

chart *n.* ti⁴ t'u² 地圖.

charter *n.* t'e⁴ hsü³ chuang⁴ 特許狀.

chase *v.* chui¹ pu³ 追捕; *n.* (*hunting*) lieh⁴ 獵.

chassis *n.* ch'e¹ chia⁴ 車架.

chat *v.* hsien² t'an² 閒談.

chauffeur *n.* ch'i⁴ ch'e¹ fu¹ 汽車夫.

cheap *a.* chia⁴ lien² te¹ 價廉的.

cheat *v.* ch'i¹ p'ien¹ 欺騙.

check *v.* (*hold back*) tsu² chih³ 阻止, (*examine*)
chiao⁴ tui⁴ 校對; *n.* (*bank*) chih¹ p'iao⁴ 支票.

41

checkbook n. chih¹ p'iao⁴ pen³ 支票本.

checkerboard n. ch'i² p'an² 棋盤.

cheek n. chia² 頰.

cheer v. (*shout*) huan¹ hu¹ 歡呼.

cheerful a. yü² k'uai⁴ te¹ 愉快的.

cheese n. kan¹ lo⁴ 乾酪.

chemical n. hua⁴ hsüeh² chih⁴ p'in³ 化學製品; a. hua⁴ hsüeh² te¹ 化學的; **~ warfare,** hua⁴ hsüeh² chan⁴ 化學戰(軍).

chemist n. hua⁴ hsüeh² chia¹ 化學家.

chemistry n. hua⁴ hsüeh² 化學.

cherry n. (*blossom*) ying¹ t'ao² 櫻桃, (*tree*) ying¹ t'ao² shu⁴ 櫻桃樹.

chess n. ch'i² 棋.

chest n. hsiung¹ 胸, (*box*) hsiang¹ 箱.

chestnut n. li⁴ tzu¹ 栗子.

chew v. chüeh² 嚼.

chicken n. hsiao³ chi¹ 小雞; **~ pox,** shui³ tou⁴ 水痘.

chief n. shou² ling³ 首領.

child n. hsiao³ hai² 小孩.

childhood n. yu⁴ nien² shih² tai⁴ 幼年時代.

chill n. han² leng³ 寒冷.

chime n. (*bell*) chung¹ sheng¹ 鐘聲; v. chung¹ ming² 鐘鳴.

chimney n. yen¹ ch'uang¹ 煙窗.

chin n. k'o² 頦.

china n. tz'u² ch'i⁴ 磁器.

chip n. hsiao³ p'ien⁴ 小片; v. ch'ieh¹ sui⁴ 切碎.

chisel n. tsao² 鑿.

chlorine n. lü⁴ ch'i⁴ 氯氣.

chloroform n. mi² meng² yao⁴ 迷蒙藥.

chocolate n. (*candy*) ch'iao¹ k'o³ lü⁴ t'ang² 巧可律糖.

choice n. hsüan³ tse² 選擇.

choir n. (*church*) ch'ang⁴ shih¹ pan¹ 唱詩班, ch'ang⁴ ko¹ tui⁴ 唱歌隊.

choke v. chih⁴ hsi² 窒息.

cholera n. huo⁴ luan⁴ 霍亂(醫).

choose v. hsüan³ tse² 選擇.

chop v. (*cut*) ch'ieh¹ sui⁴ 切碎.

chopsticks n. k'uai⁴ tzu¹ 筷子.

chorus n. ho² ch'ang⁴ tui⁴ 合唱隊, (*composition*) ho² ch'ang⁴ ch'ü² 合唱曲.

Christ n. chi¹ tu¹ 基督.

Christian *n.* chi¹ tu¹ chiao⁴ t'u² 基督教徒.

Christianity *n.* chi¹ tu¹ chiao⁴ 基督教.

Christmas *n.* sheng⁴ tan⁴ chieh² 聖誕節; ~**card,** sheng⁴ tan⁴ k'a³ 聖誕卡; ~ **carol** sheng⁴ tan⁴ sung⁴ ko¹ 聖誕頌歌; ~**Day,** sheng⁴ tan⁴ jih⁴ 聖誕日; ~ **Eve,** sheng⁴ tan⁴ ch'ien¹ hsi¹ 聖誕前夕; ~ **present,** sheng⁴ tan⁴ li³ wu⁴ 聖誕禮物.

chrysanthemum *n.* chü² hua¹ 菊花.

chuckle *n.,* *v.* ch'ih¹ chih¹ erh² hsiao⁴ 吃吃而笑.

church *n.* chiao⁴ t'ang² 教堂.

cicada *n.* ch'an² 蟬.

cider *n.* p'in² kuo³ chih¹ 蘋果汁.

cigar *n.* hsüeh³ ch'ieh² yen¹ 雪茄煙.

cigarette *n.* chih³ yen¹ 紙煙, hsiang¹ yen¹ 香煙.

cinder *n.* mei² cha¹ 煤渣.

cinema *n.* huo² tung⁴ tien⁴ ying³ 活動電影.

cinemascope *n.* hsin¹ i⁴ tsung⁴ ho² t'i³ tien⁴ ying³ 新藝綜合體電影. 「hsing² 流行.

circle *n.* yüan² chou¹ 圓周; *v.* (*trip*) huan²

circuit *n.* hsün² hui² 巡迴, (*electric*) tien⁴ lu⁴ 電路.

circular *a.* yüan² te¹ 圓的.

circulate *v.* hsün² huan² 循環.

circulation *n.* hsün² huan² 循環.

circumference *n.* yüan² chou¹ 圓周.

circumstance *n.* ching³ yü⁴ 境遇.

circus *n.* ma³ hsi⁴ 馬戲.

cistern *n.* chi¹ shui³ ch'u⁴ 積水處.

cite *v.* yin³ yung⁴ 引用. 「嘉獎.

citation *n.* (*for outstanding service*) chia¹ chiang³

citizen *n.* kuo² min² 國民, kung¹ min² 公民.

citizenship *n.* kung¹ min² ch'üan² 公民權.

city *n.* shih⁴ 市.

civil *a.* kuo² nei⁴ te¹ 國內的, (*polite*) yu² li³ te¹ 有禮的; ~ **Aeronautics Board (US),** min² yung⁴ hang² k'ung¹ chü² 民用航空局(美).

civilian *n.* p'ing² min² 平民.

civilization *n.* wen² ming² 文明.

civilize *v.* chiao⁴ hua⁴ 教化.

claim *n.* ch'üan² li⁴ 權利; *v.* (*demand*) yao¹ ch'iu² 要求, (*insist*) chien¹ ch'ih² 堅持.

clam *n.* ko² 蛤, pang⁴ 蚌.

clan *n.* t'ung² tsung¹ 同宗.

clap *n.* (*applause*) ku² chang³ 鼓掌.

clash *v.* p'eng⁴ chi¹ 碰擊.

clasp *v.* chin³ wo⁴ 緊握.

class *n.* (*sort*) chung³ lei⁴ 種類, (*school*) pan¹ 班, (*rank of society*) chieh¹ chi² 階級, (*grade*) teng³ chi² 等級; ～ **struggle****, chieh¹ chi² tou⁴ cheng¹ 階級鬥爭**.

classification *n.* fen¹ lei⁴ 分類.

classify *v.* fen¹ lei⁴ 分類.

classmate *n.* t'ung² pan¹ t'ung² hsüeh¹ 同班同學.

clause *n.* (*in an agreement*) t'iao² k'uan³ 條款.

claw *n.* chua³ 爪.

clay *n.* nien² t'u³ 黏土. ┌ch'ing¹ 使潔淨.

clean *a.* ch'ing¹ chieh² te¹ 清潔的; *v.* shih³ chieh²

cleanliness *n.* ch'ing¹ chieh² 清潔.

cleanse *v.* shih³ ch'ing¹ chieh² 使清潔.

clear *a.* ch'ing² lang³ te¹ 晴朗的, (*easily understood*) ming² pai² te¹ 明白的; *v.* ch'eng² ch'ing¹ 澄

clearly *adv.* ming² liao³ ti² 明瞭地. └清.

clench *v.* chin³ wo⁴ 緊握.

clergyman *n.* mu⁴ shih¹ 牧師. ┌書記.

clerk *n.* (*store*) tien⁴ yüan² 店員, (*office*) shu¹ chi⁴

clever *a.* ts'ung¹ ming² te¹ 聰明的.

cleverness *n.* ts'ung¹ ming² 聰明. ┌k'o⁴ 顧客.

client *n.* tang¹ shih⁴ jen² 當事人, (*customer*) ku⁴

cliff *n.* hsüan² ai² 懸崖, chüeh² pi⁴ 絕壁.

climate *n.* ch'i⁴ hou⁴ 氣候.

climax *n.* ting² tien³ 頂點.

climb *v.* p'an¹ teng¹ 攀登.

cling *v.* chin³ t'ieh¹ 緊貼.

clip *n.* (*gun*) tan⁴ chia¹ 彈夾.

clique *n.* hsi⁴ 系, tang³ 黨.

cloak *n.* wai⁴ t'ao⁴ 外套.

clock *n.* chung¹ 鐘.

close *v.* kuan¹ pi⁴ 關閉; *a.* chieh¹ chin⁴ te¹ 接近的, (*intimate*) ch'in¹ je⁴ te¹ 親熱的; ～ **combat**, chin⁴ chan⁴ 近戰(軍).

closet *n.* (*toilet*) pien⁴ so³ 便所.

clot *v.* ning² chieh² 凝結.

cloth *n.* pu⁴ 布.

clothe *v.* ch'uan¹ 穿.

clothes *n.* i¹ fu² 衣服.

clothing *n.* i¹ fu² 衣服.

cloud *n.* yün² 雲.

cloudless *a.* wu² yün¹ te¹ 無雲的.

cloudy *a.* yu² yün² te¹ 有雲的.

clown *n.* hsiao² ch'ou³ 小丑.

club *n.* chü¹ le⁴ pu⁴ 俱樂部.

clue *n.* hsien⁴ so³ 線索.

clumsy *a.* cho¹ lieh⁴ te¹ 拙劣的.

cluster *n.* i⁴ ch'ün² 一羣; *v.* ch'eng² ch'ün² 成羣.

coach *n.* ta⁴ ma³ ch'e¹ 大馬車, (*railway*) k'o⁴ ch'e¹ 客車, (*athletic*) chih² tao² che³ 指導者.

coal *n.* mei² 煤.

coalition *n.* lien² ho² 聯合; ～ **government,** lien² ho² cheng⁴ fu³ 聯合政府.

coarse *a.* ts'u¹ ta⁴ te¹ 粗大的.

coast *n.* hai³ pin¹ 海濱; ～ **artillery,** hai³ an⁴ p'ao⁴ ping¹ 海岸砲兵.

coat *n.* shang⁴ i¹ 上衣.

cobbler *n.* pu³ hsieh² chiang⁴ 補鞋匠.

cobweb *n.* chu¹ wang³ 蛛網.

cock *n.* hsiung² chi¹ 雄雞.

cocoa *n.* k'o² k'o² fen³ 可可粉.

cocoon *n.* chien³ 繭.

cod *n.* min³ 鰵. 「密碼.

code *n.* (*standard*) fa² tien³ 法典, (*secret*) mi⁴ ma³

coeducation *n.* nan² nü³ t'ung² hsüeh² 男女同學.

coffee *n.* k'a¹ fei¹ 咖啡.

coffin *n.* kuan¹ 棺.

coil *v.* p'an² jao⁴ 盤繞; *n.* hsien⁴ ch'üan¹ 線圈.

coin *n.* huo⁴ pi⁴ 貨幣.

coincide *v.* (*correspond*) i² chih⁴ 一致.

coincidence *n.* i² chih⁴ 一致.

cold *a.* han² leng³ te¹ 寒冷的; *n.* shang¹ han² 傷寒, kan³ mao⁴ 感冒. 「章.

collar *n.* ling³ 領; ～ **insignia,** ling³ chang¹ 領

colleague *n.* t'ung² liao² 同僚, t'ung² shih⁴ 同事.

collect *v.* shou¹ chi² 收集. 「集款.

collection *n.* sou¹ chi² 蒐集, (*offering*) chi² k'uan³

collective *a.* chi² ho² te¹ 集合的; ～ **Farm****,

chi² t'i³ nung² ch'ang³ 集體農場**; ～ **security,** chi² t'i³ an¹ ch'üan² 集體安全.

college n. hsüeh² yüan⁴ 學院.

collide v. p'eng⁴ chuang¹ 碰撞.

collision n. p'eng⁴ chuang¹ 碰撞.

colloquial a. t'u³ hua⁴ te¹ 土話的.

colonel n. shang⁴ hsiao⁴ 上校.

colonist n. chih² min² 殖民.

colony n. chih² min² ti⁴ 殖民地.　　　「染色.

color n. yen² se⁴ 顏色, (flag) ch'i² 旗; v. jan³ se⁴

color-blind a. se⁴ mang² te¹ 色盲的.

colt n. hsiao² ma³ 小馬.　　　　　　　「tui⁴ 隊.

column n. yüan² chu⁴ 圓柱, (formation) tsung¹

comb n. mu⁴ shu¹ 木梳.

combat n. chan⁴ tou⁴ 戰鬪; ～ **area,** chan⁴ tou⁴ ti⁴ yü⁴ 戰鬪地域(軍); ～ **order,** chan⁴ tou⁴ ming⁴ ling⁴ 戰鬪命令(軍); ～ **team.** chan⁴ tou⁴ ch'ün² 戰鬪群(軍).

combination n. lien² ho² 聯合.

combine v. chieh¹ ho² 結合, lien² ho² 聯合.

come v. lai² 來.

comedian n. pan⁴ yen² hsi³ chü⁴ che³ 扮演喜劇者.

comedy n. hsi³ chü⁴ 喜劇.

comfort n., v. an¹ wei⁴ 安慰.

comfortable a. shu¹ shih⁴ te¹ 舒適的.

comic a. hsi³ chü⁴ te¹ 喜劇的.

comma n. tou⁴ tien³ 逗點.

command n. ming⁴ ling⁴ 命令; v. chih³ hui¹ 指揮; ～ **car,** chih³ hui¹ ch'e¹ 指揮車(軍).

commander n. chih³ hui¹ kuan¹ 指揮官, ssu¹ ling⁴ kuan¹ 司令官, (navy) chung¹ hsiao⁴ 中校(海).

commemorate v. chi⁴ nien⁴ 紀念.

commence v. k'ai¹ shih³ 開始.

commencement n. ch'i² shih³ 起始, (school) pi⁴ 「yeh⁴ li³ 畢業禮.

commend v. t'ui¹ chien⁴ 推薦.

comment v. p'i¹ p'ing² 批評.

commerce n. shang¹ yeh⁴ 商業.

commercial a. shang¹ yeh⁴ te¹ 商業的.

commission n. wei³ jen⁴ 委任, (committee) wei³ yüan² hui⁴ 委員會, (pay) yung⁴ chin¹ 佣金; ～ **of Legislative Affairs****, fa³ chih⁴ wei³ yüan² hui⁴ 法制委員會**; ~ **of Nationalties Affairs****, min² tsu² shih⁴ wu⁴ wei³ yüan² hui⁴ 民族事務委員會**; ~ **of Overseas Chinese Affairs****, hua² ch'iao² shih⁴ wu⁴ wei³ yüan² hui⁴ 華僑事務委員會**; ~ **of Physical Calture****, t'i³ yü⁴ yün⁴ tung⁴ wei³ yüan² hui⁴ 體育運動委員會**; ~ **for Eliminating Illiteracy****, sao³ ch'u² wen² mang² kung¹ tso⁴ wei³ yüan² hui⁴ 掃除文盲工作委員會**.

commissioner n. wei³ yüan² 委員.

commit v. (deliver) fu⁴ t'o¹ 付託, (confine) chien¹ chin⁴ 監禁, (do something wrong) fan⁴ 犯.

committee n. wei³ yüan² hui⁴ 委員會; ~ **of Cultural and Education Affairs****, wen² hua² chiao⁴ yü⁴ wei³ yüan² hui⁴ 文化教育委員會**; ~ **of Financial and Economics Affairs****, ts'ai² cheng⁴ ching¹ chi⁴ wei³ yüan² hui⁴ 財政經濟委員會**; ~ **of People's Control****, jen² min² chien¹ ch'a² wei³ yüan² hui⁴ 人民監察委員會**; ~ **of Political and Legal Affairs****, cheng⁴ chih⁴ fa³ lü⁴ wei³ yüan² hui⁴ 政治法律委員會**.

commodity n. huo⁴ wu⁴ 貨物, shang¹ p'in³ 商品.

commodore n. chun³ chiang⁴ 准將(海).

common a. (mutual) kung¹ t'ung² te¹ 共同的, (ordinary) p'u³ t'ung¹ te¹ 普通的; ~ **Programme****, kung¹ t'ung² kang¹ ling³ 共同綱領; ~ **sense**, ch'ang² shih⁴ 常識.

commonplace a. p'ing² fan² te¹ 平凡的.

commonwealth n. lien² pang¹ 聯邦, (republic) kung⁴ ho² cheng⁴ chih⁴ 共和政治.

communicate v. (pass along) ch'uan² pu⁴ 傳布, (by writing, telephone, etc) t'ung¹ hsun¹ 通訊.

communication n. (transfer) ch'uan² pu⁴ 傳布, (letter, message) t'ung¹ hsun¹ 通訊.

communion n. (church) hui⁴ yu³ 會友.

communism n. kung⁴ ch'an² chu³ i⁴ 共產主義.

communist n. kung⁴ ch'an² tang³ yüan² 共產黨員; ~ **party**, kung⁴ ch'an² tang³ 共產黨.

community n. she⁴ hui⁴ 社會.

compact a. ch'ou² mi⁴ te¹ 稠密的.

companion n. pan⁴ lü³ 伴侶.

company n. (business) kung¹ ssu¹ 公司, (army)

47

lien² 連, (*in certain special units*) chung¹ tui⁴ 中隊; ~ **commander**, lien² chang³ 連長, (*in certain special units*) chung¹ tui⁴ chang³ 中隊長; ~ **headquarters**, lien² pu⁴ 連部, (*in certain special units*) chung¹ tui⁴ pu⁴ 中隊部.

comparatively *adv.* pi³ chiao⁴ ti¹ 比較地.

compare *v.* pi³ chiao⁴ 比較.

comparison *n.* pi³ chiao⁴ 比較.

compartment *n.* hsiao³ fang² chien¹ 小房間.

compass *n.* lo² chen¹ 羅針.

compassion *n.* lien² min³ 憐憫.

compel *v.* ch'iang² p'o⁴ 強迫.

compensate *v.* pu³ ch'ang² 補償.

compete *v.* ching⁴ cheng¹ 競爭.

competent *a.* (*able*) yu³ neng² li⁴ te¹ 有能力的, (*qualified*) ho² ko² te¹ 合格的.

competition *n.* ching⁴ cheng¹ 競爭.

competitive *a.* ching⁴ cheng¹ te¹ 競爭的.

compile *v.* pien¹ tsuan³ 編纂.

complain *v.* k'ung¹ su⁴ 控訴. 「t'ung⁴ 苦痛.

complaint *n.* pao⁴ yüan⁴ 抱怨, (*sickness*) k'u³

complete *v.* wan² ch'eng² 完成.

complex *a.* ts'o⁴ tsung¹ 錯綜的.

complicate *v.* shih³ fu⁴ tsa² 使複雜.

complication *n.* fu⁴ tsa² 複雜.

compliment *n.* k'o⁴ t'ao⁴ 客套.

complimentary *a.* wen⁴ hou⁴ te¹ 問候的.

comply *v.* shun⁴ ts'ung² 順從. 「hsieh³ tso⁴ 寫作.

compose *v.* (*make up*) kou⁴ ch'eng² 構成, (*write*)

composer *n.* (*music*) tso⁴ ch'ü³ chia¹ 作曲家.

composition *n.* kou⁴ ch'eng² 構成, (*musical work*) tso⁴ ch'ü³ 作曲, (*written*) tso⁴ wen² 作文.

compound *v.* tsu³ ho² 組合.

compress *v.* ya¹ so¹ 壓縮.

compromise *n.* t'o³ hsieh² 妥協.

compulsion *n.* ch'iang³ chih⁴ 強制.

compulsory *a.* ch'iang³ p'o⁴ te¹ 強迫的.

comrade *n.* t'ung² chih⁴ 同志.

conceal *v.* yin³ ni⁴ 隱匿.

concede *v.* ch'eng² jen⁴ 承認.

conceit *n.* tzu⁴ fu⁴ 自負.

conceive v. (*imagine*) hsiang³ hsiang⁴ 想像, (*child*) huai² yün⁴ 懷孕.

concentrate v. chi² chung¹ 集中. 「nien⁴ 掛念.

concern n. (*matter*) shih⁴ wu⁴ 事務, (*worry*) kua⁴

concerning prep. kuan¹ yü² 關於.

concert n. yin¹ yüeh⁴ hui⁴ 音樂會.

concession n. tsu¹ chieh⁴ 租界.

concise a. chien³ chieh² te¹ 簡潔的.

conclude v. t'ui¹ tuan⁴ 推斷.

conclusion n. chieh² lun⁴ 結論.

concrete a. shih² tsai⁴ te¹ 實在的.

concubine n. ch'ieh⁴ 妾.

concussion n. chen⁴ tung⁴ 震動.

condemn v. (*pronounce guilty*) ting⁴ tsui⁴ 定罪.

condense v. ning² chieh² 凝結.

condition n. (*state*) ch'ing² hsing² 情形, (*in an agreement*) t'iao² chien⁴ 條件, ti⁴ wei⁴ 地位.

condole v. tiao⁴ wei⁴ 弔慰.

condolence n. tiao⁴ wei⁴ 弔慰.

conduct n. hsing² wei² 行為; v. (*direct*) chih³ hui¹ 指揮, (*lead*) yin² tao³ 引導.

conductor n. (*music*) chih³ hui¹ che³ 指揮者, (*bus*) shou⁴ p'iao⁴ yüan² 售票員.

cone n. yüan² chui¹ t'i³ 圓錐體. 「授給.

confer v. hsiang¹ shang¹ 相商, (*give*) shou⁴ chi¹

conference n. hui⁴ i⁴ 會議.

confess v. tzu⁴ jen⁴ 自認.

confession n. ch'eng² jen⁴ 承認.

confide v. shin⁴ jen⁴ 信任.

confidence n. hsin⁴ jen⁴ 信任.

confidential a. chi¹ mi⁴ te¹ 機密的, (*security classification*) mi⁴ 密.

confine v. chien¹ chin⁴ 監禁.

confirm v. cheng² shih² 證實.

confiscate v. ch'ung¹ kung¹ 充公.

conflict n. ch'ung¹ t'u² 衝突. 「te¹ 孔子的.

Confucian a. ju² chiao⁴ te¹ 儒教的, k'ung² tzu³

Confucianism n. ju² chiao⁴ 儒教. k'ung³ chiao⁴

confuse v. k'un⁴ huo⁴ 困惑. 「孔教.

confusion n. k'un⁴ huo⁴ 困惑.

congratulate v. ch'ing² ho⁴ 慶賀.

49

congratulation *n.* ch'ing² ho⁴ 慶賀.

congress *n.* kuo² hui⁴ 國會.

conjunction *n.* (*grammar*) lien² chieh¹ tz'u¹ 連接詞.

connect *v.* lien² chieh¹ 連接.

connection *n.* lien² chieh¹ 連接.

connotation *n.* han² hsü⁴ 含蓄.

conquer *v.* k'o⁴ fu² 克服.

conqueror *n.* chan⁴ sheng⁴ che³ 戰勝者.

conquest *n.* cheng¹ fu² 征服.

conscience *n.* liang² hsin¹ 良心.

conscientious *a.* pen³ yü² liang² hsin¹ te¹ 本於良心的.

conscious *a.* chih¹ chüeh² te¹ 知覺的.

consciousness *n.* chih¹ chüeh² 知覺.

consent *v., n.* t'ung² i⁴ 同意.

consequence *n.* chieh² kuo³ 結果.

consider *v.* k'ao³ lü⁴ 考慮.

considerable *a.* chung⁴ yao⁴ te¹ 重要的.

consign *v.* chiao¹ fu⁴ 交付.

consignment *n.* wei³ t'o¹ 委託.

consist *v.* tsu³ ch'eng² 組成.

consolation *n.* an¹ wei⁴ 安慰.

consolidation *n.* t'uan² chieh² 團結.

consonant *n.* fu³ yin¹ 輔音.

conspiracy *n.* yin¹ mou² 陰謀.

constable *n.* hsün² ching³ 巡警.

constabulary *n.* ching³ ch'a² tui⁴ 警察隊, (*state police*) kuo² chia¹ ching³ ch'a² 國家警察.

constant *a.* (*same*) pu² pien⁴ te¹ 不變的, (*continuous*) pu² tuan⁴ te¹ 不斷的.

constellation *n.* hsing¹ tso⁴ 星座.

constituent *n.* yao⁴ su⁴ 要素, ch'eng² fen⁴ 成分, (*political*) hsüan² chü³ che³ 選舉者.

constitution *n.* cheng⁴ t'i³ 政體, (*government*) hsien⁴ fa³ 憲法.

construct *v.* chien⁴ chu² 建築, chien⁴ she⁴ 建設.

construction *n.* (*making*) kou⁴ tsao⁴ 構造.

constructive *a.* chien⁴ chu² hsing⁴ te¹ 建築性的.

consul *n.* ling³ shih⁴ 領事.

consulate *n.* ling³ shih⁴ kuan³ 領事館.

consult *v.* tzu¹ hsün² 諮詢.

consume *v.* hao⁴ fei⁴ 耗費.

consumption *n.* hao⁴ fei⁴ 耗費.

contact *n.* chieh¹ ch'u⁴ 接觸.

contagious *a.* ch'uan² jan³ te¹ 傳染的.

contain *v.* pao¹ k'uo⁴ 包括.

contaminate *v.* jan³ wu¹ 染汚.

contempt *n.* ch'ing¹ shih⁴ 輕視.

contend *v.* li⁴ cheng¹ 力爭.

content *a.* man³ i⁴ te¹ 滿意的; *n.* man³ i⁴ 滿意, (*contents*) nei⁴ jung² 內容.

contentment *n.* man³ tsu² 滿足.

contest *n.* ching⁴ cheng¹ 競爭.

context *n.* shang⁴ hsia⁴ wen² 上下文.

continent *n.* ta⁴ lu⁴ 大陸.

continual *a.* chi⁴ hsü⁴ te¹ 繼續的.

continue *v.* chi⁴ hsü⁴ 繼續. 「tuan⁴ te¹ 不間斷的.

continuous *a.* lien² hsü⁴ te¹ 連續的, pu² chien⁴

contraband *n.* wei² chin⁴ p'in³ 違禁品; *a.* chin⁴

contract *n.* shou¹ so¹ 收縮. 「chih³ te¹ 禁止的.

contradict *v.* (*deny*) fou³ jen⁴ 否認.

contradictorily *adv.* mao² tun⁴ ti⁴ 矛盾地.

contralto *n.* (*voice*) nü³ ti¹ yin¹ 女低音.

contrary *a.* fan³ tui⁴ te¹ 反對的.

contrast *n.* tui⁴ pi³ 對比.

contribute *v.* chüan¹ chu⁴ 捐助.

contribution *n.* chüan¹ chu⁴ 捐助.

control *v., n.* kuan² li³ 管理; ~ **Yuan***, chien¹ ch'a² yüan²* 監察院*.

convenience *n.* pien⁴ li⁴ 便利.

convenient *a.* pien⁴ li⁴ te¹ 便利的. 「an¹ 尼庵

convent *n.* hsiu¹ tao⁴ yüan⁴ 修道院, (*Chinese*) ni²

convention *n.* hui⁴ i⁴ 會議.

conversation *n.* hui⁴ hua⁴ 會話.

convert *v.* kai³ pien⁴ 改變.

convertible *a.* k'o² kai³ pien⁴ te¹ 可改變的.

convince *v.* shuo¹ fu² 說服.

convoy *n.* hu⁴ sung⁴ 護送.

cook *v., n.* p'eng¹ t'iao² 烹調.

cool *a.* liang² te¹ 涼的; *v.* shih³ liang² 使涼.

coolie, cooly *n.* hsiao³ kung¹ 小工, k'u³ li⁴ 苦力.

coop *n.* lung² 籠.

copper *n.* t'ung² 銅.

copy *v.* ch'ao¹ hsieh³ 抄寫.

coral *n.* shan¹ hu² 珊瑚.

cord *n.* sheng² 繩.

cordial *a.* ch'eng² hsin¹ te¹ 誠心的.

core *n.* hsin¹ 心.

cork *n.* juan³ mu⁴ sai¹ 軟木塞.

corn *n.* yü⁴ shu² shu³ 玉蜀黍, *(toe)* chi¹ yen³ 雞眼.

corner *n.* chiao³ 角.　　　　　「現有之 " 軍 ").

corps *n.* *(army)* chün¹ t'uan² 軍團(美編制約等中國

corpse *n.* shih¹ shou³ 屍首.　　　　「te¹ 正確的.

correct *v.* kai³ cheng⁴ 改正; *a.* cheng⁴ ch'üeh⁴

correspond *v.* fu² ho² 符合.　　「t'ung¹ hsin¹ 通信

correspondence *n.* fu² ho² 符合, *(letter writing)*

corridor *n.* tsou³ lang² 走廊.　　　　「海盜船

corsair *n.* hai³ tao⁴ 海盜, *(ship)* hai³ tao⁴ ch'uan²

cost *n.* chih² 值; *n.* fei⁴ yung⁴ 費用.

costly *a.* ang² kuei⁴ te¹ 昂貴的.

costume *n.* fu² chuang¹ 服裝.

cot *n.* mao² she⁴ 茅舍, hsiao³ wu¹ 小屋.

cottage *n.* hsiao³ wu¹ 小屋.

cotton *n.* mien² hua¹ 棉花, *(cloth)* mien² pu⁴ 棉布.

couch *n.* ch'uang² 牀, t'a⁴ 榻.

cough *n., v.* k'o² sou⁴ 咳嗽.

council *n.* p'ing² i⁴ hui⁴ 評議會; ～ of Economic
　Advisers (US), ching¹ chi⁴ ku⁴ wen⁴ wei³ yüan²
　hui⁴ 經濟顧問委員會(美).

counsel *n.* hui⁴ t'an² 會談, *(advice)* chung¹ kao⁴
　忠告; *v.* *(advise)* chung¹ kao⁴ 忠告, *(consult)*

count *v.* chi⁴ suan⁴ 計算.　　[shang¹ liang² 商量.

counter *n.* kuei⁴ t'ai² 櫃臺.

counteract *v.* fan³ tui⁴ 反對.

counterfeit *a.* chia³ te¹ 假的.

countersign *v.* fu⁴ shu³ 副署.　　　　「chia¹ 國家.

country *n.* hsiang¹ chien¹ 鄉間, *(nation)* kuo²

county *n.* chün⁴ 郡.　　　　　　「fu¹ fu⁴ 夫婦.

couple *n.* *(pair)* i² tui⁴ 一對, *(husband and wife)*

courage *n.* yung³ ch'i⁴ 勇氣.

course *n.* *(route)* t'u² ching⁴ 途徑, *(school)* k'o⁴
　ch'eng² 課程.　　　　　　　「法庭.

court *n.* *(palace)* kung¹ tien⁴ 宮殿, *(law)* fa³ t'ing²

court-martial *n.* chün¹ fa³ ts'ai² p'an⁴ 軍法裁判.

courtesy *n.* li³ mao⁴ 禮貌.

courtyard *n.* t'ing² yüan² 庭院.

cover *v.* che¹ kai⁴ 遮蓋; *n.* che¹ kai⁴ wu⁴ 遮蓋物.

cow *n.* p'in³ niu² 牝牛.

coward *n.* no⁴ fu¹ 懦夫.

cowardice *n.* tan³ ch'üeh⁴ 膽怯.

cower *v.* wei⁴ so¹ 畏縮.

cozy *a.* shu¹ shih⁴ te¹ 舒適的.

crab *n.* hsieh⁴ 蟹.

crack *n.* lieh⁴ hsi⁴ 裂隙; *v.* p'o⁴ lieh⁴ 破裂.

cracker *n.* (*biscuit*) lo⁴ ping³ kan¹ 酪餅干, (*fire-cracker*) pao⁴ chu² 爆竹.

cradle *n.* yao² lan² 搖籃.

craft *n.* (*skill*) chi¹ ch'iao³ 技巧, (*trade*) shou³ i⁴ 手藝.

craftsman *n.* shou³ i⁴ che³ 手藝者, kung¹ chiang⁴ 工匠.

crafty *a.* chiao³ hua² te¹ 狡猾的.

crane *n.* (*machine*) ch'i³ chung⁴ chi¹ 起重機, (*bird*) hao² 鶴.

crash *n.*, *v.* (*collision*) p'eng¹ chuang⁴ 碰撞.

crate *n.* lan² 籃.

crater *n.* (*volcano*) huo³ shan¹ k'ou³ 火山口.

crave *v.* k'o³ wang⁴ 渴望.

crawl *v.* p'u² fu² 匍匐.

crayon *n.* se⁴ fen² pi³ 色粉筆.

crazy *a.* feng¹ k'uang² te¹ 瘋狂的.

creak *v.* chan³ ya⁴ 輾軋.

cream *n.* ju³ lo⁴ 乳酪.

create *v.* ch'uang⁴ tsao⁴ 創造.

creator *n.* ch'uang⁴ tsao⁴ che³ 創造者.

creature *n.* sheng¹ wu⁴ 生物.

credential *n.* hsin⁴ jen⁴ chuang⁴ 信任狀.

credit *n.* (*belief*) hsin⁴ yung⁴ 信用, (*money*) chi⁴ chang⁴ 記賬.

creditable *a.* yu³ ling⁴ ming² te¹ 有令名的.

creek *n.* hsiao³ ho² 小河, hsiao³ wan¹ 小灣.

creep *v.* p'a² 爬.

cremate *v.* huo³ tsang⁴ 火葬.

crescent *n.* hsin¹ yüeh⁴ 新月.

crevice *n.* lieh⁴ feng⁴ 裂縫.

crew *n.* (*of ship*) ch'uan² yüan² 船員, (*working together*) ch'eng² yüan² 乘員, (*group*) ch'ün² 群.

cricket *n.* hsi¹ shuai⁴ 蟋蟀, (*game*) pan³ ch'iu² hsi⁴ 板球戲.

crime *n.* wei² fa³ 違法.

criminal *a.* fan⁴ tsui⁴ te¹ 犯罪的.

crimson *n.* shen¹ hung² se⁴ 深紅色.

cripple *n.* po³ tzu¹ 跛子.

crisis *n.* wei² chi¹ 危機.

crisp *a.* ts'ui⁴ te¹ 脆的.

crisscross *n.* shih² tzu⁴ hsing² 十字形; *a.* shih² tzu⁴ hsing² te¹ 十字形的.

critical *a.* p'ing² lun⁴ te¹ 評論的, (*crisis*) wei² chi² te¹ 危急的.

criticism *n.* p'i¹ p'ing² 批評.

criticize *v.* p'i¹ p'ing² 批評.

crocodile *n.* e⁴ 鱷.

crop *n.* shou¹ huo⁴ 收獲.

cross *n.* shih² tsu⁴ hsing² 十字形, (*Christ*) shih² tzu⁴ chia⁴ 十字架; *a.* heng² te¹ 橫的; *v.* chiao¹ ch'a¹ 交叉.

crossing *n.* chiao¹ ch'a¹ tien³ 交叉點.

crossroads *n.* shih² tzu⁴ chieh¹ 十字街.

crouch *v.* tun¹ fu² 蹲伏.

crow *n.* ya¹ 鴉; *v.* (*cock*) chi¹ ming² 雞鳴.

crowd *n.* ch'ün² chung⁴ 羣衆; *v.* ch'ün² chi² 羣集.

crown *n.* huang² kuan¹ 皇冠; *v.* chia¹ mien³ 加晃; ～ **prince,** huang² t'ai⁴ tzu³ 皇太子.

crucify *v.* sha¹ hai⁴ 殺害.

crude *a.* ts'u¹ ts'ao¹ te¹ 粗糙的.

cruel *a.* ts'an² jen³ te¹ 殘忍的, pei¹ ts'an³ te¹ 悲慘的.

cruise *v.* hsün² hang² 巡航.

cruiser *n.* hsün² yang² chien⁴ 巡洋艦(軍).

crumb *n.* mien⁴ pao¹ p'ien⁴ 麵包片.

crusade *n.* shih² tzu⁴ chün¹ 十字軍.

crush *v.* ya¹ sui⁴ 壓碎.

crust *n.* mien⁴ pao¹ p'i² 麵包皮.

crutch *n.* kuai³ chang⁴ 枴杖.

cry *v.* chiao⁴ han³ 叫喊, (*weep*) ai¹ k'u¹ 哀哭.

crystal *n.* shui² ching¹ 水晶.

cub *n.* (*bear*) hsiao³ hsiung² 小熊, (*fox*) hsiao³ hu² 小狐, (*lion*) hsiao³ shih¹ 小獅.

cube *n.* li⁴ fang¹ t'i³ 立方體; *v.* (*mathematics*) san¹ tz'u⁴ ch'eng² 三次乘; ～ **root,** li⁴ fang¹ ken¹ 立方根; ～ **sugar,** fang¹ t'ang² 方糖.

cuckoo *n.* tu⁴ chüan¹ 杜鵑.

cucumber *n.* huang² kua¹ 黄瓜, hu² kua¹ 胡瓜.

cuff *n.* (*of sleeve*) hsiu⁴ k'ou³ 袖口.

culprit *n.* fan⁴ jen² 犯人.

cultivate *v.* keng¹ chung⁴ 耕種.

cultivation *n.* keng¹ tso⁴ 耕作.

culture *n.* (*civilization*) wen² hua⁴ 文化.

cup *n.* pei¹ 杯.

cupboard *n.* shih² ch'u² 食厨.

cure *n.* i¹ chih⁴ 醫治; *v.* chih⁴ liao² 治療.

curfew *n.* chieh⁴ yen² 戒嚴.

curiosity *n.* hao⁴ ch'i² hsin¹ 好奇心.

curious *a.* hao⁴ ch'i² te¹ 好奇的.

curl *n.* ch'üan² fa³ 鬈髮; *v.* ch'üan² ch'ü¹ 鬈曲.

curly *a.* yu³ ch'üan² fa³ te¹ 有鬈髮的.

currant *n.* hsiao³ p'u² t'ao² kan¹ 小葡萄乾.

current *n.* (*electric*) tien⁴ liu² 電流; *a.* liu² t'ung¹ 流通的. ⌐te¹ 流通的.

curtain *n.* ch'uang¹ wei² 窗帷.

curve *n.* ch'ü¹ hsien⁴ 曲線.

cushion *n.* tso⁴ tien⁴ 坐墊.

custody *n.* k'an¹ kuan³ 看管.

custom *n.* feng¹ su² 風俗, (*customs*) kuan¹ shui⁴ 關稅, (*office*) hai³ kuan¹ 海關; ∼ **Administration****, hai³ kuan¹ tsung² shu³ 海關總署; ∼ **house,** hai³ kuan¹ 海關.

customer *n.* ku⁴ k'o⁴ 顧客. ⌐ko¹ 割.

cut *n.* ch'ieh¹ k'ou³ 切口, (*style*) ts'ai² fa³ 裁法; *v.*

cutlery *n.* li⁴ ch'i⁴ 利器.

cycle *n.* chou¹ ch'i¹ 周期.

cylinder *n.* yüan² chu⁴ t'i³ 圓柱體.

cystitis *n.* p'ang² kuang¹ yen² 膀胱炎.

D

dabble *v.* (*splash*) chien⁴ shih¹ 濺濕, (*work a little*) she¹ lieh⁴ 涉獵.

daffodil *n.* shui³ hsien¹ 水仙(植).

dagger *n.* pi² shou³ 匕首.

dahlia *n.* t'ien¹ chu² mu³ tan¹ 天竺牡丹(植).

daily *adv.* mei³ jih⁴ ti⁴ 每日地; *a.* mei³ jih⁴ te¹ 每日的, 「te¹ 美味的」 *(delicious)* mei⁴ wei⁴

dainty *a.* yu¹ mei³ te¹ 優美的, *(delicious)* mei⁴ wei⁴

dairy *n.* chih⁴ lo⁴ ch'ang³ 製酪場.

daisy *n.* ch'u² chü² 雛菊.

dam *n.* ti¹ 堤; *v.* chu² ti¹ 築堤.

damage *n.* sun³ hai⁴ 損害; *v.* hui³ shang¹ 毀傷.

damp *a.* shih¹ te¹ 濕的.

dampen *v.* (*moisten*) pien⁴ shih¹ 變濕, (*depress*) chü³ sang⁴ 沮喪.

dance *n.* wu³ tao⁴ 舞蹈; *v.* t'iao⁴ wu³ 跳舞.

dancer *n.* wu³ tao⁴ chia¹ 舞蹈家.

dandelion *n.* p'u² kung¹ ying¹ 蒲公英(植).

danger *n.* wei² hsien³ 危險.

dangerous *a.* wei² hsien³ te¹ 危險的.

dare *v.* kan³ 敢, (*challenge*) t'iao³ chan⁴ 挑戰.

dark *a.* an⁴ te¹ 暗的, (*sad*) pu⁴ yü² k'uai⁴ te¹ 不愉快的; *n.* hei¹ an⁴ 黑暗, (*ignorance*) yü² mei⁴ 愚昧.

darken *v.* pien⁴ wei² hei¹ 變為黑暗.

darkroom *n.* an⁴ fang² 暗房(攝).

darling *a.* ch'in¹ ai⁴ te¹ 親愛的; *n.* ai⁴ jen² 愛人.

darn *v.* chih¹ pu³ 織補; *n.* chih¹ pu³ ch'u⁴ 織補處.

dart *n.* t'ou² ch'iang¹ 投鎗, (*rush*) t'u² chin⁴ 突進.

dash *v.* (*splash*) p'o¹ chien⁴ 潑濺, (*rush*) t'u² chin⁴ 突進, (*smash*) ch'ung¹ chuang⁴ 衝撞.

date *n.* jih⁴ ch'i¹ 日期, (*fruit*) tsao³ 棗.

daughter *n.* nü³ erh² 女兒.

dawn *n.* li² ming² 黎明.

day *n.* jih⁴ chien¹ 日間.

daybreak *n.* p'o⁴ hsiao³ 破曉, li² ming² 黎明.

daylight *n.* jih⁴ kuang¹ 日光.

dazzle *v.* mu⁴ hsüan² 目眩.

dead *a.* ssu³ te¹ 死的.　　　　　　　「命的.

deadly *a.* chih⁴ ssu³ te¹ 致死的, chih⁴ ming⁴ te¹ 致

deaf *a.* lung² te¹ 聾的.

deafen *v.* shih³ lung² 使聾.

deal *v.* (*have to do*) lun⁴ chi² 論及, (*take action*) ch'u³ chih⁴ 處置, (*do business*) ching¹ ying² 經營, (*give*) chi² i³ 給以, (*distribute*) fen¹ p'ei⁴ 分配; *n.* (*trade*) chiao¹ i⁴ 交易, (*distribution*) fen¹ p'ei⁴ 分配, (*amount*) liang⁴ 量.

dealer *n.* (*merchant*) shang¹ jen² 商人, (*distributor*) fen¹ p'ei⁴ che³ 分配者.

dear *a.* ch'in¹ ai⁴ te¹ 親愛的, (*costly*) ang² kuei⁴ te¹

death *n.* ssu³ 死, ssu³ wang² 死亡.　　　　　「昂貴的.

debate *v.* cheng¹ lun⁴ 爭論, t'ao³ lun⁴ 討論.

debt *n.* chai⁴ 債, fu⁴ chai⁴ 負債.

decay *v.* (*rot*) fu³ lan⁴ 腐爛, shuai¹ t'ui⁴ 衰退; *n.* (*rotting*) fu³ pai⁴ 腐敗, shuai¹ wei² 衰微.

decease *v.* ssu³ 死.

deceit *n.* kan¹ chi² 奸計, ch'i¹ p'ien⁴ 欺騙.

deceive *v.* ch'i¹ cha⁴ 欺詐.

December *n.* shih² erh⁴ yüeh⁴ 十二月.

decent *a.* ho² li³ te¹ 合禮的.

decide *v.* chüeh² ting⁴ 決定.

decision *n.* chüeh² ting⁴ 決定, chüeh² hsin¹ 決心.

deck *n.* chia² pan³ 甲板, (*cards*) i⁴ tsu² chih³ p'ai² 一組紙牌.　　　　　　　　　「宣言書.

declaration *n.* hsüan¹ yen² 宣言, hsüan¹ yen² shu¹

declare *v.* hsüan¹ kao⁴ 宣告.

decline *v.* (*refuse*) hsieh⁴ chüeh² 謝絕, (*bend down*) fu³ ch'ü¹ 俯屈, (*decay*) shuai¹ lao⁴ 衰落.

decorate *v.* chuang¹ shih⁴ 裝飾.

decoration *n.* chuang¹ shih⁴ p'in³ 裝飾品.

decrease *v.*, *n.* chien² shao³ 減少.

decree *n.* ming⁴ ling⁴ 命令.

dedicate *v.* feng¹ hsien⁴ 奉獻, hsien⁴ shen¹ 獻身.

deed *n.* (*act*) hsing² wei² 行為, (*agreement*) ch'i⁴ chü¹ 契據.

deem *v.* jen⁴ wei² 認為, i³ wei² 以為.

deep *a.* shen¹ te¹ 深的.

deer *n.* lu⁴ 鹿.

defeat *n.* pai⁴ pei³ 敗北; *v.* chi¹ pai⁴ 擊敗.

defect *n.* (*fault*) kuo⁴ shih¹ 過失, (*short*) pu⁴ tsu² 不足.

defend *v.* pao³ hu⁴ 保護, (*lawsuit*) k'ang⁴ pien⁴ 抗辯.

defendant *n.* pei⁴ kao⁴ 被告. (律).

defense *n.* fang² yü⁴ 防禦, (*law*) pien⁴ hu⁴ 辯護.

defensive *a.* fang² yü⁴ te¹ 防禦的; *n.* (*strategically*) shou³ shih⁴ 守勢, (*tactics*) fang² yü⁴ 防禦; ~ **offensive**, shou³ shih⁴ kung¹ chi¹ 守勢攻擊; ~ **position**, fang² yü⁴ chen⁴ ti⁴ 防禦陣地; ~ **tactics**, fang² yü⁴ chan⁴ shu⁴ 防禦戰術.

defer *v.* yen² ko¹ 延擱.

defiance *n.* (*resistance*) fan³ k'ang⁴ 反抗, (*challenge*) t'iao³ chan⁴ 挑戰.

deficit *n.* pu⁴ tsu² 不足.

definite *a.* (*clear*) chien³ chieh² te¹ 簡潔的, (*restricted*) hsien⁴ ting⁴ te¹ 限定的.

deformity *n.* chi¹ hsing² 畸形. 「chan⁴ 挑戰.

defy *v.* (*resist*) fan³ k'ang⁴ 反抗, (*challenge*) t'iao³

degree *n.* (*extent*) ch'eng² tu⁴ 程度, (*title*) hsüeh² wei⁴ 學位, (*rank*) teng³ chi² 等級.

deity *n.* shen² ming² 神明.

delay *v.* yen² ko¹ 延擱, (*hinder*) tsu² chih³ 阻止; *n.* yen² ch'i¹ 延期, yen² chih⁴ 延滯.

delegate *n.* tai⁴ piao³ 代表.

delegation *n.* wei³ p'ai⁴ 委派, (*group of delegates*) tai⁴ piao³ t'uan² 代表團. 「考慮.

deliberate *a.* shen³ shen³ te¹ 審慎的; *v.* k'ao³ lü⁴

delicate *a.* mei³ wei⁴ te¹ 美味的, (*of fine make*) ching¹ hsi⁴ te¹ 精細的.

delicious *a.* mei³ wei⁴ te¹ 美味的.

delight *v.* k'uai⁴ lo⁴ 快樂, shih⁴ hsi³ yüeh⁴ 使喜悦.

delinquent *n.* k'uang⁴ chih² 曠職.

deliver *v.* (*distribute*) sung⁴ ti⁴ 送遞, (*hand over*) chiao¹ fu⁴ 交付, (*speak*) ch'en² shu⁴ 陳述.

deliverance *n.* shih⁴ fang⁴ 釋放.

delivery *n.* ti⁴ sung⁴ 遞送, (*release*) shih⁴ fang⁴ 釋放, (*speech, etc*) fa¹ yen² 發言.

delude *v.* ch'i¹ p'ien⁴ 欺騙.

demand *v.* yao¹ ch'iu² 要求; *n.* hsü¹ yao⁴ 需要.

democracy *n.* min² chu³ cheng⁴ chih⁴ 民主政治, min² chu² chu³ i⁴ 民主主義.

democratic *a.* min² chu³ te¹ 民主的.

demonstrate *v.* cheng⁴ ming² 證明, (*example*) shih⁴ fan⁴ 示範.

demonstration *n.* (*proof*) cheng⁴ ming² 證明, (*parade*) shih⁴ wei¹ yün⁴ tung⁴ 示威運動.

den *n.* tung⁴ k'u¹ 洞窟.

denote *v.* chih³ shih⁴ 指示, piao³ shih⁴ 表示.

denounce *v.* (*condemn*) fei¹ nan² 非難, (*accuse*) kao⁴ fa¹ 告發.

dense *a.* hou⁴ te¹ 厚的, ch'ou² mi⁴ te¹ 稠密的.

dentist *n.* ya² k'o¹ i¹ sheng¹ 牙科醫生.

deny *v.* fan³ po² 反駁, fou³ jen⁴ 否認.

depart *v.* li² ch'ü⁴ 離去.

department *v.* pu⁴ 部, ch'ang² so³ 場所; ~ of **Agriculture** (US), nung² yeh⁴ pu⁴ 農業部(美); ~ of **Commerce** (US), shang¹ wu⁴ pu⁴ 商務部(美); ~ of **Defence** (US), kuo² fang² pu⁴ 國防部(美); ~ of **Justice** (US), ssu¹ fa³ pu⁴ 司法部(美); ~ of **Labor** (US), lao² kung¹ pu⁴ 勞工部(美); ~ of **State** (US), kuo² wu⁴ yüan⁴ 國務院(美); ~ of **the Air Force** (US), k'ung¹ chün¹ pu⁴ 空軍部(美); ~ of **the Army** (US), lu⁴ chün¹ pu⁴ 陸軍部(美); ~ of **the Interior** (US), nei⁴ cheng⁴ pu⁴ 內政部(美); ~ of **the Navy** (US), hai³ chün¹ pu⁴ 海軍部(美); ~ of **the Post Office** (US), yu² cheng⁴ pu⁴ 郵政部(美); ~ of **the Treasury** (US), ts'ai³ cheng⁴ pu⁴ 財政部(美).

departure *n.* fen¹ pieh² 分別.

depend *v.* hsin⁴ lai⁴ 信賴, i¹ k'ao⁴ 依靠.

dependent *n.* (*family*) chuan⁴ shu³ 眷屬.

deposit *n.* ts'un² k'uan³ 存款, pao² kuan³ wu⁴ 保管物; *v.* ts'un² fang⁴ 存放, ts'un² ch'u⁴ 存儲.

depress *v.* ch'en¹ hsia⁴ 沈下. 「wa¹ ti⁴ 凹地.

depression *n.* (*sadness*) chü³ sang⁴ 沮喪, (*hollow*)

deprive *v.* po¹ to² 剝奪, to² ch'ü⁴ 奪去.

depth *n.* shen¹ 深, shen¹ ch'u⁴ 深處.

deputy *n.* tai⁴ piao³ 代表.

derail *v.* ch'u¹ kuei³ 出軌. 「源.

derive *v.* (*obtain*) te² lai² 得來, (*trace*) su⁴ yüan² 溯

descend *v.* (*go down*) hsia⁴ chiang⁴ 下降.

descendant *n.* tzu³ sun¹ 子孫.

59

descent *n.* (*going down*) chiang⁴ hsia⁴ 降下, (*slope*) hsieh² p'o¹ 斜坡, (*family line*) chia¹ shih⁴ 家世, (*attack*) hsi² chi¹ 襲擊.

describe *v.* hsü² shu⁴ 敍述.

description *n.* hsü² shu⁴ 敍述, chung³ lei² 種類.

desert *n.* sha¹ mo⁴ 沙漠; *v.* (*forsake*) p'ao¹ ch'i¹ 抛棄, (*army*) t'ao² wang² 逃亡(軍).

deserter *n.* (*army*) t'ao² ping¹ 逃兵(軍).

deserve *v.* ying¹ te² 應得. 「yang⁴ 打樣.

design *n.* t'u² an⁴ 圖案; *v.* she⁴ chi⁴ 設計, ta³

desire *n.* yü⁴ wang⁴ 慾望; *v.* hsi¹ chi⁴ 希冀, k'o³ wang⁴ 渴望.

desk *n.* shu¹ cho¹ 書桌. 「望.

despair *n.* chüeh² wang⁴ 絕望; *v.* shih¹ wang⁴ 失

desperate *a.* (*hopeless*) chüeh² wang⁴ te¹ 絕望的.

despise *v.* ch'ing¹ shih⁴ 輕視.

dessert *n.* ts'an¹ hou⁴ te¹ tien³ hsin¹ 餐後的點心.

destination *n.* mu⁴ ti⁴ ti⁴ 目的地. 「te¹ 貧窮的.

destitute *a.* ch'üeh¹ fa² te¹ 欠乏的, p'in² ch'iung²

destroy *v.* hui³ huai⁴ 毀壞.

destroyer *n.* p'o⁴ huai⁴ che³ 破壞者, (*warship*) ch'ü¹ chu² chien⁴ 驅逐艦(海).

destruction *n.* hui³ mieh⁴ 毀滅, p'o⁴ huai⁴ 破壞.

detail *v.* hsiang² shu⁴ 詳述. 「liu² 扣留.

detain *v.* (*delay*) tsu² chih³ 阻止, (*confine*) k'ou⁴

detect *v.* fa¹ hsien⁴ 發現.

detective *n.* chen¹ t'an⁴ 偵探.

determination *n.* chüeh² ting⁴ 決定.

determine *v.* chüeh² i⁴ 決意, tuan⁴ ting⁴ 斷定.

develop *v.* (*grow*) fa¹ chan³ 發展, (*display*) p'u⁴ lu⁴ 暴露, (*photography*) ch'ung¹ hsi³ 沖洗(攝).

development *n.* fa¹ chan³ 發展, fa¹ yü⁴ 發育.

device *n.* (*machine*) chi¹ hsieh⁴ 機械, (*plan*) chi⁴ hua⁴ 計劃, (*drawing*) shih⁴ yang⁴ 式樣.

devil *n.* mo² kuei³ 魔鬼.

devise *v.* fa¹ ming² 發明.

devote *v.* feng⁴ hsien⁴ 奉獻. 「誠.

devotion *n.* hsien⁴ shen¹ 獻身, ch'ien² ch'eng² 虔

devour *v.* (*eat*) t'un¹ 吞, (*waste*) hao⁴ fei⁴ 耗費.

dew *n.* lu⁴ 露.

dial *n.* chung¹ (piao³) mien⁴ 鐘(錶)面, jih⁴ kuei¹ 日

規; *v.* po¹ tien⁴ hua⁴ hao⁴ ma³ 撥電話號碼.

dialect *n.* fang¹ yen² 方言, t'u² yü³ 土語.

dialogue *n.* hui⁴ hua⁴ 會話, tui⁴ t'an² 對談.

diameter *n.* chih² ching⁴ 直徑.

diamond *n.* (*precious stone*) chin¹ kang¹ tsuan⁴ 金鋼鑽, (*figure*) ling² hsing² 菱形, (*playing cards*) fang¹ k'uai⁴ 方塊.

diarrhea *n.* li⁴ chi² 痢疾.

diary *n.* jih⁴ chi⁴ 日記.

dictate *v.* (*stenography*) mo⁴ hsieh³ 默寫.　「令.

dictation *n.* mo⁴ hsieh³ 默寫, (*orders*) fa¹ ling⁴ 發

dictator *n.* tu² ts'ai² che³ 獨裁者.

dictatorship *n.* tu² ts'ai² 獨裁.

dictionary *n.* tzu⁴ tien³ 字典.

die *v.* ssu³ 死, wei¹ hsieh⁴ 萎謝.　　「國會.

diet *n.* (*food*) yin³ shih² 飲食, (*assembly*) kuo² hui⁴

differ *v.* ch'a¹ i⁴ 差異.

difference *n.* pu⁴ t'ung² 不同, hsiang¹ i⁴ 相異.

different *a.* pu⁴ t'ung² te¹ 不同的, hsiang¹ i⁴ te¹ 相

difficult *a.* k'un⁴ nan² te¹ 困難的.　　　「異的.

difficulty *n.* nan² 難, nan² shih⁴ 難事.

dig *v.* chüeh² 掘.

digest *v.* hsiao¹ hua⁴ 消化.　　　　　　「力.

digestion *n.* hsiao¹ hua⁴ 消化, hsiao¹ hua⁴ li⁴ 消化

dignified *a.* kao¹ kuei⁴ te¹ 高貴的.

dignity *n.* (*stateliness*) tsun¹ yen² 尊嚴, (*high office*) kao¹ wei⁴ 高位, (*nobleness*) kao¹ kuei⁴ 高貴.

dike, dyke *n.* ti¹ 堤.

diligence *n.* ch'in² mien³ 勤勉.

diligent *a.* ch'in² mien³ te¹ 勤勉的.

diligently *adv.* ch'in² mien³ ti⁴ 勤勉地.

dim *a.* po² an¹ te¹ 薄暗的.

dimension *n.* t'i³ chi¹ 體積.

diminish *v.* chien² shao³ 減少.

dimple *n.* yeh⁴ 靨, (*hollow place*) wa¹ ch'u⁴ 凹處.

din *n.* hsüan¹ sheng¹ 喧聲.

dine *v.* shih² 食, chin⁴ shan⁴ 進膳.

dining-car *n.* ts'an¹ ch'e¹ 餐車(火車上).

dining-room *n.* ts'an¹ t'ing¹ 餐廳.

dining-table *n.* ts'an¹ cho¹ 餐桌.

dinner *n.* (*main meal*) cheng⁴ ts'an¹ 正餐, (*formal*

meal) yen⁴ hui⁴ 宴會.

dip *v.* chin⁴ 浸, chi² ch'ü³ 汲取.

diphtheria *n.* pai² hou² 白喉(醫).

diploma *n.* wen² p'ing² 文憑, cheng⁴ shu¹ 證書.

diplomacy *n.* wai⁴ chiao¹ 外交.

diplomat *n.* wai⁴ chiao¹ chia¹ 外交家.

dipper *n.* chü² ch'ü² che³ 掬取者, shao² 杓.

direct *a.* chih² chieh¹ te¹ 直接的, (*frank*) t'an³ pai² te¹ 坦白的; *v.* chih² tao³ 指導, (*order*) ming⁴ ling⁴ 命令; ~ **current**, chih² liu² tien⁴ 直流電; ~ **fire**, chih² chieh¹ she⁴ chi¹ 直接射擊; ~ **hit**, ming⁴ chung⁴ tan⁴ 命中彈.

direction *n.* fang¹ hsiang⁴ 方向, (*guidance*) chien¹ tu¹ 監督; ~ **of attack**, kung¹ chi¹ fang¹ hsiang⁴ 攻擊方向.

directly *adv.* chih² chieh¹ ti¹ 直接地.

director *n.* (*movie*) tao² yen³ 導演, (*company*) li³ shih⁴ 理事. 「所名簿.

directory *n.* jen² min² chu⁴ so³ ming² pu⁴ 人民住

dirt *n.* wu¹ wu⁴ 汚物. 「sun³ shih¹ 損失.

dirty *a.* wu¹ hui⁴ te¹ 汚穢的.

disadvantage *n.* (*unfavorable*) pu² li⁴ 不利, (*loss*)

disagree *v.* (*differ*) hsiang¹ i⁴ 相異, (*quarrel*) cheng¹ chih² 爭執, (*be harmful*) pu² i² 不宜.

disagreeable *a.* t'ao³ yen⁴ te¹ 討厭的.

disappear *v.* pu² chien⁴ 不見, hsiao¹ mieh⁴ 消滅.

disappoint *v.* shih³ shih¹ wang⁴ 使失望.

disappointment *n.* shih¹ wang⁴ 失望. 「反對.

disapprove *v.* pu² tsan⁴ ch'eng² 不贊成, fan³ tui⁴

disarm *v.* (*completely disarm*) chiao³ hsieh⁴ 繳械, (*reduce or limit*) ts'ai² ping¹ 裁兵, (*remove suspicion*) shih⁴ i² 釋疑.

disaster *n.* tsai¹ nan⁴ 災難, pu² hsing⁴ 不幸.

disastrous *a.* to¹ tsai¹ nan⁴ te¹ 多災難的, pu² hsing⁴ te¹ 不幸的.

disband *v.* chieh³ san⁴ 解散.

discharge *v.* (*electric*) fang⁴ she⁴ 放射, (*release*) mien³ ch'u² 免除, (*unload*) hsieh⁴ ch'ü⁴ 卸去, (*from army*) t'ui⁴ i⁴ 退役(軍).

disciple *n.* men² t'u² 門徒.

discipline *n.* (*training*) hsün⁴ lien⁴ 訓練, (*order*)

62

chi⁴ lü⁴ 紀律, (*punishment*) ch'eng² chieh² 懲戒.

disclose v. p'u⁴ lou⁴ 暴露.

discontent n. pu⁴ man³ 不滿.

discount v. che² k'ou⁴ 折扣, t'ieh¹ hsien⁴ 貼現.

discourage v. shih² chü³ sang⁴ 使沮喪.

discover v. fa¹ hsien⁴ 發現.

discovery n. fa¹ hsien⁴ 發現.

discretion n. chen¹ cho² 斟酌, shen³ shen⁴ 審慎.

discriminate v. ch'ü¹ pieh² 區別, ch'i² tai⁴ 岐待.

discrimination n. ch'ü¹ pieh² 區別, ch'a¹ pieh² 差別.

discuss v. t'ao³ lun⁴ 討論.

discussion n. t'ao³ lun⁴ 討論.

disgrace v. ch'ih³ ju⁴ 耻辱; n. (*shame*) ch'ih³ ju⁴ 耻辱, (*loss of favor*) shih¹ ch'ung³ 失寵.

disguise v. chia³ chuang¹ 假裝; n. pien⁴ chuang¹ 變裝.

disgust n. hsien² wu⁴ 嫌惡.

dish n. tieh² 碟, (*food*) ts'ai⁴ yao² 菜餚.

dishonest a. pu⁴ ch'eng² shih² te¹ 不誠實的.

dishonesty n. pu⁴ ch'eng² shih² 不誠實.

dishonor n. pu⁴ ming² yü⁴ 不名譽; v. shih³ ju⁴ 使耻辱.

disinclination n. pu² chung⁴ i⁴ 不中意.

disinterested a. (*fair*) kung¹ p'ing² te¹ 公平的.

disk n. yüan² p'an² 圓盤.

dislike n., v. hsien² wu⁴ 嫌惡.

disloyal a. pu⁴ chung¹ te¹ 不忠的.

dismal a. i⁴ yü⁴ te¹ 抑鬱的, ch'i¹ liang² te¹ 凄涼的.

dismay n. sang⁴ tan³ 喪膽; v. ching¹ k'ung³ 驚恐.

dismiss v. ch'ien³ san⁴ 遣散, mien³ chih² 免職, ch'e⁴ chih² 撤職.

dismount v. (*unhorse*) hsia⁴ ma³ 下馬.

disobedience n. pu² shun⁴ ts'ung² 不順從.

disobedient a. k'ang⁴ ming⁴ te¹ 抗命的.

disobey v. wei² pei⁴ 違背.

disorder n. (*lack of order*) wu² chih⁴ hsü⁴ 無秩序, (*public disturbance*) sao¹ luan⁴ 騷亂, (*sickness*) chi² ping⁴ 疾病.

dispatch n. (*letter*) fa¹ sung⁴ 發送, (*message*) kung¹ wen² 公文; v. p'ai⁴ ch'ien³ 派遣, su² sung⁴ 速送.

disperse v. fen¹ san³ 分散.

dispersion n. (*gunnery*) san¹ fei¹ 散飛.

display n., v. ch'en² lieh⁴ 陳列.

disposal *n.* (*sale*) ch'u¹ shou⁴ 出售, (*settlement*) ch'u² li³ 處理, (*display*) ch'en² lieh⁴ 陳列.

dispose *v.* (*arrange*) p'ei⁴ chih⁴ 配置, (*settle*) ch'u² li³ 處理. 「hsing⁴ ch'ing² 性情.

disposition *n.* (*order*) chih⁴ hsü⁴ 秩序, (*nature*)

dispute *n.* pien⁴ lun⁴ 辯論; *v.* (*quarrel*) cheng¹ cheng¹ 爭論.

disregard *v.* hu¹ lüeh⁴ 忽略. 「lun⁴ 爭論.

disrespect *n.* pu² ching⁴ 不敬.

disrespectful *a.* pu² ching⁴ te¹ 不敬的.

dissatisfy *v.* shih³ pu⁴ man³ tsu² 使不滿足.

dissipate *v.* (*scatter*) hsiao¹ san³ 消散, (*waste*) lang⁴ fei⁴ 浪費.

dissipated *a.* (*wasted*) hao⁴ lang⁴ fei⁴ te¹ 好浪費的.

dissolve *v.* jung² chieh³ 溶解, (*end*) ch'ü³ hsiao¹ 取消.

distance *n.* chü⁴ li² 距離. 「取消.

distant *a.* yüan³ fang¹ 遠方的.

distasteful *a.* wu² wei⁴ te¹ 無味的.

distinct *a.* (*clear*) ch'ing¹ ch'u³ te¹ 清楚的, (*separate*) ko⁴ pieh² te¹ 各別的.

distinctly *adv.* ming² pai² ti⁴ 明白地.

distinguish *v.* ch'ü¹ pieh² 區別, (*make famous*) shih³ hsien³ yang² 使顯揚. 「te¹ 有名的.

distinguished *a.* cho¹ yüeh⁴ te¹ 卓越的, yu³ ming²

distort *v.* (*twist*) niu³ wai¹ 扭歪, (*falsify*) ch'ü¹ chieh³ 曲解.

distract *v.* mi² luan⁴ 迷亂. 「chieh³ 曲解.

distress *n.* t'ung⁴ k'u³ 痛苦, tsai¹ nan⁴ 災難.

distribute *v.* (*divide*) fen¹ p'ei⁴ 分配, (*spread*) san⁴ pu⁴ 散佈, (*classify*) lei⁴ pieh² 類別.

distribution *n.* fen¹ p'ai⁴ 分派, fen¹ p'ei⁴ 分配; ~ of fire, fen¹ huo³ 分火; ~ of troops, ping¹ li⁴ p'ei⁴ pei⁴ 兵力配備.

district *a.* ti⁴ fang¹ 地方, ch'ü¹ 區.

disturb *v.* jao³ luan⁴ 擾亂, fang² hai⁴ 妨害.

ditch *n.* kou¹ 溝. 「俯衝(航).

dive *v.* ch'ien² shui³ 潛水, (*airplane*) fu³ ch'ung¹

divest *v.* po¹ to² 剝奪, lüeh⁴ to² 掠奪.

divide *v.* fen¹ 分.

divine *a.* shen² te¹ 神的, shang⁴ ti⁴ te¹ 上帝的.

division *n.* ch'ü¹ fen¹ 區分, (*mathematics*) ch'u² fa³ 除法, (*army*) shih¹ 師.

divorce *n.* li² hun¹ 離婚; *v.* li² hun¹ 離婚.

dizzy *a.* hsüan² yün⁴ te¹ 眩暈的.

do *v.* hsing² 行, wei² 為.

docile *a.* hsün² liang² te¹ 馴良的.

dock *n.* ma³ t'ou² 碼頭, ch'uan² wu⁴ 船塢.

dockyard *n.* tsao⁴ ch'uan² ch'ang³ 造船廠.

doctor *n.* i¹ sheng¹ 醫生; *v.* chih⁴ liao² 治療.

doctrine *n.* chiao⁴ i⁴ 教義, chu³ i⁴ 主義.

document *n.* kung¹ wen² 公文, wen² chien⁴ 文件.

dodge *v.* to³ pi⁴ 躲避.

doe *n.* (*deer*) p'in³ lu⁴ 牝鹿, (*antelope*) p'in³ yang² 牝羊, (*rabbit*) p'in³ t'u⁴ 牝兔.

dog *n.* ch'uan³ 犬, kou³ 狗.

doleful *a.* pei¹ ai¹ te¹ 悲哀的.

doll *n.* wan² ou³ 玩偶, yang² wa² wa² 洋娃娃.

dollar *n.* yin² yüan² 銀圓.

dolmen *n.* shih² pei¹ mu⁴ 石碑墓.

dome *n.* yüan² wu¹ ting³ 圓屋頂.

domestic *a.* (*family*) chia¹ t'ing² te¹ 家庭的, (*country*) kuo² nei⁴ te¹ 國內的.

dominate *v.* kuan² li³ 管理, t'ung³ chih⁴ 統治.

dominion *n.* (*authority*) chu³ ch'üan² 主權, (*territory*) ling³ t'u³ 領土.

donkey *n.* lü² tzu¹ 驢子.

doom *n.* (*fate*) ming⁴ yün⁴ 命運, (*ruin*) mieh⁴ wang² 滅亡, (*sentence*) p'an⁴ chüeh² 判決; *v.* (*fate*) ting⁴ ming⁴ yün⁴ 定命運, (*sentence*) p'an⁴ [chüeh² 判決.

door *n.* men² 門.

dormitory *n.* su⁴ she⁴ 宿舍.

dose *n.* i⁴ fu² 一服; *v.* ling⁴ fu² yao⁴ 令服藥.

dot *n.* tien³ 點; *v.* ju² tien³ 如點.

double *a.* pei⁴ 倍; *v.* pei⁴ 倍; ~ **envelopment,** liang³ i⁴ pao¹ wei² 兩翼包圍; "~ **time march!**" p'ao³ pu⁴ tsou³ 跑步走!; ~ **track,** shuang¹ kuei³ 雙軌(鐵).

doubt *n.* huai² i² 懷疑; *v.* i² huo⁴ 疑惑.

doubtful *a.* k'o³ i² te¹ 可疑的.

doubtless *adv.* wu² i² 無疑, pi⁴ ting⁴ 必定.

dove *n.* ko¹ 鴿.

down *adv.* hsia⁴ 下, tzu⁴ ku³ i³ lai² 自古以來; *prep.* hsiang⁴ hsia⁴ 向下, ~ **with,** ta² tao³ 打倒.

downcast *a.* (*sad*) chü³ sang⁴ te¹ 沮喪的.

65

downstairs *n.* lou² hsia⁴ 樓下.

downtown *a.*, *a.* tsai⁴ ch'eng² li³ 在城裡.

downward *adv.* hsiang⁴ hsia⁴ te¹ 向下的.

dowry *n.* chia⁴ lien² 嫁奩.

doze *v.* hsiao³ shui⁴ 小睡, chia³ mei⁴ 假寐.

dozen *n.* i⁴ ta³ 一打.

draft, draught *n.* (*rough copy*) ts'ao² kao³ 草稿, (*bank*) hui⁴ p'iao⁴ 匯票, (*of a boat*) ch'ih¹ shui³ 吃水, (*conscription*) cheng¹ chi² 徵集(軍); *v.* (*sketch*) hui⁴ 繪, (*write*) ch'i² kao³ 起稿, (*select*) hsüan³ pa² ⌐選拔.

draftsman *n.* hui⁴ t'u² yüan² 繪圖員.

drag *v.* t'o¹ yeh⁴ 拖曳, ch'ien¹ yin¹ 牽引.

dragon *n.* lung² 龍.

dragonfly *n.* ch'ing¹ t'ing² 蜻蜓.

drain *n.* kou¹ ch'ü¹ 溝渠, *v.* p'ai² shui³ 排水.

drake *n.* hsiung² ya¹ 雄鴨.

drama *n.* hsi⁴ chü⁴ 戲劇.

dramatic *a.* hsi⁴ chü⁴ hsing⁴ te¹ 戲劇性的.

draw *v.* (*pull*) ch'ien¹ yin¹ 牽引, (*attract*) yin³ yu⁴ 引誘, (*receive*) chih¹ ch'ü³ 支取, (*picture*) hui⁴ 繪.

drawback pu² li⁴ 不利, fang² ai⁴ 防礙.

drawer *n.* (*bank*) chih¹ k'uan² che³ 支款者, (*picture*) hui⁴ t'u² che² 繪圖者, (*box*) ch'ou¹ t'i⁴ 抽屜.

dread *n.* k'ung³ pu⁴ 恐怖; *v.* k'ung³ pu⁴ 恐怖.

dreadful *a.* k'o³ pu² te¹ 可怖的. ⌐chien¹ 夢現.

dream *n.* meng⁴ 夢, huan⁴ hsiang³ 幻想; *v.* meng⁴

dreary *a.* yu¹ yü⁴ te¹ 憂鬱的.

dredge *v.* (*machine*) i³ wa¹ ni² chi¹ wa¹ ch'ü³ 以挖泥機挖取, (*net*) i² wang³ lao¹ ch'ü³ 以網撈取.

dredger *n.* san² fen³ hsia³ 糝粉匣.

dress *n.* i¹ fu² 衣服; *v.* (*decorate*) chuang¹ shih⁴ 裝飾, (*comb*) shu¹ fa³ 梳髮. ⌐(軍)

drift *v.* p'iao¹ liu² 飄流, (*gunnery*) p'ien¹ liu² 偏流.

drill *n.* (*tool*) chui¹ 錐, (*training*) ts'ao¹ lien⁴ 操練; (*pierce*) ch'uan¹ 穿, (*train*) chiao⁴ lien⁴ 教練; ～ **ground,** ts'ao¹ ch'ang³ 操場.

drink *v.* yin³ 飲.

drip *v.* ti¹ hsia⁴ 滴下.

drive *v.* chia⁴ yü⁴ 駕御.

driver *n.* ch'e¹ fu¹ 車夫, yü⁴ shou³ 取手.

drizzle *n.* hsi⁴ yü³ 細雨.

droop v. (*bend down*) hsia⁴ ch'ui² 下垂, (*become weak*) wei¹ tun⁴ 萎頓.

drop v. ti¹ lao² 滴落; ～ **anchor,** hsia⁴ mao² 下錨; ～ **bombs,** t'ou² tan⁴ 投彈.

drown v. ni⁴ ssu³ 溺死, (*flood*) fan⁴ lan⁴ 氾濫, (*suppress*) hsiao¹ mieh¹ 消滅.

drowsy a. yü⁴ shui¹ te¹ 欲睡的. 「藥品.

drug n. (*medicine*) yao⁴ p'in³ 藥品; v. t'ou² yao⁴ 投

drum n. ku³ 鼓, (*gasoline*) ch'i⁴ yu² t'ung³ 汽油桶, (*magazine*) tzu³ tan⁴ hsia² 子彈匣(軍).

drummer n. ku² shou³ 鼓手.

drunk a. tsui⁴ te¹ 醉的.

drunkard n. chiu³ t'u² 酒徒.

drunken a. tsui⁴ te¹ 醉的, hao⁴ chiu³ te¹ 好酒的.

dry v. shih³ kan¹ 使乾; a. kan¹ tsao³ te¹ 乾燥的, (*no rain*) wu² yü³ te¹ 無雨的, (*without tears*) wu² lei⁴ te¹ 無淚的, (*thirsty*) k'o³ te¹ 渴的; ～ **cell,** kan¹ tien⁴ ch'ih¹ 乾電池.

duck n. ya¹ 鴨.

due a. (*debt*) so³ fu⁴ te¹ 所負的, (*proper*) shih⁴ tang¹

dull a. tun⁴ te¹ 鈍的. 「te¹ 適當的.

duly adv. shih⁴ tang¹ 適當.

dumb a. (*not able to speak*) ya³ te¹ 啞的, (*silent*) ch'en² mo⁴ te¹ 沈默的.

dumb-bell n. ya³ ling² 啞鈴.

duplicate n. fu⁴ pen³ 副本; v. tso⁴ fu⁴ pen³ 作副本.

duration n. ch'i¹ chien¹ 期間.

during prep. tang¹ 當(其時).

dusk n. huang² hun¹ 黃昏, (*shade*) yin¹ an⁴ 陰暗.

dust n. ch'en² 塵 v. fu² ch'ü⁴ ch'en² ai¹ 拂去塵埃.

duster n. (*person*) fu² ch'en² jen² 拂塵人, (*thing*) fu² ch'en² ch'i⁴ 拂塵器.

dusty a. ch'en² ai¹ man³ pu⁴ te¹ 塵埃滿佈的.

dutiful a. chin⁴ tse² te¹ 盡責的, (*obedient*) fu² ts'ung² te¹ 服從的.

duty n. (*responsibility*) tse² jen⁴ 責任, i⁴ wu⁴ 義務, (*work*) chih³ wu⁴ 職務, (*tax*) ch'üan¹ shui⁴ 捐稅.

dwarf n. (*person*) ai³ jen² 矮人. 「細論.

dwell v. (*live*) chü¹ chu⁴ 居住, (*discuss*) hsi⁴ lun⁴

dye v. jan³ se⁴ 染色; n. jan³ liao⁴ 染料.

dynamite n. cha⁴ yao⁴ 炸藥.

67

dynamo *n.* chih² liu² fa¹ tien⁴ chi¹ 直流發電機.

dysentery *n.* li⁴ chi² 痢疾.

E

each *pron.* mei³ 每, ko⁴ ko⁴ 各個.

eager *a.* k'o³ wang⁴ te¹ 渴望的.

eagle *n.* (*bird*) ying¹ 鷹.

ear *n.* (*body*) erh³ 耳, (*plants*) sui⁴ 穗.

earl *n.* po² chüeh² 伯爵.　　　　　　　　　「早的.

early *adv.* tsao³ 早, chi² shih² 及時; *a.* tsao³ te¹

earmark *n.* chi⁴ hao⁴ 記號.

earn *v.* chuan⁴ 賺, huo² te² 獲得; *n.* hsin¹ shui³
薪水, kung¹ tzu¹ 工資.　　　　　　　　　「真誠的.

earnest *a.* je⁴ hsin¹ te¹ 熱心的, chen¹ ch'eng² te¹

earphone *n.* erh³ chi¹ 耳機.

earshot *n.* t'ing¹ chü⁴ 聽距.　　　　　　　　「地.

earth *n.* (*planet*) ti⁴ ch'iu² 地球, (*land*) t'u³ ti⁴ 土

earthquake *n.* ti⁴ chen⁴ 地震.

ease *n.* an¹ lo⁴ 安樂, shu¹ shih⁴ 舒適; *v.* shih³ an¹
i⁴ 使安逸, shih³ shu¹ shih⁴ 使舒適.

easel *n.* hua⁴ chia⁴ 畫架.

east *n.* tung¹ 東.

Easter *n.* fu⁴ huo² chieh² 復活節.

easy *a.* jung² i⁴ te¹ 容易的.

eat *v.* ch'ih¹ 喫.

eaves *n.* yen² 簷.

eavesdropper *n.* t'ou¹ t'ing¹ che³ 偷聽者.

ebb *v.,* *n.* (*tide*) t'ui⁴ ch'ao² 退潮, (*decline*) shuai¹
　　　　　　　　　　　　　　　　　　　　　　「lao⁴ 衰落.

ebony *n.* wu¹ mu⁴ 烏木.

ebullient *a.* fen⁴ chi¹ te¹ 奮激的, (*boiling*) fei⁴
t'eng² te¹ 沸騰的.　　　　　　　　　　　　「騰.

ebullition *n.* chi¹ ang² 激昂, (*boiling*) fei⁴ t'eng² 沸

eccentric *a.* ku³ kuai⁴ te¹ 古怪的.

echo *n.* hui² sheng¹ 回聲; *v.* hui² sheng¹ 回聲,
fan³ hsiang³ 反響.　　　　　　　　　　　　「折衷的.

eclectic *a.* hsüan³ tse² te¹ 選擇的, che² chung¹ te¹

eclipse *n.* (*sun*) jih⁴ shih² 日蝕, (*moon*) yüeh⁴
shih² 月蝕.

economic *a.* ching¹ chi⁴ te¹ 經濟的, ching¹ chi⁴ hsüeh² te¹ 經濟學的.

economical *a.* ching¹ chi⁴ te¹ 經濟的, chieh² chien³ te¹ 節儉的.

economics *n.* ching¹ chi⁴ hsüeh² 經濟學.

economist *n.* ching¹ chi⁴ hsüeh² chia¹ 經濟學家, ching¹ chi⁴ chia¹ 經濟家. 「節儉.

economize *v.* sheng³ yung⁴ 省用, chieh² chien²

economy *n.* chieh² chien³ 節儉, ching¹ chi⁴ 經濟.

ecru *n.* tan⁴ ho² se⁴ 淡褐色.

ecstasy *n.* k'uang² hsi³ 狂喜.

ecumenical *a.* p'u³ pien⁴ te¹ 普遍的.

eczema *n.* shih¹ chen³ 濕疹(醫).

eddy *n.* hsuan¹ wo¹ 旋渦; *v.* hsuan¹ liu² 旋流.

edge *n.* (*knife*) tao¹ k'ou³ 刀口, (*sharpness*) jui⁴ li⁴ 銳利, (*brink*) pien¹ yüan² 邊緣.

edible *a.* k'o³ shih² te¹ 可食的.

edict *n.* kao⁴ shih⁴ 告示, ming⁴ ling⁴ 命令.

edifice *n.* ta⁴ hsia⁴ 大廈.

edify *v.* (*instruct*) chiao⁴ hsün⁴ 教訓.

edit *v.* pien¹ chi² 編輯.

educate *v.* chiao⁴ yü⁴ 教育.

educe *v.* yin³ ch'u¹ 引出, fa¹ sheng¹ 發生.

eel *n.* man² 鰻(魚).

efface *v.* ch'ieh¹ ch'ü⁴ 揩去, t'u² hsiao¹ 塗消.

effect *v.* shih² hsing² 實行; *n.* chieh² kuo³ 結果.

effective *a.* yu³ hsiao⁴ te¹ 有效的; **～ range**, yu³ hsiao⁴ she⁴ ch'eng² 有效射程.

effectual *a.* yu³ hsiao⁴ te¹ 有效的. 「嬌弱的.

effeminate *a.* nü³ hsing⁴ te¹ 女性的, chiao¹ jo⁴ te¹

effervesce *v.* (*bubble*) ch'i¹ p'ao⁴ 起泡, (*be excited*) hsing¹ fen⁴ 興奮.

efficacy *n.* hsiao⁴ li⁴ 效力.

efficient *a.* yu³ hsiao⁴ te¹ 有效的.

effigy *n.* hsiao⁴ hsiang⁴ 肖像.

effluvium *n.* ch'ou⁴ ch'i⁴ 臭氣.

effort *n.* nu³ li⁴ 努力.

effrontery *n.* hou⁴ yen² 厚顏, wu² ch'ih³ 無恥.

effulgent *a.* kuang¹ chao⁴ te¹ 光照的.

effuse *v.* ch'ing¹ ch'u¹ 傾出.

egg *n.* lan³ 卵, tan⁴ 蛋, (*of hen*) chi¹ tan⁴ 雞蛋.

eggplant *n.* ch'ieh² tzu¹ 茄子.

ego *n.* tzu⁴ wo³ 自我.

egoism *n.* li⁴ chi² chu³ i⁴ 利己主義.

egotism *n.* tzu⁴ tsun¹ 自尊, tzu⁴ ao⁴ 自傲.

egress *n.* (*going out*) li² ch'ü¹ 離去, (*exit*) ch'u¹ k'ou³ 出口.

eight *n.* pa¹ 八; *a.* pa¹ te¹ 八的. 「八.

eighteen *a.* shih² pa¹ te¹ 十八的; *n.* shih² pa¹ 十

eighty *a.* pa¹ shih² te¹ 八十的; *n.* pa¹ shih² 八十.

either *a.* erh⁴ che³ chih¹ i⁴ 二者之一的, mei³ i⁴ te¹ 每一的. 「fa¹ te¹ 突發的.

ejaculate *v.* t'u² jan² shuo¹ ch'u¹ 突然說出, t'u²

eject *v.* chih¹ ch'u¹ 擲出.

ejector *n.* p'ao¹ k'o² t'ing³ 拋殼挺(兵).

eke *v.* tseng¹ chia¹ 增加.

elaborate *v.* hsin¹ k'u³ tso⁴ ch'eng² 辛苦作成.

elapse *v.* kuo⁴ ch'ü⁴ 過去, ching¹ kuo⁴ 經過.

elastic *a.* t'an² hsing⁴ te¹ 彈性的.

elate *v.* shih³ te² i⁴ 使得意.

elbow *n.* chou³ 肘, chou³ hsing² wu⁴ 肘形物.

elder *a.* chiao⁴ lao³ te¹ 較老的.

elderly *a.* shao¹ lao³ te¹ 稍老的. 「擇.

elect *v.* hsüan² chü³ 選舉, (*choose*) hsüan³ tse² 選

election *n.* hsüan³ tse² 擇選, (*by vote*) hsüan² chü³ 「選舉.

electricity *n.* tien⁴ 電.

electrify *v.* shih² kan³ tien⁴ 使感電, (*excite*) chi¹ 「tung⁴ 激動.

electro *n.* tien⁴ pan³ 電版.

electrocute *v.* shih¹ tien⁴ hsing² 施電刑.

electrode *n.* tien⁴ chi² 電極.

electrolysis *n.* tien⁴ chieh³ 電解.

electrolyte *n.* tien⁴ chieh³ chih² 電解質.

electromagnet *n.* tien⁴ tz'u² t'ieh³ 電磁鐵.

electromotive *a.* fa¹ tien⁴ te¹ 發電的.

electron *n.* tien⁴ tzu³ 電子.

electroplate *v.* tien⁴ tu⁴ 電鍍.

electroscope *n.* yen⁴ tien⁴ ch'i⁴ 驗電器. 「鑄術.

electrotype *n.* tien⁴ pan³ 電版, tien⁴ chu⁴ shu⁴ 電

elegant *a.* yu¹ mei³ te¹ 優美的, wen² ya³ te¹ 文雅 「的.

elegy *n.* wan³ shih¹ 輓詩. 「的.

element *n.* yüan² su⁴ 原素, yao⁴ su⁴ 要素.

elementary *a.* yüan² chih² te¹ 原質的, ch'u¹ pu⁴

70

te¹ 初步的; ~ **school,** hsiao³ hsüeh² hsiao 小學 ⌐校.

elephant *n.* hsiang⁴ 象.

elevate *v.* chü² ch'i³ 舉起, sheng¹ kao¹ 升高.

elevation *n.* (*artillery*) she⁴ chiao³ 射角(軍), (*top*) piao¹ kao¹ 標高; ~ **sight,** kao¹ ti¹ miao² chun³ chü⁴ 高低瞄準具.

eleven *n.* shih² i¹ 十一; *a.* shih² i⁴ te¹ 十一的.

elf *n.* kuei³ kuai⁴ 鬼怪.

elicit *v.* yin³ ch'u¹ 引出, yu⁴ ch'u¹ 誘出.

elide *v.* ko¹ ch'ü⁴ 割去, sheng³ lüeh⁴ 省略 ⌐的.

eligible *a.* shih⁴ i² te¹ 適宜的, k'o² ch'ü³ te¹ 可取

eliminate *v.* ch'u² ch'ü⁴ 除去.

elite *n.* ching¹ hua² 精華.

elk *n.* mi² 麋.

ellipse *n.* t'o³ yüan² hsing² 橢圓形.

ellipsis *n.* sheng³ lüeh⁴ fa³ 省略法. ⌐的.

elliptic, elliptical *a.* t'o³ yüan² hsing² te¹ 橢圓形

elm *n.* yü² shu⁴ 楡樹(植).

elocution *n.* yen³ shuo¹ shu⁴ 演說術.

elongate *v.* yen² ch'ang² 延長.

eelop *v.* ssu¹ pen¹ 私奔.

eloquent *a.* hsiung² pien⁴ te¹ 雄辯的.

else *a.,* *pron.* pieh² te¹ 別的, ling⁴ wai⁴ 另外.

elsewhere *adv.* pieh² ch'u⁴ 別處, t'a¹ ch'u⁴ 他處.

elucidate *v.* shuo¹ ming² 說明.

elude *v.* t'ao² pi⁴ 逃避.

Elysium *n.* t'ien¹ t'ang² 天堂.

emaciate *v.* shih³ shou⁴ 使瘦.

emanate *v.* liu² ch'u¹ 流出, fa¹ ch'u¹ 發出.

emancipate *v.* shih⁴ fang⁴ 釋放.

embalm *v.* pao³ ts'un² 保存.

embank *v.* chu² ti¹ 築堤.

embargo *n.* t'ing² chih³ 停止, chin¹ yün⁴ 禁運.

embark *v.* (*ship*) shang⁴ ch'uan² 上船, (*start*) ts'ung² shih⁴ 從事.

embarrass *v.* k'un⁴ huo⁴ 困惑, (*hinder*) fang² ai⁴ 妨礙, (*debt*) shih³ ch'iung² p'o⁴ 使窮迫.

embassy *n.* ta⁴ shih² kuan³ 大使館.

embellish *v.* chuang¹ shih⁴ 裝飾.

ember *n.* yü² huo³ 餘火.

embezzle *v.* tao⁴ yung⁴ 盜用.

71

embitter v. shih³ k'u³ 使苦.

emblem n. piao³ chi⁴ 表記.　　　　　「形成一體.

embody v. ho² ping⁴ 合併, hsing² ch'eng² i⁴ t'i³

embolden v. ku³ li⁴ 鼓勵.　　　　　　　「包括.

embrace v. yung³ pao⁴ 擁抱, (*contain*) pao³ k'uo⁴

embrocate v. t'u² ts'a¹ 塗擦.

embroider v. tz'u⁴ hsiu⁴ 刺繡.　　　　　「亂.

embroil v. shih³ cheng¹ tou⁴ 使爭鬭, tao³ luan⁴ 搗

embryo n. p'ei¹ t'ai¹ 胚胎.

emend v. kai³ cheng⁴ 改正.

emerald n. lü³ pao³ shih² 綠寶石, lü⁴ yü⁴ 綠玉.

emerge v. ch'u¹ hsien⁴ 出現.

emergency n. wei² chi² 危急, chi² shih⁴ 急事.

emeritus a. ming² yü⁴ t'ui⁴ chih² te¹ 名譽退職的.

emery n. chin¹ kang¹ sha¹ 金鋼砂.

emetic a. chih⁴ t'u⁴ te¹ 致吐的.

emigrate v. i² chü¹ 移居.　　　　　　　「高位的.

eminent a. chu⁴ ming² te¹ 著名的, kao¹ wei⁴ te¹

emissary n. mi⁴ shih³ 密使.

emission n. fa¹ she⁴ 發射, fang⁴ she⁴ wu⁴ 放射物.

emit v. fa¹ ch'u¹ 發出, she⁴ ch'u¹ 射出.

emollient a. shih³ jou² juan³ te¹ 使柔軟的, yu²
hua² te¹ 油滑的.

emolument n. li⁴ i⁴ 利益, pao⁴ ch'ou² 報酬.

emotion n. kan³ ch'ing² 感情.

emperor n. huang² ti⁴ 皇帝.　　　　　「chung⁴ 加重.

emphasis n. chia¹ chung⁴ yü³ shih⁴ 加重語勢, chia¹

empire n. ti⁴ kuo² 帝國, kuo² t'u³ 國土.

empirical a. ching¹ yen⁴ te¹ 經驗的.

employ v. (*use*) shih³ yung⁴ 使用, (*hire*) ku⁴ yung⁴

employee n. ku⁴ yüan² 僱員.　　　　　　「僱用.

employer n. ku⁴ chu³ 僱主.

employment n. chih² yeh⁴ 職業, ku⁴ yung⁴ 僱用.

empower v. shou⁴ ch'üan² 授權.　　　　「女皇.

empress n. huang² hou⁴ 皇后, (*ruler*) nü³ huang²

empty a. k'ung¹ te¹ 空的, k'ung¹ hsü¹ te¹ 空虛的.

emulate v. ching⁴ cheng¹ 競爭, k'ang⁴ heng² 抗
衡.　　　　　　　　　　　　　　　　「乳狀液.

emulsify v. pien⁴ ch'eng² ju³ chuang⁴ yeh⁴ 變成

emulsion n. ju³ chuang⁴ yeh⁴ t'i³ 乳狀液體.

enable v. shih³ neng² 使能, shou⁴ ch'üan² 授權.

enact *v.* chih⁴ ting⁴ 制定.

enamel *n.* fa⁴ lang² chih² 珐瑯質.

encamp *v.* cha³ ying² 紮營, chu⁴ ying² 駐營.

enchain *v.* so³ chu⁴ 鎖住.

enchant *v.* mi² huo⁴ 迷惑.

encipher *v.* fan¹ ch'eng² mi⁴ ma³ 翻成密碼.

encircle *v.* wei² jao⁴ 圍繞.   「入.

enclose *v.* pao¹ wei² 包圍, (*envelop*) feng¹ ju⁴ 封

encompass *v.* huan² jao⁴ 環繞.

encore *adv.* tsai¹ i² tz'u⁴ 再一次.   「chan⁴ 會戰.

encounter *v.* (*meet*) yü² chien⁴ 遇見, (*battle*) hui⁴

encourage *v.* ku³ li⁴ 鼓勵.

encroach *v.* ch'in¹ chan⁴ 侵佔.   「ho⁴ 負荷.

encumber *v.* (*obstruct*) tsu³ ai⁴ 阻礙, (*burden*) fu⁴

encyclopedia *n.* pai³ k'o¹ ch'üan² shu¹ 百科全書.

end *n.* chung¹ tien³ 終點, wan² chieh² 完結; *v.* chung¹ liao³ 終了.

endanger *v.* mao⁴ hsien³ 冒險.

endear *v.* shih² k'o³ ai⁴ 使可愛.

endeavor *n.* nu³ li⁴ 努力; *v.* ch'ang² shih⁴ 嘗試.

endive *n.* chü² chü⁴ 菊距(植).

endorse *v.* (*check*) pei⁴ ch'ien¹ 背簽, (*approve*) tsan⁴ chu⁴ 贊助.   「*etc*)fu⁴ yü² 賦與.

endow *v.* chi³ i² pu³ chu⁴ chin¹ 給以補助金,(*talent,*

endure *v.* chi⁴ hsü⁴ 繼續, ch'ih² chiu³ 持久.

enema *n.* kuan¹ ch'ang² 灌腸(醫), kuan¹ ch'ang² 「chi⁴ 灌腸劑.

enemy *n.* ch'ou² ti² 仇敵.

energize *v.* chu⁴ shih⁴ 助勢, yung⁴ li⁴ 用力.

energy *n.* (*vigor*) neng² li⁴ 能力, (*power*) shih⁴ li⁴ 「勢力.

enervate *v.* chih⁴ jo⁴ 致弱.

enfeeble *v.* shih³ jo⁴ 使弱.

enfilade *v.* chih² chi¹ 直擊, tsung¹ she⁴ 縱射.

enforce *v.* shih² hsing² 實行, ch'iang³ p'o⁴ 強迫.

enfranchise *v.* (*free*) shih⁴ fang⁴ 釋放.   「戰.

engage *v.* yüeh¹ ting⁴ 約定, (*battle*) hui⁴ chan⁴ 會

engaging *a.* tung⁴ jen² te¹ 動人的.

engender *v.* ch'an³ sheng¹ 產生, yin³ ch'i³ 引起.

engine *n.* chi¹ ch'i⁴ 機器, yin³ ch'ing² 引擎.

engineer *n.* kung¹ ch'eng² shih¹ 工程師.

engrave *v.* tiao¹ k'o¹ 彫刻.

engross *v.* hsi¹ shou¹ 吸收, lung³ tuan⁴ 壟斷.

engulf v. t'un¹ ju⁴ 吞入, hsien⁴ ju⁴ 陷入.

enhance v. tseng¹ chia¹ 增加, chia¹ ta⁴ 加大.

enigma n. mi² 謎. 「chih³ 禁止.

enjoin v. (order) ming⁴ ling⁴ 命令, (forbid) chin⁴

enjoy v. hsiang³ le⁴ 享樂.

enkindle v. tien² huo³ 點火, hsing¹ fen⁴ 興奮.

enlarge v. tseng¹ chia¹ 增加, fang⁴ ta⁴ 放大.

enlighten v. ch'i¹ fa¹ 啓發, chiao⁴ tao³ 教導.

enlist v. (military service) ju⁴ wu³ 入伍(軍).

enliven v. shih³ huo² tung⁴ 使活動, shih³ k'uai⁴
le⁴ 使快樂.

enmity n. ch'ou² hen⁴ 仇恨, yüan⁴ hen⁴ 怨恨.

ennoble v. shih² hsien³ ta² 使顯達.

enormous a. chü⁴ ta⁴ te¹ 巨大的.

enormity n. ta⁴ tsui⁴ 大罪, ta⁴ e⁴ 大惡.

enough a. ch'ung¹ tsu² te² 充足的.

enquire v. hsün⁴ wen⁴ 詢問, ch'a² chiu¹ 查究.

enrage v. ch'u⁴ nu⁴ 觸怒.

enrapture v. shih³ k'uang² hsi³ 使狂喜.

enrich v. shih³ fu⁴ 使富.

enroll v. chu⁴ ts'e⁴ 註册, (enlist) ying⁴ mu⁴ 應募.

ensign n. ch'i² chih⁴ 旗幟, (rank) shao⁴ wei⁴ 少尉
└(海).

enslave v. nu² i⁴ 奴役.

ensue v. (follow) chui¹ sui² 追隨.

ensure v. pao³ cheng⁴ 保證, pao² hsien³ 保險.

entangle v. lien² lei⁴ 連累.

enter v. chin⁴ ju⁴ 進入.

enteric a. ch'ang² te¹ 腸的.

enterprise n. ch'i⁴ yeh⁴ 企業. 「的.

enterprising a. chü⁴ ch'i⁴ yeh⁴ hsin¹ te¹ 具企業心

entertain v. k'uan³ tai⁴ 款待, yü² le⁴ 娛樂.

enthrall, enthral v. shih³ wei² nu² li⁴ 使爲奴隸.

enthrone v. chi² wei⁴ 卽位.

enthusiasm n. je⁴ hsin¹ 熱心, je⁴ ch'ing² 熱情.

entice v. yu⁴ huo⁴ 誘惑.

entire a. wan² cheng³ te¹ 完整的; ～ **front,**
ch'üan² hsien⁴ 全線.

entitle v. (qualify) shou⁴ i³ ch'üan² li⁴ 授以權利,
(name) tsun¹ ch'eng¹ 尊稱.

entity n. shih² tsai⁴ wu⁴ 實在物.

entomb v. tsang⁴ 葬.

entomology *n.* k'un¹ ch'ung² hsüeh² 昆蟲學.

entrails *n.* nei⁴ tsang⁴ 內臟.

entrain *v.* ch'eng² hou³ ch'e¹ 乘火車.

entrance *n.* (*door*) ju⁴ k'ou³ 入口.

entrap *v.* ching² pu³ 阱捕.

entreat *v.* k'en³ ch'iu² 懇求.

entry *n.* ju⁴ 入, (*list*) teng¹ lu⁴ 登錄.

entwine *v.* ch'an² jao⁴ 纏繞.

enumerate *v.* chi⁴ shu⁴ 計數.

enunciate *v.* ch'en² shu⁴ 陳述, (*pronounce*) fa¹ yin¹ 發音.

envelop *v.* (*wrap*) feng¹ 封, (*surround*) pao¹ wei² 包圍.

envelope *n.* (*letter*) hsin⁴ feng¹ 信封.

envenom *v.* hsia⁴ tu² 下毒, (*hate*) shih³ k'u³ 使苦.

envious *a.* chi⁴ tu⁴ te¹ 嫉妒的.

environ *v.* wei² 圍, huan² jao⁴ 環繞.

environment *n.* wei² jao⁴ 圍繞, huan² ching⁴ 環境.

envoy *n.* chuan¹ shih³ 專使.

envy *n.* chi⁴ tu⁴ 嫉妒, hsien⁴ mu⁴ 羨慕.

epaulet *n.* chien¹ chang¹ 肩章.

ephemeral *a.* tuan³ ming⁴ te¹ 短命的.

epidemic *a.* p'u³ t'ung⁴ te¹ 普通的, (*disease*) liu² hsing² ping⁴ te¹ 流行病的.

epidermis *n.* (*skin*) piao³ p'i² 表皮, shu⁴ p'i² 樹皮.

epiglottis *n.* ch'i⁴ kuan³ men² 氣管門(醫).

epigram *n.* ching² yü³ 警語.

epilepsy *n.* tien¹ hsien² 癲癇(醫).

Epiphany *n.* chu² hsien³ chieh¹² 主顯節.

episode *n.* ou³ jan² te¹ shih⁴ 偶然的事.

epistle *n.* shu¹ hsin⁴ 書信.

epitaph *n.* mu⁴ chih⁴ ming² 墓誌銘.

epitome *n.* yao³ ling³ 要領, chai¹ yao⁴ 摘要.

epoch *n.* shih² tai⁴ 時代, chi⁴ yüan² 紀元.

equable *a.* i² lü⁴ te¹ 一律的.

equal *a.* hsiang¹ teng³ te¹ 相等的.

equalize *v.* shih³ hsiang¹ teng³ 使相等.

equanimity *n.* chen⁴ ching⁴ 鎮靜.

equation *n.* fang¹ ch'eng² shih⁴ 方程式.

equator *n.* ch'ih⁴ tao⁴ 赤道.

equiangular *a.* teng² chiao¹ te¹ 等角的.

equidistant *a.* teng³ chü¹ te¹ 等距的.

equilateral *a.* teng³ pien¹ te¹ 等邊的.

75

equilibrium *n.* p'ing² heng² 平衡.

equip *v.* she⁴ pei⁴ 設備.

equipment *n.* chuang¹ pei⁴ 裝備(軍).

equipoise *n.* p'ing² heng² 平衡.

equity *n.* kung¹ p'ing² 公平.

equivalent *a.* hsiang¹ teng³ te¹ 相等的.

era *n.* shih² tai⁴ 時代, chi⁴ yüan² 紀元.

eradicate *v.* pa² ch'u² 拔除.

erase *v.* mo³ ch'ü⁴ 抹去, ts'a¹ ch'ü⁴ 擦去.

ere *prep., conj.* i³ ch'ien² 以前. 「chien⁴ li⁴ 建立.

erect *a.* chih² li⁴ te¹ 直立的; *v.* chih² li⁴ 直立.

erode *v.* fu³ shih² 腐蝕.

erotic *a.* ai¹ te¹ 愛的, lien⁴ ai¹ te¹ 戀愛的.

err *v.* mi² lu⁴ 迷路, ch'a¹ wu⁴ 差誤.

errand *n.* shih³ ming⁴ 使命.

errant *a.* yu² tang⁴ te¹ 遊蕩的.

erratic *a.* (*uncertain*) pu² ting⁴ te¹ 不定的, (*queer*) ku³ kuai⁴ te¹ 古怪的.

erratum *n.* ts'o⁴ tzu⁴ 錯字.

erroneous *a.* ts'o⁴ wu⁴ te¹ 錯誤的.

error *n.* (*mistake*) ts'o⁴ wu⁴ 錯誤, (*sin*) tsui⁴ 罪.

erstwhile *adv.* wang³ hsi¹ 往昔.

erudite *a.* po² hsüeh² te¹ 博學的. 「tung⁴ 暴動.

erupt *v.* pao⁴ fa¹ 爆發, ch'ung¹ ch'u¹ 衝出, pao⁴

escalade *n.* teng¹ ch'iang² 登牆.

escapade *n.* t'o¹ t'ao² 脫逃, t'ao² wang² 逃亡.

escape *v.* t'ao² tsou³ 逃走.

escheat *n.* kuei¹ huan² ch'an³ yeh⁴ 歸還產業.

eschew *v.* kuei¹ pi⁴ 規避, pi⁴ mien³ 避免.

escort *n.* hu⁴ shung⁴ che³ 護送者. 「枪.

escritoire *n.* shu¹ cho¹ 書桌, hsieh³ tzu⁴ t'ai² 寫字

esculent *a.* k'o³ shih² te¹ 可食的.

esophagus *n.* shih² tao⁴ 食道, shih² kuan³ 食管.

especial *a.* t'e⁴ pieh² te¹ 特別的.

Esperanto *n.* shih⁴ chieh⁴ yü³ 世界語.

espionage *n.* chen¹ t'an⁴ 偵探, chien⁴ tieh² 間諜.

esplanade *n.* kuang² ch'ang³ 廣場, k'ung¹ ti⁴ 空地.

espy *v.* (*see*) chien⁴ 見, (*spy*) chen¹ t'an⁴ 偵探.

essay *n.* (*composition*) lun⁴ wen² 論文, (*try*) ch'ang² shih⁴ 嘗試; *v.* ch'ang² shih⁴ 嘗試.

essential *a.* pi⁴ hsü¹ te¹ 必需的.

establish *v.* ch'uang⁴ li⁴ 創立.

establishment *n.* ch'uang⁴ li⁴ 創立, (*institution*) tsu³ chih¹ 組織. 「shen¹ fen⁴ 身份.

estate *n.* (*possessions*) ts'ai² ch'an³ 財産, (*status*)

esteem *v.* (*value*) ku¹ chia⁴ 估價, (*regard highly*) chung⁴ shih⁴ 重視, (*consider*) shih⁴ wei² 視為.

ester *n.* yu³ chi¹ yen² 有機鹽.

estimable *a.* k'o³ ching⁴ te¹ 可敬的.

estimate *v.* p'in⁴ p'ing⁴ 品評; *n.* (*of cost*) ku¹ chia⁴ 估價; ~ **of terrain,** ti⁴ hsing² p'an⁴ tuan⁴ 地形判斷; ~ **of the enemy situation,** ti² ch'ing² p'an⁴ tuan⁴ 敵情判斷; ~ **of the situation,** ch'ing² k'uang⁴ p'an⁴ tuan⁴ 情況判斷.

estop *v.* tsu³ ai⁴ 阻礙, tsu² chih³ 阻止. 「間.

estrange *v.* shih³ su¹ yüan³ 使疏遠, li² chien⁴ 離

et cetera *n.* teng³ teng³ 等等, ch'i² yü² 其餘.

etch *v.* shih³ k'o⁴ 蝕刻. 「sheng¹ 永生.

eternal *a.* yung² yüan³ te¹ 永遠的; ~ **life,** yung³

eternity *n.* yung² yüan³ 永遠.

ether *n.* mi² 醚, i³ t'ai¹ 以太, (*clear sky*) t'ai⁴ k'ung¹ 太空.

ethics *n.* lun² li³ hsüeh⁴ 倫理學. 「種族的.

ethnic *a.* jen² chung³ te¹ 人種的, chung³ tsu² te¹

ethnography *n.* jen² chung³ chih⁴ 人種誌.

ethnology *n.* jen² chung³ hsüeh² 人種學.

ethyl *n.* erh¹ wan² chi¹ 二烷基(化).

etiquette *n.* li³ i² 禮儀. 「yüan² 字源.

etude *n.* yen² chiu¹ 研究.

etymology *n.* tzu⁴ yüan² hsüeh² 字源學, tzu⁴

Eucharist *n.* sheng⁴ ts'an¹ 聖餐.

eugenics *n.* yu¹ sheng¹ hsüeh² 優生學.

eulogy *n.* sung⁴ yang² 頌揚.

eunuch *n.* yen¹ jen² 閹人, t'ai⁴ chien⁴ 太監.

euphemism *n.* wan³ tz'u² 婉辭.

evacuate *v.* (*withdraw*) ch'e⁴ t'ui⁴ 撤退.

evade *v.* pi⁴ mien³ 避免, t'ao² pi⁴ 逃避.

evanescent *a.* hsiao¹ mieh⁴ te¹ 消滅的, fei¹ san³ te¹ 飛散的.

evangelist *n.* ch'uan² tao⁴ che³ 傳道者.

evangelize *v.* shih³ hsin⁴ yeh¹ su¹ chiao⁴ 使信耶

蘇敎. 「shih¹ 消失.

evaporate *v.* cheng¹ fa¹ 蒸發, (*vanish*) hsiao¹

eve *n.* chieh² jih⁴ te¹ ch'ien² hsi 節日的前夕.

even *a.* p'ing² te¹ 平的, kuang¹ hua² te¹ 光滑的; *adv.* ch'üeh⁴ jan² 確然.

evening *n.* wan³ 晚; ~ **dress**, yeh⁴ li³ fu² 夜禮服; ~ **paper**, wan³ pao⁴ 晚報.

event *n.* fa¹ sheng¹ 發生, shih⁴ pien⁴ 事變.

eventful *a.* to¹ shih⁴ te¹ 多事的.

eventual *a.* tsui⁴ hou⁴ te¹ 最後的.

eventuate *v.* chieh² kuo² 結果.

ever *adv.* ching¹ ch'ang² 經常.

everglade *n.* shih¹ ti⁴ 濕地.

evergreen *a.* ch'ang² lü⁴ te¹ 常綠的.

everlasting *a.* wu² ch'iung² te¹ 無窮的.

evermore *adv.* yung² yüan³ 永遠. 「個.

every *a.* mei³ i⁴ te¹ 每一的; *pron.* mei³ i² ko⁴ 每一

everybody *n.* ko⁴ jen² 各人.

everyone *n.* ko⁴ jen² 各人.

everything *n.* mei³ shih⁴ 每事, mei³ wu⁴ 每物.

everywhere *adv.* ch'u⁴ ch'u⁴ 處處.

evict *v.* ch'ü¹ chu² 驅逐.

evidence *n.* cheng⁴ chü⁴ 證據, (*law*) cheng⁴ yen² 證言; *v.* cheng⁴ ming² 證明. 「惡.

evil *a.* e⁴ te¹ 惡的; *n.* tsai¹ hai⁴ 災害, hsieh² e⁴ 邪

evince *v.* ming² shih⁴ 明示.

evolution *n.* (*growth*) fa¹ yü⁴ 發育 (*biology*) chin⁴

evolve *v.* chan³ k'ai¹ 展開. 「hua⁴ 進化.

ewe *n.* tz'u² yang² 雌羊.

ewer *n.* ta⁴ shui³ p'ing² 大水瓶. 「so³ 强索.

exact *a.* cheng⁴ ch'üeh⁴ te¹ 正確的; *v.* ch'iang²

exactitude *n.* ching¹ ch'üeh⁴ 精確.

exaggerate *v.* k'ua¹ chang¹ 誇張.

examination *n.* k'ao³ shih⁴ 考試; ~ **Yuan***, k'ao³ shih⁴ yüan⁴ 考試院*.

examine *v.* ch'a² wen⁴ 查問, k'ao³ ch'a² 考察.

example *n.* hsien¹ li⁴ 先例, mo² fan⁴ 模範.

excavate *v.* fa¹ chüeh² 發掘.

excavation *n.* hsüeh⁴ 穴, tung⁴ 洞.

exceed *v.* (*go beyond*) ch'ao¹ yüeh⁴ 超越, (*surpass*) yu¹ yüeh⁴ 優越.

exceeding *a.* (*very great*) chi² ta⁴ te¹ 極大的, (*surpassing*) yu¹ yüeh⁴ te¹ 優越的.

excel *v.* yu¹ sheng⁴ 優勝, ch'ao¹ yüeh⁴ 超越.

excellent *a.* yu¹ yüeh⁴ te¹ 優越的, tsui⁴ chia¹ te¹ 最佳的. 「te¹ 較上的.

excelsior *a.* keng⁴ kao¹ te¹ 更高的, chiao⁴ shang⁴

except *v.* ch'u² ch'ü⁴ 除去; *prep.* ch'u² wai⁴ 除外.

exception *n.* ch'u² wai⁴ 除外, (*objection*) i⁴ i⁴ 異議.

excerpt *n.* chai¹ lu⁴ 摘錄, hsüan³ lu⁴ 選錄.

exchange *v.* chiao¹ huan⁴ 交換, chiao¹ i⁴ 交易; *n.* chiao¹ i⁴ so³ 交易所; ~ **of prisoners,** chiao¹ huan⁴ chan⁴ fu² 交換戰俘.

exchequer *n.* kuo² k'u⁴ 國庫.

excise *n.* (*tax*) shui⁴ 稅.

excite *v.* chi¹ tung⁴ 激動, hsing¹ fen⁴ 興奮.

exclaim *v.* hu¹ ch'u¹ 呼出.

exclamation *n.* hu¹ han³ 呼喊. 「wai⁴ 除外.

exclude *v.* chu² ch'u¹ 逐出, p'ai² ch'ih⁴ 排斥, ch'u²

excrement *n.* p'ai² hsieh⁴ wu⁴ 排泄物.

excrescence *n.* liu² 瘤, chui⁴ jou⁴ 贅肉.

excrete *v.* p'ai² hsieh⁴ 排泄.

excruciate *v.* chia¹ i³ t'ung⁴ k'u³ 加以痛苦.

exculpate *v.* cheng⁴ ming² wu² tsui⁴ 證明無罪.

excursion *n.* (*trip*) lü³ hsing² 旅行; ~ **ticket,** yu² lan³ ch'üan⁴ 遊覽券; ~ **train,** yu² lan³ lieh⁴ ch'e¹ 遊覽列車. 「消遣的.

excursive *a.* man⁴ yu² te¹ 漫遊的, hsiao¹ yao² te¹

excusable *a.* k'o³ shu⁴ te¹ 可恕的.

excuse *v.* yüan² liang⁴ 原諒, (*apologize*) yu⁴ shu⁴ 宥恕, she⁴ mien³ 赦免; *n.* li³ yu² 理由, (*apology*) shu⁴ yu⁴ 恕宥. 「ch'u³ chüeh¹ 處決.

execute *v.* (*carry out*) chih² hsing² 執行, (*punish*)

executioner *n.* kuei⁴ tzu¹ shou³ 劊子手.

executive *a.* chih² hsing² te¹ 執行的; *n.* (*office*) hsing² cheng⁴ pu⁴ 行政部, (*person*) hsing² cheng⁴ kuan¹ 行政官; ~ **Yuan***, hsing² cheng⁴ yüan⁴ 行政院*.

executor *n.* chih² hsing² che³ 執行者.

exegesis *n.* chu⁴ chieh³ 註解.

exemplar *n.* fang² pen³ 倣本, yang⁴ tzu¹ 樣子.

exempt *a.* huo⁴ mien³ te¹ 豁免的, mien³ ch'u² te¹

免除的; *n.* mien³ ch'u² che³ 免除者.

exemption *n.* huo⁴ mien⁴ 豁免, mien³ ch'u² 免除; ~ **from service,** mien³ i⁴ 免役.

exercise *n.* (*use*) shih³ yung⁴ 使用, (*physical*) t'i³ ts'ao¹ 體操, (*practice*) yen³ hsi² 演習; *v.* (*use*) shih³ yung⁴ 使用, (*train*) ts'ao¹ lien⁴ 操練, (*annoy*) k'un⁴ nao³ 困惱.

exert *v.* yung⁴ li⁴ 用力, nu³ li⁴ 努力.

exhale *v.* hu¹ ch'u¹ 呼出, cheng¹ fa¹ 蒸發.

exhaust *v.* ch'ou¹ chin⁴ 抽盡, shih³ k'ung⁴ 使空; ~ **pipe,** p'ai² ch'i⁴ kuan³ 排氣管; ~ **valve,** p'ai² ch'i⁴ men² 排氣門. 「ch'e⁴ te¹ 透徹的.

exhaustive *a.* ch'ou¹ k'ung¹ te¹ 抽空的, t'ou⁴

exhibit *v.* ch'en² lieh⁴ 陳列, chan² lan³ 展覽.

exhibition *n.* (*display*) ch'en² lieh⁴ 陳列, (*public show*) chan² lan³ hui⁴ 展覽會. 「p'o¹ 使活潑.

exhilarate *v.* shih³ yü² k'uai⁴ 使愉快, shih³ huo²

exhort *v.* ch'üan⁴ wei² shan⁴ 勸爲善, ch'in² mien³

exhume *v.* fa¹ chüeh² 發掘. 「勉勉.

exigency *n.* chi² hsü¹ 急需, chin³ chi² 緊急.

exigent *a.* p'o⁴ ch'ieh¹ te¹ 迫切的, wei² chi² te¹ 危急的. 「chu² 放逐.

exile *n.* fang⁴ chu² 放逐, liu² fan⁴ 流犯; *v.* fang⁴

exist *v.* ts'un² tsai⁴ 存在, sheng¹ ts'un² 生存; *n.* sheng¹ ts'un² 生存, ts'un² tsai⁴ wu⁴ 存在物.

exit *n.* (*way out*) ch'u¹ k'ou³ 出口, (*departure*) wai⁴ ch'u¹ 外出, (*stage*) t'ui⁴ ch'ang³ 退場.

exodus *n.* ch'u¹ hsing² 出行.

exonerate *n.* mien³ tsui⁴ 免罪.

exorbitant *a.* kuo⁴ fen⁴ te¹ 過分的.

exotic *a.* wai⁴ kuo² te¹ 外國的, wai⁴ lai² te¹ 外來的; *n.* wai⁴ lai² wu⁴ p'in³ 外來物品.

expand *v.* chan³ k'ai¹ 展開, fa¹ chan³ 發展.

expanse *n.* kuang³ ta⁴ te¹ mien⁴ chi¹ 廣大的面積.

expatriate *v.* fang⁴ chu² 放逐; *n.* liu² fan⁴ 流犯.

expect *v.* yü⁴ ch'i¹ 預期, hsi¹ wang⁴ 希望.

expectorate *v.* t'u⁴ 吐, t'o⁴ 唾, t'u⁴ t'an² 吐痰.

expedient *a.* te² ts'e⁴ te¹ 得策的; *n.* chi⁴ mou² 計 「謀.

expedite *v.* ts'ui¹ ts'u⁴ 催促.

expedition *n.* (*prompt action*) su² pan⁴ 速辦, (*journey*) yüan³ cheng¹ 遠征.

expel *v.* ch'ü¹ chu² 驅逐, fa¹ fang⁴ 發放.

expend *v.* hao² fei⁴ 耗費.

expense *n.* tai⁴ chia⁴ 代價, fei⁴ yung⁴ 費用.

expensive *a.* fei⁴ ch'ien² te¹ 費錢的, ang² kuei⁴ te¹ 昂貴的.

experience *n.* ching¹ yen⁴ 經驗, yüeh⁴ li⁴ 閱歷; *v.* ching¹ li⁴ 經歷, tsao¹ yü⁴ 遭遇.

experienced *a.* yu³ ching¹ yen⁴ te¹ 有經驗的.

experiment *n.* shih⁴ yen⁴ 試驗, shih² yen⁴ 實驗; *v.* shih⁴ yen⁴ 試驗.

expert *a.* lao³ lien⁴ te¹ 老練的, chi⁴ ch'iao³ te¹ 技巧的; chuan¹ chia¹ 專家, lao² shou³ 老手.

expiate *v.* shu² 贖(罪).

expire *v.* (*end*) man³ ch'i¹ 滿期, (*die*) ssu³ 死, (*breathe out*) hu¹ ch'u¹ 呼出.

explain *v.* chieh⁴ shih⁴ 解釋, chiang³ ming² 講明.

explicate *v.* (*explain*) chieh⁴ shih⁴ 解釋.

explicit *a.* ming² pai⁴ te¹ 明白的, ming² liao³ te¹ 明瞭的.

explode *v.* pao⁴ cha⁴ 爆炸, pao⁴ fa¹ 爆發.

exploit *n.* kung¹ yeh⁴ 功業, wei³ yeh⁴ 偉業.

explore *v.* t'an¹ ch'a² 探查, t'an¹ hsien³ 探險.

explosion *n.* pao⁴ cha⁴ 爆炸.

explosive *n.* cha⁴ yao⁴ 炸藥.

export *v.* shu¹ ch'u¹ 輸出, ch'u¹ k'ou³ 出口; *n.* (*article*) ch'u¹ k'ou³ huo⁴ 出口貨, (*exporting*) ch'u¹ k'ou³ yeh⁴ 出口業.

expose *v.* (*uncover*) p'u⁴ lou⁴ 暴露, (*display*) chan² lan³ 展覽, (*reveal*) hsien³ shih⁴ 顯示.

expostulate *v.* ch'üan¹ kao⁴ 勸告.

exposure *n.* p'u⁴ lou⁴ 暴露.

expound *v.* shuo¹ ming² 說明, chieh³ shih⁴ 解釋.

express *v.* (*indicate*) piao³ ming² 表明, (*press out*) cha⁴ ch'u¹ 榨出, (*message*) k'uai⁴ ti⁴ 快遞; *a.* (*clear*) ming² pai⁴ te¹ 明白的, (*exact*) k'u⁴ hsiao⁴ te¹ 酷肖的, (*fast*) chi² su⁴ te¹ 急速的, (*special*) t'e⁴ pieh² te¹ 特別的; *n.* (*message*) chuan¹ ch'ai¹ 專差, (*sending quick*) t'e⁴ k'uai⁴ yu² 特郵, (*traveling fast*) t'e⁴ pieh² k'uai⁴ ch'e¹ 特別快車; ~ **tickєt**, t'e⁴ k'uai⁴ ch'e¹ p'iao⁴ 特快車票; ~ **train**, t'e⁴ k'uai⁴ ch'e¹ 特快車.

expression v. piao³ pai² 表白, tz'u² chü⁴ 辭句.

expressive a. piao³ shih⁴ te¹ 表示的.

expulsion n. fang⁴ chu² 放逐, ch'u² ming² 除名.

expulsive a. chu² ch'u¹ te¹ 逐出的.

expunge v. mo³ ch'ü⁴ 抹去, t'u² ch'ü⁴ 塗去.

expurgate v. shan¹ cheng⁴ 删正.

exquisite a. (*delicate*) chüeh² mei³ te¹ 絕美的, (*sharp*) chi⁴ lieh⁴ te¹ 劇烈的.

extant a. ts'un² tsai⁴ te¹ 存在的.

extemporaneous a. lin² shih² te¹ 臨時的.

extempore a. lin² shih² te¹ 臨時的.

extend v. shen¹ chan³ 伸展, ta² 達, (*formation*) su³ k'ai¹ 疏開(軍).

extension n. shen¹ chan³ 伸展, k'uo⁴ chang¹ 擴張; ~ **course**, han² shou⁴ pan¹ 函授班(軍).

extent n. fan⁴ wei² 範圍, ta⁴ hsiao³ 大小.

extenuate v. chien³ ch'ing¹ 減輕, chien² shao³ 減少; a. chien³ ch'ing¹ te¹ 減輕的, chien² shao³ te¹ 減少的. 「表的; ~ **lines,** wai⁴ hsien⁴ 外線.

exterior a. wai⁴ mien⁴ te¹ 外面的, wai⁴ piao³ te¹ 外

exterminate v. mieh⁴ chüeh² 滅絕, ch'üan² hui³ 全毀. 「薄的.

external a. wai⁴ pu⁴ te¹ 外部的, ch'ien³ po² te¹ 淺

extinct a. hsi² mieh⁴ te¹ 熄滅的, pu⁴ ts'un² tsai⁴ te¹ 不存在的. 「hui³ mieh⁴ 毁滅.

extinguish v. (*quench*) hsi² mieh⁴ 熄滅, (*destroy*)

extirpate v. pa² ch'u² 拔除, chüeh² mieh⁴ 絕滅.

extol, extoll v. sung⁴ yang² 頌揚.

extort v. le¹ so³ 勒索.

extra a. e² wai⁴ te¹ 額外的; n. (*newspaper*) lin² shih² tseng¹ k'an¹ 臨時增刊, hao⁴ wai⁴ 號外, (*movie*) lin² shih² yen² yüan² 臨時演員.

extract n. (*substance*) ch'ou¹ ch'u¹ wu⁴ 抽出物, (*passage*) t'i² yao⁴ 提要; v. ch'ou¹ ch'u¹ 抽出.

extraction n. t'i² ch'u¹ 提出, (*descent*) chia¹ hsi⁴ 家

extradite v. yin³ tu⁴ 引渡. 「系.

extradition n. yin³ tu⁴ tsui⁴ fan⁴ 引渡罪犯.

extraneous a. wai⁴ lai² te¹ 外來的.

extraordinary a. fei¹ ch'ang² te¹ 非常的.

extravagant a. (*excessive*) kuo⁴ tu⁴ te¹ 過渡的, (*wasteful*) lang⁴ fei⁴ te¹ 浪費的.

82

extreme *a.* chi² tuan¹ te¹ 極端的; ～ **range**, tsui⁴ ta⁴ she⁴ ch'eng² 最大射程.

extricate *v.* chieh³ ch'u² 解除, p'ai² nan² 排難.

extrinsic *a.* wai¹ lai² te¹ 外來的.

extrude *v.* ch'u¹ chu² 驅逐.　　　　　　「豐富的.

exuberant *a.* fan² sheng⁴ te¹ 繁盛的, feng¹ fu⁴ te¹

exude *v.* liu² ch'u¹ 流出, shen⁴ ch'u¹ 滲出.

exult *v.* ta⁴ hsi³ 大喜.　　　　　　　　　　「觀察.

eye *n.* yen³ 眼, mu⁴ 目; *v.* k'an⁴ 看, kuan¹ ch'a²

eyeball *n.* yen³ ch'iu² 眼球.

eyebrow *n.* mei² 眉, mei² mao² 眉毛.

eyeglass *n.* yen³ ching² 眼鏡.

eyelash *n.* chieh² mao² 睫毛.

eyelid *n.* yen² chien³ 眼瞼, yen³ p'i² 眼皮.

eyesight *n.* mu⁴ kuang¹ 目光, yen³ li⁴ 眼力, shih⁴ li⁴ 視力.　　　　　　　　　　「che³ 目睹者.

eyewitness *n.* chien⁴ cheng⁴ jen² 見證人, mu⁴ tu²

F

fable *n.* shen² kuai⁴ hsiao³ shuo¹ 神怪小說, yü⁴ yen² 寓言; *v.* nieh¹ tsao⁴ 捏造, tu⁴ chuan¹ 杜撰.

fabulous *a.* yü⁴ yen² te¹ 寓言的, wu² chi¹ te¹ 無稽 的.

face *n.* mien⁴ mao⁴ 面貌, mien⁴ 面, (*surface*) piao³ mien⁴ 表面; *v.* (*toward*) mien⁴ hsiang⁴ 面向, (*oppose*) tui⁴ k'ang⁴ 對抗.　　　　　　　　「稽的.

facetious *a.* hui¹ hsieh² te¹ 詼諧的, hua² chi¹ te¹ 滑

facile *a.* jung² i⁴ te¹ 容易的.　　　「pien⁴ 使輕便.

facilitate *v.* shih³ jung² i⁴ 使容易, shih³ ch'ing¹

facility *n.* ch'ing¹ i⁴ 輕易, shou² lien⁴ 熟練.

fact *n.* (*truth*) shih³ shih² 事實, (*act*) tung⁴ tso⁴ 動 作.　　　　　　　　　　　　　　　「突.

faction *n.* tang³ p'ai⁴ 黨派, (*strife*) ch'ung¹ t'u² 衝

factor *n.* (*element*) yao⁴ su⁴ 要素, (*mathematics*) yin¹ su⁴ 因素, (*agent*) tai⁴ li³ jen² 代理人.

factory *n.* kung¹ ch'ang³ 工廠, chih⁴ tsao⁴ so³ 製造

factotum *n.* tsa² i⁴ 雜役.　　　　　　　　　　「所.

faculty *n.* (*ability*) neng² li⁴ 能力, ts'ai² neng² 才

能, chih⁴ li⁴ 智力, (teachers) chiao⁴ yüan² t'uan² 致員團

fade v. (wither) k'u¹ wei³ 枯萎, (lose color) t'un⁴ se⁴ 褪色, (disappear) hsiao¹ mieh⁴ 消滅.

fag v. ch'in² lao² 勤勞, shih³ p'i² lao² 使疲勞.

fagot n. i² shu⁴ hsin¹ 一束薪.　　　　　　「表.

Fahrenheit n. hua² shih⁴ wen¹ tu⁴ piao³ 華氏溫度

fail v. shih¹ pai⁴ 失敗; n. shih¹ pai⁴ 失敗.

failure n. (failing) shih¹ pai⁴ te¹ 失敗.

fain a. ch'ing¹ yüan⁴ te¹ 情願的, hsi³ yüeh⁴ te¹ 喜悅的; adv. hsi³ yüeh⁴ ti⁴ 喜樂地, ta⁴ hsi³ ti⁴ 大喜地.

faint a. (timid) tan³ ch'üeh⁴ te¹ 膽怯的, (weak) shuai¹ jo⁴ te¹ 衰弱的; v. hun¹ yün² 昏暈.

fair a. (just) kung¹ p'ing² 公平, (average) chung¹ teng³ te¹ 中等的, (light) tan⁴ se⁴ te¹ 淡色的, (sunny) ch'ing² lang³ te¹ 晴朗的, (beautiful) mei² hao³ te¹ 美好的, (clean) ch'ing¹ pai² te¹ 清白的, (open) k'ai¹ k'uo⁴ te¹ 開闊的, (plain) ming² hsi¹ te¹ 明晰的; n. chih⁴ chi² 市集, (charity) tz'u² shan⁴ shih⁴ 慈善事; ～ **play,** kung¹ p'ing² ch'u³ chih⁴ 公平處置.　　　　　　　　　　　　　　「ch'ing¹ 妖精.

fairy n. (good) hsiao³ hsien¹ nü³ 小仙女, (evil) yao¹

faith n. hsin⁴ jen⁴ 信任, hsin⁴ yang³ 信仰, chung¹

falcon n. ying¹ 鷹.　　　　　　　　「ch'eng² 忠誠.

fall v. (drop down) hsia⁴ chiang⁴ 下降, (droop) ch'ui² hsia⁴ 垂下, (be captured) hsien⁴ lao⁴ 陷落, (be killed) ssu³ wang² 死亡, (happen) fa¹ sheng¹ 發生, (price) tieh⁴ lao⁴ 跌落, (look sad) tso⁴ pu² yü⁴ se⁴ 作不豫色; n. chiang⁴ hsia⁴ 降下, (capture) hsien⁴ lao⁴ 陷落, (price) tieh¹ chia⁴ 跌價, (slope) hsieh² p'o² 斜坡, (autumn) ch'iu¹ chi⁴ 秋季.

fallacy n. miu⁴ lun⁴ 謬論.

fallow a. tan⁴ huang² te¹ 淡黃的, wei⁴ k'en³ te¹ 未墾的; n. hsiu² keng¹ ti⁴ 休耕地.

false a. pu⁴ chen¹ shih² te¹ 不眞實的, ch'i¹ cha⁴ te¹ 欺詐的, wei³ tsao⁴ te¹ 僞造的; ～ **alarm,** hsü¹ ching¹ 虛驚; ～ **hair,** chia² fa³ 假髮; ～ **tooth,** chia² ch'ih³ 假齒器.

fame n. ming² yü⁴ 名譽, sheng¹ wang⁴ 聲望.

familiar a. (intimate) ch'in¹ mi⁴ te¹ 親密的, (well-acquainted) shou² hsi² te¹ 熟悉的, (well-known)

84

wen² ming² te¹ 聞名的.   「**name,** hsing⁴ 姓.

family *n.* chia¹ t'ing² 家庭, chia¹ tsu² 家族; ~

famine *n.* chi¹ huang¹ 饑荒, chi¹ e⁴ 饑餓.

famous *a.* chu⁴ ming² te¹ 著名的.

fan *n.* shan⁴ 扇, shan⁴ hsing² wu⁴ 扇形物; *v.* shan⁴
tung⁴ 扇動, ch'ui⁴ fu² 吹拂.

fanatic *n.* k'uang² je⁴ che³ 狂熱者.

fancy *n.* (*imagination*) huan⁴ hsiang³ 幻想, huan⁴
hsiang⁴ 幻象, (*fondness*) shih⁴ hao⁴ 嗜好; *v.* (*imagine*) huan⁴ hsiang³ 幻想, (*like*) hsi³ hao⁴ 喜好; ~
ball, hua⁴ chuang¹ t'iao⁴ wu³ hui⁴ 化裝跳舞會;
~ **procession,** hua⁴ chuang¹ yu² hsing² 化裝遊
行.

fantastic *a.* ch'i² huan⁴ te¹ 奇幻的, kuai⁴ i⁴ te¹ 怪
異的, hsiang³ hsiang⁴ te¹ 想像的.

fantasy *n.* huan⁴ hsiang³ 幻想, kuai⁴ hsiang³ 怪想.

far *a.* liao² yüan⁴ te¹ 遼遠的, chiu² yüan³ te¹ 久遠
的; ~ **East,** yüan³ tung¹ 遠東.

farad *n.* fa⁴ la¹ 法拉(電量單位).

farce *a.* hua⁴ chi¹ chü⁴ 滑稽劇, ch'ü⁴ chü⁴ 趣劇.

fare *n.* (*money*) ch'e¹ fei⁴ 車費, (*passenger*) ch'eng²
k'o⁴ 乘客, (*food*) shih² wu⁴ 食物; *v.* (*travel*) lü³
hsing² 旅行, (*happen*) tsao¹ feng² 遭逢, (*eat*)
hsiang³ yin³ shih² 享飲食.

farewell *n.* kao⁴ pieh² 告別, tsai⁴ hui⁴ 再會.

farm *n.* t'ien² ti⁴ 田地, nung² ch'ang³ 農場; *v.*
[keng¹ yün⁴ 耕耘.

farmer *n.* nung² fu¹ 農夫.

farmhouse *n.* t'ien² she⁴ 田舍.

farrow *n.* yu⁴ t'un² 幼豚; *v.* sheng¹ yü⁴ 生育.

farther *a.* keng⁴ yüan³ te¹ 更遠的, chin⁴ i² pu⁴ te¹

farthest *a.* tsui⁴ yüan³ te¹ 最遠的. 「進一步的.

fascinate *v.* mi² huo⁴ 迷惑.

fashion *n.* liu² hsing² 流行, shih² shang⁴ 時尚,
shih⁴ yang⁴ 式樣; *v.* kou⁴ ch'eng² 構成.

fast *a.* (*swift*) hsün⁴ su⁴ te¹ 迅速的, (*wild*) fang⁴
tang⁴ te¹ 放蕩的, (*firm*) chien¹ ku⁴ te¹ 堅固的,
(*loyal*) chung¹ shih² te¹ 忠實的; *adv.* (*quickly*)
k'uai⁴ su⁴ ti⁴ 快速地, (*firmly*) chien¹ ting⁴ ti⁴ 堅定
地.

fasten *v.* shih³ ku⁴ ting⁴ 使固定, fu² chu⁴ 縛住.

fastidious *a.* ch'ui¹ mao² ch'iu² tz'u¹ te¹ 吹毛求疵

85

的, nan² yü³ ch'ü³ yüeh⁴ te¹ 難於取悅的.

fastness *n.* yao² sai⁴ 要塞, p'ao¹ t'ai² 砲臺, hsün²
su² 迅速.

fat *n.* chih¹ fang¹ 脂肪, tsui⁴ liang² pu⁴ fen⁴ 最良部
份; *a.* fei² p'an⁴ te¹ 肥胖的.　　　　「祥的.

fatal *a.* chih⁴ ming⁴ te¹ 致命的, pu⁴ hsiang² te¹ 不

fate *n.* ming⁴ yün⁴ 命運, ting⁴ shu⁴ 定數, t'ien¹
ming⁴ 天命.　　　　　　　　　　　　　　　　「的.

fated *a.* ming⁴ ting⁴ te¹ 命定的, chu⁴ ting⁴ te¹ 註定

fatherland *n.* tsu³ kuo² 祖國.

fatigue *n.* p'i² lao² 疲勞; *v.* shih³ p'i² lao² 使疲勞.

fatten *v.* shih³ fei² 使肥, pien⁴ fei² 變肥.

fatuous *a.* yü² pen⁴ te¹ 愚笨的.

faucet *n.* shui³ lung² t'ou² 水龍頭.

fault *n.* (*mistake*) kuo⁴ shih¹ 過失.

favor *n.* en¹ tse² 恩澤, en¹ hui⁴ 恩惠: *v.* ch'ung³
ai⁴ 寵愛, (*approve*) tsan⁴ hsü³ 贊許, (*support*)
pang¹ chu⁴ 幫助, (*look like*) mao⁴ ssu⁴ 貌似.

favorite *a.* pei¹ ai⁴ hao³ te¹ 被愛好的.

favoritism *n.* p'ien¹ ai⁴ 偏愛, hsün² ssu¹ 徇私.

fawn *n.* yu⁴ lu⁴ 幼鹿; *v.* e¹ yü² 阿諛; *a.* tan³ ho²
se⁴ te¹ 淡褐色的.

fealty *n.* shun⁴ fu² 順服, chung¹ ch'eng² 忠誠.

fear *n.* k'ung³ chü⁴ 恐懼.

feast *n.* yen⁴ hui⁴ 宴會, (*festival*) chieh² ch'i¹ 節期.

feat *n.* kung¹ yeh⁴ 功業, shih⁴ yeh⁴ 事業, (*skill*)
chi⁴ i⁴ 技藝.

feather *n.* yü³ mao² 羽毛.

feature *n.* (*face*) mien⁴ mao⁴ 面貌, (*quality*) t'e⁴
se⁴ 特色.

febrifuge *n.* chieh³ je⁴ chi⁴ 解熱劑(醫).

febrile *a.* fa¹ je⁴ te¹ 發熱的 je⁴ ping⁴ te¹ 熱病的.

February *n.* erh⁴ yüeh⁴ 二月.

federal *a.* lien² meng² te¹ 聯盟的, lien² pang¹ kuo²
chia¹ te¹ 聯邦國家的.

federalize *v.* shih³ ch'eng² lien² pang¹ 使成聯邦.

federated *a.* lien² pang¹ te¹ 聯邦的, t'ung² meng²
te¹ 同盟的.

fee *n.* (*charge*) fei⁴ 費, ch'ou² chin¹ 酬金, (*tip*)
shang³ chin¹ 賞金, (*fief*) feng¹ t'u³ 封土.

feeble *a.* shuai¹ jo⁴ te¹ 衰弱的.

feed *v.* (*give food to*) wei⁴ ssu⁴ 喂飼; *n.* (*food for* *animals*) shih² liao⁴ 食料.

feel *v.* (*touch*) ch'u⁴ chih¹ 觸知, (*feeling*) kan³ chüeh² 感覺; *n.* (*sense of touch*) ch'u⁴ chüeh² 觸覺, (*a feeling*) kan³ chüeh² 感覺. 「kan³ 情感.

feeling *a.* jui⁴ kan³ te¹ 銳感的; *n.* (*emotion*) ch'ing²

feint *n.* (*attack*) yang² kung¹ 佯攻, (*pretense*) chia³ t'o¹ 假託; ∼ **attack,** yang² kung¹ 佯攻.

felicitate *v.* chu⁴ ho⁴ 祝賀. 「hsing³ fu² 幸福.

felicity *n.* (*happiness*) k'uai⁴ le⁴ 快樂, (*fortune*)

fellow *n.* (*man*) jen² 人, (*companion*) pan⁴ lü³ 伴侶.

felony *n.* chung⁴ tsui⁴ 重罪.

female *n.* (*for people*) nü³ hsing⁴ 女性, (*for animals*) tz'u² tung⁴ wu⁴ 雌動物.

fence *n.* (*wall*) wei² ch'ang² 圍場; *v.* (*enclose*) wei² hu⁴ 圍護, (*defend*) fang² wei² 防衛, (*fight with swords*) wu³ chien⁴ 舞劍.

fencing *n.* chien⁴ shu⁴ 劍術.

fend *v.* fang² yü⁴ 防禦.

ferment *n.* chiao⁴ mu³ 酵母, (*unrest*) sao¹ jao³ 騷擾; *v.* shih³ fa¹ chiao⁴ 使發酵, (*unrest*) sao¹ tung⁴ 騷動. 「tung⁴ 騷動.

fermentation *n.* fa¹ chiao⁴ 發酵, (*unrest*) sao¹

fern *n.* yang² ch'ih³ lei² chih² wu⁴ 羊齒類植物.

ferocious *a.* hsiung¹ pao⁴ te¹ 兇暴的, yeh³ man² te¹ 野蠻的.

ferocity *n.* ts'an² jen⁴ 殘忍, hsiung¹ pao⁴ 兇暴.

ferret *v.* sou¹ hsün² 搜尋; *n.* hsüeh³ tiao¹ 雪貂.

ferruginous *a.* t'ieh³ te¹ 鐵的, t'ieh³ hsiu⁴ se⁴ te¹

ferrule *n.* chin¹ shu³ huan⁴ 金屬環. 「鐵銹色的.

ferry *n.* (*steam ferry*) lun² tu⁴ 輪渡, (*place*) tu⁴ k'ou³ 渡口, (*boat*) tu⁴ ch'uan² 渡船.

fertile *a.* to¹ ch'an³ te¹ 多產的, fu⁴ jao² te¹ 富饒的.

fertilizer *n.* fei² liao⁴ 肥料.

ferule *n.* chieh⁴ ch'ih³ 戒尺; *v.* chieh⁴ tse² 戒責.

fervent *a.* (*hot*) je⁴ te¹ 熱的, (*earnest*) je⁴ ch'ing² te¹ 熱情的. 「熱的.

fervid *a.* je⁴ hsin¹ te¹ 熱心的, (*hot*) cho² je⁴ te¹ 灼

fervor *n.* (*emotion*) je⁴ ch'ing² 熱情.

festal *a.* chieh² jih⁴ te¹ 節日的. 「節期.

festival *a.* chieh² ch'i¹ te¹ 節期的; *n.* chieh² ch'i¹

festoon *n.* hua¹ ts'ai³ 花綵.

87

fetch v. (*go and get*) ch'ü³ lai² 取來, (*bring*) hsieh² lai² 携來.

fete n. sheng⁴ yen² 盛筵, chieh² jih⁴ 節日, chu⁴ tien³ 祝典; v. yen² hsiang³ 宴享.

fetid a. ch'ou⁴ te¹ 臭的, fu³ ch'ou⁴ te¹ 腐臭的.

fetish n. ou³ hsiang⁴ 偶像.

fetter n. (*chain*) chiao³ liao³ 脚鐐, (*restraint*) chi¹ pan⁴ 羈絆.

fetus n. t'ai² erh² 胎兒.

feud n. su⁴ ch'ou² 宿仇.

feudal a. feng³ chien⁴ te¹ 封建的.

fever n. je⁴ ping⁴ 熱病.

few a. shao³ shu⁴ te¹ 小數的, pu⁴ to¹ te¹ 不多的.

fez n. chan¹ mao³ 氈帽(無邊沿之).

fiat n. ming⁴ ling⁴ 命令, fa³ ling⁴ 法令.

fib n. huang² yü³ 謊語; v. shuo¹ huang³ 說謊.

fiber, fibre n. hsien¹ wei² 纖維, hsien¹ wei² chih⁴ 纖維質.

fickle a. i⁴ pien⁴ te¹ 易變的, wu² heng² te¹ 無恒的.

fiction n. hsü¹ kou⁴ 虛構, hsiao³ shuo¹ 小說.

fidelity n. (*faithfulness*) chung¹ ch'eng² 忠誠, (*accuracy*) chun³ ch'üeh⁴ 準確.

fidget v. pu⁴ an¹ 不安; n. pu⁴ an¹ ching⁴ 不安靜; a. pu⁴ an¹ ching⁴ te¹ 不安靜的.

fiduciary n. shou⁴ t'o¹ jen² 受託人; a. shou⁴ t'o¹ te¹ 受託的.

fief n. ts'ai³ se⁴ 采色, feng¹ t'u³ 封土.

field n. (*land*) t'ien² ti⁴ 田地, (*battle*) chan⁴ ch'ang² 戰場; ~ **army,** yeh³ chan⁴ chün¹ 野戰軍; ~ **artillery,** yeh³ p'ao⁴ ping¹ 野砲兵(軍); ~ **exercises,** yeh³ wai⁴ yen³ hsi² 野外演習(軍); ~ **glass,** wang⁴ yüan³ ching⁴ 望遠鏡; ~ **gun,** yeh³ p'ao⁴ 野炮; ~ **hospital,** yeh³ chan⁴ i¹ yüan⁴ 野戰醫院 (軍); ~ **howitzer,** yeh³ chan⁴ liu² tan⁴ p'ao⁴ 野戰榴彈砲(軍); ~ **manual,** ts'ao¹ tien³ 操典(軍); ~ **officer,** hsiao⁴ kuan¹ 校官(軍).

fieldpiece n. yeh³ chan⁴ p'ao⁴ 野戰礟.

fiend n. mo² kuei³ 魔鬼, e⁴ jen² 惡人.

fierce a. meng³ lieh⁴ te¹ 猛烈的, hsiung¹ pao⁴ te¹ 兇暴的, ts'an³ jen³ te¹ 殘忍的.

fiery a. ju² huo³ te¹ 如火的, chi¹ nu⁴ te¹ 激怒的 yung² meng³ te¹ 勇猛的.

fife n. ti² 笛.

fig *n.* wu² hua¹ kuo³ 無花果, (tree) wu² hua¹ kuo³ shu⁴ 無花果樹.

fight *v.* tou⁴ ou³ 鬬毆, (*war against*) chan⁴ cheng¹ 戰爭.

figure *n.* (*numeral*) shu⁴ tzu⁴ 數字, (*person*) jen² wu⁴ 人物, (*human form*) feng¹ tu⁴ 風度, (*design*) t'u² yang⁴ 圖樣, (*price*) chia⁴ ko² 價格.

figurehead *n.* (*ship*) ch'uan² t'ou² hsiang⁴ 船頭像, (*person*) kua⁴ ming² ling³ hsiu⁴ 掛名領袖.

filament *n.* (*thread*) hsien⁴ 線, hsien¹ wei² 纖維, (*bulb*) tien⁴ teng¹ ssu¹ 電灯絲.

filch *v.* t'ou¹ ch'ieh⁴ 偷竊.

file *n.* (*tool*) ts'o⁴ tao¹ 銼刀, (*documents*) tang⁴ an⁴ 檔案, (*of men*) wu³ 伍(軍); *v.* (*smooth*) ts'o⁴ p'ing² 銼平, (*documents*) kuei¹ tang⁴ 歸檔, (*march*) lieh⁴ tui⁴ erh² hsing² 列隊而行, (*application*) shang⁴ ch'eng² 上呈.

fill *v.* chuang¹ man³ 裝滿, ch'ung¹ man³ 充滿.

film *n.* (*layer*) po² mo⁴ 薄膜, (*photography*) juan³ p'ien⁴ 軟片.

filter *n.* lü⁴ yeh⁴ ch'i⁴ 濾液器; *v.* lü⁴ ch'ing¹ 濾清, lü⁴ kuo⁴ 濾過, shen⁴ kuo⁴ 滲過.

fin *n.* ch'i² 鰭.

final *a.* tsui⁴ hou⁴ te¹ 最後的, chung¹ chieh² te¹ 終結的, chung¹ chü² te¹ 終局的.

finale *n.* mo⁴ tuan⁴ 末段, chung¹ ch'ang³ 終場, chieh² chü² 結局.

finance *n.* ts'ai² cheng⁴ 財政.

financial *a.* ts'ai² cheng⁴ te¹ 財政的; ~ **crisis**, chin¹ jung² k'ung³ huang¹ 金融恐慌; ~ **year**, k'uai⁴ chi⁴ nien² tu⁴ 會計年度.

find *v.* (*discover*) fa¹ hsien⁴ 發見, (*obtain*) huo⁴ te² 獲得, (*reach*) ta² tao⁴ 達到.

fine *a.* (*thin*) ching¹ hsi⁴ te¹ 精細的, (*excellent*) yu¹ liang² te¹ 優良的; *n.* (*punishment*) fa² chin¹ 罰金; *v.* (*punish*) k'o¹ i³ fa² chin¹ 科以罰金.

fineness *n.* yu¹ liang² 優良, ching¹ mei³ 精美.

finery *n.* yen⁴ fu² 艷服.

finger *n.* shou³ chih³ 手指.

finis *n.* chung¹ chü² 終局.

finish *v.* wan² pi⁴ 完畢, chung¹ chieh² 終結, kao⁴ chün⁴ 告峻.

finished *a.* wan² pi⁴ te¹ 完畢的, wan² mei³ te¹ 完美的.

finite *a.* hsien⁴ ting⁴ te¹ 限定的, yu⁴ hsien⁴ te¹ 有限的.

fiord *n.* hsia⁴ chiang¹ 峽江, shen¹ wan¹ 深灣.

fir *n.* ts'ung¹ shu⁴ 樅樹(植).

fire *n.* (*burning*) huo³ 火, (*conflagration*) huo³ tsai¹ 火災, (*gunnery*) she⁴ chi¹ 射擊; *v.* (*burn*) tien³ huo³ yü³ 點火於, (*shoot*) fa¹ she⁴ 發射, (*from job*) k'ai¹ ch'u² 開除; ~ **alarm,** huo² ching³ 火警; ~ **command,** she⁴ chi¹ k'ou³ ling⁴ 射擊口令; ~ **control,** she⁴ chi¹ chih³ hui¹ 射擊指揮; ~ **discipline,** she⁴ chi¹ chün¹ chi⁴ 射擊軍紀; ~ **distribution,** fen¹ huo³ 分火; ~ **effect,** she⁴ chi¹ hsiao³ kuo³ 射擊效果; ~ **extinguisher,** mieh⁴ huo³ ch'i¹ 滅火器; ~ **for effect,** hsiao³ li⁴ she⁴ 效力射; ~ **power,** huo³ li⁴ 火力; ~ **support,** huo³ li⁴ chih¹ yüan² 火力支援.

firebrand *n.* (*wood*) huo³ pa⁴ 火把.

firefly *n.* ying² 螢.

fireman *n.* (*at a furnace*) huo³ fu¹ 火夫, (*he who puts out fire*) chiu⁴ huo³ yüan² 救火員.

firework *n.* yen¹ huo³ 煙火.

firm *a.* ku⁴ ting⁴ te¹ 固定的, chien¹ shih² te¹ 堅實的; *n.* shang¹ tien⁴ 商店, kung¹ ssu¹ 公司.

firmament *n.* ch'iung² ts'ang¹ 穹蒼, t'ien¹ 天.

first *a.* ti⁴ i⁴ te¹ 第一的; ~ **aid,** chi² chiu⁴ 急救; ~ **class,** t'ou² teng³ 頭等.

fiscal *a.* ts'ai² cheng⁴ te¹ 財政的.

fish *n.* yü² 魚; *v.* pu³ yü² 捕魚.

fisherman *n.* yü² fu¹ 漁夫.

fishery *n.* yü² yeh⁴ 漁業.

fishing *n.* tiao⁴ yü² 釣魚, pu³ yü² 捕魚.

fissile *a.* i⁴ p'o⁴ te¹ 易破的.

fissure *n.* lieh⁴ k'ou³ 裂口, lieh⁴ feng² 裂縫; *v.* p'o⁴ lieh⁴ 破裂.

fist *n.* ch'üan² 拳.

fit *n.* (*disease*) chi² ping⁴ 急病; *a.* ho² i⁴ te¹ 合宜的; *v.* shih³ shih⁴ ho² 使適合, shih¹ ying⁴ 適應.

fitful *a.* fan³ fu⁴ pu² ting⁴ te¹ 反覆不定的.

fitting *a.* shih⁴ i² te¹ 適宜的, hsiang¹ tang¹ te¹ 相當的.

five *n.* wu³ 五; *a.* wu³ te¹ 五的.

fix *v.* chieh¹ lao² 結牢, ku⁴ ting⁴ 固定; "~ **bayo-**

90

nets! " shang⁴ tz'u⁴ tao¹ 上刺刀(軍). 「弛的.

flabby a. jou² juan³ te¹ 柔軟的, sung⁴ ch'ih³ te¹ 鬆

flaccid a. juan³ jo⁴ te¹ 軟弱的.

flag n. ch'i² 旗; ～ **at half-mast,** pan⁴ ch'i² 半旗; ～ **of truce,** pai² ch'i² 白旗; ～ **semaphore,** ch'i² yü³ 旗語(軍). 「的.

flagitious a. chi² e⁴ te¹ 極惡的, ts'an² jen³ te¹ 殘忍

flagpole n. ch'i² kan¹ 旗桿. 「chi² e⁴ te¹ 極惡的.

flagrant a. lieh⁴ chi¹ chao¹ chang¹ te¹ 劣跡昭彰的,

flagship n. ch'i² chien⁴ 旗艦(軍).

flagstone n. shih² pan³ 石板.

flail n. ta³ ho² chü⁴ 打禾具.

flake n. p'ien⁴ 片, po² p'ien⁴ 薄片, sui⁴ p'ien⁴ 碎片; v. shih³ ch'eng² po² p'ien⁴ 使成薄片.

flambeau n. huo³ pa⁴ 火把, chung⁴ yu² huo³ chü⁴ 重油火炬. 「te¹ 華美的.

flamboyant a. ts'an⁴ lan⁴ te¹ 燦爛的, hua² mei³

flame n. huo³ yen⁴ 火焰; ～ **thrower,** huo³ yen⁴ fang⁴ she⁴ ch'i⁴ 火焰放射器.

flamingo n. hung² hao⁴ 紅鶴.

flank n. ts'e⁴ mien⁴ 側面; ～ **guard,** ts'e⁴ wei¹ 側衞; ～ **security,** ts'e⁴ mien⁴ ching³ chieh⁴ 側面 「警戒.

flannel n. fa² lan² jung² 法蘭絨.

flap n. (birds) p'u¹ i⁴ 撲翼, (envelope) hsin⁴ feng¹ kai¹ 信封蓋, (airplane) tsu² pan³ 阻板; v. p'u¹ chi⁴ 撲繫, (birds) ku³ i⁴ 鼓翼.

flapjack n. hsiao³ po² ping³ 小薄餅.

flare n. shan³ shuo⁴ 閃爍, (illuminating) chao⁴ ming² tan⁴ 照明彈(軍), (signal) hsin⁴ hao⁴ tan⁴ 信 號彈(軍). 「閃光.

flash v. fa¹ shan³ kuang¹ 發閃光; n. shan³ kuang¹

flashlight n. (by batteries) shou³ tien⁴ t'ung³ 手電 筒. 「hsü¹ shih⁴ te¹ 虛飾的.

flashy a. (flashing) shan³ shuo⁴ te¹ 閃爍的, (gaudy)

flask n. ch'ang² ching³ p'ing² 長頸瓶.

flat a. (even) p'ing² t'an³ te¹ 坪坦的, (without interest) fa² wei⁴ te¹ 乏味的, (music) ti¹ yü² cheng⁴ yin¹ te¹ 低於正音的(樂); n. (land) p'ing² ti⁴ 平地. ～ **trajectory,** ti¹ shen¹ tan⁴ tao⁴ 低伸彈道.

flatiron n. yün⁴ tou³ 熨斗.

flatten v. shih³ p'ing² 使平, pien⁴ p'ing² 變平.

flatter v. ch'an³ mei⁴ 詔媚.

flattery n. e¹ yü² 阿諛.

flatulent a. ch'i⁴ chang⁴ te¹ 氣脹的.

flaunt v. hsüan⁴ yüeh⁴ 炫燿. 「味.

flavor n. wei⁴ 味, mei³ wei¹ 美味; v. t'iao² wei¹ 調

flaw n. (crack) lieh⁴ k'ou³ 裂口, (fault) ch'üeh¹
tien³ 缺點, (gust) k'uang² feng¹ 狂風.

flax n. ya³ ma² 亞蔴, ya³ ma² chih⁴ wu⁴ 亞蔴織物.

flaxen a. ya³ ma² se⁴ te¹ 亞蔴色的, ya³ ma² chih⁴
ch'eng² te¹ 亞蔴製成的.

flay v. pao¹ p'i² 剝皮.

flea n. tsao³ 蚤.

flection n. wan¹ ch'ü¹ 彎曲. 「mao² 生羽毛.

fledge v. kung¹ i² yü³ mao¹ 供以羽毛, sheng¹ yü³

flee v. t'ao² pi⁴ 逃避. 「剪羊毛.

fleece n. yang² mao² 羊毛; v. chien³ yang² mao²

fleecy a. jou² juan³ te¹ 柔軟的, ju² yang² mao² te¹
如羊毛的.

fleer v. ch'ao² nung⁴ 嘲弄, ch'ao² hsiao⁴ 嘲笑; n.
ch'ao² nung⁴ 嘲弄, ch'ao² hsiao⁴ 嘲笑.

fleet n. chien⁴ tui⁴ 艦隊; v. chi² ch'ih⁴ 疾馳; a.
hsün⁴ su² te¹ 迅速的.

fleeting a. chi² kuo⁴ te¹ 疾過的.

flesh n. (meat) jou⁴ 肉.

flexible a. jou² jen⁴ te¹ 柔靱的.

flexor n. ch'ü¹ chin¹ 屈筋.

flexure n. wan¹ ch'ü¹ 彎曲, ch'ü¹ hsien⁴ 曲線.

flicker v. (wavering light) fa¹ shan³ kuang¹ 發閃
光; n. (woodpecker) cho² mu⁴ niao³ 啄木鳥.

flight n. (flying) fei¹ hsing² 飛行, (unit) fen¹ tui⁴ 分
隊(軍). 「的.

flimsy a. ch'an² jo⁴ te¹ 孱弱的, ts'ui⁴ jo⁴ te¹ 脆弱

flinch v. t'ui⁴ so¹ 退縮, wei³ so¹ 畏縮.

fling v. (throw) t'ou² 投, chih¹ ch'ung¹ 衝; n.
(throw) t'ou² chih¹ 投擲, (dance) chi² wu³ 急舞.

flint n. ta² huo³ shih² 打火石.

flippant a. ch'ing¹ shuai¹ te¹ 輕率的. 「擲.

flirt v., n. t'iao² ch'ing² 調情, (toss) chi² chih¹ 急

flit v. chi² fei¹ 疾飛, lüeh¹ kuo⁴ 掠過. 「浮物.

float v. p'iao¹ fu² 漂浮, p'iao¹ liu² 漂流; n. fu² wu⁴

flocculent a. ssu⁴ yang² mao² te¹ 似羊毛的.

flock *n.* ch'ün² 群, (*cavalry*) san⁴ ping¹ ch'ün² 散兵群(騎); *v.* ch'ün² chi² 群集.

floe *n.* fu² ping¹ k'uai⁴ 浮冰塊.

flog *v.* pien¹ t'a⁴ 鞭撻, ch'iang³ p'o⁴ 強迫.

flood *v.* fan¹ i⁴ 氾溢; *n.* hung² shui³ 洪水.

floor *n.* ti⁴ pan³ 地板, (*story*) lou² ts'eng² 樓層; *v.* p'u⁴ ti⁴ pan³ 鋪地板.

floral *a.* hua¹ te¹ 花的, ssu⁴ hua¹ te¹ 似花的.

floret *n.* (*small flower*) hsiao³ hua¹ 小花.

florist *n.* hua¹ shang¹ 花商.

flotation *n.* fu² 浮.

flotilla *n.* pu⁴ lei² t'ing³ tui⁴ 佈雷艇隊.

flounce *n.* (*dress*) chou⁴ pien¹ 皺邊.

flounder *n.* (*flatfish*) tieh² yü² 鰈魚.

flour *n.* mien⁴ fen³ 麵粉.

flourish *v.* (*thrive*) mao⁴ sheng⁴ 茂盛, (*display*) hsüan⁴ yüeh⁴ 炫燿.

flow *v.* liu² tung⁴ 流動.

flower *n.* hua¹ 花.

flowery *a.* to¹ hua¹ te¹ 多花的.

fluctuate *v.* po¹ tung⁴ 波動, ch'i³ fu² 起伏.

fluctuation *n.* po¹ tung⁴ 波動, ch'i³ fu² 起伏.

fluent *a.* (*flowing*) liu² tung⁴ te¹ 流動的, (*language*) liu² li⁴ te¹ 流利的.

fluid *n.* yeh⁴ t'i³ 液體, liu² chih⁴ 流質; *a.* yeh⁴ t'i³ te¹ 液體的, liu² chih² te¹ 流質的.

flurry *n.* (*gust*) k'uang² feng¹ 狂風.

flush *v.* (*blush*) fa¹ hung² 發紅, (*wash*) ch'ung¹ hsi³ 冲洗, (*excite*) chi¹ fa¹ 激發.

flute *n.* ti² 笛.

flutter *v.* p'iao¹ tung⁴ 飄動, (*flap*) ku³ i⁴ 鼓翼, (*excite*) chi¹ tung⁴ 激動.

fly *n.* ts'ang¹ ying² 蒼蠅; *a.* fei¹ 飛.

flywheel *n.* fei¹ lun² 飛輪(機).

foam *n.* p'ao⁴ mo⁴ 泡沫; *v.* shih³ ch'i³ p'ao⁴ 使起泡.

focus *n.* chiao¹ tien³ 焦點; *v.* chi² chung¹ 集中.

fodder *n.* mo⁴ ch'u² 秣芻, ch'u² ts'ao³ 芻草.

foe *n.* ch'ou² jen² 仇人, ti² jen² 敵人.

fog *n.* wu⁴ 霧.

fogy, fogey *n.* ku² pan³ che³ 古板者, shou³ chiu⁴ che³ 守舊者.

foil *v.* cho² pai⁴ 拙敗.

fold *n.* (*sheep*) yang² lan² 羊欄; *v.* ho² lung³ 合攏, che² tieh² 摺疊.

foliage *n.* ts'u⁴ yeh⁴ 簇葉.

93

folk *n.* (*people*) jen² min² 人民, (*nation*) min² tsu² 民族.　　　　「kuo³ 結果.

follow *v.* (*go after*) ken¹ sui² 跟隨, (*result*) chieh⁴

follower *n.* ken¹ sui² che³ 跟隨者.

folly *n.* yü² ch'un³ 愚蠢.　　　「ai⁴ te¹ 溺愛的.

fond *a.* hsi⁴ ai⁴ te¹ 喜愛的, tz'u² ai⁴ te¹ 慈愛的, ni⁴

font *n.* hsi³ li³ p'en² 洗禮盆.

food *n.* shih² wu⁴ 食物, liang² shih² 糧食.

fool *n.* yü² jen² 愚人, (*clown*) hsiao³ ch'ou³ 小丑; *v.*

foolery *n.* yü² hsing² 愚行.　　「yü² nung⁴ 愚弄.

foolish *a.* yü² pen⁴ te¹ 愚笨的.

foot *n.* (*animal*) tsu² 足, (*measure*) ch'ih³ 呎, (*base*) chi¹ pu⁴ 基部; *v.* (*walk*) pu⁴ hsing² 步行.

football *n.* tsu² ch'iu² 足球.

footlights *n.* chiao³ teng¹ 脚燈(戲臺前).

footman *n.* nan² p'u² 男僕.

footpath *n.* jen² hsing² tao⁴ 人行道.

footstep *n.* (*sound*) chiao³ sheng¹ 脚聲, (*footprint*) tsu² chi¹ 足跡.

footstool *n.* t'a⁴ chiao³ teng⁴ 踏脚凳.

for *prep.* (*in place of*) tai⁴ t'i⁴ 代替, (*in support of*) tsan⁴ ch'eng² 贊成, (*time*) ta² 達, (*because of*) yin¹ wei⁴ 因爲, (*to get to*) hsiang⁴ 向; ~ **example**, li⁴ ju² 例如; ~ **good**, yung² chiu³ 永久; ~ **the time being**, mu⁴ hsia⁴ 目下.

forage *n.* ch'u² mo⁴ 芻秣, ssu⁴ liao⁴ 飼料.

forbearance *n.* (*self-control*) tzu⁴ chih⁴ 自制.

forbid *v.* chin⁴ chih³ 禁止.　　　「p'o⁴ 強迫.

force *n.* t'i³ li⁴ 體力, ching¹ li⁴ 精力; *v.* ch'iang³

ford *n.* ch'ien³ t'an¹ 淺灘, t'u² she⁴ ch'ang³ 徒涉場 (軍); *v.* (*on foot*) t'u² she⁴ 徒涉.

fordable *a.* k'o³ t'u² she⁴ te¹ 可徒涉的.

forecast *n.* yü⁴ kao⁴ 預告.

forefather *n.* tsu³ tsung¹ 祖宗.

forefinger *n.* shih² chih³ 食指.

forefront *n.* tsui⁴ ch'ien² pu⁴ 最前部.

forego, forgo *v.* ch'i⁴ chüeh² 棄絕, fei⁴ ch'i⁴ 廢棄.

foreground *n.* ch'ien² ching³ 前景.

forehead *n.* e² 額.

foreign *a.* wai⁴ kuo² te¹ 外國的; ~ **capital**, wai⁴ tzu¹ 外資; ~ **debt**, wai⁴ chai⁴ 外債; ~ **ex-**

change, wai⁴ hui⁴ 外匯; ~ **goods,** po² lai² p'in³ 舶來品; ~ **minister,** wai⁴ chiao¹ pu⁴ chang³ 外 〔交部長.

foreigner *n.* wai⁴ kuo² jen² 外國人.

foreland *n.* chia⁸ 岬.

foreman *n.* kung¹ t'ou² 工頭, chien¹ kung¹ 監工.

foremost *a.* tsui⁴ hsien¹ te¹ 最先的.

foresee *v.* hsien¹ chih¹ 先知, yü⁴ liao⁴ 預料.

foresight *n.* hsien¹ chien⁴ 先見, yüan² lü⁴ 遠慮.

forest *n.* sen¹ lin² 森林.

foretell *v.* yü⁴ kao⁴ 預告, yü⁴ yen² 預言.

forewarn *v.* yü⁴ hsien¹ ching³ kao⁴ 預先警告.

forfeit *n.* mo⁴ shou¹ wu⁴ 沒收物; *v.* mo⁴ shou¹ 沒收, sang⁴ shih¹ 喪失.

forge *n.* tuan⁴ t'ieh⁸ lu² 煅鐵爐; *v.* (*metal*) tuan⁴ yeh³ 煅冶, (*counterfeit*) wei⁴ tsao⁴ 偽造.

forgery *n.* wei⁴ tsao⁴ 偽造.

forget *v.* wang⁴ chi⁴ 忘記.

forgetful *a.* chien⁴ wang⁴ te¹ 健忘的.

forget-me-not *n.* hsiang¹ ssu¹ ts'ao⁸ 相思草(植).

forgive *v.* yüan² yu⁴ 原宥.

forgiveness *n.* yüan² yu⁴ 原宥.

fork *n.* ch'a¹ 叉, (*road*) ch'a¹ lu⁴ 叉路.

forlorn *a.* (*deserted*) chien⁴ ch'i⁴ te¹ 見棄的.

form *n.* hsing² chuang⁴ 形狀, hsing² shih⁴ 形式; *v.* hsing² ch'eng² 形成.

formal *a.* (*of form*) hsing² shih⁴ shang⁴ te¹ 形式上 的, (*methodical*) cheng⁴ shih⁴ te¹ 正式的.

formality *n.* li³ chieh² 禮節, chü¹ ni⁴ hsing² shih⁴ 拘泥形式.

formation *n.* hsing² shih⁴ 形式, (*order*) tui⁴ hsing² 隊形; ~ **flying,** pien¹ tui⁴ fei¹ hsing² 編隊飛行.

former *a.* tsai⁴ hsien¹ te¹ 在先的, i³ ch'ien² te¹ 以 〔前的.

formula *n.* kung¹ shih⁴ 公式.

fornication *n.* ssu¹ t'ung¹ 私通.

forsake *v.* i² ch'i⁴ 遺棄.

forsaken *a.* i² ch'i⁴ te¹ 遺棄的.

forswear *v.* shih⁴ pu⁴ ch'eng² jen⁴ 誓不承認.

fort *n.* yao⁴ sai⁴ 要塞, p'ao⁴ t'ai² 礮臺.

forth *adv.* (*forward*) hsiang⁴ ch'ien² 向前, (*away*) wai⁴ ch'u¹ 外出.

forthwith *adv.* li⁴ k'o⁴ 立刻.

fortification *n.* (*fortifying*) chu² ch'eng² 築城軍), (*forts*) yao⁴ sai⁴ 要塞.

fortify *v.* chu² ch'eng² 築城.

fortitude *n.* chien¹ i⁴ 堅毅, kang¹ ch'iang² 剛強.

fortress *n.* yao⁴ sai⁴ 要塞, pao² lei³ 堡壘.

fortunate *a.* hsing⁴ yün⁴ te¹ 幸運的.

fortune *n.* (*fate*) ming⁴ yün⁴ 命運, (*good luck*) hsing⁴ yün⁴ 幸運, (*wealth*) ts'ai⁴ fu⁴ 財富.

forward *a.* ch'ien² te¹ 前進的;*adv.* hsiang⁴ ch'ien² 向前; *v.* (*mail*) ch'uan² ti⁴ 傳遞; " ~ **march!** " (*on foot*) ch'i² pu⁴ tsou³ 齊步走 (步), (*mounted*) ch'ien² chin⁴ tsou³ 前進走 (騎).

fossil *a., n.* hua⁴ shih² 化石, (*person*) shou³ chiu⁴ 守舊者.

foster *v.* fu² yang³ 撫養.

foul *a.* pu⁴ chieh⁴ te¹ 不潔的, wu¹ cho² te¹ 污濁的; *v.* chien⁴ li⁴ 建立. 使污.

found *v.* chien⁴ li⁴ 建立.

foundation *n.* (*base*) ken¹ chi¹ 根基, (*fund*) chi¹ chin¹ 基金.

founder *n.* (*person*) ch'uang² pan⁴ jen² 創辦人.

foundling *n.* ch'i⁴ hai² 棄孩.

foundry *n.* chu⁴ t'ieh² ch'ang³ 鑄鐵廠, fan¹ sha¹ ch'ang³ 翻砂廠. 噴泉.

fount, fountain *n.* ch'üan² 泉, yüan² 源, p'en¹

four *n.* ssu⁴ 四; *a.* ssu⁴ te¹ 四的. 禽肉.

fowl *n.* (*large birds*) chia¹ ch'in² 家禽, (*flesh*) ch'in²

fox *n.* hu² li² 狐狸; ~ **hole**, san⁴ ping¹ k'eng¹ 散

foxglove *n.* mao² ti⁴ huang² 毛地黃(植). 兵坑.

foxy *a.* (*crafty*) chiao³ hua² te¹ 狡猾的.

fraction *a.* (*a part*) pu⁴ fen⁴ 部份, (*mathematics*) fen¹ shu⁴ 分數. 骨斷.

fracture *n.* (*crack*) p'o⁴ lieh⁴ 破裂, (*bone*) ku³ tuan⁴

fragile *a.* i⁴ sui⁴ te¹ 易碎的.

fragment *n.* sui⁴ hsieh⁴ 碎屑, hsiao³ p'ien⁴ 小片.

fragrance *n.* fen¹ fang¹ 芬芳.

fragrant *a.* fen¹ fang¹ te¹ 芬芳的.

frail *a.* nen⁴ jo⁴ te¹ 嫩弱的, i⁴ sui⁴ te¹ 易碎的.

frailty *n.* ts'ui⁴ jo⁴ 脆弱, i⁴ sui⁴ 易碎.

frame *n.* kou⁴ tsao⁴ wu⁴ 構造物.

framework *n.* ku³ chia⁴ 骨架, chieh² kou⁴ 結構.

franchise *n.* (*privilege*) t'e⁴ ch'üan² 特權, (*right to vote*) hsüan² chü³ ch'üan² 選舉權.

frank *a.* t'an³ pai² te¹ 坦白的, chih² shuai⁴ te¹ 直率的, ch'eng² k'en³ te¹ 誠懇的.

fraternize *v.* ch'in¹ mu⁴ 親睦.

fraud *n.* ch'i¹ cha⁴ 欺詐.

fraudulent *a.* ch'i¹ cha⁴ te¹ 欺詐的.

fray *n.* cheng¹ tou⁴ 爭鬪, hsüan¹ ch'ao¹ 喧吵; *v.* mo² shang¹ 磨傷, ts'a¹ sun³ 擦損.

freak *n.* huan⁴ hsiang³ 幻想, wang⁴ hsiang³ 妄想.

freckle *n.* ch'iao³ pan¹ 雀班.

free *a.* tzu⁴ yu² te¹ 自由的, (*without cost*) mien³ fei⁴ te¹ 免費的; *v.* huo⁴ mien³ 豁免; ~ **balloon,** p'iao¹ liu² ch'i⁴ ch'iu² 飄流氣球; ~ **love,** tzu⁴ yu² lien⁴ ai⁴ 自由戀愛; ~ **marriage,** tzu⁴ yu² chieh² hun¹ 自由結婚; ~ **of charge,** mien³ fei⁴ te¹ 免費的; ~ **of duty,** mien³ shui⁴ te¹ 免稅的; ~ **port,** tzu⁴ yu² chiang³ 自由港; ~ **trade,** tzu⁴ yu² mao⁴ i⁴ 自由貿易; ~ **translation,** i⁴ i⁴ 意譯.

freedom *n.* tzu⁴ yu² 自由.　　　　　　「會員.

Freemason *n.* kung⁴ chi⁴ hui⁴ hui⁴ yüan² 共濟會

freeze *v.* chieh² ping¹ 結冰.　　　　　　「運費.

freight *n.* (*cargo*) huo⁴ wu⁴ 貨物, (*charge*) yün⁴ fei⁴

frenzy *n.* k'uang² luan⁴ 狂亂.

frequency *n.* lü³ tz'u⁴ 屢次, chou¹ lü⁴ 週率.

frequent *a.* ching¹ ch'ang² te¹ 經常的.

fresh *a.* hsin¹ hsien¹ te¹ 新鮮的.

fret *v.* (*be worried*) fan² nao³ 煩惱, (*rub*) mo² hao⁴

fretful *a.* nao³ nu⁴ te¹ 惱怒的.　　　　　　「耗損.

friable *a.* i⁴ p'o⁴ sui⁴ te¹ 易破碎的.

friction *n.* mo² ts'a¹ li⁴ 磨擦力, mo² ts'a¹ 磨擦.

Friday *n.* hsing¹ ch'i² wu³ 星期五.

friend *n.* p'eng² yu³ 朋友.　　　　「chün¹ 友軍.

friendly *a.* yu³ shan⁴ te¹ 友善的; ~ **troops,** yu³

friendship *n.* yu³ i² 友誼.

fright *n.* k'ung³ pu⁴ 恐怖, ching¹ hai⁴ 驚駭.

frighten *v.* shih³ ching¹ hai⁴ 使驚駭.

frightful *a.* k'o³ ching¹ te¹ 可驚的.

frigid *a.* leng³ te¹ 冷的, (*in feeling*) hsing⁴ ch'ing² leng³ tan⁴ te¹ 性情冷淡的.

fringe *n.* sui⁴ 繸.

frisk *v.* huan¹ yao⁴ 歡躍.　　「huo² p'o¹ te¹ 活潑的.

frisky *a.* (*playful*) hsi¹ hsi⁴ te¹ 嬉戲的, (*lively*),

frog *n.* wa¹ 蛙.

frolic *n.* hsi¹ hsi⁴ 嬉戲.

frolicsome *a.* hao⁴ hsi¹ hsi⁴ te¹ 好嬉戲的.

from *prep.* ts'ung² 從, tzu⁴ 自, (*because of*) yin¹ wei⁴ 因爲.

front *n.* (*foremost part*) ch'ien² mien⁴ 前面, ch'ien² pu⁴ 前部, cheng⁴ mien⁴ 正面, (*opposite to rear*) ch'ien² fang¹ 前方, (*line of battle*) chan⁴ hsien⁴ 戰線, chan⁴ ch'ang³ 戰場; ~ **line,** chan⁴ hsien⁴ 戰線; ~ **sight,** chun³ hsing¹ 準星(兵).

frontage *n.* cheng⁴ mien⁴ 正面; ~ **in attack,** kung¹ chi¹ cheng⁴ mien⁴ 攻擊正面(軍).

frontier *n.* pien¹ chieh⁴ 邊界.

frost *n.* shuang¹ 霜.

frosty *a.* chiang⁴ shuang¹ te¹ 降霜的.

froth *n.* p'ao⁴ mo⁰ 泡沫; *v.* ch'i³ p'ao⁴ 起泡.

frothy *a.* ssu⁴ p'ao⁴ mo⁴ te¹ 似泡沫的.

froward *a.* kang¹ pi⁴ te¹ 剛愎的.

frown *n.* p'in² mei⁴ 顰眉, ts'u⁴ e² 蹙額.

frozen *a.* chieh² ping¹ te¹ 結冰的.

frugal *a.* chieh² chien³ te¹ 節儉的.

frugality *n.* chieh² chien³ 節儉.

fruit *n.* shui² kuo³ 水果, (*result*) chieh² kuo³ 結果.

fruiterer *n.* shui² kuo³ shang¹ 水果商.

fruitless *a.* (*barren*) pu⁴ chieh² kuo³ te¹ 不結果的, (*useless*) wu² yung⁴ te¹ 無用的.

frustrate *v.* ts'o⁴ che² 挫折, shih¹ pai⁴ 失敗.

fry *v.* yu² chien¹ 油煎.　　　　「屬(植).

fuchsia *n.* tiao² chung¹ hai³ t'ang² shu³ 弔鐘海棠

fuel *n.* jan² liao⁴ 燃料; ~ **gauge,** yu² piao³ 油表(汽); ~ **tank,** yu² hsiang¹ 油箱(汽).

fugitive *a.* t'ao² wang² te¹ 逃亡的; *n.* wang² ming² che³ 亡命者; (*ish*) wan² ch'eng² 完成.

fulfill, fulfil *v.* (*carry out*) shih² hsing² 實行, (*fin-*

full *a.* ch'ung¹ man³ te¹ 充滿的, fu⁴ tsu² te¹ 富足的, wan² ch'üan² te¹ 完全的.

fulsome *a.* k'o³ yen⁴ te¹ 可厭的.

fun *n.* wan² hsiao⁴ 玩笑.

function *n.* chi¹ neng² 機能.

fund *n.* chi¹ chin¹ 基金.　　　　「te¹ 主要的.

fundamental *a.* chi¹ pen³ te¹ 基本的, chu³ yao⁴

98

funeral *n.* (*ceremonies*) tsang³ li¹ 葬禮, (*procession*) sung⁴ pin¹ hsing² lieh⁴ 送殯行列.

fungus *n.* chün⁴ 菌. 「t'ung³ 煙筒.

funnel *n.* (*pouring*) lou⁴ tou³ 漏斗-, (*boat*) yen¹

funny *a.* hua² chi¹ te¹ 滑稽的, k'o³ hsiao⁴ te¹ 可笑 「的.

fur *n.* mao² p'i² 毛皮.

furbish *v.* (*polish*) ts'a¹ liang⁴ 擦亮.

furious *a.* (*raging*) sheng⁴ nu⁴ te¹ 盛怒的.

furl *v.* chüan² ch'i³ 捲起.

furnace *n.* lu² 爐.

furnish *v.* kung¹ chi³ 供給.

furniture *n.* chia¹ chü⁴ 家具.

furrier *n.* p'i² huo⁴ shang¹ 皮貨商.

furrow *n.* kou¹ 溝.

further *a.* keng⁴ yüan³ te¹ 更遠的; *adv.* keng⁴ chin⁴ i² pu⁴ ti⁴ 更進一步地; *v.* tseng¹ chin⁴ 增進.

furtherance *n.* ts'u⁴ chin⁴ 促進, t'ui¹ chin⁴ 推進.

furtive *a.* kuei³ pi⁴ te¹ 詭祕的.

fury *n.* pao⁴ nu⁴ 暴怒.

fuse *v.* jung² ho² 鎔合, jung² chieh³ 鎔解; *n.* (*electric*) pao⁴ hsien³ ssu¹ 保險絲, (*ordnance*) yin³ hsin⁴ 引信, hsin⁴ kuan³ 信管; ～ **setter**, ting³ miao³ ch'i⁴ 定秒器. 「身.

fuselage *n.* (*airplane*) fei¹ chi¹ chi¹ shen¹ 飛機機

fusible *a.* i⁴ jung² te¹ 易熔的.

fuss *n.* hsiao³ t'i² ta⁴ tso⁴ 小題大做.

fusty *a.* e⁴ ch'ou⁴ te¹ 惡臭的, (*out-of-date*) lao³ shih⁴ te¹ 老式的.

futile *a.* wu² yung⁴ te¹ 無用的.

futility *n.* (*uselessness*) wu² yung⁴ 無用.

future *a.* chiang¹ lai² te¹ 將來的.

futurity *n.* wei⁴ lai² 未來, chiang¹ lai² 將來.

G

gaff *n.* ta⁴ yü² kou¹ 大魚鉤.

gag *n.* sai¹ k'ou³ wu⁴ 塞口物; *v.* sai⁴ k'ou³ 塞口.

gaiety *n.* yü² k'uai⁴ 愉快.

gaily, gayly *adv.* k'uai⁴ le⁴ ti¹ 快樂地.

gain *n.* li⁴ i⁴ 利益; *v.* huo⁴ te² 獲得.

gainsay *v.* (*deny*) fou³ jen⁴ 否認, (*dispute*) k'ang⁴ pien⁴ 抗辯.

gait *n.* pu⁴ t'ai⁴ 步態, pu⁴ fa³ 步法; ~ **of march,** hsing² chin⁴ pu⁴ tu⁴ 行進步度(軍).

gala *n.* chieh² jih⁴ 節日.

gale *n.* pao⁴ feng¹ 暴風.

gallant *a.* hua² li⁴ te² 華麗的.

gallery *n.* tsou³ lang⁴ 走廊, yang² t'ai² 洋臺, (*indoor range*) shih⁴ nei⁴ she⁴ chi¹ ch'ang³ 室內射擊場.

galley *n.* (*rowboat*) hua² ch'uan² 划船, (*kitchen*) ch'uan² shang⁴ ch'u² fang² 船上廚房.

gallon *n.* chia¹ lun² 加倫.

gallop *n.* ch'ih² ma³ 馳馬; *v.* chi³ ch'ih² 疾馳.

gallows *n.* chiao³ chia⁴ 絞架.　　「套鞋.

galosh, galoshes *n.* hsiang⁴ p'i² t'ao⁴ hsieh² 橡皮

galvanism *n.* (*medical*) tien⁴ liao² fa³ 電療法.

galvanize *v.* tien⁴ tu⁴ 電鍍.

gamble *v.* tu³ po² 賭博.

gambler *n.* tu³ t'u² 賭徒.

game *n.* (*amusement*) yu² hsi⁴ 游戲, (*contest*) ching⁴ sai⁴ 競賽, (*plan*) chi⁴ hua⁴ 計劃.

gamester *n.* tu³ t'u² 賭徒.

gamut *n.* ch'üan² yin¹ chieh¹ 全音階(樂).

gander *n.* hsiung² e² 雄鵝.

gang *n.* i⁴ ch'ün² 一群, i² tui⁴ 一隊.

gangway *n.* (*passageway*) t'ung¹ lu⁴ 通路, (*ship*) hsien² men² 舷門, (*gangplank*) t'iao⁴ pan³ 跳板.

gap *n.* lieh⁴ k'ou³ 裂口, (*in line of battle*) chien⁴ hsi⁴ 間隙, (*in wire entanglement*) t'ung¹ lu⁴ 通路.

gape *v.* (*yawn*) ta³ ho¹ ch'ien⁴ 打呵欠, (*open wide*) chang¹ k'ai¹ 張開.

garage *n.* ch'i⁴ ch'e¹ fang² 汽車房, (*for repairing*) ch'i⁴ ch'e¹ hsiu¹ li² ch'ang³ 汽車修理廠.

garbage *n.* la¹ hsi¹ 拉圾.

garden *n.* (*flowers*) hua¹ yüan² 花園; ~ **city,** hua¹ yüan² shih⁴ 花園市; ~ **party,** yüan² yu² hui⁴ 園遊會.

gardener *n.* yüan² ting¹ 園丁.　　「喉.

gardening *n.* yüan² i⁴ 園藝.

gargle *n.* shu⁴ hou² yao⁴ 漱喉藥; *v.* shu⁴ hou² 漱

garlic *n.* ta⁴ suan⁴ 大蒜.

garment *n.* i¹ fu² 衣服.

garner *n.* ku³ ts'ang¹ 穀倉; *v.* chu⁴ ts'ang² 貯藏.

garnish *v.* chuang¹ shih⁴ 裝飾.

garret *n.* ting³ lou² 頂樓, ko² lou² 閣樓.

garrison *n.* chu⁴ chün¹ 駐軍; *v.* wei⁴ shu⁴ 衞戍; ~ **commander,** ching³ pei⁴ ssu¹ ling⁴ 警備司令, wei⁴ shu⁴ ssu¹ ling⁴ 衞戍司令; ~ **headquarters,** ching³ pei⁴ ssu¹ ling⁴ pu⁴ 警備司令部, wei⁴ shu⁴ ssu¹ ling⁴ pu⁴ 衞戍司令部.

garrulous *a.* to¹ tsui³ te¹ 多嘴的.

garter *n.* tiao⁴ wa⁴ tai⁴ 吊襪帶.

gas *n.* ch'i⁴ t'i³ 氣體, (*poison gas*) tu² ch'i⁴ 毒氣 (軍), (*for heating*) wa³ ssu¹ 瓦斯, (*gasoline*) ch'i⁴ yu² 氣油; ~ **alarm,** tu² ch'i⁴ ching³ pao⁴ 毒氣警報(軍); ~ **attack,** tu² ch'i⁴ kung¹ chi¹ 毒氣攻擊 (軍); ~ **bomb,** tu² ch'i⁴ cha⁴ tan⁴ 毒氣炸彈(軍); ~ **mask,** fang² tu² mien⁴ chü⁴ 防毒面具(軍); ~ **shell,** tu² ch'i⁴ tan⁴ 毒氣彈(軍); ~ **stove,** wa³ ssu¹ lu² 瓦斯爐.

gaseous *a.* ch'i⁴ t'i³ te¹ 氣體的.

gash *n.* shang¹ hen² 傷痕; *v.* ko¹ shang¹ 割傷.

gasket *n.* juan⁴ tien⁴ 軟墊, tien⁴ huan² 墊環.

gasoline *n.* ch'i⁴ yu² 氣油; ~ **consumption,** ch'i⁴ yu² hsiao¹ hao⁴ 氣油消耗; ~ **station,** ch'i⁴ yu² chan⁴ 氣油站. 「ch'uan³ ch'i⁴ 喘氣.

gasp *n.* ch'uan³ ch'i⁴ 喘氣; *v.* hsiao¹ ch'uan³ 哮喘.

gate *n.* men² k'ou³ 門口.

gather *v.* (*assemble*) chi² ho² 集合, (*get together*) shou¹ ts'ai³ 收採.

gathering *n.* chü⁴ ho² 聚合.

gaudy *a.* hsüan⁴ shih⁴ te¹ 炫飾的. 「liang² 估量.

gauge, gage *n.* ts'e⁴ liang² piao³ 測量表; *v.* ku¹

gaunt *a.* shou⁴ hsiao¹ te¹ 瘦削的.

gauze *n.* sha¹ pu⁴ 紗布.

gay *a.* yü² k'uai⁴ te¹ 愉快的.

gaze *n.* ning² shih⁴ 凝視; *v.* ning² shih⁴ 凝視.

gazette *n.* (*newspaper*) hsin¹ wen² pao⁴ 新聞報, (*official*) kung¹ pao⁴ 公報.

gear *n.* (*wheel*) ch'ih³ lun² 齒輪, (*machinery*) chi¹ kuan¹ 機關, (*equipment*) chuang¹ chih⁴ 裝置.

gearbox *n.* ch'ih³ lun² hsiang¹ 齒輪箱(機).

gelatin, gelatine *n.* chiao¹ chih² 膠質.

gem *n.* pao³ shih² 寶石.

gender *n.* hsing⁴ pieh² 性別.

general *a.* i⁴ pan¹ te¹ 一般的; *n.* (*rank*) shang⁴ chiang⁴ 上將; ~ **anesthetic**, ch'üan² shen¹ ma² tsui⁴ fa³ 全身麻醉法(醫); ~ **attack**, tsung³ kung¹ chi¹ 總攻擊(軍); ~ **headquarters**, tsung³ ssu¹ ling⁴ pu⁴ 總司令部(軍); ~ **mobilization**, tsung³ tung⁴ yüan² 總動員; ~ **of the Army** (US), yuan² shuai⁴ 元帥; ~ **officer**, chiang⁴ kuan¹ 將官(軍); ~ **reserve**, tsung³ yü⁴ pei⁴ tui⁴ 總預備隊(軍).

generalization *n.* kai⁴ k'uo⁴ 概括, t'ung¹ lun⁴ 通論.

generalize *v.* kai⁴ k'uo⁴ 概括, kuei¹ na⁴ 歸納.

generate *v.* ch'an³ sheng¹ 產生, tsao⁴ ch'eng² 造成.

generation *n.* shih⁴ tai⁴ 世代.

generator *n.* fa¹ tien⁴ chi¹ 發電機.

generosity *n.* k'ang² k'ai³ 慷慨.

generous *a.* k'ang² k'ai³ te¹ 慷慨的.

genius *n.* t'ien¹ ts'ai² 天才.

genteel *a.* yu³ li³ mao⁴ te¹ 有禮貌的.

gentian *n.* lung² tan³ shu³ chih² wu⁴ 龍膽屬植物.

gentle *a.* ch'u¹ shen¹ kao¹ kuei⁴ te¹ 出身高貴的, wen¹ wen² te¹ 溫文的.

gentleman *n.* shen¹ shih⁴ 紳士, chün¹ tzu³ 君子.

genuine *a.* chen¹ shih² te¹ 真實的.

geography *n.* ti⁴ li³ hsüeh² 地理學.

geology *n.* ti⁴ chih² hsüeh² 地質學.

geometry *n.* chi³ ho² hsüeh² 幾何學.

germ *n.* (*disease*) wei¹ sheng¹ chün⁴ 微生菌, (*seed*) chung³ tzu¹ 種子, (*origin*) yüan² shih³ 原始.

germinate *v.* shih³ fa¹ ya² 使發芽.

gesticulate *v.* tso⁴ shou³ shih⁴ 作手勢, tso⁴ tzu¹ shih⁴ 做姿勢.

gesture *n.* shou³ shih⁴ 手勢, tzu¹ shih⁴ 姿勢.

get *v.* te² 得, huo⁴ 獲, ying² 贏.

ghastly *a.* (*horrible*) k'o³ p'a⁴ te¹ 可怕的, (*deathly pale*) hui¹ pai² se⁴ te¹ 灰白色的.

ghost *n.* kuei³ 鬼.

giant *n.* chü⁴ jen² 巨人.

gibbet *n.* chiao³ chia⁴ 絞架.

gibe *v.* ch'ao³ nung⁴ 嘲弄.

giddy *a.* (*dizzy*) hsüan⁴ yün⁴ te¹ 眩暈的, (*flighty*) ch'ing¹ shuai¹ te¹ 輕率的. 「天才.

gift *n.* (*present*) li³ wu⁴ 禮物, (*talent*) t'ien¹ ts'ai² 天才的.

gifted *a.* t'ien¹ ts'ai² te¹ 天才的.

gigantic *a.* ssu⁴ chü⁴ jen² te¹ 似巨人的, shih¹ ta⁴ te¹ 碩大的. 「te¹

gild *v.* tu⁴ chin¹ 鍍金.

gill *n.* (*fish*) sai¹ 鰓.

gimlet *n.* shou³ tsuan⁴ 手鑽.

gin *n.* (*drink*) tu⁴ sung¹ tzu¹ chiu³ 杜松子酒, (*machine*) ya⁴ mien² chi¹ 軋棉機.

ginger *n.* chiang¹ 薑.

gingerbread *n.* chiang¹ ping³ 薑餅.

gipsy *n.* chi¹ p'u³ sai⁴ jen² 吉普賽人.

giraffe *n.* ch'ang² t'ou² lu⁴ 長頭鹿, pao⁴ lu⁴ 豹鹿.

gird *v.* su⁴ fu² 束縛.

girdle *n.* yao¹ tai⁴ 腰帶. 「chün¹ 女童子軍.

girl *n.* nü³ hai² 女孩; ～ **scout**, nü³ t'ung² tzu³

girth *n.* (*for horse*) ma¹ tu⁴ tai⁴ 馬肚帶.

give *v.* chi³ 給.

glacial *a.* ping¹ tung⁴ te¹ 冰凍的.

glacier *n.* ping¹ ho² 冰河, ping¹ ch'uan¹ 冰川.

glad *a.* k'uai¹ le⁴ te¹ 快樂的.

glade *n.* k'ung¹ ti⁴ 空地(森林中). 「kuang¹ 閃光.

glance *v.* (*look*) p'ieh¹ chien⁴ 瞥見, (*gleam*) shan³

gland *n.* hsien⁴ 腺. 「shan³ yao⁴ 閃耀.

glare *n.* (*light*) hsüan⁴ kuang¹ 眩光; *v.* (*shine*)

glaring *a.* (*dazzling*) hsüan⁴ mu⁴ te¹ 眩目的.

glass *n.* po¹ li² 玻璃.

glaze *v.* chuang¹ i³ po¹ li² 裝以玻璃.

glazier *n.* po¹ li² chiang⁴ 玻璃匠.

gleam *n.* shan¹ kuang¹ 閃光; *v.* fa¹ kuang¹ 發光.

glean *v.* shou¹ shih² 收拾, shou¹ chi² 收集.

glee *n.* (*joy*) huan¹ le⁴ 歡樂.

gleeful *a.* huan¹ le⁴ te¹ 歡樂的.

glen *n.* hsia² ku³ 狹谷, yu¹ ku³ 幽谷.

glide *v.* (*glider only*) hua² hsiang² 滑翔, (*descend*) hsia⁴ hua² 下滑; ～ **landing**, hua² hsiang² chiang⁴ lo⁴ 滑翔降落.

glider *n.* (*aircraft*) hua² hsiang² chi¹ 滑翔機.

glimmer *n.* wei¹ kuang¹ 微光; *v.* fa¹ wei¹ kuang¹ 發微光.

glimpse *n.* i⁴ p'ieh¹ 一瞥, p'ieh¹ chien⁴ 瞥見.

glisten *v.* shan³ shuo⁴ 閃爍.

glitter *v.* shan³ shuo⁴ 閃爍.

gloat *v.* ning² shih⁴ 凝視.

globe *n.* (*sphere*) ch'iu² t'i³ 球體, (*earth*) ti⁴ ch'iu² 地球, (*planet*) hsing² hsing² 行星.

globular *a.* ch'iu² chuang⁴ te¹ 球狀的.

globule *n.* hsiao³ ch'iu² 小球.　「ch'ou² 憂愁.

gloom *n.* (*darkness*) hun¹ an⁴ 昏暗, (*sadness*) yu¹

gloomy *a.* (*dark*) hun¹ an⁴ te¹ 昏暗的, (*sad*) ch'i¹ ts'an³ te¹ 悽慘的.

glorify *v.* (*give glory to*) shih³ kuang¹ jung² 使光榮, (*praise*) tsan⁴ mei³ 讚美.

glorious *a.* kuang¹ jung² te¹ 光榮的.

glory *n.* kuang¹ jung² 光榮.

glossary *n.* tzu⁴ hui⁴ 字彙.

glove *n.* shou³ t'ao⁴ 手套.

glow *n.* chih⁴ je⁴ 熾熱; *v.* fa¹ chih⁴ je⁴ 發熾熱.

glowing *a.* fa¹ chih⁴ je⁴ te¹ 發熾熱的.

glowworm *n.* ying² huo³ ch'ung² 螢火蟲.

glucose *n.* p'u² t'ao² t'ang² 葡萄糖.

glue *n.* chiao¹ 膠; *v.* chiao¹ chan¹ 膠粘.

glutinous *a.* nien² hsing⁴ te¹ 黏性的, ju² chiao¹ te¹ 如膠的.

glutton *n.* t'an¹ shih² che³ 貪食者.

gluttony *n.* yin³ shih² kuo⁴ tu⁴ 飲食過度.

glycerin, glycerine *n.* kan¹ yu² 甘油.

gnat *n.* wen² 蚊, jui⁴ 蚋.

gnaw *v.* yao³ 咬, nieh⁴ 嚙.

go *v.* hsing² 行, ch'ü⁴ 去; ~ **abroad**, ch'u¹ yang² 出洋; ~ **ahead**, ch'ien² chin⁴ 前進; ~ **away**, ch'ü⁴ 去, fan³ 返; ~ **down**, hsia⁴ ch'ü⁴ 下去; ~ **on**, chi⁴ hsü⁴ chin⁴ hsing² 繼續進行; ~ **up**, shang⁴ 上.　「mu⁴ piao¹ 目標.

goal *n.* (*race*) chung¹ tien³ 終點, (*thing wanted*)

goat *n.* shan¹ yang² 山羊.

goblin *n.* e⁴ mo² 惡魔.

god *n.* shang⁴ ti⁴ 上帝, shen² 神.

godchild *n.* chiao⁴ tzu³ 敎子.

goddess *n.* (*female god*) nü³ shen² 女神, (*beautiful woman*) chüeh² shih⁴ mei³ jen² 絕世美人.

godfather *n.* chiao⁴ fu⁴ 教父.

godlike *a.* ssu⁴ shen² te¹ 似神的.

godmother *n.* chiao⁴ mu³ 教母.

goggles *n.* feng¹ ching⁴ 風鏡.

gold *n.* chin¹ 金; ～ **coin,** chin¹ pi⁴ 金幣; ～ **reserve,** hsien⁴ chin¹ chun³ pei⁴ 現金準備; ～ **standard,** chin¹ pen³ wei⁴ 金本位; ～ **leaf,** chin¹ po² 金箔.

golden *a.* chin¹ te¹ 金的.

goldsmith *n.* chin¹ chiang⁴ 金匠.

gondola *n.* p'ing² ti³ ch'uan² 平底船 (威尼斯).

gonorrhea, gonorrhoea *n.* lin⁴ ping⁴ 淋病.

good *a.* liang² hao³ te¹ 良好的.

good-by, good-bye *int.*, *n.* tsai⁴ hui⁴ 再會.

good-natured *a.* ho² ai³ te¹ 和藹的.

goodness *n.* shan⁴ liang² 善良.

goods *n.* (*belongings*) tung⁴ ch'an³ 動產, (*wares*) huo⁴ wu⁴ 貨物.

goose *n.* e² 鵝.

gooseberry *n.* ts'u⁴ li⁴ 醋栗.

gorge *n.* hsia⁴ 峽; *v.* t'an¹ shih² 貪食.

gorgeous *a.* hua² li⁴ te¹ 華麗的.

gory *a.* hsüeh³ jan³ te¹ 血染的.

gospel *n.* fu² yin¹ 福音.

gossip *n.* hsien² t'an² 閒談, (*person*) hsien² t'an² che³ 閒談者; *v.* hsien² t'an² 閒談.

gourd *n.* hu² lu² 葫蘆, hu² lu² p'iao² 葫蘆瓢.

gout *n.* (*disease*) t'ung⁴ feng¹ 痛風.

gouty *a.* huan⁴ t'ung⁴ feng¹ te¹ 患痛風的.

govern *v.* kuan³ li³ 管理.

governess *n.* chia¹ t'ing² nü³ chiao⁴ shih¹ 家庭女教師.

government *n.* cheng⁴ fu³ 政府; ～ **Administration Council****, cheng⁴ wu⁴ yüan⁴ 政務院**; ～ **property,** kung¹ ch'an³ 公產.

governor *n.* (*US*) chou¹ chang³ 州長(美), (*CHINA*) sheng² chu³ hsi² 省主席(中), (*device*) t'iao² su⁴ ch'i⁴ 調速器(機).

grace *n.* (*favor*) en¹ hui⁴ 恩惠, (*before or after a meal*) ch'i² tao³ 祈禱.

graceful *a.* yu¹ ya³ te¹ 優雅的.

gracious *a.* jen² ai⁴ te¹ 仁愛的, ch'ien¹ pei¹ te¹ 謙卑的.

gradation n. chieh¹ chi² 階級, teng³ chi² 等級.

grade n. (*quality*) teng³ chi² 等級, (*rank*) chieh¹ chi² 階級, (*slope*) hsieh² tu⁴ 斜度.

gradient n. (*rate of change*) pien⁴ lü⁴ 變率, (*slope*) p'o¹ tu⁴ 坡度.

gradual a. chu² chien⁴ te¹ 逐漸的.

graduate n. pi⁴ yeh⁴ sheng¹ 畢業生; v. pi⁴ yeh⁴

graduation n. pi⁴ yeh⁴ 畢業.   畢業.

graft n. chieh¹ chih¹ 接枝, (*money*) t'an¹ wu¹ 貪汚.

grain n. ku³ li⁴ 穀粒.

grammer n. wen² fa³ 文法.

grammatical a. wen² fa³ te¹ 文法的.

gramophone n. liu² sheng¹ chi² 留聲機.

granary n. (*storehouse*) ku³ ts'ang¹ 穀倉, (*region*) ch'an² ku³ ti⁴ 產穀地.

grand a. (*main*) shou⁴ yao⁴ te¹ 首要的, (*fine*) hua² li⁴ te¹ 華麗的; ~ **Canal**, ta⁴ yün⁴ ho² 大運河; ~ **piano**, ta⁴ kang¹ ch'in² 大鋼琴.

granite n. hua¹ kang¹ shih² 花崗石(礦).

grant n. tseng⁴ p'in³ 贈品; v. yün³ hsü³ 允許.

grantee n. shou⁴ jang⁴ jen² 受讓人.

grantor n. jang⁴ tu⁴ jen² 讓渡人.

grape n. p'u² t'ao² 葡萄.

grasp n. chin³ wo⁴ 緊握; v. chin³ wo⁴ 緊握.

grass n. ts'ao³ 草.

grasshopper n. cha⁴ meng³ 蚱蜢.

grassy a. ssu⁴ ts'ao³ te¹ 似草的.

grate n. lu² ch'uang² 爐牀; v. chuang¹ ko² 裝格.

grateful a. kan³ hsieh⁴ te¹ 感謝的.

gratification n. yü² k'uai⁴ 愉快, man³ i⁴ 滿意.

gratify v. shih³ yü² k'uai⁴ 使愉快, shih² man³ i⁴ 使滿意.

gratitude n. kan³ hsieh⁴ 感謝, kan³ en¹ 感恩.

gratuity n. (*tip*) shang³ chin¹ 賞金, (*present*) li³ wu⁴ 禮物, (*for dead and wounded*) fu³ hsü⁴ chin¹ 撫卹金.

grave n. fen² mu⁴ 墳墓; a. (*important*) chung⁴ ta⁴ te¹ 重大的, (*solemn*) chuang¹ yen² te¹ 莊嚴的.

gravel n. sui⁴ shih² 碎石, sha¹ li⁴ 砂礫; ~ **pit**, li⁴ k'eng¹ 礫坑.

gravelly a. to¹ sha¹ li⁴ te¹ 多砂礫的.

106

gravestone *n.* mu⁴ pei¹ 墓碑, mu⁴ shih² 墓石.

graveyard *n.* mu⁴ ti⁴ 墓地.

gravitate *v.* ch'ing¹ hsiang⁴ 傾向.

gravity *n.* hsi¹ li⁴ 吸力, (*weight*) chung⁴ liang⁴ 重量, (*seriousness*) yen² chung⁴ 嚴重.

gravy *n.* jou⁴ chih¹ 肉汁, lu³ chih¹ 滷汁.

gray *a.* hui¹ se⁴ te¹ 灰色的, (*dark*) yin¹ an⁴ te¹ 陰暗的.

graze *v.* ssu⁴ ts'ao³ 飼草, (*rub*) ts'a¹ 擦.

grease *n.* yu² chih¹ 油脂; *v.* ts'a¹ yu² 擦油, yu² 油; ~ **cup,** huang² yu² pei¹ 黃油杯; ~ **gun,** huang² yu² ch'iang¹ 黃油槍.

greasy *v.* han² yu² te¹ 含油的, t'u² te¹ 塗的.

great *a.* chü⁴ ta⁴ te¹ 巨大的, (*remarkable*) wei³ ta⁴ te¹ 偉大的.

greatness *n.* chü⁴ ta⁴ 巨大, wei³ ta⁴ 偉大.

greedy *a.* t'an¹ lan² te¹ 貪婪的, (*piggish*) t'an¹ shih² te¹ 貪食的.

green *a.* lü⁴ se⁴ te¹ 綠色的, (*unripe*) wei⁴ ch'eng² shou² te¹ 未成熟的; *n.* lü⁴ se⁴ 綠色, (*ground*) ts'ao³ ti⁴ 草地.

greenhouse *n.* yang³ hua¹ shih¹ 養花室, nuan³ fang² 暖房.

greet *v.* huan¹ ying² 歡迎.

greeting *n.* wen⁴ hou⁴ 問候, huan¹ ying² 歡迎.

gregarious *a.* ch'ün² chü⁴ te¹ 群居的, hao⁴ ch'ün² te¹ 好群的.

grenade *n.* shou³ liu² tan⁴ 手榴彈, (*fire*) mieh⁴ huo³ p'ing² 滅火瓶.

grid *n.* (*electric*) cha⁴ 柵, cha⁴ chi² 柵極; ~ **north,** fang¹ ko² pei² 方格北.

grief *n.* pei¹ shang¹ 悲傷, t'ung⁴ k'u³ 痛苦.

grievance *n.* k'u³ ch'ing² 苦情.

grieve *v.* pei¹ ai¹ 悲哀, t'ung⁴ k'u³ 痛苦.

grievous *a.* pei¹ shang¹ te¹ 悲傷的, t'ung⁴ k'u³ te¹ 痛苦的.

grill *v.* pei⁴ k'ao³ 焙烤.

grim *a.* hsiung¹ pao⁴ te¹ 兇暴的.

grin *v.* lou⁴ ch'ih³ erh² hsiao⁴ 露齒而笑.

grind *v.* yen² sui³ 研碎.

grindstone *n.* ti³ shih² 砥石.

grip *n.* chin³ wo⁴ 緊握, chʻo¹ lao² 捉牢; *v.* chin³ wo⁴ 緊握.

grisly *a.* k'o³ p'a⁴ te¹ 可怕的.

gristle *n.* juan² ku³ 軟骨.

grit *n.* sha¹ li⁴ 砂礫.

107

gritty *a.* yu³ sha¹ li⁴ te¹ 有砂礫的.

groan *v.* shen¹ yin² 呻吟.

grocer *n.* tsa² huo⁴ shang¹ 雜貨商.

grocery *n.* tsa² huo⁴ tien⁴ 雜貨店.

groin *n.* fu⁴ ku³ kou¹ 腹股溝(蹊).

groom *n.* (*horse*) ma³ fu¹ 馬夫, (*bridegroom*) hsin¹ lang² 新郎; **~ a horse,** shua¹ ma³ 刷馬(騎).

groove *n.* kou¹ ts'ao² 溝槽, (*rifling*) yin¹ hsien⁴ 陰線(兵); *v.* tso⁴ ts'ao² 作槽.

grope *v.* mo² so³ 摸索.

gross *a.* (*whole*) tsung³ shu⁴ te¹ 總數的; *n.* tsung³ shu⁴ 總數, (*twelve dozen*) i⁴ lo² 一籮; **~ tonnage,** tsung³ tun⁴ shu⁴ 總頓數; **~ weight,** ch'üan² chung⁴ 全重.

grotesque *a.* kuai⁴ tan⁴ te¹ 怪誕的.

grotto *n.* tung⁴ t'ien¹ 洞天, tung³ fu³ 洞府.

ground *n.* ti⁴ 地, (*reason*) li³ yu² 理由, i¹ chü⁴ 依據, (*electric*) ti⁴ hsien⁴ 地線; *v.* (*run aground*) ko¹ ch'ien³ 擱淺, (*electric*) chieh¹ ti⁴ 接地; **~ crew,** ti⁴ ch'in² jen² yüan² 地勤人員; **~ level,** ti⁴ p'ing² mien⁴ 地平面; **~ observation,** ti⁴ mien⁴ kuan¹ ts'e⁴ 地面觀測; **~ reconnaissance,** ti⁴ mien⁴ sou¹ so³ 地面搜索.

groundless *a.* wu² ken¹ chü⁴ te¹ 無根據的.

group *n.* tsu³ 組, ch'ün² 群, huo³ 夥, (*AF*) ta⁴ tui⁴ 大隊(航); **~ commander,** ta⁴ tui⁴ chang³ 大隊長(航); **~ life,** t'uan² t'i³ sheng¹ huo² 團體生活.

grouse *n.* sung¹ chi¹ 松鷄.

grove *n.* ts'ung² shu⁴ 叢樹.

grovel *v.* p'u² fu² 匍匐, fu² hsing² 伏行.　「栽培.

grow *v.* sheng¹ chang² 生長, (*cultivate*) tsai¹ p'ei²

growl *v.* su⁴ k'u³ 訴苦, tzu⁴ pao⁴ hsiao¹ 咆哮.

growth *n.* sheng¹ chang³ 生長, chung⁴ chih² 種植.

grub *n.* yu⁴ ch'ung² 幼蟲; *v.* chüeh² 掘.

gruel *n.* chou¹ 粥, hsi¹ fan⁴ 稀飯.

gruff *v.* kuai¹ li⁴ te¹ 乖戾的, ts'u¹ pao⁴ te¹ 粗暴的.

grumble *v.* su⁴ yüan⁴ 訴怨.

grunt *n.* chu¹ chiao⁴ sheng¹ 猪叫聲; *v.* tso⁴ chu¹ chiao⁴ sheng¹ 作猪叫聲.

guarantee *n.* pao³ cheng⁴ 保證; *v.* tan¹ pao³ 擔保; **~ fund,** pao³ cheng⁴ chin¹ 保證金.

guard *n.* wei⁴ ping¹ 衛兵; *v.* shou³ wei⁴ 守衛; ～ **commander,** wei⁴ ping¹ ssu¹ ling² 衛兵司令; ～ **duty,** wei⁴ ping¹ ch'in² wu⁴ 衛兵勤務; ～ **of honor,** i² chang⁴ tui⁴ 儀仗隊.

guardhouse *n.* (*guard quarters*) wei⁴ ping¹ shih⁴ 衛兵室, (*for confinement*) chin⁴ pi⁴ shih⁴ 禁閉室.

guardian *n.* (*law*) pao³ hu⁴ jen² 保護人(律).

guerrilla, guerilla *n.* yu² chi¹ tui⁴ 遊擊隊; ～ **tactics,** yu² chi¹ chan⁴ shu⁴ 遊擊戰術; ～ **warfare,** yu² chi¹ chan⁴ 遊擊戰.

guess *n.* ts'ai¹ ts'e⁴ 猜測; *v.* t'ui¹ ts'e⁴ 推測.

guest *n.* k'o⁴ jen² 客人, (*hotel*) lü³ k'o⁴ 旅客.

guidance *n.* ling² tao³ 領導, chih³ hui¹ 指揮.

guide *n.* (*person*) hsiang⁴ tao³ 嚮導, (*guidebook*) lü³ hsing² chih³ nan² 旅行指南; *v.* yin³ tao³ 引導, chih³ tao³ 指導.

guidebook *n.* lü³ hsing² chih³ nan² 旅行指南.

guild *n.* hsieh² hui⁴ 協會.

guile *n.* chiao³ hua² 狡猾.

guilt *n.* fan⁴ tsui⁴ 犯罪.

guiltless *a.* wu² tsui⁴ te¹ 無罪的.

guilty *a.* fan⁴ tsui⁴ te¹ 犯罪的, tsui⁴ e⁴ te¹ 罪惡的.

guitar *n.* liu⁴ hsien² ch'in² 六弦琴.

gulf *n.* ta⁴ hai³ wan¹ 大海灣.

gull *n.* (*bird*) hai³ ou¹ 海鷗(鳥), (*person*) i⁴ ch'i¹ che³ 易欺者.

gum *n.* shu⁴ chiao¹ 樹膠; *v.* chiao¹ ho² 膠合.

gummy *a.* chiao¹ chan¹ te¹ 膠粘的.

gun *n.* (*cannon*) p'ao⁴ 礮, (*rifle*) ch'iang¹ 鎗; ～ **crew,** p'ao⁴ shou³ 砲手; ～ **park,** p'ao⁴ ch'ang³ 砲礮.

gunboat *n.* p'ao⁴ t'ing³ 礮艇.

gunner *n.* p'ao⁴ shou³ 砲手, (*artillery*) miao² chun² shou³ 瞄準手(砲), 射擊法.

gunnery *n.* she⁴ chi¹ hsüeh² 射擊學, she⁴ chi¹ fa³.

gunpowder *n.* huo³ yao⁴ 火藥.

gush *v.* yung³ ch'u¹ 湧出.

gust *n.* k'uang² feng¹ 狂風.

gusty *a.* k'uang² feng¹ te¹ 狂風的.

gut *n.* ch'ang² 腸, nei⁴ tsang⁴ 內臟.

guttapercha *n.* ma³ lai² shu⁴ chiao¹ 馬來樹膠.

gutter *n.* shui³ ts'ao² 水槽, (*ditch*) shui³ kou¹ 水溝.

guttural *a., n.* yen¹ hou² te¹ 咽喉的, hou² yin¹ te¹ 喉音的.

gymnasium *n.* chien⁴ shen¹ fang² 健身房, t'i³ yü⁴ kuan³ 體育館.

gymnastic *a.* t'i³ ts'ao¹ te¹ 體操的.

gymnastics *n.* t'i³ ts'ao¹ 體操.

H

habit *n.* hsi² kuan⁴ 習慣.

habitable *a.* k'o³ chü¹ chu⁴ te¹ 可居住的.

habitation *n.* (*inhabiting*) chü¹ chu⁴ 居住, (*place*) chu⁴ so³ 住所.

habitual *a.* hsi² kuan⁴ te¹ 習慣的.

habituate *v.* shih³ kuan⁴ yü⁴ 使慣於. 「乾咳.

hack *v.* (*cut*) luan⁴ ch'ieh¹ 亂切, (*cough*) kan¹ k'o²

haft *n.* tao¹ ping³ 刀柄. 「(*witch*) nü³ wu¹ 女巫.

hag *n.* (*ugly woman*) ch'ou² lao³ yü⁴ 醜老嫗,

haggard *a.* ch'iao² ts'ui⁴ te 憔悴的, hsiao¹ shou⁴

haggle *v.* (*price*) lun⁴ chia⁴ 論價. 「te¹ 消瘦的.

hail *n.* pao² 雹, (*cheer*) huan¹ hu¹ 歡呼; *v.* hsia⁴ pao² 下雹, (*greet*) huan¹ ying² 歡迎.

hair *n.* mao² fa³ 毛髮.

hairpin *n.* fa³ chia¹ 髮夾.

hairy *a.* yu³ mao² te¹ 有毛的. 「te¹ 平靜的.

halcyon *a.* t'ai⁴ p'ing² te¹ 太平的, p'ing² ching⁴

hale *a.* k'ang¹ chien⁴ te¹ 康健的.

half *n.* i² pan⁴ 一半, erh⁴ fen¹ chih¹ i¹ 二分之一; *a.* i² pan⁴ te¹ 一半的.

half-breed *n.* hun⁴ hsüeh⁴ erh² 混血兒.

half-tone *n.* chao⁴ hsiang⁴ pan³ 照像板.

hall *n.* (*corridor*) tsou³ lang² 走廊, (*auditorium*) hui⁴ t'ang² 會堂.

hallucination *n.* huan⁴ hsiang⁴ 幻像, huan⁴ chüeh² 幻覺. 「靈光.

halo *n.* (*sun*) yün⁴ lun² 暈輪, (*saint*) ling² kuang¹

halt *n.* chih³ pu⁴ 止步, (*challenge*) chan⁴ chu⁴ 站住, (*military command*) li⁴ ting⁴ 立定(軍).

halter *n.* lung² t'ou² 籠頭.

ham *n.* huo² t'ui³ 火腿.

hamlet *n.* hsiao³ ts'un¹ 小村.

hammer *n.* ch'ui² 鎚; *v.* ch'ui² ta³ 鎚打.

hammock *n.* tiao⁴ ch'uang² 吊牀.

hamper *v.* tsu² ai⁴ 阻礙; *n.* shih² wu⁴ lan² 食物籃.

hand *n.* shou³ 手; *v.* ti⁴ 遞; **~ brake,** shou³ ch'a⁴ ch'e¹ 手刹車; **~ grenade,** shou³ liu² tan⁴ 手榴彈; **~ over,** (*an office*) i² chiao¹ 移交; **~ salute,** chü² shou² li³ 舉手禮.

handbill *n.* ch'uan² tan¹ 傳單.　　「nan² 指南.

handbook *n.* shou³ ts'e⁴ 手册, (*guidebook*) chih³

handbrake *n.* shou³ ch'a⁴ ch'e¹ 手刹車(汽).

handcuff *n.* shou² k'ao³ 手銬.

handful *n.* i⁴ pa³ 一把, i² wo⁴ 一握.　　「工業.

handicraft *n.* shou³ i⁴ 手藝, shou³ kung¹ yeh⁴ 手

handkerchief *n.* shou³ p'a⁴ 手帕.

handle *n.* ping³ 柄; *v.* (*touch*) fu³ mo² 撫摩, (*deal with*) ch'u² li³ 處理.

handsome *a.* mei³ kuan¹ te¹ 美觀的.

handy *a.* li³ pien⁴ te¹ 利便的.　　「ssu³ 絞死.

hang *v.* hsüan² kua⁴ 懸掛, (*die by hanging*) chiao²

hangar *n.* p'eng² ch'ang² 棚廠.

hangman *n.* kuei⁴ tzu¹ shou³ 劊子手.

hanker *v.* je⁴ wang⁴ 熱望.

happen *v.* fa¹ sheng¹ 發生.

happiness *n.* yü² k'uai⁴ 愉快, hsi³ yüeh⁴ 喜悅.

happy *a.* hsi³ yüeh⁴ te¹ 喜悅的.

harangue *n.* kao¹ sheng¹ yen³ shuo¹ 高聲演說; *v.* tso⁴ kao¹ sheng¹ yen³ shuo¹ 作高聲演說.

harass *v.* (*harry*) jao³ luan⁴ 擾亂, (*worry*) yu¹ lü⁴ 憂慮.　　「chiang³ fang² 港防.

harbor *n.* chiang² k'ou³ 港口; **~ defence,**

hard *a.* (*not soft*) chien¹ ying⁴ te¹ 堅硬的, (*persistent*) fen⁴ mien³ te¹ 奮勉的, (*difficult*) k'un⁴ nan² te¹ 困難的.

harden *v.* shih³ chien¹ ying⁴ 使堅硬.

hard-hearted *a.* wu² ch'ing² te¹ 無情的, ts'an² jen³ te¹ 殘忍的.

hardship *n.* chien¹ k'u³ 艱苦.

hardware *n.* chin¹ shu³ ch'i⁴ 金屬器.

hardy *a.* nai⁴ k'u³ te¹ 耐苦的.

hare *n.* yeh³ t'u⁴ 野兔.

111

harlequin *n.* ch'ou² chiao³ 丑角.

harlot *n.* ch'ang¹ chi¹ 娼妓.

harm *n.* sun³ hai⁴ 損害; *v.* sun³ shang¹ 損傷.

harmful *a.* yu³ hai⁴ te¹ 有害的.

harmless *a.* wu² hai⁴ te¹ 無害的.

harmonious *a.* t'iao² ho² te¹ 調和的.

harmonize *v.* ho² ho² 和合, ho² hsieh² 和諧.

harmony *n.* ho² hsieh² 和諧, (*music*) ho² sheng¹ 和聲.

harness *n.* (*horse*) an¹ chü¹ 鞍具, (*soldier*) chia⁴ 「chou³ 甲冑. [胄.

harp *n.* shu⁴ ch'in² 豎琴; *v.* t'an² shu⁴ ch'in² 彈豎 [琴.

harrow *v.* p'a² 耙.

harsh *a.* ts'u¹ ts'ao¹ te¹ 粗糙的.

hart *n.* hsiung² ch'ih⁴ lu⁴ 雄赤鹿. 「結果.

harvest *n.* shou¹ huo⁴ 收穫, (*result*) chieh² kuo⁴

hash *n.* tsa² sui⁴ shih² p'in³ 雜碎食品; *v.* ch'ieh¹ [sui⁴ 切碎.

hasp *n.* ta¹ niu³ 搭扭, kou¹ 鉤.

hassock *n.* p'u² t'uan² 蒲團.

haste *n.* hsün² su² 迅速, ts'ung¹ ts'u⁴ 匆促.

hasten *v.* shih³ hsün⁴ su² 使迅速, kan³ k'uai⁴ 趕 [快.

hasty *a.* hsün⁴ su² te¹ 迅速的.

hat *n.* mao⁴ 帽; ~ **insignia,** mao⁴ hui¹ 帽徽.

hatch *v.* fu¹ hua⁴ 孵化, (*plan*) chi⁴ hua⁴ 計劃.

hatchet *n.* hsiao² fu³ 小斧.

hate *n.* tseng¹ e⁴ 憎惡; *v.* t'ung⁴ hen⁴ 痛恨.

hateful *a.* k'o³ hen⁴ te¹ 可恨的.

hatred *n.* hsien² hen⁴ 嫌恨.

hatter *n.* chih⁴ mao⁴ shang¹ 製帽商.

haughtiness *n.* ao⁴ man⁴ 傲慢.

haughty *a.* ao⁴ man⁴ te¹ 傲慢的.

haul *n.* meng³ t'o¹ 猛拖; *v.* t'o¹ 拖, la¹ 拉.

haunch *n.* yao¹ pu⁴ 腰部. 「ch'ang² tao⁴ 常到.

haunt *n.* ch'ang² tao⁴ chih¹ ti⁴ 常到之地; *v.*

have *v.* (*own*) yu³ 有, (*be endowed with*) chü¹ yu³

haversack *n.* kan¹ liang² tai⁴ 乾糧袋.

havoc *n.* jou² lin⁴ 蹂躪. 「lieh⁴ 以鷹行獵.

hawk *n.* (*bird*) ying¹ 鷹; *v.* (*hunt*) i³ ying¹ hsing²

hawker *n.* (*peddler*) hsiao³ fan⁴ 小販.

hawser *n.* kang¹ so³ 鋼索.

hawthorn *n.* shan¹ cha¹ shu⁴ 山楂樹.

hay *n.* kan¹ ts'ao³ 乾草.

haystack *n.* kan¹ ts'ao³ tui¹ 乾草堆.

hazard *n.* mao⁴ hsien³ 冒險.

hazardous *a.* mao⁴ hsien³ te¹ 冒險的.

haze *n.* mai² 霾.

hazel *n.* chen¹ 榛 (植), (*color*) hung⁴ ho² se⁴ 紅褐色; *a.* (*color*) hung⁴ ho² se⁴ te¹ 紅褐色的.

hazy *a.* yu³ wu⁴ te¹ 有霧的.

he *pron.* t'a¹ 他.

head *n.* t'ou² 頭, (*leader*) shou² ling³ 首領; *v.* shuai⁴ ling³ 率領; ~ **wind,** ni⁴ feng¹ 逆風.

headache *n.* t'ou² t'ung⁴ 頭痛.

headdress *n.* t'ou² shih⁴ 頭飾.

headland *n.* chia³ 岬.

headlight *n.* ch'ien¹ teng¹ 前燈, ch'e¹ t'ou² teng¹ 車頭燈.

headline *n.* piao¹ t'i² 標題(新聞).

headmaster *n.* ssu¹ li⁴ hsüeh² hsiao⁴ hsiao⁴ chang³ 私立學校校長.

headstrong *a.* wan² ku⁴ te¹ 頑固的, kang¹ pi⁴ te¹ 剛愎的.

heal *v.* chih⁴ yü⁴ 治愈.

health *n.* chien⁴ k'ang¹ 健康.

healthful *a.* wei⁴ sheng¹ te¹ 衛生的.

healthy *a.* chien⁴ k'ang¹ te¹ 健康的, yu³ i⁴ chien⁴ k'ang¹ te¹ 有益健康的.

heap *n.* tui¹ 堆, (*large amount*) to¹ liang⁴ 多量; *v.* tui¹ chi¹ 堆積.

hear *v.* t'ing¹ 聽, wen² 聞.

hearer *n.* t'ing¹ che³ 聽者.

hearing *n.* t'ing¹ chüeh² 聽覺.

hearken *v.* ti⁴ t'ing¹ 諦聽.

hearse *n.* chiu⁴ ch'e¹ 柩車.

heart *n.* hsin¹ 心, hsin¹ tsang⁴ 心臟.

heartily *adv.* ch'eng³ k'en³ ti⁴ 誠懇地.

hearty *a.* ch'eng² i⁴ te¹ 誠意的, je⁴ lieh⁴ te¹ 熱烈的.

heat *n.* je⁴ 熱; *v.* shih³ je⁴ 使熱; ~ **indicator,** wen¹ tu⁴ piao³ 溫度表.

heater *n.* ch'ü² nuan³ ch'i⁴ 取暖器.

heathen *a.* i⁴ chiao⁴ te¹ 異教的; *n.* i⁴ chiao⁴ t'u² 異教徒.

heave *v.* (*lift*) chü⁴ ch'i³ 舉起, (*throw*) t'i² chih⁴ 提擲, (*pull*) t'o¹ yeh⁴ 拖曳.

heaven *n.* t'ien¹ t'ang² 天堂.

heavenly *a.* t'ien¹ k'ung¹ te¹ 天空的, t'ien¹ kuo² te¹ 天國的; *adv.* ling² hsiao¹ 靈霄, ju² t'ien¹ 如天.

heavy *a.* chung⁴ te¹ 重的; ～ **artillery**, chung⁴ p'ao⁴ ping¹ 重砲兵(軍); ～ **bomber**, chung⁴ hung¹ cha⁴ chi¹ 重轟炸機(航); ～ **burden**, chung⁴ fu⁴ 重負; ～ **machine gun**, chung⁴ chi¹ kuan¹ ch'iang¹ 重機關鎗(軍); ～ **weapon**, chung⁴ ping¹ ch'i⁴ 重兵器(軍).

heckle *v.* yen² chieh² 嚴詰.   「籬笆.

hedge *n.* ai³ shu⁴ li² 矮樹籬; *v.* wei² i³ li² pa¹ 圍以

hedgehog *n.* tz'u⁴ wei² 刺蝟.

heed *n. v.* chu⁴ i⁴ 注意, kuan¹ hsin¹ 關心.

heedless *a.* pu² chu⁴ i⁴ te¹ 不注意的.

heel *n.* ken¹ 跟.   「炸高(砲).

height *n.* kao¹ tu⁴ 高度; ～ **of burst**, cha⁴ kao¹

heighten *v.* shih³ kao¹ 使高.

heinous *a.* hsiung¹ pao⁴ te¹ 兇暴的.

heir *n.* hou⁴ ssu⁴ 後嗣, chi⁴ ch'eng² jen² 繼承人.

heirloom *n.* tsu³ ch'uan² wu⁴ 祖傳物.

helicopter *n.* chih² sheng¹ fei¹ chi¹ 直昇飛機.

heliport *n.* chih² sheng¹ chi¹ ch'ang³ 直昇機場.

hell *n.* ming² fu³ 冥府, ti⁴ yü⁴ 地獄.

helm *n.* to⁴ ping³ 舵柄.

helmet *n.* t'ou⁴ k'uei¹ 頭盔, kang¹ k'uei¹ 鋼盔.

helmsman *n.* to⁴ kung¹ 舵工.

help *n., v.* pang¹ chu⁴ 幫助.

helpful *a.* yu³ chu⁴ te¹ 有助的.

helpless *a.* wu² chu⁴ te¹ 無助的.

hem *n.* i¹ pien¹ 衣邊; *v.* hsiang¹ pien¹ 鑲邊.

hemisphere *n.* pan⁴ ch'iu² 半球.

hemlock *n.* tu² ch'in² 毒芹.

hemorrhage *n.* liu² hsüeh¹ 流血.

hemorrhoids *n.* chih⁴ ch'uang¹ 痔瘡.

hemp *n.* ta⁴ ma² 大蔴.

hen *n.* p'in³ chi¹ 牝鷄.

hence *adv.* ts'ung² tz'u³ 從此, chin¹ hou⁴ 今後.

henceforth *adv.* chin¹ hou⁴ 今後.

hencoop *n.* chi¹ lung² 鷄籠.

henpeck *v.* chü⁴ nei⁴ 懼內.

her *pron.* t'a¹ 她; *a.* t'a¹ te¹ 她的.

herb *n.* ts'ao² pen³ chih² wu⁴ 草本植物.

herculean *a.* li⁴ shih⁴ te¹ 力士的.   「ch'ün² 成群.

herd *n.* (*animal*) shou⁴ ch'ün² 獸群; *v.* ch'eng²

114

here *adv.* tsai⁴ tz'u³ ti⁴ 在此地, tao⁴ tz'u³ ti⁴ 到此地.

hereafter *adv.* tz'u³ hou⁴ 此後.

hereby *adv.* yu² shih⁴ 由是.

hereditary *a.* tsu³ ch'uan² te¹ 祖傳的, i² ch'uan² te¹ 遺傳的.

herein *adv.* yü² tz'u³ 於此.

hereof *adv.* kuan¹ yü² tz'u³ 關於此.

hereon *adv.* yü² tz'u³ 於此.

heresy *n.* i⁴ shuo¹ 異說, i⁴ tuan¹ 異端.

heretic *n.* i⁴ chiao⁴ t'u² 異敎徒.

heretofore *adv.* wang³ hsi² 往昔.

herewith *adv.* tsai⁴ tz'u³ 在此.

heritage *n.* i² ch'an³ 遺產.

hermit *n.* yin³ shih⁴ 隱士.

hero *n.* ying¹ hsiung² 英雄.

heroic *a.* ying¹ hsiung² te¹ 英雄的.

heroine *n.* nü³ ying¹ hsiung² 女英雄.

heroism *n.* ying¹ hsiung² ch'i⁴ kai⁴ 英雄氣概, ying¹ hsiung² hsing² wei² 英雄行爲.

heron *n.* pai² lu⁴ 白鷺.

herring *n.* fei¹ 鯡.

hers *pron.* t'a¹ te¹ 她的.

herself *pron.* t'a¹ tzu⁴ chi³ 她自己.

hesitate *v.* ch'ou² ch'u² 躊躇, ch'ih² i² 遲疑.

hesitation *n.* ch'ou² ch'u² 躊躇, ch'ih² i² 遲疑.

heterodox *a.* i⁴ tuan¹ te¹ 異端的, i⁴ chiao⁴ te¹ 異敎的.

heterogeneous *a.* ko⁴ chung³ te¹ 各種的, pu⁴ t'ung² te¹ 不同的.

hew *v.* chan³ 斬, k'an³ 砍, p'i¹ 劈.

hide *n.* shou⁴ p'i² 獸皮; *v.* yin³ ts'ang² 隱藏, (oneself) tzu⁴ ni⁴ 自匿.

hideous *a.* k'o³ tseng¹ te¹ 可憎的, t'ao³ yen⁴ te¹ 討厭的.

high *a.* kao¹ te¹ 高的; ～ **gear**, san¹ tang³ 三檔 (汽); ～ **ground**, kao¹ ti⁴ 高地; ～ **school**, kao¹ teng³ hsüeh² hsiao⁴ 高等學校; ～ **seas**, kung¹ hai³ 公海.

highly *adv.* kao¹ 高.

highness *n.* kao¹ 高, (*royal families*) tien¹ hsia⁴ 殿下.

highroad *n.* kung¹ lu⁴ 公路.

hilarity *n.* k'uang² hsi³ 狂喜.

hill *n.* hsiao³ shan¹ 小山, ch'iu¹ ling² 丘陵.

hilly *a.* to¹ hsiao³ shan¹ te¹ 多小山的.

hilt *n.* (*sword*) tao¹ ping³ 刀柄, (*dagger*) chien⁴

him *pron.* t'a¹ 他.　　　　　　　　　　　⌐ping³ 劍柄.

himself *pron.* t'a¹ tzu⁴ chi³ 他自己.

hinder *v.* fang² ai⁴ 妨礙, tsu³ ai⁴ 阻礙.

hindrance *n.* fang² ai⁴ 妨礙, tsu³ chang⁴ 阻障.

hinge *n.* chiao³ lien⁴ 鉸鏈; *v.* ting¹ chiao³ lien⁴ 釘

hint *n.*, *v.* an⁴ shih⁴ 暗示.　　　　　　　　⌐鉸鏈.

hip *n.* k'uan¹ 髖.

hire *v.* (*thing*) tsu¹ chieh⁴ 租借, (*person*) ku⁴ yung⁴
僱用; *n.* (*thing*) tsu¹ chin¹ 租金, (*person*) kung¹

his *a.*, *pron.* t'a¹ te¹ 他的.　　　　　　　⌐tzu¹ 工資.

hiss *n.* ch'ih¹ sheng¹ 嗤聲; *v.* tso⁴ ssu¹ ssu¹ sheng¹
作嘶嘶聲.　　　　　　　　　　　　⌐chia¹ 史學家.

historian *n.* li⁴ shih³ chia¹ 歷史家, shih³ hsüeh²

history *n.* li⁴ shih³ 歷史.

hit *v.* chi¹ chung⁴ 擊中.　　　　　　　　　⌐繫住.

hitch *v.* (*harness*) t'ao⁴ chia⁴ 套架, (*tie*) hsi⁴ chu⁴

hither *adv.* chih⁴ tz'u³ ch'u⁴ 至此處, tz'u³ ch'u⁴

hive *n.* feng¹ fang² 蜂房.　　　　　　　　　⌐此處.

hoard *n.* ch'u² ts'ang² 儲藏; *v.* ch'u² ts'ang² 儲藏.

hoarse *a.* ts'u¹ se⁴ te¹ 粗澀的.

hobble *v.* (*limp*) po³ hsing² 跛行.

hobby *n.* shih⁴ hao⁴ 嗜好.

hock *n.* chiao³ huai² kuan¹ chieh² 脚踝關節.

hoe *n.* ch'u² 鋤.

hog *n.* (*pig*) chu¹ 豬.

hoist *v.* chü² ch'i³ 舉起, la¹ ch'i³ 拉起.

hold *v.* chin³ wo⁴ 緊握; *n.* huo⁴ ts'ang¹ 貨艙.

holder *n.* chih² yu⁴ che³ 執有者, ch'ih² yu⁴ che³

hole *n.* tung⁴ hsüeh⁴ 洞穴.　　　　　　　　⌐持有者.

holiday *n.* chia⁴ jih⁴ 假日, hsiu¹ hsi² jih⁴ 休息日.

holiness *n.* shen² sheng⁴ 神聖.

hollow *a.* k'ung¹ hsü¹ te¹ 空虛的; *n.* (*hole*) tung⁴
hsüeh⁴ 洞穴, (*valley*) ku³ 谷; *v.* shih³ k'ung¹ 使
空.

holster *n.* shou³ ch'iang¹ p'i² t'ao⁴ 手鎗皮套.

holy *a.* shen² sheng⁴ te¹ 神聖的, sheng⁴ chieh² te¹

homage *n.* (*respect*) tsun¹ ching⁴ 尊敬.　⌐聖潔的.

home *n.* (*live*) chia¹ 家, (*born*) ku⁴ hsiang¹ 故鄉;
~ life, chia¹ t'ing² sheng¹ huo² 家庭生活.

homeless *a.* wu² chia¹ te¹ 無家的.

116

homely *a.* p'u¹ su⁴ te¹ 樸素的, p'ing² fan² te¹ 平凡
homesick *a.* ssu¹ chia¹ ping⁴ te¹ 思家病的.　　⌐的.
homeward *adv.* hsiang⁴ chia¹ 向家.
homicide *n.* hsiung¹ fan⁴ 凶犯.
hone *n.* mo² tao¹ shih² 磨刀石.
honest *a.* ch'eng² shih² te¹ 誠實的.
honesty *n.* ch'eng² shih² 誠實.
honey *n.* mi⁴ 蜜.
honeymoon *n.* mi⁴ yüeh⁴ 蜜月.
honeysuckle *n.* jen³ tung¹ 忍冬(植).
honorary *a.* ming² yü⁴ te¹ 名譽的; ～ **degree,**
　ming² yü⁴ hsüeh² wei⁴ 名譽學位.
honor *n.* kuang¹ jung² 光榮; *v.* tsun¹ ching⁴ 尊敬.
honorable *a.* k'o³ tsun¹ ching⁴ te¹ 可尊敬的; ～
　discharge, jung² yü⁴ t'ui⁴ i⁴ 榮譽退役.
hood *n.* t'ou² tou¹ 頭兜.
hoodwink *v.* yu⁴ hung¹ 誘哄, ch'i¹ p'ien⁴ 欺騙.
hoof *n.* t'i² 蹄, (*foot*) tsu² 足.
hook *n.* kou¹ 鈎; *v.* kou¹ chu⁴ 鈎住.
hooked *n.* kou¹ hsing² te¹ 鈎形的.
hoop *n.* huan² ku¹ 環箍; *v.* chia¹ ku¹ 加箍.
hop *n.* t'iao⁴ yüeh⁴ 跳躍; *v.* tu² chiao³ t'iao⁴ 獨脚
hope *n.,* *v.* hsi¹ wang⁴ 希望.　　　　　　⌐跳.
hopeful *a.* yu³ hsi¹ wang⁴ te¹ 有希望的.
hopeless *a.* wu² hsi¹ wang⁴ te¹ 無希望的.
horizon *n.* ti⁴ p'ing² hsien⁴ 地平線.
horizontal *a.* ti⁴ p'ing² te¹ 地平的, p'ing² hsing²
　hsien⁴ te¹ 平行線的.
horn *n.* chiao³ 角, hao⁴ chiao³ 號角.
hornet *n.* ta⁴ huang² feng¹ 大黃蜂.　　　⌐騷的.
horrible *a.* k'o³ pu⁴ te¹ 可怖的, ching¹ hai⁴ te¹ 驚
horrid *a.* k'o³ pu⁴ te¹ 可怖的.
horror *n.* k'ung³ pu⁴ 恐怖, (*dislike*) tseng¹ e⁴ 憎惡.
horse *n.* ma³ 馬; ～ **artillery,** ch'i² p'ao⁴ ping¹
　騎砲兵; ～ **feed,** fu⁴ liao⁴ 麩料.
horseback *n.* ma³ pei³ 馬背.
horsefly *n.* ma³ mang² 馬虻, ma³ ying² 馬蠅.
horsehair *n.* ma³ tsung¹ mao² 馬鬃毛.
horsemanship *n.* ch'i² shu⁴ 騎術.
horsepower *n.* ma³ li⁴ 馬力(力之單位).
horseradish *n.* la⁴ lo² po¹ 辣蘿蔔.

horseshoe n. ma³ t'i² t'ieh² 馬蹄鐵.

horticulturul a. yüan² i⁴ te¹ 園藝的.

horticulture n. yüan² i⁴ 園藝.

horticulturist n. yüan² i⁴ chia¹ 園藝家.

hose n. (stockings) ch'ang² t'ung³ mo⁴ 長襪.

hosier n. wa⁴ shang¹ 襪商.

hospitable a. k'uan³ tai⁴ te¹ 款待的.

hospital n. i¹ yüan⁴ 醫院, ping⁴ yüan⁴ 病院.

hospitality n. k'uan³ tai⁴ 款待.　　　　　　 「大群.

host n. chu³ jen² 主人, (large number) ta⁴ ch'ün²

hostage n. (person) jen² chih² 人質, (security) tan¹ pao² p'in³ 擔保品.

hostess n. nü³ chu³ jen² 女主人.

hostile a. ch'ou² ti² te¹ 仇敵的.

hot a. (temperature) je⁴ te¹ 熱的, (taste) hsin¹ la⁴

hotel n. lü³ kuan³ 旅館.　　　　 「te¹ 辛辣的.

hound n. lieh⁴ ch'üan³ 獵犬.　　　　 「陌.

hour n. shih² chien¹ 時間, (o'clock) hsiao³ shih² 小

hourly a. mei² hsiao³ shih² te¹ 每小時的; adv. shih² ch'ang² 時常.

house n. fang² wu¹ 房屋; v. liu² su⁴ 留宿; ~ of call, chih² yeh⁴ chieh⁴ shao⁴ so³ 職業紹介所; ~ of Representatives (US), chung⁴ i⁴ yüan⁴ 衆議院(美).

household a. chia¹ nei⁴ te¹ 家內的; n. (family) chia¹ shu³ 家屬, (affairs) chia¹ wu⁴ 家務.

householder n. chia¹ chu³ 家主.

housekeeper n. kuan³ chia¹ fu⁴ 管家婦.

housemaid n. nü³ p'u² 女僕, pei⁴ nü³ 婢女.

housewife n. chu³ fu⁴ 主婦.

hovel n. lou⁴ shih⁴ 陋室.

how adv. ju² ho² 如何.

however adv. wu² lun⁴ ju² ho² 無論如何.

howitzer n. liu² tan⁴ p'ao⁴ 榴彈砲.

howl n., v. ai¹ hao⁴ 哀號.

hub n. lun² ku³ 輪轂.

hubbub n. hsüan¹ jang³ 喧嚷, ts'ao² tsa² 嘈雜.

huddle v. fen¹ chi¹ 紛集, yung³ chi³ 擁擠.

hue n. (color) se⁴ 色, (shouting) hsüan¹ jang³ 喧嚷.

hug v. yung³ pao⁴ 擁抱, chin³ pao⁴ 緊抱.

huge a. chü⁴ ta⁴ te¹ 巨大的.

hull *n.* (*rice*) mi³ k'o² 米殼, (*fruit*) kuo³ p'i² 果皮, (*ship*) ch'uan² shen¹ 船身; *v.* (*rice*) ch'ü⁴ k'o² 去殼, (*fruit*) ch'ü⁴ p'i² 去皮, (*ship*) kuan⁴ ch'uan¹ 貫穿.

hum *n.* tso⁴ weng¹ weng¹ sheng¹ 作嗡嗡聲.

human *a.* jen² lei⁴ te¹ 人類的; ~ **nature,** jen² hsing⁴ 人性.

humane *a.* jen² tz'u² te¹ 仁慈的. 「者.

humanitarian *n.* jen² tao⁴ chu³ i⁴ che⁸ 人道主義

humanity *n.* jen² ch'ing² 人情, jen² hsing⁴ 人性, jen² tz'u² 仁慈.

humble *a.* (*not grand*) ti¹ wei¹ te¹ 低微的, (*modest*) ch'ien¹ jang⁴ te¹ 謙讓的.

humbug *n.* ch'i¹ p'ien¹ 欺騙.

humid *a.* ch'ao² shih¹ te¹ 潮濕的.

humidity *n.* ch'ao² shih¹ 潮濕.

humiliate *v.* i⁴ chih⁴ 抑制, pien⁸ ti¹ 貶低.

humiliation *n.* ch'ü¹ ju³ 屈辱.

humility *n.* ch'ien¹ sun⁴ 謙遜.

humor *n.* yu¹ mo⁴ 幽默, hui¹ hsieh² 詼諧.

humorist *n.* yu¹ mo⁴ chia¹ 幽默家, hua² chi¹ che³ 滑稽者. 「幽默的.

humorous *a.* hui¹ hsieh² te¹ 詼諧的, yu¹ mo¹ te¹

hump *n.* lung² jou⁴ 隆肉, (*mound*) yüan² ch'iu¹ 圓

humpback *n.* t'o³ pei⁴ 駝背. 「丘.

hundred *n.* pai³ 百; *a.* pai³ te¹ 百的.

hunger *n.* chi¹ e⁴ 飢餓.

hungry *a.* chi¹ e⁴ te¹ 飢餓的. 「sou¹ so³ 搜索.

hunt *n.* ta³ lieh⁴ 打獵; *v.* chui¹ lieh⁴ 追獵, (*search*)

hunter *n.* (*person*) lieh⁴ jen² 獵人, (*dog*) lieh⁴

hurdle *n.* t'iao² lan² 跳欄. 「ch'üan³ 獵犬.

hurl *v.* meng³ chih¹ 猛擲.

hurricane *n.* chü⁴ feng¹ 颶風, hsüan⁴ feng¹ 旋風.

hurried *a.* chi² ts'u⁴ te¹ 急促的.

hurry *n.* ts'ung¹ ts'u⁴ 忽促; *v.* ts'ui¹ ts'u⁴ 催促.

hurt *n.* shang¹ 傷; *v.* sun³ hai⁴ 損害.

hurtful *a.* shang¹ hai⁴ te¹ 傷害的.

husband *n.* chang⁴ fu¹ 丈夫.

hush *v.* wu⁴ hsiang³ 勿響.

hut *n.* hsiao³ wu¹ 小屋, mao² she⁴ 茅舍.

hyacinth *n.* feng¹ hsin⁴ tzu¹ 風信子(植), feng¹ hsin⁴ tzu¹ shih² 風信子石.

hydraulic *a.* shui³ li⁴ te¹ 水力的.

hydraulics *n.* shui³ li⁴ hsüeh² 水力學.　　　　　「彈.

hydrogen *n.* ching¹ 氫; ~ **bomb,** ching¹ tan⁴ 氫

hydrophobia *n.* k'ung² shui³ ping⁴ 恐水病, wen¹ ch'üan³ ping⁴ 瘋犬病.

hygiene *n.* wei⁴ sheng¹ hsüeh² 衛生學.

hymen *n.* ch'u² nü³ mo⁴ 處女膜.

hymeneal *a.* hun¹ yin¹ te¹ 婚姻的.

hymn *n.* tsan⁴ mei³ shih¹ 讚美詩.

hyperbole *n.* k'ua¹ chang¹ fa³ 誇張法.

hyphen *n.* tuan³ hua⁴ 短劃.

hypnotism *n.* ts'ui¹ mien² shu⁴ 催眠術.

hypocrisy *n.* chia³ tao⁴ hsüeh² 假道學, wei⁴ shan⁴ 僞善.　　　　　　　　　　　「tzu³ 僞君子.

hypocrite *n.* chiao³ shih⁴ che³ 矯飾者, wei⁴ chün¹

hypothesis *n.* chia³ she⁴ 假設, chia³ ting⁴ 假定.

hysteria *n.* i⁴ ping⁴ 癔病.

I

I *pron.* wo³ 我.

ice *n.* ping¹ 冰; ~ **cream,** ping¹ ch'i² lin² 冰淇淋; ~ **house,** ping¹ k'u⁴ 冰庫; ~ **water,** ping¹ leng³ shui³ 冰冷水.

iceberg *n.* ping¹ shan¹ 冰山.

icebox *n.* ping¹ hsiang¹ 冰箱.

iced *a.* ping¹ tung⁴ te¹ 冰凍的.

icicle *n.* ping¹ chu⁴ 冰柱.

icy *a.* ssu⁴ ping¹ te¹ 似冰的, yen² han⁴ te¹ 嚴寒的.

idea *n.* kuan¹ nien⁴ 觀念.

ideal *a.* li² hsiang³ te¹ 理想的; *n.* li² hsiang³ 理想.

identical *a.* hsiang¹ t'ung² te¹ 相同的.

identification *n.* shih⁴ pieh² 識別, (mark) piao¹ chih⁴ 標誌; ~ **card (US),** shen¹ fen⁴ cheng² 身份證(美); ~ **light,** shih⁴ pieh² teng¹ 識別燈(軍); ~ **mark,** piao¹ chih⁴ 標誌; ~ **panel,** hsin⁴ hao⁴ pu⁴ pan³ 信號布板(軍); ~ **papers,** cheng⁴ ming² wen² chien⁴ 證明文件; ~ **tags (US),** shih⁴ pieh² p'ai² 識別牌(美).

identify v. pien² pieh² 辨別, shih⁴ pieh² 識別.

identity n. (of military personnel) hsing⁴ ming² chieh¹ chi² 姓名階級, (of unit) fan¹ hao⁴ 番號, (nationality of airplane) kuo² pieh² 國別.

idiom n. ch'eng² yü³ 成語.

idiomatic a. ch'eng² yü³ te¹ 成語的.

idiot n. ch'ih² tzu¹ 痴子.

idle a. (not busy) k'ung⁴ hsien² te¹ 空閒的, (lazy) lan³ tai⁴ te¹ 懶怠的.

idol n. ou³ hsiang⁴ 偶像.

idolater n. ou³ hsiang⁴ ch'ung² pai⁴ che³ 偶像崇拜者.　　　　　　　　　　　　　　　　　「像的.

idolatrous a. ch'ung² pai⁴ ou³ hsiang⁴ te¹ 崇拜偶

idolatry n. ou³ hsiang⁴ ch'ung² pai⁴ 偶像崇拜.

idolize v. ch'ung² pai⁴ 崇拜, tsun¹ ching⁴ 尊敬.

if conj. chia² shih³ 假使.

ignite v. jan² shao¹ 燃燒, tien² huo³ 點火.

ignition n. tien² huo³ 點火, (motor) yin² huo³ 引火; ～ **cartridge,** tien² huo³ yao⁴ t'ung³ 點火藥筒 (軍); ～ **spark,** huo³ hua¹ 火花; ～ **switch,** tien⁴ men² 電門.

ignoble a. ch'u¹ shen¹ ti¹ wei¹ te¹ 出身低微的.

ignominious a. k'o² ch'ih³ te¹ 可恥的.

ignominy n. ch'ih³ ju³ 恥辱.

ignorance n. wu² chih¹ 無知, yü² mei⁴ 愚昧.

ignorant a. wu² chih¹ shih⁴ te¹ 無知識的.

ignore v. pu⁴ li³ 不理.

ill a. (sick) yu³ ping⁴ te¹ 有病的; adv. (badly) e⁴ lieh⁴ ti⁴ 惡劣地; n. (sickness) chi² ping⁴ 疾病.

illegal a. wei² fa³ te¹ 違法的.

illegality n. wei² fa³ 違法.

illegible a. nan² tu² te¹ 難讀的.　　　　「違法的.

illegitimate a. ssu¹ sheng¹ te¹ 私生的, wei² fa³ te¹

illicit a. fei¹ fa³ te¹ 非法的, fan⁴ chin¹ te¹ 犯禁的.

illiteracy n. wen² mang² 文盲.

illiterate a. wu² chiao¹ yü⁴ te¹ 無教育的.

illness n. chi² ping⁴ 疾病.

illogical a. pu⁴ ho² li³ lun⁴ te¹ 不合理論的.

illuminate v. (light up) chao⁴ yao⁴ 照耀.

illusion n. huan⁴ ying³ 幻影.

illustrate v. shuo¹ ming² 說明, li⁴ chieh³ 例解.

illustration *n.* chiang² chieh³ 講解.

illustrative *a.* shuo¹ ming² te¹ 說明的, t'u² chieh³ te¹ 圖解的.

illustrious *a.* cho² ming² te¹ 著名的.

image *n.* hsiao⁴ hsiang⁴ 肖像.

imaginable *a.* k'o² hsiang³ hsiang⁴ te¹ 可想像的.

imaginary *a.* hsiang³ hsiang⁴ te¹ 想像的; ～ enemy, chia² she⁴ ti² 假設敵.

imagination *n.* hsiang³ hsiang⁴ li⁴ 想像力.

imaginative *a.* hsiang³ hsiang⁴ te¹ 想像的.

imagine *v.* hsiang³ hsiang⁴ 想像.

imbibe *v.* (*drink*) yin³ 飲, (*absorb*) hsi¹ ju⁴ 吸入.

imitate *v.* mo² fang³ 模倣.

imitation *n.* mo² fang³ 模倣.

imitative *a.* mo² fang³ te¹ 模倣的.

imitator *n.* mo² fang³ che³ 模倣者.

immaculate *a.* wu² hsia² tz'u¹ te¹ 無瑕疵的.

immaterial *a.* (*insignificant*) pu² chung⁴ yao⁴ te¹ 不重要的, (*spiritual*) ching¹ shen² shang⁴ te¹ 精神上的.

immediate *a.* li⁴ k'o⁴ te¹ 立刻的.

immemorial *a.* pu⁴ neng² chi⁴ i⁴ te¹ 不能記憶的.

immense *a.* kuang³ ta⁴ te¹ 廣大的.

immensity *n.* kuang³ ta⁴ 廣大, wu² hsien⁴ 無限.

immigrant *n.* i² min² 移民.

immigrate *a.* ch'ien³ i² 遷移.

immigration *n.* i² min² 移民.

imminent *a.* wei² p'o⁴ te¹ 危迫的.

immobility *n.* ku⁴ ting⁴ 固定.

immoderate *a.* wu² chieh² chih⁴ te¹ 無節制的, kuo⁴ tu⁴ te¹ 過度的.

immodest *a.* (*indecent*) fei¹ li³ te¹ 非禮的.

immolate *v.* tsai³ hsien⁴ 宰獻, hsien⁴ chi⁴ 獻祭.

immoral *a.* pu² tao⁴ te² te¹ 不道德的, fang⁴ tang⁴ te¹ 放蕩的.

immortal *a.* yung³ sheng¹ te¹ 永生的.

immortality *n.* yung³ sheng¹ 永生.

immortalize *v.* shih² yung³ sheng¹ 使永生.

immovable *a.* pu⁴ neng² i² tung⁴ te¹ 不能移動的; ～ property, pu² tung⁴ ch'an³ 不動產.

immunity *n.* (*disease*) mien³ i⁴ hsing⁴ 免疫性.

immure *v.* chü³ chin⁴ 拘禁, yu¹ pi⁴ 幽閉.

imp *n.* (*devil*) hsiao² kuei¹ 小鬼, (*child*) wan² t'ung² 頑童.

impair *v.* sun³ shang¹ 損傷.

impale *v.* kuan⁴ ch'uan¹ 貫穿.

impart *v.* (*give*) fen¹ chi³ 分給, (*tell*) kao⁴ chih¹ 告知.

impartial *a.* kung¹ cheng⁴ 公正.

impartiality *n.* kung¹ cheng⁴ 公正的.

impassable *a.* pu⁴ neng² t'ung¹ kuo⁴ te¹ 不能通過.

impassible *a.* wu² kan³ chüeh¹ te¹ 無感覺的, ma² mu⁴ te¹ 麻木的.

impassioned *a.* je⁴ ch'ing² te¹ 熱情的.

impatience *n.* wu² jen⁴ nai⁴ hsing⁴ 無忍耐性.

impatient *a.* pu² nai⁴ fan² te¹ 不耐煩的.

impeach *v.* (*accuse*) k'ung⁴ su⁴ 控訴.

impede *v.* tsu³ ai⁴ 阻礙.

impediment *n.* chang⁴ ai⁴ wu⁴ 障礙物.

impel *v.* t'ui¹ chin⁴ 推進.

impenitent *v.* pu⁴ hui³ wu⁴ te¹ 不悔悟的.

imperative *a.* (*urgent*) p'o⁴ ch'ieh⁴ te¹ 迫切的, (*peremptory*) ming⁴ ling⁴ te¹ 命令的.

imperceptible *a.* pu⁴ neng² pien¹ pieh² te¹ 不能辨別的, (*very slight*) chi² hsi¹ wei¹ te¹ 極細微的.

imperfect *a.* pu⁴ wan² ch'üan² te¹ 不完全的.

imperfection *n.* pu⁴ wan² ch'üan² 不完全, (*defect*) ch'üeh¹ tien³ 缺點.

imperial *a.* ti⁴ kuo² te¹ 帝國的.

imperious *a.* (*haughty*) chü⁴ ao⁴ te¹ 倨傲的, (*urgent*) chin³ chi² te¹ 緊急的.

imperishable *a.* pu⁴ hsiu³ te¹ 不朽的, pu² mieh⁴ te¹ 不滅的.

impermeable *a.* pu⁴ neng² shen⁴ t'ou⁴ te¹ 不能滲透的.

impersonal *a.* pu⁴ chih³ jen² te¹ 不指人的.

impersonate *v.* pan⁴ yen³ 扮演.

impertinence *n.* wu² li³ 無禮.

impertinent *a.* (*saucy*) lu² mang³ te¹ 鹵莽的.

imperturbable *a.* chen⁴ ching⁴ te¹ 鎮靜的.

impetus *n.* tung⁴ li⁴ 動力.

impiety *n.* pu² ching⁴ shen² ming² 不敬神明.

impious *a.* pu² ching⁴ shen² te¹ 不敬神的.

implacable *a.* pu⁴ k'o³ shu⁴ te¹ 不可恕的.

implement *n.* kung¹ chü⁴ 工具, yung⁴ chü⁴ 用具.

implicate v. (*involve*) ch'ien¹ she⁴ 牽涉, (*imply*) an⁴ shih⁴ 暗示.

implicit a. (*absolute*) chüeh² tui⁴ te¹ 絕對的, (*implied*) an⁴ shih⁴ te¹ 暗示的.

implore v. k'en³ ch'iu² 懇求, ch'i² ch'iu² 祈求.

imply v. an⁴ shih⁴ 暗示.

impolite a. wu² li³ te¹ 無禮的.

import v. chin⁴ k'ou³ 進口, shu¹ ju⁴ 輸入; ～ **duty,** chin⁴ k'ou³ shui⁴ 進口稅; ～ **trade,** chin⁴ k'ou³ mao⁴ i⁴ 進口貿易.

importance n. chung⁴ ta⁴ 重大, chin³ yao⁴ 緊要.

important a. chung⁴ ta⁴ te¹ 重大的, chin³ yao⁴ te¹ 緊要的.

importer n. chin⁴ k'ou³ shang¹ 進口商.

impossibility n. pu⁴ k'o³ neng² 不可能.

impossible a. pu⁴ k'o³ neng² te¹ 不可能的.

impost n. kuan¹ shui⁴ 關稅. 「p'ien¹ tzu³ 騙子.

impostor n. chia³ mao⁴ che³ 假冒者, (*deceiver*)

imposture n. ch'i¹ p'ien⁴ 欺騙.

impotence n. shuai¹ jo⁴ 衰弱, wu² li⁴ 無力.

impotent a. shuai¹ jo⁴ te¹ 衰弱的, (*sexual power*) yang² wei¹ te¹ 陽萎的.

impoverish v. shih³ p'in² fa² 使貧乏.

impracticable a. pu⁴ neng² shih² hsing¹ te¹ 不能

imprecate v. tsu³ chou⁴ 詛咒. 「實行的.

impregnable a. nan² kung¹ hsien⁴ te¹ 難攻陷的.

impregnate v. shih³ huai² yün⁴ 使懷孕.

impress v. shih² kan³ tung¹ 使感動.

impression n. yin⁴ hsiang⁴ 印象. 「感人的.

impressive a. tung⁴ jen² te¹ 動人的, kan³ jen² te¹

imprint v. kai⁴ yin⁴ 蓋印; n. (*publisher*) ch'u¹ pan³ chia¹ ming² ch'eng¹ 出版家名稱.

imprison v. hsia⁴ yü⁴ 下獄, chien¹ chin⁴ 監禁.

imprisonment n. chien¹ chin⁴ 監禁.

improbable a. pu⁴ i² ting⁴ te¹ 不一定的, wei⁴ pi⁴ jan² te¹ 未必然的.

improper a. (*not correct*) pu⁴ chun³ ch'üeh⁴ te¹ 不準確的, (*not suitable*) pu² shih⁴ i² te¹ 不適宜的, (*not decent*) pu² cheng⁴ tang¹ te¹ 不正當的.

impropriety n. pu² cheng⁴ tang¹ 不正當.

improve v. kai³ shan⁴ 改善.

improvement *n.* kai³ chin¹ 改進.

improvident *a.* (*lacking foresight*) wu² hsien¹ chien⁴ te¹ 無先見的, (*careless*) pu⁴ liu² i⁴ te¹ 不留意的, (*not thrifty*) lang⁴ fei⁴ te¹ 浪費的.

imprudence *n.* lu² mang³ 鹵莽.

imprudent *a.* lu² mang³ te¹ 鹵莽的.

impudence *n.* hou⁴ yen² 厚顏.

impudent *a.* hou⁴ yen² te¹ 厚顏的.

impulse *n.* ch'ung¹ tung⁴ 衝動.

impulsive *a.* ch'ung¹ tung⁴ te¹ 衝動的.

impunity *n.* mien³ fa² 免罰.

impure *a.* pu⁴ chieh² te¹ 不潔的.

impurity *n.* pu⁴ chieh² 不潔.

impute *v.* kuei¹ wei³ 歸委.

in *prep.* tsai⁴ nei⁴ 在內, tsai⁴ chung¹ 在中; ～ **advance**, yü¹ hsien¹ 預先; ～ **a few words**, chien³ yen² chih¹ 簡言之; ～ **a moment**, li⁴ chi² 立卽; ～ **behalf of**, tai⁴ 代; ～ **case**, chia³ jo⁴ 假若; ～ **charge of**, kuan³ li³ 管理; ～ **conclusion**, chieh² kuo³ 結果; ～ **fact**, shih² tsai⁴ 實在; ～ **favor of**, tsan⁴ ch'eng² 贊成; ～ **general**, ta⁴ kai⁴ 大概; ～ **no respect**, hao² pu⁴ 毫不; ～ **order**, yu³ chih⁴ hsü⁴ te¹ 有秩序的; ～ **place of**, tai⁴ t'i⁴ 代替; ～ **regard to**, kuan¹ yü² 關於; ～ **short**, tsung³ chih¹ 總之; ～ **spite of**, pu² ku⁴ 不顧; ～ **time**, chun³ shih² 準時; ～ **turn**, shun⁴ tz'u⁴ 順次; ～ **vain**, t'u² jan² 徒然; ～ **view of**, chien¹ yü² 鑒於.

inability *n.* wu² ts'ai² 無才, wu² neng² 無能.

inaccessible *a.* nan² chieh¹ chin⁴ te¹ 難接近的.

inaccuracy *n.* ts'o⁴ wu⁴ 錯誤, pu⁴ chun³ ch'üeh⁴ 不準確. 「不確的.

inaccurate *a.* ts'o⁴ wu⁴ te¹ 錯誤的, pu⁴ ch'üeh⁴ te¹

inaction *n.* pu⁴ huo² tung⁴ 不活動, lan³ to⁴ 懶惰.

inactive *a.* pu⁴ huo² tung⁴ te¹ 不活動的, lan³ to⁴ te¹ 懶惰的.

inadequate *a.* (*not enough*) pu⁴ tsu² te¹ 不足的.

inadmissible *a.* pu⁴ jung² hsü³ te¹ 不容許的.

inadvertence *n.* pu² chu⁴ i⁴ 不注意, su¹ hu¹ 疏忽.

inadvertent *a.* pu² chu⁴ i⁴ te¹ 不注意的, su¹ hu¹ te¹ 疏忽的.

inalienable *a.* pu⁴ k'o³ i² jang¹ te¹ 不可移讓的.

inanimate *a.* (*lifeless*) wu² sheng¹ ming¹ te¹ 無生命的, (*dull*) pu⁴ huo² p'o¹ te¹ 不活潑的.

inanity *n.* k'ung¹ hsü¹ 空虛, k'ung¹ t'an² 空談, wu² wei¹ chih¹ hsing² wei² 無謂之行爲.

inapplicable *a.* pu⁴ ho² i² te¹ 不合宜的, pu² shih⁴ yung⁴ te¹ 不適用的.

inappropriate *a.* pu² shih⁴ i² te¹ 不適宜的.

inaptitude *n.* pu² shih⁴ ho² 不適合.

inattention *n.* su¹ hu¹ 疏忽, pu² chu⁴ i⁴ 不注意.

inattentive *a.* su¹ hu¹ te¹ 疏忽的, pu² chu⁴ i⁴ te¹ 不注意的.

inaudible *a.* t'ing¹ pu⁴ ch'ing¹ te¹ 聽不清的.

inaugurate *v.* chiu⁴ chih⁴ li³ 就職禮, (*begin*) k'ai¹ shih³ 開始.

inauguration *n.* chiu⁴ chih⁴ 就職, (*beginning*) 「shih³ 開始.

inauspicious *a.* pu⁴ chi² te¹ 不吉的. 「的.

incalculable *a.* pu⁴ k'o³ sheng¹ chi⁴ te¹ 不可勝計

incandescent *a.* fa¹ pai² je⁴ te¹ 發白熱的, kuang¹ hui¹ te¹ 光輝的.

incapable *a.* wu² neng² te¹ 無能的.

incapacity *n.* wu² neng² 無能, (*disqualification*) wu² tzu¹ ko² 無資格.

incautious *a.* lu² mang³ te¹ 鹵莽的, pu⁴ chin³ shen⁴ te¹ 不謹慎的.

incendiary *n.* (*arsonist*) tsung⁴ huo² che³ 縱火者, (*bomb*) jan² shao¹ tan⁴ 燃燒彈; *a.* (*setting fire*) tsung⁴ fang⁴ te¹ 縱放的, (*causing fires*) jan² shao¹ te¹ 燃燒的. 「香.

incense *n.* hsiang¹ liao⁴ 香料; *v.* fen² hsiang¹ 焚

incentive *a.* chi¹ ang² te¹ 激昂的, ts'u⁴ chi¹ te¹ 刺激的. 「覆的.

incessant *a.* chi⁴ hsü⁴ te¹ 繼續的, fan³ fu⁴ te¹ 反

inch *n.* ts'un⁴ 吋, ying¹ ts'un⁴ 英寸.

incident *n.* i⁴ wai² shih⁴ ku⁴ 意外事故. 「雕刻.

incise *v.* (*cut*) ch'ieh¹ ko¹ 切割, (*carve*) tiao¹ k'o¹

incite *v.* (*urge*) ts'ui¹ ts'u⁴ 催促, (*stir*) chi¹ tung⁴ 激

inclination *n.* ch'ing¹ hsiang⁴ 傾向. 「動.

incline *n.* (*slope*) ch'ing¹ hsieh² 傾斜; *v.* (*be favorable*) ch'ing¹ hsiang⁴ 傾向.

include *v.* pao¹ han² 包含, pao¹ k'uo⁴ 包括.

inclusive *a.* pao¹ han² te¹ 包含的, pao¹ k'uo⁴ te¹ 包括的.

incoherent *a.* pu⁴ lien² kuan⁴ te¹ 不連貫的.

income *n.* shou¹ ju⁴ 收入, chin⁴ i⁴ 進益; ~ **tax,** so³ te² shui⁴ 所得稅.

incomparable *a.* wu² ti² te¹ 無敵的, wu² pi³ te¹ 無比的.

incomplete *a.* pu⁴ wan² ch'üan² te¹ 不完全的, yu³ ch'üeh¹ tien³ te¹ 有缺點的.

incomprehensible *a.* pu⁴ neng² li³ hui⁴ te¹ 不能理會的.

inconceivable *a.* pu⁴ k'o² hsiang³ hsiang⁴ te¹ 不可想像的.

inconclusive *a.* wei⁴ chüeh² ting⁴ te¹ 未決定的.

incongruous *a.* pu⁴ hsiang¹ p'ei⁴ te¹ 不相配的.

inconsequent *a.* wu² lun² tz'u⁴ te¹ 無論次的, chih¹ li² te¹ 支離的.

inconsiderable *a.* pu⁴ tsu² chu⁴ i⁴ te¹ 不足注意的.

inconsiderate *a.* pu⁴ t'i³ liang⁴ te¹ 不體諒的.

inconsistency *n.* mao² tun⁴ 矛盾, pu⁴ i² chih⁴ 不一致. 「te¹ 不一致的.

inconsistent *a.* mao² tun⁴ te¹ 矛盾的, pu⁴ i² chih⁴

inconsolable *a.* wu² k'o³ wei⁴ chieh⁴ te¹ 無可慰籍的. 「heng² hsing⁴ 無恒性.

inconstancy *n.* fan³ fu⁴ wu² ch'ang² 反覆無常, wu²

inconstant *a.* fan³ fu⁴ wu² ch'ang² te¹ 反覆無常的.

incontinent *a.* pu⁴ neng² tzu⁴ chih⁴ te¹ 不能自制的.

incontrovertible *a.* wu² k'o³ cheng¹ pien⁴ te¹ 無可爭辯的. 「可爭辯的.

inconvenience *n.* pu² pien⁴ 不便.

inconvenient *a.* pu² pien⁴ te¹ 不便的.

inconvertible *a.* (*paper currency*) pu⁴ neng² tui⁴ huan⁴ te¹ 不能兌換的.

incorrect *a.* pu² ch'üeh⁴ te¹ 不確的, (*not proper*) pu² shih⁴ tang⁴ te¹ 不適當的. 「的.

incorrigible *a.* pu⁴ neng² kan³ hua⁴ te¹ 不能感化的.

increase *n., v.* tseng¹ chia¹ 增加.

incredibility *n.* pu⁴ k'o³ hsin⁴ 不可信.

incredible *a.* pu⁴ k'o³ hsin⁴ te¹ 不可信的.

incredulity *n.* huai² i² 懷疑.

incredulous *a.* huai² i² te¹ 懷疑的.

incur *v.* tsao¹ feng² 遭逢, chao¹ je⁴ 招惹.

incurable *a.* pu⁴ k'o³ chiu⁴ yao⁴ te¹ 不可救藥的.

incursion *n.* ch'in¹ ju⁴ 侵入, lai² fan⁴ 來犯.

indebted *a.* (*money*) fu⁴ chai⁴ te¹ 負債的, (*gratitude*) kan³ en¹ te¹ 感恩的.

indecent *a.* (*improper*) pu² shih⁴ i² te¹ 不適宜的, (*obscene*) yin² wei³ te¹ 淫猥的.

indeed *adv.* shih² tsai⁴ 實在, ti² ch'üeh⁴ 的確.

indefatigable *a.* pu⁴ p'i² chüan⁴ te¹ 不疲倦的.

indefinite *a.* (*unlimited*) wu² hsien⁴ chih⁴ te¹ 無限制的.

indemnity *n.* p'ei² k'uan³ 賠款.

independence *n.* tu² li⁴ 獨立, tzu⁴ yu² 自由; ～ **Day** (US), tu² li⁴ chi⁴ nien⁴ jih⁴ 獨立記念日(美).

independent *a.* tu² li⁴ te¹ 獨立的, tzu⁴ yu² te¹ 自由的.

indescribable *a.* nan² i³ hsing² jung² te¹ 難以形容的.

indestructible *a.* pu⁴ neng² p'o⁴ huai⁴ te¹ 不能破壞的.

indeterminate *a.* pu⁴ ting⁴ te¹ 不定的, nan² chüeh² te¹ 難決的.

index *n.* so² yin³ 索引, (*finger*) shih² chih³ 食指.

indicate *v.* chih³ shih⁴ 指示.

indication *n.* chih³ shih⁴ 指示.

indicative *a.* chih³ ming² te¹ 指明的.

indict *v.* k'ung⁴ su⁴ 控訴.

indifference *n.* pu⁴ kuan¹ hsin¹ 不關心.

indifferent *a.* pu⁴ kuan¹ hsin¹ te¹ 不關心的.

indigestible *a.* pu⁴ hsiao¹ hua⁴ te¹ 不消化的.

indigestion *n.* hsiao¹ hua⁴ pu⁴ liang² 消化不良.

indignant *a.* fen⁴ k'ai³ te¹ 憤慨的.

indignation *n.* fen⁴ nu⁴ 憤怒.

indignity *n.* wu³ ju⁴ 侮辱. 、   「深藍色.

indigo *n.* tien⁴ ch'ing¹ 靛青, (*color*) shen¹ lan² se⁴

indirect *a.* chien⁴ chieh¹ te¹ 間接的; ～ **fire**, chien⁴ chieh¹ she⁴ chi¹ 間接射擊(軍); ～ **laying**, chien⁴ chieh¹ miao² chun³ 間接瞄準(軍); ～ **observation**, chıen⁴ chieh¹ kuan¹ ts'e⁴ 間接觀測; ～ **tax**, chien⁴ chieh¹ shui⁴ 間接稅.

indiscreet *a.* pu⁴ liu² i⁴ te¹ 不留意的.

indiscretion *n.* pu⁴ shen³ ch'a² 不審察.   「別的.

indiscriminate *a.* pu⁴ k'o³ pien⁴ pieh² te¹ 不可辯

indispensable *a.* pi⁴ yao⁴ te¹ 必要的.

indisposed *a.* (*ill*) hsiao³ ping⁴ te¹ 小病的.

indisposition *n.* (*illness*) hsiao³ ping⁴ 小病.

indisputable *a.* wu² k'o³ cheng¹ pien⁴ te¹ 無可爭辯的.「解的.

indissoluble *a.* pu⁴ neng² jung² chieh³ te¹ 不能溶

indistinct *a.* pu⁴ ch'ing¹ hsi¹ te¹ 不清晰的.

individual *a.* tan¹ tu² te¹ 單獨的, ko⁴ pieh⁴ te¹ 個別的; *n.* ko⁴ jen² 個人.

induce *v.* ch'üan¹ yu⁴ 勸誘 chao¹ chih⁴ 招致.

inducement *n.* yu⁴ huo⁴ 誘惑.「(軍).

induct *v.* (*enroll in military service*) ju⁴ ying² 入營

induction *n.* (*electric*) kan³ ying⁴ tso⁴ yung⁴ 感應作用, (*process of enlistment*) ju⁴ ying² shih¹ 入營

indulgent *a.* fang⁴ tsung⁴ te¹ 放縱的.「式(軍).

industrial *a.* kung¹ yeh⁴ te¹ 工業的.

industrious *a.* ch'in² mien³ te¹ 勤勉的.

industry *n.* kung¹ yeh⁴ 工業, (*diligence*) ch'in² mien³ 勤勉.

ineffectual *a.* wu² hsiao⁴ kuo³ te¹ 無效果的, wu² yung⁴ te¹ 無用的.

inelegant *a.* pu⁴ yu¹ ya³ te¹ 不優雅的.

ineligible *a.* pu⁴ ho² tzu¹ ko² te¹ 不合資格的.

inequality *n.* (*amount*) pu⁴ hsiang¹ teng³ 不相等.

inert *a.* (*lifeness*) wu² sheng¹ ch'i⁴ te¹ 無生氣的, (*slow*) ch'ih² huan³ te¹ 遲緩的.

inestimable *a.* nan² p'ing² chia⁴ te¹ 難評價的.

inevitable *a.* pu⁴ k'o³ pi⁴ mien³ te¹ 不可避免的, pi⁴ jan² te¹ 必然的.

inexact *a.* pu⁴ chun³ ch'üeh⁴ te¹ 不準確的.

inexcusable *a.* pu⁴ neng² yüan² liang⁴ te¹ 不能原諒的.「chin⁴ te¹ 不盡的.

inexhaustible *a.* wu² ch'iung² te¹ 無窮的, pu²

inexorable *a.* ying⁴ hsin¹ ch'ang² te¹ 硬心腸的, shuo¹ pu² tung⁴ te¹ 說不動的.

inexperience *n.* wu- ching¹ yen⁴ 無經驗, shao³ yüeh⁴ li⁴ 少閱歷.

infallibility *n.* wu² wu⁴ 無誤, chun³ ch'üeh⁴ 準確.

infallible *a.* wu² wu⁴ te¹ 無誤的, chun³ ch'üeh⁴ te¹ 準確的.

infamy *n.* e⁴ ming² 惡名, ch'ou³ hsing² 醜行.

infant *n.* ying¹ hai² 嬰孩.

infantry *n.* pu⁴ ping¹ 步兵; ~ **division,** pu⁴ ping¹ shih¹ 步兵師(軍); ~ **gun,** pu⁴ ping¹ p'ao⁴ 步兵砲

(軍); ～ **school,** pu⁴ ping¹ hsüeh² hsiao⁴ 步兵學

infect v. (*disease*) ch'uan² jan³ 傳染.　　　└校(軍).

infection n. ch'uan² jan³ 傳染.

infectious a. ch'uan² jan³ hsing⁴ te¹ 傳染性的.

infer v. ch'uai³ tu⁴ 揣度, t'ui¹ lun⁴ 推論.

inference n. t'ui¹ ts'e⁴ 推測.

inferior a. hsia⁴ chi² te¹ 下級的.

inferiority n. hsia⁴ chi² 下級; ～ **complex,** tzu⁴ pei¹ kan³ 自卑感.

infernal a. ti⁴ yü⁴ te¹ 地獄的.

infest v. (*trouble*) sao¹ jao³ 騷擾.

infidel n. pu² hsin⁴ tsung¹ chiao⁴ che³ 不信宗敎者.

infinite a. wu² hsien⁴ te¹ 無限的.

infinitive n. pu² ting⁴ shih¹ 不定式.

infirm a. (*weak*) hsü¹ jo⁴ te¹ 虛弱的.

infirmary n. ping⁴ yüan⁴ 病院, i¹ yüan⁴ 醫院.

inflammable a. i⁴ jan² te¹ 易燃的, (*easily excited*) i⁴ chi¹ tung⁴ te¹ 易激動的.

inflammation n. (*disease*) fa¹ yen² 發炎(醫).

inflate v. (*tube of tire*) ta³ ch'i⁴ 打氣, (*balloon*) kuan⁴ ch'i⁴ 灌氣.　　　└通貨膨脹.

inflation n. (*currency*) t'ung¹ huo⁴ p'eng² chang⁴

inflexible a. pu⁴ ch'ü¹ te¹ 不屈的.

inflict v. k'o¹ hsing² 科刑, chia¹ fa² 加罰.

infliction n. k'o¹ hsing² 科刑, chia¹ fa² 加罰.

influence n. ying² hsiang³ 影響, shih⁴ li⁴ 勢力; v. kan³ hua⁴ 感化.

influential a. yu³ shih⁴ li⁴ te¹ 有勢力的.

influenza n. liu² hsing² hsing⁴ kan³ mao⁴ 流行性

influx n. liu² ju⁴ 流入.　　　└感冒.

inform v. (*units of same level*) t'ung¹ pao⁴ 通報 (軍), (*units of lower echelon*) t'ung¹ chih¹ 通知(軍), (*units of higher echelon*) pao⁴ kao⁴ 報告(軍).

informal a. fei¹ cheng⁴ shih⁴ te¹ 非正式的.

information n. (*knowledge*) chih¹ shih⁴ 知識, (*news*) hsin¹ wen² 新聞, (*law*) kao⁴ fa¹ 告發, (*by espionage*) tieh² pao⁴ 諜報, ch'ing² pao⁴ 情報.

infringe v. wei² fan⁴ 違犯, (*trespass*) ch'in¹ chan⁴ 侵佔.

infuse v. kuan⁴ shu¹ 灌輸.　　　　└劑.

infusion n. chu⁴ ju⁴ 注入, (*medicine*) chin⁴ chi⁴ 浸

ingenuous *a.* t'ien¹ chen¹ te¹ 天眞的, t'an³ pai² te¹ 坦白的. 「金銀錠.

ingot *n.* chin¹ shu³ k'uai⁴ 金屬塊, chin¹ yin² ting⁴

ingratitude *n.* wang⁴ en¹ fu⁴ i⁴ 忘恩負義.

ingredient *n.* ch'eng² fen⁴ 成分.

ingress *n.* chin⁴ ju⁴ 進入.

inhabit *v.* chü¹ chu⁴ 居住.

inhabitant *n.* chu⁴ min² 住民, chü¹ min² 居民.

inhale *v.* hsi¹ ju⁴ fei⁴ nei⁴ 吸入肺內.

inharmonious *a.* pu² ho² hsieh² te¹ 不和諧的.

inherent *a.* ku⁴ yu³ te¹ 固有的.

inherit *v.* chi⁴ ch'eng² 繼承.

inheritance *n.* chi⁴ ch'eng² 繼承.

inhospitable *a.* pu² hao³ k'o⁴ te¹ 不好客的.

inhuman *a.* wu² jen² tao⁴ te¹ 無人道的, ts'an² jen³ te¹ 殘忍的.

inhumanity *n.* wu² jen² tao⁴ 無人道, ts'an² jen³ 殘

inimical *a.* (*hostile*) ch'ou² shih⁴ te¹ 仇視的, (*harmful*) yu³ hai⁴ te¹ 有害的.

inimitable *a.* pu⁴ k'o³ mo² fang³ te¹ 不可摹倣的.

initial *a.* tsui⁴ ch'u¹ te¹ 最初的; *n.* shou³ tzu⁴ mu³ 首字母; *v.* ch'ien¹ hsing⁴ ming² shou³ tzu⁴ mu³ yü² 簽姓名首字母於.

initiate *v.* ch'uang⁴ shih³ 創始.

initiation *n.* fa¹ ch'i³ 發起.

initiative *n.* (*military*) chu³ tung⁴ 主動(軍).

inject *v.* chu⁴ she⁴ 注射, ta³ chen¹ 打針.

injection *n.* chu⁴ she⁴ 注射, ta³ chen¹ 打針.

injunction *n.* ming⁴ ling⁴ 命令, chin¹ ling⁴ 禁令.

injure *v.* shang¹ hai⁴ 傷害.

injury *n.* shang¹ hai⁴ 傷害.

injustice *n.* pu⁴ kung¹ p'ing² 不公平.

ink *n.* mo⁴ shui³ 墨水.

inkstand *n.* mo⁴ shui³ chia⁴ 墨水架, (*container*) mo⁴ shui³ p'ing² 墨水瓶.

inland *a.* nei⁴ ti⁴ te¹ 內地的; *n.* nei⁴ ti⁴ 內地.

inlet *n.* hai² k'ou³ 海口, (*entrance*) chin⁴ k'ou³ 進口.

inn *n.* k'o⁴ chan⁴ 客棧, hsiao³ lü² kuan³ 小旅館.

innate *a.* t'ien¹ fu⁴ te¹ 天賦的.

inner *a.* nei⁴ pu⁴ te¹ 內部的.

131

innkeeper *n.* lü² kuan² chu³ jen² 旅館主人.

innocence *n.* wu² ku¹ 無辜, wu² tsui¹ 無罪.

innocent *a.* wu² ku¹ te¹ 無辜的, wu² tsui¹ te¹ 無罪

innocuous *a.* wu² hai⁴ te¹ 無害的. 　　 　[的.

innovation *n.* ko² hsin¹ 革新.

innumerable *a.* wu² shu⁴ te¹ 無數的.

inoculate *v.* chu⁴ she⁴ 注射, chieh¹ chung⁴ 接種.

inoculation *n.* chu⁴ she⁴ 注射, chieh¹ chung⁴ 接種.

inopportune *a.* pu⁴ ho² shih² i² te¹ 不合時宜的.

inordinate *a.* wu² chieh² chih⁴ te¹ 無節制的, kuo⁴

inquest *n.* shen³ hsun⁴ 審訊. 　　 　[tu⁴ te¹ 過度的.

inquire *v.* hsün² wen⁴ 詢問, p'an² chieh¹ 盤詰.

inquiry *n.* hsün² wen⁴ 詢問, chih⁴ wen⁴ 質問.

inquisitive *a.* hao⁴ wen⁴ te¹ 好問的, (*curious*) hao⁴
ch'i² te¹ 好奇的.

inroad *n.* ju⁴ k'ou⁴ 入寇, ch'in¹ lüeh⁴ 侵掠.

insane *a.* ching¹ shen² ts'o⁴ luan⁴ te¹ 精神錯亂的;
∼ **asylum,** ching¹ shen² ping⁴ yuan⁴ 精神病院
(醫). 　　 　　 　[精神病.

insanity *n.* tien¹ k'uang² 癲狂, ching¹ shen² ping⁴

inscribe *v.* (*write*) shu¹ hsieh³ 書寫, (*engrave*) tiao¹

inscription *n.* k'o¹ tzu⁴ 刻字. 　　 　[k'o¹ 雕刻.

insect *n.* k'un¹ ch'ung² 昆蟲.

insecure *a.* pu⁴ an¹ ch'üan² te¹ 不安全的.

insecurity *n.* pu⁴ an¹ ch'üan² 不安全.

insensible *a.* wu² chih¹ chüeh² te¹ 無知覺的.

insert *v.* ch'a¹ ju⁴ 插入, ch'ien¹ ju⁴ 嵌入, t'ien² ju⁴

insertion *n.* ch'a¹ ju⁴ wu⁴ 插入物. 　　 　[填入.

inside *a.* nei⁴ pu⁴ te¹ 內部的; *adv.* tsai⁴ nei⁴ mien⁴
在內面; *n.* nei⁴ pu⁴ 內部; ∼ **information,** nei⁴
mu⁴ hsin¹ wen² 內幕新聞.

insight *n.* tung⁴ ch'a² 洞察.

insignia *n.* hui¹ chang¹ 徽章.

insignificance *n.* pu² chung⁴ yao⁴ 不重要, (*mean-
inglessness*) wu² i⁴ i⁴ 無意義.

insignificant *a.* pu² chung⁴ yao⁴ te¹ 不重要的,
(*meaningless*) wu² i⁴ te¹ 無意義的.

insincere *a.* hsü¹ wei⁴ te¹ 虛偽的, pu⁴ t'an³ pai³

insist *v.* chien¹ ch'ih² 堅持. 　　 　[te¹ 不坦白的.

insolent *a.* (*insulting*) wu³ ju⁴ te¹ 侮辱的, (*boldly
rude*) chiao¹ heng² te¹ 驕橫的.

132

insoluble *a.* (*not dissolve*) nan² jung² chieh³ te¹ 難溶解的, (*problem*) nan² chieh³ chüeh² te¹ 難解決的.

inspect *v.* (*barracks*) chien³ ch'a² 檢查, (*troops*) hsiao⁴ yüeh⁴ 校閱(軍), (*in an official tour*) shih⁴ ch'a² 視察.

inspection *n.* (*troops*) hsiao⁴ yüeh⁴ 校閱(軍).

inspector *n.* (*troops*) hsiao⁴ yüeh⁴ kuan¹ 校閱官, shih⁴ ch'a² kuan¹ 視察官.

inspiration *n.* kan³ tung⁴ 感動.

inspire *v.* kan³ tung⁴ 感動, ku³ wu³ 鼓舞.

install *v.* (*for use*) she⁴ chih⁴ 設置.

installment, instalment *n.* (*debt*) fen¹ ch'i¹ fu⁴ k'uan³ 分期付款.

instance *n.* li⁴ cheng⁴ 例證; *v.* chü³ li⁴ 舉例.

instant *a.* (*immediate*) chi² k'o⁴ te¹ 即刻的, (*urgent*) chin³ chi² te¹ 緊急的, (*present*) hsien⁴ tsai⁴ te¹ 現在的; *n.* ch'ing³ k'o⁴ 頃刻.

instantly *adv.* li⁴ k'o⁴ 立刻.

instead *prep.* tai⁴ t'i⁴ 代替.

instep *n.* tsu² pei¹ 足背.

instigate *v.* shan¹ tung⁴ 煽動.

instigation *n.* shan¹ tung⁴ 煽動.　「te¹ 本能的.

instinctive *a.* t'ien¹ hsing⁴ te¹ 天性的, pen³ neng²

institute *v.* chien⁴ li⁴ 建立.

institution *n.* (*organization*) she⁴ t'uan² 社團.

instruct *v.* (*teach*) chiao⁴ shou⁴ 教授, (*order*) hsün⁴ ling⁴ 訓令.　　　　　「hsün⁴ ling⁴ 訓令.

instruction *n.* (*teaching*) chiao⁴ shou⁴ 教授, (*order*)

instructive *a.* yu³ i⁴ te¹ 有益的.

instructor *n.* chiao⁴ kuan¹ 教官.

instrument *n.* (*tool*) ch'i⁴ chü⁴ 器具, (*document*) wen² chien⁴ 文件; ~ **of credit**, hsin⁴ yung⁴ cheng⁴ ch'üan⁴ 信用證券.

insufficient *a.* pu⁴ tsu² te¹ 不足的.

insular *a.* hai² tao³ te¹ 海島的, (*narrow-minded*) pien³ hsia² te¹ 褊狹的.

insulate *v.* ko² li² 隔離.

insult *n.* wu³ ju⁴ 侮辱; *v.* wu³ ju⁴ 侮辱.　「過的.

insuperable *a.* pu⁴ neng² sheng⁴ kuo⁴ te¹ 不能勝

insupportable *a.* nan² k'an¹ te¹ 難堪的.

insurance *n.* pao² hsien³ 保險; ～ **company,** pao² hsien³ kung¹ ssu¹ 保險公司; ～ **policy,** pao² hsien³ tan¹ 保險單.

insure *v.* pao² hsien³ 保險.

insurgent *a., n.* p'an⁴ luan⁴ te¹ 叛亂的.

insurrection *n.* fan³ p'an⁴ 反叛, p'an⁴ luan⁴ 叛亂.

intact *a.* wei⁴ ch'u⁴ tung⁴ te¹ 未觸動的.

integrity *n.* (*completeness*) wan² cheng³ 完整.

intellect *n.* chih⁴ li⁴ 智力, (*person*) chih⁴ shih⁴ chieh¹ chi² 智識階級.

intellectual *a.* chih⁴ li⁴ te¹ 智力的; ～ **class,** chih⁴ shih⁴ chieh¹ chi² 智識階級.

intelligence *n.* chih⁴ hui⁴ 智慧, (*military*) ch'ing² pao⁴ 情報; ～ **school,** ch'ing² pao⁴ hsüeh² hsiao⁴ 情報學校; ～ **test,** chih⁴ li⁴ ts'e⁴ yen⁴ 智力測驗.

intelligent *a.* ts'ung¹ ming² te¹ 聰明的.

intend *v.* ch'i⁴ t'u² 企圖.

intense *a.* ch'iang² lieh⁴ te¹ 强烈的.

intensity *n.* ch'iang² tu⁴ 强度.

intent *a.* chu⁴ i⁴ te¹ 注意的, chuan¹ hsin¹ te¹ 專心的; n. i⁴ hsiang⁴ 意向.

intention *n.* ch'i⁴ t'u² 企圖, i⁴ t'u² 意圖.

intentional *a.* ts'un² hsin¹ te¹ 存心的, ku⁴ i⁴ te¹ 故意的.

intercept *v.* (*tactical*) chieh² chi² 截擊, (*electronics*) ch'ieh⁴ t'ing¹ 竊聽.

intercession *n.* t'iao² chieh³ 調解.

interchange *v.* chiao¹ huan⁴ 交換, keng¹ tieh⁴ 更迭.

interchangeable *a.* k'o³ chiao¹ huan⁴ te¹ 可交換的, k'o³ keng¹ tieh⁴ te¹ 可更迭的.

intercourse *n.* chiao¹ t'ung¹ 交通, (*sexual connection*) hsing⁴ chiao¹ 性交.

interdict *v.* tsu² chih³ 阻止.

interest *n.* ch'ü⁴ wei⁴ 趣味, (*money*) li⁴ hsi² 利息.

interested *a.* yu³ hsing⁴ wei⁴ te¹ 有興味的.

interesting *a.* yu³ ch'ü⁴ te¹ 有趣的.

interfere *v.* (*clash*) ch'ung¹ t'u² 衝突, (*meddle*) kan¹ she⁴ 干涉.

interference *n.* (*signal*) jao³ luan⁴ 擾亂.

interim *n.* (*meantime*) t'ung² shih² 同時.

interior *a.* nei⁴ pu⁴ te¹ 內部的; n. nei⁴ pu⁴ 內部; ～ **lines,** nei⁴ hsien⁴ 內線(軍).

interlude *n.* ch'a¹ ch'ü¹ 插曲.

interment *n.* mai² tsang⁴ 埋葬.

interminable *a.* wu² chin¹ te¹ 無盡的.　　「歇.

intermission *n.* t'ing² tun⁴ 停頓, chien⁴ hsieh¹ 間

intermittent *a.* tuan⁴ hsü⁴ te¹ 斷續的, chien⁴ hsieh⁴ te¹ 間歇的.

intermix *v.* hun⁴ ho² 混合.

internal *a.* nei⁴ pu⁴ te¹ 內部的.

international *a.* kuo² chi⁴ te¹ 國際的; ～ **conference,** kuo² chi⁴ hui⁴ i⁴ 國際會議; ～ **law,** kuo² chi⁴ fa³ 國際法; ～ **Red Cross Committee,** kuo² chi⁴ hung² shih² tzu⁴ hui⁴ 國際紅十字會.

interpolate *v.* ts'uan⁴ kai¹ 竄改.

interpose *v.* (*insert*) ch'a¹ ju⁴ 插入.

interpret *v.* chieh³ shih⁴ 解釋, chieh³ i⁴ 解譯.

interpretation *n.* (*analysis*) chieh³ shih⁴ 解釋, (*translation*) fan¹ i⁴ 繙譯.

interpreter *n.* (*translator*) i⁴ yüan² 譯員.

interrogate *v.* shen³ wen⁴ 審問.

interrogation *n.* shen³ wen⁴ 審問.

interrupt *v.* tsu³ tuan⁴ 阻斷.

interruption *n.* tsu³ tuan⁴ 阻斷.

intersect *v.* chiao¹ ch'ieh¹ 交切, heng² tuan⁴ 橫斷.

intervene *v.* (*settle*) kan¹ she⁴ 干涉, t'iao² t'ing² 調停.

interview *n.* hui⁴ t'an² 會談.　　　　　　　「停.

intestine *n.* ch'ang² 腸.

intimate *a.* ch'in¹ mi⁴ te¹ 親密的; *v.* (*hint*) an⁴ shih⁴ 暗示.

intimation *n.* (*hint*) an⁴ shih⁴ 暗示.

intimidate *v.* wei¹ ho⁴ 威嚇, hsieh² p'o⁴ 脅迫.

intimidation *n.* wei¹ ho⁴ 威嚇, hsieh² p'o⁴ 脅迫.

into *prep.* chin⁴ ju⁴ 進入.　　「nan² k'an¹ te¹ 難堪的.

intolerable *a.* pu⁴ neng² jung² jen³ te¹ 不能容忍的,

intolerant *a.* pu⁴ neng² jung² jen³ te¹ 不能容忍的.

intoxicate *v.* shih³ tsui⁴ 使醉.

intoxication *n.* (*drunkenness*) ch'en² tsui⁴ 沈醉, (*poisoning*) chung⁴ tu² 中毒.

intravenous *a.* ching⁴ mo⁴ nei⁴ te¹ 靜脈內的; ～ **injection,** ching⁴ mo⁴ chu⁴ she⁴ 靜脈注射(醫).

intrepid *a.* yung² kan³ te¹ 勇敢的, wu² wei¹ te¹ 無畏的.

intricacy *n.* ts'o⁴ tsung⁴ 錯綜.　　　　「畏的.

introduce v. chieh⁴ shao⁴ 介紹, (*bring in*) yin³ chin⁴ 引進. 「lun⁴ 緒論.

introduction n. chieh⁴ shao⁴ 介紹, (*in book*) hsü⁴

introductory a. chieh⁴ shao⁴ te¹ 介紹的.

intrude v. ch'iang² ju⁴ 強入, shan⁴ ju⁴ 擅入.

intuition n. chih² chüeh² 直覺, liang² chih¹ 良知.

intuitive a. chih² chüeh² te¹ 直覺的, liang² chih¹ te¹ 良知的.

invade v. ch'in¹ chan⁴ 侵佔, ch'in¹ fan⁴ 侵犯.

invader n. ch'in¹ lüeh⁴ che³ 侵略者.

invalid a. (*not valid*) wu² hsiao⁴ te¹ 無效的.

invalidate v. shih³ wu² hsiao⁴ 使無效.

invaluable a. wu² chia⁴ te¹ 無價的.

invariable a. pu² pien⁴ te¹ 不變的.

invasion n. ch'in¹ ju⁴ 侵入, ch'in¹ hsi² 侵襲, ch'in¹ 「lüeh⁴ 侵略.

invent v. fa¹ ming² 發明.

invention n. fa¹ ming² 發明.

inventive a. fa¹ ming² te¹ 發明的.

inventor n. fa¹ ming² chia¹ 發明家.

inventory n. huo⁴ wu⁴ ch'ing¹ tan¹ 貨物清單, chin⁴ huo⁴ 進貨.

inverse a. tien¹ tao³ te¹ 顛倒的.

invert v. tien¹ tao³ 顛倒.

invest v. (*capital*) t'ou² tzu¹ 投資.

investigate v. yen² chiu⁴ 研究, tiao⁴ ch'a² 調查.

investigation n. yen² chiu⁴ 研究, tiao⁴ ch'a² 調查.

investiture n. shou⁴ chih² 授職.

investment n. (*capital*) t'ou² tzu¹ 投資.

inveterate a. hsi² jan² i³ shen¹ te¹ 習染已深的.

invincible a. pu⁴ neng² k'o⁴ fu² te¹ 不能克服的.

inviolable a. pu⁴ k'o³ ch'in¹ fan⁴ te¹ 不可侵犯的.

inviolate a. pu⁴ k'o³ ch'in¹ fan⁴ te¹ 不可侵犯的.

invisible a. pu⁴ neng² chien⁴ te¹ 不能見的.

invitation n. yao¹ ch'ing³ 邀請.

invite v. yao¹ ch'ing³ 邀請.

invoice n. fa¹ p'iao⁴ 發票, huo⁴ tan¹ 貨單.

involuntary a. fei¹ pen³ i⁴ te¹ 非本意的; ～ **man-slaughter**, wu² i⁴ sha¹ jen² tsui⁴ 無意殺人罪.

involve v. pao¹ k'uo⁴ 包括, ch'ien¹ lien² 牽連.

invulnerable a. pu⁴ neng² sun³ hai⁴ te¹ 不能損害的.

136

inward *a.* hsiang⁴ nei⁴ te¹ 向內的; *adv.* hsiang⁴ nei⁴ 向內.

iodine, iodin *n.* tien³ hua⁴ wu⁴ 碘化物.

iris *n.* (*plant*) ch'ang¹ p'u² 菖蒲(植), (*eye*) hung² mo⁴ 虹膜, yin² lien² 銀鹽.

irksome *a.* ling² jen² p'i² fa² te¹ 令人疲乏的.

iron *a.* t'ieh³ chih⁴ te¹ 鐵製的; *n.* t'ieh³ 鐵; *v.* (*press*) yun⁴ p'ing² 熨平.

irony *n.* chi¹ tz'u⁴ 譏刺.

irradiate *v.* kuang¹ chao⁴ 光照.

irrational *a.* wu² li³ hsing⁴ te¹ 無理性的, pei⁴ li⁴ te¹ 悖理的.

irredeemable *a.* pu⁴ k'o² chiao³ cheng⁴ te¹ 不可矯正的, chüeh² wang⁴ te¹ 絕望的.

irregular *a.* pu⁴ kuei¹ tse² te¹ 不規則的.

irregularity *n.* pu⁴ kuei¹ tse² 不規則, pien⁴ t'ai⁴ 變態.

irrelevant *a.* pu² shih⁴ ch'ieh⁴ te¹ 不適切的, pu⁴ hsiang¹ kan¹ te¹ 不相干的.

irreligious *a.* fan³ tsung¹ chiao⁴ te¹ 反宗敎的.

irremediable *a.* wu² k'o³ chiu⁴ yao⁴ te¹ 無可救藥的.

irreparable *a.* pu⁴ neng² pu³ chiu⁴ te¹ 不能補救的.

irresistible *a.* pu⁴ k'o² ti³ k'ang⁴ te¹ 不可抵抗的.

irresolute *a.* ch'ou² ch'u² pu⁴ chüeh² te¹ 躊躇不決的.

irrespective *a.* pu² ku⁴ te¹ 不顧的, pu⁴ chü¹ te¹ 不拘的.

irresponsible *a.* pu² fu⁴ tse² te¹ 不負責的.

irreverent *a.* pu⁴ tsun¹ chung⁴ te¹ 不尊重的.

irrevocable *a.* pu⁴ neng² keng¹ kai³ te¹ 不能更改的.

irrigate *v.* kuan⁴ kai⁴ 灌漑.　　　　　　　し的.

irritability *n.* i⁴ chi¹ nu⁴ 易激怒.

irritable *a.* i⁴ chi¹ nu⁴ te¹ 易激怒的.

irritate *v.* chi¹ nu⁴ 激怒.

irritation *n.* chi¹ nu⁴ 激怒.

irruption *n.* ch'in¹ ju⁴ 侵入, ch'ung⁴ ju⁴ 衝入.

isinglass *n.* yü² chiao¹ 魚膠, (*mica*) yün² mu³ 雲母.

island *n.* tao³ 島.

islander *n.* tao³ min² 島民.

isle *n.* hsiao³ tao³ 小島.

137

-ism *n.* (*suffix*) chu³ i⁴ 主義(接尾語).

isolate *v.* ko² li² 隔離, shih³ ku¹ li⁴ 使孤立.

issue *n.* fa¹ hsing² 發行; *v.* (*send out*) fa¹ ch'u¹ 發出, (*come out*) liu² ch'u¹ 流出, (*supplies*) fa¹ chi³ 發給, (*orders*) hsia⁴ ta² 下達.

-ist *n.* (*suffix*) che³ 者(接尾語).

isthmus *n.* ti⁴ hsia⁴ 地峽.

it *pron.* t'a¹ 它, t'a¹ 牠.

italics *n.* hsieh² t'i³ tzu⁴ 斜體字.

itch *n.* hsien³ 癬; *v.* fa¹ yang³ 發癢.

item *n.* t'iao² hsiang⁴ 條項, hsiang¹ mu⁴ 項目.

iterate *v.* ch'ung² fu⁴ 重複.

itinerant *v.* yu² li⁴ te¹ 遊歷的.

its *pron.* t'a¹ te¹ 它的, t'a¹ te¹ 牠的.

itself *pron.* t'a¹ tzu⁴ chi³ 它自己.

ivory *n.* hsiang⁴ ya² 象牙.

ivy *n.* ch'ang² ch'un¹ t'eng² 常春藤(植).

J

jab *v.* lu⁴ tz'u⁴ 戮刺.

jack *n.* (*man*) jen² 人, (*sailor*) shui² shou³ 水手, (*tool*) ch'i³ chung⁴ chi¹ 起重機.

jackdaw *n.* hsüeh⁴ wu¹ 穴烏(鳥).

jacket *n.* tuan³ wai⁴ i¹ 短外衣, (*covering*) t'ao⁴ 套.

jade *n.* yü⁴ 玉.

jagged *a.* chü⁴ ch'ih³ hsing² te¹ 鋸齒形的.

jail *n.* chien¹ yü⁴ 監獄.

jailer, jailor *n.* yü⁴ li⁴ 獄吏.

jam *n.* (*passage*) yung¹ chi³ 擁擠, (*fruit*) kuo³ chiang⁴ 果醬, (*firearms*) ku⁴ chang⁴ 故障; *v.* (*passage*) yung¹ chi³ 擁擠, (*radio*) kan¹ jao³ 干擾, (*firearms*) fa¹ sheng¹ ku⁴ chang⁴ 發生故障.

janitor *n.* kuan³ men² che³ 管門者.

January *n.* i² yüeh⁴ 一月.

jar *n.* p'ing² 瓶.

jasmine, jasmin *n.* mo⁴ li⁴ 茉莉(植); ～ **tea,** mo⁴ li⁴ hsiang¹ ch'a² 茉莉香茶, hsiang¹ p'ien⁴ 香片.

jaundice *n.* (*disease*) huang² tan⁴ ping⁴ 黃疸病.

138

jaw n. han³ 頷.

jay n. (bird) hsi³ ch'iao¹ 喜鵲.

jazz n. chüeh² shih⁴ yin¹ yüeh⁴ 爵士音樂.

jealous a. chi⁴ tu⁴ te¹ 媢妒的.

jealousy n. tu⁴ chi⁴ 妒忌.

jeer v. ch'ao² nung⁴ 嘲弄, chi¹ hsiao⁴ 譏笑.

jelly n. kuo³ tzu¹ tung⁴ 果子凍.

jeopardy n. mao⁴ hsien³ 冒險.

jerk v. (pull) chi² la¹ 急拉; ～ **the trigger,** meng³ k'ou⁴ pan³ chi¹ 猛扣板機; v. ch'ao² nung⁴ 嘲弄.

jest n. hsiao⁴ ping¹ 笑柄; v. ch'ao² nung⁴ 嘲弄.

jester n. hsi¹ nüeh⁴ che³ 戲謔者.

Jesus n. chiu⁴ chu³ 救主, yeh¹ su¹ 耶穌.

jet n. (spout) she⁴ k'ou³ 射口; v. p'en¹ she⁴ 噴射, she⁴ ch'u¹ 射出; ～ **bomber,** p'en¹ she⁴ shih⁴ hung¹ cha⁴ chi¹ 噴射式轟炸機; ～ **fighter,** p'en¹ she⁴ chan⁴ tou⁴ chi¹ 噴射式戰鬥機; ～ **plane,** p'en¹ she⁴ chi¹ 噴射機; ～ **propulsion,** p'en¹ she⁴ t'ui¹ chin⁴ 噴射推進.

jetty n. (breakwater) fang² lang⁴ ti¹ 防浪堤, (pier) ma³ t'ou² 碼頭.

jewel n. pao³ shih² 寶石, chu¹ pao³ 珠寶.

jeweler n. chu¹ pao³ shang¹ 珠寶商.

jewelry n. chu¹ pao³ yeh⁴ 珠寶業.

jingle v. tso⁴ ting¹ tang¹ hsiang³ 作叮噹響.

jinrikisha, jinricksha n. jen² li⁴ ch'e¹ 人力車.

job n. (piece of work) pao¹ kung¹ 包工, (employment) chih² yeh⁴ 職業.

jockey n. ch'i² shih¹ 騎師.

jocose a. hui¹ hsieh² te¹ 詼諧的.

jocular a. hua² chi¹ te¹ 滑稽的.

join v. (connect) lien² chieh¹ 連接, (assemble) chieh² ho² 結合, (take part) ts'an¹ chia¹ 參加, (to report to a unit) pao⁴ tao⁴ 報到.

joint n. (inanimate) chieh¹ t'ou² 接頭, kuan¹ chieh¹ 關接; a. kung⁴ t'ung² te¹ 共同的; ～ **operations,** lien² ho² tso⁴ chan⁴ 聯合作戰.

joke n. hsiao⁴ hua⁴ 笑話; v. ch'ao² hsiao⁴ 嘲笑.

jolly a. yü² k'uai⁴ te¹ 愉快的.

jolt v. chen⁴ tung⁴ 震動, tien¹ po³ 顛簸.

journal n. (diary) jih⁴ chi⁴ 日記, (newspaper) jih⁴

pao⁴ 日報, (*magazine*) tsa² chih⁴ 雜誌.

journalism *n.* hsin¹ wen² shih⁴ yeh⁴ 新聞事業.

journalist *n.* hsin¹ wen² chi⁴ che³ 新聞記者.

journey *n.* (*trip*) lü³ hsing² 旅行, (*distance*) lü³ ch'eng² 旅程; *v.* lü³ hsing² 旅行.

journeyman *n.* chih² kung¹ 職工, ku⁴ kung¹ 傭工.

joy *n.* huan¹ le⁴ 歡樂.

joyful *a.* huan¹ le⁴ te¹ 歡樂的.

joyless *a.* yu¹ ch'ou² te¹ 憂愁的.

jubilant *a.* huan¹ le⁴ te¹ 歡樂的.

jubilation *n.* huan¹ le⁴ 歡樂.

judge *n.* (*law court*) fa³ kuan¹ 法官, (*game*) ts'ai² p'an⁴ yüan² 裁判員; *v.* ts'ai² p'an⁴ 裁判; **~ advocate,** chun¹ fa³ kuan¹ 軍法官.

judgment *n.* ts'ai² p'an⁴ 裁判, p'an⁴ tuan⁴ 判斷.

judicial *a.* ssu¹ fa³ te¹ 司法的; **~ Yuan*,** ssu¹ fa³ yüan² 司法院*.

judicious *a.* ming² tuan⁴ te¹ 明斷的.

jug *n.* p'ing² 瓶, hu² 壺.

juggle *v.* pien⁴ hsi⁴ fa³ 變戲法.

juggler *n.* pien⁴ hsi⁴ fa² che³ 變戲法者.

juice *n.* chih¹ 汁, yeh⁴ 液.

juicy *a.* to¹ chih¹ te¹ 多汁的.

July *n.* ch'i² yüeh⁴ 七月.

jumble *n.* hun⁴ ho² wu⁴ 混合物; *v.* hun⁴ ho² 混合.

jump *v.* t'iao⁴ yüeh⁴ 跳躍.

junction *n.* (*joining*) lien² chieh¹ 連接, (*railroad*) chiao¹ ch'a¹ tien³ 交叉點.

June *n.* liu⁴ yüeh⁴ 六月.　　　　　　「chan⁴ 森林戰.

jungle *n.* sen¹ lin² 森林; **~ warfare,** sen¹ lin²

junior *n.* shao⁴ nien² 少年; *a.* nien² yu⁴ te¹ 年幼的, (*of low position*) tzu¹ ch'ien³ te¹ 資淺的; **~ officer,** (*company officer*) wei⁴ kuan¹ 尉官.

juniper *n.* kuei⁴ shu³ kuan⁴ mu⁴ 檜屬灌木.

junk *n.* (*ship*) fan¹ ch'uan² 帆船.

Jupiter *n.* (*planet*) mu⁴ hsing¹ 木星.　　　「法律上的.

juridical *a.* ssu¹ fa³ te¹ 司法的, fa³ lü⁴ shang⁴ te¹

jurisdiction *n.* (*law*) ssu¹ fa³ 司法, ssu¹ fa³ ch'üan² 司法權, (*control*) kuan³ hsia² ch'ü¹ yü⁴ 管轄區域.

jurisprudence *n.* fa³ hsüeh² 法學.

juror *n.* p'ei² shan³ yüan² 陪審員.

jury *n.* p'ei² shen³ t'uan² 陪審團.

just *a.* kung¹ p'ing² te¹ 公平的.

justice *n.* (*just conduct*) kung¹ p'ing² shen³ p'an⁴ 公平審判, (*judge*) fa³ kuan¹ 法官.

justifiable *a.* k'o³ pien⁴ hu⁴ te¹ 可辯護的.

justification *n.* cheng⁴ ming² cheng⁴ tang¹ 證明正常.

justify *v.* cheng⁴ ming² cheng⁴ tang¹ 證明正常, pien⁴ hu⁴ 辯護.

jut *v.* t'u² ch'u¹ 突出.

juvenile *a.* shao⁴ nien² te¹ 少年的; *n.* shao⁴ nien² jen² 少年人.

K

kale *n.* chüan³ yeh⁴ ts'ai¹ 捲葉菜, kan¹ lan² 甘藍.

kangaroo *n.* tai⁴ shu³ 袋鼠.

keel *n.* lung² ku³ 龍骨.

keen *a.* chien¹ jui⁴ te¹ 尖銳的, min³ jui⁴ 敏銳.

keenness *n.* min³ jui⁴ 敏銳.

keep *v.* (*promise*) pao² shou³ 保守, (*observe*) tsun¹ shou³ 遵守, (*guard*) pao³ wei⁴ 保衛, (*raise*) ssu⁴ yang³ 飼養, (*retain*) pao³ ch'ih² 保持, (*employ*) ku⁴ yung⁴ 雇用, (*refrain*) i⁴ chih¹ 抑制, (*maintain*) wei² ch'ih² 維持, (*preserve*) ts'ang² chih⁴ 藏置, (*stay*) liu² chu⁴ 留住; ~ **accounts**, chi⁴ chang⁴ 記帳; ~ **away**, pi⁴ k'ai¹ 避開; ~ **back**, (*prevent*) fang² chih³ 防止; ~ **down**, i⁴ chih⁴ 抑制; ~ **from**, chin⁴ chieh⁴ 禁戒; ~ **off**, li² k'ai¹ 離開; ~ **on**, chi⁴ hsü⁴ 繼續; ~ **out**, chü⁴ ju⁴ 拒入; ~ **promise**, tsun¹ shou³ no⁴ yen² 遵守諾言; ~ **secret**, pao² shou³ pi⁴ mi⁴ 保守祕密; ~ **silence**, an¹ ching⁴ 安靜; ~ **time**, shou³ shih² 守時; ~ **under**, (*control*) k'ung⁴ chih⁴ 控制; ~ **up**, (*maintain*) wei² ch'ih² 維持.

keeper *n.* k'an¹ shou³ che³ 看守者.

keepsake *n.* chi⁴ nien⁴ p'in³ 紀念品.

kennel *n.* kou³ k'o¹ 狗窩.

kernel *n.* (*nut*) ho² jen² 核仁.

kerosene *n.* mei² yu² 煤油, yang² yu² 洋油.

kettle *n.* kuo¹ 鍋, hu² 壺.

key *n.* yao⁴ shih² 鑰匙, (*telegraphic*) tien⁴ chien⁴ 電鍵, (*cipher*) tien⁴ ma² piao³ 電碼表; ~ **point,**

keyboard *n.* chien⁴ p'an² 鍵盤. 「chü tien³ 據點.

keyhole *n.* yao⁴ k'ung³ 鑰孔.

keystone *n.* kung³ hsin¹ shih² 拱心石.

khaki *a.* ts'ao³ huang² se⁴ te¹ 草黄色的; *n.* (*uniform*) ts'ao³ huang² se⁴ chih⁴ fu² 草黄色制服.

kick *n.*, *v.* t'i¹ 踢, ts'u⁴ 蹴.

kid *n.* (*goat*) hsiao³ shan¹ yang² 小山羊, (*child*) hai² tzu¹ 孩子.

kidnap *v.* kuai³ yu⁴ 拐誘, pang³ p'iao⁴ 綁票.

kidney *n.* shen⁴ 腎. 「遭

kill *v.* sha¹ ssu³ 殺死; ~ **time,** hsiao¹ ch'ien³ 消

kiln *n.* lu² 爐, tsao² 竈, yao² 窯; ~ **yard,** yao³

kilocycle *n.* ch'ien¹ chou¹ 千週. 「ch'ang³ 窯場

kilowatt *n.* ch'ien¹ wa³ t'e⁴ 千瓦特.

kin *n.* ch'in¹ shu³ 親屬. 「切的

kind *a.* jen² tz'u² te¹ 仁慈的, ch'in¹ ch'ieh⁴ te¹ 親

kindergarten *n.* yu⁴ chih⁴ yüan² 幼稚園.

kindle *v.* (*burn*) jan² shao¹ 燃燒.

kindness *n.* jen² tz'u² 仁慈.

kindred *n.* ch'in¹ shu³ 親屬; *a.* ch'in¹ shu³ kuan¹ hsi⁴ te¹ 親屬關係的.

king *n.* kuo² wang² 國王.

kingdom *n.* wang² kuo² 王國.

kingfisher *n.* ts'ui⁴ niao³ 翠鳥.

kingly *a.* kuo² wang² te¹ 國王的.

kinsman *n.* nan² ch'in¹ ch'i¹ 男親戚.

kiss *n.* chieh¹ wen³ 接吻; *v.* chieh¹ wen³ 接吻.

kit *n.* chuang¹ chü⁴ 裝具.

kichen *n.* ch'u² fang² 廚房.

kite *n.* feng¹ cheng¹ 風箏, chih³ yüan¹ 紙鳶; ~ **balloon,** yüan¹ shih⁴ ch'i⁴ ch'iu² 鳶式氣球.

kitten *n.* hsiao³ mao¹ 小貓.

knack *n.* shou² lien⁴ 熟練.

knapsack *n.* pei⁴ nang² 背囊. 「摩

knead *v.* jou² k'ung⁴ 揉控, (*massage*) an⁴ mo² 按

knee *n.* hsi¹ 膝.

kneel *v.* ch'ü¹ hsi¹ 屈膝, hsia⁴ kuei⁴ 下跪.

knell *n.* chung¹ sheng¹ 鐘聲, sang¹ chung¹ 喪鐘; *v.* ming² chung¹ 鳴鐘.

knife *n.* hsiao³ tao¹ 小刀.

knight *n.* ch'i² shih⁴ 騎士, wu³ shih⁴ 武士.

knit *v.* pien¹ chih¹ 編織.

knob *n.* (*lump*) yüan² k'uai¹ 圓塊, (*handle*) nieh¹ shou³ 揑手, ping³ t'ou² 柄頭, (*hill*) yüan² ch'iu¹ 圓丘, yüan² shan¹ 圓山. 「ch'iao¹ 敲.

knock *n.* k'ou⁴ men² 叩門; *v.* chi¹ 擊, k'ou⁴ 叩,

knoll *n.* hsiao³ yüan² ch'iu¹ 小圓丘.

knot *n.* chieh² 結, (*nautical mile*) hai² li³ 海里; *v.* ta³ chieh² 打結. 「nan² te¹ 困難的.

knotty *a.* to¹ chieh² te¹ 多節的, (*difficult*) k'un⁴

know *v.* jen⁴ shih⁴ 認識.

knowing *a.* t'ung¹ hsiao³ te¹ 通曉的.

knowledge *n.* chih¹ shih⁴ 知識, hsüeh² wen⁴ 學問.

knuckle *n.* chih³ chieh² ku³ 指節骨, hsi¹ chieh² 膝節.

L

label *n.* ch'ien¹ t'iao² 籤條; *v.* piao¹ ming² 標明.

labor *v.* lao² kung¹ 勞工; *n.* lao² tung⁴ 勞動; ～ **day,** lao² tung⁴ chieh² 勞動節, ～ **party,** lao² tung⁴ tang³ 勞動黨.

laboratory *n.* shih² yen⁴ shih⁴ 實驗室.

laborer *n.* lao² tung⁴ che³ 勞動者.

laborious *a.* lao² k'u³ te¹ 勞苦的.

lace *n.* hsien⁴ tai¹ 線帶, hua¹ pien¹ 花邊; *v.* shih⁴ i³ hua¹ pien¹ 飾以花邊. 「hai⁴ 傷害.

lacerate *v.* (*tear*) ssu¹ lieh⁴ 撕裂, (*hurt*) shang¹

lack *n.*, *v.* ch'üeh¹ fa² 缺乏, pu⁴ tsu² 不足.

laconic *a.* chien³ ming² te¹ 簡明的.

lacquer *n.* ch'i¹ 漆; *v.* t'u² ch'i¹ 塗漆.

lacrimator *n.* ts'ui¹ lei⁴ chi¹ 催淚劑; ～ **gas,** ts'ui¹ lei⁴ hsing⁴ tu² ch'i¹ 催淚性毒氣.

lad *n.* nan² hai² 男孩, shao⁴ nien² 少年.

ladder *n.* t'i¹ 梯.

lade *v.* (*load*) chuang¹ tsai⁴ 裝載.

lading *n.* tsai⁴ huo⁴ 載貨, chuang¹ tsai⁴ 裝載.

ladle *n.* chi² shui³ shao² 汲水杓.

lady *n.* nü² chu³ jen² 女主人, kuei⁴ fu⁴ 貴婦, fu¹ jen² 夫人.

lag *v.* ch'ih² huan³ 遲緩, lao⁴ hou⁴ 落後.

laggard *a.* chih² huan³ te¹ 遲緩的, lao⁴ hou⁴ te¹ 落後的; *n.* ch'ih² huan² che⁴ 遲緩者, lao⁴ hou⁴ che³ 落後者.

lair *n.* shou⁴ hsüeh⁴ 獸穴.

lake *n.* hu² 湖.

lamb *n.* kao¹ yang² 羔羊.

lame *a.* po³ te¹ 跛的; *v.* shih² po³ 使跛.

lameness *n.* po³ 跛.

lament *n.* ai¹ tao⁴ 哀悼, (*poem*) wan³ shih¹ 輓詩; *v.* pei¹ shang¹ 悲傷, ai¹ tao⁴ 哀悼.

lamentable *a.* pei¹ shang¹ te¹ 悲傷的, ai¹ tao⁴ te¹ 哀悼的.

lamentation *n.* pei¹ shang¹ 悲傷, ai¹ tao⁴ 哀悼.

lamp *n.* teng¹ 燈.

lance *n.* mao² 矛; *v.* i³ mao² tz'u⁴ 以矛刺.

lancet *n.* liu³ yeh⁴ tao¹ 柳葉刀.

land *n.* lu⁴ ti⁴ 陸地, (*in firearms*) yang² hsien⁴ 陽線 (兵); *v.* (*to touch the ground*) lao⁴ ti⁴ 落地, (*from the air*) chiang⁴ lao⁴ 降落, (*from water*) teng¹ lu⁴ 登陸; ~ **mine**, ti⁴ lei² 地雷.

landholder *n.* ti⁴ chu³ 地主, tien⁴ hu⁴ 佃戶.

landlady *n.* nü³ ti⁴ chu³ 女地主, (*inn*) lü² kuan² chu³ fu⁴ 旅館主婦.

landlord *n.* ti⁴ chu³ 地主, (*inn*) lü² kuan² chu³ jen² 旅館主人.

landmark *n.* pei¹ 碑, chieh⁴ shih² 界石.

landscape *n.* feng¹ ching³ 風景, (*picture*) feng¹ ching³ hua⁴ 風景畫.

landslide *n.* peng¹ t'u³ 崩土.

lanyard *n.* (*gun*) la¹ huo³ sheng² 拉火繩.

lane *n.* hsia² lu⁴ 狹路, li³ 里, hsiang⁴ 巷.

language *n.* (*written*) wen² tzu⁴ 文字, (*spoken*) yü³ yen² 語言.

languid *a.* shuai¹ jo⁴ te¹ 衰弱的.

languish *v.* wei³ tun⁴ 委頓.

languor *n.* p'i² pai⁴ 疲憊.

lank *a.* shou⁴ ch'ang² te¹ 瘦長的.

lantern *n.* teng¹ lung² 燈籠, (*magic*) huan⁴ teng¹ 幻燈.

lap *n.* hsi¹ pu⁴ 膝部; *v.* (*over*) ch'ao¹ kuo⁴ 超過, (*drink*) shih³ 舐.

lapdog *n.* hsiao³ ch'üan³ 小犬.

lapidary *n.* pao³ shih² chiang⁴ 寶石匠.

144

lapse v. (*backslide*) to⁴ lao⁴ 墮落, (*time*) ching¹ kuo⁴ 經過. 「盜罪.

larceny n. ch'ieh⁴ tao⁴ 竊盜, ch'ieh⁴ tao⁴ tsui⁴ 竊

larch n. lo⁴ yeh⁴ sung¹ 落葉松.

lard n. chu¹ yu² 豬油. 「t'uan² 大兵團.

larder n. shih² ch'u² 食廚.

large a. chü⁴ ta⁴ te¹ 巨大的; ～ **units**, ta⁴ ping¹

lark n. pai³ ling² niao³ 百靈鳥.

lascivious a. yin² tang⁴ te¹ 淫蕩的.

lash n. tai⁴ 帶; v. pien¹ chi¹ 鞭擊, (*tie*) i³ sheng² fu² 以繩縛; ～ **rope**, k'un³ pao¹ sheng² 捆包繩.

lass n. (*girl*) shao⁴ nü³ 少女, (*sweetheart*) ch'ing² fu⁴ 情婦.

lassitude n. p'i² lao² 疲勞, tai⁴ chüan⁴ 怠倦.

last a. tsui⁴ hou⁴ te¹ 最後的; n. tsui⁴ hou⁴ che³ 最後者; adv. tsui⁴ hou⁴ ti¹ 最後地. 「久的.

lasting a. yung³ chiu³ te¹ 永久的, nai⁴ chiu³ te¹ 耐

latch n. shuan¹ 閂.

late a. ch'ih² te¹ 遲的, (*dead*) i³ ku⁴ te¹ 已故的.

lately adv. hsin¹ chin⁴ 新近, chin³ lai² 近來.

latent a. ch'ien² fu² te¹ 潛伏的.

lateral a. ts'e⁴ mien⁴ te¹ 測面的.

lath n. t'iao² pan³ 條板. 「鏇床(机).

lathe n. ch'e¹ ch'uang² 車牀(机), hsüan⁴ ch'uang²

lather n. (*soap*) fei² tsao³ p'ao⁴ mo⁴ 肥皂泡沫, (*sweat*) han⁴ chu¹ 汗珠.

latin a. la¹ ting¹ te¹ 拉丁的; n. (*language*) la¹ ting¹ yü³ 拉丁語, (*people*) la¹ ting¹ jen² 拉丁人.

latitude n. wei⁴ tu⁴ 緯度. 「的.

latter a. hou⁴ che³ te¹ 後者的, ch'i² tz'u⁴ te¹ 其次

lattice n. ko² tzu¹ 格子.

laud v. tsan⁴ mei³ 讚美, ko¹ fan² 歌煩.

laudable a. k'o³ tsan⁴ fan² te¹ 可讚煩的.

laudanum n. ya¹ p'ien⁴ chi⁴ 鴉片劑.

laugh n., v. hsiao⁴ 笑.

laughable a. k'o³ hsiao⁴ te¹ 可笑的.

laughter n. ta⁴ hsiao⁴ 大笑.

launch n. ta⁴ t'ing³ 大艇(軍艦所屬); v. (*ship*) ju⁴ shui³ 入水, (*start*) k'ai¹ shih³ 開始; ～ **the attack**, k'ai¹ shih³ kung¹ chi¹ 開始攻擊.

laundress n. hsi³ i¹ fu⁴ 洗衣婦.

145

laundry n. hsi³ i¹ chü² 洗衣局.

laurel n. yüeh⁴ kuei⁴ shu⁴ 月桂樹, yüeh⁴ kuei⁴ 月桂冠.

lava n. huo³ shan¹ shih² 火山石, jung² yen² 熔岩.

lavatory n. kuan⁴ hsi³ shih⁴ 盥洗室, (toilet) ssu⁴ so³ 廁所.

lave v. hsi³ cho² 洗濯.

lavish a. lan⁴ fei⁴ te¹ 濫費的; v. lan⁴ fei⁴ 濫費.

law n. fa³ lü⁴ 法律.

lawful a. ho² fa³ te¹ 合法的.

lawn n. ts'ao³ ti⁴ 草地, (cloth) hsi⁴ ma² pu⁴ 細麻布.

lawsuit n. su⁴ sung⁴ 訴訟.

lawyer n. lü⁴ shih¹ 律師.

lax a. (slack) k'uan¹ shih³ te¹ 寬弛的, (careless) su¹ hu¹ te¹ 疏忽的, (vague) han² hu² te¹ 含糊的.

laxative n. ch'ing¹ hsieh⁴ chi⁴ 輕瀉劑.

lay v. (put) an¹ fang⁴ 安放, (egg) sheng¹ tan⁴ 生蛋.

layman n. wai⁴ hang² 外行.

lazy a. lan³ to⁴ te¹ 懶惰的, tai⁴ to⁴ te¹ 怠惰的.

lead v. (guide) yin³ tao³ 引導, (a large unit) t'ung³ shuai⁴ 統率, (a small unit) shuai⁴ ling³ 率領; ～ horse, ch'ien² ma³ 前馬(軍).

lead n. (metal) ch'ien¹ 鉛.

leader n. ling³ hsiu⁴ 領袖, (editorial) she⁴ lun⁴ 社論.

leaf n. (plant) yeh⁴ 葉, (a sheet of paper) shu¹ yeh⁴ 書頁.

leafy a. to¹ yeh⁴ te¹ 多葉的.

league n. lien² meng² kuo² chia¹ 聯盟國家, t'ung² meng² 同盟.

leak n. lou⁴ tung⁴ 漏洞, lou⁴ hsieh⁴ 漏洩; v. lou⁴ 漏, hsieh⁴ 洩; ～ out, hsieh⁴ lou⁴ 洩漏.

leakage n. lou⁴ 漏, hsieh⁴ 洩.

leaky a. lou⁴ te¹ 漏的.

lean a. wu² chih¹ fang¹ te¹ 無脂肪的, (scant) p'in¹ fa² te¹ 貧乏的; v. (bend) ch'ing¹ hsieh² 傾斜, (on) i¹ lai⁴ 依賴.

leap n. t'iao⁴ 跳; v. t'iao⁴ 跳.

learn v. hsüeh² hsi² 學習, (hear) te² hsi² 得悉.

learned a. po² hsüeh² te¹ 博學的.

learning n. hsüeh² shih⁴ 學識, po² hsüeh² 博學.

lease n. tsu¹ yüeh¹ 租約; v. tsu¹ tai⁴ 租貸.

leash n. hsi⁴ shou⁴ p'i² t'iao² 繫獸皮條; v. yung⁴ p'i² tai⁴ fu² chu⁴ 用皮帶縛住.

least a. tsui⁴ hsiao³ te¹ 最小的.

leather n. p'i² ko² 皮革.

leathern *a.* ko² chih⁴ te¹ 革製的.

leave *v.* li² k'ai¹ 離開, (*remain*) i² liu² 遺留; *n.* chia⁴ 假; ～ out i² lou⁴ 遺漏.　　　　「發酵.

leaven *n.* chiao⁴ mu³ 酵母; *v.* shih³ fa¹ chiao⁴ 使

lecture *n., v.* yen² chiang³ 演講.

lecturer *n.* yen² chiang² che³ 演講者, chiang³ 　　　　　　　　　　　　　　「shih¹ 講師.

ledge *n.* chia⁴ 架.

ledger *n.* tsung³ chang⁴ pu⁴ 總賬簿.

leech *n.* shui³ chih⁴ 水蛭, (*person*) ch'iang¹ so²

leek *n.* chiu³ 韭.　　　　　　　「che¹¹ 强索者.

leer *n.* hsieh² shih⁴ 斜視; *v.* hsieh² shih⁴ 斜視, sung⁴ ch'iu¹ po¹ 送秋波.

leeward *n.* pei⁴ feng¹ te¹ 背風的.

left *a.* tso³ pien¹ te¹ 左邊的; *adv.* hsiang⁴ tso³ 向 　　　　　　　　　　　「左; *n.* tso³ 左.

leg *n.* t'ui³ 腿.

legacy *n.* i² ch'an³ 遺產.

legal *a.* fa³ lü⁴ te¹ 法律的.

legalize *a.* shih³ ho² fa³ 使合法.

legatee *n.* i² ch'an³ chi⁴ ch'eng² che³ 遺產繼承者.

legend *n.* pai⁴ shih³ 稗史, ch'uan² ch'i² 傳奇, (*of a map*) t'u² li⁴ 圖例.　　　　　「te¹ 傳奇的.

legendary *a.* pai⁴ shih³ te¹ 稗史的, ch'uan² ch'i²

legible *a.* i⁴ tu² te¹ 易讀的.

legislate *v.* li⁴ fa³ 立法.

legislation *n.* li⁴ fa³ 立法.

legislative *a.* li⁴ fa³ te¹ 立法的; ～ Yuan*, li⁴ fa³ yüan⁴ 立法院*.

legislator *n.* li⁴ fa² che³ 立法者.

legislature *n.* li⁴ fa³ yüan⁴ 立法院.

legitimacy *n.* ho² fa³ 合法, cheng⁴ tang¹ 正當.

legitimate *a.* ho² fa³ te¹ 合法的, cheng⁴ tang¹ te¹ 正當的; ～ child, ti² tzu³ 嫡子.

leisure *n.* chien⁴ hsia² 間暇.　　　　「te¹ 從容的.

leisurely *a.* chien⁴ hsia² te¹ 間暇的, ts'ung¹ jung²

lemon *n.* ning² meng² 檸檬.

lemonade *n.* ning² meng² shui³ 檸檬水.

lend *v.* chieh³ yü² 借與.

length *n.* ch'ang² 長; ～ of bore, t'ang² ch'ang² 膛長; ～ of projectile, tan⁴ ch'ang² 彈長.

lengthen *v.* shih³ ch'ang² 使長, pien⁴ ch'ang² 變

lengthy *a.* ch'ang² te¹ 長的.　　　　　　「長.

lenient *a.* wen² ho⁴ te¹ 溫和的, k'uan¹ hou⁴ te¹ 寬厚的.

lens *n.* t'ou⁴ ching⁴ 透鏡.

lent *n.* ssu⁴ hsün² ch'i² 四旬齊.

lentil *n.* pien³ tou⁴ 扁豆.

leopard *n.* pao⁴ 豹.

leper *n.* ma² feng¹ ping⁴ jen² 麻瘋病人.

leprosy *n.* ma² feng¹ 麻瘋.

less *a.* chiao⁴ hsiao³ (-shao³) te¹ 較小(少)的; *adv.* chiao⁴ hsiao³ (-shao³) ti⁴ 較小(少)地.

lessee *n.* tsu¹ hu⁴ 租戶.

lessen *v.* chien² shao³ 減少, pien⁴ hsiao³ 變小.

lesson *n.* kung¹ k'o⁴ 功課.

lessor *n.* yeh⁴ chu³ 業主.

lest *conj.* wei² k'ung³ 維恐.

let *v.* *(allow)* jung² hsü³ 容許.

lethargy *n.* mi² shui⁴ 迷睡, hun¹ shui⁴ 昏睡.

letter *n.* shu¹ hsin⁴ 書信; ～ **of credit,** hsin⁴ yung⁴ chuang⁴ 信用狀; ～ **of instruction,** hsin⁴ ling⁴ 訓令.

lettuce *n.* wan⁴ chü⁴ 萬苣.

levee *n.* fang² shui³ ti¹ 防水堤.

level *a.* ti⁴ p'ing² te¹ 地平的, shui³ p'ing² te¹ 水平的; *n.* shui³ p'ing² 水平; *v.* shih³ p'ing² 使平.

lever *n.* kang¹ kan³ 槓桿.

levy *n.* *(tax)* cheng¹ shou¹ 徵收, *(man)* chao¹ chi² 招集.

lewd *a.* hao⁴ se⁴ te¹ 好色的, yin² tang⁴ te¹ 淫蕩的.

liable *a.* *(responsible)* fu⁴ tse² te¹ 負責的.

liaison *n.* lien² lo⁴ 聯絡; ～ **officer,** lien² lo⁴ kuan¹ 聯絡官.

liar *n.* shuo¹ huang² che³ 說謊者.

libel *n.* hui³ pang⁴ wen² 毀謗文; *v.* hui³ pang⁴ 毀謗.

libelous *a.* fei³ pang⁴ te¹ 誹謗的.

liberal *a.* *(generous)* k'ang¹ k'ai³ te¹ 慷慨的, *(plentiful)* ta⁴ liang⁴ te¹ 大量的; ～ **party,** tzu⁴ yu² tang³ 自由黨; ～ **translation,** i⁴ i⁴ 意譯.

liberate *v.* chieh³ fang⁴ 解放.

liberty *n.* tzu⁴ yu² 自由; ～ **of conscience,** hsin⁴ chiao⁴ tzu⁴ yu² 信敎自由; ～ **of the press,** ch'u¹ pan³ tzu⁴ yu² 出版自由; ～ **of speech,** yen² lun⁴ tzu⁴ yu² 言論自由.

librarian *n.* t'u² shu¹ kuan² kuan² li³ yüan² 圖書館管理員.

148

library *n.* ts'ang² shu¹ shih⁴ 藏書室, t'u² shu¹ kuan³ 圖書館. 「k'o³ 許可.

licence, license *n.* chih² chao⁴ 執照; *v.* hsü²

lick *v.* shih³ 舐.

lid *n.* kai⁴ 蓋.

lie *n.* huang² yü³ 謊語; *v.* shuo¹ huang³ 說謊, (*recline*) t'ang² wo⁴ 躺臥; ~ **down,** t'ang³ hsia⁴ 躺

lieu *n.* ti⁴ wei⁴ 地位, ch'ang² so³ 場所.   「下.

lieutenant *n.* (*first*) chung¹ wei⁴ 中尉, (*second*) shao⁴ wei⁴ 少尉, (*navy*) shang⁴ wei⁴ 上尉; ~ **colonel,** chung¹ hsiao⁴ 中校; ~ **commander,** shao⁴ hsiao⁴ 少校(海); ~ **general,** chung¹ chiang⁴ 中將; ~ **junior grade,** chung¹ wei⁴ 中尉(海).

life *n.* sheng¹ ming⁴ 生命; ~ **annuity,** chung¹ shen¹ nien² chin¹ 終身年金; ~ **belt,** chiu⁴ sheng¹ tai⁴ 救生帶; ~ **insurance,** jen² shou⁴ pao² hsien³ 人壽保險; ~ **preserver,** chiu⁴ sheng¹ chü 救生具; ~ **sentence,** wu² ch'i¹ t'u² hsing² 無期徒刑.

lifeboat *n.* chiu⁴ sheng¹ t'ing² 救生艇.

lifeless *a.* wu² sheng¹ ming⁴ te¹ 無生命的.

lifelong *a.* pi⁴ sheng¹ te¹ 畢生的.

lifetime *n.* i⁴ sheng¹ 一生.

lift *n.* tien⁴ t'i¹ 電梯; *v.* chü² ch'i³ 舉起.

ligament *n.* jen⁴ tai⁴ 靭帶.

light *a.* (*having light*) kuang¹ ming² te¹ 光明的, (*not heavy*) ch'ing¹ te¹ 輕的; *n.* kuang¹ 光, (*lamp*) teng¹ 燈; *v.* (*fire*) tien³ teng¹ 點燈, (*light*) chao⁴ yao⁴ 照耀, (*alight*) chiang⁴ hsia⁴ 降下.

lighten *v.* shih³ kuang¹ ming² 使光明, (*reduce*) chien³ ch'ing¹ 減輕.

lighter *n.* (*cigarette*) ta² huo³ chi¹ 打火機, (*boat*) po² ch'uan² 駁船.

lighthouse *n.* teng¹ t'a³ 燈塔.

lightly *adv.* ch'ing¹ ch'ing¹ ti⁴ 輕輕地.

lightning *n.* tien⁴ kuang¹ 電光, shan³ tien⁴ 閃電.

like *a.* hsiang¹ ssu⁴ te¹ 相似的; *adv.* t'ung² yang⁴ ti⁴ 同樣地; *n.* hsiang¹ ssu⁴ che³ 相似者; *v.* ai⁴ hao³ 愛好.

likelihood *n.* k'o³ neng² hsing⁴ 可能性.

149

likely *a.* (*probable*) huo⁴ yü³ te¹ 或有的, (*promising*) yu³ wang⁴ te¹ 有望的; *adv.* huo⁴ hsü³ 或許.

liken *v.* pi² ni³ 比擬.

likeness *n.* hsiang¹ ssu⁴ hsing⁴ 相似性.

likewise *adv.* i⁴ 亦, t'ung² yang⁴ 同樣.

lilac *n.* tzu³ ting¹ hsiang¹ 紫丁香(植).

lily *n.* pai³ ho² hua¹ 百合花.

limb *n.* ssu⁴ chih¹ 四肢, (*tree*) ta⁴ chih¹ 大枝.

lime *n.* shih² hui¹ 石灰.

limekiln *n.* shih² hui¹ yao² 石灰窯.

limit *n.* chieh⁴ hsien⁴ 界限; *v.* hsien⁴ chih⁴ 限制.

limitation *n.* chieh⁴ hsien⁴ 界限, hsien⁴ chih⁴ 限制.

limited *a.* yu³ hsien⁴ te¹ 有限的; ～ **attack,** yu³ hsien⁴ kung¹ chi¹ 有限攻擊; ～ **objective,** yu³ hsien⁴ mu⁴ piao¹ 有限目標.

limousine *n.* hua² kuei⁴ ch'i⁴ ch'e¹ 華貴汽車.

limp *n.* po³ hsing² 跛行; *v.* po³ 跛; *a.* jou² juan³ 柔軟的.

limpid *a.* t'ou⁴ ming² te¹ 透明的.

line *n.* hsien⁴ 線; *v.* hua⁴ hsien⁴ 畫線; ～ **of defence,** fang² yü⁴ hsien⁴ 防禦線.

lineage *n.* chia¹ hsi⁴ 家系, hsüeh³ t'ung³ 血統.

lineal *a.* chih² hsi⁴ te¹ 直系的, cheng⁴ t'ung³ te¹ 正統的.

lineament *n.* hsiang¹ mao⁴ 相貌, wai⁴ hsing² 外形.

linen *n.* ma² pu⁴ 麻布; *a.* ma² chih⁴ te¹ 麻製的.

linger *v.* tan¹ ko¹ 躭擱.

linguist *n.* yü³ yen² hsüeh² chia¹ 語言學家.

liniment *n.* ts'a¹ chi⁴ 擦劑.

lining *n.* chia² li³ 夾裏.

link *v.* lien² chieh¹ 連接, chieh² pan⁴ 結伴.

linnet *n.* mei² hua¹ ch'iao³ 梅花雀(鳥).

linseed *n.* ya³ ma² tzu¹ 亞麻子.

lint *n.* juan³ pu² 軟布, jung² pu⁴ 絨布.

lion *n.* shih¹ 獅.

lioness *n.* p'in³ shih¹ 牝獅.

lip *n.* ch'un² 脣.

lipstick *n.* k'ou³ hung² 口紅, ch'un² kao¹ 脣膏.

liquid *a.* liu² tung⁴ te¹ 流動的; *n.* yeh⁴ t'i³ 液體.

liquidate *v.* ch'ing¹ suan⁴ 清算.

liquidation *n.* ch'ing¹ suan⁴ 清算.

liquor *n.* chiu³ 酒.

lisp *v.* fa¹ yin¹ han² hu² 發音含糊.

list *n.* (*in sheets*) piao³ ko² 表格, (*in booklet form*) piao³ ts'e⁴ 表册, (*ship*) ch'uan² chih¹ ch'ing¹ ts'e⁴ ⌊船之傾側.

listen *v.* ch'ing¹ t'ing¹ 傾聽.

literal *a.* chun³ ch'üeh⁴ te¹ 準確的, chih² chieh³ te¹ 直解的; ~ **translation**, chih² i⁴ 直譯.

literary *a.* wen² hsüeh² te¹ 文學的.

literature *n.* wen² hsüeh² 文學.

lithographer *n.* shih² yin⁴ chiang⁴ 石印匠.

lithography *n.* shih² yin⁴ shu⁴ 石印術.

litigation *n.* su⁴ sung⁴ 訴訟, chin⁴ hsing² su⁴ sung⁴ 進行訴訟.

litter *n.* (*disorder*) san³ luan⁴ 散亂, (*stretcher*) tan¹ chia⁴ 担架; ~ **bearer**, tan¹ chia⁴ ping¹ 担架兵.

little *a.* (*amount*) shao² te¹ 少的, (*size*) hsiao³ te¹ 小的; *n.* shao² hsü³ 少許.

live *v.* (*dwell*) chü¹ chu⁴ 居住; *a.* (*alive*) yu³ sheng¹ ming⁴ te¹ 有生命的; ~ **ammunition**, ⌊shih² tan⁴ 實彈.

livelihood *n.* sheng¹ chi⁴ 生計.

living *n.* sheng¹ chi⁴ 生計; ~ **Buddha (Mongolian)**, huo² fo² 活佛(蒙古); ~ **room**, ch'i³ chü¹ chien¹ 起居間.

livelong *a.* i⁴ sheng¹ te¹ 一生的, yu¹ chiu³ te¹ 悠久

lively *a.* huo² p'o¹ te¹ 活潑的.

liver *n.* kan¹ 肝.

lizard *n.* hsi¹ i⁴ 蜥蜴.

load *n.* chuang⁴ ho⁴ 重荷; *v.* (*ammunition*) chuang¹ t'ien² 裝填, (*transportation*) chuang¹ tsai⁴ 裝載.

loam *n.* jang² t'u³ 壤土, nien² t'u³ 黏土.

loan *n.* tai⁴ k'uan³ 貸款.

lobby *n.* chieh¹ tai⁴ shih⁴ 接待室.

lobster *n.* lung² hsia¹ 龍蝦.

local *a.* pen³ ti⁴ te¹ 本地的, chü² pu⁴ te¹ 局部的; ~ **anesthesia**, chü² pu⁴ ma² tsui⁴ fa³ 局部麻醉法; ~ **attack**, chü² pu⁴ kung¹ chi¹ 局部攻擊.

locate *v.* ch'üeh⁴ ting⁴ ti⁴ tien³ 確定地點, she⁴ chih⁴ 設置.

lock *n.* so³ 鎖, (*water*) shui³ cha² 水閘.

locksmith *n.* so³ chiang⁴ 鎖匠.

locomotion *n.* i² tung⁴ 移動.

locomotive *n.* huo³ ch'e¹ t'ou² 火車頭.

locust *n.* huang² ch'ung² 蝗蟲.

lodge *n.* su⁴ so³ 宿所; *v.* yü⁴ chü¹ 寓居.

lodger *n.* yü⁴ k'o⁴ 寓客.

lodging *n.* yü⁴ so³ 寓所.

loft *n.* wu¹ ting³ lou² 屋頂樓.

lofty *a.* (*high*) kao¹ sung³ te¹ 高聳的.

log *n.* ta⁴ mu⁴ liao⁴ 大木料, (*ship*) hang² hsing² jih⁴ chi⁴ 航行日記.

logarithm *n.* tui⁴ shu⁴ 對數.

logic *n.* lun⁴ li³ hsüeh² 論理學.

logical *a.* ho² lun⁴ li³ te¹ 合論理的.

logician *n.* lun⁴ li³ hsüeh² chia¹ 論理學家.

logistics *n.* hou⁴ fang¹ ch'in² wu⁴ 後方勤務.

logwood *n.* su¹ fang¹ mu⁴ 蘇方木(植).

loin *n.* yao¹ 腰, (*meat*) yao¹ jou⁴ 腰肉.

loiter *v.* p'ai² hui² 徘徊.

lonely *a.* ku¹ tu² te¹ 孤獨的.

lonesome *a.* chüeh² ku¹ chi¹ te¹ 覺孤寂的, ch'i¹ liang² te¹ 凄涼的.

long *a.* (*size*) ch'ang² te¹ 長的, (*time*) chiu³ te¹ 久的, (*distance*) yüan³ te¹ 遠的; *v.* (*desire*) k'o³ wang⁴ 渴望. ~ **ago**, ts'ung² ch'ien² 從前; ~ **before**, pu⁴ chiu² i³ ch'ien² 不久以前; ~ **distance telephone**, ch'ang² t'u² tien⁴ hua⁴ 長途電話; ~ **wave**, ch'ang² po¹ 長波.

longevity *n.* ch'ang² shou⁴ 長壽.

longing *n.* k'o³ wang⁴ 渴望.

longitude *n.* ching¹ tu⁴ 經度.

look *n.* i² k'an⁴ 一看; *v.* k'an⁴ 看; ~ **after**, chao⁴ fu² 照拂; ~ **as if**, hao³ ssu⁴ 好似; ~ **back**, chui¹ hsiang³ 追想; ~ **for**, hsün² chao³ 尋找; ~ **forward to**, yü⁴ ch'i¹ 預期; ~ **on**, chu⁴ i⁴ 注意; ~ **out**, chu⁴ i⁴ 注意; ~ **round**, hsün² mi⁴ 尋覓; ~ **sharp**, liu² hsin¹ 留心; ~ **to**, chu⁴ i⁴ 注意.

loom *n.* chih¹ pu⁴ chi¹ 織布機.

loop *n.* hsien⁴ ch'üan¹ 線圈.

loose *a.* pu⁴ chin³ te¹ 不緊的, k'uan¹ te¹ 寬的.

loosen *v.* shih³ k'uan¹ sung¹ 使寬鬆.

lop *v.* (*cut*) k'an³ fa² 砍伐.

lord *n.* (*god*) shang⁴ ti⁴ 上帝, (*Christ*) yeh¹ su¹ 耶穌, (*noble*) kuei⁴ tsu² 貴族.

lore *n.* hsüeh² wen⁴ 學問.

lose *v.* sun³ shih¹ 損失, (*fail to win*) shih¹ pai⁴ 失敗; ～ **temper,** fa¹ nu⁴ 發怒; ～ (**one's**) **way,** 「mi² lu⁴ 迷路.

loser *n.* fu⁴ fang¹ 負方.

loss *n.* sun³ shih¹ 損失.

lost *a.* (*astray*) mi² lu⁴ te¹ 迷路的, (*sensing*) pu² chien⁴ tan⁴ 不見彈(砲), (*horse*) t'ao² shih¹ 逃失.

lot *n.* (*fortune*) ming⁴ yün⁴ 命運, (*house*) ti⁴ ch'ü¹ 地區.

lotion *n.* hsi³ cho² yao⁴ shui³ 洗濯藥水.

lottery *n.* ts'ai³ p'iao⁴ 彩票, chiang³ ch'üan⁴ 獎券.

loud *a.* hsüan¹ hsiao¹ te¹ 喧嚣的.

louse *n.* shih¹ 虱.

lovable *a.* k'o³ ai⁴ te¹ 可愛的.

love *n.* ai⁴ ch'ing² 愛情; *v.* ai⁴ 愛.

lovely *a.* mei³ li⁴ te¹ 美麗的.

lover *n.* ai⁴ jen² 愛人.

low *a.* (*not high*) ti¹ te¹ 低的; ～ **gear,** t'ou² tang⁴ 頭檔; ～ **ground,** ti¹ ti⁴ 低地.

lower *v.* (*let down*) chiang⁴ hsia⁴ 降下; ～ **classes,** hsia⁴ ts'eng² chieh¹ chi² 下層階級.

lowly *a.* hsia⁴ chi² te¹ 下級的, (*humble*) ch'ien¹ sun⁴ te¹ 謙遜的.

low-spirited *a.* chü³ sang⁴ te¹ 沮喪的.

loyal *a.* chung¹ hsin¹ te¹ 忠心的.

loyalty *n.* chung¹ ch'eng² 忠誠.

lozenge *n.* hsieh² tao¹ hsing² 斜刀形.

lubricate *v.* jun⁴ hua² 潤滑.

luck *n.* hsing⁴ yün⁴ 幸運.

lucky *a.* hsing⁴ yün⁴ te¹ 幸運的.

lucrative *a.* huo⁴ li⁴ te¹ 獲利的.

ludicrous *a.* k'o³ hsiao⁴ te¹ 可笑的.

lug *v.* t'o¹ la¹ 拖拉.

luggage *n.* hsing² li³ 行李.

lukewarm *a.* wen¹ je⁴ te¹ 溫熱的.

lull *n.* chan⁴ shih² p'ing² ching⁴ 暫時平靜; *v.* shih² p'ing² ching⁴ 使平靜.

lullaby *n.* ts'ui¹ mien² ko¹ 催眠歌.

lumbago *n.* yao¹ t'ung⁴ 腰痛.

lumber *n.* mu⁴ ts'ai² 木材.

luminous *a.* fa¹ kuang¹ te¹ 發光的.

lump *n.* i⁴ t'uan² 一團.

lunacy *n.* feng¹ tien¹ 瘋癲.

lunar *a.* yüeh⁴ te¹ 月的, yüeh⁴ hsing² te¹ 月形的; ～ **eclipse,** yüeh⁴ shih² 月蝕.

lunatic *a.* tien¹ k'uang² te¹ 癲狂的; ～ **asylum** *n.* feng¹ jen² yüan⁴ 瘋人院.

lunch *n.* wu⁴ ts'an¹ 午餐; *v.* chin⁴ wu³ ts'an¹ 進 「午餐.

lung *n.* fei⁴ 肺.

lure *n.*, *v.* yin³ yu⁴ 引誘, yu⁴ huo⁴ 誘惑.

lurk *v.* ch'ien² fu² 潛伏.

luscious *a.* kan¹ mei³ te¹ 甘美的.

lust *n.* (*sex*) se⁴ yü⁴ 色慾.

lute *n.* p'i² p'a² 琵琶. 「shui⁴ 奢侈稅.

luxury *n.* she¹ ch'ih³ 奢侈; ～ **tax,** she¹ ch'ih³

lye *n.* chien² shui³ 鹼水.

lymph *n.* lin² pa¹ yeh⁴ 淋巴液.

lynx *n.* shan¹ mao⁴ 山貓.

lyre *n.* ch'i¹ hsien² ch'in² 七弦琴.

lyric *a.* shu¹ ch'ing² te¹ 抒情的.

M

macadam *n.* sui⁴ shih² 碎石.

macaroni *n.* t'ung¹ hsin¹ fen³ 通心粉.

machination *n.* yin¹ mou² 陰謀.

machine *n.* chi¹ hsieh⁴ 機械; ～ **gun,** chi¹ kuan¹ ch'iang¹ 機關槍; ～ **gun company,** chi¹ kuan¹ ch'iang¹ lien² 機關槍連; ～ **gun emplacement,** chi¹ kuan¹ ch'iang¹ yen² t'i³ 機關槍掩體; ～ **gun position,** chi¹ kuan¹ ch'iang¹ chen⁴ ti⁴ 機關槍陣地; ～ **shop,** hsieh⁴ ch'ang³ 械廠.

machinery *n.* chi¹ hsieh⁴ 機械.

machinist *n.* chi¹ shih¹ 機師, chi¹ hsieh⁴ chiang⁴ 「機械匠.

mackerel *n.* ch'ing¹ 鯖.

mad *a.* feng¹ tien¹ te¹ 瘋癲的.

madam *n.* fu¹ jen² 夫人.

madman *n.* feng¹ jen² 瘋人.

madness *n.* tien¹ k'uang² 癲狂.

154

magazine *n.* tsa² chih⁴ 雜誌.

maggot *n.* ch'ü¹ 蛆.

magic *n.* (*art*) mo² shu⁴ 魔術, (*power*) mo² li⁴ 魔力；
～ **lantern,** huan⁴ teng¹ 幻燈.

magical *a.* mo² shu⁴ te¹ 魔術的, mo² li⁴ te¹ 魔力的.

magician *n.* mo² shu⁴ chia¹ 魔術家.

magistrate *n.* chang³ kuan¹ 長官, (*judge*) shen³
p'an⁴ kuan¹ 審判官.

magnanimity *n.* kao¹ shang⁴ 高尚, ta⁴ liang⁴ 大量.

magnanimous *a.* kao¹ shang⁴ te¹ 高尚的, ta⁴
liang⁴ te¹ 大量的.

magnate *n.* wei³ jen² 偉人, (*important person*)
yao⁴ jen² 要人.

magnet *n.* tz'u² t'ieh³ 磁鐵, tz'u² shih² 磁石.

magnetic *a.* tz'u² hsing⁴ te¹ 磁性的；～ **field,**
tz'u² ch'ang³ 磁場；～ **north,** tz'u² pei³ 磁北.

magnetism *n.* tz'u² hsing⁴ 磁性.　　　　「吸引.

magnetize *v.* tz'u² hua⁴ 磁化, (*attract*) hsi¹ yin³

magneto *n.* tz'u² t'ieh³ fa¹ tien⁴ chi¹ 磁鐵發電機.

magnificence *n.* hung² ta⁴ 宏大, chuang⁴ li⁴ 壯
麗, fei¹ fan² 非凡.

magnificent *a.* hung² ta⁴ te¹ 宏大的, chuang⁴ li⁴
te¹ 壯麗的, fei¹ fan² te¹ 非凡的.

magnify *v.* k'uo⁴ ta⁴ 擴大, k'ua¹ ta⁴ 誇大.

magnitude *n.* (*size*) ta⁴ hsiao³ 大小, (*importance*)
chung⁴ yao⁴ 重要.　　　　　　　　「饒舌者.

magpie *n.* (*bird*) ch'iao¹ 鵲, (*person*) jao⁴ she² che³

mahogany *n.* (*wood*) t'ao² hua¹ hsin¹ mu⁴ 桃花心
木, (*color*) hung² tsung¹ se⁴ 紅棕色.

maid *n.* wei⁴ chia⁴ chih¹ nü³ tzu¹ 未嫁之女子.

maiden *a.* (*girl*) shao⁴ nü³ 少女, (*virgin*) ch'u² nü³
處女.　　　　　　　　　　　　　　「處女.

maidservant *n.* nü³ p'u² 女僕.

mail *n.* yu² chien⁴ 郵件.

mailbox *n.* hsin⁴ hsiang¹ 信箱.

mailman *n.* yu² ch'ai¹ 郵差.

maim *v.* shih³ ch'eng² ts'an² fei⁴ 使成殘廢.

main *a.* chu³ yao⁴ te¹ 主要的, chung⁴ yao⁴ te¹ 重要
的；～ **attack,** chu³ kung¹ 主攻(軍)；～ **force,**
chu³ li⁴ 主力(軍)；～ **line of resistance,** chu³
ti³ k'ang⁴ hsien⁴ 主抵抗線；～ **line,** (*railway*)
kan⁴ hsien⁴ 幹線.

mainland *n.* ta⁴ lu⁴ 大陸. 「大概.

mainly *adv.* chu³ yao⁴ pu⁴ fen¹ 主要部分, ta⁴ kai⁴

maintain *v.* (*keep up*) wei² ch'ih² 維持, (*insist*) chien¹ ch'ih² 堅持.

maize *n.* yü⁴ shu² shu³ 玉蜀黍. 「高貴的.

majestic *a.* tsun¹ yen² te¹ 尊嚴的, kao¹ kuei⁴ te¹

majesty *n.* (*nobility*) kao¹ kuei⁴ 高貴, (*stateliness*) tsun¹ yen² 尊嚴, (*title*) pi⁴ hsia⁴ 陛下.

major *a.* chu³ yao⁴ te¹ 主要的; *n.* shao⁴ hsiao⁴ 少校; ~ **general,** shao⁴ chiang¹ 少將; ~ **operation** (*medical*), ta⁴ shou³ shu⁴ 大手術.

majority *n.* ta⁴ to¹ shu⁴ 大多數.

make *v.* chih⁴ tso⁴ 製做.

maker *n.* chih⁴ tso⁴ che³ 製作者.

malady *n.* ping⁴ cheng⁴ 病症.

malaria *n.* nüeh⁴ chi² 瘧疾.

male *a.* nan² hsing⁴ te¹ 男性的, (*of animals*) hsiung² hsing⁴ te¹ 雄性的.

malediction *n.* tsu³ chou⁴ 詛咒.

malefactor *n.* tsui⁴ fan⁴ 罪犯.

malevolence *n.* e⁴ i⁴ 惡意, yüan⁴ tu² 怨毒.

malice *n.* tu² hen⁴ 毒恨, e⁴ i⁴ 惡意.

malicious *a.* tu² hen⁴ te¹ 毒恨的, e⁴ i⁴ te¹ 惡意的.

malign *v.* hui³ pang⁴ 毀謗. 「惡性的.

malignant *a.* hsiung¹ e⁴ te¹ 兇惡的, e⁴ hsing⁴ te¹

malignity *n.* hsiung¹ e⁴ 兇惡, e⁴ i⁴ 惡意.

mallet *n.* mu⁴ ch'ui² 木槌.

mallow *n.* chin³ k'uei² 錦葵(植).

malnutrition *n.* ying² yang³ pu⁴ liang² 營養不良.

malt *n.* mai⁴ ya² 麥芽.

maltreat *v.* nüeh⁴ tai⁴ 虐待.

mamma *n.* ma¹ ma¹ 媽媽, mu³ ch'in¹ 母親.

mammoth *n.* ku³ tai⁴ chü⁴ hsiang⁴ 古代巨象.

man *n.* (*person*) jen² 人, (*male*) nan² tzu¹ 男子.

manacle *n.* liao⁴ k'ao⁴ 鐐銬.

manage *v.* kuan² li³ 管理.

manageable *a.* k'o³ kuan² li³ te¹ 可管理的.

management *n.* kuan² li³ 管理.

manager *n.* ching¹ li³ 經理.

mandate *n.* hsün⁴ ling⁴ 訓令, (*trusteeship*) wei³ t'o¹ shu¹ 委託書.

mandolin *n.* man⁴ t'o² lin² ch'in² 曼陀琳琴.

mane *n.* tsung¹ mao² 鬃毛.

maneuver, manoeuver *n.* (*in movements*) tiao⁴ tung⁴ 調動, (*in operations*) yün⁴ yung⁴ 運用, (*military*)yen³ hsi² 演習.

manful *a.* (*brave*) yung² kan³ te¹ 勇敢的.

mange *n.* ch'u⁴ hsien³ 蓄癬.

manger *n.* ma³ ts'ao³ 馬槽.

manhood *n.* ch'eng² nien² 成年.

maniac *n.* tsao⁴ k'uang² che³ 躁狂者.

manifest *a.* hsien³ ming² te¹ 顯明的; *v.* hsien³ shih¹ 顯示, (*prove*)cheng⁴ ming² 證明; *n.* ch'uan² huo⁴ tan¹ 船貨單.

manifestation *n.* hsien³ shih⁴ 顯示, (*demonstration*) shih⁴ wei¹ yün⁴ tung⁴ 示威運動.

manifesto *n.* hsüan¹ yen² 宣言.

manifold *a.* to¹ chung³ te¹ 多種的.

mankind *n.* jen² lei⁴ 人類.

manly *a.* yung² kan³ te¹ 勇敢的.

manner *n.* t'ai⁴ tu⁴ 態度.   「俗.

manners *n.* li³ mao² 禮貌, (*customs*) feng¹ su² 風

mannerly *a.* yu²-li³ mao² te¹ 有禮貌的, ho² i² te¹

man-of-war *n.* chan⁴ chien⁴ 戰艦.   「合宜的.

mansion *n.* ta⁴ hsia⁴ 大廈.

manslaughter *n.* sha¹ jen² 殺人.

mantis *n.* t'ang² lang² 螳螂.

mantle *n.* p'i¹ feng¹ 披風.

manual *a.* shou³ te¹ 手的, shou³ chih⁴ te¹ 手製的; *n.* shou³ ts'e⁴ 手册; ~ **training**, shou³ kung¹ 手工.

manufactory *n.* chih⁴ tsao⁴ ch'ang³ 製造廠.

manufacture *n.* chih⁴ tsao⁴ 製造, (*thing manufactured*) chih⁴ tsao⁴ p'in³ 製造品; *v.* chih⁴ tsao⁴ 製造.   「ch'ang² chu³ 廠主.

manufacturer *n.* chih⁴ tsao⁴ che³ 製造者, (*owner*)

manure *n.* (*refuse*) fen⁴ 糞, (*fertilizer*) fei² liao⁴ 肥料; *v.* shih¹ fei² liao⁴ 施肥料.

manuscript *n.* shou² kao³ 手稿, ch'ao¹ pen³ 抄本.

many *a.* chung⁴ to¹ te¹ 衆多的.

map *n.* ti⁴ t'u² 地圖; ~ **case**, t'u² nang² 圖囊.

maple *n.* feng¹ 楓.

mar v. shang¹ hai⁴ 傷害.　　　「li³ shih² 大理石.

marble a. ta⁴ li³ shih² chih⁴ te¹ 大理石製的; n. ta⁴

march v. hsing² chün¹ 行軍; n. (March) san¹ yüeh⁴ 三月; ~ **in review,** fen¹ lieh⁴ shih⁴ 分列式(軍); ~ **off,** k'ai¹ pa² 開拔.

mare n. p'in² ma³ 牝馬.

margin n. (border) pien¹ chieh⁴ 邊界, (blank space) yeh⁴ pien¹ 頁邊, (extra) yü² pai² 餘白.

marigold n. wan⁴ shou⁴ chü² 萬壽菊(植).

marine a. (of the sea) hai³ yang² te¹ 海洋的, (of navy) hai³ chün¹ te¹ 海軍的; n. (soldier) shui³ ping¹ 水兵, (shipping) ch'uan² po⁴ 船舶; ~ **corps** (US), hai³ chün¹ lu⁴ chan⁴ tui⁴ 海軍陸戰隊(美); ~ **insurance,** hai³ shang⁴ pao² hsien³ 海上保險; ~ **policy,** hai³ shang⁴ pao² hsien³ tan¹ 海上保險單.

mariner n. shui² shou³ 水手, hai³ yüan² 海員.

maritime a. pin¹ hai³ te¹ 濱海的, shu² hai³ te¹ 屬海的.

mark n. chi⁴ hao⁴ 記號, (grade) fen¹ shu⁴ 分數; v. piao¹ shih⁴ 標示, (rate) chi⁴ fen¹ 記分.

market n. shih⁴ ch'ang³ 市場, shang¹ ch'ang³ 商場; ~ **place,** shih⁴ ch'ang³ 市場; ~ **price,** shih⁴ chia⁴ 市價.

marketable a. k'o³ ch'u¹ mai⁴ te¹ 可出賣的.

marksmanship n. she⁴ chi¹ chi⁴ neng² 射擊技能(軍).

marmalade n. kuo³ chiang⁴ 果醬(多爲橘類).

marquee n. ta⁴ ying² chang⁴ 大營帳.

marquis n. hou² chüeh² 侯爵.

marriage n. hun¹ yin¹ 婚姻, chieh² hun¹ 結婚.

marriageable a. k'o³ chieh² hun¹ te¹ 可結婚的.

married a. i³ hun¹ te¹ 已婚的.

marrow n. ku² sui³ 骨髓.

marry v. chieh² hun¹ 結婚, (for man) ch'ü³ 娶, (for woman) chia⁴ 嫁.

Mars n. (planet) huo³ hsing¹ 火星.

marsh n. chao³ tse² 沼澤.

marshal n. (military title) yüan² shuai⁴ 元帥.

marten n. tiao¹ 貂.

martial a. chan⁴ cheng¹ te¹ 戰爭的, (warlike)

shang⁴ wu³ te¹ 尚武的; ~ **law,** chieh⁴ yen²

martin *n.* yen² 燕. 「ling² 戒嚴令.

martyr *n.* hsün¹ chiao⁴ che³ 殉教者.

marvel *n.* ch'i² shih⁴ 奇事; *v.* ch'i² i⁴ 奇異.

marvelous, marvellous *a.* ch'i² i⁴ te¹ 奇異的.

mascot *n.* fu² hsing¹ 福星, chi² jen² 吉人.

masculine *a.* nan² hsing⁴ te¹ 男性的.

mask *n.* chia³ mien⁴ chü⁴ 假面具; *v.* tai⁴ chia³ mien⁴ chü⁴ 戴假面具, (*disguise*) ch'iao² chuang¹ 喬裝.

mason *n.* ni² shui³ chiang⁴ 泥水匠.

mass *n.* (*quantity*) ta⁴ liang⁴ 大量, (*bulk*) jung² liang⁴ 容量, (*majority*) ta⁴ pu⁴ 大部, (*group*) ch'ün² chi² 群集, (*Catholic*) mi² sa² 彌撒; ~ **marriage,** chi² t'uan² chieh² hun¹ 集團結婚; ~ **production,** ta⁴ liang⁴ sheng¹ ch'an³ 大量生產.

massacre *n.* t'u² sha¹ 屠殺.

massive *a.* chü⁴ ta⁴ te¹ 巨大的.

mast *n.* wei² 桅.

master *n.* chu³ jen² 主人; ~ **of arts,** wen² k'o¹ shih⁴ shih⁴ 文科碩士; ~ **of science,** li³ k'o¹ shih⁴ shih⁴ 理科碩士; ~ **of ceremonies,** ssu¹ i² 司儀.

masterpiece *n.* chieh² tso⁴ 傑作.

mastery *n.* (*control*) chih¹ p'ei⁴ 支配, (*upper hand*) yu¹ shih⁴ 優勢, (*skill*) ching¹ t'ung¹ 精通.

mastiff *n.* ao² ch'üan³ 獒, meng³ ch'üan³ 猛犬.

match *n.* huo³ ch'ai² 火柴, (*athletic*) ti² shou³ 敵手; *v.* p'i³ ti² 匹敵.

matchmaker *n.* chih⁴ huo³ ch'ai² che³ 製火柴者.

mate *n.* (*marriage*) p'ei⁴ ou³ 配偶, (*companion*) pan⁴ lü³ 伴侶. 「原料.

material *a.* wu⁴ chih² te¹ 物質的; *n.* yüan² liao⁴

materiel *n.* (*equipment*) ch'i⁴ ts'ai² 器材.

maternal *a.* mu³ te¹ 母的, mu³ hsi⁴ te¹ 母系的.

maternity *n.* mu³ hsing⁴ 母性.

mathematical *a.* shu⁴ hsüeh² te¹ 數學的. 「學.

mathematics *n.* suan⁴ shu⁴ 算術, shu⁴ hsüeh² 數

matriculate *v.* hsü³ ju⁴ ta⁴ hsüeh² 許入大學.

matrimony *n.* hun¹ yin¹ 婚姻.

matter *n.* (*material*) wu⁴ chih² 物質, (*affair*) shih⁴ chien⁴ 事件; *v.* kuan¹ hsi⁴ 關係.

mattock *n.* hao² tsui³ ch'u² 鶴嘴鋤.

mattress *n.* tien⁴ ju⁴ 墊褥.

mature *a.* (*people*) ch'eng² shou² te¹ 成熟的, (*things*) tao⁴ ch'i¹ te¹ 到期的.

maul *v.* ta³ shang¹ 打傷.

maxim *n.* chen¹ yen² 箴言, ko² yen² 格言.

maximum *a.* (*largest*) tsui⁴ ta⁴ te¹ 最大的, (*highest*) tsui⁴ kao¹ te¹ 最高的; ~ **price**, tsui⁴ kao¹ chia⁴ ko² 最高價格.　　　　　　　「yüeh⁴ 五月.

may *v. aux.* neng² 能, k'o³ 可; *n.* (*May*) wu³

mayor *n.* shih⁴ chang³ 市長.

me *pron.* wo³ 我.

meadow *n.* ts'ao³ yüan² 草原.

meager, meagre *a.* (*thin*) shou⁴ chi¹ te¹ 瘦脊的, (*scanty*) pu⁴ feng¹ te¹ 不豐的.

meal *n.* ts'an¹ 餐, shan⁴ shih² 膳食.

mean *a.* (*poor*) ti¹ teng³ te¹ 低等的, (*average*) chung¹ yung¹ te¹ 中庸的.

meaning *n.* i⁴ i⁴ 意義.　　　　　　　　　「時.

meantime *adv.* t'ung² shih² 同時, ch'i² shih² 其

measles *n.* ma² chen³ 麻疹.

measurable *a.* k'o³ tu⁴ liang² te¹ 可度量的.

measure *n.* tu⁴ liang² 度量, *v.* ts'e⁴ liang² 測量.

meat *n.* jou⁴ 肉, jou⁴ lei⁴ 肉類.

mechanic *n.* chi⁴ shih¹ 技師, chi¹ chiang⁴ 機匠.

mechanical *a.* chi¹ hsieh⁴ te¹ 機械的; ~ **engineering**, chi¹ hsieh⁴ kung¹ ch'eng² hsüeh² 機械工程學.　　　　　　　　「紀念章

medal *n.* chiang³ chang¹ 獎章, chi⁴ nien⁴ chang¹

meddle *v.* kan¹ yü⁴ 干預.

mediate *v.* t'iao² t'ing² 調停, chung⁴ ts'ai¹ 仲裁.

mediation *n.* t'iao² t'ing² 調停, chung⁴ ts'ai¹ 仲裁.

mediator *n.* t'iao² t'ing² che³ 調停者, chung⁴ ts'ai² che³ 仲裁者.

medical *a.* i¹ yao⁴ te¹ 醫藥的; ~ **practitioner**, i¹ sheng¹ 醫生; ~ **profession**, i¹ yeh⁴ 醫業.

medicine *n.* (*drug*) yao⁴ p'in³ 藥品, (*science*) i¹ shu⁴ 醫術.　　　　　　　　　　「庸

mediocrity *n.* p'ing² ch'ang² 平常, fan² yung¹ 凡

meditate *v.* mo⁴ hsiang³ 默想, (*intend*) ch'i² t'u² 企圖

meditation *n.* ch'en² ssu¹ 沈思.　　　　「企圖

meditative *a.* ch'en² ssu¹ te¹ 沈思的.

medium a. chung¹ teng³ te¹ 中等的; n. chung¹ yung¹ 中庸; ~ **artillery,** chung¹ p'ao⁴ ping¹ 中砲兵(軍).

meek a. wen¹ shun⁴ te¹ 溫順的, ch'ien¹ jang⁴ te¹ 謙讓的.

meet v. yü⁴ chien⁴ 遇見.

meeting n. chi² hui⁴ 集會.

melancholy a. yu¹ yü⁴ te¹ 憂鬱的, chü³ sang⁴ te¹ 沮喪的; n. yu¹ yü⁴ 憂鬱, chü³ sang⁴ 沮喪.

mellow a. jou² shou⁴ te¹ 柔熟的; v. shih³ ch'eng² shou² 使成熟.

melodious a. yüeh⁴ erh³ te¹ 悅耳的.

melody n. hsüan² lü⁴ 旋律, ch'ü³ tiao⁴ 曲調.

melon n. kua¹ 瓜, t'ien² kua¹ 甜瓜.

melt v. jung² hua⁴ 融化.

member n. hui⁴ yüan² 會員, (animal) chih¹ t'i³ 肢體.

membrane n. mo⁴ 膜.

memento n. chi⁴ nien⁴ p'in³ 紀念品.

memoir n. (biography) ch'uan² chi⁴ 傳記.

memorable a. chih² te² chi⁴ i⁴ te¹ 值得記憶的.

memorandum n. pei⁴ wang⁴ lu⁴ 備忘錄.

memorial a. i³ tzu¹ chi⁴ nien⁴ te¹ 以資紀念的; n. chi⁴ nien⁴ wu⁴ 紀念物.

memory n. chi⁴ i⁴ li⁴ 記憶力, chi⁴ i⁴ 記憶.

menace n. wei¹ ho⁴ 威嚇; v. tung⁴ ho⁴ 恫嚇.

mend v. (repair) hsiu¹ pu³ 修補, (improve) kai³ shan⁴ 改善.

meningitis n. nao³ mo⁴ yen² 腦膜炎.

mental a. (of mind) ching¹ shen² te¹ 精神的.

mention v. shuo¹ chi² 說及, ch'en² shu⁴ 陳述.

mercantile a. (commercial) shang¹ yeh⁴ te¹ 商業的.

mercenary n. (soldier) mu⁴ ping¹ 募兵.

merchandise n. huo⁴ wu⁴ 貨物, shang¹ p'in³ 商品.

merchant n. shang¹ jen² 商人.

merciful a. lien² min³ te¹ 憐憫的, k'uan¹ shu⁴ te¹ 寬恕的.

merciless a. yen² k'u⁴ te¹ 嚴酷的, ts'an² jen³ te¹ 殘忍的.

mercury n. shui³ yin² 水銀, (planet) shui³ hsing¹ 水星.

mercy n. lien² min³ 憐憫, k'uan¹ shu⁴ 寬恕.

mere a. chin³ chin³ 僅僅, pu² kuo⁴ 不過.

merger n. ho² ping⁴ 合併.

meridian *n.* tzu² wu³ hsien⁴ 子午線.

merit *n.* kung¹ chi¹ 功績, kung¹ kuo⁴ 功過; *v.* ying¹ te² 應得. 「稱贊的.

meritorious *a.* ying¹ shou⁴ ch'eng¹ tsan⁴ te¹ 應受

merry *a.* k'uai⁴ le⁴ te¹ 快樂的.

mess *n.* (*meal*) chü⁴ ts'an¹ 聚餐; ～ **call**, k'ai¹ fan⁴ hao⁴ 開飯號(軍); ～ **kit**, fan⁴ ho² 飯盒(軍); ～ **sergeant**, chi² yang³ chün¹ shih⁴ 給養軍士(軍).

message *n.* hsin⁴ hsi² 信息.

messenger *n.* hsin⁴ ch'ai⁴ 信差, shih² che⁸ 使者.

Messiah *n.* mi² sai⁴ ya³ 彌賽亞.

metal *n.* chin¹ shu³ 金屬.

metallic *a.* chin¹ shu³ te¹ 金屬的.

metallurgy *n.* yeh³ chin¹ shu³ 冶金術.

metaphor *n.* yin³ yü⁴ 隱喻, an⁴ pi³ 暗比.

meteor *n.* yün³ hsing¹ 隕星, liu² hsing¹ 流星.

meter *n.* mi³ t'u² 米突, kung¹ ch'ih³ 公尺, (*meas-* **method** *n.* fang¹ fa³ 方法. 「*urer*) chi⁴ 計.

methodical *a.* ho² fa³ tse² te¹ 合法則的.

metropolis *n.* ta⁴ tu¹ shih⁴ 大都市.

mew *v.* mao¹ chiao⁴ 貓叫.

mica *n.* yün³ mu³ 雲母.

microphone *n.* ch'uan² hua⁴ ch'i⁴ 傳話器, sheng¹ yin¹ fang⁴ ta⁴ ch'i⁴ 聲音放大器.

microscope *n.* hsien³ wei¹ ching⁴ 顯微鏡.

midday *n.* chung¹ wu³ 中午.

middle *a.* chung¹ chien¹ te¹ 中間的; ～ **ages**, chung¹ shih⁴ chi⁴ 中世紀; ～ **class**, chung¹ teng³ she⁴ hui⁴ 中等社會; ～ **life**, chung¹ nien² 中年; ～ **school**, chung¹ hsüeh² hsiao⁴ 中學校.

middleway *adv.* pan⁴ t'u² te¹ 半途的, chung¹ t'u²

midnight *n.* wu³ yeh⁴ 午夜. 「te¹ 中途的.

midst *n.* chung¹ pu⁴ 中部, chung¹ chien¹ 中間.

midsummer *n.* chung⁴ hsia⁴ 仲夏; *a.* chung⁴ hsia⁴ te¹ 仲夏的. 「*fu*⁴ 助產婦.

midwife *n.* chieh¹ sheng¹ p'o² 接生婆, chu⁴ ch'an⁸

mien *n.* i² piao³ 儀表, t'ai⁴'t'u⁴ 態度.

might *n.* li⁴ 力.

mighty *a.* yu³ li⁴ te¹ 有力的, chü⁴ ta⁴ te¹ 巨大的.

migrate *v.* i² chü¹ 移居.

migration *n.* ch'ien¹ i² 遷移.

162

mil *n.* mi⁴ wei⁴ 密位.

mild *a.* wen¹ ho² te¹ 溫和的.

mildew *n.* mei² chün⁴ 霉菌.

mile *n.* li³ 哩, ying¹ li³ 英里.

military *a.* chün¹ shih⁴ te¹ 軍事的; *n.* (*soldier*) shih⁴ ping¹ 士兵, (*army*) chün¹ tui⁴ 軍隊; ~ **academy,** chün¹ kuan¹ hsüeh² hsiao⁴ 軍官學校; ~ **affairs,** chün¹ wu⁴ 軍務; ~ **age,** cheng¹ ping¹ nien² ling² 徵兵年齡; ~ **attache,** lu⁴ chün¹ wu³ kuan¹ 陸軍武官; ~ **authority,** chün¹ shih⁴ tang¹ chü² 軍事當局; ~ **correspondent,** sui² chün¹ chi⁴ che³ 隨軍記者; ~ **courtesy,** lu⁴ chün¹ li³ chieh² 陸軍禮節; ~ **discipline,** chün¹ chi⁴ 軍紀; ~ **education,** chün¹ shih⁴ chiao⁴ yü⁴ 軍事教育; ~ **expenditure,** chün¹ fei⁴ 軍費; ~ **government,** chün¹ cheng¹ fu³ 軍政府; ~ **history,** chan⁴ shih³ 戰史; ~ **intelligence,** chün¹ shih⁴ ch'ing² pao⁴ 軍事情報; ~ **mission,** chün¹ shih⁴ tai⁴ piao³ t'uan² 軍事代表團; ~ **police,** hsien⁴ ping¹ 憲兵; ~ **review,** yüeh¹ ping¹ 閱兵; ~ **secret,** chün¹ shih⁴ pi⁴ mi⁴ 軍事祕密; ~ **service,** ping¹ i⁴ 兵役; ~ **system,** chün¹ chih⁴ 軍制.

militia *n.* min² ping¹ 民兵, min² chün¹ 民軍.

milk *n.* niu² ju³ 牛乳, (*mother's*) ju³ 乳; *v.* chi² ju³ 擠乳.

milkman *n.* mai⁴ niu² ju² che³ 賣牛乳者.

milky *a.* ju³ pai² se⁴ te¹ 乳白色的.

mill *n.* (*machine*) mo² ku³ chi¹ 磨穀機, (*manufactory*) chih⁴ tsao⁴ ch'ang³ 製造廠.

millet *n.* shu³ 黍.

million *n.* pai³ wan⁴ 百萬; *a.* pai³ wan⁴ te¹ 百萬的.

millionaire, millionnaire *n.* pai³ wan⁴ fu⁴weng¹ 百萬富翁.

mimeograph *v.* fu⁴ yin⁴ 複印.

mimic *v.* mo² fang³ 摹倣.

mimicry *n.* mo² fang³ 摹倣.

mince *v.* ch'ieh¹ sui⁴ 切碎.

mind *n.* hsin¹ 心; *v.* (*take notice*) chu⁴ i⁴ 注意.

mindful *a.* liu² i⁴ te¹ 留意的.

mine *pron.* wo³ te¹ 我的; *n.* k'uang⁴ 礦, ti⁴ lei² 地雷; ~ **detector,** ti⁴ lei² sou³ so³ ch'i⁴ 地雷搜索器(軍); ~ **layer,** pu⁴ lei² t'ing³ 佈雷艇(軍).

163

miner *n.* k'uang⁴ kung¹ 礦工.

mineral *n.* k'uang⁴ wu⁴ 礦物; *a.* han² k'uang⁴ wu⁴ te¹ 含礦物的.

mineralogy *n.* k'uang⁴ wu⁴ hsüeh² 礦物學.

mingle *v.* hun⁴ ho² 混合.

mining *n.* ts'ai³ k'uang⁴ 採礦.

minister *n.* (*church*) mu⁴ shih¹ 牧師, (*government*) pu⁴ chang³ 部長, (*foreign country*) kung¹ shih³ 公使.

ministry *n.* (*department*) pu⁴ 部; ～ **of Communication***, chiao¹ t'ung¹ pu⁴ 交通部*; ～ **of Economics***, ching¹ chi⁴ pu⁴ 經濟部*; ～ **of Education***, chiao⁴ yü⁴ pu⁴ 教育部*; ～ **of Finance***, ts'ai² cheng⁴ pu⁴ 財政部*; ～ **of Foreign Affairs***, wai⁴ chiao¹ pu⁴ 外交部*; ～ **of Justice***, ssu¹ fa³ hsing² cheng⁴ pu⁴ 司法行政部*; ～ **of National Defense***, kuo² fang² pu⁴ 國防部*; ～ **of the Interior***, nei⁴ cheng⁴ pu⁴ 內政部*.

minor *a.* (*smaller*) chiao⁴ hsiao³ te¹ 較小的, (*lesser*) chiao⁴ shao³ te¹ 較少的; *n.* wei⁴ ch'eng² nien² 〔che³ 未成年者.

minority *n.* shao³ shu⁴ 少數.

mint *n.* po⁴ ho² 薄荷, (*money*) tsao⁴ pi⁴ ch'ang³ 造幣廠; *v.* tsao⁴ pi⁴ 造幣.

minute *n.* fen¹ 分, (*short time*) p'ien¹ k'o⁴ 片刻; *a.* hsi⁴ wei¹ te¹ 細微的.

miracle *n.* ch'i² chi⁴ 奇跡.

miraculous *a.* ch'i² miao⁴ te¹ 奇妙的, shen² ch'i² te¹ 神奇的. 〔ching⁴ 幻境.

mirage *n.* hai³ shih⁴ ch'en² lou² 海市蜃樓, huan⁴

mire *n.* juan³ ni² 軟泥.

mirror *n.* ching⁴ 鏡.

mirth *n.* yü² k'uai⁴ 愉快.

mirthful *a.* yü² k'uai⁴ te¹ 愉快的.

misapply *v.* wu⁴ yung⁴ 誤用, ts'o⁴ yung⁴ 錯用.

misbehave *v.* hsing² wei² pu² cheng⁴ 行為不正.

miscalculate *v.* wu⁴ suan⁴ 誤算.

miscalculation *n.* wu⁴ suan⁴ 誤算.

miscarriage *n.* (*failure*) shih¹ pai⁴ 失敗.

miscarry *v.* shih¹ pai⁴ 失敗.

miscellaneous *a.* ling² sui⁴ te¹ 零碎的.

mischance *n.* e⁴ yün⁴ 惡運, pu² hsing⁴ 不幸.

mischief *n.* (*injury*) sun³ hai⁴ 損害.

mischievous *a.* sun³ hai⁴ te¹ 損害的.

misconduct *n.* p'in³ hsing⁴ pu⁴ tuan¹ 品行不端.

misdeed *n.* e⁴ hsing² 惡行.

miser *n.* shou³ ts'ai² nu² 守財奴.

miserable *a.* k'o³ lien² te¹ 可憐的.

miserly *a.* lin⁴ se⁴ te¹ 吝嗇的.

misery *n.* t'ung⁴ k'u³ 痛苦.

misfortune *n.* pu² hsing⁴ 不幸, e⁴ yün⁴ 惡運.

misgiving *n.* i² chü⁴ 疑懼, pu² an¹ 不安.

mishap *n.* hsiao³ tsai¹ 小災, hsiao³ huo⁴ 小禍.

mislead *v.* wu⁴ tao³ 誤導, (*deceive*) ch'i¹ p'ien⁴ 欺騙. 「pan⁴ ts'o⁴ 辦錯.

mismanage *v.* ch'u³ chih⁴ shih¹ tang⁴ 處置失當,

misprint *n.* wu⁴ yin⁴ 誤印.

misquote *v.* wu⁴ yin³ yung⁴ 誤引用.

misrepresent *v.* wu⁴ shu⁴ 誤述.

misrepresentation *n.* wei⁴ yen² 偽言.

miss *v.* (*not seize*) shih¹ ch'üeh⁴ 失却; *n.* (*Miss, only put before a girl's or unmarried woman's name*) nü³ shih⁴ 女士, hsiao² chieh³ 小姐.

missile *a.* k'o³ chih² te¹ 可擲的, k'o³ she⁴ te¹ 可射

missing *a.* (*in action*) shih¹ tsung¹ 失踪(軍). 「的.

mission *n.* shih³ ming⁴ 使命, (*church*) ch'uan² chiao⁴ shih⁴ 傳教士. 「chiao⁴ shih⁴ 宣教師.

missionary *n.* ch'uan² chiao⁴ shih⁴ 傳教士, hsüan⁴

missive *n.* han² chien⁴ 函件.

mist *n.* wu⁴ 霧.

mistake *n.* ts'o⁴ wu⁴ 錯誤; *v.* wu⁴ chieh³ 誤解.

mister *n.* hsien¹ sheng¹ 先生, ko² hsia⁴ 閣下.

mistress *n.* chu³ fu⁴ 主婦.

mistrust *v.* huai² i² 懷疑.

misty *a.* yu³ wu⁴ te¹ 有霧的.

misunderstand *v.* wu⁴ chieh³ 誤解.

misunderstanding *n.* wu⁴ chieh³ 誤解.

misuse *n.* lan⁴ yung⁴ 濫用; *v.* lan⁴ yung⁴ 濫用, (*abuse*) nüeh⁴ tai⁴ 虐待.

mitigate *v.* chien³ ch'ing¹ 減輕.

mix *v.* hun⁴ ho² 混合.

mixture *n.* hun⁴ ho² wu⁴ 混合物.

moan v. shen¹ yin² 呻吟, pei¹ ch'i⁴ 悲泣.

moat n. hao² kou¹ 壕溝.

mob n. min² chung⁴ 民眾, (*lawless crowd*) pao⁴ t'u² 暴徒.

mobile a. i² tung⁴ te¹ 移動的; ~ **troops,** chi¹ tung⁴ pu⁴ tui⁴ 機動部隊.

mobility n. chi¹ tung⁴ hsing⁴ 機動性.

mobilization n. tung⁴ yüan² 動員; ~ **order,** tung⁴ yüan² ling⁴ 動員令; ~ **plan,** tung⁴ yüan² chi⁴ hua⁴ 動員計劃.

mobilize v. tung⁴ yüan² 動員.

mock a. mo² fang⁴ te¹ 摹倣的; v. ch'ao⁴ hsiao⁴ 嘲笑.

model n. (*pattern*) mo² hsing² 模型, (*ideal*) mo² fan⁴ 模範.

moderate a. chung¹ yung¹ te¹ 中庸的.

moderation n. chung¹ yung¹ 中庸.

modern a. hsien⁴ tai⁴ te¹ 現代的, hsin¹ shih⁴ te¹ 新式的.

modest a. ch'ien⁴ sun⁴ te¹ 謙遜的.

modesty n. ch'ien⁴ sun⁴ 謙遜.

modification n. (*change*) hsiu¹ cheng⁴ 修正.

modify v. hsiu¹ cheng⁴ 修正.

modulate v. t'iao² chieh⁴ 調節.

Mohammedan n. hui² chiao⁴ t'u² 回教徒; a. hui² chiao⁴ te¹ 回教的.

moist a. ch'ao² shih¹ te¹ 潮濕的. 潮潤.

moisten v. shih³ ch'ao² shih¹ 使潮濕, ch'ao² jun² 潮潤.

moisture n. shih¹ ch'i⁴ 濕氣.

mold n. mo² hsing² 模型; v. mo² tsao⁴ 模造.

molder n. peng¹ huai⁴ 崩壞.

moldy a. sheng¹ mei² te¹ 生霉的.

mole n. chih⁴ 痣, (*animal*) yen² shu³ 鼹鼠.

molest v. fan² jao³ 煩擾.

molestation n. fan² jao³ 煩擾.

mollify v. chen⁴ ching⁴ 鎮靜, k'uan¹ wei⁴ 寬慰.

molt v. t'o¹ huan⁴ 脫換.

moment n. ch'ing³ k'o⁴ 頃刻.

momentary a. ch'ing³ k'o⁴ te¹ 頃刻的.

momentous a. chung⁴ yao⁴ te¹ 重要的.

monarch n. chün¹ chu³ 君主.

monarchic, monarchical a. chün¹ chu⁸ te¹ 君主的, chuan¹ chih⁴ chün¹ chu⁸ te¹ 專制君主的.

monarchy *n.* chün¹ chu³ cheng⁴ t'i³ 君主政體, chün¹ chu³ kuo² 君主國.

monastery *n.* (*monks*) ho² shang⁴ miao⁴ 和尚廟, (*Chinese nuns*) ni² an¹ 尼庵.

Monday *n.* hsing¹ ch'i² i¹ 星期一.

money *n.* ch'ien² pi⁴ 錢幣, ts'ai² fu⁴ 財富; ~ **market,** chin¹ jung² shih⁴ ch'ang³ 金融市場.

Mongolian *a.* meng³ ku¹ jen² te¹ 蒙古人的, (*language*) meng³ ku¹ yü³ te¹ 蒙古語的; ~ **and Tibetan Affairs Commission***, meng³ tsang⁴ wei³ yüan² hui⁴ 蒙藏委員會*.

mongrel *a.* tsa² chung³ te¹ 雜種的.

monk *n.* seng¹ 僧.

monkey *n.* hou² 猴.

monoplane *n.* tan¹ i⁴ fei¹ chi¹ 單翼飛機.

monopoly *n.* chuan¹ mai⁴ 專賣.

monosyllable *n.* tan¹ yin¹ chieh² tzu⁴ 單音節字.

monotonous *a.* tan¹ tiao⁴ te¹ 單調的.

monotony *n.* tan¹ tiao⁴ 單調.

monster *n.* kuai⁴ wu⁴ 怪物.

monstrous *a.* (*huge*) chü⁴ ta⁴ te¹ 巨大的.

month *n.* yüeh⁴ 月.

monument *n.* chi⁴ nien⁴ wu⁴ 紀念物.

mood *n.* hsin¹ ching⁴ 心境.

moody *a.* kuai⁴ li⁴ te¹ 乖戾的, i⁴ yü⁴ te¹ 抑鬱的.

moon *n.* yüeh⁴ 月.

moonlight *n.* yüeh⁴ kuang¹ 月光.

moor *n.* huang¹ yeh³ 荒野; *v.* ting⁴ po² 碇泊.

moorings *n.* chi⁴ ch'uan² chü⁴ 繫船具.

mop *n.* t'o¹ chou³ 拖帚; *v.* sa² sao³ 洒掃.

moral *a.* tao⁴ te² te¹ 道德的; *n.* chiao⁴ hsün⁴ 教訓.

morale *n.* (*military*) shih⁴ ch'i⁴ 士氣.

morality *n.* tao⁴ te² 道德.

morals *n.* p'in³ hsing² 品行.

morass *n.* chao³ ti⁴ 沼地.

morbid *n.* pu⁴ chien⁴ ch'üan² te¹ 不健全的, ping⁴ t'ai⁴ te¹ 病態的.

more *adv.* chiao⁴ ta⁴ te¹ 較大的, chiao⁴ to¹ te¹ 較多的; ~ **or less,** ch'a¹ pu⁴ to¹ 差不多; ~ **and more,** yüeh⁴ chia¹ 越加; ~ **than ever,** yüeh⁴ fa¹ 越發.

moreover *adv.* erh² ch'ieh³ 而且, tsai⁴ che³ 再者.

morning *n.* tsao³ ch'en² 早晨.

morphine, morphia *n.* ma³ fei¹ 嗎啡.

morrow *n.* ming² t'ien¹ 明天.

morsel *n.* i⁴ k'ou³ 一口, i⁴ hsieh¹ 一些.

mortal *a.* pu⁴ neng² mien³ ssu³ te¹ 不能免死的; *n.* fan² jen² 凡人.

mortar *n.* hui¹ ni² 灰泥, (*gun*) chiu⁴ p'ao⁴ 臼礮, p'o⁴ chi¹ p'ao⁴ 迫擊砲. 「典質, ti³ ya¹ 抵押.

mortgage *n.* ti³ ya¹ p'in³ 抵押品; *v.* tien³ chih³

mortgagee *n.* shou⁴ ti³ ya¹ che³ 受抵押者.

mortuary *a.* mai² tsang⁴ te¹ 埋葬的.

mosaic *n.* ch'ien¹ kung¹ 嵌工.

mosque *n.* hui² chiao⁴ t'ang² 回教堂, ch'ing¹ chen¹ ssu⁴ 清真寺.

mosquito *n.* wen² 蚊; ~ **net,** wen² chang⁴ 蚊帳.

moss *n.* hsien³ t'ai² 蘚苔.

mossy *a.* sheng¹ t'ai² te¹ 生苔的, ssu⁴ t'ai² te¹ 似 「苔的.

most *adv.* tsui⁴ 最.

moth *n.* e² 蛾.

mother *n.* mu³ ch'in¹ 母親; ~ **country,** tsu³ kuo² 祖國; ~ **tongue,** pen³ kuo² yü³ yen² 本國語言.

mother-of-pearl *n.* chen¹ chu¹ mu³ 真珠母.

motherless *a.* wu² mu³ te¹ 無母的.

motherly *a.* ju² mu³ te¹ 如母的.

motion *n.* yün⁴ tung⁴ 運動.

motionless *a.* pu² tung⁴ te¹ 不動的.

motive *n.* tung⁴ chi¹ 動機.

motor *n.* fa¹ tung⁴ chi¹ 發動機. 「踏車.

motorcar *n.* ch'i⁴ ch'e¹ 汽車.

motorcycle *n.* chi¹ ch'i⁴ chiao³ t'a⁴ ch'e¹ 機器脚

motorist *n.* chia⁴ tzu⁴ tung⁴ ch'e¹ che³ 駕自動車 「者.

motto *n.* chen¹ yen² 箴言, ko² yen² 格言.

mound *n.* t'u³ ti¹ 土堤, t'u³ tun¹ 土墩.

mount *v.* (*go up*) teng¹ 登, (*horse*) ch'i² 騎.

mount *n.* kao¹ shan¹ 高山.

mountain *n.* kao¹ shan¹ 高山; ~ **artillery,** shan¹ p'ao⁴ ping¹ 山砲兵; ~ **gun,** shan¹ p'ao⁴ 山砲; ~ **range,** shan¹ mo⁴ 山脈; ~ **ridge,** shan¹ chi³ 山脊; ~ **warfare,** shan¹ ti⁴ chan⁴ 山地戰.

mountaineer *n.* shan¹ chü¹ che³ 山居者.

mountainous *a.* to¹ shan¹ te¹ 多山的.

mourn *v.* ai¹ t'ung⁴ 哀慟, pei¹ shang¹ 悲傷.

mourner *n.* ai¹ t'ung⁴ che³ 哀慟者. 「悲傷的.

mournful *a.* ai¹ t'ung⁴ te¹ 哀慟的, pei¹ shang¹ te¹

mourning *n.* pei¹ shang¹ 悲傷, ai¹ tao⁴ 哀悼.

mouse *n.* hsiao² shu³ 小鼠.

moustache *n.* hu² tzu¹ 鬍子.

mouth *n.* k'ou³ 口, tsui³ 嘴.

mouthful *n.* i⁴ k'ou³ 一口, shao³ liang⁴ 少量.

movable *a.* k'o³ i² tung⁴ te¹ 可移動的.

move *v.* i² tung⁴ 移動.

movement *n.* yün⁴ tung⁴ 運動.

movie *n.* huo² tung⁴ tien⁴ ying³ 活動電影; ～ **fan,** ying³ mi² 影迷.

moving *a.* tung⁴ te¹ 動的. 「tui¹ 禾堆(割禾).

mow *n.* (*grass*) ts'ao³ tui¹ 草堆(刈草), (*grain*) ho²

much *a.* to¹ te¹ 多的; *adv.* shen² 甚.

mucous *a.* nien² yeh⁴ te¹ 黏液的.

mucus *n.* nien² yeh⁴ 黏液.

mud *n.* ni² 泥.

muddy *a.* ni² ning⁴ te¹ 泥濘的.

muff *n.* nuan³ shou² t'ung³ 煖手筒.

muffler *n.* wei² chin¹ 圍巾, (*motor*) hsiao¹ yin¹

mufti *n.* pien⁴ i¹ 便衣. 「ch'i⁴ 消音器.

mug *n.* pei¹ 杯. 「色.

mulberry *n.* sang¹ 桑, (*color*) an⁴ ch'ih⁴ se⁴ 暗赤

mule *n.* lo² 騾. 「fu⁴ te¹ 很豐富的.

multifarious *a.* to¹ chung³ te¹ 多種的, hen³ feng¹

multiplication *n.* fan² chih² 繁殖, (*mathematics*) ch'eng² fa³ 乘法.

multiplicity *n.* to¹ yang⁴ 多樣, hsü³ to¹ 許多.

multiply *v.* (*increase*) tseng¹ to¹ 增多, (*time*) ch'eng² 乘. 「群衆.

multitude *n.* to¹ shu⁴ 多數, (*crowd*) ch'ün² chung⁴

mummery *n.* chia³ mien⁴ ch'ü⁴ chü⁴ 假面趣劇, hua² chi¹ piao³ yen³ 滑稽表演.

mummy *n.* mu⁴ nai³ i¹ 木乃伊, kan¹ shih¹ 乾屍.

mumps *n.* liu² hsing² hsing² sai¹ hsien⁴ yen² 流行性腮腺炎. 「的.

municipal *a.* shih⁴ te¹ 市的, shih⁴ cheng⁴ te¹ 市政

169

municipality *n.* shih⁴ 市.

munificence *n.* po² shih¹ 博施.

munificent *a.* po² shih¹ te¹ 博施的.

munition *n.* chün¹ huo³ 軍火.

murder *n.* mou² sha¹ 謀殺; *v.* mou² sha¹ 謀殺.

murderer *n.* hsiung¹ shou³ 凶手, an⁴ sha¹ che¹ 暗殺者. ⌐的.

murky *a.* hei⁴ an⁴ te¹ 黑暗的, yin¹ ch'en² te¹ 陰沉

murmur *n.* ch'an² ch'an² chih¹ sheng¹ 潺潺之聲; ⌐*v.* ti¹ yü³ 低語.

muscle *n.* chin¹ jou⁴ 筋肉.

muscular *a.* chin¹ jou⁴ te¹ 筋肉的, (*strong*) ch'iang² chuang⁴ te¹ 強壯的.

muse *v.* mo⁴ ssu¹ 默思, ch'en² hsiang³ 沉想.

mushroom *n.* chün⁴ 菌.

music *n.* yin¹ yüeh⁴ 音樂.

musical *a.* yin¹ yüeh⁴ te¹ 音樂的; ~ **instrument,** yüeh⁴ ch'i⁴ 樂器.

musician *n.* yin¹ yüeh⁴ chia¹ 音樂家.

musk *n.* she⁴ hsiang¹ 麝香.

muslin *n.* po² mien² pu⁴ 薄綿布, yang² sha¹ 洋紗.

must *n.* (*grape wine*) hsin¹ p'u² t'ao² chiu³ 新葡萄酒; *v. aux.* pi⁴ hsü¹ 必須, pi⁴ ting⁴ 必定.

mustard *n.* chieh⁴ 芥, chieh⁴ fen³ 芥粉; ~ **gas,** chieh⁴ tzu¹ ch'i⁴ 芥子氣.

musty *a.* fa¹ mei² te¹ 發霉的, hsiu² fu³ te¹ 朽腐的.

mute *a.* (*silent*) chien¹ mo⁴ te¹ 緘默的; *n.* ya³ tzu¹ 啞子.

mutilate *v.* ch'ieh¹ tuan⁴ 切斷.

mutilation *n.* ch'ieh¹ tuan⁴ 切斷.

mutinous *a.* pei⁴ p'an⁴ te¹ 背叛的.

mutiny *n.* pei⁴ p'an⁴ 背叛, ping¹ pien⁴ 兵變.

mutter *v.* nan² nan² ti¹ yü³ 喃喃低語, su⁴ yüan⁴ 訴怨.

mutton *n.* yang² jou⁴ 羊肉.

mutual *a.* hsiang¹ hu⁴ te¹ 相互的, kung⁴ t'ung² te¹ 共同的; ~ **support,** hu⁴ hsiang¹ chih¹ yüan² 互相支援.

muzzle *n.* (*gun*) huo³ shen¹ k'ou³ 火身口; ~ **cap,** ch'iang¹ k'ou³ mao⁴ 槍口帽; ~ **velocity,** ch'u¹ su⁴ 初速.

my *pron.* wo³ te¹ 我的.

myself *pron.* wo³ tzu⁴ chi³ 我自己.

mysterious *a.* shen² mi⁴ te¹ 神祕的, ch'i² miao⁴ te¹ 奇妙的.

mystery *n.* shen² mi⁴ 神祕.

myth *n.* shen² hua⁴ 神話.
mythology *n.* shen² hua⁴ chi² 神話集.

N

nail *n.* ting¹ 釘, (*finger*) chih¹ chia³ 指甲; *v.* ting¹
naked *a.* ch'ih¹ lo³ te¹ 赤裸的. ⌈lao³ 釘牢.
name *n.* ming² tzu⁴ 名字; *v.* ch'ü³ ming² 取名.
nameless *a.* wu² ming² te¹ 無名的.
namely *adv.* chi² shih⁴ 即是.
nap *n.* hsiao³ shui⁴ 小睡; *v.* chia³ mei⁴ 假寐.
nape *n.* t'ou² pei⁴ 頭背.
naphtha *n.* shih² yu² ching¹ 石油精.
napkin *n.* ts'an¹ chin¹ 餐巾. ⌈麻醉劑.
narcotic *a.* ma² tsui⁴ te¹ 麻醉的; *n.* ma² tsui⁴ chi⁴
narrate *v.* chiang³ 講, hsü⁴ shu⁴ 敘述.
narration *n.* chi⁴ shih⁴ wen² 記事文.
narrative *n.* (*story*) ku⁴ shih⁴ 故事.
narrow *a.* hsia² chai³ te¹ 狹窄的; *v.* shih³ hsia²
hsiao³ 使狹小; ～ **front,** hsia² chai³ cheng⁴
mien⁴ 狹窄正面.
nasal *a.* pi² te¹ 鼻的, pi² yin¹ te¹ 鼻音的.
nasturtium *n.* chin¹ lien² hua⁴ 金蓮花(植).
nasty *a.* (*dirty*) wu¹ hui⁴ te¹ 汚穢的. ⌈tsu² 民族.
nation *n.* (*country*) kuo² chia¹ 國家, (*people*) min²
national *a.* kuo² chia¹ te¹ 國家的, min² tsu² te¹ 民
族的; ～ **anthem,** kuo² ko¹ 國歌; ～ **Assembly,**
kuo² min² ta⁴ hui⁴ 國民大會; ～ **Congress (US),**
kuo² hui⁴ 國會(美); ～ **debt,** kuo² chai⁴ 國債; ～
defence, kuo² fang² 國防; ～ **government,**
kuo² min² cheng⁴ fu³ 國民政府; ～ **holiday,**
kuo² ting⁴ chieh² jih⁴ 國定節日; ～ **policy,** kuo²
nationality *n.* kuo² chi² 國籍. ⌈ts'e⁴ 國策.
native *n.* pen³ ti⁴ jen² 本地人; *a.* pen³ ti⁴ te¹ 本地
的.
natural *a.* tzu⁴ jan² te¹ 自然的; ～ **cover,** t'ien¹
jan² yen³ pi⁴ 天然掩蔽(軍).
nature *n.* tzu⁴ jan² 自然.
naughty *a.* wan² p'i² te¹ 頑皮的.

nausea *n.* e³ hsin¹ 惡心(醫).

nauseous *a.* e³ te¹ 惡的.　　　　　　「li³ 海里.

nautical *a.* ch'uan² po⁴ te¹ 船舶的; ~ **mile,** hai²

naval *a.* hai³ chün¹ te¹ 海軍的; ~ **Academy**
(US), hai³ chün¹ hsüeh² hsiao⁴ 海軍學校(美); ~
attache, hai³ chün¹ wu³ kuan¹ 海軍武官; ~
base, hai³ chün¹ chi¹ ti⁴ 海軍基地(軍); ~ **blockade,** hai³ chün¹ feng¹ so³ 海軍封鎖(軍); ~ **man-
oeuvres,** hai³ chün¹ yen³ hsi² 海軍演習(軍).

navigable *a.* k'o³ hang² te¹ 可航行的.

navigate *v.* hang² hsing² 航行.

navigation *n.* hang² hsing² 航行.

navigator *n.* (*sea*) hang² hai³ chia¹ 航海家, (*air*)
ling³ hang² che³ 領航者.

navy *n.* hai³ chün¹ 海軍; ~ **blue,** shen¹ lan² se⁴ 深
藍色; ~ **Department** (US), hai³ chün¹ pu⁴ 海
軍部(美); ~ **yard,** hai³ chün¹ tsao⁴ ch'uan² so³
海軍造船所.

near *prep.* chieh¹ chin⁴ 接近; *a.* chin⁴ te¹ 近的;
adv. chin⁴ ti⁴ 近地; ~ **horse,** fu² ma³ 服馬(軍).

nearness *n.* chieh¹ chin² 接近.

neat *a.* cheng³ chieh² te¹ 整潔的.

necessarily *adv.* pi⁴ ting⁴ 必定.

necessary *a.* pi⁴ hsü¹ te¹ 必需的.

necessitate *v.* shih³ pi⁴ hsü¹ 使必需.

necessity *n.* pi⁴ hsü¹ 必需.

neck *n.* ching³ pu⁴ 頸部.

necklace *n.* hsiang⁴ lien⁴ 項鍊.

need *n., v.* pi⁴ yao⁴ 必要, hsü¹ yao⁴ 需要.

needful *a.* hsü¹ yao⁴ te¹ 需要的.

needle *n.* chen¹ 針.

needless *a.* wu² hsü¹ te¹ 無須的.

nefarious *a.* hsiung¹ e⁴ te¹ 兇惡的.

negative *a.* (*saying no*) fou³ jen⁴ te¹ 否認的, (*not
positive*) fan³ mien⁴ te¹ 反面的; *n.* (*film*) ti³
p'ien⁴ 底片(攝).

neglect *n., v.* hu¹ lüeh⁴ 忽略.

negligence *n.* su¹ hu¹ 疏忽.

negligent *a.* su¹ hu¹ te¹ 疏忽的.

negotiable *a.* k'o³ ts'o¹ shang¹ te¹ 可磋商的.

negotiate *v.* chiao¹ she⁴ 交涉, ts'o¹ shang¹ 磋商.

negotiation *n.* ts'o¹ shang¹ 磋商, shang¹ liang² 商

negress *n.* nü³ hei¹ jen² 女黑人. ⌐量.

negro *n.* hei¹ jen² 黑人.

neigh *n.* ma³ ssu¹ sheng¹ 馬嘶聲; *v.* ssu¹ 嘶(馬).

neighbor *n.* lin² chü¹ 鄰居.

neighborhood *n.* lin² chü¹ 鄰居.

neighboring *a.* lin² chin⁴ te¹ 鄰近的.

neighborly *a.* lin² chin⁴ te¹ 鄰近的.

neither *pron.* chün¹ pu⁴ 均不.

nerve *n.* shen² ching¹ 神經; ~ **war,** shen² ching¹
chan⁴ 神經戰.

nervous *a.* shen² ching¹ te¹ 神經的, shen² ching¹
kuo⁴ min³ te¹ 神經過敏的; ~ **breakdown,** shen²
ching¹ shih¹ ch'ang² 神經失常.

nest *n.* ch'ao² 巢, wo¹ 窩, hsüeh⁴ 穴.

net *n.* wang³ 網; *a.* (*business*) ch'un² ching⁴ te¹ 純
淨的; ~ **price,** shih² chia⁴ 實價; ~ **profit,**
ching⁴ li⁴ 淨利; ~ **weight,** ching⁴ chung⁴ 淨重.

nettle *n.* hsin² ma² chen³ 蕁麻疹(醫), feng¹ chen³
k'uai⁴ 風疹塊(醫).

network *n.* wang³ 網.

neuralgia *n.* shen² ching¹ t'ung⁴ 神經痛.

neuter *a.* chung¹ li⁴ te¹ 中立的, (*gender*) wu²
hsing⁴ te¹ 無性的.

neutral *a.* chung¹ li⁴ te¹ 中立的.

neutrality *n.* chung¹ li⁴ 中立.

neutralize *v.* shih³ chung¹ li⁴ 使中立.

never *adv.* ts'ung² pu⁴ 從不, yung³ pu⁴ 永不.

nevertheless *adv.* jan² erh² 然而.

new *a.* hsin¹ te¹ 新的; ~ **guard,** chieh¹ pan¹
wei⁴ ping¹ 接班衛兵(軍).

newly *adv.* (*recently*) hsin¹ chin⁴ te¹ 新近的.

news *n.* hsin¹ wen² 新聞, hsiao¹ hsi² 消息.

newspaper *n.* hsin¹ wen² chih³ 新聞紙, pao⁴
chih³ 報紙.

next *a.* ch'i² tz'u⁴ te¹ 其次的. ⌐chih³ 報紙.

nice *a.* mei³ hao³ te¹ 美好的.

nickel *n.* nieh⁴ 鎳, nieh⁴ pi⁴ 鎳幣.

nickname *n.* pieh² hao⁴ 別號, hsiao³ ming² 小名.

niggardly *a.* lin⁴ se⁴ te¹ 吝嗇的.

night *n.* yeh⁴ 夜; ~**attack,** yeh⁴ chien¹ kung¹
chi¹ 夜間攻擊(軍); ~ **blindness,** yeh⁴ mang² 夜

盲(瘠); ~ **bombing,** yeh⁴ chien¹ hung¹ cha⁴ 夜間轟炸(軍); ~ **club,** yeh⁴ tsung³ hui⁴ 夜總會; ~ **letter,** yeh⁴ tien¹ pao⁴ 夜電報; ~ **march,** yeh⁴ hsing² chün¹ 夜行軍(軍); ~ **school,** yeh⁴ hsiao⁴ 夜校; ~ **withdrawal,** yeh⁴ chien¹ ch'e⁴ t'ui⁴ 夜間撤退(軍).

nightcap n. shui⁴ mao⁴ 睡帽.

nightdress n. shui⁴ i¹ 睡衣.

nightingale n. yeh⁴ ying¹ 夜鶯.

nightshirt n. nan² shui⁴ i¹ 男睡衣.

nightly a. mei³ yeh⁴ te¹ 每夜的, (at night) yeh⁴ chien¹ te¹ 夜間的; adv. mei³ yeh⁴ 每夜, (at night) tsai⁴ yeh⁴ chien¹ 在夜間.

nightmare n. meng⁴ yen³ 夢魘.

nimble a. ch'ing¹ k'uai⁴ te¹ 輕快的.

nine n. chiu³ 九; a. chiu³ te¹ 九的.

nip v. (bite) yao³ 咬.

nipple n. ju⁸ t'ou² 乳頭.

no a. pu² shih⁴ te¹ 不是的; adv. pu⁴ 不, pu² shih⁴ 不是.

nobility n. (nobleman) kuei⁴ tsu² 貴族.

noble a. kao⁴ kuei⁴ te¹ 高貴的, kuei⁴ tsu² te¹ 貴族的, kao¹ shang⁴ te¹ 高尚的.

nobleman n. kuei⁴ tsu² 貴族.

nobody pron. wu² jen² 無人.

nocturnal a. yeh⁴ chien¹ 夜間.

nod n. tien³ t'ou² 點頭; v. tien³ t'ou² 點頭.

noise n. hsiang³ sheng¹ 響聲, hsüan¹ hua² 喧嘩.

noisy a. hsüan¹ tsao⁴ te¹ 喧噪的.

nominal a. kua⁴ ming² te¹ 掛名的.

nominate v. t'i² ming² 提名, (appoint) jen⁴ ming⁴ 任命.

nomination n. jen⁴ ming⁴ 任命.

nominee n. pei⁴ jen⁴ ming⁴ che³ 被任命者.

noncommissioned a. wu² wei³ ling⁴ te¹ 無委令狀的.

none pron. (person) wu² jen² 無人, (not any) hao² wu² 毫無.

nonprofit a. wu² li⁴ te¹ 無利的.

nonsense n. hao² wu² i⁴ i⁴ 毫無意義.

nonstop a. pu⁴ t'ing² te¹ 不停的.

nook n. chiao³ 角, (hidden spot) yin³ so³ 隱所.

noon n. cheng⁴ wu³ 正午.

noose n. huo² chieh² 活結.

nor conj. i⁴ fei¹ 亦非.

normal *a.* cheng⁴ ch'ang² te¹ 正常的.

north *n.* pei³ fang¹ 北方; *a.* pei³ fang¹ te¹ 北方的; ～ **latitude,** pei³ wei⁴ 北緯; ～ **Pole,** pei³ chi² 北極; ～ **Star,** pei³ chi² hsing¹ 北極星.

nose *n.* pi² 鼻, (*airplane*) chi¹ t'ou² 機頭, (*ship*) ch'uan² shou³ 船首, (*projectile*) tan⁴ t'ou² 彈頭; ～ **dive,** ch'ui³ chih² fu³ ch'ung¹ 垂直俯衝(軍); ～ **fuse,** tan⁴ t'ou² hsin⁴ kuan³ 彈頭信管(軍).

nostril *n.* pi² k'ung³ 鼻孔.

not *adv.* pu⁴ 不.

notable *a.* k'an¹ chu⁴ i⁴ te¹ 堪注意的.

notary *n.* kung¹ cheng⁴ jen² 公證人.

notch *v.* k'o¹ wa¹ 刻凹.

note *n.* (*memo*) pi³ chi⁴ 筆記, (*notice*) chu⁴ i⁴ 注意, (*music*) yin¹ fu² 音符; *v.* (*write*) chi⁴ lu⁴ 記錄, (*see*) chu⁴ mu⁴ yü² 注目於.

noted *a.* cho² ming² te¹ 著名的.

nothing *n.* wu² 無; *adv.* hao² wu² 毫無.

notice *n.* (*attention*) liu² hsin¹ 留心, (*information*) t'ung¹ chih¹ 通知; *v.* (*take notice of*) chu⁴ i⁴ 注意, (*give notice to*) t'ung¹ chih¹ 通知.

notify *v.* t'ung¹ kao⁴ 通告.

notion *n.* (*idea*) kai¹ nien⁴ 概念. 「的.

notorious *a.* lieh⁴ chi¹ chao¹ chang¹ te¹ 劣跡昭彰

notwithstanding *conj.* sui¹ jan² 雖然.

noun *n.* ming² tz'u² 名詞.

nourish *v.* tzu¹ yang³ 滋養.

nourishment *n.* (*food*) shih² wu⁴ 食物. 「說.

novel *a.* hsin¹ ch'i² te¹ 新奇的; *n.* hsiao³ shuo¹ 小

novelist *n.* hsiao³ shuo¹ chia¹ 小說家.

novelty *n.* hsin¹ ch'i² 新奇.

November *n.* shih² i² yüeh¹ 十一月.

novice *n.* (*beginner*) sheng¹ shou³ 生手.

now *adv.* hsien⁴ chin¹ 現今, tz'u³ k'o¹ 此刻.

nowhere *adv.* wu² ch'u⁴ 無處.

nowise *adv.* ch'üan² pu⁴ 全不, hao² pu⁴ 毫不.

noxious *a.* (*poisonous*) yu³ tu² te¹ 有毒的, (*harmful*) yu³ hai³ te¹ 有害的.

nucleus *n.* (*central*) ho² hsin¹ 核心.

nude *a.* ch'ih⁴ lo³ te¹ 赤裸的.

nudity *n.* ch'ih⁴ lo³ 赤裸.

nuisance *n.* jao³ jen² shih⁴ wu⁴ 擾人事物.

null *a.* wu² hsiao⁴ te¹ 無效的; ~ **and void,** tso⁴

nullity *n.* wu² hsiao⁴ 無效. ⌐fei⁴ 作廢.

numb *a.* ma² mu⁴ te¹ 麻木的, shih¹ kan³ chüeh² te¹ 失感覺的.

number *n.* (*figure*) shu⁴ mu⁴ 數目, (*series*) hao⁴ ma³ 號碼, (*suffix*) hao⁴ shu⁴ 號數; ~ **of hits,** ming⁴ chung⁴ shu⁴ 命中數(軍).

numberless *a.* wu² shu⁴ te¹ 無數的.

numerical *a.* shu⁴ te¹ 數的, piao³ shu⁴ te¹ 表數的.

numerous *a.* wu² shu⁴ te¹ 無數的. ⌐nü³ 修道女.

nun *n.* (*Chinese*) ni² ku¹ 尼姑, (*Western*) hsiu¹ tao⁴

nunnery *n.* (*Chinese*) ni² an¹ 尼庵, (*Western*) nü³ hsiu¹ tao⁴ yüan⁴ 女修道院.

nurse *n.* (*hospital*) hu⁴ shih⁴ 護士, (*family*) pao² mu³ 保姆; *v.* (*hospital*) k'an¹ hu⁴ 看護, (*wet*)

nursery *n.* yü⁴ ying¹ so³ 育嬰所. ⌐ju² pu³ 乳哺.

nut *n.* chien¹ kuo³ 堅果, (*of bolt*) lo² mu³ 螺母(機).

nutcracker *n.* chien¹ kuo³ ch'ien² 堅果鉗.

nutmeg *n.* jou⁴ tou⁴ k'ou⁴ 肉荳蔻(植). ⌐餐料.

nutriment *n.* shih² wu⁴ 食物, tzu¹ yang³ liao⁴ 滋

nutrition *n.* shih² wu⁴ 食物.

nutritious *a.* tzu¹ yang³ te¹ 滋養的.

nutshell *n.* chien¹ kuo³ k'o² 堅果殼.

O

oak *n.* hsiang⁴ shu⁴ 橡樹.

oaken *a.* hsiang⁴ mu⁴ chih⁴ te¹ 橡木製的.

oakum *n.* ma² ken¹ 麻根.

oar *n.* chiang³ 槳.

oasis *n.* lü⁴ chou¹ 綠洲, sha¹ mo⁴ wo⁴ ti⁴ 沙漠沃地.

oats *n.* yen⁴ mai⁴ 燕麥.

oath *n.* shih⁴ yen² 誓言. ⌐燕麥片.

oatmeal *n.* yen⁴ mai⁴ fen³ 燕麥粉, yen⁴ mai⁴ p'ien⁴

obdurate *a.* ying⁴ hsin¹ ch'ang² te¹ 硬心腸的.

obedience *n.* shun⁴ ts'ung² 順從.

obedient *a.* fu² ts'ung² te¹ 服從的.

obey *v.* shun⁴ ts'ung² 順從, fu² ts'ung² 服從.

176

object *n.* (*thing*) wu⁴ 物, (*aim*) mu⁴ ti⁴ 目的, (*grammar*) shou⁴ tz'u² 受詞; *v.* fan³ tui⁴ 反對.

objection *n.* fan³ tui⁴ 反對.

objectionable *a.* i⁴ ch'i² fan³ tui⁴ te¹ 易起反對的.

objective *a.* mu⁴ piao¹ 目標.

obligation *n.* i⁴ wu⁴ 義務.　　　　　　　　　「的.

obligatory *a.* pi⁴ hsü¹ te¹ 必須的, i⁴ wu⁴ te¹ 義務

oblige *v.* (*force*) ch'iang³ chih⁴ 強制, (*do a favor*) shih⁴ en¹ 施恩.　　　　　　　　　　「射(軍).

oblique *a.* hsieh² te¹ 斜的; ～ **fire,** hsieh⁴ she⁴ 斜

obliterate *v.* t'u² mo³ 塗抹, hsiao¹ mieh⁴ 消滅.

oblivion *n.* mai² mo⁴ 埋沒, wang¹ ch'üeh¹ 忘却.

oblong *a.* ch'ang² hsing² te¹ 長形的, ch'ang² fang¹ hsing² te¹ 長方形的.　　　　　　　　「yen⁴ te¹ 可厭的.

obnoxious *a.* i⁴ ch'i² fan³ tui⁴ te¹ 易起反對的, k'o³

obscene *a.* yin² hsieh² te¹ 淫褻的.

obscure *a.* pu⁴ ch'ing¹ ch'u³ te¹ 不清楚的.

obscurity *n.* mo² hu² 模糊, (*unknown*) pu⁴ cho² ming² 不著名.

obsequies *n.* tsang⁴ i² 葬儀.

observance *n.* (*obey*) tsun¹ shou³ 遵守.

observant *a.* (*observing*) kuan¹ ch'a² te¹ 觀察的.

observation *n.* kuan¹ ch'a² 觀察; ～ **airplane,** kuan¹ ts'e⁴ chi¹ 觀測機(軍); ～ **aviation,** kuan¹ ts'e⁴ fei¹ hsing² 觀測飛行(軍); ～ **ballon,** kuan¹ ts'e⁴ ch'i⁴ ch'iu² 觀測氣球(軍); ～ **of fire,** she⁴ chi¹ kuan¹ ts'e⁴ 射擊觀測(軍); ～ **post,** kuan¹ ts'e⁴ so³ 觀測所(軍).　　　　　　「文臺.

observatory *n.* (*astronomical*) t'ien¹ wen² t'ai² 天

observe *v.* (*see*) kuan¹ ch'a² 觀察, (*obey*) tsun¹ shou³ 遵守.

observer *n.* kuan¹ ch'a² che³ 觀察者, (*artillery*) kuan¹ ts'e⁴ yüan² 觀測員.

obsolete *a.* fei⁴ ch'i⁴ te¹ 廢棄的.

obstacle *n.* chang⁴ ai⁴ 障礙, chang⁴ ai⁴ wu⁴ 障礙物; ～ **race,** chang⁴ ai⁴ ching¹ tsou³ 障礙競走.

obstinacy *n.* ku⁴ chih² 固執, wan² ku⁴ 頑固.

obstinate *a.* ku⁴ chih² te¹ 固執的.

obstruct *v.* tsu³ ai⁴ 阻礙, tsu³ sai⁴ 阻塞.

obstruction *n.* tsu³ ai⁴ 阻礙, tsu³ sai⁴ 阻塞.

obtain *v.* ch'ü³ te² 取得.

obtainable *a.* k'o³ te² te¹ 可得的.

obtrusive *a.* ch'uang⁴ ju⁴ te¹ 闖入的.

obtuse *a.* tun⁴ te¹ 鈍的.

obviate *v.* hsiao¹ ch'u² 消除. 「白的.

obvious *a.* hsien³ jan² te¹ 顯然的, ming² pai² te¹ 明

occasion *n.* shih² chi¹ 時機. 「然的.

occasional *a.* sui² shih² te¹ 隨時的, ou³ jan² te¹ 偶

occult *a.* shen² mi⁴ te¹ 神祕的, shen¹ ao⁴ te¹ 深奧

occupant *n.* chan⁴ yu² che³ 佔有者. 「的.

occupation *n.* (*work*) chih⁴ yeh⁴ 職業, (*military*) chan⁴ ling³ 佔領; ~ **of a position,** chen⁴ ti⁴ chan⁴ ling³ 陣地佔領(軍).

occupy *v.* chan⁴ yu³ 佔有; ~ **a position,** chan⁴ ling³ chen⁴ ti⁴ 佔領陣地(軍).

occur *v.* fa¹ sheng¹ 發生.

occurrence *n.* tsao¹ yü⁴ 遭遇, (*event*) i⁴ wai⁴ chih¹ shih¹ 意外之事.

ocean *n.* hai³ yang² 海洋.

octagon *n.* pa¹ pien¹ hsing² 八邊形, pa¹ chiao³ hsing² 八角形.

octagonal *a.* pa¹ pien¹ hsing² te¹ 八邊形的, pa¹ chiao³ hsing² te¹ 八角形的.

October *n.* shih² yüeh⁴ 十月.

oculist *n.* yen³ k'o¹ i¹ sheng¹ 眼科醫生, yen³ k'o¹ chuan¹ chia¹ 眼科專家.

odd *a.* (*not even*) ch'i² shu⁴ te¹ 奇數的, (*strange*) t'e⁴ i⁴ te¹ 特異的; ~ **number,** ch'i² shu⁴ 奇數.

odds *n.* chi¹ shih⁴ 優勢.

ode *n.* shu¹ ch'ing² tuan³ shih¹ 抒情短詩.

odious *a.* tseng¹ wu⁴ te¹ 憎惡的.

odium *n.* tseng¹ wu⁴ 憎惡.

odor *n.* ch'i⁴ wei⁴ 氣味.

odoriferous *a.* yu³ hsiang¹ ch'i⁴ te¹ 有香氣的, fen¹ fang¹ te¹ 芬芳的.

of *prep.* (*belonging to*) chih¹ 之, te¹ 的, (*made from*) i³ 以, (*containing*) han² yu³ 含有, (*away from*) chü⁴ 距, (*through*) yu² yü² 由於; ~ **course,** tang¹ jan² 當然.

off *prep.* (*not on*) ts'ung²...t'o¹ li² 從...脫離, (*away from*) li² k'ai¹ 離開, (*seaward from*) tsai⁴...te¹ hai³ chung¹ 在...的海中; ~ **one's head,** ching¹ shen² ts'o⁴ luan⁴ 精神錯亂; ～ **horse,** ts'an¹ ma³ 驂馬.

offend v. mao⁴ fan⁴ 冒犯. 「(軍).

offense n. (*attack*) kung¹ chi¹ 攻擊, (*fault*) kuo⁴ shih⁴ 過失.

offensive a. mao⁴ fan⁴ te¹ 冒犯的, (*attacking*) kung¹ chi¹ te¹ 攻擊的; n. kung¹ shih⁴ 攻勢, (*attack*) kung¹ chi¹ 攻擊; ～ **defensive,** kung¹ shih⁴ fang² yü⁴ 攻勢防禦(軍); ～ **spirit,** kung¹ chi¹ ching¹ shen² 攻擊精神.

offer v. (*present*) feng⁴ hsien⁴ 奉獻, (*price*) ch'u¹ chia⁴ 出價. 「祭品.

offering n. (*church*) kung¹ hsien⁴ 供獻, chi¹ p'in³

office n. (*room*) pan⁴ kung¹ shih⁴ 辦公室, (*position*) chih² wu⁴ 職務.

officer n. chün¹ kuan¹ 軍官; ～ **in charge,** chu³ kuan³ chün¹ kuan¹ 主管軍官(軍); ～ **of the day,** chih² jih⁴ kuan¹ 值日官(軍).

official a. kung¹ wu⁴ te¹ 公務的; n. kuan¹ li⁴ 官吏; ～ **correspondence,** kung¹ wen² 公文.

officious a. to¹ shih⁴ te¹ 多事的.

oft, often adv. shih² ch'ang² 時常.

oil n. yu² 油; v. chia¹ yu² 加油; ～ **tank** (*large*), yu² t'a³ 油塔, (*portable*) yu² hsiang¹ 油箱; ～ **tanker,** yu² chien⁴ 油艦. 「滑的.

oily a. to¹ yu² te¹ 多油的, (*slippery*) yu² hua² te¹ 油

ointment n. juan³ kao¹ 軟膏, yu² kao¹ 油膏.

old a. (*person*) lao³ te¹ 老的, chiu⁴ te¹ 舊的; ～ **guard,** chiao¹ pan¹ wei⁴ ping⁴ 交班衛兵.

olive n. kan² lan³ 橄欖; ～ **oil,** kan² lan³ yu² 橄欖 「油.

omelet n. ch'ao³ tan⁴ 炒蛋.

omen n. yü⁴ chao⁴ 預兆. 「te¹ 不祥的.

ominous a. hsiung¹ chao⁴ te¹ 兇兆的, pu⁴ hsiang²

omission n. sheng³ lüeh⁴ 省略.

omit v. sheng³ lüeh⁴ 省略.

omnipotence n. wan⁴ neng² 萬能.

omnipotent a. wan⁴ neng² te¹ 萬能的.

omniscient a. ch'üan² chih¹ te¹ 全知的.

on prep. (*place*) tsai⁴...shang⁴ 在...上, (*time*) tsai⁴ 在; ～ **all accounts,** wu² lun⁴ ju² ho² 無論如何; ～ **credit,** kua⁴ chang⁴ 掛賬; ～ **demand,** chi² fu⁴ 即付; ～ **foot,** pu⁴ hsing² 步行; ～ **hand,**

hsien⁴ yu³ 現有; ~ **leave,** ch'ing³ chia⁴ chung¹ 請假中; ~ **the contrary,** fan³ chih¹ 反之; ~ **time,** chun³ shih² 準時.

once *adv.* i² tz'u⁴ 一次.

one *n., a.* i¹ 一; ~ **after another,** lu⁴ hsü⁴ ti⁴ 陸續地; ~ **by one,** chu² i¹ 逐一; ~ **way traffic,** i⁴ fang¹ t'ung¹ hsing² 一方通行.

onerous *a.* fan² chung⁴ te¹ 繁重的.

onion *n.* yang² ts'ung¹ 洋葱.

only *a.* wei² i¹ te¹ 唯一的; *adv.* wei² i¹ 唯一.

onset *n.* kung¹ chi¹ 攻擊.

onslaught *n.* meng³ chi¹ 猛擊.

onward *a.* hsiang⁴ ch'ien² te¹ 向前的; *adv.* hsiang⁴ ch'ien² 向前.

onyx *n.* t'iao² wen² ma² nao³ 條紋瑪瑙.

opal *n.* tan⁴ pai² shih² 蛋白石.

opaque *a.* pu² t'ou⁴ ming² te¹ 不透明的.

open *a.* k'ai¹ te¹ 開的; *v.* k'ai¹ 開; ~ **air,** hu⁴ wai⁴ 戶外; ~ **city,** pu² she⁴ fang² ch'eng² shih⁴ 不設防城市; ~ **fire,** k'ai¹ shih³ she⁴ chi¹ 開始射擊; ~ **mind,** hsiung¹ wu² ch'eng² chu² te¹ 胸無成竹的; ~ **terrain,** k'ai¹ k'uo⁴ ti⁴ 開闊地.

opening *n.* (*gap*) k'ai¹ k'ou³ 開口, (*beginning*) k'ai¹ shih³ 開始, (*meeting*) k'ai¹ mu⁴ 開幕, (*opportunity*)

opera *n.* ko¹ chü⁴ 歌劇.   ⌈chi¹ hui⁴ 機會.

operate *v.* (*machine*) kung¹ tso⁴ 工作, (*manage*) kuan³ li³ 管理.

operation *n.* (*military*) tso⁴ chan⁴ 作戰, (*surgical*) shou³ shu⁴ 手術; ~ **order,** tso⁴ chan⁴ ming⁴ ling⁴ 作戰命令(軍).   ⌈有效的.

operative *a.* tung⁴ tso⁴ te¹ 動作的, yu³ hsiao⁴ te¹

operator *n.* tung⁴ tso⁴ che³ 動作者, shih¹ shou³ shu⁴ che³ 施手術者.

ophthalmia *n.* yen³ yen² 眼炎.

opinion *n.* i⁴ chien⁴ 意見.

opium *n.* ya¹ p'ien⁴ 鴉片.

opponent *n.* tui⁴ shou³ 對手, ti² shou³ 敵手.

opportune *a.* hsing⁴ yün⁴ te¹ 幸運的.

opportunity *n.* chi¹ hui⁴ 機會.

oppose *v.* fan³ tui⁴ 反對.   ⌈相反的.

opposite *a.* hsiang¹ tui⁴ te¹ 相對的, hsiang¹ fan³ te¹

opposition *n.* fan³ k'ang⁴ 反抗, *(party)* fan³ tui⁴ ⌈tang³ 反對黨.

oppress *v.* ya¹ p'o⁴ 壓迫.

oppression *n.* ya¹ p'o⁴ te¹ 壓迫的.

oppressive *a.* ya¹ p'o⁴ te¹ 壓迫的.

oppressor *n.* ya¹ p'o⁴ che² 壓迫者.

optical *a.* yen³ te¹ 眼的, *(of vision and light)* kuang¹ hsüeh² te¹ 光學的.

optimist *n.* le⁴ kuan¹ chu³ i⁴ che³ 樂觀主義者.

option *n.* hsüan³ tse² 選擇.

optional *a.* sui² i⁴ te¹ 隨意的.

opulence *n.* ts'ai² fu⁴ 財富.

opulent *a.* fu⁴ tsu² te¹ 富足的.

or *conj.* huo⁴ che³ 或者.

oracle *n.* shen² yü⁴ 神諭.

oral *a.* k'ou³ shu⁴ te¹ 口述的. ⌈se⁴ 橙黃色.

orange *n.* kuang³ kan¹ 廣柑; *a.* ch'eng² huang²

oration *n.* yen³ shuo¹ 演說.

orator *n.* yen³ shuo¹ chia¹ 演說家.

oratorical *a.* yen³ shuo¹ chia¹ te¹ 演說家的.

orchard *n.* kuo³ yüan² 果園, kuo³ shu⁴ lin² 果樹林.

orchestra *n.* kuan³ hsien² yüeh⁴ tui⁴ 管弦樂隊.

orchid *n.* lan² shu³ chih² wu⁴ 蘭屬植物.

ordain *v.* kuei¹ ting⁴ 規定, *(church)* shou⁴ sheng⁴ chih² 授聖職.

order *n.* *(command)* ming⁴ ling⁴ 命令, *(arrangement)* shun⁴ hsü⁴ 順序; *v.* *(command)* ming⁴ ling⁴ 命令, *(goods)* ting⁴ huo⁴ 定貨; ~ **of battle,** chan⁴ tou⁴ hsü⁴ lieh⁴ 戰鬪序列(軍); ~ **of march,** hsing² chün¹ hsü⁴ lieh⁴ 行軍序列(軍).

orderly *a.* i¹ tz'u⁴ te¹ 依次的; *n.* ch'uan² ling⁴ ping¹ 傳令兵(軍).

ordinance *n.* fa³ ling⁴ 法令. ⌈te¹ 平凡的.

ordinary *a.* t'ung¹ ch'ang² te¹ 通常的, p'ing² fan²

ordnance *n.* *(branch of army)* ping¹ kung¹ 兵工; ~ **depot,** chün¹ hsieh⁴ k'u⁴ 軍械庫; ~ **materiel,** chün¹ huo³ 軍火; ~ **officer,** chün¹ hsieh⁴ kuan¹ 軍械官.

ore *n.* k'uang⁴ shih² 鑛石. ⌈ch'in² 風琴.

organ *n.* *(of body)* ch'i⁴ kuan¹ 器官, *(music)* feng¹

organic *a.* ch'i⁴ kuan¹ te¹ 器官的, *(produced by animal or plant)* yu³ chi¹ te¹ 有機的; ~ **unit,**

181

chien⁴ chih⁴ tan¹ wei⁴ 建制單位(軍).

organist *n.* feng¹ ch'in² shih¹ 風琴師.

organization *n.* (*function*) chi¹ kou⁴ 機構，(*internal structure*) tsu³ chih¹ 組織，(*military*) pien¹ chih¹ 編制；～ **of fire**, huo³ hsien⁴ kou⁴ ch'eng² 火線構成(軍)；～ **of position**, chen⁴ ti⁴ pien¹ ch'eng² 陣地編成(軍).

organize *v.* (*company, club, etc*) tsu³ chih¹ 組織，(*unit*) pien¹ ch'eng² 編成.

orient *n.* tung¹ fang¹ 東方；*v.* (*directions*) ting¹ fang¹ wei⁴ 定方位，(*map*) piao¹ ting⁴ 標定，(*position*) ts'e⁴ ting⁴ wei⁴ chih¹ 測定位置，(*personnel*) chih² tao³ 指導.

oriental *a.* tung¹ fang¹ te¹ 東方的；*n.* tung¹ fang¹ jen² 東方人.

orifice *n.* k'ou³ 口, k'ung³ 孔.

origin *n.* ch'i³ yüan² 起源, (*birth*) chia¹ hsi⁴ 家系.

original *a.* ch'i³ tuan¹ te¹ 起端的.

originality *n.* k'ai¹ ch'uang⁴ 開創.

originate *v.* (*invent*) shou³ ch'uang⁴ 首創, (*begin*) fa¹ tuan¹ 發端.

ornament *n.* chuang¹ shih⁴ p'in³ 裝飾品；*v.* chuang¹ shih⁴ 裝飾.

ornamental *a.* chuang¹ shih⁴ te¹ 裝飾的.

ornithology *n.* niao³ lei⁴ hsüeh⁴ 鳥類學.

orphan *n.* ku¹ erh² 孤兒.

orthodox *a.* (*religion*) cheng⁴ chiao⁴ te¹ 正教的.

orthography *n.* p'in¹ tzu⁴ fa³ 拼字法.

oscillate *v.* chen⁴ tang⁴ 振盪.

oscillation *n.* chen⁴ tang⁴ 振盪.

osier *n.* liu³ chih¹ 柳枝.　　　　　「te¹ 顯出的.

ostensible *a.* piao³ mien⁴ te¹ 表面的, hsien³ ch'u¹

ostentation *n.* hsü¹ shih⁴ 虛飾.

ostentatious *a.* hsü¹ shih⁴ te¹ 虛飾的.

ostler *n.* ma³ fu¹ 馬夫, chiu¹ tsu² 廄卒.

ostrich *n.* t'o² niao³ 鴕鳥.

other *a.* ch'i² t'a¹ te¹ 其他的.

otter *n.* shui³ t'a³ 水獺.

ought *v. aux.* ying¹ tang¹ 應當, pi⁴ hsü¹ 必須.

ounce *n.* ang⁴ ssu¹ 盎司.

our *pron.* wo³ men² te¹ 我們的.

ourselves *pron.* wo³ men² tzu⁴ chi³ 我們自己.

out *adv.* tsai⁴ wai⁴ 在外, pu⁴ tsai⁴ 不在; ~ **of date,** pu⁴ ho² shih² i² 不合時宜.

outbid *v.* ch'u¹ kao¹ chia⁴ 出高價(拍賣時).

outbreak *n.* pao⁴ fa¹ 爆發.

outcast *n.* liu² lang⁴ che⁴ 流浪者.

outcome *n.* chieh² kuo³ 結果.

outdo *v.* sheng¹ kuo⁴ 勝過.

outer *a.* wai⁴ mien⁴ te¹ 外面的, wai⁴ kuan¹ te¹ 外觀的; ~ **garment,** wai⁴ i¹ 外衣.

outfit *n.* pi² hsü¹ p'in³ 必須品.

outflank *v.* pao¹ ch'ao¹ 包抄(軍).

outgoing *a.* li² k'ai¹ te¹ 離開的.

outgrow *v.* sheng¹ chang³ chiao⁴ su² yü² 生長較速於. 「.

outlaw *n.* (*lawless person*) pu⁴ fa³ chih¹ t'u² 不法之

outlay *n.* fei⁴ yung⁴ 費用, hsiao¹ hao⁴ 消耗.

outlet *n.* ch'u¹ lu⁴ 出路, ch'u¹ k'ou³ 出口.

outline *n.* lun² k'uo⁴ 輪廓, (*rough draft*) ta⁴ kang¹ 大綱; *v.* miao² lun² k'uo⁴ 描輪廓, (*sketch*) tso⁴ kang¹ yao⁴ 作綱要.

outlive *v.* shou⁴ chang³ yü² 壽長於.

outpost *n.* ch'ien² shao⁴ 前哨; ~ **line,** ch'ien² shao⁴ hsien⁴ 前哨線(軍); ~ **position,** ch'ien² shao⁴ chen⁴ ti⁴ 前哨陣地(軍).

output *n.* sheng¹ ch'an³ e² 生產額.

outrage *n.* pao⁴ hsing² 暴行; *v.* mao⁴ fan⁴ 冒犯.

outrageous *a.* ch'iang² pao⁴ te¹ 强暴的.

outside *n.* wai⁴ mien⁴ 外面; *a.* wai⁴ pu⁴ te¹ 外部的; *adv., prep.* tsai⁴ wai⁴ 在外.

outward *a.* hsiang⁴ wai⁴ te¹ 向外的; *adv.* hsiang⁴ wai⁴ 向外.

oval *a.* luan³ hsing² te¹ 卵形的.

oven *n.* yao² lu² 窰爐. 「過.

over *prep.* tsai⁴ shang⁴ 在上; *adv.* yüeh⁴ kuo⁴ 越

overboard *adv.* tsai⁴ ch'uan² wai⁴ 在船外.

overcast *v.* yin³ pi⁴ 隱蔽.

overcoat *n.* wai⁴ t'ao⁴ 外套, ta⁴ i¹ 大衣.

overcome *v.* k'o⁴ fu² 克服.

overdue *a.* kuo⁴ ch'i¹ te¹ 過期的, t'o¹ ch'ien⁴ te¹ 拖欠的.

overflow *v.* fan⁴ lan⁴ 汜濫.

overgrown *a.* sheng¹ chang³ kuo⁴ su² 生長過速, ts'ung¹ sheng¹ 叢生.

overhead *adv.* tsai⁴ shang⁴ 在上; ~ **fire**, ch'ao¹ yüeh⁴ she¹ chi¹ 超越射擊.

overhear *v.* ch'ieh⁴ t'ing¹ 竊聽.

overload *v.* chuang¹ tsai⁴ kuo⁴ chung⁴ 裝載過重.

overlook *v.* fu³ k'an⁴ 俯瞰.

overpower *v.* cheng¹ fu² 征服, ya¹ tao³ 壓倒.

overrun *v.* man⁴ yen² 蔓延.

oversea, overseas *adv.* tsai⁴ hai³ wai⁴ 在海外; *a.* hai³ wai⁴ te¹ 海外的; ~ **edition**, hai³ wai⁴ pan³ 海外版; ~ **Chinese Affairs Commission***, ch'iao² wu⁴ wei³ yüan² hui⁴ 僑務委員會*; ~ **expedition**, hai³ wai⁴ yüan³ cheng¹ 海外遠征.

overseer *n.* chien¹ tu¹ che³ 監督者.

oversight *n.* shih¹ ch'a² 失察.

overtake *v.* chui¹ chi² 追及.

overthrow *n.* t'ui¹ fan¹ 推翻; *v.* t'ui¹ fan¹ 推翻.

overture *n.* (*proposal*) t'i² i⁴ 提議, (*music*) ch'ien² tsou⁴ ch'ü³ 前奏曲.

overturn *v.* t'ui¹ fan¹ 推翻, ch'ing¹ fu⁴ 傾覆.

overweight *n.* kuo⁴ chung⁴ 過重.

owe *v.* fu⁴ chai⁴ 負債.

owl *n.* hsiao¹ 鴞.

own *a.* tzu⁴ chi³ te¹ 自己的; *v.* yu³ 有.

owner *n.* so² yu³ che³ 所有者.

ox *n.* kung¹ niu² 公牛.

oxygen *n.* yang³ ch'i⁴ 養氣.

oyster *n.* mu³ li⁴ 牡蠣, hao² 蠔; ~**plant**, p'o² lo² men² shen¹ 婆羅門參(植).

P

pace *n.* (*rate*) pu⁴ fa¹ 步伐, (*step*) pu⁴ 步; *v.* (*set the pace for*) cheng³ ch'i² pu⁴ fa¹ 整齊步伐.

pacific *a.* hao⁴ ho² p'ing² te¹ 好和平的, t'ai⁴ p'ing² te¹ 太平的; ~ **Ocean**, t'ai⁴ p'ing² yang² 太平洋.

pacify *v.* fu³ wei⁴ 撫慰.

pack *n.* pao¹ kuo³ 包裹; *v.* pao¹ cha² 包紮; ~

artillery, t'o² tsai⁴ p'ao⁴ ping¹ 駄載砲兵(軍); 〜 **howitzer,** t'o² tsai⁴ liu² tan⁴ p'ao⁴ 駄載榴彈砲 (軍).

package *n.* pao¹ kuo³ 包裹, pao¹ chien⁴ 包件.

packet *n.* hsiao³ pao¹ kuo³ 小包裹.

pad *n.* tien⁴ 墊, (*cavalry*) an¹ ju⁴ 鞍褥, (*paper*) p'ai¹ chih³ pu⁴ 拍紙簿; *v.* t'ien² sai⁴ 填塞.

padding *n.* t'ien² liao⁴ 填料.

paddock *n.* wei² ch'ang³ 圍場.

padlock *n.* lien⁴ so³ 鏈鎖.

pagan *n.* i⁴ chiao⁴ t'u² 異教徒.

page *n.* yeh⁴ 頁, (*servant*) t'ung² p'u² 僮僕.

pagoda *n.* t'a³ 塔.

pail *n.* shui³ t'ung³ 水桶, t'i² t'ung³ 提桶.

pain *n.* t'ung⁴ k'u³ 痛苦, k'u³ ch'u³ 苦楚.

painful *a.* t'ung⁴ k'u³ te¹ 痛苦的.

paint *n.* yu² ch'i¹ 油漆; *v.* (*house*) yu² ch'i¹ 油漆, (*picture*) tso⁴ hua⁴ 作畫. 「chiang⁴ 漆匠.

painter *n.* (*picture*) hua⁴ chia¹ 畫家, (*house*) ch'i¹

painting *n.* yu² hua⁴ 油畫.

pair *n.* i² 一對, i⁴ shuang¹ 一雙; *v.* shih³ ch'eng² tui⁴ 使成對, ch'eng² shuang¹ 成雙.

palace *n.* huang² kung¹ 皇宮. 「口的.

palatable *a.* mei⁴ wei⁴ te¹ 美味的, k'o² k'ou³ te¹ 可

palate *n.* e⁴ 腭.

palatial *a.* wang² kung¹ te¹ 王宮的.

pale *a.* ts'ang¹ pai² te¹ 蒼白的; *n.* chuang¹ 樁; *v.* chuan³ wei² ts'ang¹ pai² 轉爲蒼白.

paleness *n.* ts'ang¹ pai² 蒼白.

palette *n.* t'iao² se⁴ pan³ 調色板.

pallid *a.* ts'ang¹ pai² te¹ 蒼白的.

palm *n.* shou² chang³ 手掌, (*tree*) tsung¹ lü² 棕櫚.

palmistry *n.* shou³ hsiang⁴ shu⁴ 手相術.

palpable *a.* k'o³ chieh¹ ch'u⁴ te¹ 可接觸的, (*obvious*) hsien³ fan² te¹ 顯然的.

palpitate *v.* t'iao⁴ tung⁴ 跳動, chi⁴ tung⁴ 悸動.

palpitation *n.* hsin¹ chi⁴ 心悸.

paltry *v.* (*worthless*) wu² chia⁴ chih² te¹ 無價值的, (*trifling*) so³ hsieh⁴ te¹ 瑣屑的.

pamper *v.* (*indulge*) ts'ung¹ jung² 從容.

pamphlet *n.* hsiao³ ts'e⁴ tzu¹ 小册子.

185

pan *n.* p'an² 盤.

panacea *n.* wan⁴ ying⁴ yao⁴ 萬應藥.

pancake *n.* po² chien¹ ping³ 薄煎餅.

pane *n.* i² k'uai¹ po¹ li² 一塊玻璃.

panel *n.* ch'ien¹ pan³ 嵌板.

pang *n.* chi¹ t'ung⁴ 劇痛.

panic *n.* k'ung³ huang¹ 恐慌, ching¹ huang² 驚惶.

pansy *n.* san¹ se⁴ chin³ 三色菫(植).

pant *n.* ch'uan³ hsi² 喘息; *v.* ch'uan³ ch'i⁴ 喘氣.

panther *n.* pao⁴ 豹.

pantomime *n.* ya³ chü⁴ 啞劇.

pantry *n.* shih² ch'i⁴ shih⁴ 食器室.

paper *n.* chih³ 紙.

par *n.* t'ung³ teng³ 同等, *(face value)* p'iao⁴ mien⁴ chia⁴ e² 票面價額; ~ **value,** p'iao⁴ mien⁴ chia⁴ 「ko² 票面價格.

parable *n.* yü² yen² 寓言.

parachute *n.* chiang⁴ lao⁴ san³ 降落傘; ~ **flare,** chiang⁴ lao⁴ san³ chao⁴ ming² tan⁴ 降落傘照明彈 (軍); ~ **tower,** t'iao⁴ san³ t'a³ 跳傘塔(軍); ~ **troops,** chiang⁴ lao⁴ san³ pu⁴ tui⁴ 降落傘部隊(軍).

parachutist *n.* san³ ping¹ 傘兵.

parade *n.* yu² hsing² 遊行, *(troops)* fen¹ lieh⁴ shih⁴ 分列式(軍); *v.* lieh⁴ tui⁴ yu² hsing² 列隊遊行; ~ **ground,** ts'ao¹ ch'ang³ 操場(軍).

paradise *n.* t'ien¹ t'ang² 天堂, *(place of happiness)* le⁴ yüan² 樂園.

parallel *a.* p'ing² hsing² te¹ 平行的.

paralysis *n.* t'an¹ huan⁴ 癱瘓, ma² pi⁴ 麻痺.

paralytic *a.* t'an¹ huan⁴ te¹ 癱瘓的, ma² pi⁴ te¹ 麻痺的.

paramount *a.* *(chief in importance)* shou³ yao⁴ te¹ 首要的, *(above others)* chiao⁴ kao¹ te¹ 較高的.

paramour *n.* *(male)* chien¹ fu¹ 姦夫, *(female)* yin² 「fu⁴ 淫婦.

parapet *n.* tuan³ ch'iang² 短牆.

parasite *n.* chi⁴ sheng¹ wu⁴ 寄生物.

parasol *n.* t'ai⁴ yang² san³ 太陽傘.

parcel *n.* pao¹ kuo³ 包裹.

parch *v.* hung¹ kan¹ 烘乾.

parchment *n.* yang² p'i² chih³ 羊皮紙.

pardon *n., v.* yüan² liang⁴ 原諒.

pardonable *a.* k'o³ jao² shu⁴ te¹ 可饒恕的.

pare *v.* ch'ü⁴ p'i² 去皮.

paregoric *n.* chen⁴ t'ung⁴ yao⁴ 鎮痛藥, chang¹ nao³ ya¹ p'ien¹ ting¹ 樟腦鴉片酊.

parent *n.* shuang¹ ch'in¹ 雙親, fu⁴ mu³ 父母.

parentage *n.* chia¹ shih⁴ 家世, men² ti⁴ 門第.

parenthesis *n.* k'uo⁴ hu² 括弧.

parish *n.* chiao⁴ ch'ü¹ 教區.

parishioner *n.* chiao⁴ ch'ü¹ chü¹ min² 教區居民.

park *n.* kung¹ yüan² 公園.

parley *n.* t'an² p'an⁴ 談判; *v.* t'an² p'an⁴ 談判.

parliament *n.* kuo² kui⁴ 國會. 「廳.

parlor *n.* ying⁴ chieh¹ shih⁴ 應接室, k'o⁴ t'ing¹ 客

parole *n.* shih⁴ yen² 誓言, (*release*) chia⁴ shih⁴ 假釋.

parquetry *n.* ch'ien¹ mu⁴ hsi⁴ kung¹ 嵌木細工.

parrot *n.* ying¹ wu³ 鸚鵡.

parry *v.* (*evade*) shan³ pi⁴ 閃避.

parse *v.* fen¹ hsi¹ 分析(字句).

parsimonious *a.* chieh² chien³ te¹ 節儉的, (*stingy*) lin⁴ se⁴ te¹ 吝嗇的. 「se⁴ 吝嗇.

parsimony *n.* chieh² chien³ 節儉, (*stinginess*) lin⁴

parsley *n.* ho² lan² ch'in¹ 荷蘭芹.

parson *n.* chiao⁴ ch'ü¹ chang³ 教區長.

part *n.* i² pu⁴ fen¹ 一部分; *v.* (*divide*) fen¹ k'ai¹ 分開, (*separate*) fen¹ pieh² 分別.

partial *a.* pu⁴ fen¹ te¹ 部分的.

partiality *n.* p'ien¹ hao³ 偏好, p'ien¹ ssu¹ 偏私.

participate *v.* ts'an¹ yü⁴ 參與, ts'an¹ chia¹ 參加.

participation *n.* ts'an¹ yü⁴ 參與, ts'an¹ chia¹ 參加.

particle *n.* (*physics*) fen⁴ tzu³ 分子.

particular *a.* t'e⁴ pieh² te¹ 特別的; *n.* shih⁴ hsiang⁴ 事項.

parting *n.* fen¹ k'ai¹ 分開, li² pieh² 離別.

partisan, partizan *n.* yu³ p'ien¹ chien⁴ te¹ 有偏見的. 「見的.

partition *n.* kua¹ fen¹ 瓜分.

partly *adv.* pu⁴ fen¹ ti⁴ 部分地.

partner *n.* huo³ pan⁴ 夥伴, (*wife or husband*) p'ei¹ ou³ 配偶; ~ **for life**, chung¹ shen¹ pan⁴ lü³ 終身伴侶.

partnership *n.* ho² huo³ 合夥. 「伴侶.

partridge *n.* che¹ ku¹ 鷓鴣.

party *n.* hui⁴ 會, (*political*) tang³ p'ai⁴ 黨派.

pass *n.* t'ung¹ kuo⁴ 通過, (*a permit*) t'ung¹ hsing² cheng⁴ 通行證; *v.* t'ung¹ kuo⁴ 通過.

passable *a.* shang⁴ k'o⁸ te¹ 尚可的, (*can be passed*) k'o³ t'ung¹ kuo⁴ te¹ 可通過的.

passage *n.* tsou³ lang² 走廊.

passenger *n.* ch'eng² k'o⁴ 乘客.

passion *n.* ch'ing² hsü⁴ 情緒.

passionate *a.* i⁴ chi¹ tung⁴ te¹ 易激動的.

passive *a.* pei⁴ tung⁴ te¹ 被動的; **~ air defense**, hsiao¹ chi² fang² k'ung¹ 消極防空(軍); **~ defense**, hsiao¹ chi² fang² yü⁴ 消極防禦(軍).

passport *n.* hu⁴ chao⁴ 護照.

password *n.* k'ou³ ling⁴ 口令(軍).

past *a.* kuo⁴ ch'ü⁴ te¹ 過去的; *prep.* kuo⁴ 過; *n.* kuo⁴ ch'ü⁴ 過去.

paste *n.* chiang¹ hu² 漿糊; *v.* chan¹ t'ieh¹ 黏貼.

pastime *n.* yü² le⁴ 娛樂.

pastor *n.* mu⁴ shih¹ 牧師.

pastoral *a.* (*of country life*) t'ien² yeh³ te¹ 田野的, (*of shepherds*) mu⁴ jen² te¹ 牧人的; **~ poetry**, t'ien² yüan² shih¹ 田園詩.

pastry *n.* ping³ 餅.

pasture *n.* mu⁴ ch'ang³ 牧場.

pasty *a.* ju² chiang¹ hu² te¹ 如漿糊的.

patch *n.* pu⁴ k'uai⁴ 布塊; *v.* pu³ chui⁴ 補綴.

patent *n.* t'e⁴ hsü³ chuang⁴ 特許狀, chuan¹ mai⁴ cheng⁴ 專賣證; *v.* t'e⁴ hsü³ 特許, chuan¹ mai⁴ 專賣.

paternal *a.* fu⁴ te¹ 父的.

paternity *n.* fu⁴ tao⁴ 父道, fu⁴ hsi⁴ 父系.

path *n.* hsiao³ lu⁴ 小路.

pathetic *a.* tung⁴ jen² lien² min³ te¹ 動人憐憫的.

pathos *n.* pei¹ ai¹ 悲哀, ch'i¹ ts'an³ 悽慘.

patience *n.* jen³ nai⁴ 忍耐.

patient *a.* jen³ nai⁴ te¹ 忍耐的; *n.* ping⁴ jen² 病人.

patriot *n.* ai⁴ kuo² che³ 愛國者.

patriotic *a.* ai⁴ kuo² te¹ 愛國的.

patriotism *n.* ai⁴ kuo² hsin¹ 愛國心.

patrol *n.* hsün² lo² 巡邏, (*military*) ch'ih⁴ hou² 斥候(軍); *v.* hsün² ch'a² 巡察.

patron *n.* lao² chu³ ku⁴ 老主顧, (*support*) tsan⁴ chu⁴ che³ 贊助者.

patronage *n.* kuang¹ ku⁴ 光顧, (*support*) tsan⁴ chu⁴ 贊助.

patroness *n.* nü² chu³ ku⁴ 女主顧, (*support*) nü³ tsan⁴ chu⁴ che³ 女贊助者.

patronize *v.* ch'ui² ku⁴ 垂顧, (*support*) tsan⁴ chu⁴ 贊助.

pattern *n.* yang⁴ pen³ 樣本, (*model*) mo² hsing² 模型.

pauper *n.* ch'iung² jen² 窮人, p'in² min² 貧民.

pause *n.*, *v.* hsiu¹ chih³ 休止.

pave *v.* p'u⁴ ch'i⁴ 鋪砌.

pavement *n.* (*material*) p'u⁴ liao⁴ 鋪料, ch'i⁴ liao⁴ 砌料.

pavilion *n.* chang⁴ p'eng² 帳篷, hsüan¹ wu¹ 軒屋, t'ing² 亭.

paw *n.* chua³ 爪; *v.* sao¹ p'a² 搔爬.

pawn *n.* chih⁴ wu⁴ 質物; *v.* tien³ chih³ 典質.

pawnbroker *n.* tien³ tang⁴ shang¹ 典當商.

pay *n.* pao⁴ ch'ou² 報酬; *v.* fu⁴ chi³ 付給; **~ in advance**, yü⁴ fu⁴ 預付.

payable *a.* k'o³ fu⁴ te¹ 可付的.

payee *n.* shou¹ k'uan³ jen² 收款人.

payer *n.* fu⁴ k'uan³ jen² 付款人.

payment *n.* fu⁴ k'uan³ 付款.

pea *n.* wan³ tou⁴ 豌豆.

peace *n.* ho² p'ing² 和平.

peaceful *a.* ho² p'ing² te¹ 和平的.

peach *n.* t'ao² tzu¹ 桃子.

peacock *n.* hsiung² k'ung² ch'iao³ 雄孔雀.

peak *n.* shan¹ tien¹ 山巔.

peal *n.* (*thunder*) lei² ming² sheng¹ 雷鳴聲, (*bell*) chung¹ sheng¹ 鐘聲.

pear *n.* li² 梨.

pearl *n.* chen¹ chu¹ 眞珠.

peasant *n.* nung² fu¹ 農夫.

peasantry *n.* nung² fu¹ 農夫.

peat *n.* ni² mei² 泥煤.

pebble *n.* hsiao³ shih² luan³ 小石卵.

peck *v.* hui⁴ cho² 喙啄.

peculiar *a.* t'e⁴ shu¹ te¹ 特殊的, ch'i² i⁴ te¹ 奇異的.

peculiarity *n.* t'e⁴ hsing⁴ 特性, t'e⁴ chih² 特質.

pecuniary *a.* chin¹ ch'ien² te¹ 金錢的.

pedal *n.* t'a⁴ pan³ 踏板.

pedantic *a.* yü¹ ju² te¹ 迂儒的.

peddler, pedlar *n.* hsiao³ fan⁴ 小販.

pedestal *n.* t'ai² tso⁴ 臺座.

pedestrian *a.* t'u² pu⁴ te¹ 徒步的; *n.* pu⁴ hsing⁻ che³ 步行者.

pedigree *n.* chia¹ p'u³ 家譜, shih⁴ hsi⁴ 世系.

peel *n.* p'i² 皮; *v.* pao¹ p'i² 剝皮.

peep *n.* k'uei¹ shih⁴ 窺視; *v.* ch'ieh⁴ shih⁴ 竊視.

peer *n.* (*title*) kuei⁴ tsu² 貴族; *v.* ning² shih⁴ 凝視.

peerage *n.* chüeh² wei⁴ 爵位.

peerless *a.* wu² pi³ te¹ 無比的, wu² p'i³ te¹ 無匹的.

peevish *a.* kuai² chang¹ te¹ 乖張的, i⁴ nu⁴ te¹ 易怒的.

peg *n.* mu⁴ ting¹ 木釘; *v.* ting⁴ shuan¹ 釘栓.

pell-mell *adv.* hun⁴ luan⁴ 混亂.

pen *n.* (*brush*) mao² pi³ 毛筆, (*steel*) kang¹ pi³ 鋼筆, (*fountain*) tzu⁴ lai² shui² pi³ 自來水筆, (*cage*) shou⁴ lan² 獸欄.

penal *a.* hsing² fa² te¹ 刑罰的.

penalty *n.* hsing² fa² 刑罰.

pencil *n.* ch'ien¹ pi³ 鉛筆.

pending *a.* tai⁴ chüeh² te¹ 待決的.

pendulum *n.* pai³ 擺.

penetrable *a.* k'o³ ch'uan¹ ju⁴ te¹ 可穿入的.

penetrate *v.* t'ou⁴ ju⁴ 透入, (*shells*) kuan⁴ ch'uan¹ 貫穿, (*troops*) t'u² p'o⁴ 突破.

peninsula *n.* pan⁴ tao³ 半島.

penis *n.* yang² chü¹ 陽具.

penitence *n.* hui³ tsui⁴ 悔罪, ch'an⁴ hui³ 懺悔.

penitent *a.* hui³ tsui⁴ te¹ 悔罪的, ch'an⁴ hui³ te¹ 懺悔的.

penknife *n.* hsiao³ tao¹ 小刀.

penniless *a.* ch'ih⁴ p'in² 赤貧的.

pension *n.* yang² lao³ chin¹ 養老金, en¹ feng⁴ 恩俸.

pensive *a.* yu¹ ssu¹ te¹ 憂思的.

people *n.* jen² min² 人民; ~'s Procurator-General's Office** , tsui⁴ kao¹ jen² min² chien³ ch'a² shu³ 最高人民檢察署** ; ~'s Revolutionary Military Council** , jen² min² ko² ming⁴ chün¹ shih⁴ wei³ yuan² hui⁴ 人民革命軍事委員會** .

pepper *n.* hu² chiao¹ 胡椒.

peppermint *n.* po⁴ ho² 薄荷.

per *prep.* (*for each*) mei³ 每; ～ **diem,** (*allowance*) ch'u¹ ch'ai¹ fei⁴ 出差費. 「百分比.

percentage *n.* pai³ fen¹ lü 百分率, pai³ fen¹ pi³

perceptible *a.* k'o³ chih¹ chüeh¹ te¹ 可知覺的, k'o²
ling³ wu⁴ te¹ 可領悟的. 「悟力的

perception *n.* chih¹ chüeh² 知覺, ling³ wu⁴ li⁴ 領

perch *n.* (*hell*) hsi¹ mu⁴ 棲木; *v.* hsi¹ hsi² 棲息.

perdition *n.* (*hell*) ti⁴ yü⁴ 地獄.

perennial *a.* yung² chiu³ te 永久的.

perfect *a.* wan² ch'üan² te¹ 完全的, li² hsiang³ te¹
理想的; *v.* shih⁴ wan² ch'üan² 使完全.

perfection *n.* wan² ch'üan² 完全, wan² mei³ 完美.

perfidious *a.* pu² i⁴ te¹ 不義的.

perfidy *n.* pu² i⁴ 不義.

perforate *v.* ch'uan¹ k'ung³ 穿孔.

perforation *n.* tsuan² k'ung³ 鑽孔.

perform *v.* (*do*) tso⁴ 作, (*carry out*) li³ hsing²
行, (*music*) piao² yen³ 表演.

performance *n.* (*of duty*) chih² hsing² 執行,
(*show*) piao² yen³ 表演, (*characteristics*) hsing⁴
neng² 性能. 「shui³ 香水.

perfume *n.* hsiang¹ ch'i⁴ 香氣, (*liquid*) hsiang¹

perhaps *adv.* huo⁴ che³ 或者.

peril *n.* wei² hsien³ 危險, mao⁴ hsien³ 冒險.

perilous *a.* wei² hsien³ te¹ 危險的, mao⁴ hsien³ te¹
冒險的. 「點號.

period *n.* (*time*) shih² ch'i¹ 時期, (*dot*) tien³ hao⁴

periodical *a.* ting⁴ ch'i¹ te¹ 定期的.

periscope *n.* ch'ien² wang⁴ ching⁴ 潛望鏡.

perish *v.* ssu³ wang² 死亡.

perishable *a.* i⁴ ssu³ wang² te¹ 易死亡的.

peritonitis *n.* fu⁴ mo⁴ yen² 腹膜炎(醫).

perjure *v.* fa¹ wei² shih⁴ 發偽誓, tso⁴ wang⁴
cheng⁴ 作妄證.

perjury *n.* wei² shih⁴ 偽誓, wang⁴ cheng⁴ 妄證.

permanent *a.* yung² chiu³ te¹ 永久的; ～ **station,**
yung² chiu³ chu⁴ ti⁴ 永久駐地(軍).

permeable *a.* k'o³ t'ou⁴ ju⁴ te¹ 可透入的.

permeate *v.* t'ou⁴ ju⁴ 透入.

permissible *a.* k'o³ chun³ hsü³ te¹ 可准許的.

permission *n.* hsü³ k'o³ 許可.

permit *n.* hsü² k'o³ cheng⁴ 許可證; *v.* chun² hsü³
　　　　　　　　　　　　　　　　　　　　　　　　　　　└准許.
pernicious *a.* p'o⁴ huai⁴ te¹ 破壞的.
perpendicular *a.* ch'ui² chih² te¹ 垂直的; *n.*
　(*line*) ch'ui² chih² hsien⁴ 垂直線.
perpetrate *v.* tso⁴ (惡), fan⁴ (罪).
perpetration *n.* tso⁴ e⁴ 作惡, fan⁴ tsui⁴ 犯罪.
perpetual *a.* yung² chiu³ te¹ 永久的.
perpetuate *v.* shih³ yung² chiu³ 使永久.
perpetuity *n.* yung² chiu³ hsing² 永久性.
perplex *v.* shih³ mi² luan⁴ 使迷亂, shih³ fu⁴ tsa²
　使複雜.
perplexity *n.* mi² luan⁴ 迷亂, fu⁴ tsa² 複雜.
persecute *v.* ya¹ p'o⁴ 壓迫, p'o⁴ hai⁴ 迫害.
persecution *n.* ya¹ p'o⁴ 壓迫, p'o⁴ hai⁴ 迫害.
persecutor *n.* p'o⁴ hai⁴ che³ 迫害者.
perseverance *n.* chien¹ jen³ 堅忍.
persevere *v.* chien¹ ch'ih² 堅持, chien¹ jen³ 堅忍.
persist *v.* chien¹ ch'ih² 堅持.
persistent *a.* chien¹ ch'ih² te¹ 堅持的.
person *n.* jen² 人.　　　　　　　　　　　　└的.
personal *a.* ko⁴ jen² te¹ 個人的, ssu¹ jen² te¹ 私人
personnel *n.* jen² yüan² 人員; ～ **roster,** jen²
　yüan² ming² ts'e⁴ 人員名册.
perspective *n.* t'ou⁴ shih⁴ hua⁴ fa³ 透視畫法,
　yüan² chin⁴ p'ei⁴ ching³ 遠近配景.
perspiration *n.* han⁴ 汗.
perspire *v.* ch'u¹ han⁴ 出汗.
persuade *v.* shuo¹ fu² 說服.
persuasion *n.* shuo¹ fu² 說服.
persuasive *a.* tung⁴ t'ing¹ te¹ 動聽的.　　└的.
pert *a.* lu² mang³ te¹ 鹵莽的, t'ang² t'u² te¹ 唐突
pertinacious *a.* wan² ch'iang² te¹ 頑强的, chih²
　niu⁴ te¹ 執拗的.　　　　　　　　　└te¹ 貼切的.
pertinent *a.* shih⁴ tang¹ te¹ 適當的, t'ieh¹ ch'ieh⁴
perusal *n.* hsiang² tu² 詳讀.
peruse *v.* hsi⁴ tu² 細讀.
pervade *v.* pien⁴ pu⁴ 遍佈.
perverse *a.* hsieh² p'i⁴ te¹ 邪僻的, chüeh¹
　ch'iang² te¹ 倔强的, kang¹ pi⁴ te¹ 剛愎的.　└解.
perversion *n.* p'ien¹ hsieh² 偏邪, ch'ü¹ chieh³ 曲
pest *n.* e⁴ i⁴ 惡疫, i⁴ ping⁴ 疫病.

pestilence *n.* i⁴ 疫.

pestilent *a.* chih⁴ ssu³ te¹ 致死的.

pestle *n.* ch'u³ 杵, yen² pang⁴ 研棒.

pet *a.* (*favorite*) pei⁴ ch'ung³ ai⁴ te¹ 被寵愛的; *n.* ai⁴ wu⁴物 愛物; *v.* ch'ung³ ai⁴ 寵愛.

petal *n.* hua¹ pan⁴ 花瓣.

petition *n.* ch'ing³ yüan⁴ 請願; *v.* k'en² ch'ing³ 懇請.

petrify *v.* hua⁴ ch'eng² shih² 化成石.

petroleum *n.* shih² yu² 石油.

petticoat *n.* ch'en⁴ ch'ün² 襯裙, (*skirt*) ch'ün² 裙.

pettish *a.* i⁴ nu⁴ te¹ 易怒的.

petty *a.* pu² chung⁴ yao⁴ te¹ 不重要的, (*lower*) hsia⁴ chi² te¹ 下級的.

petulance *n.* i⁴ nu⁴ 易怒.

petulant *a.* i⁴ nu⁴ te¹ 易怒的.

pew *n.* chiao⁴ t'ang² chung¹ chih¹ tso⁴ hsi² 教堂中之座席.

phantom *n.* huan⁴ hsiang⁴ 幻像, (*ghost*) ju² kuei³ 如鬼的.

pharmaceutic *a.* chih⁴ yao⁴ shu⁴ te¹ 製藥術的.

pheasant *n.* chih⁴ 雉, yeh³ chi¹ 野雞.

phenomenon *n.* hsien⁴ hsiang⁴ 現象.

philanthropy *n.* tz'u² shan⁴ 慈善.

philosopher *n.* che² hsüeh² chia¹ 哲學家.

philosophy *n.* che² hsüeh² 哲學.

phlegm *n.* t'an² 痰.

phlegmatic *a.* ch'ih² tun⁴ te¹ 遲鈍的.

phosphate *n.* lin² suan¹ yen² 燐酸鹽.

phosphorus *n.* lin² 燐.

photograph *n.* chao⁴ p'ien⁴ 照片.

photographer *n.* she⁴ ying³ chia¹ 攝影家.

photography *n.* she⁴ ying³ shu⁴ 攝影術.

phrase *n.* p'ien⁴ yü³ 片語.

phraseology *n.* yung⁴ tzu⁴ 用字.

phrenology *n.* ku³ hsiang¹ hsüeh² 骨相學.

physic *n.* (*drug*) i¹ yao⁴ 醫藥.

physical *a.* shen¹ t'i³ te¹ 身體的; ~ **drill,** t'i³ ts'ao¹ 體操; ~ **education,** t'i³ yü⁴ 體育; ~ **inspection,** t'i³ ko² chien³ ch'a² 體格檢查.

physician *n.* i¹ sheng¹ 醫生, nei⁴ k'o¹ i¹ sheng¹ 內科醫生.

physiology *n.* sheng¹ li³ hsüeh² 生理學.

pianist *n.* kang¹ ch'in² chia¹ 鋼琴家.

piano *n.* kang¹ ch'in² 鋼琴.

pick *n.* (*choice*) hsüan³ tse² 選擇, (*tool*) hao² tsui³ ch'u² 鶴嘴鋤; *v.* (*choose*) hsüan³ tse² 選擇, (*flower*) chai¹ ts'ai³ 摘採.

pickle *n.* yen² chih¹ 鹽汁.

pickpocket *n.* p'a² shou³ 扒手.

picture *n.* t'u² hua⁴ 圖畫; *v.* hui⁴ hua⁴ 繪畫.

picturesque *a.* ju² hua⁴ te¹ 如畫的.

pie *n.* p'ai² 排(外來語). 「份.

piece *n.* (*bit*) hsiao³ p'ien⁴ 小片, (*part*) pu⁴ fen⁴ 部

piecemeal *adv.* tuan⁴ p'ien⁴ ti¹ 斷片地, ling² sui⁴ ti¹ 零碎地.

pier *n.* ma³ t'ou² 碼頭.

pierce *v.* tz'u⁴ ju⁴ 刺入, (*hole*) ch'uan¹ k'ung³ 穿

piety *n.* ch'ien² ch'eng² 虔誠. 「孔.

pig *n.* chu¹ 豬.

pigeon *n.* ko¹ 鴿.

pike *n.* mao² 矛.

pile *n.* i⁴ tui¹ 一堆; *v.* tui¹ chi¹ 堆積.

pilfer *v.* t'ou¹ ch'ieh⁴ 偷竊.

pilgrim *n.* hsiang¹ k'o⁴ 香客.

pilgrimage *n.* ch'ao² pai⁴ sheng⁴ ti⁴ 朝拜聖地.

pill *n.* wan² chi¹ 丸劑, yao⁴ wan² 藥丸.

pillage *n.* chieh² lüeh⁴ 劫掠; *v.* chieh² lüeh⁴ 劫掠.

pillar *n.* chu⁴ 柱.

pillow *n.* chen³ t'ou² 枕頭.

pillowcase *n.* chen³ t'ou² t'ao⁴ 枕頭套.

pilot *n.* (*ship*) to⁴ fu¹ 舵夫, (*plane*) fei¹ chi¹ chia¹ shih³ yüan² 飛機駕駛員.

pimple *n.* hsiao³ ch'iu¹ chen³ 小丘疹(醫).

pin *n.* pieh² chen¹ 別針; *v.* chen¹ chu⁴ 針住.

pincers *n.* ch'ien² tzu¹ 鉗子.

pinch *n.*, *v.* k'ung⁴ 控.

pine *n.* sung¹ 松; *v.* (*yearn*) ch'ieh⁴ wang⁴ 切望.

pineapple *n.* po¹ lo² mi⁴ 波蘿蜜, feng⁴ li² 鳳梨.

pink *a.* fen³ hung² se⁴ te¹ 粉紅色的; *n.* fen³ hung² se⁴ 粉紅色.

pious *a.* je⁴ hsin¹ tsung¹ chiao⁴ te¹ 熱心宗教的.

pipe *n.* yen¹ tou³ 烟斗.

pippin *n.* p'ing² kuo³ lei⁴ 蘋果類.

pique *n.* yün⁴ nu⁴ 慍怒; *v.* shih³ yün⁴ nu⁴ 使慍怒.

piracy *n.* hai² shang⁴ ch'iang³ chieh² 海上搶劫.

pirate *n.* hai³ tao⁴ 海盜; *v.* tang¹ hai³ tao³ 當海盜.

piratical *a.* hai³ tao⁴ te¹ 海盜的.

pistol *n.* shou³ ch'iang¹ 手鎗.

piston *n.* huo² sai³ 活塞.

pit *n.* k'eng¹ 坑.

pitch *n.* t'ou² chih³ 投擲, (*point*) ting² tien³ 頂點; *v.* p'ao¹ chih² 拋擲, (*set up*) shu⁴ ch'i³ 豎起.

pitcher *n.* shui³ p'ing² 水瓶, (*baseball*) t'ou² shou³ 投手.

piteous *a.* k'o³ lien² te¹ 可憐的.

pitiful *a.* k'o³ lien² te¹ 可憐的.

pitiless *a.* wu² tz'u² pei¹ hsin¹ te¹ 無慈悲心的.

pity *n., v.* lien² min³ 憐憫.

pivot *n.* shu¹ chou² 樞軸.

placard *n.* chao¹ t'ieh¹ 招貼.

place *n.* ch'ang² so³ 場所; *v.* fang⁴ chih⁴ 放置.

placid *a.* p'ing² ching⁴ te¹ 平靜的.

plague *n.* wen¹ i⁴ 瘟疫(疫).

plain *a.* ch'ing¹ ch'u³ te¹ 清楚的; *n.* p'ing² yüan² 平原.

plaint *n.* su⁴ k'u³ 訴苦.

plaintiff *n.* yüan² kao⁴ 原告.

plaintive *a.* pei¹ ai¹ te¹ 悲哀的.

plan *n., v.* chi⁴ hua⁴ 計劃.

plane *n.* p'ing² mien⁴ 平面, (*airplane*) fei¹ chi¹ 飛機, (*carpenter*) pao⁴ 鉋.

planet *n.* hsing² hsing¹ 行星.

plank *n.* pan³ 板.

plant *n.* chih² wu⁴ 植物; *v.* chung¹ chih² 種植.

plantation *n.* shu⁴ lin² 樹林, chung¹ chih² ti⁴ 種植地, chih² min² ti⁴ 殖民地.

plaster *n.* hui¹ ni² 灰泥; *v.* t'u² i³ hui¹ ni² 塗以灰泥.

plastic *a.* chiao¹ chih² te¹ 膠質的.

plate *n.* p'an² 盤.

platform *n.* t'ai² 臺, (*station*) yüeh⁴ t'ai² 月臺.

platinum *n.* pai² chin¹ 白金, po² 鉑.

platoon *n.* p'ai² 排, (*in certain special units*) ch'ü¹ tui² 區隊.

platter *n.* ta⁴ p'an² 大盤.

plausible *a.* ssu⁴ yu² li³ te¹ 似有理的.

play *n.* yu² hsi⁴ 遊戲; *v.* wan² shua³ 玩耍.

player *n.* yen³ chi⁴ che⁴ 演技者.

playful *a.* hsi¹ hsi⁴ te¹ 嬉戲的.

playhouse *n.* wan² chü⁴ shih⁴ 玩具室.

plea *n.* k'en³ ch'iu² 懇求.

plead *v.* pien⁴ hu⁴ 辯護.

pleasant *a.* ling⁴ jen² yü² k'uai⁴ te¹ 令人愉快的.

please *v.* shih⁴ hsi³ yüeh⁴ 使喜悅.

pleasing *a.* yü² k'uai⁴ te¹ 愉快的.

pleasure *n.* yü² k'uai⁴ 愉快.

pledge *n.* shih⁴ yüeh¹ 誓約.

plenipotentiary *n.* ch'üan² ch'üan² tai⁴ piao³ 全權代表; *a.* yu³ ch'üan² ch'üan² te¹ 有全權的.

plenitude *n.* wan² ch'üan² 完全.

plentiful *a.* feng¹ fu⁴ te¹ 豐富的.

plenty *n.* feng¹ fu⁴ 豐富.

pleurisy *n.* hsiung¹ mo⁴ yen² 胸膜炎(醫).

pliable *a.* i⁴ ch'ü¹ te¹ 易曲的, jou² juan³ te¹ 柔軟的.

pliers *n.* ch'ien² tzu¹ 鉗子.

plight *n.* ch'ing² hsing² 情形, ching³ k'uang⁴ 景況.

plod *v.* chung⁴ pu⁴ erh² hsing² 重步而行.

plot *n.* yin¹ mou² 陰謀, (*ground*) ti⁴ ch'ü¹ 地區.

plover *n.* chü¹ chiu¹ 雎鳩.

plow, plough *n.* ch'u² 鋤, (*snow*) p'ai³ hsüeh³ chi¹ 排雪機.

plowman, ploughman *n.* nung² fu¹ 農夫.

plowshare, ploughshare *n.* li² t'ou² 犁頭.

pluck *v.* (*pick*) chai¹ 摘, (*pull*) t'o¹ la¹ 拖拉.

plug *n.* sai¹ tzu¹ 塞子; *v.* sai¹ chu⁴ 塞住.

plum *n.* mei² 梅.

plumage *n.* yü³ mao² 羽毛.

plumb *adv.* hsüan² ch'ui² 懸錘.

plumber *n.* ch'ien¹ chiang⁴ 鉛匠.

plume *n.* yü³ mao² 羽毛; *v.* shih¹ i² yü³ mao² 飾以羽毛.

plummet *n.* ch'ien¹ ch'ui² hsien⁴ 鉛錘線.

plump *a.* fei² man² te¹ 肥滿的.

plunder *n.* lüeh⁴ to² wu⁴ 掠奪物; *v.* ch'iang³ chieh² 搶劫.

plunge *v.* t'u² chin⁴ 突進.

plural *n.* fu⁴ shu⁴ 複數.

plus *prep.* chia¹ 加.

plush *n.* ssu¹ jung² 絲絨.

pneumonia *n.* fei⁴ yen² 肺炎.

pocket *n.* i¹ tai⁴ 衣袋.

pocketbook *n.* hsiao³ p'i² chia¹ 小皮夾.

pod *n.* tou⁴ chia¹ 豆莢.

196

poem *n.* shih¹ 詩.

poet *n.* shih¹ jen² 詩人.

poetical *a.* shih¹ te¹ 詩的, shih¹ jen² te¹ 詩人的.

poetry *n.* shih¹ 詩.

point *n.* (*dot*) tien³ 點; *v.* (*punctuate*) chia¹ piao² 加標點.

pointed *a.* chien¹ jui⁴ te¹ 尖銳的.

poise *v.* p'ing² heng² 平衡.

poison *n.* tu² wu⁴ 毒物; *v.* ling⁴ chung⁴ tu² 令中毒.

poisonous *a.* yu³ tu² te¹ 有毒的.

poke *v.* ch'ung¹ 衝.

poker *n.* (*card*) p'ai² hsi¹ 牌戲.

pole *n.* kan¹ 竿, (*South*) nan² chi² 南極, (*North*) pei³ chi² 北極, (*positive*) yang² chi² 陽極, (*negative*) yin¹ chi² 陰極.

polestar *n.* pei³ chi² hsing¹ 北極星.

police *n.* ching³ ch'a² 警察.

policeman *n.* hsün² ching³ 巡警, ching³ kuan¹ 警官.

policy *n.* cheng⁴ ts'e⁴ 政策.

polish *n.* kuang¹ hua² 光滑; *v.* ts'a¹ liang⁴ 擦亮.

polite *a.* yu³ li³ te¹ 有禮的.

politeness *n.* li³ mao⁴ 禮貌.

political *a.* cheng⁴ chih⁴ te¹ 政治的.

politician *n.* cheng⁴ chih⁴ chia¹ 政治家.

politics *n.* cheng⁴ chih⁴ hsüeh¹ 政治學.

poll *n.* t'ou² p'iao⁴ shu⁴ 投票數.

pollute *v.* wu¹ cho² 汙濁.

pollution *n.* tien⁴ wu¹ 玷汙, jan³ wu¹ 染汙(水).

pomade *n.* sheng¹ fa³ yu² 生髮油.

pomegranate *n.* shih² liu² 石榴.

pomp *n.* hua² li⁴ 華麗.

pompous *a.* tzu⁴ fu⁴ te¹ 自負的, k'ua¹ chang¹ te¹ 誇張的.

pond *n.* ch'ih² 池.

ponder *v.* k'ao³ lü⁴ 考慮, ch'en² ssu¹ 沈思.

ponderous *a.* pen⁴ chung⁴ te¹ 笨重的.

pontiff *a.* (*the Pope*) chiao⁴ huang² 教皇.

pony *n.* hsiao² ma³ 小馬.

pool *n.* ch'ih² 池.

poor *a.* p'in² ch'iung² te¹ 貧窮的.

Pope, pope *n.* lo² ma³ chiao⁴ huang² 羅馬教皇.

poplar *n.* pai² yang² 白楊(植).

poppy *n.* ying¹ su⁴ 罌粟.

197

populace *n.* p'ing² min² 平民.

popular *a.* (*well-liked*) fu² chung⁴ wang⁴ te¹ 孚衆望的, (*common*) t'ung¹ su² te¹ 通俗的.

popularity *n.* jen² wang⁴ 人望.

populate *v.* chü¹ chu⁴ 居住.

population *n.* jen² k'ou³ 人口.

populous *a.* jen² k'ou³ ch'ou² mi⁴ te¹ 人口稠密的.

porcelain *n.* tz'u² ch'i⁴ 瓷器.

porch *n.* ju⁴ k'ou³ 入口.

pore *n.* mao² k'ung³ 毛孔, hsi⁴ k'ung³ 細孔.

pork *n.* chu¹ jou⁴ 豬肉.

porous *a.* yu³ hsi⁴ k'ung³ te¹ 有細孔的.

porphyry *n.* yün² pan¹ shih² 雲斑石.

porridge *n.* chou¹ 粥.

port *n.* chiang² k'ou³ 港口; ~ of debarkation, hsieh⁴ yün⁴ chiang² k'ou³ 卸運港口; ~ of embarkation, chuang¹ yün⁴ chiang² k'ou³ 裝運港口.

portable *a.* k'o³ hsieh² tai⁴ te¹ 可攜帶的.

portal *n.* men² 門, (*entrance*) ju⁴ k'ou³ 入口.

portend *v.* yü⁴ shih⁴ 預示.

portent *n.* hsiung¹ chao⁴ 凶兆.

portentous *a.* hsiung¹ chao⁴ te¹ 兇兆的, pu⁴ hsiang² te¹ 不祥的. 「jen² 守門人.

porter *n.* t'iao¹ fu¹ 挑夫, (*doorkeeper*) shou³ men²

port-hole *n.* ch'uan² ts'e⁴ chih¹ p'ao⁴ men² 船側之礮門, chuang¹ huo⁴ k'ou³ 裝貨口, hsien² ch'uang¹ 舷窗.

portion *n.* i² pu⁴ fen¹ 一部分.

portrait *n.* hsiao⁴ hsiang⁴ 肖像.

position *n.* wei⁴ chih⁴ 位置; ~ warfare, chen⁴ ti⁴ chan⁴ 陣地戰(軍).

positive *a.* ch'üeh⁴ ting⁴ te¹ 確定的.

possess *v.* chan⁴ yu³ 佔有.

possession *n.* chan⁴ yu³ 佔有.

possessor *n.* wu⁴ chu³ 物主, so² yu² che³ 所有者.

possibility *n.* k'o³ neng² hsing⁴ 可能性.

possible *a.* k'o³ neng² te¹ 可能的.

post *n.* (*mail*) yu² chien⁴ 郵件; *v.* (*mail*) yu² chi⁴ 郵寄, (*fasten up*) chang¹ t'ieh¹ 張貼; ~ card, ming² hsin⁴ p'ien⁴ 明信片; ~ exchange, chün¹ chung¹ ho² tso⁴ she³ 軍中合作社(軍); ~ office, yu² cheng⁴ chü² 郵政局.

postage *n.* yu² tzu¹ 郵資.

postdate *v.* yü⁴ t'ien² jih⁴ ch'i¹ 預填日期.

poster *n.* chao¹ t'ieh¹ 招貼.

posterity *n.* hou⁴ tai⁴ 後代.

posthaste *adv.* chi² su² te¹ 極速的.

postman *n.* yu² ch'ai¹ 郵差.

postmark *n.* yu² ch'o¹ 郵戳.

postmaster *n.* yu² cheng⁴ chü² chang³ 郵政局長.

postpaid *a.* yu² fei⁴ i³ ch'i⁴ te¹ 郵費已訖的.

postpone *v.* tan¹ ko¹ 耽擱, yen³ ch'i¹ 延期.

postscript *n.* tsai⁴ ch'i³ 再啓, fu⁴ pai² 附白.

posture *n.* tzu¹ shih⁴ 姿勢.

postwar *a.* chan⁴ hou⁴ te¹ 戰後的.

pot *n.* hu² 壺.

potato *n.* ma³ ling² shu³ 馬鈴薯.

potent *a.* yu³ li⁴ te¹ 有力的.

potter *n.* t'ao² kung¹ 陶工.

pottery *n.* t'ao² ch'i⁴ 陶器.

pouch *n.* tai⁴ 袋.

poultry *n.* chia¹ ch'in² 家禽. 「chin⁴ ku⁴ 禁錮.

pound *n.* pang⁴ 磅; *v.* chung⁴ chi¹ 重擊, (*confine*)

pour *v.* ch'ing¹ chu⁴ 傾注.

poverty *n.* p'in² ch'iung² 貧窮. 「樂.

powder *n.* fen³ mo⁴ 粉末, (*explosive*) huo³ yao⁴ 火

power *n.* li⁴ 力; ~ **plant,** tien⁴ li⁴ ch'ang³ 電力廠.

powerful *a.* yu³ li⁴ te¹ 有力的.

powerless *a.* wu² li⁴ te¹ 無力的. 「yung⁴ 可用.

practicability *n.* k'o³ shih² hsing² 可實行, k'o³

practicable *a.* k'o³ shih² hsing² te¹ 可實行的, k'o³ yung⁴ te¹ 可用的.

practical *a.* shih² hsing² te¹ 實行的; ~ **joke,** e⁴ tso⁴ chü⁴ 惡作劇.

practice *n.* lien⁴ hsi² 練習, (*habit*) hsi² kuan⁴ 習慣.

practise *v.* lien⁴ hsi² 練習.

practitioner *n.* ts'ao¹ yeh⁴ che³ 操業者.

praise *n., v.* tsan⁴ mei³ 讚美.

praiseworthy *a.* k'o³ chia¹ chiang³ te¹ 可嘉獎的.

prank *n.* hsi⁴ nung⁴ 戲弄. 「tao³ 祈禱.

pray *v.* (*entreat*) k'en³ ch'iu² 懇求, (*to God*) ch'i²

prayer *n.* ch'i² tao³ 祈禱.

preach *v.* chiang³ tao⁴ 講道, ch'uan² chiao⁴ 傳教.

preacher *n.* mu⁴ shih¹ 牧師.

preamble *n.* hsü⁴ yen² 序言.

precaution *n.* yü⁴ fang² 預防, yü⁴ fang² fa³ 預防法.

precede *v.* hsien¹ hsing² 先行.

precedent *n.* hsien¹ li⁴ 先例.

precept *n.* chen¹ yen² 箴言.

precinct *n.* ch'ü⁴ yü⁴ 區域.

precious *a.* pao³ kuei⁴ te¹ 寶貴的.

precipice *n.* chüeh¹ pi⁴ 絕壁.

precipitate *a.* ts'ung¹ ts'u⁴ te¹ 忽促的.

precise *a.* ching¹ ch'üeh⁴ te¹ 精確的.

precision *n.* ching¹ ch'üeh⁴ 精確, chun¹ ch'üeh⁴ 準確; ～ **firing,** ching¹ mi⁴ she⁴ chi¹ 精密射擊 (軍).

preclude *v.* tsu² chih² 阻止, yü⁴ fang² 預防.

precocious *a.* tsao³ shou² te¹ 早熟的.

predecessor *n.* ch'ien² jen⁴ che³ 前任者, (*ancestor*) tsu³ hsien¹ 祖先.

predict *v.* yü⁴ yen² 預言, yü⁴ kao⁴ 預告.

predilection *n.* ai⁴ hao³ 愛好, p'ien¹ ai⁴ 偏愛.

predominant *a.* chan⁴ yu¹ shih⁴ te¹ 佔優勢的.

predominate *v.* chan⁴ yu¹ shih⁴ 佔優勢.

preeminent *a.* cho¹ yüeh⁴ te¹ 卓越的.

preface *n.* hsü⁴ yen² 序言; *v.* tso⁴ hsü⁴ 作序.

prefer *v.* ai⁴ hao³ 愛好.

preferable *a.* chiao⁴ yu¹ te¹ 較優的.

preference *n.* p'ien¹ ai⁴ 偏愛.

preferment *n.* cho² sheng¹ 擢升.

prefix *n.* tzu⁴ shou³ 字首.

pregnancy *n.* huai² yün⁴ 懷孕.

pregnant *a.* yu³ yün⁴ te¹ 有孕的. 「斷.

prejudice *n.* p'ien¹ chien⁴ 偏見; *v.* wu³ tuan⁴ 武

prelate *n.* chu³ chiao⁴ 主教.

preliminary *a.* ch'u¹ pu⁴ te¹ 初步的. 「te¹ 過早的.

premature *a.* tsao³ shou² te¹ 早熟的, kuo⁴ tsao³

premeditate *v.* yü⁴ ssu¹ 預思, yü⁴ chi⁴ 預計.

premeditation *n.* yü⁴ ssu¹ 預思, yü⁴ chi⁴ 預計.

premier *a.* ti⁴ i¹ te¹ 第一的, shou³ yao⁴ te¹ 首要的; *n.* shou³ hsiang⁴ 首相.

premium *n.* (*prize*) chiang² p'in³ 獎品, (*insurance*) pao² hsien³ fei⁴ 保險費.

preparation *n.* yü⁴ pei⁴ 預備.

preparatory *a.* yü⁴ pei⁴ te¹ 預備的; ～ **command,** yü⁴ ling⁴ 預令(軍); ～ **fire,** shih⁴ she⁴ 試射(軍).

prepare *v.* yü⁴ pei⁴ 預備.

prepay *v.* yü⁴ fu⁴ 預付.

preponderate *v.* sheng⁴ kuo⁴ 勝過.

preposition *n.* ch'ien² chih⁴ tz'u² 前置詞, chieh⁴ hsi⁴ tz'u² 介系詞.

prepossession *n.* ch'eng² chien⁴ 成見, p'ien¹ ai⁴ 偏愛.

preposterous *a.* huang¹ miu⁴ te¹ 荒謬的.

prerogative *n.* t'e⁴ ch'üan² 特權.

prescribe *v.* (*order*) chih³ ling⁴ 指令, (*medical advice*) k'ai¹ yao⁴ fang¹ 開藥方.

prescription *n.* (*order*) ming⁴ ling⁴ 命令, (*medicine*) yao⁴ fang¹ 藥方.

presence *n.* tsai⁴ ch'ang³ 在場.

present *a.* tsai⁴ ch'ang³ te¹ 在場的, (*now*) hsien⁴ tsai⁴ te¹ 現在的; *n.* hsien⁴ tsai⁴ 現在, (*gift*) li³ wu⁴ 禮物; *v.* tseng⁴ sung⁴ 贈送.

presently *adv.* pu⁴ chiu³ 不久.

preservation *n.* pao³ ts'un² 保存, pao³ ch'üan² 保全.

preserve *v.* pao³ ts'un² 保存.

president *n.* hui⁴ chang³ 會長, (*of country*) tsung² t'ung³ 總統.

press *n.* (*newspapers*) hsin¹ wen² chih³ 新聞紙, (*machine*) yin⁴ shua¹ chi¹ 印刷機; *v.* ya¹ p'o⁴ 壓迫.

pressing *a.* chi² p'o⁴ te¹ 急迫的.

pressure *n.* ya¹ li⁴ 壓力.

presumable *a.* k'o³ i⁴ tuan⁴ te¹ 可憶斷的, k'o² chia³ ting⁴ te¹ 可假定的.

presume *v.* (*suppose*) t'ui¹ tuan⁴ 推斷, (*dare*) tan² kan³ 膽敢.

pretend *v.* chia³ chuang¹ 假裝.

pretext *n.* chieh⁴ k'ou³ 藉口, chia³ t'o¹ 假託.

pretty *a.* mei³ li⁴ te¹ 美麗的.

prevail *v.* liu² hsing² 流行.

prevalence *n.* sheng⁴ hsing² 盛行.

prevalent *a.* liu² hsing² te¹ 流行的.

prevaricate *v.* t'ui¹ t'o¹ 推託.

prevarication *n.* t'ui¹ t'o¹ 推託, tun⁴ tz'u² 遁辭.

prevent *v.* fang² chih³ 防止.

prevention *n.* fang² chih³ 防止.

preventive *a.* yü⁴ fang² te¹ 預防的.　　「以前的.
previous *a.* tsai⁴ hsien¹ te¹ 在先的, i³ ch'ien² te¹
prey *v.* lieh⁴ pu³ 獵捕.
price *n.* chia⁴ chih² 價值.
priceless *a.* wu² chia⁴ te¹ 無價的.
prick *v.* chien¹ tz'u⁴ 尖刺.
pride *n.* tzu⁴ tsun¹ 自尊.
priest *n.* mu⁴ shih¹ 牧師, chiao⁴ shih⁴ 教士.
priestly *a.* mu⁴ shih¹ te¹ 牧師的, chiao⁴ shih⁴ te¹
教士的.
primary *a.* tsui⁴ ch'u¹ te¹ 最初的, (*chief*) chu³
yao⁴ te¹ 主要的; ～ **education,** ch'u¹ chi² chiao⁴
yü⁴ 初級教育; ～ **school,** hsiao³ hsüeh² hsiao⁴
小學校.
prime *a.* shou³ yao⁴ te¹ 首要的.
primer *n.* ch'u¹ chi² tu² pen³ 初級讀本, (*gunpowder*) lei² kuan³ 雷管.
primitive *a.* yüan² shih³ te¹ 原始的.
primrose *n.* ying¹ ts'ao³ hua¹ 櫻草花.
prince *n.* huang² t'ai⁴ tzu³ 皇太子, (*ruler*) wang²
王(小國).　　　　　　　　　「fei¹ tzu¹ 妃子.
princess *n.* kung¹ chu³ 公主, (*wife of a prince*)
principal *a.* chu³ yao⁴ te¹ 主要的, shou³ yao⁴ te¹
首要的; *n.* hsiao⁴ chang³ 校長.
principle *n.* yüan² tse² 原則.
print *n.*, *v.* yin⁴ shua¹ 印刷.
printer *n.* yin⁴ shua¹ che³ 印刷者.
printing *n.* yin⁴ shua¹ 印刷, yin⁴ shua¹ shu⁴ 印刷
prior *a.* tsai⁴ ch'ien² te¹ 在前的.　　　　　「術.
priority *n.* yu¹ hsien¹ 優先.　　　　　　「三稜鏡.
prism *n.* leng² chu⁴ t'i³ 稜柱體, san¹ leng² ching⁴
prismatic *a.* san¹ leng² hsing² te¹ 三稜形的.
prison *n.* chien¹ yü⁴ 監獄.
prisoner *n.* ch'iu² fan⁴ 囚犯.
private *a.* ssu¹ jen² te¹ 私人的; *n.* shih⁴ ping¹ 士
兵; ～ **enterprise,** ssu¹ jen² ch'i⁴ yeh⁴ 私人企業;
～ **school,** ssu¹ li⁴ hsüeh² hsiao⁴ 私立學校; ～
teacher, ssu¹ jen² chiao⁴ shou⁴ 私人教授.
privilege *n.* t'e⁴ ch'üan² 特權.　　　　　　　「賞.
prize *n.* chiang² p'in³ 獎品; *v.* chiang² shang³ 獎
probability *n.* huo⁴ jan² hsing⁴ 或然性.

202

probable *a.* huo⁴ yu³ te¹ 或有的.

probation *n.* shih⁴ yen⁴ 試驗.

probity *n.* cheng⁴ chih² 正直.

problem *n.* wen⁴ t'i² 問題.

procedure *n.* shou³ hsü⁴ 手續.

proceed *v.* chin⁴ hsing² 進行; *n.* (*plural*) shou¹ ju⁴ 收入, shou¹ i⁴ 收益.

process *n.* kuo⁴ ch'eng² 過程.

procession *n.* hsing² lieh⁴ 行列.

proclaim *v.* hsüan¹ kao⁴ 宣告, kung¹ pu⁴ 公佈.

proclamation *n.* hsüan¹ kao⁴ 宣告, kung¹ pu⁴ 公佈.　　　　　　　　　　　　「偏向.

proclivity *n.* ch'ing¹ hsiang⁴ 傾向, p'ien¹ hsiang⁴

procrastinate *v.* yen² ko¹ 延擱, yen² ch'i¹ 延期

procrastination *n.* yen² ko¹ 延擱, yen² ch'i¹ 延期.

procure *v.* huo⁴ te² 獲得.

prodigal *a.* lang⁴ fei⁴ te¹ 浪費的.

prodigality *n.* lang⁴ fei⁴ 浪費, she¹ ch'ih³ 奢侈.

prodigious *a.* i⁴ ch'ang² te¹ 異常的, chü⁴ ta⁴ te¹ 巨

prodigy *n.* ch'i² shih⁴ 奇事.　　　　　　　　「大的.

produce *n.* sheng¹ ch'an³ wu⁴ 生產物; *v.* (*make*) sheng¹ ch'an³ 生產.

producer *n.* sheng¹ ch'an² che³ 生產者, (*movie*) yen³ ch'u¹ che³ 演出者.

product *n.* sheng¹ ch'an³ wu⁴ 生產物.

production *n.* (*manufacture*) sheng¹ ch'an³ 生產, (*product*) sheng¹ ch'an³ wu⁴ 生產物.

productive *a.* sheng¹ ch'an³ te¹ 生產的.

profanation *n.* hsieh⁴ tu⁴ shen² sheng⁴ 褻瀆神聖.

profane *a.* fei¹ shen² sheng⁴ te¹ 非神聖的; *v.* hsieh⁴ tu⁴ 褻瀆.

profanity *n.* hsieh⁴ tu⁴ 褻瀆.

profess *v.* hsüan¹ ch'eng¹ 宣稱.

profession *n.* chih² yeh⁴ 職業.

professional *a.* chuan¹ men² te¹ 專門的.

professor *n.* chiao⁴ shou⁴ 教授.

proffer *v.* feng⁴ hsien⁴ 奉獻.

proficiency *n.* shou² lien⁴ 熟練.　　　　　「chia¹ 專家.

proficient *a.* shou² lien⁴ te¹ 熟練的; *n.* chuan¹

profile *n.* p'ou¹ mien⁴ 剖面, (*outline*) lun² k'uo⁴ 輪

profit *n.* li⁴ i⁴ 利益.　　　　　　　　　　　　「廓.

203

profitable *a.* yu³ li⁴ te¹ 有利的.

profligate *a.* fang⁴ tang⁴ te¹ 放蕩的.

profound *a.* shen¹ te¹ 深的.

profuse *a.* po² shih¹ te¹ 博施的, to¹ ch'an³ te¹ 多產的, feng¹ fu⁴ te¹ 豐富的.

progeny *n.* hou⁴ i⁴ 後裔.

program *n.* chieh² mu⁴ 節目.

progress *a., v.* chin⁴ pu⁴ 進步.

progressive *a.* ch'ien²chin⁴ te¹ 前進的, chin⁴ pu⁴ te¹ 進步的.

prohibit *v.* chin⁴ chih³ 禁止.

prohibition *n.* chin⁴ chih³ 禁止.

prohibitive *a.* chin⁴ chih³ te¹ 禁止的.

project *n.* chi⁴ hua⁴ 計畫; *v.* (*on screen*) t'ou² ying³ 投影, (*stick out*) t'u² ch'u¹ 突出.

projectile *n.* she⁴ tan⁴ 射彈.

prolific *a.* to¹ ch'an³ te¹ 多產的.

prolix *a.* jung³ ch'ang² te¹ 冗長的.

prologue, prolog *n.* (*by actor*) k'ai¹ ch'ang³ pai² 開場白, (*preface*) hsü⁴ yen² 序言.

prolong *v.* yen² ch'ang² 延長.

promenade *n.* san³ pu⁴ 散步.

prominent *a.* ch'u¹ chung⁴ te¹ 出衆的.

promiscuous *a.* hun⁴ luan⁴ te¹ 混亂的.

promise *n.* no⁴ yen² 諾言; *v.* ta¹ ying⁴ 答應.

promissory *a.* yüeh¹ ch'i¹ te¹ 約期的.

promote *v.* t'i² sheng¹ 提升, (*help to develop*) ts'u⁴ chin⁴ 促進.

promotion *n.* tiao⁴ sheng¹ 調升, (*development*) ts'u⁴ chin⁴ 促進.

prompt *a.* hsün⁴ su² te¹ 迅速的; *v.* chi¹ li⁴ 激勵.

pronoun *n.* tai⁴ ming² tz'u² 代名詞.

pronounce *v.* fa¹ yin¹ 發音. 「法.

pronunciation *n.* fa¹ yin¹ 發音, tu² yin¹ fa³ 讀音

proof *n.* cheng⁴ ming² 證明, (*of book*) chiao⁴ yang⁴ 校樣.

prop *v.* chih¹ ch'ih² 支持. 「校樣.

propagate *v.* fan² chih² 繁殖.

propel *n.* t'ui¹ chin⁴ 推進.

propeller *n.* lo² hsüan² chiang³ 螺旋槳.

proper *a.* shih⁴ tang¹ te¹ 適當的.

property *n.* ts'ai² ch'an³ 財產, (*quality*) hsing⁴ chih² 性質.

prophecy *n.* yü⁴ yen² 預言. 「chih² 性質.

prophesy *v.* yü⁴ yen² 預言.

prophet *n.* yü⁴ yen² chia¹ 預言家.

prophetic *a.* yü⁴ yen² te¹ 預言的.

proportion *n.* pi³ li⁴ 比例.

proportionate *a.* an⁴ pi³ li⁴ te¹ 按比例的.

proposal *n.* t'i² i⁴ 提議.

propose *v.* t'i² i⁴ 提議.

proposition *n.* t'i² i⁴ 提議.

proprietor *n.* so² yu² che³ 所有者.

propriety *n.* shih⁴ tang¹ 適當.

prose *n.* san³ wen² 散文.

prosecute *v.* k'ung⁴ su⁴ 控訴.

prosecution *n.* k'ung⁴ su⁴ 控訴.

prosecutor *n.* k'ung⁴ su⁴ che³ 控訴者.

prospect *n.* ch'i¹ wang⁴ 期望.

prospective *a.* ch'i¹ wang⁴ te¹ 期望的.

prosper *v.* (*flourish*) hsing¹ sheng⁴ 興盛.

prosperity *n.* hsing¹ sheng⁴ 興盛.

prosperous *a.* hsing¹ sheng⁴ te¹ 興盛的.

prostrate *v.* fu³ fu² 俯伏.

protect *v.* pao³ hu⁴ 保護.

protection *n.* pao³ hu⁴ 保護.

protector *n.* pao³ hu⁴ che³ 保護者.

protest *n.* k'ang⁴ i⁴ 抗議.

protestation *n.* k'ang⁴ i⁴ 抗議.

protrude *v.* shen¹ ch'u¹ 伸出, t'u² ch'u¹ 凸出.

proud *a.* ao⁴ man⁴ te¹ 傲慢的. 「ting⁴ 檢定.

prove *v.* shih⁴ yen⁴ 試驗, cheng⁴ shih² 證實, chien³

proverb *n.* ko² yen² 格言, yen⁴ yü³ 諺語.

proverbial *a.* ko² yen² te¹ 格言的, yen⁴ yü³ te¹ 諺

provide *v.* kung¹ chi³ 供給. 「語的.

providence *n.* t'ien¹ ming⁴ 天命.

provident *a.* hsien¹ chien⁴ te¹ 先見的.

providential *a.* t'ien¹ ming⁴ te¹ 天命的.

province *n.* sheng³ 省.

provincial *a.* sheng³ te¹ 省的. 「糧食.

provision *n.* kuei¹ ting⁴ 規定, (*plural*) liang² shih²

provisional *a.* chan⁴ shih² te¹ 暫時的.

provoke *v.* chi¹ nu⁴ 激怒.

prow *n.* ch'uan² shou³ 船首.

prowess *n.* yung² kan³ 勇敢.

prowl *v.* an⁴ so³ 暗索.

proximity *n.* chieh¹ chin⁴ 接近.

prudent *a.* shen¹ lü⁴ te¹ 深慮的.

prune *n.* niao³ mei² 鳥梅; *v.* hsiu¹ chien³ 修剪.

psalm *n.* sheng⁴ ko¹ 聖歌, tsan⁴ mei² shih¹ 讚美詩.

psychoanalysis *n.* hsin¹ li³ fen¹ hsi¹ 心理學分析.

psychology *n.* hsin¹ li³ hsüeh² 心理學.

psychosis *n.* ching¹ shen² ping⁴ 精神病(醫).

psychotherapy *n.* hsin¹ li³ liao² fa³ 心理療法(醫).

public *a.* kung¹ chung⁴ te¹ 公衆的, (*open to all*) kung¹ k'ai¹ te¹ 公開的; ~ **enemy,** kung¹ ti² 公敵; ~ **opinion,** kung¹ lun⁴ 公論.

publication *n.* ch'u¹ pan³ 出版, (*announcement*) kung¹ pu⁴ 公佈.

publicity *n.* hsüan¹ ch'uan² 宣傳.

publish *v.* ch'u¹ pan³ 出版, fa¹ hsing² 發行.

publisher *n.* ch'u¹ pan³ chia¹ 出版家, fa¹ hsing² [jen² 發行人.

pudding *n.* pu⁴ ting¹ 布丁(糕餅類).

puddle *n.* wu¹ shui³ ch'ih² 污水池.

puff *n.*, *v.* ch'ui¹ 吹.

pugnacious *a.* hao⁴ cheng¹ tou⁴ te¹ 好爭鬪的.

pull *v.* t'o¹ la¹ 拖拉.

pulley *n.* hua² ch'e¹ 滑車.

pulp *n.* sui³ 髓.

pulpit *n.* chiang³ t'an² 講壇.

pulsation *n.* t'uan² tung⁴ 搏動, t'iao⁴ tung⁴ 跳動.

pulse *n.* mo⁴ t'uan² 脈搏, (*beans*) tou⁴ lei⁴ 豆類.

pulverize *v.* yen² mo⁴ 研末, fen³ sui⁴ 粉碎.

pumice *n.* fu² shih² 浮石.

pump *n.* chi¹ t'ung³ 唧筒; *v.* yung⁴ chi² t'ung³ ch'ou¹ shui³ 用唧筒抽水, (*blow air into*) ch'ung¹ i³ k'ung¹ ch'i⁴ 充以空氣.

pumpkin *n.* nan² kua¹ 南瓜.

pun *n.* shuang¹ kuan¹ yü³ 雙關語. [眼.

punch *v.* (*hit*) ch'üan² ta³ 拳打, (*hole*) ta² yen² 打

punctual *a.* (*on time*) chun³ shih² te¹ 準時的.

punctuation *n.* piao¹ tien³ 標點, piao¹ tien² fa³ 標 [點法.

puncture *v.* tz'u⁴ k'ung³ 刺孔.

punish *v.* ch'u³ fa² 處罰.

punishment *n.* ch'u³ fa² 處罰.

puny *a.* jo⁴ hsiao³ te¹ 弱小的.

pupil *n.* hsüeh² sheng¹ 學生.

206

puppet *n.* k'uei² lei² 傀儡. 「tzu¹ 絨袴子.

puppy *n.* (*dog*) hsiao² kou³ 小狗, (*man*) wan² k'u⁴

purchase *n.*, *v.* kou⁴ mai³ 購買.

purchaser *n.* kou⁴ mai² che³ 購買者.

pure *a.* ch'un² ts'ui⁴ te¹ 純粹的

purgative *n.* hsieh⁴ yao⁴ 瀉藥. 「通便.

purge *v.* ch'ing¹ ch'u² 清除, (*bowel*) t'ung¹ pien⁴

purification *n.* chieh³ ching⁴ 潔淨, ch'eng² ch'ing¹

purify *v.* shih³ ch'ing¹ chieh² 使清潔. 「澄清.

purity *n.* ch'un² chieh² 純潔.

purloin *v.* t'ou¹ 偷, ch'ieh⁴ 竊.

purple *a.* tzu³ se⁴ te¹ 紫色的; *n.* tzu³ se⁴ 紫色.

purpose *n.* mu⁴ ti⁴ 目的.

purposely *adv.* ku⁴ i⁴ ti⁴ 故意地.

purse *n.* ch'ien² tai⁴ 錢袋, p'iao⁴ chia¹ 票夾.

purser *n.* k'uai⁴ chi⁴ yüan² 會計員.

pursue *v.* chui¹ pu³ 追捕.

pursuit *n.* chui¹ pu³ 追捕.

purvey *v.* pei⁴ pan⁴ 備辦.

pus *n.* nung² 膿(醫).

push *v.* ts'ui¹ ts'u⁴ 催促. 「hsiao³ te¹ 膽小的.

pusillanimous *a.* ch'üeh⁴ no⁴ te¹ 怯懦的, tan³

put *v.* an¹ chih⁴ 安置.

putrefy *v.* shih³ fu³ lan⁴ 使腐爛.

putrid *a.* fu³ ch'ou⁴ te¹ 腐臭的. 「惑.

puzzle *n.* nan² t'i² 難題; *v.* shih³ mi² huo⁴ 使迷

pyramid *n.* leng² chui¹ t'i³ 稜錐體, (*Egyptian*)
chin¹ tzu¹ t'a³ 金字塔.

Q

quack *n.* ya¹ chiao⁴ sheng¹ 鴨叫聲; *v.* tso⁴ ya¹
chiao⁴ 作鴨叫. 「hsing² 方形.

quadrangle *n.* ssu⁴ chiao³ hsing² 四角形, fang¹

quadrant *n.* (*instrument*) hsiang⁴ hsien⁴ i² 象限儀
(兵). 「曲.

quadrille *n.* fang¹ wu³ 方舞, fang¹ wu² ch'ü⁴ 方舞

quadruped *n.* ssu⁴ tsu² shou⁴ 四足獸, ssu⁴ tsu²
tung⁴ wu⁴ 四足動物.

quadruple *a.* ssu⁴ pei⁴ te¹ 四倍的. 「憺怕.

quail *n.* an¹ ku¹ 鵪鶉; *v.* wei² so¹ 畏縮, chü¹ p'a⁴

quaint *a.* ch'i² kuai⁴ te¹ 奇怪的, li³ ch'i² te¹ 離奇的.

quake *v.* yao² tung⁴ 搖動, chan⁴ li⁴ 戰慄.

Quaker *n.* chiao¹ yu³ p'ai⁴ chiao⁴ t'u² 教友派教徒.

qualification *n.* tzu¹ ko² 資格, (*limitation*) hsien⁴ chih⁴ 限制; ~ **course**, chen¹ pieh² she⁴ chi¹ 甄

qualified *a.* ho² ko² te¹ 合格的. 「別擊擊(軍).

qualify *v.* shih³ shih⁴ ho² 使適合.

quality *n.* hsing⁴ chih² 性質, (*of a force*) su⁴ chih²

quantity *n.* shu⁴ liang⁴ 數量. 「素質.

quarantine *n.* (*preventive*) fang² i⁴ ko² li² 防疫隔離, (*examination of incoming ship*) chien³ i⁴ ko² li² 檢疫隔離.

quarrel *n.* k'ou² chiao³ 口角; *v.* cheng¹ lun⁴ 爭論.

quarrelsome *a.* hao⁴ cheng¹ lun⁴ te¹ 好爭論的.

quarry *n.* shih² k'uang⁴ 石礦; *v.* ts'ai³ 採(石).

quart *n.* k'ua¹ erh³ 夸脫(量名).

quarter *n.* (*one fourth*) ssu⁴ fen¹ chih¹ i¹ 四分之一, (*25 cents*) erh⁴ chiao³ wu³ fen¹ 二角五分, (*time*) shih³ wu³ fen¹ chung¹ 十五分鐘, i² k'o⁴ chung¹ 一刻鐘, (*region*) ch'ü¹ yü⁴ 區域, (*quarters*) su⁴ she⁴ 宿舍; *v.* fen¹ wei² ssu⁴ fen⁴ 分爲四份, (*live*) chu⁴

quarterly *a.* mei³ chi⁴ te¹ 每季的. 「su⁴ 住宿.

quartermaster *n.* chün¹ hsü¹ kuan¹ 軍需官.

quartet, quartette *n.* (*for singers*) ssu⁴ ch'ung² ch'ang⁴ 四重唱, (*for players*) ssu⁴ ch'ung² tsou⁴ 四重奏, (*for music*) ssu⁴ pu⁴ ch'ü³ 四部曲.

quarto *n.* ssu⁴ k'ai¹ 四開, (*book*) ssu⁴ k'ai¹ pen³ 四

quartz *n.* shih² ying¹ 石英. 「開本.

quash *v.* chen⁴ ya¹ 鎭壓, (*make void*) tso⁴ fei⁴ 作廢.

quaver *n.* chan⁴ sheng¹ 顫聲; *v.* yao² tung⁴ 搖動, chan⁴ li⁴ 戰慄.

quay *n.* ma³ t'ou² 碼頭. 「皇.

queen *n.* huang² hou⁴ 皇后, (*ruler*) nü³ huang² 女

queer *a.* ch'i² kuai⁴ te¹ 奇怪的.

quell *v.* t'an² ya¹ 彈壓, chih⁴ fu² 制服.

quench *v.* mieh⁴ hsi¹ 滅熄.

querulous *a.* ming² pu⁴ p'ing² te¹ 鳴不平的, pao⁴ yüan⁴ te¹ 抱怨的.

question *n.* wen⁴ t'i² 問題, wen⁴ chü⁴ 問句; *v.*

hsün² wen⁴ 詢問, fei¹ nan⁴ 非難; ~ **mark,** wen⁴

questionable *a.* k'o³ i² te¹ 可疑的. └hao⁴ 問號.

questionaire *n.* i⁴ tsu³ wen¹ t'i² 一組問題.

quick *a.* hsün² su² te¹ 迅速的, shun⁴ hsi² te¹ 瞬息
的; ~ **fire,** su² she⁴ 速射; ~ **fuse,** shun⁴ fa¹
hsin⁴ kuan² 瞬發信管(軍).

quicken *v.* chia¹ su² 加速, shih³ hsün⁴ su² 使迅速.

quicklime *n.* sheng¹ shih² hui¹ 生石灰.

quicksilver *n.* shui³ yin⁴ 水銀.

quiet *a.* an¹ ching⁴ te¹ 安靜的; *n.* p'ing² ching⁴ 平
靜; *v.* shih³ p'ing² ching⁴ 使平靜.

quilt *n.* pei¹ ju⁴ 被褥; *v.* t'ien² sai⁴ 填塞.

quince *n.* wu⁴ po² 榲桲(植).

quinine *n.* k'uei² ning² 奎寧(醫), chi¹ na⁴ 鷄納(醫).

quinsy *n.* nung² hsing⁴ yen¹ men¹ yen² 膿性咽門
炎.

quire *n.* i⁴ tao¹ chih³ 一刀紙.

quit *v.* (*stop*) t'ing² chih³ 停止, (*leave*) li² k'ai¹ 離
開, (*pay back*) ch'ang² huan² 償還.

quite *adv.* wan² ch'üan² 完全, shih² fen¹ 十分.

quiver *n.* chan⁴ tung⁴ 顫動, (*case*) chien⁴ nang² 箭
囊; *v.* chan⁴ li⁴ 戰慄.

quoit *n.* t'ieh³ huan² 鐵環.

quota *n.* ting¹ e² 定額.

quotation *n.* yin³ yung⁴ 引用, yin³ cheng⁴ 引證;
~ **mark,** yin³ hao⁴ 引號.

quote *v.* yin³ yung⁴ 引用, yin³ cheng⁴ 引證.

quotient *n.* shang¹ shu⁴ 商數.

R

rabbit *n.* t'u⁴ 兔.

rabble *n.* pao⁴ t'u² 暴徒.

rabid *a.* k'uang² pao⁴ te¹ 狂暴的.

rabies *n.* chi¹ yao³ ping⁴ 瘈咬病(醫), feng¹
ch'üan² yao³ 瘋犬咬(醫).

race *n.* sai⁴ p'ao³ 賽跑; (*people*) chung³ tsu² 種族.

rack *n.* chia⁴ 架. └*v.* sai⁴ p'ao³ 賽跑.

racket, racquet *n.* wang³ ch'iu² p'ai¹ 網球拍.

radiance *n.* fu² she⁴ 輻射, fa¹ she⁴ 發射.

radiant *a.* fu² she⁴ te¹ 輻射的, fa¹ she⁴ te¹ 發射的.

radiate *v.* fu² she⁴ 輻射, fa¹ she⁴ 發射.

radiator *n.* san⁴ je⁴ ch'i⁴ 散熱器, (*automobile*) shui³ hsiang¹ 水箱.

radio *n.* wu² hsien⁴ tien⁴ 無線電; ～ **station,** wu² hsien⁴ tien⁴ t'ai² 無線電臺.

radioactive *a.* fang⁴ she⁴ hsing⁴ te¹ 放射性的.

radioactivity *n.* fang⁴ she⁴ hsing⁴ 放射性.

radiography *n.* fu² she⁴ hsüeh² 輻射學, fang⁴ she⁴ hsüeh² 放射學.

radiogram *n.* wu² hsien⁴ tien⁴ pao⁴ 無線電報.

radiotelegraphy *n.* wu² hsien⁴ tien⁴ pao⁴ shu⁴ 無線電報術.

radiotherapy *n.* fu² she⁴ hsing⁴ chih⁴ liao² shu⁴ 輻射性治療術.

radish *n.* lo² po² 蘿蔔.

radium *n.* kuang¹ lei² 鐳.

radius *n.* pan⁴ ching⁴ 半徑.

raffle *n.* ch'ou¹ chiang³ 抽獎.

raft *n.* fa² 筏, mu⁴ pai⁴ 木排.

rag *n.* p'o⁴ pu⁴ 破布.

rage *n., v.* sheng¹ nu⁴ 盛怒.

ragged *a.* lan² lü³ te¹ 襤褸的.

raid *n., v.* t'u² chi¹ 突擊.

rail *n.* (*fence*) lan² kan¹ 欄干, (*track*) kuei³ tao⁴ 軌道, (*railroad*) t'ieh³ lu⁴ 鐵路.

raillery *n.* ch'ao² hsiao⁴ 嘲笑.

railroad, railway *n.* t'ieh³ lu⁴ 鐵路, t'ieh³ tao⁴ 鐵道.

rain *n.* yü³ 雨; *v.* hsia⁴ yü³ 下雨.

rainbow *n.* hung² 虹.

rainy *a.* yü³ te¹ 雨的.

raise *v.* (*lift up*) chü⁴ ch'i³ 舉起, (*rear*) yang³ yü⁴ 養育.

raisin *n.* p'u² t'ao² kan¹ 葡萄乾.

rake *n.* p'a² 把; *v.* sao³ ch'u² 掃除.

ram *n.* kung¹ yang² 公羊; *v.* li⁴ chuang⁴ 力撞.

ramble *v.* san³ pu⁴ 散步.

rambling *a.* san³ pu⁴ te¹ 散步的, man⁴ yu² te¹ 漫遊的.

rampart *n.* ch'eng² lei³ 城壘, pao² lei³ 保壘.

random *a.* wu² mu⁴ ti⁴ 無目的.

range *n.* (*extent*) fan⁴ wei² 範圍, (*gun*) she⁴ ch'eng² 射程, (*place*) pa² ch'ang³ 靶場, (*mountain*) shan¹ mo⁴ 山脈; ～ **finder,** ts'e⁴ yüan³ chi¹ 測遠器

測遠機.

rank *n.* (*row*) hang² lieh⁴ 行列, (*grade*) chieh¹ chi²
階級; **~ and file,** hang² wu³ 行伍.

ransack *v.* sou¹ hsün² 搜尋.

ransom *n.* shu² chin¹ 贖金; *v.* shu² hui² 贖回.

rapacious *a.* ch'iang³ chieh² te¹ 搶劫的. ┌姦.

rape *n.* chieh² lüeh⁴ 劫掠, (*sex*) ch'iang³ chien¹ 强

rapid *a.* hsün² su² te¹ 迅速的; **~ march,** chi²
hsing² chün¹ 急行軍.

rapine *n.* chieh² lüeh⁴ 劫掠.

rare *a.* han² yu³ te¹ 罕有的.

rarefy *v.* shih³ hsi¹ po² 使稀薄.

rascal *n.* liu² mang² 流氓, e⁴ t'u² 惡徒.

rash *a.* lu² mang³ te¹ 鹵莽的; *n.* chen³ 疹.

rasher *n.* (*bacon*) hsien² jou⁴ p'ien¹ 鹹肉片, (*ham*)
huo² t'ui³ p'ien¹ 火腿片.

rasp *n.* mu⁴ ts'o⁴ 木銼.

raspberry *n.* fu⁴ p'en² tzu¹ 覆盆子(植).

rat *n.* shu³ 鼠.

rate *n.* pi³ lü⁴ 比率, (*speed*) su² tu⁴ 速度.

rather *adv.* ning² k'o³ 寧可.

ratify *v.* (*confirm*) cheng⁴ shih² 證實, (*approve*) p'i¹
┌chun³ 批准.

ration *n.* k'ou³ liang² 口糧.

rational *a.* ho² li³ te¹ 合理的.

rattle *v.* tso⁴ tuan³ jui⁴ sheng¹ 作短銳聲.

ravage *v.* hui² mieh⁴ 毀滅.

raven *n.* tu⁴ niao³ 渡鳥.

ravenous *a.* chi¹ e⁴ te¹ 飢餓的.

ravine *n.* shan¹ hsia² 山峽.

raw *a.* (*not cooked*) sheng¹ te¹ 生的.

ray *n.* kuang¹ hsien⁴ 光線.

raze *v.* ch'an³ p'ing² 剷平.

razor *n.* t'i⁴ tao¹ 剃刀.

reach *v.* tao² ta² 到達.

read *v.* tu² 讀.

readily *adv.* hsün⁴ su² ti¹ 迅速地.

reading *n.* tu² 讀.

ready *a.* yu² chun³ pei¹ te¹ 有準備的; **" ~,
front ! "** hsiang⁴ ch'ien² k'an¹ 向前看(軍).

real *a.* chen¹ shih² te¹ 眞實的.

reality *n.* chen¹ shih² 眞實.

211

realize *v.* li² chieh³ 理解.

really *adv.* shih² tsai⁴ ti⁴ 實在地.

realm *n.* wang² kuo² 王國.

reap *v.* shou¹ ko¹ 收割.

rear *a.* hou⁴ fang¹ te¹ 後方的; *n.* hou⁴ mien⁴ 後面; *v.* yang³ yü⁴ 發育; ～ **admiral,** shao⁴ chiang⁴ 少將(海); ～ **guard,** hou⁴ wei⁴ 後衛(軍); ～ **sight,** piao² ch'ih³ 表尺(兵).

reason *n.* (*cause*) li³ yu² 理由, yüan² yin¹ 原因.

reasonable *a.* ho² li³ te¹ 合理的.

rebel *n.* p'an⁴ t'u² 叛徒; *v.* fan³ p'an⁴ 反叛.

rebellion *n.* fan³ p'an⁴ 反叛.

rebellious *a.* fan³ p'an⁴ te¹ 反叛的.

rebuke *v.* ch'ih⁴ tse² 斥責, ch'ien³ tse² 譴責.

recall *v.* (*order back*) chao⁴ hui² 召回, (*remember*) hui² i⁴ 回憶.

recant *v.* shou¹ hui² 收回.

recantation *n.* shou¹ hui² 收回.

recede *v.* (*go backward*) t'ui⁴ hou⁴ 退後.

receipt *n.* shou¹ chü⁴ 收據.

receive *v.* shou¹ shou⁴ 收受.

receiver *n.* shou¹ shou⁴ che³ 收受者.

recent *a.* hsin¹ chin⁴ te¹ 新近的.

reception *n.* chao¹ tai⁴ 招待, (*party*) chao¹ tai⁴ hui⁴ 招待會.

recess *n.* chan⁴ hsi² 暫息.

recipe *n.* shih² p'u³ 食譜.

recipient *n.* shou¹ shou⁴ che³ 收受者.

reciprocal *a.* hu⁴ hsiang¹ te¹ 互相的.

recital *n.* (*singing*) tu² ch'ang⁴ hui⁴ 獨唱會, (*playing*) tu² tsou⁴ hui⁴ 獨奏會.

recitation *n.* lang³ sung⁴ 朗誦.

recite *v.* lang³ sung⁴ 朗誦.

reckless *a.* mao⁴ hsien³ te¹ 冒險的.

reckon *v.* (*count*) chi⁴ suan⁴ 計算.

reclaim *v.* chiao³ cheng⁴ 矯正.

recline *v.* hsieh² i³ 斜倚, ts'e⁴ wo⁴ 側臥.

recognition *n.* (*admission*) ch'eng² jen⁴ 承認, (*know*) jen⁴ shih⁴ 認識.

recognize *v.* (*admit*) ch'eng² jen⁴ 承認, (*knowing*) jen⁴ shih⁴ 認識.

recoil *v.* t'ui⁴ hui² 退回; ～ **mechanism,** chih⁴ t'ui⁴ chi¹ 制退機(兵), (*ber*) hui² i⁴ 回憶.

recollect *v.* (*collect again*) tsai⁴ chi² 再集, (*remem-*

recommend v. (*suggest*) chien⁴ i⁴ 建議, (*a person*) t'ui¹ chien⁴ 推薦.

recommendation n. t'ui¹ chü³ 推舉.

recompense v. (*pay back*) p'ei² ch'ang² 賠償, (*reward*) pao⁴ ta² 報答.

reconcile v. shih³ ho² hao³ 使和好.

reconnoiter, reconnoitre v. chen¹ ch'a² 偵察.

reconsider a. tsai⁴ k'ao³ lü⁴ 再考慮, fu⁴ i⁴ 複議.

record v. chi⁴ lu⁴ 記錄; n. chi⁴ lu⁴ 記錄, (*for phonograph*) ch'ang⁴ p'ien⁴ 唱片.

recourse n. ch'iu² yüan² 求援.

recover v. (*from illness*) fu⁴ yüan² 復原, (*position*)

recovery n. fu⁴ yüan² 復元.   ⌊shou¹ fu⁴ 收復.

recreant a. ch'üeh⁴ jo⁴ te¹ 怯弱的.

recreation n. yü² le⁴ 娛樂.

recriminate v. fan³ k'ung⁴ 反控.

recrimination n. fan³ k'ung⁴ 反控.

recruit n. hsin¹ ping¹ 新兵; v. chao¹ ping¹ 招兵.

rectify v. kai³ cheng⁴ 改正.

rectitude n. cheng⁴ chih² 正直, cheng⁴ i⁴ 正義.

recumbent a. hsieh² i³ te¹ 斜倚的, yen³ wo⁴ te¹ 偃 ⌊臥的.

recuperate v. fu⁴ yüan² 復元.

red a. hung² se⁴ te¹ 紅色的; ~ **Cross,** hung² shih² tzu⁴ hui⁴ 紅十字會.

redeem v. shu² hui² 贖囘.

redeemable a. k'o³ shu² hui² te¹ 可贖囘的.

redemption n. shu² hui² 贖囘.

red-hot a. ch'ih⁴ je⁴ te¹ 赤熱的.

redoubt n. pao² lei³ 保壘.

redoubtable a. k'o³ p'a⁴ te¹ 可怕的.

reduce v. chien³ ti¹ 減低.

reduction n. chien² shao³ 減少.

reed n. lu² wei³ 蘆葦.

reef n. an⁴ chiao¹ 暗礁.

reek n. (*vapor*) cheng¹ ch'i⁴ 蒸氣.

reel n. fang³ ch'e¹ 紡車, chüan³ hsien⁴ ch'e¹ 捲線車; v. hsüan² chuan³ 旋轉.

re-elect v. ch'ung² hsüan³ 重選.

re-establish v. ch'ung² chien⁴ 重建.

refer v. (*turn for information*) ts'an¹ k'ao³ 參考; ~ **to higher authority,** ch'ing³ shih⁴ 請示.

reference n. ts'an¹ k'ao³ 參考.

refine v. ching¹ lien⁴ 精鍊.

refinement n. wen² ya³ 文雅.

reflect v. fan³ she⁴ 反射.

reflection n. fan³ she⁴ 反射.

reflector n. fan³ she⁴ ch'i² 反射器.

reform n. kai³ liang² 改良; v. kai³ ko² 改革.

refractory a. ch'iang² wan⁴ te¹ 強頑的.

refrain v. tsu² chih³ 阻止.

refresh v. t'i² shen² 提神.

refreshment n. t'i² shen² 提神, (refreshments)
ch'a² tien³ 茶點.

refrigerator n. ping¹ hsiang¹ 冰箱.

refuge n. pi⁴ nan⁴ so³ 避難所.

refusal n. chü⁴ chüeh⁴ 拒絕.

refuse v. chü⁴ chüeh² 拒絕; n. la⁴ hsi¹ 垃圾.

regal a. huang² chia¹ te¹ 皇家的.

regard n. (consideration) ku⁴ lü⁴ 顧慮; v. (consider) k'ao³ lü⁴ 考慮.

regardless a. pu² ku⁴ lü⁴ te¹ 不顧慮的.

regatta n. sai⁴ ch'uan² 賽船.

regenerate a. ko² hsin¹ te¹ 革新的; v. ko² hsin¹

regeneration n. ko² hsin¹ 革新.　　　　　　〔革新.

regent a. she⁴ cheng⁴ te¹ 攝政的.

regiment n. t'uan² 團.

region n. ti⁴ ch'ü¹ 地區.

register n. (record) teng² chi⁴ pu⁴ 登記簿; v.
(write in record) chi⁴ lu⁴ 記錄, (school) chu⁴ ts'e¹
註册, (mail) kua⁴ hao⁴ 掛號.

registrar n. (of school) chu⁴ ts'e⁴ yüan² 註册員.

regret n. i² han⁴ 遺憾; v. pao⁴ ch'ien⁴ 抱歉.

regular a. (usual) ch'ang² li⁴ te¹ 常例的; ~ army,
cheng⁴ kuei¹ chün¹ 正規軍.

regulate v. kuei¹ ting⁴ 規定.

regulation n. kuei¹ ting⁴ 規定.

rehearsal n. yü⁴ yen³ 預演.

rehearse v. yü⁴ yen³ 預演.

reign n. ch'ao² tai⁴ 朝代; v. t'ung³ chih⁴ 統治.

reimburse v. ch'ang² huan² 償還.

rein n. chiang¹ 韁.

reindeer n. hsün² lu⁴ 馴鹿.

reinforce v. (*another unit*) tseng¹ yüan² 增援, (*the strength of a unit*) chia¹ ch'iang² 加强.

reiterate v. fan³ fu⁴ 反復.

reject v. chü⁴ chüeh¹ 拒絕.

rejoice v. shih² hsi³ yüeh⁴ 使喜悅.

relate v. hsü⁴ shu⁴ 敘述.

relation n. kuan¹ hsi⁴ 關係.

relative a. ch'in¹ shu³ te¹ 親屬的.

relax v. sung¹ ch'ih² 鬆弛.

relay v. chiao¹ t'i⁴ shu¹ sung⁴ 交替輸送.

release v. (*let go*) shih⁴ fang⁴ 釋放.

relent v. pien⁴ k'uan¹ ho² 變寬和.

relentless a. ts'an² jen³ te¹ 殘忍的.

relevant a. shih⁴ ch'ieh¹ te¹ 適切的.

reliance n. hsin⁴ t'o¹ 信托.

relief n. (*aid*) chiu⁴ chi⁴ 救濟.

relieve v. (*aid*) yüan² chiu⁴ 援救, (*take over*) chieh¹ fang² 接防, (*of one's command*) mien³ chih² 免職.

religion n. tsung¹ chiao⁴ 宗敎.

religious a. tsung¹ chiao⁴ te¹ 宗敎的.

relinquish v. fang⁴ ch'i⁴ 放棄.

relish n. mei³ wei⁴ 美味; v. t'iao² wei⁴ 調味.

reluctance n. pu² yüan⁴ 不願.

reluctant a. pu² yüan⁴ te¹ 不願的.

rely v. hsin⁴ t'o¹ 信託.

remain v. liu² chü¹ 留居, (*be left over*) i² liu² 遺留.

remainder n. yü² shu⁴ 餘數.

remand v. ya¹ hui² 押回.

remark v. pei⁴ k'ao³ 備考, (*say*) shuo¹ 說.

remarkable chih² te² ch'u⁴ i⁴ te¹ 值得注意的, (*unusual*) fei¹ ch'ang² te¹ 非常的.

remedy n. pu³ chiu⁴ 補救.

remember v. chi⁴ te² 記得.

remembrance n. chi⁴ i⁴ 記憶, (*souvenir*) chi⁴ nien⁴ wu⁴ 紀念物.

remind v. t'i² hsing³ 提醒.

reminiscence n. chi⁴ i⁴ 記憶, chui¹ hsiang³ 追想.

remiss a. su¹ hu¹ te¹ 疏忽的.

remit v. (*send money*) hui⁴ k'uan³ 匯款.

remittance n. hui⁴ chi⁴ 匯寄.

remnant a. ts'an² yü² 殘餘.

215

remonstrance *n.* k'ang⁴ i⁴ 抗議.

remonstrate *v.* k'ang⁴ i⁴ 抗議.

remorse *n.* t'ung⁴ hui³ 痛悔.

remote *a.* yüan³ li² te¹ 遠離的.

removal *n.* ch'e⁴ ch'ü⁴ 撤去.

remove *v.* i² ch'ü⁴ 移去.

remunerate *v.* pao⁴ ch'ou² 報酬.

remuneration *n.* pao⁴ ch'ou² 報酬.

rend *v.* ssu¹ p'o⁴ 撕破. 「fan¹ i⁴ 翻譯.

render *v.* (*give in return*) pao⁴ ta² 報答, (*translate*)

renew *v.* keng¹ hsin¹ 更新.

renewal *n.* keng¹ hsin¹ 更新.

renounce *v.* fang⁴ ch'i⁴ 放棄.

renovate *v.* keng¹ hsin¹ 更新.

renovation *n.* keng¹ hsin¹ 更新.

renown *n.* ming² yü⁴ 名譽, sheng¹ wang⁴ 聲望.

rent *n.* tsu¹ chin¹ 租金; *v.* (*from*) tsu¹ yung⁴ 租用,
(*to*) ch'u¹ tsu¹ 出租.

renunciation *n.* fang⁴ ch'i⁴ 放棄.

reorganize *v.* (*within unit*) cheng² li² 整理, (*into
new units*) kai³ pien¹ 改編.

repair *n.* hsiu¹ li³ 修理; *v.* hsiu¹ li³ 修理.

reparation *n.* pu³ ch'ang² 補償.

repast *n.* (*meal*) ts'an¹ 餐.

repay *v.* fu⁴ huan² 付還.

repayment *n.* fu⁴ huan² 付還.

repeal *n.* fei⁴ chih³ 廢止.

repeat *v.* ch'ung² fu⁴ 重複.

repeatedly *adv.* fan³ fu⁴ 反復.

repel *v.* ch'ü¹ t'ui⁴ 驅退.

repent *v.* ao⁴ hui³ 懊悔.

repentance *n.* ao⁴ hui³ 懊悔.

repentant *a.* ao⁴ hui³ te¹ 懊悔的.

repetition *n.* ch'ung² fu⁴ 重複.

replace *v.* tai⁴ t'i⁴ 代替.

replenish *v.* tsai⁴ pu³ ch'ung¹ 再補充.

reply *n.* hui² ta² 回答; *v.* hui² ta² 回答.

report *n.* pao⁴ kao⁴ 報告; *v.* pao⁴ kao⁴ 報告.

reprehensible *a.* k'o³ ch'ih⁴ tse² te¹ 可斥責的.

represent *v.* (*stand for*) tai⁴ piao³ 代表.

representation *n.* tai⁴ piao³ 代表.

representative *a.* tai⁴ piao³ te¹ 代表的; *n.* tai⁴ piao³ 代表.

reprieve *n., v.* huan³ hsing² 緩刑.　　「責.

reprimand *v.* ch'eng² chieh⁴ 懲戒, ch'ih⁴ tse² 斥

reproach *n., v.* ch'ih⁴ tse² 斥責.

reproduce *v.* tsai⁴ sheng¹ 再生.

reproof *n.* ch'ih⁴ tse² 叱責.

reprove *v.* ch'ien³ tse² 譴責.

reptile *n.* p'a² ch'ung² 爬蟲.

republic *n.* kung⁴ ho² kuo² 共和國.

repudiate *v.* chü⁴ chüeh² 拒絕.

repulse *v.* ch'ü¹ hui² 驅回.

reputation *n.* ming² yü⁴ 名譽.

repute *n.* ming² yü⁴ 名譽; *v.* jen⁴ wei² 認爲.

request *n., v.* yao¹ ch'iu² 要求.

require *v.* hsü¹ yao⁴ 需要.

requisite *a.* hsü¹ yao⁴ te¹ 需要的; *n.* hsü¹ yao⁴ p'in³ 需要品.

requisition *n.* ch'ing³ chiu² 請求.

requite *v.* pao⁴ ta² 報答.

rescind *v.* fei⁴ chih³ 廢止.

rescue *v.* chiu⁴ chu⁴ 救助.

research *n.* yen² chiu¹ 研究.

resemblance *n.* hsiang¹ ssu⁴ 相似.

resemble *v.* hsiang¹ ssu⁴ 相似.

resent *v.* fen⁴ nu⁴ 憤怒.

reservation *n.* (*keep*) yü⁴ yüeh¹ 預約.

reserve *n.* (*fund*) chun³ pei⁴ chin¹ 準備金, (*troops*) yü⁴ pei⁴ tui⁴ 預備隊, (*inactive duty*) yü⁴ pei⁴ i⁴ 預備役; *v.* (*keep back*) pao³ liu² 保留, (*save*) chu³ ts'ang² 貯藏.

reserved *a.* pao³ liu² te¹ 保留的.

reservoir *n.* chu² shui³ ch'ih² 貯水池.

reside *v.* chü¹ chu⁴ 居住.

residence *n.* chu⁴ chai² 住宅.　　「民.

resident *a.* chü¹ chu⁴ te¹ 居住的; *n.* chü¹ min² 居

resign *v.* tz'u² chih² 辭職.

resignation *n.* tz'u² chih² 辭職.

resin *n.* sung¹ hsiang¹ 松香.

resist *v.* ti³ k'ang⁴ 抵抗.

resistance *n.* ti³ k'ang⁴ 抵抗.

resistless *a.* wu² k'o² ti³ k'ang⁴ te¹ 無可抵抗的.

resolute *a.* chüeh² ting⁴ te¹ 決定的.

resolve *v.* (*decide*) chüeh² ting⁴ 決定.

resort *v.* (*go often*) ch'ang² wang³ 常往.

resource *n.* tzu¹ yüan² 資源.

respect *n.*, *v.* tsun¹ ching⁴ 尊敬.

respectable *a.* k'o³ ching⁴ te¹ 可敬的.

respectful *a.* kung¹ ching⁴ te¹ 恭敬的.

respective *a.* ko⁴ pieh² te¹ 個別的.

respiration *n.* hu¹ hsi¹ 呼吸.

respire *v.* hu¹ hsi¹ 呼吸.

resplendent *a.* shan³ shuo⁴ te¹ 閃爍的.

respond *v.* hui² ta² 回答.

respondent *n.* hui² ta² che³ 回答者.

response *n.* hui² ta² 回答.

responsibility *n.* fu⁴ tse² 負責.

responsible *a.* fu⁴ tse² te¹ 負責的.

rest *n.* hsiu¹ hsi¹ 休息, (*remainder*) ch'i² yü² 其餘;
v. hsiu¹ hsi¹ 休息.

restaurant *n.* fan⁴ tien⁴ 飯店, chiu² kuan³ 酒舘.

restless *a.* pu⁴ neng² shui⁴ mien² te¹ 不能睡眠的.

restoration *n.* hui¹ fu⁴ 恢復.

restore *v.* hui¹ fu⁴ 恢復.

restrain *v.* e⁴ chih³ 遏止, (*confine*) chien¹ chin¹ 監〔禁.

restrict *v.* hsien⁴ chih⁴ 限制, shu⁴ fu² 束縛.

restricted *a.* (*security classification*) hsien⁴ yüeh⁴
限閱.

restriction *n.* hsien⁴ chih⁴ 限制, shu⁴ fu² 束縛.

result *n.*, *v.* chieh² kuo³ 結果.

resume *v.* tsai⁴ tso⁴ 再作.

resurrection *n.* fu⁴ huo² 復活.

retail *n.*, *v.* ling² shou⁴ 零售.

retailer *n.* ling² shou⁴ shang¹ 零售商.

retain *v.* pao³ ch'ih² 保持.

retaliate *v.* pao⁴ fu⁴ 報復.

retaliation *n.* pao⁴ fu⁴ 報復.

retard *v.* ch'ih² yen² 遲延.

retention *n.* pao³ liu² 保留.

reticence *n.* ch'en² mo⁴ 沈默.

retinue *n.* shih⁴ ts'ung² 侍從, sui² yüan² 隨員.

retire *v.* (*from office*) t'ui⁴ chih² 退職, (*go to bed*) chiu⁴ ch'in³ 就寢, *(from military service)* t'ui⁴ i⁴ 退役, *(movement)* t'ui⁴ ch'üeh⁴ 退卻.

retract *v.* ch'e⁴ hui² 撤回.

retreat *n.*, *v.* t'ui⁴ ch'üeh⁴ 退卻.

retrench *v.* chieh² sheng³ 節省, chien³ so¹ 減縮.

retribution *n.* pao⁴ ying⁴ 報應.

retrieve *v.* *(get again)* hsün² te² 尋得.

retrograde *a.* t'ui⁴ hou⁴ te¹ 退後的.

return *v.* *(go back)* hui² lai² 回來, *(give back)* kuei¹

reunion *n.* ch'ung² chü⁴ 重聚.　　　[huang² 鄰邊.

reunite *v.* ch'ung² chü⁴ 重聚.

reveal *v.* hsieh⁴ lou⁴ 洩露.

reveille *n.* ch'i³ ch'uang² hao⁴ 起床號.

revelation *n.* hsieh⁴ lou⁴ 洩露.

revenge *v.* pao⁴ ch'ou² 報仇.

revengeful *a.* pao⁴ ch'ou² te¹ 報仇的.

revenue *n.* *(income)* shou¹ ju⁴ 收入.

reverberate *v.* fan² hsiang³ 反響.

revere *v.* tsun¹ ching⁴ 尊敬.

reverence *n.* tsun¹ ching⁴ 尊敬.

reverend *a.* k'o³ tsun¹ ching⁴ te¹ 可尊敬的.

reverent *a.* kung¹ ching⁴ te¹ 恭敬的.

review *v.* *(lessons)* wen¹ hsi² kung¹ k'o⁴ 溫習功課, *(troops)* chiao⁴ yüeh⁴ 校閱, *(book)* p'i¹ p'ing² 批評.

revise *v.* chiao⁴ ting⁴ 校訂.

revision *n.* chiao⁴ ting⁴ 校訂.

revival *n.* fu⁴ huo² 復活.

revive *v.* shih³ fu⁴ huo² 使復活.

revoke *v.* ch'ü³ hsiao¹ 取消.

revolt *n.* pei⁴ p'an⁴ 背叛; *v.* fan³ p'an⁴ 反叛.

revolution *n.* *(rebellion)* ko² ming⁴ 革命.

revolve *v.* hsüan² chuan³ 旋轉.

revolver *n.* tso³ lun² shou³ ch'iang¹ 左輪手鎗 (兵).

reward *n.* ch'ou² pao⁴ 酬報; *v.* chiang² shang³ 獎

rheumatism *n.* feng¹ shih¹ cheng⁴ 風濕症.　　[賞.

rhododendron *n.* tu⁴ chüan¹ hua¹ shu³ 杜鵑花屬.

rhubarb *n.* ta⁴ huang² 大黃 (醫).

rib *n.* lei⁴ ku³ 肋骨.

ribbon *n.* ssu¹ tai⁴ 絲帶.

rice *n.* mi³ 米.

rich *a.* fu⁴ yu³ te¹ 富有的.

219

riches *n.* ts'ai² fu⁴ 財富.

rick *n.* kan¹ ts'ao³ tui¹ 乾草堆.

rickets *n.* chü¹ lou² ping² 痀僂病.

ricochet *n.* t'iao⁴ tan⁴ 跳彈(兵).

rid *v.* chieh³ t'o¹ 解脫.

riddle *n.* mi² yü³ 謎語.

ride *n.*, *v.* (*horseback*) ch'i² ma³ 騎馬.

ridge *n.* shan¹ mo⁴ 山脈.

ridicule *n.* ch'ao² nung⁴ 嘲弄.

rifle *n.* pu⁴ ch'iang¹ 步鎗.

rifleman *n.* pu⁴ ch'iang¹ ping¹ 步鎗兵.

rifling *n.* lai² fu⁴ hsien⁴ 來復線(兵).

right *a.* (*correct*) pu² ts'o⁴ te¹ 不錯的; *adv.* (*correctly*) wu² wu⁴ ti⁴ 無誤地; *n.* cheng⁴ tang¹ 正當, (*privilege*) ch'üan² li⁴ 權利, (*direction*) yü⁴ mien¹ 右面; "~ **face!**" hsiang⁴ yu⁴ chuan³ 向右轉 〔(軍).

righteous *a.* cheng⁴ chih² te¹ 正直的.

rightful *a.* ho² fa³ te¹ 合法的.

rim *n.* pien¹ 邊, yüan² 緣.

ring *n.* (*circle*) ch'üan¹ 圈, (*finger*) chieh⁴ chih³ 戒指; *v.* (*bell*) yao² ling² 搖鈴.

ringleader *n.* tao⁴ k'uei² 盜魁.

rinse *v.* hsi³ ti² 洗滌.

riot *n.* pao⁴ tung⁴ 暴動; *v.* pao⁴ luan⁴ 暴亂.

riotous *a.* pao⁴ tung⁴ te¹ 暴動的.

rip *v.* ch'e³ k'ai¹ 扯開.

ripe *a.* ch'eng² shou² te¹ 成熟的.

ripen *v.* ch'eng² shou² 成熟.

ripple *n.* wei¹ po¹ 微波.

rise *v.* ch'i³ li⁴ 起立, (*ascend*) shang⁴ sheng¹ 上升.

risk *n.* mao⁴ hsien³ 冒險; *v.* mao⁴ hsien³ ts'ung² shih⁴ yü² 冒險從事於.

rite *n.* i² shih⁴ 儀式.

rival *n.* ti² shou³ 敵手; *v.* ching⁴ cheng¹ 競爭.

river *n.* ho² 河, chiang¹ 江.

rivet *n.* mao³ ting¹ 鉚釘.

rivulet *n.* hsiao³ hsi¹ 小溪.

road *n.* kung¹ lu⁴ 公路; ~ **sign**, lu⁴ piao¹ 路標; ~ **space**, hsing² chün¹ ch'ang² ching⁴ 行軍長徑 〔(軍).

roam *v.* man⁴ yu² 漫游.

roar *n.* hou³ chiao⁴ 吼叫.

roast *n.* k'ao³ jou⁴ 烤肉; *v.* k'ao³ 烤.

rob *v.* ch'iang³ chieh² 搶劫.

robber *n.* ch'iang³ tao⁴ 強盜.

robbery *n.* ch'iang³ chieh² 搶劫.

robe *n.* ch'ang³ p'ao² 長袍; *v.* ch'uan¹ chao⁴ 穿著.

robust *a.* ch'iang² chuang⁴ te¹ 強壯的.　　　　「勁.

rock *n.* shih² k'uai⁴ 石塊; *v.* (*sway*) yao² tung⁴ 搖

rocket *n.* huo³ chien⁴ 火箭; ～ **gun,** huo³ chien⁴ p'ao⁴ 火箭砲.

rocky *a.* to¹ yen² shih² te¹ 多巖石的.

rod *n.* kan³ 桿.

rogue *n.* liu² mang² 流氓.

roguery *n.* chiao³ hua² 狡猾.

roguish *a.* chiao³ hua² te¹ 狡猾的.

roll *n.* (*list of names*) hua¹ ming² ts'e⁴ 花名册; ～ **call,** tien³ ming² 點名.

roller *n.* ya⁴ lun² 軋輪, kun³ tzu¹ 滾子.

romance *n.* yen⁴ shih⁴ 艷事.

romantic *a.* yen⁴ shih⁴ te¹ 艷事的.

roof *n.* (*house*) wu¹ ting³ 屋頂.

rook *n.* pai² tsui³ ya¹ 白嘴鴉.

room *n.* fang² 房, shih⁴ 室.

roost *n.* hsi² mu⁴ 棲木.

rooster *n.* hsiung² chi¹ 雄雞.

root *n.* ken¹ 根.

rope *n.* sheng² 繩.

ropy *a.* nien² ch'ou² hsing⁴ 粘稠性.

rosary *n.* (*Buddhist*) nien⁴ fo² chu¹ 念佛珠.

rose *n.* mei² kuei¹ 玫瑰.

rosemary *n.* mi² tieh² hsiang¹ 迷迭香(植).

rosin *n.* sung¹ hsiang¹ 松香.

rosy *a.* ju² mei² kuei¹ te¹ 如玫瑰的.

rot *n.* hsiu³ huai⁴ 朽壞.

rotate *v.* hsüan² chuan³ 旋轉.　　　　「lun² liu² 輪流.

rotation *n.* hsüan² chuan³ 旋轉, (*change in turn*)

rotten *a.* hsiu³ huai⁴ te¹ 朽壞的.

rough *a.* ts'u¹ ts'ao¹ te¹ 粗糙的.

roughness *n.* ts'u¹ ts'ao¹ 粗糙.

round *a.* yüan² te¹ 圓的; *n.* (*of ammunition*) fa¹ 發; *adv., prep.* huan² jao⁴ 環繞.

rouse *v.* huan⁴ hsing³ 喚醒.

221

rout *n.* hui⁴ pai⁴ 潰敗.

route *n.* lu⁴ hsien² 路線.

routine *n.* ch'ang² kuei¹ 常規；~ **matters,** (*official*) li⁴ hsing² kung¹ shih⁴ 例行公事；~ **order,** jih⁴ jih⁴ ming⁴ ling⁴ 日日命令(軍).

rove *v.* man⁴ yu² 漫遊.

row *n.* p'ai² lieh⁴ 排列, (*disturbance*) jao³ luan⁴ 擾亂；*v.* hua² ch'uan² 划船.

royal *a.* wang² chia¹ te¹ 王家的.

royalist *n.* wang² tang³ 王黨.

royalty *n.* wang² tsu² 王族, (*rights*) pan³ shui⁴ 版稅.

rub *v.* mo² ts'a¹ 摩擦.

rubber *n.* hsiang⁴ p'i² 橡皮.

rubbish *n.* fei⁴ wu⁴ 廢物.

ruby *n.* hung² pao³ shih² 紅寶石.

rudder *n.* to⁴ 舵.

ruddy *a.* hung² jun⁴ te¹ 紅潤的.

rude *a.* ts'u¹ yeh³ te¹ 粗野的.

rudeness *n.* t'su¹ ts'ao¹ 粗糙.

rudiment *n.* ch'u¹ pu⁴ 初步.

rudimentary *a.* ch'u¹ pu⁴ te¹ 初步的.

rue *v.* hui³ hen⁴ 悔恨.

rueful *a.* pei¹ ai¹ te¹ 悲哀的.

rug *n.* ti⁴ t'an³ 地毯.

ruin *n., v.* hui³ mieh⁴ 毀滅.

ruinous *a.* mieh⁴ wang² te¹ 滅亡的.

rule *n.* kuei¹ tse² 規則；*v.* (*decide*) ts'ai¹ chüeh² 裁決.

ruler *n.* t'ung³ chih⁴ che³ 統制者, (*used in measuring*) ch'ih³ 尺.

rum *n.* t'ang² chiu³ 糖酒.

rumble *v.* tso⁴ lung² lung² sheng¹ 作隆隆聲.

rumor *n.* yao² yen² 謠言；*v.* yao² ch'uan² 謠傳.

run *n., v.* p'ao³ 跑.

runaway *n.* t'ao² wang² che³ 逃亡者.

runway *n.* lu⁴ ching⁴ 路徑, (*of airport*) p'ao³ tao⁴ 跑道.

rupture *n., v.* p'o⁴ lieh⁴ 破裂.

rural *a.* hsiang¹ ts'un¹ te¹ 鄉村的.

rush *n., v.* t'u² chin⁴ 突進.

rust *n.* t'ieh³ hsiu⁴ 鐵銹；*v.* sheng¹ hsiu⁴ 生銹.

rustic *a.* hsiang¹ ts'un¹ te¹ 鄉村的.

rustle *n.* sha¹ sha¹ sheng¹ 沙沙聲；*v.* tso⁴ sha¹ sha¹ sheng¹ 作沙沙聲.

rusty *a.* sheng¹ hsiu⁴ te¹ 生銹的.
rye *n.* lo³ mai⁴ 稞麥.

S

Sabbath *n.* an¹ hsi² jih⁴ 安息日.
sable *n.* hei¹ tiao¹ 黑貂.
sabotage *n.* tai⁴ kung¹ 怠工.
sabre *n.* chün¹ tao¹ 軍刀.
sack *n.* tai⁴ 袋.
sacrament *n.* sheng⁴ li³ 聖禮.
sacred *a.* shen² sheng⁴ te¹ 神聖的.
sacrifice *n.* kung⁴ hsien⁴ 供獻.
sacrilege *n.* tu² shen² 瀆神.
sad *a.* pei¹ ai¹ te¹ 悲哀的.
saddle *n.* ma³ an¹ 馬鞍.
saddler *n.* an¹ chiang⁴ 鞍匠.
sadness *n.* pei¹ shang¹ 悲傷.
safe *a.* an¹ ch'üan² te¹ 安全的; *n.* pao² hsien³ hsiang¹ 保險箱.
safety *n.* an¹ ch'üan² 安全, (*firearm locking device*) pao² hsien³ 保險.
sage *a.* ts'ung¹ ming² te¹ 聰明的; *n.* sheng⁴ jen² 聖人.
sail *n.* fan¹ 帆; *v.* fan¹ hang² 帆航.
sailor *n.* shui² shou³ 水手, (*navy*) shui³ ping¹ 水兵.
saint *n.* sheng⁴ jen² 聖人.
sake *n.* yüan² yin¹ 原因.
salad *n.* sheng¹ ts'ai⁴ shih² p'in³ 生菜食品.
salary *n.* hsin¹ feng⁴ 薪俸.
sale *n.* ch'u¹ mai⁴ 出賣.
salesman *n.* shou⁴ huo⁴ yüan² 售貨員.
saliva *n.* t'o⁴ yeh⁴ 唾液.
sallow *a.* ping² huang⁴ se⁴ 病黃色.
sally *n.*, *v.* t'u² chi¹ 突擊.
salmon *n.* kuei¹ 鮭.
saloon *n.* chiu³ tien⁴ 酒店.
salt *a.* shih² yen² te¹ 食鹽的; *n.* yen² 鹽; *v.* yen¹ i³ yen² 醃以鹽.
saltcellar *n.* yen² p'ing² 鹽瓶.

223

saltpeter, saltpetre *n.* hsiao¹ shih² 硝石.

salubrious *a.* tseng¹ chin⁴ chien⁴ k'ang¹ te¹ 增進健康的.

salubrity *n.* tseng¹ chin⁴ chien⁴ k'ang¹ 增進健康, shih⁴ yü² wei⁴ sheng¹ 適於衛生.

salutary *a.* tseng¹ chin⁴ chien⁴ k'ang¹ te¹ 增進健康的, yu³ i⁴ te¹ 有益的.

salutation *n.* chih⁴ ching⁴ 致敬.

salute *n., v.* chih⁴ ching⁴ 致敬.

salvage *n.* chiu⁴ hu⁴ 救護.

salvation *n.* cheng³ chiu⁴ 拯救, ch'ao¹ tu⁴ 超度; ～ **Army,** chiu⁴ shih⁴ chün¹ 救世軍.

salve *n.* yu² kao¹ 油膏, juan³ kao¹ 軟膏.

salver *n.* p'an² 盤.

salvo *n.* (*artillery, in turn*) i⁴ tz'u⁴ she⁴ 翼次射, (*artillery, all at once*) ch'i² she⁴ 齊射.

same *a.* hsiang¹ t'ung² te¹ 相同的.

sampan *n.* shan¹ p'an¹ 舢舨.

sample *n.* yang¹ p'in³ 樣品.

sanction *n.* p'i¹ chun³ 批准; *v.* jen⁴ k'o³ 認可.

sanctity *n.* shen² sheng⁴ 神聖.

sanctuary *n.* sheng⁴ ti⁴ 聖地.

sand *n.* sha¹ 沙; ～ **table exercise,** sha¹ p'an² yen³ hsi² 沙盤演習(軍).

sandwich *n.* san¹ ming² chih⁴ 三明治.

sandy *a.* han² sha¹ te¹ 含沙的.

sanguinary *a.* liu² hsüeh⁴ te¹ 流血的, (*combat*) ts'an³ lieh⁴ te¹ 慘烈的.

sanguine *a.* hsüeh⁴ hung² te¹ 血紅的.

sanity *n.* t'ou² nao³ ch'ing¹ ch'u⁴ 頭腦清楚.

sap *n.* shu⁴ yeh⁴ 樹液; *v.* (*approach*) p'o⁴ chin¹ 迫近.

sarcastic *a.* ch'ao² ma² te¹ 嘲罵的.

sash *n.* tai⁴ 帶, (*frame*) ch'uang¹ k'uang¹ 窗框.

satchel *n.* hsiao³ tai⁴ 小袋.

satellite *n.* wei⁴ hsing¹ 衛星.

satin *n.* tuan⁴ 緞.

satire *n.* feng⁴ tz'u⁴ 諷刺.

satisfaction *n.* man³ i⁴ 滿意.

satisfactory *a.* shih³ jen² man³ i⁴ te¹ 使人滿意的.

satisfied *a.* man³ i⁴ te¹ 滿意的.

satisfy *v.* shih² man³ i⁴ 使滿意.

224

saturate v. pao³ ho² 飽和.

Saturday n. hsing¹ ch'i² liu⁴ 星期六.

Saturn n. (planet) t'u³ hsing¹ 土星.

sauce n. chiang⁴ yu² 醬油.

saucepan n. cheng¹ kuo¹ 蒸鍋.

saucer n. tieh⁴ 碟.

saucy a. ts'u¹ yeh³ te¹ 粗野的.

saunter v. hsien² yu² 閒遊.

sausage n. la⁴ ch'ang² 臘腸.

savage a. yeh³ man¹ te¹ 野蠻的.

save v. cheng³ chiu⁴ 拯救.

saving a. (economical) chieh² sheng³ te¹ 節省的; n. (plural) ch'u² chin¹ 儲金.

savior n. chiu⁴ chu³ 救主.

savory a. mei³ wei⁴ te¹ 美味的.

saw n. chü⁴ 鋸; v. chü⁴ k'ai¹ 鋸開.

say v. shuo¹ 說.

saying n. shuo¹ 說.

scab n. chia¹ 痂.

scabbard n. tao¹ ch'iao⁴ 刀鞘.

scabies n. chieh⁴ ch'uang¹ 疥瘡.

scaffold n. chien⁴ chu² chia⁴ 建築架, (for criminals) tuan⁴ t'ou² t'ai² 斷頭臺.

scald n., v. t'ang⁴ shang¹ 燙傷.

scale n. (fish) lin² 鱗, (scales) t'ien¹ ch'eng⁴ 天秤, (map) pi³ li⁴ ch'ih³ 比例尺.

scallop n. shan⁴ ling² 扇蛤(魚).

scaly a. yü³ lin² te¹ 有鱗的.

scamper v. chi² p'ao³ 疾跑.

scandal n. ch'ou³ hsing² 醜行.

scandalous a. ch'ou³ hsing² te¹ 醜行的.

scanty a. pi⁴ lin⁴ te¹ 鄙吝的.

scar n. pan¹ hen² 瘢痕.

scarce a. han³ yu³ te¹ 罕有的.

scarcity n. hsi¹ shao³ 稀少.

scare v. k'ung³ ho⁴ 恐嚇.

scarecrow n. tao⁴ ts'ao³ jen² 稻草人.

scarf n. wei² chin¹ 圍巾.

scarlet n. hsing¹ hung² se⁴ 猩紅色; ~ fever, hsing¹ hung² je⁴ 猩紅熱.

scatter v. shih³ fen¹ san³ 使分散.

scavenger *n.* ch'ing¹ tao⁴ fu¹ 清道夫.

scene *n.* (*play*) mu⁴ 幕, (*theater*) mu⁴ ching³ 幕景.

scenery *n.* (*theater*) wu³ t'ai² pu⁴ ching³ 舞臺佈景, (*landscape*) feng¹ ching³ 風景.

scent *n.* ch'i⁴ wei⁴ 氣味.

schedule *n.* piao³ 表.

scheme *n.* chi⁴ hua⁴ 計畫.

scholar *n.* hsüeh² che³ 學者.

school *n.* hsüeh² hsiao⁴ 學校.

schoolfellow *n.* t'ung² hsüeh² 同學.

schoolmaster *n.* chiao⁴ chih² yüan² 敎職員.

sciatica *n.* tso⁴ ku³ shen² ching¹ t'ung⁴ 坐骨神經痛.

science *n.* k'o¹ hsüeh² 科學.

scientific *a.* k'o¹ hsüeh² te¹ 科學的.

scissors *n.* chien³ tao¹ 剪刀.

scold *v.* tse² ma⁴ 責罵.

scope *n.* fan⁴ wei² 範圍.

scorch *v.* shao¹ chiao¹ 燒焦.

score *n.* tien³ shu⁴ 點數; *v.* te² fen¹ 得分.

scorn *n., v.* ch'ing¹ mieh² 輕蔑.

scornful *a.* ch'ing¹ mieh⁴ te¹ 輕蔑的.

scoundrel *n.* wu² lai⁴ 無賴.

scour *v.* mo² kuang¹ 磨光.

scourge *n.* pien¹ 鞭; *v.* ch'eng² fa² 懲罰.

scout *n.* chien⁴ tieh² 間諜; *v.* chen¹ t'an⁴ 偵探.

scowl *n.* nu³ 怒; *v.* chou⁴ mei² 皺眉.

scraggy *a.* shou⁴ chi² te¹ 瘦瘠的.

scramble *n.* p'u² fu² 匍匐; *v.* p'an¹ yüan² 攀緣.

scrap *n.* hsiao³ k'uai⁴ 小塊.

scrape *v.* mo² ts'a¹ 磨擦; *n.* mo² ts'a¹ sheng¹ 磨擦聲.

scratch *v.* chua¹ 抓; *n.* sao¹ hen² 搔痕.

scrawl *n.* liao² ts'ao³ shu¹ hsieh³ 潦草書寫; *v.* luan¹ hsieh³ 亂寫.

scream *n.* chien¹ sheng¹ hu¹ han³ 尖聲呼喊; *v.*

screen *n.* wei² p'ing² 圍屏, (*films*) mu⁴ 幕.

screw *n.* lo² ting¹ 螺釘; *v.* hsüan² chuan³ 旋轉.

script *n.* (*money*) chün¹ p'iao⁴ 軍票.

scripture *n.* sheng¹ ching¹ 聖經.

scrofula *n.* lo³ li⁴ 瘰癧(瘵).

scrub *v.* hsi³ ts'a¹ 洗擦.

scrupulous *a.* chü¹ chin³ te¹ 拘謹的.

scrutiny *n.* hsiang² ch'a² 詳察.

scuffle *n., v.* cheng¹ tou⁴ 爭鬪.

sculptor *n.* tiao¹ k'o¹ chia¹ 彫刻家.

sculpture *n.* tiao¹ k'o¹ shu⁴ 彫刻術.

scum *n.* p'ao⁴ mo⁴ 泡沫.

scurrilous *a.* ts'u¹ pi³ te¹ 粗鄙的.

scurvy *n.* huai⁴ hsüeh⁴ ping⁴ 壞血病(醫).

scythe *n.* lien² tao¹ 鐮刀.

sea *n.* hai³ 海.

seal *n.* (*animal*) hai³ pao⁴ 海豹, (*mark*) t'u² chang¹ 圖章; *v.* kai¹ yin⁴ 蓋印.

seam *n.* hsien⁴ feng² 線縫; *v.* feng² ho² 縫合.

seaman *n.* hai³ yüan² 海員, shui³ shou³ 水手.

seamstress *n.* nü³ ts'ai² feng² 女裁縫.

seaplane *n.* shui³ shang⁴ fei¹ chi¹ 水上飛機.

search *v.* hsün² mi⁴ 尋覓.

searchlight *n.* t'an⁴ chao⁴ teng¹ 探照燈.

seasickness *n.* yün⁴ ch'uan² 暈船.

season *n.* chi⁴ 季; *v.* (*flavor*) chia¹ wei⁴ 加味, (*wood*) shih³ kan¹ tsao⁴ 使乾燥.

seasonable *a.* shih⁴ shih² te¹ 適時的.

seat *n.* tso⁴ wei⁴ 座位.

seaweed *n.* hai² tsao³ 海藻.

secede *v.* t'o¹ 脫.

seclusion *n.* yin³ t'ui⁴ 隱退.

second *a.* ti⁴ erh⁴ te¹ 第二的; *v.* tsan⁴ ch'eng² 贊成; *n.* (*unit of time*) miao³ 秒; ~ **gear,** erh⁴ tang⁴ 二檔(汽).

secondary *a.* ti⁴ erh⁴ te¹ 第二的, (*less importance*) tz'u⁴ yao⁴ te¹ 次要的; ~ **education,** chung¹ teng³ chiao⁴ yü⁴ 中等教育.

second-hand *a.* chiu⁴ te¹ 舊的.

secrecy *n.* pi⁴ mi⁴ 祕密.

secret *a.* pi⁴ mi⁴ te¹ 祕密的 (*security classification*) chi¹ mi⁴ 機密; *n.* pi⁴ mi⁴ 祕密; ~ **cipher,** mi⁴ ma³ 密碼; ~ **service,** t'e⁴ wu⁴ 特務; ~ **servicemen,** t'e⁴ wu⁴ jen² yüan² 特務人員.

secretary *n.* pi⁴ shu¹ 祕書.

secrete *v.* yin³ ts'ang² 隱藏.

sect *n.* tsung¹ p'ai⁴ 宗派.

section *n.* (*part*) tuan⁴ lo⁴ 段落, (*unit*) pan¹ 班.

227

sector *n.* shan⁴ hsing² 扇形(幾何學).

secular *a.* shih⁴ su² te 世俗的.

secure *a.* an¹ ch'üan² te¹ 安全的; *v.* shih³ an¹ ch'üan² 使安全, (*obtain*) ch'ü te² 取得.

security *n.* an¹ ch'üan⁴ 安全.

sedate *a.* chen⁴ ching⁴ te¹ 鎮靜的.

sedentary *a.* chiu³ tso⁴ te¹ 久坐的.

sediment *n.* ch'en² tien² wu⁴ 沈澱物.

sedition *n.* mou² p'an⁴ 謀叛.

seditious *a.* shan¹ luan⁴ te¹ 煽亂的.

seduce *v.* yu⁴ huo⁴ 誘惑.

seduction *n.* yin³ yü⁴ 引誘.

seductive *a.* yin³ yü⁴ te¹ 引誘的.

see *v.* k'an⁴ chien⁴ 看見.

seed *n.* chung³ tzu¹ 種子.

seek *v.* hsün² ch'iu² 尋求.

seem *v.* ssu⁴ hu¹ 似乎.

seethe *v.* (*boil*) fei⁴ t'eng² 沸騰.

seize *v.* (*spies*) pu³ huo⁴ 捕獲, (*materiel and animals*) to² ch'ü 奪取, (*a position*) chan⁴ ling³ 佔領.

seizure *n.* pu³ huo⁴ 捕獲.

seldom *adv.* hsi¹ yu³ 希有.

select *v.* hsüan³ tse² 選擇.

selection *n.* hsüan³ tse² 選擇.

self *n.* tzu⁴ chi³ 自己.

self-denial *n.* tzu⁴ chih⁴ 自制.

selfish *a.* tzu⁴ ssu¹ te¹ 自私的.

self-love *n.* tzu⁴ ai⁴ 自愛.

sell *v.* shou⁴ mai⁴ 售賣.

semicolon *n.* pan⁴ chih¹ tien³ 半支點.

Senate *n.* (*US*) ts'an¹ i⁴ yüan⁴ 參議院(美).

senator *n.* ts'an¹ i⁴ yüan² 參議員(美).

send *v.* p'ai⁴ ch'ien³ 派遣.

senior *n.* (*older*) chang² che³ 長者, (*chief*) chang³ kuan¹ 長官.

sensation *n.* kan³ chüeh² 感覺.

sense *n.* (*five senses*) wu³ kuan¹ 五官, (*good.sense*) li³ hsing⁴ 理性, (*common sense*) ch'ang² shih⁴ 常識, (*moral sense*) te² hsing⁴ 德性; ～ **of hearing**, t'ing¹ chüeh² 聽覺; ～ **of sight**, shih⁴ chüeh² 視覺; ～ **of smell**, hsiu⁴ chüeh² 嗅覺; ～ **of taste**, wei⁴ chüeh² 味覺; ～ **of touch,** ch'u⁴ chüeh² 觸覺.

senseless *a.* (*unconscious*) wu² chih¹ chüeh² li⁴ te¹ 無知覺力的, (*meaningless*) wu² i⁴ i⁴ te¹ 無意義的.

sensibility *n.* chih¹ chüeh² neng² 知覺能.

sensible *a.* min² kan³ te¹ 敏感的.

sensitive *a.* min² kan³ hsing⁴ te¹ 敏感性的.

sensual *a.* jou⁴ yü⁴ te¹ 肉慾的.

sensuality *n.* jou⁴ yü⁴ 肉慾.

sentence *n.* chü¹ tzu¹ 句子, (*for crime*) p'an⁴ chüeh² 判決; *v.* hsüan¹ p'an⁴ 宣判.

sentiment *n.* kan³ ch'ing² 感情.

sentimental *a.* to¹ kan³ ch'ing² te¹ 多感情的.

sentinel *n.* shao⁴ ping¹ 哨兵.

sentry *n.* shao⁴ ping¹ 哨兵.

separable *a.* k'o³ fen¹ li² te¹ 可分離的.

separate *a.* fen¹ li² te¹ 分離的; *v.* fen¹ li² 分離.

separation *n.* fen¹ li² 分離.

September *n.* chiu³ yüeh⁴ 九月.

sequence *n.* chieh² kuo³ 結果.

serenade *n.* yeh⁴ ch'ü⁴ 夜曲.

serene *a.* ch'en² ching⁴ te¹ 沈靜的.

serenity *n.* ch'en² ching⁴ 沈靜.

serf *n.* nung² nu² 農奴.

serge *n.* hsieh² wen² pu⁴ 斜紋布.

sergeant *n.* chün¹ shih⁴ 軍士.

serial *a.* lien² hsü⁴ te¹ 連續的; ～ **number,** (*military*) jen² yüan² pien¹ hao⁴ 人員編號(軍).

serious *a.* yen² su⁴ te¹ 嚴肅的.

sermon *n.* chiang³ tao⁴ 講道, shuo¹ chiao⁴ 說教.

serpent *n.* she² 蛇.

serum *n.* chiang¹ yeh⁴ 漿液, hsüeh⁴ ch'ing¹ 血清.

servant *n.* p'u² i⁴ 僕役.

serve *v.* fu² wu⁴ 服務.

service *n.* fu³ i⁴ 服役.

serviceable *a.* k'o³ yung⁴ te¹ 可用的.

servile *a.* nu² li⁴ te¹ 奴隸的.

servitude *n.* nu² i⁴ 奴役.

session *n.* hui⁴ i⁴ 會議.

set *v.* (*put*) fang⁴ chih⁴ 放置, (*go down*) ch'en² io⁴ 沈落, (*table*) pu⁴ chih⁴ 佈置.

settle v. (*determine*) chüeh² ting⁴ 決定, (*arrange*) cheng³ tun⁴ 整頓, (*take up residence*) an¹ chü¹ 安居; ~ **down,** an¹ chia¹ 安家.

settlement n. (*place*) tsu¹ chieh⁴ 租界.

seven n. ch'i¹ 七; a. ch'i¹ te¹ 七的.

sever v. fen¹ li² 分離.

several a. shu⁴ ko⁴ te¹ 數個的.

severe a. yen² li⁴ te¹ 嚴厲的.

severity n. yen² li⁴ 嚴厲.

sew v. feng² jen⁴ 縫紉.

sewer n. yin¹ kou¹ 陰溝.

sewerage n. kou¹ tao⁴ p'ai² wu¹ fa³ 溝道排污法.

sewing a. feng² jen⁴ te¹ 縫紉的; ~ **kit,** chen¹ hsien⁴ pao¹ 針線包; ~ **machine,** feng² jen⁴ chi¹ 縫紉機.

sex n. hsing⁴ 性; ~ **appeal,** hsing⁴ kan³ 性感; ~ **education,** hsing⁴ chiao⁴ yü⁴ 性教育.

sexton n. chiao⁴ t'ang² k'an¹ shou³ yüan² 教堂看守員.

sexual a. hsing⁴ te¹ 性的.

sexy a. hsing⁴ kan³ te¹ 性感的.

shabby a. lan² lü³ te¹ 襤褸的.

shackle v. chia¹ liao⁴ 加鐐.

shade n. yin¹ 陰, yin⁴ 蔭.

shadow n. ying³ 影.

shadowy a. to¹ ying³ te¹ 多影的.

shady a. to¹ ying³ te¹ 多影的.

shaft n. (*arrow*) chien⁴ kan³ 箭桿, (*spear*) mao² kan³ 矛桿.

shake v. (*hands*) wo⁴ shou³ 握手, (*tremble*) chan⁴ li⁴ 顫慄.

shallow a. ch'ien³ te¹ 淺的.

sham n. (*pretense*) chia³ chuang¹ 假裝, (*fraud*) ch'i¹ cha⁴ 欺詐.

shame n. ch'ih² ju³ 耻辱; v. shih³ hsiu¹ ch'ih³ 使羞耻.

shameful a. ch'ih² ju³ te¹ 耻辱的.

shameless a. pu⁴ chih¹ ch'ih³ te¹ 不知耻的.

shank n. ching⁴ ku³ 脛骨, hsiao² t'ui³ 小腿.

shape n. yang⁴ shih⁴ 樣式.

share n. ku³ fen⁴ 股份; v. fen¹ hsiang³ 分享.

shareholder n. ku³ tung¹ 股東.

shark n. chiao¹ 鮫.

sharp a. chien¹ jui⁴ te¹ 尖銳的.

sharpen v. shih³ chien¹ jui⁴ 使尖銳.

shatter v. shih³ sui⁴ 使碎.

shave v. t'i¹ 剃.

shawl n. chien¹ chin¹ 肩巾.

she pron. t'a¹ 她.

sheaf n. i² su⁴ 一束.

shear v. chien³ 剪, ko¹ 割.

shears n. chien³ tao¹ 剪刀.

sheath n. tao¹ ch'iao⁴ 刀鞘.

shed n. ch'ang³ 場; v. liu² ch'u¹ 流出.

sheep n. yang² 羊.

sheet n. (cloth) pei¹ tan¹ 被單, (newspaper) hsin¹ wen² chih³ 新聞紙.

shelf n. chia⁴ 架.

shell n. k'o² 殼, (gun) p'ao⁴ tan⁴ 砲彈.

shelter n. pi⁴ hu⁴ wu⁴ 庇護物; v. pao³ hu⁴ 保護.

shepherd n. mu⁴ yang² jen² 牧羊人.

shield n. tun⁴ 盾; v. pao³ hu⁴ 保護.

shin n. ching⁴ 脛.

shine v. fa¹ kuang¹ 發光, (polish) ts'a¹ liang⁴ 擦亮.

ship n. ch'uan² 船; v. chuang¹ tsai⁴ 裝載.

shipment n. chuang¹ huo⁴ 裝貨.

shipper n. yün⁴ huo⁴ jen² 運貨人.

shipwreck n. p'o⁴ ch'uan² 破船.

shirt n. ch'en⁴ i¹ 襯衣.

shiver v. chan¹ li⁴ 戰慄.

shoal a. ch'ien³ te¹ 淺的; n. ch'ien³ t'an¹ 淺灘.

shock n. chi⁴ chen⁴ 劇震.

shoe n. hsieh² 鞋.

shoemaker n. hsieh² chiang⁴ 鞋匠.

shoot n., v. fa¹ she⁴ 發射.

shop n. tien⁴ 店.

shopkeeper n. tien⁴ chu³ 店主.

shore n. an⁴ 岸.

short a. (not long) tuan³ te¹ 短的, (not tall) ai³ te¹ 矮的; ~ circuit, tuan³ lu⁴ 短路(電).

shorten v. so¹ tuan³ 縮短.

shorthand n. su² chi⁴ fa³ 速記法.

shortly adv. pu⁴ chiu³ 不久.

short-sighted a. chin⁴ shih⁴ te¹ 近視的.

shot n. (bullets) p'ao⁴ tan⁴ 砲彈.

shoulder *n.* chien¹ 肩; *v.* fu⁴ tan¹ 負擔.

shout *n.*, *v.* han³ chiao⁴ 喊叫.

shove *v.* t'ui¹ chin¹ 推進.

shovel *n.* ch'an³ 鏟. 「顯示.

show *n.* (*display*) chan² lan³ 展覽; *v.* hsien⁴ shih⁴

shower *n.* chen⁴ yü³ 陣雨, (*bath*) lin² yü⁴ 淋浴.

shred *n.* hsiao³ p'ien⁴ 小片; *v.* ch'ieh¹ ch'eng² sui⁴ p'ien⁴ 切成碎片.

shrewd *a.* ts'ung¹ min³ te¹ 聰敏的.

shrewdness *n.* min³ jui⁴ 敏銳.

shriek *v.* chien¹ sheng¹ hu¹ han³ 尖聲呼喊.

shrill *a.* chien¹ sheng¹ te¹ 尖聲的.

shrimp *n.* hsia¹ 蝦.

shrine *n.* shen² k'an¹ 神龕.

shrink *v.* shou¹ so¹ 收縮.

shroud *n.* shou⁴ i¹ 壽衣; *v.* lien⁴ tsang⁴ 殮葬.

shrub *n.* kuan⁴ mu⁴ 灌木.

shudder *v.* chan⁴ li⁴ 戰慄.

shuffle *v.* yeh⁴ hsing² 曳行, (*card*) hsi³ p'ai² 洗牌.

shun *v.* pi⁴ mien³ 避免.

shunt *v.* chuan³ hsiang⁴ 轉向.

shut *v.* pi⁴ 閉.

shutter *n.* pai³ yeh⁴ ch'uang¹ 百葉窗.

shuttle *n.* so¹ 梭.

shy *a.* hsiu¹ ch'üeh⁴ te¹ 羞怯的.

sick *a.* chi² ping⁴ te¹ 疾病的.

sickle *n.* lien² tao¹ 鐮刀.

sickly *a.* yu³ ping⁴ te¹ 有病的.

sickness *n.* chi² ping⁴ 疾病.

side *n.* pien¹ 邊.

sideboard *n.* wan³ tieh² ch'u² 碗碟櫥.

siege *n.* wei² kung¹ 圍攻.

sigh *v.* t'an⁴ hsi² 嘆息.

sight *n.* shih⁴ li⁴ 視力.

sightless *a.* mang² mu⁴ te¹ 盲目的. 「簽名.

sign *n.* (*symbol*) chi⁴ hao⁴ 記號; *v.* ch'ien¹ ming²

signal *n.* hsin⁴ hao⁴ 信號, (*sign*) chi⁴ hao⁴ 記號; *v.* fa¹ an⁴ hao⁴ 發暗號; ～ **communication**, t'ung¹ hsin⁴ 通信; ～ **troops**, t'ung¹ hsin⁴ ping¹ pu⁴ tui¹ 通信兵部隊.

signalman *n.* t'ung¹ hsin⁴ yüan² 通信員.

signature *n.* ch'ien¹ ming² 簽名.

significance *n.* chung⁴ yao⁴ 重要.

significant *a.* (*important*) chung⁴ yao⁴ te¹ 重要的.

silence *n.* ching⁴ mo⁴ 靜默.

silent *a.* (*noiseless*) wu²' sheng¹ te¹ 無聲的, (*not speaking*) chien¹ mo⁴ te¹ 緘默的.

silk *n.* ssu¹ 絲.

silly *a.* yü² pen⁴ te¹ 愚笨的.

silver *n.* yin² 銀.

silversmith *n.* yin² chiang⁴ 銀匠.

similar *a.* hsiang¹ hsiang⁴ te¹ 相像的.

similarity *n.* hsiang¹ hsiang⁴ 相像.

simile *n.* p'i⁴ yü⁴ 譬喻.

simple *a.* chien³ tan¹ te¹ 簡單的.

simplify *v.* shih³ tan¹ ch'un² 使單純. 「發生的.

simultaneous *a.* t'ung² shih² fa¹ sheng¹ te¹ 同時

sin *n.* tsui⁴ e⁴ 罪惡; *v.* fan⁴ tsui⁴ 犯罪.

since *prep.* tzu⁴ ... i³ hou⁴ 自...以後; *conj.* (*because*) yin¹ 因, (*time*) tzu⁴ ... i³ lai² 自...以來.

sincere *a.* chen¹ ch'eng² te¹ 真誠的.

sincerity *n.* chen¹ ch'eng² 真誠.

sinful *a.* yu³ tsui⁴ te¹ 有罪的.

sing *v.* ko¹ ch'ang⁴ 歌唱.

singer *n.* ko¹ ch'ang⁴ chia¹ 歌唱家.

singing *a.* ko¹ ch'ang⁴ 歌唱.

single *a.* tan¹ i⁴ te¹ 單一的.

singular *a.* tan¹ shu⁴ te¹ 單數的.

sink *v.* (*submerge*) ch'en² mo⁴ 沈沒, (*by bomb*) cha⁴ ch'en² 炸沈, (*by gun or torpedo*) chi¹ ch'en² 擊沈.

sinner *n.* fan⁴ tsui⁴ che³ 犯罪者.

sip *v.* hsiao² yin³ 小飲.

siphon *n.* hung² hsi¹ kuan³ 虹吸管.

sit *v.* tso⁴ 坐.

site *n.* wei⁴ chih⁴ 位置.

situation *n.* (*circumstances*) ch'ing² hsing² 情形.

six *n.* liu⁴ 六; *a.* liu⁴ te¹ 六的.

size *n.* (*extent*) ta⁴ hsiao³ 大小. 「冰.

skate *n.* liu¹ ping¹ hsieh² 溜冰鞋; *v.* liu¹ ping¹ 溜

skeleton *n.* ku³ ko² 骨路.

sketch *n.* ts'ao³ t'u² 草圖. 「雪.

ski *n.* hua² hsüeh³ chi¹ 滑雪屐; *v.* hua² hsüeh³ 滑

skid *v.* hua² tsou³ 滑走.

skiff *n.* hsiao³ t'ing³ 小艇.

skillful, skilful *a.* ching¹ ch'iao³ te¹ 精巧的.

skill *n.* chi⁴ neng² 技能. 「獸皮.

skin *n.* (*human*) p'i² fu¹ 皮膚, (*animal*) shou⁴ p'i²

skip *v.* t'iao⁴ yüeh⁴ 跳躍.

skirmish *n.* hsiao³ chan⁴ 小戰.

skirt *n.* ch'ün² 裙.

sky *n.* t'ien¹ 天.

skylight *n.* t'ien¹ ch'uang¹ 天窗.

slab *n.* pan³ 板.

slack *a.* k'uan¹ sung¹ te¹ 寬鬆的.

slacken *v.* shih³ ch'ih² huan³ 使遲緩.

slander *n.* hui³ pang⁴ 毀謗.

slanderous *a.* hao⁴ hui³ pang⁴ te¹ 好毀謗的.

slang *n.* li² yü³ 俚語.

slant *v.* shih³ ch'ing¹ hsieh² 使傾斜.

slap *n., v.* chang³ chi¹ 掌擊.

slate *n.* pan³ t'iao² 板條.

slaughter *n.* t'u² sha¹ 屠殺; *v.* t'u² tsai³ 屠宰; ～ **house,** t'u² tsai² ch'ang³ 屠宰場.

slave *n.* nu² li⁴ 奴隸.

slavery *n.* nu² li⁴ shen¹ fen⁴ 奴隸身分.

slavish *a.* nu² li⁴ te¹ 奴隸的.

slay *v.* ts'an² sha¹ 殘殺.

sleep *n.* shui⁴ 睡.

sleeping *n.* shui⁴ mien² 睡眠; ～ **bag,** shui⁴ tai⁴ 睡袋; ～ **car,** wo⁴ ch'e¹ 臥車; ～ **sickness,** hun¹ shui⁴ ping⁴ 昏睡病(醫).

sleepy *a.* yü⁴ shui⁴ te¹ 欲睡的.

sleet *n.* hsien⁴ 霰.

sleeve *n.* hsiu⁴ 袖.

slender *a.* hsi⁴ ch'ang² te¹ 細長的. 「片.

slice *n.* po² p'ien⁴ 薄片; *v.* ch'ieh¹ po² p'ien⁴ 切薄

slide *v.* hua² tsou³ 滑走.

slight *a.* ch'ing¹ wei¹ te¹ 輕微的; *v.* ch'ing¹ shih⁴ 輕視.

slime *n.* nien² ni² 黏泥.

slimy *a.* nien² ni² te¹ 黏泥的.

sling *n.* (*for throwing stones*) t'ou² shih² ch'i⁴ 投石器, (*for injured arm*) san¹ chiao³ chin¹ 三角巾;

234

v. (*throw*) t'ou² chih¹ 投擲; "~ **arms!**" ch'iang¹ shang⁴ chien¹ 鎗上肩(軍).

slink *v.* ch'ien¹ t'ao² 潛逃. 「出.

slip *n.* (*mistake*) ts'o⁴ wu⁴ 錯誤; *v.* hua² ch'u¹ 滑

slipper *n.* t'o¹ hsieh² 拖鞋.

slippery *a.* hua² te¹ 滑的.

slit *n.* lieh⁴ feng² 裂縫.

sloe *n.* wu¹ ching¹ tzu¹ 烏莉子.

sloop *n.* tan¹ wei² fan¹ ch'uan² 單桅帆船.

slope *n., v.* ch'ing¹ hsieh² 傾斜.

sloth *n.* lan³ to⁴ 懶惰.

slough *n.* ni² k'eng¹ 泥坑.

sloven *n.* lan³ to⁴ che³ 懶惰者.

slovenly *a.* lan³ to⁴ te¹ 懶惰的.

slow *a.* ch'ih² man⁴ te¹ 遲漫的, yen² huan³ 延緩.

sluggard *n.* lan³ han⁴ 懶漢.

slumber *v.* shui⁴ 睡.

sly *a.* kuei³ pi⁴ te¹ 詭秘的.

small *a.* hsiao³ te¹ 小的; ~ **arms,** ch'ing¹ ping¹ ch'i⁴ 輕兵器; ~ **of the stock,** (*rifle*) ch'iang¹

smallpox *n.* t'ien¹ hua¹ 天花(醫). 「pa³ 鎗把(兵).

smart *a.* ling² li⁴ te¹ 伶俐的; *v.* chi⁴ t'ung⁴ 劇痛.

smash *v.* p'eng⁴ sui⁴ 挿碎.

smell *n.* hsiu⁴ chüeh² 嗅覺; *v.* hsiu⁴ 嗅.

smile *n., v.* wei² hsiao³ 微笑.

smith *n.* (*blacksmith*) t'ieh³ chiang⁴ 鐵匠.

smithy *n.* t'ieh³ chiang⁴ tien⁴ 鐵匠店.

smoke *n.* yen¹ 烟; *v.* ch'u¹ yen¹ 出烟, (*cigarette*) hsi¹ yen¹ 吸烟; ~ **screen,** yen¹ mu⁴ 煙幕(軍); ~ **shell,** yen¹ mu⁴ tan⁴ 煙幕彈(軍).

smoky *a.* to¹ yen¹ te¹ 多烟的. 「使滑.

smooth *a.* p'ing² t'an³ te¹ 平坦的; *v.* shih³ hua²

smoothness *n.* p'ing² hua² 平滑.

smother *v.* chih⁴ hsi¹ 窒息.

smuggle *v.* tsou³ ssu¹ 走私.

smuggler *n.* tsou³ ssu¹ che³ 走私者.

snail *n.* kua¹ niu² 蝸牛.

snake *n.* she² 蛇.

snap *n.* chi² jui⁴ sheng¹ 急銳聲; *v.* (*break*) che² tuan⁴ 折斷, (*dog*) yao⁴ 咬.

snare *n.* hsien⁴ ching³ 陷阱.

snarl *v.* p'ao² hsiao¹ 咆哮.

snatch *v.* chüeh² ch'ü³ 攫取.

sneak *v.* ch'ien² hsing² 潛行.

sneer *v.* pi⁴ i² 鄙夷; *v.* ch'ing¹ pi⁴ 輕鄙.

sneeze *n.* fen⁴ t'i⁴ 噴嚏.

sniper *n.* chü¹ chi¹ shou³ 狙擊手. 鼾聲.

snore *n.* han¹ sheng¹ 鼾聲; *v.* fa¹ han¹ sheng¹ 發

snort *v.* tso⁴ fen⁴ pi² sheng¹ 作噴鼻聲.

snout *n.* shou⁴ pi² 獸鼻.

snow *n.* hsüeh³ 雪.

snowdrop *n.* (*flower*) hsüeh³ hua¹ 雪花(植).

snowy *a.* yu² hsüeh³ te¹ 有雪的.

snuff *n.* pi² yen¹ 鼻烟; *v.* hsi¹ pi² yen¹ 吸鼻烟.

so *adv.* (*in this way*) ju² tz'u³ 如此, (*therefore*) yin¹ tz'u³ 因此; ～ **and so**, mou² mou³ 某某; ～ **far as it concerns**, chih⁴ yü² 至於; ～ **that**, pi⁴ te² 俾得.

soak *v.* chin⁴ shih¹ 浸濕.

soap *n.* fei² tsao⁴ 肥皂.

soar *v.* kao¹ fei¹ 高飛, fei¹ hsiang² 飛翔.

sob *v.* wu¹ yen¹ 嗚咽.

sober *a.* (*not drunk*) ch'ing¹ hsing³ te¹ 清醒的.

sobriety *n.* ch'ing¹ hsing³ 清醒.

sociable *a.* k'o³ chiao¹ te¹ 可交的.

social *a.* she⁴ hui⁴ te¹ 社會的; ～ **science**, she⁴ hui⁴ k'o¹ hsüeh² 社會科學; ～ **work**, she⁴ hui⁴ fu² wu⁴ 社會服務.

socialism *n.* she⁴ hui⁴ chu³ i⁴ 社會主義.

socialist *n.* she⁴ hui⁴ chu³ i⁴ che³ 社會主義者.

society *n.* she⁴ hui⁴ 社會.

sock *n.* tuan³ wa⁴ 短襪.

socket *n.* wa¹ ch'u⁴ 凹處.

sod *n.* ts'ao³ ti⁴ 草地.

soda *n.* su¹ ta³ 蘇打, t'an⁴ suan¹ na² 炭酸鈉.

soft *a.* jou² juan³ te¹ 柔軟的.

soften *v.* shih³ jou² juan³ 使柔軟.

softness *n.* jou² juan³ 柔軟.

soil *n.* ni² t'u³ 泥土.

sojourn *n.*, *v.* chi⁴ yü⁴ 寄寓.

solder *n.* han⁴ liao⁴ 焊料.

soldier *n.* chün¹ jen² 軍人.

sole n. (*fish*) tieh² 鰈, (*shoe*) hsieh² ti³ 鞋底; a. wei² i⁴ te¹ 唯一的.

solemn a. chuang¹ yen² te¹ 莊嚴的.

solemnity n. chuang¹ yen² 莊嚴.

solicitor n. ch'ing³ ch'iu² che³ 請求者.

solicitous a. chiao¹ chi² te¹ 焦急的.

solicitude n. chiao¹ chi² 焦急.

solid a. ku⁴ t'i³ te¹ 固體的.

solidarity n. hsiu¹ ch'i¹ hsiang¹ kung⁴ 休戚相共.

solidity n. chien¹ shih² 堅實.

soliloquy n. tzu⁴ yen² tzu⁴ yü³ 自言自語.

solitary a. ku¹ tu² te¹ 孤獨的.

solitude n. ku¹ tu² 孤獨.

solstice n. (*winter*) tung¹ chih⁴ 冬至, (*summer*) hsia⁴ chih⁴ 夏至.

soluble a. (*dissolve*) k'o³ jung² chieh³ te¹ 可溶解的, (*solve*) k'o² chieh³ chüeh² te¹ 可解決的.

solution n. (*of problem*) chieh³ ta² 解答, (*liquid*) jung² yeh⁴ 溶液.

solve v. chieh³ ta² 解答.

some a. (*a little*) shao² hsü³ 少許; pron. mou² 某.

somebody pron. mou³ jen² 某人; n. yao⁴ jen² 要人.

somehow adv. wu² lun² ju² ho² 無論如何.

something n. mou³ wu⁴ 某物; adv. chi² hsü³ 幾許.

sometime adv. t'o¹ jih⁴ 他日.

sometimes adv. yu⁸ shih² 有時.

somewhat adv. jo⁴ kan¹ 若干.

somewhere adv. mou³ ch'u⁴ 某處.

son n. erh² tzu³ 兒子.

song n. ko¹ ch'ü³ 歌曲.

soon adv. chi² k'o⁴ 即刻.

soot n. mei² yen¹ 煤烟.

soothe v. (*comfort*) fu³ wei⁴ 撫慰.

sorcerer n. nan² wu¹ 男巫.

sorcery n. wu¹ shu⁴ 巫術.

sordid a. pei¹ chien⁴ te¹ 卑賤的.

sore a. t'ung⁴ te¹ 痛的; n. k'uei⁴ yang² 潰瘍.

sorrel a. li⁴ se⁴ te¹ 栗色的.

sorrow n. pei¹ ai¹ 悲哀.

sorrowful a. pei¹ ai¹ te¹ 悲哀的.

sorry a. pao⁴ ch'ien⁴ te¹ 抱歉的.

sort *n.* chung³ lei⁴ 種類; *v.* fen¹ lei⁴ 分類.

soul *n.* ling² hun² 靈魂.

sound *a.* chien⁴ k'ang¹ te¹ 健康的; *n.* sheng¹ yin¹ 聲音; *v.* tso⁴ sheng¹ 作聲.

soup *n.* t'ang¹ 湯.

sour *a.* suan¹ te¹ 酸的.　　　　　「yüan² 來源.

source *n.* ken¹ yüan² 根源, (*of information*) lai²

south *n.* nan² 南.

souvenir *n.* chi⁴ nien¹ p'in³ 紀念品.

sovereign *a.* yu² chu³ ch'üan² te¹ 有主權的; *n.* ti⁴ wang² 帝王; ~ **state,** tu² li⁴ kuo² 獨立國.

sovereignty *n.* chu³ ch'üan² 主權.

sow *n.* mu³ chu¹ 母豬; *v.* po⁴ chung³ 播種.

space *n.* ti⁴ wei⁴ 地位, (*celestial*) k'ung¹ chien¹ 空

spacious *a.* k'uan¹ ch'ang³ te¹ 寬敞的.　　「間.

spade *n.* ch'u² 鋤.

span *n.* chih³ chü⁴ 指距; *v.* (*extend over*) k'ua⁴

spaniel *n.* huang² 獚(動).　　　　「kuo⁴ 跨過.

spanner *n.* pan¹ tzu¹ 搬子.

spare *a.* sheng³ yü² te¹ 剩餘的; *v.* (*save*) chieh² yung⁴ 節用; ~ **parts,** ling² chien⁴ 零件.

spark *n.* (*fire*) huo³ hua¹ 火花, (*electric*) tien⁴ hua¹

sparkle *v.* shan³ shuo⁴ 閃爍.　　　　　「電花.

sparrow *n.* ma² ch'iao³ 麻雀.

spasm *n.* ching⁴ lüan² 痙攣.

spasmodic *a.* ching⁴ lüan² te¹ 痙攣的.

spawn *n.* (*fish*) yü² lan³ 魚卵.

speak *v.* chiang³ 講, shuo¹ 說.

speaker *n.* shuo¹ hua⁴ che³ 說話者, yen³ shuo¹ che³ 演說者.　　　　　　　　「以槍刺.

spear *n.* ch'iang¹ 槍, mao³ 矛; *v.* i³ ch'iang¹ tz'u⁴

special *a.* t'e⁴ pieh² te¹ 特別的.

speciality *n.* t'e⁴ shu¹ 特殊, (*specialty*) chuan¹

specie *n.* ying⁴ pi⁴ 硬幣.　　　　　「yeh⁴ 專業.

species *n.* chung³ lei⁴ 種類.

specific *a.* (*particular*) t'e⁴ shu¹ te¹ 特殊的, (*definite*) ch'üeh² ting⁴ te¹ 確定的.

specification *n.* fen¹ men² pieh² lei⁴ 分門別類.

specify *v.* lieh⁴ chü³ 列舉.

specimen *n.* yang⁴ p'in³ 樣品, piao¹ pen³ 標本.

speck *n.* wu¹ tien³ 污點.

238

spectacle *n.* (*sight*) ch'i² kuan¹ 奇觀; (*display*)
chan² lan³ 展覽.

spectacles *n.* yen³ ching⁴ 眼鏡.

spectator *n.* p'ang² kuan¹ che³ 旁觀者.

speculate *v.* t'ui¹ lun⁴ 推論.

speculation *n.* t'ui¹ lun⁴ 推論.

speculative *a.* t'ui¹ lun⁴ te¹ 推論的.

speech *n.* yen³ shuo¹ 演說.

speed *n.* su² tu⁴ 速度; *v.* chi² hsing² 急行.

speedometer *n.* su² tu⁴ chi⁴ 速度計.

speedy *a.* hsün⁴ su² te¹ 迅速的.

spell *v.* p'in¹ tzu¹ 拼字.

spend *v.* yung⁴ 用.

spendthrift *n.* lang⁴ fei⁴ che³ 浪費者.

sphere *n.* ch'iu² t'i³ 球體, (*extent*) fan⁴ wei² 範圍.

spherical *a.* ch'iu² t'i³ te¹ 球體的.

spice *n.* hsiang¹ liao⁴ 香料; *v.* chia¹ hsiang¹ wei²
加香味.

spider *n.* chih¹ chu¹ 蜘蛛.

spike *n.* tao⁴ ting¹ 道釘.

spill *v.* shih³ i⁴ ch'u¹ 使溢出.

spin *v.* fang³ sha¹ 紡紗.

spinach *n.* po¹ ts'ai⁴ 菠菜.

spindle *n.* fang³ ch'ui² 紡錘.

spinster *n.* fang³ chih¹ nü³ 紡織女.

spiral *a.* lo² chuang⁴ hsien⁴ te¹ 螺狀線的.

spire *n.* chien¹ ting³ 尖頂.

spirit *n.* ching¹ shen² 精神.

spirited *a.* yu³ ching¹ shen² te¹ 有精神的.

spiritless *a.* chü³ sang⁴ te¹ 沮喪的.

spiritual *a.* ching¹ shen² te¹ 精神的.

spit *n.* t'o⁴ yeh⁴ 唾液; *v.* t'o⁴ t'u⁴ 唾吐.

spite *n.* e⁴ i⁴ 惡意.

spiteful *a.* yu³ e⁴ i⁴ te¹ 有惡意的.

spittle *n.* t'o⁴ yen² 唾涎.

splash *v.* chien¹ 濺, p'o¹ 潑.

splendid *a.* hua² li⁴ te¹ 華麗的.

splendor *n.* kuang¹ hui¹ 光輝.

splint *n.* chia¹ pan³ 夾板.

splinter *v.* fen¹ lieh⁴ 分裂.　　　　　「裂

split *v.* (*cut*) tsung⁴ p'i¹ 縱劈, (*divide*) fen¹ lieh⁴ 分

239

spoil n. lüeh⁴ to² p'in³ 掠奪品; v. (damage) shang¹ hai⁴ 傷害, (child) ku¹ hsi¹ 姑息.

spoliation n. lüeh⁴ to² 掠奪, ch'iang³ chieh² 搶劫.

sponge n. hai² mien² 海綿.

spontaneous a. tzu⁴ jan² te¹ 自然的.

spoon n. t'ang¹ ch'ih² 湯匙.

sport n. hu⁴ wai⁴ yün⁴ tung⁴ 戶外運動.

sportsman n. yün⁴ tung⁴ yüan² 運動員.

spot n. (dot) wu¹ tien³ 污點, (place) ti⁴ tien³ 地點; v. (get dirty) shih² yu³ wu¹ tien³ 使有污點.

spout n. p'en¹ k'ou³ 噴口; v. p'en¹ ch'u¹ 噴出.

sprain n., v. niu³ shang¹ 扭傷.

spray n. p'en¹ wu⁴ 噴霧.

spread v. san⁴ pu⁴ 散佈.

sprig n. hsiao³ chih¹ 小枝.

sprightly a. huo² p'o¹ te¹ 活潑的.

spring n. (season) ch'un¹ chi⁴ 春季, (wire) t'an² huang² 彈簧; v. t'iao⁴ ch'i³ 跳起.

sprinkle v. sa³ 灑.

sprout n. miao² 苗; v. meng² ya² 萌芽.

spruce n. chen¹ ts'ung¹ 針樅(植).   「踢」

spur n. ma³ tz'u⁴ 馬刺; v. i² ma³ tz'u⁴ t'i² 以馬刺.

spurious a. wei⁴ tsao⁴ te¹ 偽造的, chia³ te¹ 假的.

spurn v. (kick away) t'i² k'ai¹ 踢開.   「so³ 探索」

spy n. chien⁴ tieh² 間諜, chen¹ t'an⁴ 偵探; v. t'an⁴

squad n. pan¹ 班.

squadron n. (navy) fen¹ chien⁴ tui⁴ 分艦隊(海), (cavalry) ch'i² ping¹ chung¹ tui⁴ 騎兵中隊, (air force) chung¹ tui⁴ 中隊(空), (any group) tui⁴ 隊.

squalid a. wu¹ hui⁴ te¹ 污穢的.

squall n. (wind) k'uang² feng¹ 狂風.

squander v. lang⁴ fei⁴ 浪費.

square a. cheng⁴ fang¹ hsing² te¹ 正方形的; n. cheng⁴ fang¹ hsing² 正方形; v. tzu⁴ ch'eng² 自乘; ~ dance, fang¹ hsing² wu³ 方形舞.   「聲」

squeak v. tso⁴ chien¹ jui⁴ chiao⁴ sheng¹ 作尖銳叫

squeeze v. (press) ya¹ 壓.

squint v. hsieh² shih⁴ 斜視.

squirrel n. sung¹ shu³ 松鼠.

stab n., v. tz'u⁴ 刺.

stability n. ku⁴ ting⁴ 固定.

240

stable *a.* ku⁴ ting⁴ te¹ 固定的; *n.* ma³ fang² 馬房.

stack *n.* ts'ao³ tui¹ 草堆, (*chimney*) yen¹ ts'ung¹ 烟囱; "**~ arms!**" chia¹ ch'iang¹ 架鎗(軍).

staff *n.* (*officer*) ts'an¹ mou² 參謀.

stag *n.* hsiung² lu⁴ 雄鹿.

stage *n.* wu³ t'ai² 舞臺.

stagger *v.* p'an² shan¹ hsing² tsou³ 蹣跚行走.

stagnant *a.* pu⁴ liu² tung⁴ te¹ 不流動的.

stagnate *v.* ching⁴ chih³ 靜止.

staid *a.* chen⁴ ching⁴ te¹ 鎮靜的.

stain *n.* wu¹ tien³ 污點; *v.* jan³ wu¹ 染污.

stair *n.* t'i¹ chi² 梯級.

staircase *n.* lou² t'i¹ 樓梯.

stake *n.* piao¹ chuang¹ 標樁.

stale *a.* pu⁴ hsin¹ hsien¹ te¹ 不新鮮的.

stalk *n.* ching¹ 莖; *v.* ch'ien² hsing² 潛行.

stall *n.* (*for animal*) chiu⁴ chih² 廏室; *v.* (*of an airplane*) shih¹ su² 失速(空).

stammer *v.* k'ou³ ch'ih¹ 口吃.

stamp *n.* (*postage*) yu² p'iao⁴ 郵票, (*metal*) tao³ ch'ui² 搗鎚, (*seal*) yin⁴ chang¹ 印章; *v.* (*impress*) kai¹ yin¹ 蓋印, (*feet*) tun⁴ tsu² 頓足.

stand *n.* (*position*) li⁴ tsu² ti⁴ 立足地, (*support*) chia⁴ 架; *v.* chan⁴ ch'i³ 站起.

standard *a.* piao¹ chun³ te¹ 標準的; *n.* piao¹ chun³ 標準, (*flag*) ch'i² chih⁴ 旗幟; **~ language,** piao¹ chun² yü³ 標準語; **~ of living,** sheng¹ huo² ch'eng² tu⁴ 生活程度; **~ time,** piao¹ chun³ shih² 標準時.

star *n.* hsing¹ 星, (*person*) ming² hsing¹ 明星; **~ and stripes,** (*US flag*) mei³ kuo² kuo⁴ ch'i² 美國國旗, (*US Army newspaper*) hsing¹ t'iao² pao⁴ 星條報(美軍報). 「ying⁴ 堅硬.

starch *n.* tien⁴ fen³ 澱粉; *v.* (*clothes*) chiang¹

stare *n., v.* chu⁴ shih⁴ 注視. 「tung⁴ 開始行動.

start *n.* k'ai¹ shih³ 開始; *v.* k'ai¹ shih³ hsing²

startle *v.* ching¹ tung⁴ 驚動.

starvation *n.* chi¹ e⁴ 飢餓.

starve *v.* e⁴ ssu³ 餓死.

state *n.* (*condition*) ch'ing² hsing² 情形, (*nation*) kuo² 國, (*of US*) chou¹ 州; *v.* hsü² shu⁴ 敍述; **~**

241

Planning Committee**, kuo² chia¹ chi⁴ hua⁴ wei³ yüan² hui⁴ 國家計劃委員會**.

stately *a.* t'ang² huang² te¹ 堂皇的.

statement *n.* hsü⁴ shu⁴ 敍述.

statesman *n.* cheng⁴ chih⁴ chia¹ 政治家.

station *n.* chan⁴ 站; *v.* (*unit*) chu⁴ fang² 駐防, (*personnel*) p'ai⁴ tsai⁴ 派在.

stationary *a.* ku⁴ ting⁴ te¹ 固定的.

stationer *n.* wen² chü⁴ shang¹ 文具商.

stationery *n.* wen² chü⁴ 文具.

statistics *n.* t'ung³ chi⁴ 統計.

statuary *n.* tiao¹ hsiang⁴ 彫像.

statue *n.* tiao¹ hsiang⁴ 彫像.

stature *n.* t'i³ kao¹ 體高.

stay *v.* (*dwell*) chü¹ liu² 居留.

steadfast *a.* chien¹ ting⁴ te¹ 堅定的.

steady *a.* ku⁴ ting⁴ te¹ 固定的.

steak *n.* (*beefsteak*) niu² p'ai⁴ 牛排(西餐菜).

steal *v.* t'ou¹ ch'ieh⁴ 偷竊.

stealth *n.* pi⁴ mi⁴ hsing² tung⁴ 秘密行動.

stealthy *a.* pi⁴ mi⁴ hsing² tung⁴ te¹ 秘密行動的.

steam *n.* cheng¹ ch'i⁴ 蒸氣; *v.* cheng¹ chu⁴ 蒸煮.

steamboat *n.* ch'i⁴ ch'uan² 汽船.

steel *n.* kang¹ 鋼; ～ **helmet**, kang¹ k'uei¹ 鋼盔.

steep *a.* tou³ ch'iao⁴ te¹ 陡峭的; *v.* chin⁴ p'ao⁴ 浸泡. 「之尖頂」

steeple *n.* li³ pai⁴ t'ang² chih¹ chien¹ ting³ 禮拜堂

steer *v.* chia⁴ shih³ 駕駛.

steersman *n.* to⁴ shou³ 舵手.

stem *n.* ching¹ 莖.

stench *n.* ch'ou⁴ ch'i⁴ 臭氣.

step *n.* pu⁴ 步; *v.* pu⁴ hsing² 步行.

stereotype *n.* ch'ien¹ pan³ 鉛版.

sterilize *v.* sha¹ chün¹ 殺菌. 「船尾」

stern *a.* yen² li⁴ te¹ 嚴厲的; *n.* (*boat*) ch'uan² wei³

stew *n.* cheng¹ jou⁴ 蒸肉; *v.* cheng¹ chu³ 蒸煮.

stewardess *n.* (*airplane*) k'ung¹ chung¹ hsiao² chieh³ 空中小姐.

stick *n.* (*walking*) shou³ chang⁴ 手杖; *v.* (*to*) chien¹ ch'ih² 堅持, (*into*) tz'u⁴ ju⁴ 刺入, (*catch*) chan¹ t'ieh¹ 黏貼.

sticky *a.* nien² hsing⁴ te¹ 黏性的.

stiff *a.* pu² i⁴ ch'ü¹ te¹ 不易曲的.

stiffen *v.* shih³ ying⁴ 使硬.

stifle *v.* chih⁴ hsi² 窒息.

still *a.* ching⁴ te¹ 靜的; *adv.* (*time*) ch'i² chin¹ 迄今.

stimulant *n.* hsing¹ fen⁴ chi⁴ 興奮劑.

stimulate *v.* (*spur on*) chi¹ li⁴ 激勵.

sting *n.* tz'u⁴ t'ung⁴ 刺痛; *v.* tz'u⁴ 刺.

stingy *a.* pi⁴ lin² te¹ 鄙吝的.

stink *n.* ch'ou⁴ wei⁴ 臭味; *v.* fa¹ ch'ou⁴ wei⁴ 發臭

「味.

stipulate *v.* yüeh¹ ting⁴ 約定.

stipulation *n.* ting⁴ yüeh¹ 訂約.

stir *v.* shih³ tung⁴ 使動.

stirrup *n.* t'a⁴ teng⁴ 踏鐙(騎).

stitch *n.* i⁴ chen¹ 一針; *v.* feng² 縫.

stock *n.* (*things*) ts'un² huo⁴ 存貨, (*family*) chia¹ hsi⁴ 家系, (*shares*) ku³ p'iao⁴ 股票.

stockbroker *n.* cheng⁴ ch'üan⁴ ching¹ chi⁴ jen² 證
「券經紀人.

stocking *n.* ch'ang² wa⁴ 長襪.

stoker *n.* huo³ fu¹ 火夫.

stomach *n.* wei⁴ 胃.

stone *n.* shih² 石.

stony *a.* to¹ shih² te¹ 多石的.

stool *n.* teng⁴ 凳, (*bowels*) ta⁴ pien⁴ 大便.

stoop *v.* fu² shou³ 俯首.

stop *n.* t'ing² chih³ 停止; *v.* t'ing² 停.

stoppage *n.* (*weapons*) ku⁴ chang⁴ 故障.

stopper *n.* juan³ mu⁴ sai⁴ 軟木塞.

store *n.* shang¹ tien⁴ 商店; *v.* chu³ ts'ang² 貯藏.

stork *n.* hao² 鶴.

「pao⁴ 起風暴.

storm *n.* pao⁴ feng¹ yü³ 暴風雨; *v.* ch'i³ feng¹

stormy *a.* pao⁴ feng¹ yü³ te¹ 暴風雨的.

story *n.* ku⁴ shih⁴ 故事.

stout *a.* fei² p'an⁴ te¹ 肥胖的.

stove *n.* huo³ lu² 火爐.

stow *v.* pao¹ chuang¹ 包裝.

stowage *n.* pao¹ chuang¹ fa³ 包裝法.

straggle *v.* san³ lo⁴ 散落.

straight *a.* chih² te¹ 直的.

strain *v.* (*draw tight*) la¹ chin³ 拉緊, (*filter*) lü⁴ 濾, (*body*) kuo⁴ lao² 過勞.

243

strainer *n.* lü⁴ ch'i⁴ 濾器.

strait *a.* hsia² chai³ te¹ 狹窄的; *n.* hai³ hsia² 海峽.

straiten *v.* hsien⁴ chih⁴ 限制.

strand *n.* (*thread*) sheng² ku³ 繩股; *v.* (*run aground*) ko¹ ch'ien³ 擱淺, (*break a strand*) chiao² ku³ 絞股.

strange *a.* ch'i² i⁴ te¹ 奇異的.

stranger *n.* sheng¹ k'o⁴ 生客.

strangle *v.* chiao² ssu³ 絞死.

strap *n.* p'i² tai⁴ 皮帶.

strategic *a.* chan⁴ lüeh⁴ te¹ 戰略的; ~ **offensive**, chan⁴ lüeh⁴ kung¹ chi¹ 戰略攻擊(軍); ~ **withdrawal**, chan⁴ lüeh⁴ ch'e⁴ t'ui⁴ 戰略撤退(軍).

strategy *n.* chan⁴ lüeh⁴ 戰略(軍).

straw *n.* tao⁴ ts'ao³ 稻草.

strawberry *n.* ts'ao³ mei² 草莓, yang² mei² 楊梅.

stray *v.* mi² lu⁴ 迷路; ~ **bullet**, liu² tan⁴ 流彈(軍).

streak *n.* hsien⁴ t'iao² 線條.

streaky *a.* yu³ t'iao² wen² te¹ 有條紋的.

stream *n.* ho² liu² 河流.

streamline *a.* liu² hsien⁴ hsing² te¹ 流線型的.

street *n.* chieh¹ tao⁴ 街道; ~ **fighting**, hsiang⁴ chan⁴ 巷戰(軍).

strength *n.* li⁴ liang⁴ 力量, (*in men or units*) ping¹ li⁴ 兵力, (*in men and materiel*) shih² li⁴ 實力.

strengthen *v.* chia¹ ch'iang² 加强.

strenuous *a.* je⁴ hsin¹ te¹ 熱心的.

stress *n.* ya¹ p'o⁴ 壓迫.

stretch *v.* (*spread*) shen¹ chang¹ 伸張, (*elastic*) k'uo⁴ chang¹ 擴張.

stretcher *n.* t'ai² ch'uang² 舁床, tan¹ chia⁴ 担架.

strict *a.* (*severe*) yen² li⁴ te¹ 嚴厲的.

stride *v.* k'uo⁴ pu⁴ erh² hsing² 闊步而行.

strife *n.* cheng¹ lun⁴ 爭論.

strike *v.* ta³ 打, (*stop work*) pa⁴ kung¹ 罷工; *n.* (*industry*) t'ung² meng² pa⁴ kung¹ 同盟罷工; ~ **camp**, pa² ying² 拔營.

string *n.* hsi⁴ so³ 細索.

stringent *a.* sen¹ yen² te¹ 森嚴的.

strip *v.* (*undress*) t'o¹ kuang¹ 脱光, (*deprive of*) po¹ to² 剝奪; ~ **tease**, t'o¹ i¹ wu³ 脱衣舞.

stripe *n.* t'iao² wen² 條紋. 「cheng¹ 競爭.

strive *v.* (*try hard*) nu³ li⁴ 努力, (*struggle*) ching⁴

stroke *n.* (*illness*) ts'u⁴ fa¹ 猝發; *v.* fu³ mo¹ 撫摸.

stroll *n.*, *v.* san³ pu⁴ 散步.

strong *a.* ch'iang¹ te¹ 強的.

structure *n.* kou⁴ tsao⁴ 構造, (*building*) chien⁴
chu⁴ wu⁴ 建築物.

struggle *v.* nu³ li⁴ 努力, fen⁴ tou⁴ 奮鬥.

strut *n.* ao⁴ pu⁴ 傲步.

stubble *n.* ts'an² keng³ 殘梗.

stubborn *a.* wan² ch'iang² te¹ 頑強的.

stud *n.* (*nailhead*) ting¹ t'ou² 釘頭, (*horses*) ma³
hsüeh² sheng¹ 學生. 「ch'ün² 馬羣.

student *n.* hsüeh² sheng¹ 學生.

studious *a.* ch'in² hsüeh² te¹ 勤學的.

study *n.*, *v.* tu² shu¹ 讀書.

stuff *n.* ts'ai² liao⁴ 材料; *v.* t'ien² sai¹ 填塞.

stumble *v.* tien¹ chih⁴ 顛躓.

stump *n.* tuan⁴ chu¹ 斷株.

stun *v.* shih³ wu² chih¹ chüeh¹ 使無知覺.

stupefy *v.* shih³ shih¹ chih¹ chüeh² 使失知覺.

stupendous *a.* wei¹ ta⁴ te¹ 偉大的.

stupid *a.* yü² tun⁴ te¹ 愚鈍的.

stupidity *n.* yü² tun⁴ 愚鈍.

stupor *n.* pu⁴ hsing³ jen² shih⁴ 不省人事.

sturdy *a.* ch'iang² chuang⁴ te¹ 強壯的.

stutter *v.* k'ou³ ch'ih¹ 口吃.

style *n.* shih⁴ yang⁴ 式樣.

subdue *v.* cheng¹ fu² 征服.

subject *n.* (*theme*) lun⁴ t'i² 論題.

sublime *a.* kao¹ shang⁴ te¹ 高尚的.

submerge *v.* yen¹ fu⁴ 淹覆.

submission *n.* fu² ts'ung² 服從.

submit *v.* (*surrender*) ch'ü¹ fu² 屈服, (*present*)
ch'eng² ch'u¹ 呈出.

subordinate *a.* shu³ hsia⁴ te¹ 屬下的.

subscribe *v.* (*contribute*) jen⁴ chüan¹ 認捐, (*sign*)
ch'ien¹ ming² 簽名, (*magazine*) ting⁴ yüeh⁴ 定閱.

subscription *n.* (*contribution*) chüan¹ k'uan³ 捐款,
(*magazine*) ting⁴ yüeh⁴ 定閱.

subsequent *a.* hou⁴ lai² te¹ 後來的.

subside *v.* ch'en² hsia⁴ 沈下.

subsidy *a.* pu³ chu⁴ chin¹ 補助金. 「huo² 生活.

subsist *v.* ts'un² tsai⁴ 存在, (*keep alive*) sheng¹

subsistence *n.* (*living*) sheng¹ chi⁴ 生計.

substance *n.* wu⁴ chih² 物質.

substantial *a.* chen⁴ chih² te⁴ 眞實的.

substantiate *v.* cheng⁴ shih² 證實.

substitute *n.* (*thing*) tai⁴ yung⁴ p'in³ 代用品, (*person*) tai⁴ li³ che³ 代理者; *v.* tai⁴ li³ 代理.

substitution *n.* tai⁴ li³ 代理.

subtract *v.* chien³ ch'ü⁴ 減去.

subtraction *n.* chien³ ch'ü⁴ 減去.

suburb *n.* chin⁴ chiao¹ 近郊.

subversive *a.* pao⁴ tung⁴ te¹ 暴動的.

subvert *v.* t'ui¹ fan¹ 推翻. 「chi⁴ 承機.

succeed *v.* ch'eng² kung¹ 成功, (*follow*) ch'eng²

success *n.* ch'eng² kung¹ 成功.

successful *a.* ch'eng² kung¹ te¹ 成功的.

succession *n.* (*inheritance*) chi⁴ ch'eng² 繼承, (*continuation*) chi⁴ hsü⁴ 繼續.

successor *n.* chi⁴ ch'eng² che³ 繼承者.

succulent *a.* to¹ chih¹ te¹ 多汁的.

such *a.* ju² tz'u³ te¹ 如此的.

suck *v.* chün³ hsi¹ 吮吸.

suckle *v.* pu² ju³ 哺乳.

sudden *a.* t'u² jan² te¹ 突然的.

sue *v.* k'ung⁴ kao⁴ 控告.

suet *n.* niu² yang² chih¹ 牛羊脂.

suffer *v.* (*undergo*) tsao¹ yü⁴ 遭遇, (*tolerate*) jen⁴

suffering *n.* t'ung⁴ k'u³ 痛苦. 「shou⁴ 忍受.

suffice *v.* tsu² kou⁴ 足夠.

sufficiency *n.* ch'ung¹ fen¹ 充分, tsu² kou⁴ 足夠.

sufficient *a.* ch'ung¹ tsu² te¹ 充足的, tsu² kou⁴ te¹

suffocate *v.* men⁴ ssu³ 悶死. 「足夠的.

suffocation *n.* chih⁴ hsi¹ 窒息.

suffrage *n.* t'ou² p'iao⁴ 投票.

suffuse *v.* ch'ung¹ man³ 充滿.

sugar *n.* t'ang² 糖.

suggest *v.* hsiang² ch'i³ 想起, (*propose*) t'i² i⁴ 提議, (*hint*) an⁴ shih⁴ 暗示.

suggestion *n.* chien⁴ i⁴ 建議.

suicide *n.* tzu⁴ sha¹ 自殺.

suit *n.* (*of clothes*) i² t'ao⁴ 一套(衣服), (*law*) su⁴ sung⁴ 訴訟; *v.* (*make fit*) shih³ shih⁴ ho² 使適合.

suitable *a.* shih⁴ ho² te¹ 適合的, shih⁴ i² te¹ 適宜 的.

suitor *n.* ch'iu² hun¹ che² 求婚者.

sulky *a.* yün⁴ nu⁴ te¹ 慍怒的.

sullen *a.* yün⁴ nu⁴ te¹ 慍怒的.

sulphur *n.* liu² huang² 硫黃.

sulphurous *a.* liu² huang² te¹ 硫黃的.

sultan *n.* hui² chiao⁴ kuo² wang² 回教國王.

sultry *a.* men¹ je⁴ te¹ 悶熱的.

sum *n.* tsung³ shu⁴ 總數.

summary *n.* chai¹ yao⁴ 摘要.

summer *n.* hsia⁴ chi⁴ 夏季.

summit *n.* ting² tien³ 頂點.

summon *v.* chao⁴ chi² 召集, (*legal*) ch'uan² an⁴ 傳 案.

summons *n.* (*law*) ch'uan² p'iao⁴ 傳票.

sumptuous *a.* ang² kuei⁴ te¹ 昂貴的.

sun *n.* jih⁴ 日, t'ai⁴ yang² 太陽.

Sunday *n.* hsing¹ ch'i² jih⁴ 星期日.

sunny *a.* to¹ yang² kuang¹ te¹ 多陽光的.

sunrise *n.* jih⁴ ch'u¹ 日出.

sunset *n.* jih⁴ lo⁴ 日落.

sunshine *n.* jih⁴ kuang¹ 日光.

sunstroke *n.* chung⁴ shu³ 中暑(醫).

sup *v.* (*take supper*) chin⁴ wan³ ts'an¹ 進晚餐.

superabundance *n.* kuo⁴ to¹ 過多.

superabundant *a.* kuo⁴ to¹ te¹ 過多的.

superb *a.* kao¹ shang⁴ te¹ 高尚的.

superficial *a.* piao³ mien⁴ te¹ 表面的.

superfluous *a.* kuo⁴ to¹ te¹ 過多的.

superintend *v.* chien¹ tu¹ 監督.

superintendent *n.* chien¹ tu¹ 監督.

superior *a.* (*excellent*) ch'ao¹ teng³ te¹ 超等的; *n.* shang⁴ kuan¹ 上官.

superiority *n.* yu¹ yüeh⁴ 優越.

superlative *a.* tsui⁴ kao¹ chi² te¹ 最高級的.

supernatural *a.* ch'ao¹ tzu⁴ jan² te¹ 超自然的.

superstition *n.* mi² hsin⁴ 迷信.

superstitious *a.* mi² hsin⁴ te¹ 迷信的.

supervise *v.* chien¹ tu¹ 監督.

supervisor *n.* chien¹ tu¹ 監督.

supper *n.* wan³ ts'an¹ 晚餐.

supplement *a.* fu⁴ lu⁴ 附錄.

supplementary *a.* fu⁴ chia¹ te¹ 附加的.

supplicate *v.* k'en² ch'ing³ 懇請.

supply *n.* (*stock*) ts'un² huo⁴ 存貨; *v.* kung¹ chi³ 供給; ～ **sergeant,** pu² chi³ chün¹ shih⁴ 補給軍 士.

support *n.* (*troops or units*) yüan² tui⁴ 援隊, (*aid*) chih¹ yüan² 支援, (*on the flanks*) i¹ t'o¹ 依托; *v.* (*to aid*) chih¹ yüan² 支援.

supportable *a.* k'o³ chih¹ ch'ih² te¹ 可支持的.

suppose *v.* (*assume*) chia³ ting⁴ 假定, (*think*) hsiang³ hsiang⁴ 想像.

suppress *v.* chen⁴ ya¹ 鎮壓.

suppression *n.* chen⁴ ya¹ 鎮壓.

supremacy *n.* chih⁴ tsun¹ 至尊, (*power*) tsui⁴ kao¹ ch'üan² 最高權.

supreme *a.* chih⁴ kao¹ te¹ 至高的; ～ **Court,** tsui⁴ kao¹ fa³ yüan¹ 最高法院; ～ **People's Court**,** tsui⁴ kao¹ jen² min² fa³ yüan¹ 最高人民法院**.

sure *a.* ch'üeh⁴ hsin⁴ te¹ 確信的.

surf *n.* p'ai¹ an⁴ lang⁴ hua¹ 拍岸浪花.

surface *n.* piao³ mien⁴ 表面.

surgeon *n.* wai⁴ k'o¹ i¹ sheng¹ 外科醫生.　「術.

surgery *n.* wai⁴ k'o¹ hsüeh² 外科學, shou³ shu⁴ 手

surgical *a.* wai⁴ k'o¹ shu⁴ te¹ 外科術的.

surmise *v.* t'ui¹ ts'e⁴ 推測.

surname *n.* hsing⁴ 姓.

surpass *v.* sheng⁴ kuo⁴ 勝過.

surplus *n.* sheng⁴ yü² 剩餘.

surprise *n., v.* ching¹ e⁴ 驚愕.

surprising *a.* ching¹ i⁴ te¹ 驚異的.

surrender *n., v.* t'ou² hsiang² 投降.

surreptitous *a.* pi⁴ mi⁴ te¹ 秘密的.

surround *v.* pao¹ wei² 包圍.

surroundings *n.* huan² ching⁴ 環境.

survey *v.* (*measure*) ts'e⁴ liang² 測量.

survive *v.* sheng¹ ts'un² 生存.

susceptibility *n.* kan³ shou⁴ li⁴ 感受力.

susceptible *a.* i⁴ kan³ te¹ 易感的.

suspect *v.* ts'ai¹ i² 猜疑.

suspend *v.* (*hang*) hsüan² kua⁴ 懸掛, (*from office*) shih³ t'ing² chih² 使停職, (*from school*) shih³ t'ing² hsüeh² 使停學.

suspenders *n.* tiao⁴ k'u⁴ tai⁴ 吊褲帶.

suspense *n.* tiao⁴ hsüan² 吊懸.

suspicion *n.* hsüan² i² 懸疑.

suspicious *a.* hsüan² i² te¹ 懸疑的.

sustain *v.* (*keep up*) wei² ch'ih² 維持, (*support*) chih¹ ch'eng² 支撐.

swallow *n.* yen⁴ tzu¹ 燕子; *v.* t'un¹ hsia⁴ 吞下.

swamp *n.* shih¹ ti⁴ 濕地, chao³ ti⁴ 沼地.

swampy *a.* shih¹ ti⁴ te¹ 濕地的, chao³ ti⁴ te¹ 沼地的.

swan *n.* t'ien¹ e² 天鵝.

swarm *n.* feng¹ ch'ün² 蜂羣; *v.* ch'ün² chi² 羣集.

swarthy *a.* hei¹ se⁴ te¹ 黑色的.

sway *n.*, *v.* yao² pai³ 搖擺.

swear *v.* fa¹ shih⁴ 發誓.

sweat *n.* han⁴ 汗; *v.* ch'u¹ han⁴ 出汗.　　　「掃除.

sweep *n.* (*oar*) ch'ang² chiang³ 長槳; *v.* sao³ ch'u²

sweet *a.* t'ien² mi⁴ te¹ 甜密的.

sweeten *v.* shih³ t'ien² mi⁴ 使甜密.

sweetheart *n.* ai⁴ jen² 愛人.　　　「chien⁴ 密餞.

sweetmeats *n.* t'ang² kuo³ 糖果, (*preserves*) mi⁴

swell *v.* p'eng² chang⁴ 膨脹.

swelling *n.* p'eng² ta⁴ te¹ 脹大的.

swift *a.* hsün⁴ su⁴ te¹ 迅速的.

swiftness *n.* hsün⁴ su⁴ 迅速.

swim *v.* yu² yung³ 游泳.

swindle *n.*, *v.* ch'i¹ p'ien⁴ 欺騙.

swing *n.* (*seat hung from ropes*) ch'iu¹ ch'ien¹ hsi⁴ 鞦韆戲; *v.* yao² tung⁴ 搖動, (*on swing*) ta³ ch'iu¹ ch'ien¹ 打鞦韆.　　　　　　　　　　「門.

switch *n.* k'ai¹ kuan¹ 開關, (*electric*) tien⁴ men² 電

switchboard *n.* (*electric*) p'ei⁴ tien⁴ pan³ 配電板, (*telephone*) chiao¹ huan⁴ chi¹ 交換機, tsung³ chi¹

swivel *n.* chuan³ huan² 轉環.　　　　　　「總機.

swoon *v.* hun¹ yün⁴ 昏暈.

swoop *v.* hsi² chi¹ 襲擊.

sword *n.* chien⁴ 劍, tao¹ 刀.

sworn *a.* fa¹ shih⁴ te¹ 發誓的.

sycamore *n.* ta⁴ feng¹ shu⁴ 大楓樹(植).

syllable *n.* yin¹ chieh² 音節.

syllabus *n.* yao⁴ mu⁴ 要目. 「號.

symbol *n.* hsiang⁴ cheng¹ 象徵, (*mark*) fu² hao⁴ 符

symmetrical *a.* yün² ch'eng¹ te¹ 匀稱的.

symmetry *n.* yün² ch'eng¹ 匀稱.

sympathetic *a.* t'ung² ch'ing² hsin¹ te¹ 同情心的.

sympathize *v.* piao³ t'ung² ch'ing² 表同情.

sympathy *n.* t'ung² ch'ing² 同情.

symphony *n.* chiao¹ hsiang³ yüeh⁴ 交響樂, (*harmony*) t'iao² ho² 調和. ~ **orchestra,** chiao¹ hsiang³ yüeh⁴ tui⁴ 交響樂隊.

symptom *n.* (*sickness*) cheng⁴ chuang⁴ 症狀.

synagogue *n.* (*building*) yu² t'ai⁴ jen² hui⁴ t'ang² 猶太人會堂.

synonymous *a.* t'ung² i⁴ te¹ 同義的.

syphilis *n.* mei² tu² 梅毒(瘡).

syrup *n.* t'ang² chiang¹ 糖漿.

system *n.* (*relationship*) hsi⁴ t'ung³ 系統, (*organization*) chih⁴ tu⁴ 制度.

systematic *a.* hsi⁴ t'ung³ te¹ 系統的.

T

tabernacle *n.* (*tent*) chang⁴ mu⁴ 帳幕.

table *n.* cho¹ 桌; ~ **of organization,** pien¹ chih⁴ piao³ 編制表.

tablecloth *n.* cho¹ pu⁴ 桌布.

tablet *n.* (*medicine*) yao⁴ p'ien⁴ 藥片.

tacit *a.* chien¹ mo⁴ te¹ 緘默的.

tack *n.* p'ing² t'ou² ting¹ 平頭釘.

tackle *n.* (*equipment*) yung⁴ chü⁴ 用具, (*for lifting*) hua² ch'e¹ 滑車.

tactical *a.* chan⁴ shu⁴ te¹ 戰術的; ~ **exercise,** chan⁴ shu⁴ yen³ hsi² 戰術演習; ~ **march,** chan⁴ pei⁴ hsing² chün¹ 戰備行軍.

tactics *n.* chan⁴ shu⁴ 戰術.

tadpole *n.* k'o¹ tou³ 蝌蚪.

tail *n.* wei³ 尾; ~ **light,** wei³ teng¹ 尾燈.

tailor *n.* ch'eng² i¹ chiang⁴ 成衣匠.

take v. ch'ü³ 取; " ～ **arms!** " ch'ü³ ch'iang¹ 取
鎗(軍); ～ **off,** (start a flight) ch'i² fei¹ 起飛,
(leave the runway) li² ti⁴ 離地, ～ **over,** (office,
command) chieh¹ shou⁴ 接收.

talc n. hua² shih² 滑石.

tale n. ku⁴ shih⁴ 故事.

talent n. ts'ai² neng² 才能.

talented a. yu³ ts'ai² neng² te¹ 有才能的.

talk n. t'an² hua⁴ 談話; v. chiang³ 講.

talkative a. hao⁴ t'an² hua⁴ te¹ 好談話的.

tall a. kao¹ te¹ 高的.

tallow n. shou⁴ chih¹ 獸脂.

talon n. chua³ 爪.

tamarind n. lo² wang⁴ tzu¹ 羅望子(植).　　　「馴.

tame a. hsün² fu² te¹ 馴服的; v. yang³ hsün² 養

tamper v. pu² cheng⁴ tang¹ kan¹ yü⁴ 不正當干預.

tan n. (color) huang² ho² se⁴ 黃褐色; v. (leather)
hsiao¹ p'i² 硝皮.

tangibility n. k'o³ ch'u⁴ chüeh² 可觸覺.

tangible a. k'o³ ch'u⁴ chüeh² te¹ 可觸覺的.

tank n. (army) chan⁴ ch'e¹ 戰車, (for gasoline) yu²
hsiang¹ 油箱.

tanner n. chih¹ ko² chiang⁴ 製革匠.

tap v. ch'ing¹ chi¹ 輕擊; n. (water) hu² tsui³ 壺嘴,
(plural) hsi² teng¹ hao⁴ 熄燈號(軍).

tape n. hsi⁴ ch'ang² tai⁴ 細長帶; ～ **recorder,** tai⁴
lu⁴ yin¹ chi¹ 帶錄音機; ～ **recording,** tai⁴ lu⁴
yin¹ 帶錄音.

tar n. pai³ yu² 柏油, (sailor) shui³ shou³ 水手.

tardy a. huan³ man⁴ te¹ 緩慢的.

target n. (on the range) pa³ 靶, (in combat) mu⁴
piao¹ 目標; ～ **practice,** ta² pa³ 打靶; ～ **range,**
pa² ch'ang³ 靶場.

tariff n. kuan¹ shui⁴ 關稅.

tarpaulin n. yu² pu⁴ 油布.　　　　　　　「小餡餅.

tart a. (sour) suan¹ te¹ 酸的; n. hsiao³ hsien⁴ ping³

task n. (work) kung¹ tso⁴ 工作, (duty) jen⁴ wu⁴ 任

taste n. wei⁴ 味; v. ch'ang² wei⁴ 嘗味.　　　「務.

tasteful a. mei³ wei⁴ te¹ 美味的.

tasteless a. wu² wei⁴ te¹ 無味的.

tasty a. mei³ wei⁴ te¹ 美味的.

tavern *n.* chiu³ tien⁴ 酒店, (*inn*) lü² kuan³ 旅館.

tawny *a.* huang² ho² se⁴ te¹ 黃褐色的.

tax *n.* shui⁴ 稅; *v.* k'o⁴ shui⁴ 課稅.

taxi *n.* ch'u¹ tsu¹ ch'i⁴ ch'e¹ 出租汽車; *v.* ch'eng² ch'u¹ tsu¹ ch'i⁴ ch'e¹ 乘出租汽車, (*of an airplane*) hua² hsing² 滑行.

taxicab *n.* ch'u¹ tsu¹ ch'i⁴ ch'e¹ 出租汽車.

tea *n.* ch'a² 茶.

teach *v.* chiao⁴ 教.

teacher *n.* chiao⁴ yüan² 教員.

teacup *n.* ch'a² pei¹ 茶杯.

teakettle *n.* ch'a² hu² 茶壺.　　　　　「租.

team *n.* (*football*) ...tui⁴ ...隊, (*debating*) ...tsu³ ...

tear *n.* (*eye*) yen³ lei⁴ 眼淚, (*rip*) lieh⁴ feng⁴ 裂縫; *v.* ssu¹ 撕, ch'e³ 扯.

tease *v.* fan² jao³ 煩擾.

technical *a.* kung¹ i⁴ te¹ 工藝的.

tedious *a.* chih⁴ chüan⁴ te¹ 致倦的.

telegram *n.* tien⁴ pao⁴ 電報.

telegraph *n.* tien⁴ hsün⁴ 電訊; *v.* tien⁴ sung⁴ 電送, tien⁴ pao⁴ chü² 電報局.

telepathy *n.* ch'uan² hsin¹ shu⁴ 傳心術.

telephone *n.* tien⁴ hua⁴ chi¹ 電話機, tien⁴ hua⁴ 電話; *v.* ta³ tien⁴ hua⁴ 打電話; ～ **office**, tien⁴ hua⁴ chü² 電話局.

telescope *n.* wang⁴ yüan³ ching⁴ 望遠鏡.

teletypewriter *n.* tien⁴ ch'uan² ta³ tzu⁴ chi¹ 電傳

television *n.* tien⁴ shih⁴ 電視.　　　「打字機.

tell *v.* kao⁴ su⁴ 告訴.

temper *n.* hsing⁴ ch'ing² 性情; *v.* huan³ ho² 緩和.

temperance *n.* chieh² chih⁴ 節制.

temperate *a.* (*weather*) wen¹ ho² te¹ 溫和的.

temperature *n.* wen¹ tu⁴ 溫度.

tempest *n.* pao⁴ feng¹ yü³ 暴風雨.

tempestuous *a.* pao⁴ feng¹ yü³ te¹ 暴風雨的.

temple *n.* (*religious*) chiao⁴ t'ang² 教堂, (*Buddhist*) ssu⁴ yüan⁴ 寺院, (*of the forehead*) nieh⁴ ju² 顳顬.

temporary *a.* chan⁴ shih² te¹ 暫時的.

tempt *v.* yu⁴ huo⁴ 誘惑.

temptation *n.* yu⁴ huo⁴ 誘惑.

tempter *n.* yu⁴ huo⁴ che² 誘惑者.

tempting *a.* yin³ yu⁴ te¹ 引誘的.

ten *n.* shih² 十; *a.* shih² te¹ 十的.

tenant *n.* tsu¹ hu⁴ 租戶.

tend *v.* (*look after*) chao⁴ ying⁴ 照應.

tendency *n.* ch'ü² shih⁴ 趨勢.

tender *a.* jou² nen⁴ te¹ 柔嫩的; *n.* (*boat*) hsiao³ ch'uan² 小船, (*train*) mei² shui³ ch'e¹ 媒水車.

tenderness *n.* jou² nen² 柔嫩.

tendon *n.* chien⁴ 腱.

tennis *n.* wang³ ch'iu² hsi⁴ 網球戲.

tenor *n.* (*music*) nan² kao¹ yin¹ 男高音.

tense *a.* la¹ chin³ te¹ 拉緊的.

tent *n.* chang⁴ mu⁴ 帳幕.

term *n.* (*medical*) shu⁴ yü³ 術語, (*period*) ch'i¹ hsien⁴ 期限, (*condition*) t'iao² chien⁴ 條件, (*school*) hsüeh² ch'i¹ 學期.

terminal *a.* mo⁴ tuan¹ te¹ 末端的; *n.* mo⁴ tuan¹ 末端; ~ **station**, chung¹ tien³ ch'e¹ chan⁴ 終點 ⌐車站.

terminate *v.* chung¹ chieh² 終結.

termination *n.* chung¹ chih³ 終止.

terrace *n.* t'u³ t'an² 土壇.

terrible *a.* k'ung³ pu⁴ te¹ 恐怖的.

terrier *n.* keng¹ 㹴(狗).

terrific *a.* chih⁴ ching¹ k'ung³ te¹ 致驚恐的.

terrify *v.* k'ung³ ho⁴ 恐嚇.

territorial *a.* ling² t'u³ te¹ 領土的; ~ **integrity**, ling² t'u³ wan² cheng³ 領土完整; ~ **waters**,

territory *n.* ling² t'u³ 領土. ⌐ling² hai³ 領海.

terror *n.* k'ung³ pu⁴ 恐怖.

terse *a.* chien³ chieh² te¹ 簡潔的.

test *n., v.* shih⁴ yen⁴ 試驗.

testament *n.* i² chu³ 遺囑.

testicle *n.* kao¹ wan² 睾丸.

testify *v.* tso⁴ cheng⁴ 作證.

testimonial *n.* cheng⁴ ming² shu¹ 證明書.

testimony *n.* cheng⁴ shih⁴ hsüan¹ yen² 正式宣言, cheng⁴ chü⁴ 證據.

tether *n.* hsi⁴ sheng² 繫繩.

text *n.* (*main body*) pen³ wen² 本文.

textbook *n.* chiao⁴ k'o¹ shu¹ 教科書.

textile *a.* fang³ chih¹ te¹ 紡織的.

texture *n.* tsu³ chih¹ 組織.

than *conj.* pi³ 比, chiao⁴ 較.

thank *v.* hsieh⁴ hsieh⁴ 謝謝; *n.* (*plural*) kan³ 「hsieh⁴ 感謝.

thankful *a.* kan³ hsieh⁴ te¹ 感謝的.

thankless *a.* pu⁴ kan³ hsieh⁴ te¹ 不感謝的.

that *a., pron.* na⁴ 那. 「ts'ao³ 覆以茅草.

thatch *n.* ts'ao³ wu¹ ting³ 草屋頂; *v.* fu⁴ i³ mao²

thaw *n.* jung² chieh³ 融解; *v.* jung² chieh³ 融解.

the *art.* tz'u³ 此, che⁴ 這.

theater, theatre *n.* hsi⁴ yüan⁴ 戲院; ～ of war, chan⁴ ch'ang³ 戰場.

theft *n.* hsing² ch'ieh³ 行竊.

their, theirs *pron.* t'a¹ men² te¹ 他們的.

them *pron.* t'a¹ men² 他們.

theme *n.* (*subject*) t'i² mu⁴ 題目, (*composition*) lun⁴ wen² 論文, (*music*) chu³ hsüan² lü⁴ 主旋律.

themselves *pron.* t'a¹ men² tzu⁴ chi³ 他們自己.

then *adv.* tang¹ shih² 當時, (*soon afterwards*) sui² 「chi² 隨即.

theology *n.* shen² hsüeh² 神學.

theoretical *a.* li³ lun⁴ te¹ 理論的.

theory *n.* hsüeh² shuo¹ 學說, li³ lun⁴ 理論.

there *adv.* tsai⁴ pi³ ch'u⁴ 在彼處.

thereafter *adv.* ch'i² hou⁴ 其後.

thereby *adv.* yin¹ tz'u³ 因此.

therefore *adv.* yin¹ tz'u³ 因此, so² i³ 所以.

therefrom *adv.* ts'ung² tz'u³ 從此, yu² shih⁴ 由是.

thermometer *n.* han² shu⁴ piao³ 寒暑表.

they *pron.* (*male*) t'a¹ men² 他們, (*female*) t'a¹ men² 她們, (*neutral*) t'a¹ men² 牠(它)們.

thick *a.* hou⁴ te¹ 厚的; *adv.* hou⁴ ti⁴ 厚地.

thicket *n.* ts'ung¹ lin² 叢林.

thickness *n.* hou⁴ 厚.

thief *n.* tsei² 賊.

thieve *v.* t'ou¹ 偷.

thigh *n.* ku³ 股, ta⁴ t'ui³ 大腿.

thimble *n.* ting³ chen¹ 頂針, chen¹ ku¹ 針箍.

thin *a.* (*solids*) po² te¹ 薄的, (*person*) shou⁴ te¹ 瘦的, (*liquids*) tan⁴ te¹ 淡的.

thing *n.* wu⁴ 物.

think *v.* ssu¹ k'ao³ 思考.

thirst *n.* k'o³ 渴.

thirsty *a.* k'ou¹ k'o³ te¹ 口渴的.

this *a., pron.* tz'u³ 此, che⁴ 這.

thistle *n.* chi¹ 薊(植).

thong *n.* p'i² t'iao¹ 皮條.

thorn *n.* ching¹ chi⁴ 荊棘.

thorny *a.* to¹ tz'u⁴ te¹ 多刺的.

thorough *a.* wan² ch'üan² te¹ 完全的.

thoroughfare *n.* t'ung¹ lu⁴ 通路.

thoroughly *adv.* wan² ch'üan² ti⁴ 完全地.

though *adv.* jan² erh² 然而; *conj.* (*even if*) chi²
shih³ 即使, sui¹ 雖.

thought *n.* ssu¹ hsiang³ 思想.

thoughtful *a.* yu³ ssu¹ hsiang³ te¹ 有思想的.

thoughtless *a.* wu² ssu¹ hsiang⁸ te¹ 無思想的.

thousand *a.* ch'ien¹ 千; *a.* ch'ien¹ te¹ 千的.

thrash *v.* (*wheat*) ta² ku³ 打穀.

thread *n.* hsien¹ 線; *v.* ch'uan¹ hsien¹ 穿線.

threadbare *a.* lan² lü³ te¹ 襤褸的.

threat *n.* wei¹ ho⁴ 威嚇.

threaten *v.* wei¹ ho⁴ 威嚇.

three *n.* san¹ 三; *a.* san¹ te¹ 三的.

thresh *v.* ta³ ho² 打禾.

thrift *n.* chieh² chien³ 節儉.

thrifty *a.* chieh² chien³ te¹ 節儉的.

thrill *n.* chen⁴ chan⁴ 震顫.

thrive *v.* fan² sheng⁴ 繁盛.

throat *n.* yen¹ hou² 咽喉.

throb *v.* t'iao⁴ tung⁴ 跳動.

throne *n.* huang² wei⁴ 皇位.

throng *n., v.* (*crowd*) ch'ün² chung⁴ 羣衆.

throttle *n.* ch'i⁴ fa² 汽閥.

through *prep.* t'ung¹ kuo⁴ 通過; *adv.* kuan
t'ung¹ ti⁴ 貫通地; *a.* chih⁸ t'ung¹ te¹ 直通的.

throughout *prep.* pien⁴ chi² 遍及; *adv.* pien⁴ chi²
throw *v.* t'ou² 投.　　　　　　　　　　⌊ti⁴ 遍及地.

thrush *n.* (*bird*) hua⁴ mei² niao³ 畫眉鳥.

thrust *v.* t'ui¹ chin⁴ 推進.

thumb *n.* ta⁴ mu² chih⁸ 大拇指.

thunder *n.* lei² 雷; *v.* lei² ming⁴ 雷鳴.

thunderbolt *n.* lei² tien⁴ 雷電.

thunderclap *n.* lei² ming² 雷鳴.

Thursday *n.* hsing¹ ch'i² ssu⁴ 星期四.

thus *adv.* ju² tz'u³ 如此.

thwart *v.* fan³ tui⁴ 反對.

ticket *n.* p'iao⁴ 票, ch'üan⁴ 券.

tickle *v.* fa¹ yang³ 發癢.

tide *n.* ch'ao² hsi⁴ 潮汐.

tidings *n.* hsiao¹ hsi² 消息.

tidy *a.* cheng³ chieh² te¹ 整潔的.

tie *n.* (*necktie*) ling³ tai⁴ 領帶; *v.* (*bind*) fu² 縛.

tiger *n.* hu³ 虎.

tight *a.* chin³ te¹ 緊的.

tile *n.* wa³ 瓦, chuan¹ 磚.

till *prep.* ch'i⁴ 迄, chih⁴ 至; *v.* keng¹ 耕.

timber *n.* mu⁴ ts'ai² 木材.

time *n.* (*past, present*) shih² chien¹ 時間, (*amount of time*) kung¹ fu¹ 工夫, (*occasion*) tz'u⁴ 次, (*point in time*) shih² hou⁴ 時候, (*hour of day*) shih² k'o⁴ 時刻; *v.* chi⁴ shih² 計時; **~ fuse,** ting⁴ shih² hsin⁴ kuan³ 定時信管(兵).

timely *a.* ho² shih² te¹ 合時的.

timid *a.* tan³ ch'üeh⁴ te¹ 膽怯的.

timidity *n.* tan³ ch'üeh⁴ 膽怯.

tin *n.* hsi² 錫.

tincture *n.* yao⁴ chiu³ 藥酒.

tinkle *n.* ting¹ tang¹ sheng¹ 叮噹聲.

tint *n.* se⁴ 色; *v.* chao² se⁴ 著色.

tiny *a.* chi² hsiao³ te¹ 極小的.

tip *n.* mo⁴ tuan¹ 末端, (*money*) hsiao³ chang⁴ 小賬; *v.* (*over*) ch'ing¹ fu⁴ 傾覆, (*money*) fu⁴ shang³ ch'ien² 付賞錢.

tiptoe *n.* chih³ chien¹ 趾尖; *v.* i² chiao³ chien¹ hsing² tsou³ 以脚尖行走.

tire *n.* lun² t'ai¹ 輪胎; *v.* p'i² fa² 疲乏.

tired *a.* p'i² chüan⁴ te¹ 疲倦的.

tiresome *a.* p'i² chüan⁴ te¹ 疲倦的.

tissure *n.* tsu³ chih¹ 組織.

title *n.* ming² ch'eng² 名稱.

titter *v.* ch'ieh⁴ hsiao⁴ 竊笑.

to *prep.* (*direction*) hsiang⁴ 向, (*until*) ch'i⁴ 迄, (*up to and including*) ta² 達.

toad *n.* ch'an¹ ch'u² 蟾蜍(動).

256

toast *n.* t'u³ ssu¹ 土司; *v.* hung¹ kan¹ 烘乾.

tobacco *n.* yen¹ ts'ao³ 煙草.

tobacconist *n.* yen¹ ts'ao³ shang¹ 煙草商.

today, to-day *n.* chin¹ jih⁴ 今日, chin¹ t'ien¹ 今天.

toe *n.* tsu² chih³ 足趾.

together *adv.* t'ung² 同.

toil *n., v.* lao² tso⁴ 勞作. 「ts'e⁴ so³ 廁所.

toilet *n.* (*bathroom*) yü⁴ shih⁴ 浴室, (*water closet*)

toilsome *a.* lao² k'u³ te¹ 勞苦的.

token *n.* piao³ chi⁴ 表記.

tolerable *a.* k'o² jen³ shou⁴ te¹ 可忍受的.

tolerant *a.* jung² jen³ te¹ 容忍的.

tolerate *v.* jung² jen³ 容忍.

toleration *n.* jung² jen³ 容忍.

toll *n.* ming² chung¹ 鳴鐘.

tomato *n.* fan¹ ch'ieh² 番茄.

tomb *n.* fen² mu⁴ 墳墓.

tombstone *n.* mu⁴ shih² 墓石.

tom-cat *n.* hsiung² mao¹ 雄貓.

tomorrow, to-morrow *adv.* ming² jih⁴ 明日, ming² t'ien¹ 明天.

ton *n.* tun⁴ 噸.

tone *n.* yin¹ 音.

tongs *n.* ch'ien² 鉗.

tongue *n.* she² 舌, (*language*) yü³ yen² 語言.

tonic *n.* (*medicine*) pu³ yao⁴ 補藥.

tonight, to-night *adv.* chin¹ wan³ 今晚.

tonnage *n.* tun⁴ wei⁴ 噸位.

tonsil *n.* p'ien¹ t'ao² t'i³ 扁桃體.

tonsure *n.* hsüeh¹ fa³ 削髮.

too *adv.* (*also*) i⁴ 亦, (*very*) t'ai⁴ 太.

tool *n.* kung¹ chü⁴ 工具.

tooth *n.* ch'ih³ 齒.

toothache *n.* ya² t'ung⁴ 牙痛.

toothbrush *n.* ya² shua¹ 牙刷.

toothpaste *n.* ya² kao¹ 牙膏.

toothpick *n.* ya² ch'ien¹ 牙籤.

top *n.* chüeh² ting³ 絕頂, (*toy*) wan² chü⁴ 玩具; ∼ secret, (*security classification*) chi² chi¹ mi⁴ 極機 「密.

topic *n.* t'i² mu⁴ 題目.

torch *n.* huo² pa³ 火把.

torment *n.* t'ung⁴ k'u³ yüan² yin¹ 痛苦原因; *v.* shih³ t'ung⁴ k'u³ 使痛苦.

tornado *n.* k'uang² feng¹ 狂風.

torpedo *n.* yü² lei² 魚雷; ∼ **boat**, yü² lei² t'ing³ [魚雷艇(海).

torpid *a.* ma² mu⁴ te¹ 麻木的.

torpor *n.* ma² mu⁴ 麻木.

torrent *n.* chi² liu² 急流.

torrid *a.* yen² je⁴ te¹ 炎熱的.

tortoise *n.* kuei¹ 龜; ∼ **shell**, kuei¹ k'o² 龜殼.

torture *n.* k'u⁴ hsing² 酷刑; *v.* k'ao² ta³ 拷打.

toss *v.* chih⁴ 擲, p'ao¹ 拋.

total *a.* ch'üan² pu⁴ te¹ 全部的; *n.* tsung³ shu⁴ 總數; *v.* ho² chi⁴ 合計; ∼ **war**, ch'üan² mien⁴ chan⁴ cheng¹ 全面戰爭.

totality *n.* (*entirety*) ch'üan² pu⁴ 全部, (*total amount*) tsung³ shu⁴ 總數.

totter *v.* p'an² shan¹ 蹣跚.

touch *v.* (*with hands*) ch'u⁴ chüeh² 觸覺, (*contact*) chieh¹ ch'u⁴ 接觸.

touching *a.* tung⁴ jen⁴ te¹ 動人的.

tough *a.* ch'iang² jen⁴ te¹ 強韌的.

toughness *n.* ch'iang² jen⁴ 強韌.

tour *n.* lü³ hsing² 旅行. [客.

tourist *n.* lü³ hsing² kuan¹ kuang¹ k'o⁴ 旅行觀光

tournament *n.* ching⁴ chi⁴ 競技.

tow *v.* t'o¹ 拖, yeh⁴ 曳.

toward *prep.* hsiang⁴...chin⁴ hsing² 向...進行.

towel *n.* mao² chin¹ 毛巾.

tower *n.* t'a³ 塔.

town *n.* shih⁴ chen⁴ 市鎮.

toy *n.* wan² chü⁴ 玩具.

trace *n.* hen² chi⁴ 痕跡; *v.* chui¹ tsung¹ 追踪.

trachoma *n.* sha¹ yen³ 砂眼.

track *n.* (*footprint*) tsu² chi⁴ 足跡, (*mark*) hen² chi⁴ 痕跡, (*trail*) hsiao³ ching⁴ 小徑, (*car*) kuei¹ tao⁴ 軌道; *v.* (*follow*) chui¹ sui² 追隨.

tract *n.* ch'ü¹ yü⁴ 區域, (*religious*) lun⁴ wen² 論文.

tractor *n.* yeh⁴ yin³ ch'e¹ 曳引車.

trade *n.* mao² i⁴ 貿易; *v.* t'ung¹ shang¹ 通商, (*exchange*) chiao¹ i⁴ 交易.

trademark *n.* shang¹ piao¹ 商標.

258

trader *n.* mao⁴ i⁴ shang¹ 貿易商, (*ship*) shang¹ ch'uan² 商船.

tradition *n.* ch'uan² t'ung³ 傳統.

traffic *n.* chiao¹ t'ung¹ 交通; ~ **control,** chiao¹ t'ung¹ kuan³ chih⁴ 交通管制.

tragedy *n.* pei¹ chü⁴ 悲劇.

tragic, tragical *a.* pei¹ chü⁴ te¹ 悲劇的.

trail *n.* wei³ sui² 尾隨; *v.* t'o¹ 拖.

train *n.* huo³ ch'e¹ 火車; *v.* hsün⁴ lien⁴ 訓練.

traitor *n.* p'an⁴ t'u² 叛徒, mai⁴ kuo² che³ 賣國者.

tramp *n.* (*walk*) pu⁴ hsing² 步行, (*ship*) pu² ting⁴ ch'i¹ huo⁴ ch'uan² 不定期貨船; *v.* (*walk*) pu⁴ hsing² 步行.

trample *v.* chien⁴ t'a⁴ 踐踏.

transact *v.* pan⁴ li³ 辦理.

transaction *n.* ch'u² chih⁴ 處置.

transcribe *v.* ch'ao¹ lu⁴ 抄錄. 「tiao⁴ jen⁴ 調任.

transfer *n.* (*property*) chuan³ jang⁴ 轉讓, (*work*)

transform *v.* shih³ pien⁴ hsing² 使變形.

transformation *n.* pien⁴ hsing² 變形.

transformer *n.* pien⁴ ya¹ ch'i⁴ 變壓器.

transient *a.* (*fleeting*) chi² kuo⁴ te¹ 疾過的, (*temporary*) chan⁴ shih² te¹ 暫時的.

transition *n.* chuan³ pien⁴ 轉變; ~ **period,** kuo⁴ tu⁴ shih² ch'i¹ 過渡時期.

translate *v.* fan¹ i⁴ 翻譯.

translation *n.* fan¹ i⁴ 翻譯.

translator *n.* fan¹ i⁴ yüan² 翻譯員.

transmission *n.* ch'uan² ta² 傳達.

transmit *v.* ch'uan² ta² 傳達.

transparent *a.* t'ou⁴ ming² te¹ 透明的.

transplant *v.* i² chih² 移植.

transport *v.* yün⁴ shu¹ 運輸; ~ **airplane** yün⁴ shu¹ chi¹ 運輸機.

transportation *n.* yün⁴ shu¹ 運輸; ~ **troops,** yün⁴ shu¹ ping⁴ pu² tui⁴ 運輸兵部隊.

trap *n.* (*animals*) pu³ shou⁴ chi¹ 捕獸機, (*pit*) hsien⁴ ching³ 陷阱; *v.* (*set traps*) she⁴ hsien⁴ ching³ 設陷阱; ~ **door,** (*floor*) ti⁴ pan³ men² 地板門, (*roof*) t'ien¹ ch'uang¹ men² 天窗門.

travel *n., v.* lü³ hsing² 旅行.

traveler *n.* lü³ hsing² che³ 旅行者.

traverse *v.* heng² kuo⁴ 橫過.

tray *n.* ch'ien³ p'an² 淺盤.

treacherous *a.* p'an⁴ ni⁴ te¹ 叛逆的.

treachery *n.* p'an⁴ ni⁴ 叛逆.

tread *v.* pu⁴ hsing² 步行.

treason *n.* p'an⁴ ni⁴ tsui⁴ 叛逆罪.

treasure *n.* ts'ai² pao³ 財寶.

treasurer *n.* k'uai⁴ chi⁴ yüan² 會計員.

treasury *n.* kuo² k'u⁴ 國庫; ~ **Check** (US), kuo² k'u⁴ chih¹ p'iao⁴ 國庫支票(美).

treat *v.* tui⁴ tai⁴ 對待.

treatise *n.* lun⁴ wen² 論文.

treatment *n.* tai⁴ yü⁴ 待遇, (*medical*) chih⁴ liao² 治療.

treaty *n.* t'iao² yüeh¹ 條約.

tree *n.* shu⁴ 樹.

tremble *v.* chen⁴ chan⁴ 震顫.

tremendous *a.* k'o³ p'a⁴ te¹ 可怕的, (*enormous*) chung⁴ ta⁴ te¹ 重大的.

tremor *n.* chan⁴ li⁴ 戰慄.

trench *n.* chan⁴ hao² 戰壕; *v.* chüeh² hao² 掘壕.

trepidation *n.* ching¹ k'ung³ 驚恐.

trespass *v.* ch'in¹ fan⁴ 侵犯.

trestle *n.* chia⁴ 架.

trial *n.* (*law*) shen³ p'an⁴ 審判.

triangle *n.* san¹ chiao³ hsing² 三角形.

triangular *a.* san¹ chiao³ hsing² te¹ 三角形的.

tribe *n.* pu⁴ lo⁴ 部落.

tribunal *n.* fa³ t'ing² 法庭.

tributary *n.* chin¹ kung⁴ 進貢.

tribute *n.* chüan¹ k'uan⁴ 捐款.

trick *n.* kuei³ chi⁴ 詭計; *v.* ch'i¹ cha⁴ 欺詐.

trickery *n.* kuei³ chi⁴ 詭計; ch'i¹ p'ien⁴ 欺騙.

tricycle *n.* san¹ lun² tzu⁴ hsing² ch'e¹ 三輪自行車.

trifle *n.* so³ shih⁴ 瑣事; *v.* (*play with*) wan² nung⁴ 玩弄.

trigger *n.* pan³ chi¹ 板機(兵).

trill *n.* chan⁴ sheng¹ 顫聲; *v.* fa¹ chan⁴ sheng¹ 發顫聲.

trim *a.* cheng³ chieh² te¹ 整潔的.

Trinity *n.* san¹ wei⁴ i⁴ t'i³ 三位一體.

trip *n.* lü³ hsing² 旅行; *v.* tien¹ chih⁴ 顛躓.

tripod *n.* san¹ chiao³ chia⁴ 三腳架.

triumph *n.* sheng⁴ li⁴ 勝利; *v.* te² sheng⁴ 得勝.

triumphant *a.* sheng⁴ li⁴ te¹ 勝利的.

trivial *a.* pu² chung⁴ yao⁴ te¹ 不重要的.

trolley *n.* (*street car*) tien² ch'e¹ 電車.

troop *n.* chün¹ tui⁴ 軍隊, (*cavalry*) lien² 連(騎).

trophy *n.* chan⁴ li⁴ p'in² 戰利品.

tropical *a.* je⁴ tai⁴ te¹ 熱帶的.

tropics *n.* hui² kuei¹ hsien¹ 回歸線.

trot *n.* k'uai¹ pu⁴ 快步; *v.* chi² hsing² 疾行.

trouble *n.* k'u² nao² 苦惱; *v.* (*worry*) yu¹ lei⁴ 憂累.

troublesome *a.* fan² jao² te¹ 煩擾的.

trousers *n.* k'u⁴ 褲.

trout *n.* hsün² yü² 鱒魚.

trowel *n.* man² 鏝.　　　　　　　　　「談.

truce *n.* t'ing² chan⁴ 停戰; ～ **talks,** ho² t'an² 和

truck *n.* ta⁴ k'a³ ch'e¹ 大卡車.

truculent *a.* ning² e⁴ te¹ 獰惡的.

true *a.* chen¹ shih² te¹ 眞實的.

truffle *n.* sung¹ lu⁴ chün¹ 松露菌.

truly *adv.* chen¹ shih² ti⁴ 眞實地.

trump *n.* (*bridge game*) wang² p'ai² 王牌.　「大衣箱.

trumpet *n.* la³ pa¹ 喇叭.

trunk *n.* (*tree*) shu⁴ kan¹ 樹幹, (*box*) ta⁴ i¹ hsiang¹

trust *n.* (*belief*) hsin⁴ jen⁴ 信任, (*responsibility*) hsin⁴ t'o¹ 信託; *v.* hsin⁴ jen⁴ 信任.

trustee *n.* shou⁴ t'o¹ jen² 受託人.

truth *n.* chen¹ shih² 眞實.

truthful *a.* chen¹ shih² te¹ 眞實的.

try *v.* ch'ang² shih⁴ 嘗試, (*law*) shen³ wen⁴ 審問.

tub *n.* t'ung³ 桶.

tube *n.* kuan³ 管.　　　　　　　　　「癆病.

tuberculosis *n.* chieh² ho² ping⁴ 結核病, lao² ping⁴

tuck *n.* heng² che² 橫摺.

Tuesday *n.* hsing¹ ch'i² erh⁴ 星期二.

tug *n.* (*boat*) yeh⁴ ch'uan² 曳船; *v.* li⁴ yeh⁴ 力曳.

tulip *n.* yü⁴ chin¹ hsiang¹ 鬱金香(植).

tumble *v.* tieh¹ tao³ 跌倒.　　　　　　　「者.

tumbler *n.* (*acrobat*) tsou³ sheng² so³ che³ 走繩索

tumor *n.* chung³ liu² 腫瘤.

tumult *n.* sao¹ tung⁴ 騷動.

tumultuous *a.* sao¹ tung⁴ te¹ 騷動的.

tun *n.* ta⁴ t'ung³ 大桶.

261

tune *n.* ch'ü³ tiao³ 曲調; *v.* (*be in harmony*) t'iao²

tuneful *a.* ho² tiao⁴ tzu¹ te¹ 合調子的. 「ho² 調和.

tunnel *a.* sui⁴ tao⁴ 隧道; *v.* chu² sui⁴ tao⁴ 築隧道.

turbine *n.* lun² chi¹ 輪機.

turbot *n.* ta⁴ tieh² 大鰈(魚).

turbulent *a.* sao¹ tung⁴ te¹ 騷動的.

turf *n.* ts'ao² t'u³ 草土.

turkey *n.* huo³ chi¹ 火鷄.

turmoil *n.* fen¹ luan⁴ 紛亂.

turn *n.* hui² chuan³ 廻轉; *v.* hsüan³ chuan³ 旋轉.

turnip *n.* lo² po¹ 蘿蔔.

turpentine *n.* sung¹ chieh² yu² 松節油.

turquoise *n.* lan² pao³ shih² 籃寶石.

turret *n.* (*gun*) p'ao⁴ t'a³ 礮塔.

turtle *n.* kuei¹ 龜.

tusk *n.* ch'ang² ya² 長牙.

tutor *n.* chia¹ t'ing² chiao⁴ shih¹ 家庭敎師.

tweezers *n.* nieh⁴ tzu¹ 鑷子. 「的.

twelve *n.* shih² erh⁴ 十二; *a.* shih² erh⁴ te¹ 十二

twig *n.* nen⁴ chih¹ 嫩枝.

twilight *n.* shu³ kuang¹ 曙光.

twin *n.* shuang¹ sheng¹ tzu³ 雙生子, luan² sheng¹

twine *n.* sheng² 繩, so³ 索. 「tzu³ 孿生子.

twinkle *v.* shan³ shuo⁴ 閃爍.

twins *n.* shuang¹ t'ai¹ 雙胎.

twist *v.* niu² chuan³ 扭轉.

two *n.* erh⁴ 二; *a.* erh⁴ te¹ 二的.

tympanum *n.* erh² ku³ 耳鼓.

type *n.* (*sort*) yang⁴ shih⁴ 樣式, (*printing*) ch'ien¹ tzu⁴ 鉛字, (*model*) tien³ hsing² 典型; *v.* (*typewrite*) ta³ tzu⁴ 打字.

typhoid *a.* shang¹ han¹ cheng⁴ te¹ 傷寒症的; ~ **fever,** shang¹ han² 傷寒(醫).

typhus *n.* pan¹ chen³ shang¹ han² 斑疹傷寒(醫).

typical *a.* tien³ hsing² te¹ 典型的.

tyrannical *a.* pao⁴ chün¹ te¹ 暴君的.

tyrannize *v.* pao⁴ nüeh⁴ 暴虐.

tyranny *n.* pao⁴ cheng⁴ 暴政.

tyrant *n.* pao⁴ chün¹ 暴君.

U

udder *n.* ju³ fang² 乳房.

ugliness *n.* ch'ou³ lou² 醜陋.

ugly *a.* ch'ou³ lou² te¹ 醜陋的.

ulcer *n.* k'uei⁴ yang² 潰瘍.

ulcerate *v.* k'uei⁴ lan⁴ 潰爛.

ulceration *n.* k'uei⁴ lan⁴ 潰爛.

ultimate *a.* tsui⁴ hou⁴ te¹ 最後的.

ultimatum *n.* tsui⁴ hou⁴ t'ung¹ tieh² 最後通牒.

umbrella *n.* san³ 傘.

umpire *n.* kung¹ tuan⁴ jen² 公斷人, ts'ai² p'an⁴ jen² 裁判人.

unable *a.* wu² neng² li⁴ te¹ 無能力的.

unaccountable *a.* pu⁴ k'o³ chieh³ te¹ 不可解的.

unaffected *a.* p'u² shih² te¹ 樸實的.

unanimity *n.* i² chih⁴ 一致.

unanimous *a.* i² chih⁴ te¹ 一致的.

unanswerable *a.* pu⁴ neng² ta² fu⁴ te¹ 不能答覆的.

unarmed *a.* wu² wu³ chuang¹ te¹ 無武裝的.

unavailing *a.* (*not successful*) pu⁴ ch'eng² kung¹ te¹ 不成功的, (*useless*) wu² yung⁴ te¹ 無用的.

unavoidable *a.* pu⁴ k'o³ pi⁴ mien³ te¹ 不可避免的.

unaware *a.* pu⁴ chüeh² te¹ 不覺的.

unbelief *n.* pu² hsin⁴ 不信.

unbroken *a.* pu² p'o⁴ te¹ 不破的.

uncertain *a.* pu² ting⁴ te¹ 不定的.

uncertainty *n.* pu² ting⁴ 不定.

unchangeable *a.* pu² pien⁴ te¹ 不變的.

uncharitable *a.* wu² jen² tz'u² te¹ 無仁慈的.

unclean *a.* wu¹ hui⁴ te¹ 汚穢的.

uncomfortable *a.* pu⁴ shu¹ shih⁴ te¹ 不舒適的.

uncommon *a.* hsien² yu³ te¹ 鮮有的.

unconcern *n.* mo⁴ shih⁴ 漠視, leng³ tan⁴ 冷淡.

unconscious *a.* shih¹ chih¹ chüeh² te¹ 失知覺的.

uncover *v.* k'ai¹ 開, (*disclose*) hsien³ lou⁴ 顯露.

undecided *a.* wei⁴ ting⁴ te¹ 未定的, wei⁴ chüeh² te¹ 未決的.

undeniable *a.* pu⁴ neng² fou³ jen⁴ te¹ 不能否認的.

under *adv.* tsai⁴ hsia⁴ 在下; *prep.* tsai⁴...hsia⁴ 在...

下; ～ **consideration,** tsai⁴ t'ao³ lun⁴ chung¹ 在討論中; ～ **way,** tsai⁴ chin⁴ hsing² chung¹ 在進行中.

underbid v. ch'u¹ chia⁴ chiao⁴ ti¹ yü² 出價較低於.

underclothes n. nei⁴ i¹ 內衣.

undergo v. tsao¹ shou⁴ 遭受.

underground a. ti⁴ hsia⁴ te¹ 地下的; n. (activity) ti⁴ hsia⁴ huo² tung⁴ 地下活動; ～ **railroad,** ti⁴ hsia⁴ t'ieh³ lu⁴ 地下鐵路(美).

underline v. hua⁴ hsien⁴ yü²...hsia⁴ 劃線於 .. 下.

underneath adv., prep. tsai⁴ hsia⁴ mien⁴ 在下面.

undersell v. lien² shou⁴ 廉售.

understand v. liao² chieh⁴ 了解, tung³ te² 懂得.

understanding n. li² chieh³ li⁴ 理解力.

undertake v. tan¹ jen⁴ 担任.

undertaker n. ch'eng² lan² che³ 承攬者.

undervalue v. ti¹ ku¹ 低估.

underwear n. ch'en⁴ shan¹ 襯衫.

undo v. (untie) chieh³ k'ai¹ 解開.

undoubted a. wu² i² te¹ 無疑的.

undress v. t'o¹ i¹ 脫衣.

uneasy a. pu⁴ an¹ i⁴ te¹ 不安逸的.

unemployment n. shih¹ yeh⁴ 失業.

unequal a. pu⁴ teng³ te¹ 不等的.

uneven a. pu⁴ p'ing² te¹ 不平的.

unexpected a. t'u² jan² te¹ 突然的.

unexpectedly adv. i⁴ wai⁴ ti⁴ 意外地.

unfair a. (unjust) pu⁴ kung¹ p'ing² te¹ 不公平的.

unfaithful a. pu⁴ chung¹ shih² te¹ 不忠實的.

unfasten v. chieh³ k'ai¹ 解開.

unfavorable a. pu² li⁴ te¹ 不利的.

unfinished a. wei⁴ wan² ch'eng² te¹ 未完成的.

unfit a. pu² shih⁴ tang¹ te¹ 不適當的; v. shih³ pu² shih⁴ yü² 使不適於.

unfix v. fang⁴ sung¹ 放鬆; "～ **bayonets!**" hsia⁴ tz'u⁴ tao¹ 下刺刀(軍).

unfold v. chan³ k'ai¹ 展開.

unforeseen a. wei⁴ yü⁴ chih¹ te¹ 未預知的.

unfortunate a. pu² hsing⁴ te¹ 不幸的.

unfriendly a. yu³ ti² i⁴ te¹ 有敵意的.

unfurl v. chang¹ k'ai¹ 張開.

unfurnished a. pu² pei⁴ chia¹ chü⁴ te¹ 不備家具的.

ungraceful a. pu⁴ ya³ te¹ 不雅的.

unhappiness n. pu² k'uai⁴ le⁴ 不快樂.

unhappy a. pu² k'uai⁴ le⁴ te¹ 不快樂的.

unharness v. hsieh⁴ ma³ chü⁴ 卸馬具.

unhealthy a. pu² chien⁴ k'ang¹ te¹ 不健康的.

unhurt a. wei⁴ shou⁴ hai⁴ te¹ 未受害的.

uniform a. i² lü⁴ te¹ 一律的; n. chih⁴ fu² 制服.

uniformity n. t'ung² yang⁴ 同樣, i² lü⁴ 一律.

unilateral a. tan¹ fang¹ te¹ 單方的.

unimportant a. pu² chung⁴ yao⁴ te¹ 不重要的.

union n. lien² ho² 聯合.

unit n. tan¹ wei⁴ 單位, (*troop*) pu⁴ tui⁴ 部隊; ～ **commander,** pu⁴ tui⁴ chang³ 部隊長, tan¹ wei⁴ chu² kuan³ kuan¹ 單位主管官.

unite v. lien² ho² 聯合.

united a. lien² ho² te¹ 聯合的, t'uan² chieh² te¹ 團結的; ～ **Nations,** lien² ho² kuo² 聯合國; ～ **States Army,** mei³ kuo² lu⁴ chün¹ 美國陸軍; ～ **States Military Academy,** mei³ kuo² lu⁴ chün¹ kuan¹ hsüeh² hsiao⁴ 美國陸軍軍官學校; ～ **States Navy,** mei³ kuo² hai³ chün¹ 美國海軍; ～ **States of America,** mei³ li⁴ chien¹ kung¹ ho² kuo² 美利堅共和國, mei³ kuo² 美國.

universal a. p'u³ p'ien⁴ te¹ 普遍的.

universe n. yü³ chou⁴ 宇宙.

university n. ta⁴ hsüeh² 大學.

unjust a. pu⁴ kung¹ cheng⁴ te¹ 不公正的.

unkind a. pu⁴ tz'u² ai⁴ te¹ 不慈愛的.

unkindness n. pu⁴ ho² shan⁴ 不和善.

unknown a. pu⁴ chih¹ te¹ 不知的.

unlace v. chieh³ t'o¹ 解脫.

unlawful a. wei² fa³ te¹ 違法的.

unless conj. ch'u² fei¹ 除非.

unlike a. pu⁴ hsiang¹ ssu⁴ te¹ 不相似的.

unlikely a. wei⁴ pi⁴ ju² tz'u³ te¹ 未必如此的.

unlimited a. wu² hsien⁴ te¹ 無限的.

unload v. hsieh⁴ tsai⁴ 卸載.

unlucky a. pu² hsing⁴ te¹ 不幸的.

unmarried a. wei⁴ chieh² hun¹ te¹ 未結婚的.

unmerciful a. ts'an² jen³ te¹ 殘忍的.

unnecessary *a.* pu⁴ hsü¹ yao⁴ te¹ 不需要的.

unoccupied *a.* (*vacant*) k'ung⁴ te¹ 空的, (*idle*) wu² shih⁴ te¹ 無事的.

unpack *v.* ch'ai¹ k'ai¹ 拆開. 「te¹ 無匹的.

unparalleled *a.* wu² shuang¹ te¹ 無雙的, wu² p'i⁴

unpleasant *a.* ling² jen² pu² k'uai⁴ te¹ 令人不快的.

unpopular *a.* pu⁴ fu² chung⁴ wang⁴ te¹ 不孚衆望的.

unprecedented *a.* wu² hsien¹ li⁴ te¹ 無先例的.

unprepared *a.* wu² chun³ pei⁴ te¹ 無準備的.

unproductive *a.* pu⁴ sheng¹ ch'an³ te¹ 不生產的.

unprofitable *a.* wu² li⁴ i⁴ te¹ 無利益的.

unqualified *a.* pu⁴ ho² ko² te¹ 不合格的.

unquestionable *a.* ch'üeh⁴ ting⁴ te¹ 確定的.

unravel *v.* chieh³ k'ai¹ 解開.

unreasonable *a.* pu⁴ ho² li³ te¹ 不合理的.

unrelenting *a.* ts'an² jen³ te¹ 殘忍的.

unreliable *a.* pu⁴ k'o³ k'ao⁴ te¹ 不可靠的.

unreserved *a.* (*frank*) t'an³ pai⁴ te¹ 坦白的.

unripe *a.* wei⁴ ch'eng² shou² te¹ 未成熟的.

unsafe *a.* pu⁴ an¹ ch'üan² te¹ 不安全的.

unsatisfactory *a.* pu⁴ man³ i⁴ te¹ 不滿意的.

unseasonable *a.* pu⁴ ho² chi⁴ chieh³ te¹ 不合季節

unseen *a.* pu⁴ k'o³ chien⁴ te¹ 不可見的. 「的.

unselfish *a.* pu² tzu⁴ ssu¹ te¹ 不自私的. 「的.

unsociable *a.* pu² shan⁴ chiao¹ chi⁴ te¹ 不善交際

unspeakable *a.* pu⁴ k'o³ yen² yü² te¹ 不可言喻的.

unstable *a.* pu⁴ wen³ ting⁴ te¹ 不穩定的.

unsteady *a.* pu⁴ chien¹ ting⁴ te¹ 不堅定的.

unsuccessful *a.* pu⁴ ch'eng² kung¹ te¹ 不成功的.

unsuitable *a.* pu⁴ hsiang¹ p'ei⁴ te¹ 不相配的.

untie *v.* chieh³ k'ai¹ 解開.

until *prep.* ch'i⁴ 迄, chih² chih⁴ 直至.

untimely *a.* pu⁴ ho² shih² te¹ 不合時的.

untold *a.* wei⁴ shuo¹ te¹ 未說的.

untrue *a.* pu⁴ chen¹ shih² te¹ 不眞實的.

unusual *a.* fei¹ ch'ang² te¹ 非常的, han³ chien⁴ te¹

unwilling *a.* pu² yüan⁴ te¹ 不願的. 「罕見的.

unwise *a.* yü² ch'un³ te¹ 愚蠢的.

unworthy *a.* pu⁴ chih² te¹ 不值的.

up *adv., prep.* tsai⁴ shang⁴ 在上.

uphill a. shang⁴ hsieh² te¹ 上斜的.

uphold v. (*support*) wei² ch'ih² 維持.

upholsterer n. chia¹ chü⁴ shang¹ 家具商.

uplift v. chü² ch'i³ 舉起.

upon prep. tsai⁴ shang⁴ 在上.

upper a. tsai⁴ shang⁴ te¹ 在上的.

upright a. chih² li⁴ te¹ 直立的, (*honest*) ch'eng² shih² te¹ 誠實的.

uproar n. sao¹ tung⁴ 騷動.

uproot v. pa² ken¹ 拔根.

upset v. (*overturn*) ch'ing¹ fu⁴ 傾覆.

upside n. shang⁴ mien⁴ 上面; ~ **down**, tien¹ tao³ 顛倒.

upstairs n. lou² shang⁴ 樓上.

upstart n. chüeh² ch'i³ che³ 崛起者.

upward a. hsiang⁴ shang⁴ te¹ 向上的.

urbane a. yu² li³ mao⁴ te¹ 有禮貌的.

urge v. ts'ui¹ ts'u⁴ 催促.

urgency n. chi³ p'o⁴ 急迫.

urgent a. chi² p'o⁴ te¹ 急迫的.

urine n. hsiao³ pien⁴ 小便.

us pron. wo³ men² 我們.

usage a. yung⁴ fa³ 用法.

use n., v. shih³ yung⁴ 使用.

useful a. yu⁸ yung⁴ te¹ 有用的.

usefulness n. yu³ yung⁴ 有用.

useless a. wu² yung⁴ te¹ 無用的.

uselessness n. wu² yung⁴ 無用.

usher n. chao¹ tai⁴ yüan² 招待員.

usual a. kuan² ch'ang² te¹ 慣常的.

usually adv. ch'ang² ch'ang² 常常.

usurer n. fang² kao¹ li⁴ chai⁴ che³ 放高利債者.

utensil n. ch'i⁴ min³ 器皿, yung⁴ chü⁴ 用具.

utility n. hsiao⁴ yung⁴ 效用.

utilize v. li⁴ yung⁴ 利用.

utmost a. chi² tu⁴ te¹ 極度的.

utter a. wan² ch'üan² te¹ 完全的; v. shuo¹ ch'u¹ 說出.

utterance n. fa¹ yen² 發言.

utterly adv. ch'üan² jan² 全然.

V

vacancy *n.* (*position*) k'ung⁴ ch'üeh¹ 空缺.

vacant *a.* k'ung⁴ te¹ 空的.

vacate *v.* pan¹ k'ung¹ 搬空.

vacation *n.* chia⁴ ch'i¹ 假期.

vaccinate *v.* (*smallpox*) chung⁴ niu² tou⁴ 種牛痘, (*other diseases*) yü⁴ fang² chu⁴ she⁴ 預防注射.

vaccination *n.* chung⁴ tou⁴ 種痘.

vacillate *v.* ch'ou² ch'u² 躊躇.

vacillation *n.* ch'ou² ch'u² 躊躇.

vacuum *n.* chen¹ k'ung¹ 真空; ~ **tube,** chen¹ k'ung¹ kuan³ 真空管.

vagabond *n.* liu² mang² 流氓.

vagary *n.* ch'i² hsiang³ 奇想.

vagrant *n.* wu² lai⁴ 無賴.

vague *a.* han² hu² te¹ 含糊的.

vain *a.* (*of no use*) wu² hsiao⁴ te¹ 無效的, (*conceited*) tzu⁴ fu⁴ te¹ 自負的.

valet *n.* nan² p'u⁴ 男僕, shih⁴ che³ 侍者.

valiant *a.* yung² kan³ te¹ 勇敢的.

valid *a.* (*true*) chen¹ shih² te¹ 真實的.

validity *n.* (*truth*) chen¹ shih² 真實, (*effectiveness*) yu³ hsiao⁴ 有效.

valor *n.* yung² kan³ 勇敢.

valuable *a.* kuei⁴ chung⁴ te¹ 貴重的.

valuation *n.* ku¹ chia⁴ 估價.

value *n.* chia⁴ chih² 價值; *v.* ku¹ chia⁴ 估價, (*regard highly*) tsun¹ chung⁴ 尊重.

valve *n.* huo² men² 活門.

vane *n.* feng¹ piao¹ 風標.

vanish *v.* hsiao¹ shih¹ 消失, hsiao¹ san⁴ 消散.

vanity *n.* tzu⁴ fu⁴ 自負.

vanquish *v.* (*defeat*) chan⁴ sheng⁴ 戰勝, (*conquer*) cheng¹ fu² 征服.

vantage *n.* yu¹ yüeh¹ 優越.

vapor *n.* cheng¹ ch'i⁴ 蒸氣.

variable *a.* i⁴ pien⁴ te¹ 易變的.

variation *n.* pien⁴ hua² 變化.

variety *n.* pu⁴ t'ung² 不同.

various *a.* pu⁴ t'ung² te¹ 不同的.

varnish *n.* ming² yu² 明油, chao⁴ kuang¹ ch'i¹ 罩
光漆.

vary *v.* kai³ pien⁴ 改變.

vase *n.* p'ing² 瓶, (*flower*) hua¹ p'ing² 花瓶.

Vaseline *n.* fan² shih⁴ lin² yu² 凡士林油.

vassal *n.* chia¹ ch'en² 家臣.

vast *a.* chü⁴ ta⁴ te¹ 巨大的.

vat *n.* ta⁴ t'ung³ 大桶.

vault *n.* (*roof*) kung³ hsing² wu¹ ting³ 拱形屋頂,
(*jump*) ch'eng² kan¹ t'iao⁴ 撐竿跳.

vaunt *v.* chin¹ k'ua¹ 矜誇.

veal *n.* tu² jou⁴ 犢肉.

veer *v.* chuan³ hsiang⁴ 轉向(風).

vegetable *n.* su¹ ts'ai⁴ 蔬菜.

vegetate *v.* sheng¹ chang³ 生長.

vegetation *n.* chih² wu⁴ 植物.

vehicle *n.* ch'e¹ liang⁴ 車輛.

veil *n.* mien⁴ sha¹ 面紗.

vein *n.* ching⁴ mo⁴ 靜脈.

velocity *n.* su² tu⁴ 速度.

velvet *a.* t'ien¹ e² jung² te¹ 天鵝絨的; *n.* t'ien¹ e²
jung² 天鵝絨.

vender, vendor *n.* mai⁴ chu³ 賣主.

venerable *a.* k'o³ ching⁴ te¹ 可敬的.

venerate *v.* tsun¹ ching⁴ 尊敬.

veneration *n.* tsun¹ ching⁴ 尊敬.

venereal *a.* hsing⁴ chiao¹ te¹ 性交的; ~ **disease,**
hua¹ liu³ ping⁴ 花柳病.

vengeance *n.* pao⁴ ch'ou⁴ 報仇, pao⁴ fu⁴ 報復.

vengeful *a.* pao⁴ fu⁴ te¹ 報復的.

venison *n.* lu⁴ jou⁴ 鹿肉.

venom *n.* tu² yeh⁴ 毒液.

venomous *a.* yu³ tu² te¹ 有毒的.

vent *n.* (*hole*) k'ung³ 孔.

ventilation *n.* huan⁴ ch'i¹ 換氣, t'ung¹ feng¹ 通風.

ventilator *n.* (*apparatus*) t'ung¹ feng¹ ch'i¹ 通風
器.

venture *n., v.* mao⁴ hsien³ 冒險.

venturesome *a.* mao⁴ hsien³ te¹ 冒險的.

Venus *n.* (*planet*) chin¹ hsing¹ 金星.

verb *n.* tung⁴ tz'u² 動詞.

verbal *a.* k'ou³ shu⁴ te¹ 口述的.

verdict *n.* ts'ai² p'an⁴ 裁判.

verge *n.* pien¹ yüan² 邊緣.

269

verification *n.* cheng⁴ shih² 證實.

verify *v.* cheng⁴ shih² 證實.

verily *adv.* shih² tsai⁴ 實在.

veritable *a.* chen¹ shih² te¹ 眞實的.

verity *n.* chen¹ shih² 眞實.

vermilion *n.* yin² chu¹ 銀朱, chu¹ hung² 朱紅.

vermin *n.* yu³ hai⁴ tung⁴ wu⁴ 有害動物.

versatile *a.* to¹ ts'ai² to¹ i⁴ te¹ 多才多藝的.

verse *n.* shih¹ chü⁴ 詩句.

versed *a.* ching¹ t'ung¹ te¹ 精通的.

version *n.* fan¹ i⁴ 繙譯.

vertical *a.* ch'ui² chih² te¹ 垂直的; ～ **line,** ch'ui²
chih² hsien⁴ 垂直線; ～ **rudder,** fang¹ hsiang¹
to⁴ 方向舵.

very *adv.* shen² 甚; *a.* (*same*) t'ung² yang⁴ te¹ 同
樣的;～ **pistol,** hsin⁴ hao⁴ ch'iang¹ 信號槍(軍).

vessel *n.* (*boat*) ch'uan² 船, (*container*) ch'i⁴ min³
器皿.

vest *n.* pei⁴ hsin¹ 背心.

vestige *n.* hen² chi⁴ 痕跡.

veteran *n.* lao³ ping¹ 老兵.

veterinary *n.* shou⁴ i¹ 獸醫; ～ **hospital,** shou⁴
i¹ yüan⁴ 獸醫院; ～ **surgeon,** shou⁴ i¹ 獸醫.

veto *n.* fou³ jen⁴ ch'üan² 否認權.

vex *v.* nao³ nu⁴ 惱怒.

vexation *n.* nao³ nu⁴ 惱怒.

vexatious *a.* k'u² nao³ te¹ 苦惱的.

via *prep.* ching¹ kuo⁴ 經過.

vial *n.* (*bottle*) hsiao³ p'ing² 小瓶.

vibrate *v.* chen⁴ tung⁴ 震動.

vibration *n.* chen⁴ tung⁴ 震動.

vice *n.* e⁴ hsing² 惡行, (*tool*) lao² hu³ ch'ien² 老虎
鉗, (*prefix*) fu⁴... 副....

vice-admiral *n.* chung¹ chiang⁴ 中將(海).

vice-consul *n.* fu⁴ ling³ shih⁴ 副領事.

vice-president *n.* fu⁴ tsung³ t'ung³ 副總統.

viceroy *n.* tsung³ tu¹ 總督.

vicious *a.* hsieh² e⁴ te¹ 邪惡的.

victim *n.* pei⁴ hai⁴ che³ 被害者.

victor *n.* te² sheng⁴ che³ 得勝者.

victorious *a.* te² sheng⁴ te¹ 得勝的.

victory *n.* sheng⁴ li⁴ 勝利.

vie *v.* ching⁴ cheng¹ 競爭.

view *n.* (*scene*) feng¹ ching³ 風景; *v.* k'an⁴ 看.

vigilance *n.* ching² hsing³ 警醒.

vigilant *a.* ching² hsing³ te¹ 警醒的.

vigor *n.* huo² li⁴ 活力.

vigorous *a.* yu³ li⁴ te¹ 有力的.

vile *a.* (*low*) pei¹ chien⁴ te¹ 卑賤的.

villa *n.* pieh² shu⁴ 別墅.

village *n.* hsiang¹ ts'un¹ 鄉村.

villager *n.* ts'un¹ min² 村民.

villain *n.* e⁴ t'u² 惡徒. 「樹.

vine *n.* t'eng² 藤, (*grapevine*) p'u² t'ao² shu⁴ 葡萄

vinegar *n.* ts'u⁴ 醋.

vineyard *n.* p'u² t'ao² yüan² 葡萄園.

vinous *a.* p'u² t'ao² chiu³ te¹ 葡萄酒的.

violate *v.* wei² fan⁴ 違犯.

violation *n.* wei² fan⁴ 違犯.

violence *n.* chi¹ lieh⁴ 激烈.

violent *a.* meng³ lieh⁴ te¹ 猛烈的.

violet *n.* tzu³ lo² lan² 紫羅蘭(植).

violin *n.* hsiao³ t'i² ch'in² 小提琴.

violinist *n.* hsiao³ t'i² ch'in² chia¹ 小提琴家.

violoncello *n.* ta⁴ t'i² ch'in² 大提琴.

viper *n.* tu² she¹ 毒蛇.

virgin *a.* t'ung² chen¹ te¹ 童貞的, chen¹ chieh² te¹ 貞潔的; *n.* ch'u² nü³ 處女.

virginity *n.* t'ung² chen¹ 童貞.

virtual *a.* shih² chi⁴ te¹ 實際的.

virtue *n.* mei³ te² 美德.

virtuous *a.* mei³ te² te¹ 美德的.

virulent *a.* yu³ tu² te¹ 有毒的.

visage *n.* mien⁴ mao⁴ 面貌.

viscount *n.* tzu³ chüeh² 子爵.

visible *a.* k'o³ chien⁴ te¹ 可見的.

vision *n.* shih⁴ li⁴ 視力.

visit *n.*, *v.* pai⁴ fang³ 拜訪.

visitor *n.* pai⁴ fang³ che³ 拜訪者, lai² k'o⁴ 來客.

visor *n.* mao⁴ yen² 帽簷. 「pen³ te¹ 基本的.

vital *a.* sheng¹ ming⁴ te¹ 生命的, (*essential*) chi¹

vitamin, vitamine *n.* wei² t'a¹ ming⁴ 維他命, sheng¹ huo² su⁴ 生活素.

vivid *a.* sheng¹ tung⁴ te¹ 生動的.

vocabulary *n.* tzu⁴ hui⁴ 字彙. 「的.

vocal *a.* sheng¹ yin¹ te¹ 聲音的, yen² yü³ te¹ 言語

vocalist *n.* sheng¹ yüeh⁴ chia¹ 聲樂家.

vocation *n.* chih² yeh⁴ 職業.

vociferous *a.* hsüan¹ nao⁴ te¹ 喧鬧的.

vogue *n.* shih² shih⁴ 時式.

voice *n.* sheng¹ yin¹ 聲音.

void *a.* wu² hsiao⁴ te¹ 無效的.

volcano *n.* huo³ shan¹ 火山.

volley *n.* (*artillery*) ch'ün² she⁴ 群射(砲).

volt *n.* fu² t'o¹ 伏脫.

voltage *n.* tien⁴ ya¹ 電壓.

volume *n.* (*book*) shu¹ 書, (*space*) t'i³ chi¹ 體積.

voluntary *a.* chih⁴ yüan⁴ te¹ 志願的.

volunteer *n.* (*army*) chih⁴ yüan⁴ ping¹ 志願兵; *v.* tzu⁴ kao⁴ fen⁴ yung³ 自告奮勇.

vomit *v.* ou³ t'u⁴ 嘔吐.

vote *n.*, *v.* t'ou² p'iao⁴ 投票.

vouch *v.* (*guarantee*) tan¹ pao³ 擔保.

voucher *n.* (*person*) tan¹ pao³ jen² 擔保人, (*thing*) tan¹ pao² p'in³ 擔保品, (*receipt*) shou¹ chü⁴ 收據.

vow *n.* shih⁴ yen² 誓言; *v.* li⁴ shih⁴ 立誓.

vowel *n.* mu³ yin¹ 母音.

voyage *n.* hai³ ch'eng² 海程.

vulgar *a.* lou⁴ su² te¹ 陋俗的.

vulnerable *a.* k'o³ shang¹ hai⁴ te¹ 可傷害的.

vulture *n.* wu⁴ ying¹ 兀鷹(鳥).

W

wadding *n.* t'ien² sai⁴ wu⁴ 填塞物.

wade *v.* she⁴ shui³ 涉水.

wag *v.* yao² pai³ 搖擺.

wage *n.* kung¹ tzu² 工資.

wager *n.* (*bet*) tu³ 賭.

wagon *n.* huo⁴ ch'e¹ 貨車.

wagoner *n.* huo⁴ ch'e¹ fu¹ 貨車夫.

wail v. k'u¹ ch'i⁴ 哭泣, (*mourn*) pei¹ tao⁴ 悲悼.

wainscot n. hu⁴ pi⁴ pan³ 護壁板.

waist n. yao¹ 腰.

waistband n. yao¹ tai⁴ 腰帶.

wait v. teng³ hou⁴ 等候.

waiter n. (*hotel*) shih⁴ ying⁴ sheng¹ 侍應生.

waiting n. teng³ tai⁴ 等待; a. teng³ tai⁴ te¹ 等待的; ~ **room**, (*railroad station*) hou⁴ ch'e¹ shih⁴ 候車室, (*doctor's office*) hou⁴ chen¹ shih⁴ 候診室.

wake v. hsing³ 醒.

wakeful a. pu⁴ mien² te¹ 不眠的.

waken v. huan⁴ hsing³ 喚醒.

walk n., v. san³ pu⁴ 散步.

wall n. ch'iang² pi⁴ 牆壁.

wallet n. hsiao³ p'i² chia¹ 小皮夾.

wallow v. ta² kun³ 打滾.

walnut n. hu² t'ao² mu⁴ 胡桃木.

waltz n. hua² erh³ tz'u¹ wu³ 華爾滋舞; v. t'iao⁴ hua² erh³ tz'u¹ wu³ 跳華爾滋舞.

wan a. ts'ang¹ pai⁴ te¹ 蒼白的.

wand n. hsiao³ chang⁴ 小杖.

wander v. man⁴ po² 漫步.

wanderer n. p'iao¹ po² che³ 漂泊者.

want n. (*desire*) yü⁴ wang⁴ 欲望; v. (*wish*) yü⁴ 欲, (*lack*) ch'üeh¹ fa² 缺乏, (*need*) hsü¹ yao⁴ 需要.

war n. chan⁴ cheng¹ 戰爭; ~ **college**, lu⁴ chün¹ ta⁴ hsüeh² 陸軍大學; ~ **communique**, kuan¹ fang¹ chan⁴ pao⁴ 官方戰報; ~ **correspondent**, sui² chün¹ chi⁴ che³ 隨軍記者; ~ **debt**, chan⁴ chai⁴ 戰債; ~ **Department** (US), lu⁴ chün¹ pu⁴ 陸軍部(美); ~ **Department General Staff** (US), lu⁴ chün¹ pu⁴ tsung³ ts'an¹ mou² pu⁴ 陸軍部總參謀部(美); ~ **diary**, chen⁴ chung¹ jih⁴ chi⁴ 陣中日記; ~ **game**, ping¹ ch'i² 兵棋; ~ **of masses**, jen² li⁴ chan⁴ 人力戰(軍); ~ **of movement**, yün⁴ tung⁴ chan⁴ 運動戰(軍); ~ **of position**, chen⁴ ti⁴ chan⁴ 陣地戰(軍); ~ **reserves**, chan⁴ cheng¹ ch'u² ts'un² p'in³ 戰爭儲存品; ~ **strength**, chan⁴ li⁴ 戰力.

warble v. wan² chuan³ erh² ko¹ 婉轉而歌.

warder n. (*guard*) k'an¹ shou² che³ 看守者.

wardrobe *n.* i¹ ch'u² 衣櫥.

ware *n.* huo⁴ p'in² 貨品.

warehouse *n.* chan⁴ fang² 棧房.

warfare *n.* chan⁴ cheng¹ 戰爭.

wariness *n.* chu⁴ i⁴ 注意, chin³ shen⁴ 謹慎.

warlike *a.* hao⁴ chan⁴ te¹ 好戰的.

warm *a.* wen¹ nuan³ te¹ 溫暖的; *v.* shih³ wen¹ 使 ⌈溫.

warmth *n.* wen¹ nuan³ 溫暖, je⁴ ch'ing² 熱情.

warn *v.* ching³ kao⁴ 警告.

warning *n.* ching³ kao⁴ 警告; ～ **net,** ching³ pao⁴ wang³ 警報網(軍); ～ **order,** chun³ pei⁴ ming⁴ ling⁴ 準備命令(軍); ～ **signal,** ching³ pao⁴ hsin⁴ ⌈hao⁴ 警報信號(軍).

warrior *n.* chan⁴ shih⁴ 戰士.

wart *n.* liu² 瘤.

wash *n.* hsi³ ti² 洗滌; *v.* (*clothes*) hsi³ ti² 洗滌, (*self*) kuan⁴ hsi³ 盥洗.

washroom *n.* hsi² shou³ chien¹ 洗手間.

washerwoman *n.* hsi³ i¹ fu⁴ 洗衣婦.

washing *n.* hsi³ ti² 洗滌; ～ **machine,** hsi³ i¹ chi¹ 洗衣機.

washstand *n.* hsi³ mien⁴ t'ai² 洗面檯.

wasp *n.* huang² feng¹ 黃蜂.

waste *a.* lang⁴ fei⁴ te¹ 浪費的; *n.* lang⁴ fei⁴ 浪費; *v.* lang⁴ fei⁴ 浪費; ～ **paper,** fei⁴ chih³ 廢紙.

wastebasket *n.* tzu⁴ chih³ lou³ 字紙簍.

wasteful *a.* hao⁴ fei⁴ te¹ 耗費的.

watch *n.* piao³ 錶, (*lookout*) shou³ wang⁴ 守望; *v.* chien¹ shih⁴ 監視.

watchful *a.* chu⁴ i⁴ te¹ 注意的.

watchmaker *n.* piao³ chiang⁴ 錶匠.

watchman *n.* keng¹ fu¹ 更夫.

watchword *n.* t'e⁴ pieh² k'ou³ ling⁴ 特別口令.

water *n.* shui³ 水; *v.* chu⁴ i² shui³ 注以水; ～ **closet,** ts'e⁴ so³ 廁所; ～ **color,** shui³ ts'ai³ 水彩; ～ **cress,** shui³ t'ien² chieh⁴ 水田芥(植); ～ **lily,** lien² hua¹ 蓮花(植); ～ **mill,** shui³ lun² 水輪(機); ～ **polo,** shui³ ch'iu² hsi⁴ 水球戲; ～ **power,** shui³ li⁴ 水力.

watering *n.* chi² shui³ 給水; ～ **point,** chi² shui³ ch'ang³ 給水場; ～ **point for horse,** yin⁴ ma² ch'ang³ 飲馬場(軍).

waterfall *n.* pao⁴ pu⁴ 瀑布.

watermelon *n.* hsi¹ kua¹ 西瓜.

waterproof *a., n.* pu² t'ou⁴ shui³ te¹ 不透水的.

watt *n.* wa³ t'e⁴ 瓦特(電力單位).

wave *n.* (*of water, sound*) po¹ 波, (*of infantry, tanks*) p'i¹ 批; *v.* po¹ tung⁴ 波動; ~ **length**, po¹ ch'ang² 波長.

wax *n.* la⁴ 蠟; ~ **doll**, la⁴ ou³ jen² 蠟偶人.

way *n.* (*manner*) t'ai⁴ tu⁴ 態度, (*method*) fang¹ fa³ 方法, (*direction*) fang¹ hsiang⁴ 方向, (*distance*) lu⁴ ch'eng² 路程, (*road*) lu⁴ 路, (*custom*) feng¹ shang⁴ 風尚.

waylay *v.* fu² tai⁴ 伏待.

wayward *a.* jen⁴ hsing⁴ te¹ 任性的.

we *pron.* wo³ men² 我們.

weak *a.* jo⁴ te¹ 弱的.

weaken *v.* (*the enemy*) hsueh¹ jo⁴ 削弱.

weakness *n.* jo⁴ tien³ 弱點.

wealth *n.* ts'ai² fu⁴ 財富.

wealthy *a.* fu⁴ te¹ 富的.

wean *v.* shih³ tuan⁴ ju³ 使斷乳.

weapon *n.* wu³ ch'i⁴ 武器.

wear *v.* (*clothes*) ch'uan¹ 穿, (*cause damage*) hao⁴ sun³ 耗損.

weariness *n.* p'i² chüan⁴ 疲倦.

wearisome *a.* p'i² chüan⁴ te¹ 疲倦的.

weary *a.* p'i² chüan⁴ te¹ 疲倦的; *v.* shih³ chüan⁴ 使倦.

weasel *n.* ling² yu⁴ 伶鼬(動).

weather *n.* t'ien¹ ch'i⁴ 天氣.

weather-beaten *a.* pei⁴ feng¹ ch'ui¹ yü² ta³ te¹ 被風吹雨打的.

weathercock *n.* feng¹ hsin⁴ piao¹ 風信標.

weatherglass *n.* feng¹ yü³ piao³ 風雨表.

weave *v.* pien¹ chih¹ 編織.

weaver *n.* chih¹ kung¹ 織工.

web *n.* chih¹ wu⁴ 織物, (*spider*) chu¹ wang³ 蛛網.

wed *v.* chieh² hun¹ 結婚.

wedding *n.* hun¹ li³ 婚禮.

wedge *n.* hsieh⁴ 楔; *n.* p'i¹ k'ai¹ 劈開.

Wednesday *n.* hsing¹ ch'i² san¹ 星期三.

weed *n.* tsa² ts'ao³ 雜草.

week *n.* hsing¹ ch'i² 星期, chou¹ 週.

weekday *n.* chou¹ jih⁴ 週日.

weekend *n.* chou¹ mo⁴ 週末.

275

weekly *a.* i⁴ hsing¹ ch'i² te¹ 一星期的.

weep *v.* k'u¹ 哭, liu² lei¹ 流淚.

weevil *n.* hsiang⁴ pi² ch'ung² 象鼻蟲.

weigh *v.* ch'eng¹ 秤, (*anchor*) chü² ch'i³ 舉起.

weight *n.* chung⁴ liang⁴ 重量. 「yao⁴ te¹ 重要的.

weighty *a.* chung⁴ te¹ 重的, (*important*) chung⁴

welcome *n.*, *v.* huan¹ ying² 歡迎.

weld *v.* han⁴ chieh¹ 焊接.

welfare *n.* hsing⁴ fu² 幸福.

well *n.* ching³ 井; *adv.* liang² hao³ ti⁴ 良好地; ～ **to do,** hsiao³ k'ang¹ 小康.

well-bred *a.* yu³ chiao⁴ yang³ te¹ 有敎養的.

west *n.* hsi¹ fang¹ 西方; ～ **Point** (US), hsi¹ tien³ chün¹ hsiao⁴ 西點軍校(美).

western *a.* hsi¹ fang¹ te¹ 西方的.

westward *adv.* hsiang⁴ hsi¹ 向西.

wet *a.* shih¹ te¹ 濕的; *n.* shih¹ ch'i⁴ 濕氣, (*rain*) yü³ t'ien¹ 雨天; *v.* shih³ shih¹ 使濕; ～ **nurse,** 「ju² mu³ 乳母.

whale *n.* ch'ing² 鯨.

whalebone *n.* ch'ing² ku³ 鯨骨.

wharf *n.* ma³ t'ou² 碼頭; ～ **boat,** tun³ ch'uan³ 躉船. 「樣的.

what *pron.* shen² mo¹ 什麼; *a.* tsen³ yang⁴ te¹ 怎

whatever *pron.* jen⁴ ho² 任何; *a.* jen⁴ ho² te¹ 任 「何的.

wheat *n.* hsiao³ mai⁴ 小麥.

wheel *n.* lun² 輪; *v.* hsüan² chuan³ 旋轉; ～ **chair,** i³ ch'e¹ 椅車(病人用); ～ **horse,** hou⁴ ma³ 後馬.

wheelbarrow *n.* shou³ t'ui¹ hsiao³ ch'e¹ 手推小車.

wheeze *v.* ch'uan³ hsi² 喘息.

when *adv.* ho² shih² 何時.

whence *adv.* ts'ung² ho² ch'u⁴ 從何處.

whenever *adv.* wu² lun⁴ ho² shih² 無論何時.

where *adv.* tsai⁴ ho² ch'u⁴ 在何處.

whereabouts *adv.* tsai⁴ ho² ch'u⁴ 在何處.

wherever *adv.* wu² lun⁴ ho² ch'u⁴ 無論何處.

whether *conj.* i⁴ 抑, huo² 或.

which *pron.* ho² che³ 何者; *a.* na³ i² ko⁴ 那一個.

whichever *pron.* jen⁴ ho² 任何.

while *n.* shih² 時; *conj.* tang¹...shih² 當...時.

whim *n.* huan⁴ hsiang³ 幻想.

whimsical *a.* huan⁴ hsiang² te¹ 幻想的.

whine *n.* ai¹ su⁴ 哀訴.

whip *n.* pien¹ 鞭; *v.* pien¹ ta³ 鞭打.

whirl *v.* hsüan² chuan³ 旋轉.

whirlpool *n.* hsüan⁴ wo¹ 旋渦.

whirlwind *n.* hsüan⁴ feng¹ 旋風.

whiskers *n.* chia² hsü¹ 頰鬚.

whiskey *n.* wei¹ shih⁴ chi⁴ chiu³ 威士忌酒.

whisper *n., v.* erh² yü³ 耳語.

whistle *n.* (*mouth*) k'ou³ shao⁴ sheng¹ 口哨聲, (*instrument*) k'ou³ ti² 口笛; *v.* (*mouth*) ch'ui¹ k'ou³ shao⁴ 吹口哨, (*instrument*) ch'ui¹ ti² 吹笛, (*engine*) ming² ti² 鳴笛.

white *a.* pai² te¹ 白的.

whitewash *n.* shih³ hui¹ shui³ 石灰水; *v.* fen³ shua¹ 粉刷.

whither *adv.* hsiang⁴ ho² ch'u⁴ 向何處.

who *pron.* shui² 誰, ho² jen² 何人.

whoever *pron.* wu² lun⁴ ho² jen² 無論何人. 「個.

whole *a.* ch'üan² pu⁴ te¹ 全部的; *n.* cheng³ ko⁴ 整

wholesale *a.* p'i¹ fa¹ te¹ 批發的; *n.* p'i¹ fa¹ 批發.

wholesome *a.* wei⁴ sheng¹ te¹ 衞生的.

wholly *adv.* wan² ch'üan² 完全.

whom *pron.* ho² jen² 何人, shui² 誰.

whoop *n.* han³ sheng¹ 喊聲; *v.* hu¹ han³ 呼喊.

whore *n.* ch'ang¹ chi¹ 娼妓.

whose *pron.* shui² te¹ 誰的.

why *adv.* ho² ku⁴ 何故; ~ not ? wei⁴ shen² mo¹ 爲什麼; ~ so ? ho² ku⁴ 何故.

wick *n.* teng¹ hsin¹ 燈心.

wicked *a.* hsieh² e⁴ te¹ 邪惡的.

wickedness *n.* hsieh² e⁴ 邪惡.

wide *a.* k'uo⁴ te¹ 闊的.

widen *v.* shih³ k'uo⁴ 使闊.

widow *n.* kua³ fu⁴ 寡婦.

widower *n.* kuan¹ fu¹ 鰥夫.

width *n.* k'uo⁴ 闊.

wife *n.* ch'i¹ tzu¹ 妻子.

wig *n.* chia² fa³ 假髮.

wild *a.* yeh³ te¹ 野的.

wilderness *n.* huang¹ yeh³ 荒野.

wile *n.* kuei³ chi⁴ 詭計.

will v. aux. (future) chiang¹ 將, (wish) yü⁴ 欲, (must) tang¹ 當, (can) neng² 能; n. i⁴ chih⁴ 意志, (document) i² chu³ 遺屬; v. (bequeath) i² tseng⁴ 遺贈.

willful a. ku⁴ i⁴ te¹ 故意的.

willing a. ch'ing² yüan² te¹ 情願的.

willow n. liu³ 柳.

wily a. chiao³ hua² te¹ 狡猾的, chien¹ cha⁴ te¹ 奸詐的.

win v. huo⁴ sheng⁴ 獲勝.

wince v. wei⁴ so¹ 畏縮.

winch n. chiao³ ch'e¹ 絞車, chiao³ p'an² 絞盤.

wind n. feng¹ 風; v. (spring) chiao² chin³ 絞緊, (twist) ch'an² jao² 纏繞.

windlass n. chiao³ p'an² 絞盤.

windmill n. feng¹ ch'e¹ 風車.

window n. ch'uang¹ 窗.

windpipe n. ch'i⁴ kuan³ 氣管.

windward a. hsiang⁴ feng¹ te¹ 向風的; n. feng¹ hsiang⁴ 風向.

windy a. to¹ feng¹ te¹ 多風的.

wine n. chiu³ 酒.

wing n. i⁴ 翼.

wink v., n. sha⁴ yen³ 霎眼.

winner n. sheng⁴ li⁴ che³ 勝利者.

winning a. te² sheng⁴ che³ 得勝者, (attractive) chiao³ mei⁴ te¹ 嬌媚的.

winter n. tung¹ chi⁴ 冬季.

wintry a. tung¹ te¹ 冬的.

wipe v. (off) shih⁴ ching⁴ 拭淨, (eyes) shih⁴ ch'ü⁴ 拭去.

wire n. chin¹ shu³ hsien⁴ 金屬線, (electric) tien⁴ hsien⁴ 電線, (telegraph) tien² pao⁴ 電報; ~ **cutter**, t'ieh³ ssu¹ chien³ 鐵絲剪(軍); ~ **entanglement**, t'ieh³ ssu¹ wang³ 鐵絲網; ~ **laying**, (signal communication) chia⁴ hsien⁴ 架線(通信); ~ **party**, (engineer) chang¹ hsien⁴ pan¹ 張線班(工兵); ~ **recorder**, kang¹ ssu¹ lu⁴ yin¹ chi¹ 鋼絲錄音機; ~ **recording**, kang¹ ssu¹ lu⁴ yin¹ 鋼絲錄音.

wireless a. wu² hsien⁴ te¹ 無線的.

wisdom n. chih⁴ hui⁴ 智慧.

wise a. ts'ung¹ ming² te¹ 聰明的.

wish n. yüan⁴ wang⁴ 願望; v. yüan⁴ 願.

wisp n. hsiao³ shu⁴ 小束.

wisteria, wistaria n. tzu³ t'eng² 紫藤.

278

wistful *n.* (*longing*) ssu¹ mu⁴ te¹ 思慕的.

wit *n.* chih⁴ neng² 智能.

witch *n.* nü³ wu¹ 女巫.

witchcraft *n.* wu¹ shu⁴ 巫術.

with *prep.* yü³ 與, t'ung² 同.

withdraw *v.* (*draw back*) ch'e⁴ hui² 撤回, (*go a-way*) ch'e⁴ t'ui⁴ 撤退.

wither *v.* shih³ tiao¹ wei¹ 使凋萎, shih³ k'u¹ kan¹ 使枯乾.

withhold *v.* chih⁴ chih³ 制止.

within *adv.*, *prep.* tsai⁴ nei⁴ 在內.

without *adv.* tsai⁴ wai⁴ pu⁴ 在外部; *prep.* wu² 無.

withstand *v.* fan³ k'ang⁴ 反抗.

witness *n.* (*thing*) cheng⁴ chü⁴ 證據, (*person*) cheng⁴ jen² 證人; *v.* mu⁴ tu³ 目睹.

witticism *n.* hsieh² yü³ 諧語.

witty *a.* shan⁴ hui¹ hsieh² te¹ 善詼諧的.

wizard *n.* nan² wu¹ 男巫.

woe, wo *n.* pei¹ ai¹ 悲哀.

woeful, woful *a.* pei¹ shang¹ te¹ 悲傷的.

wolf *n.* lang² 狼.

woman *n.* fu⁴ jen² 婦人.

womb *n.* tzu³ kung¹ 子宮.

wonder *n.* ch'i² shih⁴ 奇事; *v.* ching¹ ya⁴ 驚訝.

wonderful *a.* ling² jen² ching¹ ch'i² te¹ 令人驚奇的.

wondrous *a.* k'o³ ching¹ te¹ 可驚的. ⌐的

woo *v.* ch'iu² ai⁴ 求愛.

wood *n.* mu⁴ 木, (*forest*) sen¹ lin² 森林.

woodbine *n.* jen³ tung¹ 忍冬(植), she² p'u² t'ao² 蛇葡萄(植).

woodcock *n.* shan¹ yü⁴ 山鷸(鳥). ⌐蛇葡萄(植).

woodcut *n.* mu⁴ k'o⁴ 木刻.

wooden *a.* mu⁴ chih⁴ te¹ 木製的; ~ **bridge,** mu⁴ ch'iao² 木橋.

woodman *n.* ch'iao² fu¹ 樵夫. ⌐ch'iao² 木橋.

woody *a.* to¹ shu⁴ mu⁴ te¹ 多樹木的.

wool *n.* yang² mao² 羊毛; ~ **blanket,** chün¹ t'an³ 軍毯.

woollen *a.* yang² mao² te¹ 羊毛的. ⌐t'an³ 軍毯.

woolly *a.* yang² mao² te¹ 羊毛的.

word *n.* tzu⁴ 字.

work *n.* (*general*) kung¹ tso⁴ 工作, (*field*) tso⁴ yeh⁴ 作業, (*duty*) chih² wu⁴ 職務.

worker *n.* kung¹ jen² 工人.

workman *n.* kung¹ jen² 工人.

workmanship *n.* shou³ i⁴ 手藝.

workshop *n.* kung¹ ch'ang³ 工廠. 「chieh⁴ 世界.

world *n.* (*physical*) ti⁴ ch'iu² 地球, (*abstract*) shih⁴

worldly *a.* hsien⁴ shih⁴ te¹ 現世的.

worm *n.* ch'ung² 蟲.

worm-eaten *a.* ch'ung² chu⁴ te¹ 蟲蛀的.

worry *n.*, *v.* yu¹ lü⁴ 憂慮. 「的.

worse *a.* keng⁴ huai⁴ te¹ 更壞的, pu⁴ hao³ te¹ 不好

worship *n.*, *v.* ch'ung² pai⁴ 崇拜.

worst *a.* tsui⁴ huai⁴ te¹ 最壞的.

worsted *n.* mao² jung² hsien⁴ 毛絨線. 「優點.

worth *a.* chih² te² te¹ 值得的; *n.* (*merit*) yu¹ tien³

worthless *a.* wu² chia⁴ chih² te¹ 無價值的.

worthy *a.* yu³ chia⁴ chih² te¹ 有價值的. 「受傷.

wound *n.* ch'uang¹ shang¹ 創傷; *v.* shou⁴ shang¹

wrangle *n.* cheng¹ lun⁴ 爭論, k'ou³ chiao³ 口角.

wrap *v.* pao¹ tsa¹ 包紮.

wrath *n.* fen⁴ nu⁴ 忿怒.

wrathful *a.* fen⁴ nu⁴ te¹ 忿怒的.

wreath *n.* hua¹ ch'üan¹ 花圈.

wreck *n.*, *v.* p'o⁴ huai⁴ 破壞.

wren *n.* ou¹ chiao¹ 鷗鷦.

wrench *n.* (*tool*) pan¹ ch'ien² 搬鉗.

wrestle *v.* chiao³ li⁴ 角力.

wrestler *n.* chiao³ li⁴ che³ 角力者.

wretch *n.* k'o³ lien² ch'ung² 可憐蟲.

wriggle *v.* wan¹ yen² 蜿蜒.

wring *v.* chiao³ 絞.

wrinkle *n.* chou⁴ wen² 皺紋; *v.* shih³ chou⁴ 使皺.

wrist *n.* wan⁴ li⁴ 腕力.

writ *n.* wen² chien⁴ 文件.

write *v.* hsieh³ 寫.

writer *n.* (*author*) chu⁴ tso⁴ chia¹ 著作家.

writhe *v.* niu² chuan³ 扭轉.

writing *n.* shu¹ hsieh³ 書寫.

wrong *a.* (*bad*) pu² tui⁴ te¹ 不對的, (*improper*) pu²
shih⁴ tang¹ te¹ 不適當的, (*mistaken*) ts'o⁴ wu⁴ te¹
錯誤的; *adv.* ts'o⁴ wu⁴ ti⁴ 錯誤地; *n.* kuo⁴ shih¹
過失; *v.* wu¹ lai⁴ 誣賴.

X

X-axis *n.* heng² chou² 橫軸.

X-coordinate *n.* heng² tso⁴ piao¹ 橫坐標.

xebec *n.* san¹ wei² ch'uan² 三桅船.

X-line *n.* heng² hsien⁴ 橫線.

Xmas *n.* sheng⁴ tan⁴ chieh² 聖誕節.

X-ray *n.* ai⁴ k'o⁴ ssu¹ kuang¹ hsien⁴ 愛克司光線; *v.* chao⁴ ai⁴ k'o⁴ ssu¹ kuang¹ hsien⁴ 照愛克司光線.

xylophone *n.* mu⁴ ch'in² 木琴.

Y

yacht *n.* yu² t'ing³ 遊艇.

yak *n.* li² niu² 犛牛.

yard *n.* t'ing² yüan⁴ 庭院, (*measure*) ma³ 碼.

yardstick *n.* ma³ ch'ih³ 碼尺. 「shih⁴ 故事.

yarn *n.* (*thread*) hsien⁴ 線, sha¹ 紗, (*story*) ku

yawn *v.* ch'ien⁴ shen¹ 欠伸, (*opening*) chang¹ k'ou³ 張口. 「實的.

yea *adv.* (*yes*) shih⁴ 是, (*indeed*) chen¹ shih² te¹ 眞

year *n.* nien² 年, (*age*) sui⁴ 歲.

yearly *adv.* mei³ nien² 每年; *a.* mei³ nien² te¹ 每 「年的.

yearn *v.* k'o³ mu⁴ 渴慕.

yeast *n.* chiao⁴ mu³ 酵母.

yell *v.* hu¹ han³ 呼喊. 「je⁴ ping⁴ 黄熱病.

yellow *a.* huang² se⁴ te¹ 黄色的; ~ **fever,** huang²

yellowish *a.* wei¹ huang² te¹ 微黄的.

yeoman *n.* (*USN*) shih⁴ kuan¹ 士官, (*landlord*) hsiao³ ti⁴ chu³ 小地主, (*attendant*) shih⁴ ts'ung² 「侍從.

yes *adv.* shih⁴ 是, jan² 然.

yesterday *n., a.* tso² jih⁴ 昨日.

yet *adv.* hsiang⁴ 像, jeng² 仍; *conj.* sui¹ 雖, tan⁴ 但, jan² tse² 然則.

yew *n.* tzu³ shan¹ mu⁴ 紫杉木.

yield *v.* (*produce*) ch'an³ sheng¹ 産生, (*grant*) yün² hsü³ 允許, (*give away*) fang⁴ ch'i⁴ 放棄, (*surren-*

der) ch'ü¹ fu² 屈服 ; *n.* (*amount*) ch'an³ e² 產額, (*product*) ch'an² p'in³ 產品.

yoke *n.* (*frame*) niu² e⁴ 牛軛, (*bond*) shu¹ fu² 束縛, (*slavery*) nu² i⁴ 奴役; *v.* chia¹ e⁴ 加軛, (*unite*) ⌊p'ei⁴ ho² 配合.

yolk *n.* tan⁴ huang² 蛋黃.

yonder *a.*, *adv.* tsai⁴ pi³ ch'u⁴ te¹ 在彼處的.

you *pron.* (*sing.*) ni³ 你, (*pl.*) ni³ men² 你們.

young *a.* nien² ch'ing¹ te¹ 年青的, yu⁴ te¹ 幼的; *n.* tzu³ nü³ 子女; ~ **Men's Christian Associa-tion** (**Y.M.C.A.**), chi¹ tu¹ chiao⁴ nan² ch'ing¹ nien² hui⁴ 基督教男青年會; ~ **Pioneers****, shao⁴ nien² erh² t'ung² tui⁴ 少年兒童**; ~ **Van-guard****, shao⁴ nien² hsien¹ feng¹ tui⁴ 少年先鋒隊**; ~ **Women's Christian Association** (**Y.W.C.A.**), chi¹ tu¹ chiao⁴ nü³ ch'ing¹ nien² hui⁴ 基督教女青年會.

youngster *n.* erh² t'ung² 兒童, shao⁴ nien² 少年.

your, yours *pron.* (*sing.*) ni³ te¹ 你的, (*pl.*) ni³ men² te¹ 你們的.

yourself *pron.* ni³ tzu⁴ chi³ 你自己.

youth *n.* shao⁴ nien² shih⁴ tai⁴ 少年時代, ch'ing¹ ch'un¹ 青春; ⌜te¹ 年青的.

youthful *a.* nien² shao³ te¹ 年少的, nien² ch'ing¹

Yule *n.* sheng⁴ tan⁴ chieh² 聖誕節.

Z

zany *n.* (*fool*) yü² jen² 愚人, (*clown*) hsiao² ch'ou³

zeal *n.* je⁴ ch'eng² 熱誠, je⁴ hsin¹ 熱心. ⌊小丑

zealot *n.* je⁴ hsin¹ che³ 熱心者.

zealous *a.* je⁴ hsin¹ te¹ 熱心的.

zebra *n.* pan¹ ma³ 斑馬.

zenith *n.* t'ien¹ ting³ 天頂, ting² tien³ 頂點.

zero *n.* ling² 零; ~ **hour,** kung¹ chi¹ k'ai¹ shih³ shih² k'o⁴ 攻擊開始時刻; ~ **shot,** shih⁴ tan⁴ 試彈; ~**reader,** ling² wei⁴ chih³ shih⁴ ch'i⁴ 零位指示器.

zest *n.* ch'ü⁴ wei⁴ 趣味, (*flavor*) hsiang¹ wei⁴ 香味.

zigzag *n.* chü⁴ ch'ih³ hsing² 鋸齒形.

zinc *n.* hsin¹ 鋅.

zone *n.* ti⁴ ch'ü¹ 地區; **~ of defense,** fang² wei⁴ ti⁴ ch'ü¹ 防衛地區(軍); **~ of action,** chan⁴ tou⁴ ti⁴ ch'ü¹ 戰鬪地區(軍); **~ of dispersion,** san⁴ pu⁴ ch'ü¹ yü⁴ 散佈區域(軍); **~ of fire,** she⁴ chi¹ ch'ü¹ 射擊區(軍); **~ of interior,** nei⁴ ti⁴ ch'ü¹ 內地區(軍).

zoological *a.* tung⁴ wu⁴ hsüeh² te¹ 動物學的.

zoology *n.* tung⁴ wu⁴ hsüeh² 動物學.

zoom *v.* sheng¹ k'ung¹ 昇空, chi² shang⁴ sheng¹ fei¹ hsing² 急上昇飛行(軍).

zymurgy *n.* niang⁴ tsao⁴ ch'ang³ 釀造場.

NUMBERS 數目 shu⁴ mu⁴

Cardinal Numbers 基數 chi¹ shu⁴

1	一	i¹
2	二	erh⁴
3	三	san¹
4	四	ssu⁴
5	五	wu³
6	六	liu⁴
7	七	ch'i¹
8	八	pa¹
9	九	chiu³
10	十	shih²
11	十一	shih² i¹
12	十二	shih² erh⁴
13	十三	shih² san¹
14	十四	shih² ssu⁴
15	十五	shih² wu³
16	十六	shih² liu⁴
17	十七	shih² ch'i¹
18	十八	shih² pa¹
19	十九	shih² chiu³
20	二十	erh⁴ shih²
21	二十一	erh⁴ shih² i¹
26	二十六	erh⁴ shih² liu⁴
30	三十	san¹ shih²
40	四十	ssu⁴ shih²
50	五十	wu³ shih²
60	六十	liu⁴ shih²
70	七十	ch'i¹ shih²
80	八十	pa¹ shih²
90	九十	chiu³ shih²
100	一百	i⁴ pai³
102	一百零二	i⁴ pai³ ling² erh⁴
1,000	一千	i⁴ ch'ien¹ ⌈shih²
1,030	一千零三十	i⁴ ch'ien¹ ling² san¹
1,950	一千九百五十	i⁴ ch'ien¹ chiu³ pai³ wu³ shih²

10,000	一萬	i² wan⁴
100,000	十萬	shih² wan⁴
1,000,000	一百萬	i⁴ pai³ wan⁴
10,000,000	一千萬	i⁴ ch'ien¹ wan⁴
100,000,000	一億 (一萬萬)	i² i⁴ (i² wan⁴ wan⁴)
1,000,000,000	十億 (十萬萬)	shih² i⁴ (shih² wan⁴ wan⁴)

NOTE: *The following are denominators frequently used with numbers:*

張　chang¹　*for chairs, desks, papers*
架　chia⁴　*for beds, machine guns, airplanes*
間　chien¹　*for houses, rooms*
件　chien⁴　*for things, objects*
炷　chu⁴　*for incense*
串　ch'uan⁴　*for pearls*
群　ch'ün²　*for animals*
份　fen⁴　*for money, refreshments, newspapers*
副　fu⁴　*for playing cards, dominoes, mahjong*
根　ken¹　*for cigarettes, matches, sticks, grasses*
個　ko⁴　*for persons, rings, houses, schools*
口　k'ou³　*for water, rice*
管　kuan³　*for pens*
塊　k'uai⁴　*for lands, stones, cakes*
筐　k'uang¹　*for threads*
捆　k'un³　*for firewood*
輛　liang⁴　*for vehicles*
門　men²　*for guns*
把　pa³　*for swords, knives, scissors, fans, locks*
盤　p'an²　*for chess, food*
本　pen³　*for books*
匹　p'i¹　*for asses, donkeys, cloth, horses*
部　pu⁴　*for vehicles, books, machines*
雙　shuang¹　*for chopsticks, shoes*
扇　shan⁴　*for doors*
帖　t'ieh¹　*for medicines*
條　t'iao²　*for cigarettes, handkerchiefs, streets, trousers*
挺　t'ing³　*for machine guns*
座　tso⁴　*for houses, mountains, theaters, cities*
堆　tsui¹　*for things, articles*

285

位 wei⁴ *for friends, teachers, professors, newsmen*

For Example: *If you want to say "a book" in Chinese, you would say " i⁴ pen³ shu¹" (一本書); but if you want to say "a horse," you should say " i⁴ p'i¹ ma³" (一匹馬) instead of " i⁴ pen² ma³." Care must be exercised in using the above denominators before specific objects.*

Ordinal Numbers 序數 hsü⁴ shu⁴

1st	第一	ti⁴ i¹
2nd	第二	ti⁴ erh⁴
3rd	第三	ti⁴ san¹
4th	第四	ti⁴ ssu⁴
5th	第五	ti⁴ wu³
6th	第六	ti⁴ liu⁴
7th	第七	ti⁴ ch'i¹
8th	第八	ti⁴ pa¹
9th	第九	ti⁴ chiu³
10th	第十	ti⁴ shih²
11th	第十一	ti⁴ shih² i¹
12th	第十二	ti⁴ shih² erh⁴
13th	第十三	ti⁴ shih² san¹
14th	第十四	ti⁴ shih² ssu⁴
15th	第十五	ti⁴ shih² wu³
16th	第十六	ti⁴ shih² liu⁴
17th	第十七	ti⁴ shih² ch'i¹
18th	第十八	ti⁴ shih² pa¹
19th	第十九	ti⁴ shih² chiu³
20th	第二十	ti⁴ erh⁴ shih²
21st	第二十一	ti⁴ erh⁴ shih² i¹
22nd	第二十二	ti⁴ erh⁴ shih² erh⁴
30th	第三十	ti⁴ san¹ shih²
40th	第四十	ti⁴ ssu⁴ shih²
50th	第五十	ti⁴ wu³ shih²
60th	第六十	ti⁴ liu⁴ shih²
70th	第七十	ti⁴ ch'i¹ shih²
80th	第八十	ti⁴ pa¹ shih²
90th	第九十	ti⁴ chiu³ shih²
100th	第一百	ti⁴ i⁴ pai³
110th	第一百一十	ti⁴ i⁴ pai³ i⁴ shih²

1,000th	第一千	ti⁴ i⁴ ch'ien¹
1,110th	第一千一百一十	ti⁴ i⁴ ch'ien¹ i⁴ pai³ i⁴ shih²
The last	最後	tsui⁴ hou⁴

Decimals 小數 hsiao³ shu⁴

.3 (*point three*) three-tenths	十分之三	shih² fen¹ chih¹ san¹
.065 (*point zero six five*) *sixty-five thousandths*	千分之六十五	ch'ien¹ fen¹ chih¹ liu⁴ shih² wu³
11.25 (*eleven point two five*) *eleven and twenty-five hundredths*	十一零百分之二十五	shih² i¹ ling² pai³ fen¹ chih¹ erh⁴ shih² wu³

Fractions 分數 fen¹ shu⁴

1/2 (*one-half; a half*)	二分之一；一半	erh⁴ fen¹ chih¹ i¹; i² pan⁴
1/3 (*one-third*)	三分之一	san¹ fen¹ chih¹ i¹
2/3 (*two-thirds*)	三分之二	san¹ fen¹ chih¹ erh⁴
1/4 (*a quarter; one-fourth*)	四分之一	ssu⁴ fen¹ chih¹ i¹
3/4 (*three quarters; three-fourths*)	四分之三	ssu⁴ fen¹ chih¹ san¹
1/10 (*one-tenth*)	十分之一	shih² fen¹ chih¹ i¹
2 7/8 (*two and seven-eighths*)	二又八分之七	erh⁴ yu⁴ pa¹ fen¹ chih¹ ch'i¹

Multiple Numbers 倍數 pei⁴ shu⁴

twofold; double; twice	二倍	erh⁴ pei⁴
threefold; triple; treble	三倍	san¹ pei⁴
fourfold; quadruple	四倍	ssu⁴ pei⁴
fivefold; quintuple	五倍	wu³ pei⁴
sixfold; sextuple	六倍	liu⁴ pei⁴
tenfold	十倍	shih² pei⁴
elevenfold	十一倍	shih² i² pei⁴

287

twentyfold	二十倍	erh⁴ shih² pei⁴	
fiftyfold	五十倍	wu³ shih² pei⁴	
hundredfold; centuple	百倍	pai³ pei⁴	

Percentage 百分率 pai³ fen¹ lü⁴

one per cent	百分之一	pai³ fen¹ chih¹ i¹
eleven per cent	百分之十一	pai³ fen¹ chih¹ shih² i¹
twenty per cent	百分之二十	pai³ fen¹ chih¹ erh⁴ shih²
fifty-one per cent	百分之五十一	pai³ fen¹ chih¹ wu³ shih² i¹
one hundred per pent	百分之百	pai³ fen¹ chih¹ pai³

The Months 月份 yüeh⁴ fen⁴

January	一 月	i² yüeh⁴
February	二 月	erh⁴ yüeh⁴
March	三 月	san¹ yüeh⁴
April	四 月	ssu⁴ yüeh⁴
May	五 月	wu³ yüeh⁴
June	六 月	liu⁴ yüeh⁴
July	七 月	ch'i² yüeh⁴
August	八 月	pa² yüeh⁴
September	九 月	chiu³ yüeh⁴
October	十 月	shih² yüeh⁴
November	十一月	shih² i² yüeh⁴
December	十二月	shih² erh⁴ yüeh⁴

The Four Seasons 四季 ssu⁴ chi⁴

Spring	春	ch'un¹	**Autumn**	秋	ch'iu¹
Summer	夏	hsia⁴	**Winter**	冬	tung¹

The Days of the Week 週日 chou¹ jih⁴

Sunday	星期日	hsing¹ ch'i² jih⁴
	禮拜天	li³ pai⁴ t'ien¹

Monday	星期一	hsing¹ ch'i² i¹
Tuesday	星期二	hsing¹ ch'i² erh⁴
Wednesday	星期三	hsing¹ ch'i² san¹
Thursday	星期四	hsing¹ ch'i² ssu⁴
Friday	星期五	hsing¹ ch'i² wu³
Saturday	星期六	hsing¹ ch'i² liu⁴

Time 時 shih²

A century	一世紀	i² shih⁴ chi⁴
A day	一 天	i⁴ t'ien¹
A fortnight	兩星期	liang³ hsing¹ ch'i²
A month	一個月	i² ko⁴ yüeh⁴
A week	一星期	i⁴ hsing¹ ch'i²
A year	一 年	i⁴ nien²
Afternoon	午 後	wu³ hou⁴
Day	日	jih⁴
Day after tomorrow	後 日	hou⁴ jih⁴
Day before yesterday	前 日	ch'ien² jih⁴
Daybreak	黎 明	li² ming²
Dusk	黃 昏	huang² hun¹
Evening	夕	hsi¹
Forenoon	午 前	wu³ ch'ien²
Last month	上 月	shang⁴ yüeh⁴
Last Year	去 年	ch'ü⁴ nien²
Morning	早 晨	tsao³ ch'en²
Next month	下 月	hsia⁴ yüeh⁴
Next week	下星期	hsia⁴ hsing¹ ch'i²
Night	夜	yeh⁴
Noon	中 午	chung¹ wu³
Today	今 日	chin¹ jih⁴
Tomorrow	明 日	ming² jih⁴
Week	星 期	hsing¹ ch'i²
Year	年	nien²
Yesterday	昨 日	tso² jih⁴

Chinese Years

Chinese years are named from the founding

289

of the Republic of China by Dr. Sun Yat-sen.
The chart below will indicate the names of the
years from 1912 on.

中華民國元年
(chung¹ hua² min² kuo² yüan² nien²)
1st year of the Republic of China   **1912**

中華民國五年
(chung¹ hua² min² kuo² wu³ nien²)
5th year of the Republic of China   **1916**

中華民國十年
(chung¹ hua² min² kuo² shih² nien²)
10th year of the Republic of China   **1921**

中華民國十五年
(chung¹ hua² min² kuo² shih² wu³ nien²)
15th year of the Republic of China   **1926**

中華民國二十年
(chung¹ hua² min² kuo² erh⁴ shih² nien²)
20th year of the Republic of China   **1931**

中華民國二十五年
(chung¹ hua² min² kuo² erh⁴ shih² wu³ nien²)
25th year of the Republic of China   **1936**

中華民國三十年
(chung¹ hua² min² kuo² san¹ shih² nien²)
30th year of the Republic of China   **1941**

中華民國三十五年
(chung¹ hua² min² kuo² san¹ shih² wu³ nien²)
35th year of the Republic of China   **1946**

中華民國四十年
(chung¹ hua² min² kuo² ssu⁴ shih² nien²)
40th year of the Republic of China   **1951**

WEIGHTS 重量 chung⁴ liang⁴

Old Standard

10 分 (fen¹)=1 錢 (ch'ien²)=*mace*
10 錢 (ch'ien²)=1 兩 (liang³)=*tael=37.8 grams*
16 兩 (liang³)=1 斤 (chin¹)=*catty=604.79 grams*

100 斤 (chin^{1})=1 擔 (tan^{4})=*picul=60.479 kilos*
=133.33 pounds

Market Standard

10 市分 (shih^{4} fen^{1}) =1 市錢 (shih^{4} ch'ien^{2})
10 市錢 (shih^{4} ch'ien^{2})=1 市兩 (shih^{4} liang^{3})
=31.25 grams
16 市兩 (shih^{4} liang^{3}) =1 市斤 (shih^{4} chin^{1})
=500 grams
100 市斤 (shih^{4} chin^{1}) =1 市擔 (shih^{4} tan^{4})
=50 kilograms
=1/2 市引 (shih^{4} yin^{3})=*110.23 pounds*

Metric System

兞=公絲 (kung^{1} ssu^{1}) =*milligram*
兣=公毫 (kung^{1} hao^{2}) =*centigram*
兝=公厘 (kung^{1} li^{2}) =*decigram*
克=公分 (kung^{1} fen^{1}) =*gram*
兙=公錢 (kung^{1} ch'ien^{2})=*decagram*
兡=公兩 (kung^{1} liang^{3}) =*hectogram*
兛=公斤 (kung^{1} chin^{1}) =*kilogram*
公噸 (kung^{1} tun^{4}) =*metric ton*

LENGTH 長度 ch'ang^{2} tu^{4}

Old Standard

10 分 (fen^{1}) =1 寸 (ts'un^{4})
10 寸 (ts'un^{4}) =1 尺 (ch'ih^{3}) =*14.1 inches*
10 尺 (ch'ih^{3}) =1 丈 (chang^{4})=*11.75 feet*
180 丈 (chang^{4})=1 里 (li^{3}) =*about 1/3 mile*

Market Standard

10 市分 (shih^{4} fen^{1}) =1 市寸 (shih^{4} ts'un^{4})
10 市寸 (shih^{4} ts'un^{4}) =1 市尺 (shih^{4} ch'ih^{3})
=0.333 meter

10 市尺 (shih⁴ ch'ih³) =1 市丈 (shih⁴ chang⁴)
150 市丈 (shih⁴ chang⁴)=1 市里 (shih⁴ li³)
=*500 meters*
=*0.31 mile*

Metric System

耗=公厘 (kung¹ li²)　　　=*millimeter*
粩=公分 (kung¹ fen¹)　　=*centimeter*
粉=公寸 (kung¹ ts'un⁴)　=*decimeter*
粃=公尺 (kung¹ ch'ih³)　=*meter*
粐=公丈 (kung¹ chang⁴)=*decameter*
粨=公引 (kung¹ yin³)　　=*hectometer*
粁=公里 (kung¹ li³)　　　=*kilometer*

VOLUME 體積 t'i³ chi¹

Old Standard

10 合 (ho²)　　=1 升 (sheng¹)=*1.09 liquid quarts*
=*1.035 liters*

10 升 (sheng¹)=1 斗 (tou³)
5 斗 (tou³)　=1 斛 (hu²)
2 斛 (hu²)　=1 石 (shih²)

Market Standard

10 市合 (shih⁴ ho²)　　=1 市升 (shih⁴ sheng¹)
=*1 liter*
10 市升 (shih⁴ sheng¹)=1 市斗 (shih⁴ tou³)
10 市斗 (shih⁴ tou³)　=1 市石 (shih⁴ shih²)

Metric System

籶=公合 (kung¹ ho²)　　=1 deciliter
籸=公升 (kung¹ sheng¹)=1 liter=*1 cubic decimeter*
籿=公斗 (kung¹ tou³)　=1 decaliter
䉻=公石 (kung¹ shih²)　=1 hectoliter
粞=公秉 (kung¹ ping³)　=1 kiloliter=*1 cubic meter*
=*1 stere*

AREA 面積 mien⁴ chi¹

Old Standard

100 方寸 (fang¹ ts'un⁴) =1 方尺 (fang¹ ch'ih³)
100 方尺 (fang¹ ch'ih³) =1 方丈 (fang¹ chang⁴)
60 方丈 (fang¹ chang⁴)=1 畝 (mu³)=0.1666 acre
100 畝 (mu³)=1 頃 (ch'ing³)
540 畝 (mu³)=1 方里 (fang¹ li³)

Market Standard

10 市毫 (shih⁴ hao²)=1 市厘 (shih⁴ li²)
10 市厘 (shih⁴ li²) =1 市分 (shih⁴ fen¹)
10 市分 (shih⁴ fen¹) =1 市畝 (shih⁴ mu³)
                    =0.1647 acre
100 市畝 (shih⁴ mu³)=1 市頃 (chih⁴ ch'ing³)
                    =16.47 acres

Metric System

勠=公分 (kung¹ fen¹)   =deciare
安=公畝 (kung¹ mu³)   =are=100 square meters
頛=公頃 (kung¹ ch'ing³)=hectare

CURRENCIES 貨幣 hou⁴ pi⁴

The money used in Nationalist China is called New Taiwan Currency (新臺幣 hsin¹ t'ai² pi⁴) (hereafter abbreviated NT) which consists of the Chinese dollar (圓 yüan²) and the dime (角 chiao³). The basic unit is the Chinese dollar, which equals ten dimes. They are divided into six denominations: ten Chinese dollars (拾圓 shih² yüan²), five Chinese dollars (伍圓 wu³ yüan²), one Chinese dollar (壹圓 i⁴ yüan²), five dimes (伍角 wu³ chiao³), two dimes (貳角 erh⁴ chiao³), and one dime (壹角 i²

chiao³). *As of the time of writing the official foreign exchange rates are as follows:**

American Foreign Exchange:

	1 US$	=NT$	15.55
Pound Sterling:	1 US£	=NT$	43.54
Hongkong Currency:	1 HK$	=NT$	2.72
Malayan Currency:	1 SS$	=NT$	5.08
Burmese Currency:	1 Kyat	=NT$	1.81
Philippines Currency:	1 Peso	=NT$	6.64
Vietnam Currency:	1 Yüan	=NT$	0.19
Siamese Currency:	1 Baht	=NT$	0.74

* *Source: Central Daily News.*

FAMILY RELATIONS

grandparent
  (*parent of one's father*)   tsu³ fu⁴ mu³   祖 父 母
  (*parent of one's mother*)
                  wai⁴ tsu³ fu⁴ mu³   外祖父母
grandfather, grandpa
  (*father of one's father*)   tsu³ fu⁴   祖   父
  (*father of one's mother*) wai⁴ tsu³ fu⁴   外 祖 父
grandmother, grandma
  (*mother of one's father*)   tsu² mu³   祖   母
  (*mother of one's mother*) wai⁴ tsu² mu³   外 祖 母
granduncle, great-uncle
  (*husband of the sister of one's father's father*)
                  ku¹ tsu³   姑   祖
  (*older brother of one's father's father*)
                  po² tsu³   伯   祖
  (*younger brother of one's father's father*)
                  shu² tsu³   叔   祖
  (*husband of the sister of one's mother's mother*)
                  i² kung¹   姨   公
  (*brother of one's mother's mother*)
                  chiu⁴ kung¹   舅   公
grandaunt, great-aunt
  (*sister of one's father's father*) ku¹ p'o²   姑   婆

(wife of the older brother of one's father's father)	po² tsu² mu³	伯祖	母
(wife of the younger brother of one's father's father)	shu² tsu² mu³	叔祖	母
(sister of one's mother's mother)	i² p'o²	姨	婆
(wife of the brother of one's mother's mother)	chiu⁴ p'o²	舅	婆
father	fu⁴ ch'in¹	父	親
stepfather	chi⁴ fu⁴	繼	父
father-in-law			
(father of one's husband)	kung¹ kung¹	公	公
(father of one's wife)	yüeh⁴ fu⁴	岳	父
mother	mu³ ch'in¹	母	親
stepmother	chi⁴ mu³	繼	母
mother-in-law			
(mother of one's husband)	p'o² p'o²	婆	婆
(mother of one's wife)	yüeh⁴ mu³	岳	母
uncle			
(older brother of one's father)	po² fu⁴	伯	父
(younger brother of one's father)	shu² fu⁴	叔	父
(brother of one's mother)	chiu⁴ fu⁴	舅	父
(husband of the sister of one's father)	ku¹ fu⁴	姑	父
(husband of the sister of one's mother)	i² fu⁴	姨	父
aunt			
(wife of the older brother of one's father)	po² mu³	伯	母
(wife of the younger brother of one's father)	shu² mu³	叔	母
(wife of the brother of one's mother)	chiu⁴ mu³	舅	母
(sister of one's father)	ku¹ mu³	姑	母
(sister of one's mother)	i² mu³	姨	母
son	erh² tzu³	兒	子
daughter-in-law	hsi¹ fu⁴	媳	婦
daughter	nü³ erh²	女	兒
son-in-law	nü³ hsü⁴	女	婿

Family Relations

stepchild	chi⁴ erh² nü³	繼兒女
stepson	chi⁴ tzu³	繼子
stepdaughter	chi⁴ nü³	繼女
brother	hsiung¹ ti⁴	兄弟
(older brother)	hsiung¹	兄
(younger brother)	ti⁴	弟
stepbrother	i⁴ fu⁴ (mu³) hsiung¹ ti⁴	異父(母)兄弟
brother-in-law		
(older brother of one's husband) ta⁴ po²		大　伯
(younger brother of one's husband)		
	hsiao³ shu²	小　叔
(older brother of one's wife)		
	nei⁴ hsiung¹	內　兄
(younger brother of one's wife) nei⁴ ti⁴		內　弟
(husband of one's older sister)		
	chieh³ fu¹	姊　夫
(husband of one's younger brother)		
	mei⁴ fu¹	妹　夫
(husband of the older sister of one's wife)		
	chin¹ hsiung¹	襟　兄
(husband of the younger sister of one's wife)		
	chin¹ ti⁴	襟　弟
(husband of the older sister of one's husband)		
	chieh³ fu¹	姊　夫
(husband of the younger sister of one's husband)		
	mei⁴ fu¹	妹　夫
sister	chieh³ mei⁴	姊　妹
(older sister)	chieh³	姐
(younger sister)	mei⁴	妹
stepsister	i⁴ fu⁴ (mu³) chieh³ mei⁴	異父(母)姊妹
sister-in-law		
(wife of the older brother of one's husband)		
	sao² sao³	嫂　嫂
(wife of the younger brother of one's husband)		
	ti⁴ mei⁴	弟妹
(wife of the older brother of one's wife)		
	ta⁴ chiu⁴ sao³	大舅嫂
(wife of the younger brother of one's wife)		
	hsiao³ chiu⁴ sao³	小舅嫂
(wife of one's older brother) sao² sao³		嫂　嫂

(*wife of one's younger brother*) ti⁴ mei⁴	弟	妹
(*older sister of one's wife*) ta⁴ i²	大	姨
(*younger sister of one's wife*) hsiao³ i²	小	姨
(*older sister of one's husband*) ta⁴ ku¹	大	姑
(*younger sister of one's husband*)		
hsiao³ ku¹	小	姑

cousin

(*older son of one's father's brother*)		
t'ang² hsiung¹	堂	兄
(*younger son of one's father's brother*)		
t'ang² ti⁴	堂	弟
(*older son of one's mother's brother*)		
chiu⁴ piao³ hsiung¹	舅表兄	
(*younger son of one's mother's brother*)		
chiu⁴ piao³ ti⁴	舅表弟	
(*older son of one's father's sister*)		
ku¹ piao³ hsiung¹	姑表兄	
(*younger son of one's father's sister*)		
ku¹ piao³ ti⁴	姑表弟	
(*older son of one's mother's sister*)		
i² piao³ hsiung¹	姨表兄	
(*younger son of one's mother's sister*)		
i² piao³ ti⁴	姨表弟	
(*older daughter of one's father's brother*)		
t'ang² chieh³	堂	姐
(*younger daughter of one's father's brother*)		
t'ang² mei⁴	堂	妹
(*older daughter of one's mother's brother*)		
chiu⁴ piao² chieh³	舅表姐	
(*younger daughter of one's mother's brother*)		
chiu⁴ piao³ mei⁴	舅表妹	
(*older daughter of one's father's sister*)		
ku¹ piao³ chieh³	姑表姐	
(*younger daughter of one's father's sister*)		
ku¹ piao³ mei⁴	姑表妹	
(*older daughter of one's mother's sister*)		
i² piao² chieh³	姨表姐	
(*younger daughter of one's mother's sister*)		
i² piao³ mei⁴	姨表妹	

nephew

(*son of one's brother*) chih² erh²	侄	兒

(*son of one's sister*)	wai⁴ sheng¹	外		甥
(*son of one's husband's brother*)				
	chih² erh²	侄		兒
(*son of one's wife's brother*)	nei⁴ chih²	內		侄
(*son of one's wife's sister*)	wai⁴ sheng¹	外		甥
(*son of one's husband's sister*)				
	wai⁴ sheng¹	外		甥

niece

(*daughter of one's brother*)	chih² nü³	侄	女
(*daughter of one's sister*)			
	wai⁴ sheng¹ nü³	外 甥 女	
(*daughter of one's husband's brother*)			
	chih² nü³	侄	女
(*daughter of one's wife's brother*)			
	nei⁴ chih² nü³	內 侄 女	
(*daughter of one's wife's sister*)			
	wai⁴ sheng¹ nü³	外 甥 女	
(*daughter of one's husband's sister*)			
	wai⁴ sheng¹ nü³	外 甥 女	

grandchild

(*child of one's son*)	sun¹ erh² nü³	孫 兒 女
(*child of one's daughter*)		
	wai⁴ sun¹ erh² nü³	外孫兒女

grandson

(*son of one's son*)	sun¹ tzu³	孫	子
(*son of one's daughter*)	wai⁴ sun¹	外	孫

granddaughter

(*daughter of one's son*)	sun¹ nü³	孫	女
(*daughter of one's daughter*)			
	wai⁴ sun¹ nü³	外 孫 女	

grandnephew

(*son of one's brother's son or daughter*)			
	chih² sun¹	侄	孫
(*son of one's sister's son or daughter*)			
	wai⁴ sun¹	外	孫
(*son of one's husband's brother's son or daugh-ter*)	chih² sun¹ erh²	侄 孫 兒	
(*son of one's wife's brother's son or daughter*)			
	nei⁴ chih² sun¹	內 侄 孫	
(*son of one's wife's sister's son or daughter*)			

298

wai⁴ sun¹ 外　孫

(*son of one's husband's sister's son or daughter*)

wai⁴ sun¹ 外　孫

grandniece

(*daughter of one's brother's son or daughter*)

chih² sun¹ nü³ 侄孫女

(*daughter of one's sister's son or daughter*)

wai⁴ sun¹ nü³ 外孫女

(*daughter of one's wife's brother's son or daughter*) nei⁴ chih² sun¹ nü³ 內侄孫女

(*daughter of one's husband's brother's son or
daughter*) wai⁴ sun¹ nü³ 外孫女

(*daughter of one's wife's sister's son or daughter*) wai⁴ sun¹ nü³ 外孫女

(*daughter of one's husband's sister's son or
daughter*) wai⁴ sun¹ nü⁴ 外孫女

IMPORTANT GEOGRAPHICAL
NAMES OF CHINA

Anhwei 安 徽

| Anching | 安 慶 | Hofei | 合 肥 |
| Wuhu | 蕪 湖 | | |

Antung 安 東

| Autung | 安 東 | Hailung | 海 龍 |
| Tunghua | 通 化 | | |

Chahar 察哈爾

Changchiakou	張家口	Hsuanhua	宣 化
(Kalgan)		Pangchiang	滂 江
Tolun	多 倫	Yuhsien	蔚 縣

Chekiang 浙 江

Chiahsing	嘉 興	Chinhua	金 華
Hangchou	杭 州	Ningpo	寧 波
Shaohsing	紹 興	Wenchou	溫 州

Geographical Names of China

Fukien 福 建

Changchou	漳 州	Changting	長 汀	
Chinmen	金 門	Chuanchou	泉 州	
Fuchou	福 州	Hsiamen	厦 門	
Yungan	永 安	(Amoy)		

Heilungkiang 黑龍江

Aihun	瑗 琿	Moho	漠 河	
Nencheng	嫩 城	Peian	北 安	

Hochiang 合 江

Chiamussu	佳木斯	Fuyuan	撫 遠	
Ilan	依 蘭	Mishan	密 山	
Tungchiang	同 江			

Honan 河 南

Anyang	安 陽	Chengchou	鄭 州	
Hsinhsiang	新 鄉	Hsinyang	信 陽	
Hsuchang	許 昌	Kaifeng	開 封	
Loyang	洛 陽	Nanyang	南 陽	
Shangchiu	商 邱			

Hopeh 河 北

Paoting	保 定	Peiping	北 平	
Shihchiachuang	石家莊			
Tangshan	唐 山	Tientsin	天 津	

Hunan 湖 南

Changsha	長 沙	Changte	常 德	
Chihchiang	芷 江	Hengyang	衡 陽	
Hsiangtan	湘 潭	Shaoyang	邵 陽	

Hupeh 湖 北

Hankow	漢 口	Ichang	宜 昌	
Shashih	沙 市	Wuchang	武 昌	

Hsingan 興 安

Hailar	海拉爾	Lupin	臚 濱	
Solun	索 倫	(Manchouli)		
Shihwei	室 韋			

Johol 熱 河

Chaoyang	朝 陽	Chengte	承 德	
Chihfeng	赤 峯	Fuhsin	阜 新	
Lingyuan	凌 源	Pingchuan	平 泉	
Weichang	圍 場			

Kansu 甘 肅
  Chiayukuan   嘉峪關   Lanchou   蘭 州

Kiangsi 江 西
  Chian   吉 安   Chingtechen   景德鎮
  Chiuchang   九 江   Kanchou   贛 州
  Nanchang   南 昌

Kiangsu 江 蘇
  Hsuchou   徐 州   Nanking   南 京
  Nantung   南 通   Pukou   浦 口
  Suchou   蘇 州   Shanghai   上 海
  Wuhsi   無 錫

Kirin 吉 林
  Changchun   長 春   Fuyu   扶 餘
  Kirin   吉 林   Tunhua   敦 化

Kwangsi 廣 西
  Kueilin   桂 林   Liuchou   柳 州
  Nanning   南 寧   Pose   百 色
  Wuchou   梧 州

Kwangtung 廣 東
  Aomen   澳 門   Chanchiang   湛 江
  (Macao)   Chaochou   潮 州
  Hainan Is.   海 南   Hsiangkang   香 港
  Kowloon   九 龍   (Hongkong)
  Shantou   汕 頭   Shaokuan   韶 關
  (Swatow)   Taishan   臺 山

Kweichow 貴 州
  Kueiyang   貴 陽

Liaoning 遼 寧
  Anshan   鞍 山   Chinchou   錦 州
  Fushun   撫 順   Liaoyang   遼 陽
  Lushun   旅 順   Penhsi   本 溪
  (Port Arthur)   Mukden   瀋 陽
  Dairen   大 連   Yingkou   營 口

Liaopei 遼 北
  Liaoyuan   遼 源   Ssuping   四 平
  Taonan   洮 南   Tungchiangkou
  Tungliao   通 遼   通江口

Nenchiang 嫩 江
  Anganghsi   昂昂溪   Hulan   呼 蘭
  Chichihaerh (Tsitsihar)   齊齊哈爾

Geographical Names of China

Ningsia 寧夏
  Yinchuan   銀川

Sikang 西康
  Yaan   雅安

Sinkiang 新疆
  Tihua   迪化

Suiyuan 綏遠
  Kueisui   歸綏   Paotou   包頭

Sungchiang 松江
  Haerhpin   哈爾濱   Hunchun   琿春
  (Harbin)   Mutanchiang   牡丹江
  Tumen   圖們   Yenchi   延吉

Shansi 山西
  Taiyuan   太源   Tatung   大同

Shantung 山東
  Tsinan   濟南   Tsingtao   青島
  Yentai   烟臺

Shensi 陝西
  Hsian   西安   Hsienyang   咸陽
  Nancheng   南鄭

Szechwan 四川
  Chengtu   成都   Chungking   重慶
  Ipin   宜賓   Kuangyuan   廣元
  Kuanhsien   灌縣   Loshan   樂山
  Tzukung   自貢   Wanhsien   萬縣

Taiwan 臺灣
  Changhua   彰化   Chiai   嘉義
  Hualien   花蓮   Hsinchu   新竹
  Ilan   宜蘭   Kaohsiung   高雄
  Keelung   基隆   Miaoli   苗栗
  Penghu   澎湖   Pingtung   屏東
  Taichung   臺中   Tainan   臺南
  Taipei   臺北   Taitung   臺東
  Taoyuan   桃源   Yuanlin   員林

Tibet (Sitsang) 西藏
  Jihkotse   日喀則   Lasa   拉薩

Tsinghai 青海
  Hsinling   西寧

Yunnan 雲南
  Kochiu   箇舊   Kunming   昆明

IMPORTANT GEOGRAPHICAL NAMES OF THE WORLD

A

Afghanistan 阿富汗
    Kabul 喀布爾
Albania 阿爾巴尼亞
    Tirana 地拉那
Argentina 阿根廷
    Buenos Aires 布宜諾斯·艾利斯
Australia 澳大利亞
    Canberra 塔培拉   Sydney 雪梨
Austria 奧地利
    Vienna 維也納

B

Belgium 比利時
    Brussels 布魯塞爾
Bolivia 玻利維亞
    La Paz 拉巴斯   Sucre 蘇克列
Brazil 巴西
    Rio de Janeiro 里約熱內盧
    Sao Paulo 聖保羅
Bulgaria 保加利亞
    Sofia 索非亞
Burma 緬甸
    Rangoon 仰光

C

Cambodia 高棉
    Pnompenh 百囍奔
Canada 加拿大
    Ottawa 渥太瓦
Ceylon 錫蘭
    Colombo 科倫波
Chile 智利
    Santiago 聖地牙哥

Colombia 哥倫比亞
    Bogota 波哥大
Costa Rica 哥斯達黎加
    San Jose 聖約瑟
Cuba 古巴
    Havana 哈瓦那
Czechoslovakia 捷克斯洛伐克
    Prague 布拉格

D

Denmark 丹麥
    Copenhagen 哥本哈根
Dominican Republic 多明尼加
    Santo Domingo 聖多明谷

E

Ecuador 厄瓜多爾
    Quito 基多
Egypt 埃及
    Alexandria 亞里山大港   Cairo 開羅
El Salvador 薩爾瓦多
    San Salvador 聖薩爾瓦多
Ethiopia (Abyssinia) 愛西屋皮亞(阿比西尼亞)
    Addis Ababa 亞的斯亞貝巴

F

Finland 芬蘭
    Helsinki 赫爾辛基
France 法國
    Lyons 里昂   Marseilles 馬賽
    Paris 巴黎   Riviera 里維耶拉
    Versailles 凡爾塞

G

Germany 德國
    Berlin 柏林   Hamburg 漢堡
Greece 希臘
    Athens 雅典
Guatemala 危地馬拉
    Guatemala 危地馬拉

H

Haiti 海地
   Port-au-Prince　太子港
Honduras 洪都拉斯
   Tegucigalpa　特古西哥爾波

I

Iceland 氷島
   Reykjavik　雷克雅未克
India, Union of 印度
   Bombay　孟曼　　　　Calcutta　加爾各答
   New Delhi　新德里
Indonesia, Republic of 印度尼西亞
   Jakarta　雅加達
Iran 伊朗
   Teheran　德黑蘭
Iraq, Irak 伊拉克
   Bagdad　巴格達
Ireland, Republic of 愛爾蘭
   Dublin　都柏林
Israel 以色列
   Tel Aviv　臺拉維夫
Italy 意大利
   Florence　佛羅稜斯　　Genoa　熱那亞
   Milan　米蘭　　　　　Naples　那不勒斯
   Rome　羅馬　　　　　Venice　威尼斯

J

Japan, Nippon 日本
   Hiroshima　廣島　　　Hokkaido　北海道
   Kobe　神戶　　　　　Kyoto　京都
   Nagasaki　長崎　　　　Nagoya　名古屋
   Osaka　大阪　　　　　Sasebo　佐世保
   Tokyo　東京　　　　　Yokohama　橫濱
   Yokosuka　橫須賀　　　Okinawa　沖繩島

K

Korea, Chosen 韓國
   Cheju Island　濟州島　　Inchon　仁川
   Kaesong　開城　　　　Koje Island　巨濟島

Munsan 汶山	Munsanni 汶山里
Panmunjon 板門店	Pusan 釜山
Pyongyang 平壤	Seoul 漢城
Taegu 大邱	

L

Laos 老撾
  Luang Prabang 郎勃
Lebanon 犁巴嫩
  Beirut 貝魯特
Liberia 利比里亞
  Monrovia 蒙羅維亞
Luxemburg 盧森堡
  Luxemburg 盧森堡

M

Mexico 墨西哥
  Mexico 墨西哥
Mongolia 蒙古
  Ulan Bator 烏蘭巴托

N

Nepal 尼泊爾
  Katmandu 加德滿都
Netherlands (Holland) 荷蘭
  The Hague 海牙
Newfoundland 紐芬蘭
  Saint John's 聖約翰
New Zealand 新西蘭
  Wellington 惠靈頓
Nicaragua 尼加拉瓜
  Managua 馬那瓜
Norway 挪威
  Oslo 奧斯陸

P

Pakistan 巴基斯坦
  Karachi 喀喇蚩
Panama 巴拿馬
  Panama 巴拿馬

Paraguay 巴拉圭
   Asuncion 亞松森

Peru 秘魯
   Lima 利馬

Philippine Islands, Philippines 菲律賓
   Baguio 碧瑤   Manila 馬尼剌

Poland 波蘭
   Warsaw 華沙

Portugal 葡萄牙
   Lisbon 里斯本

R

Romania 羅馬尼亞
   Bucharest 布加勒斯特

S

San Marino 聖馬力諾
   San Marino 聖馬力諾

Saudi Arabia 沙特阿拉伯
   Mecca 麥加   Riyadh 利雅得

Spain 西班牙
   Gibraltar 直布羅陀   Madrid 馬德里

Sweden 瑞典
   Stockholm 斯德可爾摩

Switzerland 瑞士
   Bern 伯爾尼   Geneva 日內瓦

Syria 叙利亞
   Damascus 大馬士革

T

Thailand (Siam) 泰國 (邏羅)
   Bangkok 曼谷

Transjordan 外約但
   Amman 安曼

Turkey 土耳其
   Ankara 安哥拉

U

Ukraine 烏克蘭
   Kharkov 哈科夫

World Geographical Names

Union of South Africa　南非聯邦

    Cape Town　開普敦　　Pretoria　比勒陀利亞

Union of Soviet Socialist Republics　蘇聯
(Russia, the Soviet Union)

    Moscow　莫斯科

United Kingdom　英國

    Cambridge　劍橋　　　London　倫敦
    Oxford　牛津

United States, United States of America　美國

    Alabama　亞拉巴麻　　Alaska　阿拉斯加
    　　　　　　　　　　　Juneau　哲尼亞
    Arizona　亞利桑那　　Arkansas　阿肯色
    California　加利福尼亞
    　Hollywood　好萊塢
    　Los Angeles　洛山磯
    　San Francisco　舊金山
    Colorado　可羅拉多　　Connecticut　康涅狄格
    Delaware　特拉華　　　District of Columbia
    Florida　佛羅里達　　　　　　哥命比亞特區
    Georgia　喬治亞　　　Guam　颽島
    Hawaii　夏威夷
    　Honolulu　檀香山 (火諾魯魯)
    　Pearl Harbor　珍珠港
    Idaho　愛達河　　　　Illinois　伊利諾斯
    Indiana　印第安那　　　Chicago　芝加哥
    Iowa　伊阿華　　　　Kansas　堪薩斯
    Kentucky　墾塔啓　　　Louisiana　路易斯安那
    Maine　緬因　　　　　Maryland　馬里蘭
    Massachusetts　馬臨諸塞　Michigan　密執安
    　Boston　波士頓　　　Detroit　低特律
    　　　　　　　　　　　Minnesota　明尼蘇達
    Mississippi　密士失比　Missouri　瓷蘇里
    Montana　蒙大拿　　　Nebraska　內布拉斯加
    Nevada　內華達　　　　New Hampshire
    New Jersey　紐折爾西　　　　　　紐字什爾
    New Mexico　新墨西哥　New York　紐約
    North Carolina　　　　North Dakota　北達科他
    　　　　北卡羅來納　　Ohio　俄亥俄
    Oklahoma　俄克拉何馬　Oregon　俄勒岡

Pennsylvania　Rhode Island　羅得島
　　　賓夕法尼亞　South Carolina
South Dakota　南達科他　　　　　南卡羅來納
Tennessee　田納西　Texas　塔薩斯
Utah　烏臺　Vermont　洼滿的
Virginia　味吉尼亞　Washington　華盛頓
West Virginia　　　Seattle　西雅圖
　　　西味吉尼亞　Wisconsin　威斯康星
Wyoming　歪窩民

Uruguay　烏拉圭
　Montevideo　蒙得維的亞

V

Vatican　教庭
Venezuela　委內瑞拉
　Caracas　加拉加斯
Vietnam　越南
　Hanoi　河內

W

White Russia　白俄羅斯
　Minsk　明斯克

Y

Yemen　也門
　Sana　沙那
Yugoslavia　南斯拉夫
　Belgrade　貝爾格萊德

A LIST OF COMMON CHINESE FOODS

冷盤類　Cold Dishes

1.　椒　麻　鷄　chiao^1 ma^2 chi^1
　　　　　Pepper Chicken
2.　冷　火　腿　leng^3 huo^2 t'ui^3
　　　　　Chinese Ham

309

3. 冷 蘆 筍　　leng³ lu⁴ sun³
Cold Asparagus

4. 冷 鮑 魚　　leng³ pao¹ yü²
Cold Abalone

5. 滷 猪 肝　　lu³ chu¹ kan¹
Spiced Pig's Liver

6. 滷 猪 舌　　lu³ chu¹ she²
Spiced Pig's Tongue

7. 滷 猪 肚　　lu³ chu¹ tu³
Spiced Pig's Tripe

8. 滷 牛 肉　　lu³ niu² jou⁴
Spiced Beef

9. 白 切 鷄　　pai² ch'ieh¹ chi¹
Cold Chicken

10. 棒 棒 鷄　　pang⁴ pang⁴ chi¹
Shredded Chicken w/Pepper Sauce

11. 皮　　蛋　　p'i² tan⁴
Preserved Eggs

12. 十 景 冷 盤　shih² ching² leng³ p'an²
Assorted Cold Dish

魚翅及海參類
Shark's Fins and *Beche-de-mer*

1. 鷄 翅 海 參　chi¹ ch'ih⁴ hai³ shen¹
Beche-de-mer w/Chicken Wings

2. 鷄 羢 海 參　chi¹ jung² hai³ shen¹
Beche-de-mer w/Chicken Cream

3. 鷄 羢 魚 翅　chi¹ jung² yü² ch'ih⁴
Shark's Fins w/Chicken Cream

4. 清 湯 海 參　ch'ing¹ t'ang¹ hai³ shen¹
Beche-de-mer w/Chicken Soup

5. 紅 燒 海 參　hung² shao¹ hai³ shen¹
Beche-de-mer w/Brown Sauce

6. 紅 燒 魚 翅　hung² shao¹ yü² ch'ih⁴
Shark's Fins w/Brown Sauce

7. 三 絲 魚 翅　san¹ ssu¹ yü² ch'ih⁴
Shark's Fins w/ Mushrooms, Bamboo Shoots, and Shredded Chicken

8. 酸 辣 海 參　suan¹ la⁴ hai³ shen¹

Beche-de-mer w/Sour and Chili Sauce

鮑魚類　Abalone

1. 鷄片鮑魚　chi¹ p'ien⁴ pao¹ yü²
   Abalone w/Sliced Chicken
2. 紅燒鮑魚　hung² shao¹ pao¹ yü²
   Fresh Abalone w/Brown Sauce
3. 紅燒酥鮑　hung² shao¹ su¹ pao¹
   Abalone w/Brown Sauce
4. 口蘑鮮鮑　k'ou³ mo² hsien¹ pao¹
   Fresh Abalone w/Mushrooms
5. 口蘑酥鮑　k'ou³ mo² su¹ pao¹
   Abalone w/Mushrooms
6. 麻醬鮮鮑　ma² chiang⁴ hsien¹ pao¹
   Fresh Abalone w/Sesame Sauce
7. 酸辣鮑魚　suan¹ la⁴ pao¹ yü²
   Abalone w/Sour and Chili Sauce

鷄類　Chicken

1. 紙包鷄　chih³ pao¹ chi¹
   Chicken Wrapped in Paper
2. 炒鷄鬧　ch'ao³ chi¹ nao⁴
   Fried Chicken Cream
3. 炒鷄絲　ch'ao³ chi¹ ssu¹
   Fried Shredded Chicken
4. 炒鴨片　ch'ao³ ya¹ p'ien⁴
   Fried Duck Pieces w/ Vegetable
5. 粉蒸鷄　fen³ cheng¹ chi¹
   Steamed Chicken Wrapped in Flour
6. 香酥鴨子　hsiang¹ su¹ ya¹ tzu¹
   Fried Duck
7. 掛爐鴨子　kua⁴ lu² ya¹ tzu¹
   Barbecued Duck
8. 辣子鷄丁　la⁴ tzu¹ chi¹ ting¹
   Diced Chicken w/Pepper
9. 溜炸子鷄　liu¹ cha² tzu³ chi¹
   Fried Chicken w/Sweet and Sour

Sauce

10. 子薑鴨塊　tzu³ chiang¹ ya¹ k'uai⁴
Duck w/Young Ginger

魚類　Fish

1. 炸　蝦　球　cha² hsia¹ ch'iu²
Fried Shrimps Balls

2. 椒鹽桂魚　chiao¹ yen² kuei⁴ yü²
Fried Mandarin Fish w/Pepper
and Salt

3. 炒　蝦　仁　ch'ao³ hsia¹ jen²
Fried Shrimps

4. 炒　魚　片　ch'ao³ yü² p'ien⁴
Fried Fish Pieces

5. 炒魷魚卷　ch'ao³ yu² yü² chüan³
Fried Cuttle fish

6. 炒魷魚絲　ch'ao³ yu² yü² ssu¹
Fried Shredded Cuttlefish

7. 清蒸桂魚　ch'ing¹ cheng¹ kuei⁴ yü²
Steamed Mandarin Fish

8. 清炒蝦仁　ch'ing¹ ch'ao³ hsia¹ jen²
Shrimps in Plain Sauce

9. 番茄蝦仁　fan¹ ch'ieh² hsia¹ jen²
Shrimps w/Tomato Sauce

10. 紅燒青魚　hung² shao¹ ch'ing¹ yü²
Bream w/Brown Sauce

11. 紅燒桂魚　hung² shao¹ kuei⁴ yü²
Mandarin Fish w/Brown Sauce

12. 紅燒明蝦　hung² shao¹ ming² hsia¹
Prawn Pieces w/ Brown Sauce

13. 蝦仁炒蛋　hsia¹ jen² ch'ao³ tan⁴
Shrimp Omelet

14. 干燒鯽魚　kan¹ shao¹ chi⁴ yü²
Fried Bream w/Pepper Sauce

15. 干燒黃魚　kan¹ shao¹ huang² yü²
Fried Chinese Herring w/Pepper
Sauce

16. 干燒蝦仁　kan¹ shao¹ hsia¹ jen²
Fried Shrimps w/Pepper Sauce

17. 干燒桂魚　kan¹ shao¹ kuei⁴ yü²

Fried Mandarin Fish w/Pepper Sauce

18. 干燒明蝦 kan¹ shao¹ ming² hsia¹
    Fried Prawns w/Pepper Sauce

19. 白汁桂魚 pai² chih¹ kuei¹ yü²
    Mandarin Fish w/White Sauce

20. 糖醋桂魚 t'ang² ts'u⁴ kuei⁴ yü²
    Mandarin Fish w/Sweet and sour Sauce

21. 醋溜黃魚 ts'u⁴ liu¹ huang- yü²
    Chinese Herring w/Honey Sauce

22. 脆皮桂魚 ts'ui⁴ p'i² kuei⁴ yü²
    Barbecued Mandarin Fish

蔬菜類　Vegetables

1. 鷄奶油青笋 chi¹ nai³ yu² ch'ing¹ sun³
   Spring Bamboo Shoots w/Chicken Sauce

2. 鷄油春笋 chi¹ yu² ch'un¹ sun³
   Winter Bamboo Shoots w/Chicken Sauce

3. 鷄油白菜 chi¹ yu² pai² ts'ai⁴
   Cabbage w/Chicken Sauce

4. 鷄油菜心 chi¹ yu² ts'ai⁴ hsin¹
   Tientsin Cabbage w/Chicken Sauce

5. 家常豆腐 chia¹ ch'ang² tou⁴ fu³
   Fried Bean Curd w/Onions and Mushrooms

6. 炒三冬 ch'ao³ san¹ tung¹
   Fried Bamboo Shoots w/Mushrooms and Szechwan Salted Cabbage

7. 炒双冬 ch'ao³ shuang¹ tung¹
   Fried Bamboo Shoots w/Mushrooms

8. 青豆泥 ch'ing¹ tou⁴ ni²
   Fried Sweet Green Bean Paste

9. 鳳尾青笋 feng⁴ wei³ ch'ing¹ sun³
   Fried Spring Bamboo Shoots

10. 蠔油豆腐　hao² yu² tou⁴ fu³
    Bean Curd w/Oyster Sauce
11. 蝦子春筍　hsia¹ tzu¹ ch'un¹ sun³
    Winter Bamboo Shoots w/Shrimp Eggs
12. 干燒春筍　kan¹ shao¹ ch'un¹ sun³
    Fried Winter Bamboo Shoots
13. 口磨豆腐　k'ou³ mo² tou⁴ fu³
    Bean Curd w/Mushrooms
14. 羅卜球　lo² pu³ ch'iu²
    Turnip Rolls
15. 麻婆豆腐　ma² p'o² tou⁴ fu³
    "Ma P'o" Bean Curd w/Hot Pepper
16. 奶油青筍　nai³ yu² ch'ing¹ sun³
    Fried Green Bamboo Shoots
17. 奶油白菜　nai³ yu² pai³ ts'ai⁴
    Creamed Cabbage
18. 奶油菜心　nai³ yu² ts'ai⁴ hsin¹
    Tientsin Cabbage
19. 醋溜白菜　ts'u⁴ liu² pai³ ts'ai⁴
    Cabbage w/Sweet and Sour Sauce
20. 玉蘭片　yu⁴ lan² p'ien¹
    Fried Plain Bamboo Shoots

湯類　Soup

1. 鷄羢豆花湯　chi¹ jung² tou⁴ hua¹ t'ang¹
   Chicken Cream Soup
2. 鷄片湯　chi¹ p'ien⁴ t'ang¹
   Sliced Chicken Soup
3. 青菜湯　ch'ing¹ ts'ai⁴ t'ang¹
   Tientsin Cabbage Soup w/Ham or Dried Shrimps
4. 川鯽魚湯　ch'uan¹ chi⁴ yü³ t'ang¹
   Carp Soup
5. 川竹蓀湯　ch'uan¹ chu² sun¹ t'ang¹
   Szechwan Bamboo Soup
6. 鳳瓜冬菇湯　feng⁴ kua¹ tung¹ ku¹ t'ang¹
   Chicken Feet Soup w/Mushrooms
7. 黃魚羮　huang² yü² keng¹

Chinese Herring Soup

8. 火腿冬瓜湯 huo² t'ui² tung¹ kua¹ t'ang¹
   Ham and Winter Melon Soup

9. 雪笋湯 hsüeh² sun³ t'ang¹
   Bamboo Shoot Soup w/Salted Green Cabbage

10. 口磨竹蓀湯 k'ou³ mo² chu² sun¹ t'ang¹
    Szechwan Bamboo Soup w/Mushrooms

11. 口磨豆腐湯 k'ou³ mo² tou⁴ fu³ t'ang¹
    Mushrooms and Bean Curd Soup

12. 口磨湯 k'ou³ mo² t'ang¹
    Mushroom Soup

13. 白水豆腐湯 pai² shui³ tou⁴ fu³ t'ang¹
    Plain Bean Curd Soup

14. 白菜湯 pai² ts'ai⁴ t'ang¹
    Plain Cabbage Soup w/Ham or Dried Shrimps

15. 冰汁銀耳 ping¹ chih¹ yin² erh³
    White Mushroom in Honey Sauce

16. 酸辣湯 suan¹ la⁴ t'ang¹
    Sour and Chili Soup

17. 童子雞湯 t'ung² tzu³ chi¹ t'ang¹
    Steamed Spring Chicken Soup

18. 月母雞湯 yüeh⁴ mu³ chi¹ t'ang¹
    Chicken Soup

肉類　Meat

1. 椒鹽蹄膀 chiao¹ yen² t'i² pang³
   Braised Pork Shank w/Pepper and Salt

2. 炒肉丁 ch'ao³ jou⁴ ting¹
   Fried Diced Pork

3. 炒牛肉絲 ch'ao³ niu² jou⁴ ssu¹
   Fried Beef Slices

4. 粉蒸肉 fen³ cheng¹ jou⁴
   Steamed Pork Wrapped in Flour

5. 粉蒸牛肉 fen³ cheng¹ niu² jou⁴
   Steamed Beef Wrapped in Flour

6. 蠔油牛肉 hao² yu² niu² jou⁴

Sliced Beef w/Oyster Sauce

7. 紅燒牛肉　hung² shao¹ niu² jou⁴
Beef w/Brown Sauce

8. 紅燒蹄膀　hung² shao¹ t'i² pang³
Braised Pork Shank w/Brown Sauce

9. 干燒牛肉　kan¹ shao¹ niu² jou⁴
Fried Shredded Beef w/Salted Beans

10. 古老肉　ku² lao³ jou⁴
Sweet and Sour Boneless Pork

11. 回鍋肉　hui² kuo¹ jou⁴
Fried Sliced Pork w/Green Peppers and Onions

雜類　Miscellaneous

1. 炸腼肝　cha² chun¹ kan¹
Fried Giblets

2. 叉燒火腿　ch'a¹ shao¹ huo² t'ui³
Crackling Ham

3. 炒蝦腰　ch'ao³ hsia¹ yao¹
Fried Kidney and Shrimps

4. 炒四件　ch'ao³ ssu⁴ chien⁴
Fried Chicken Liver and Giblets w/Dried Mushroom and Bamboo Shoots

5. 炒雙脆　ch'ao³ shuang² ts'ui⁴
Fried Kidney w/Pig's Tripe

6. 全家福　ch'üan² chia¹ fu²
Stewed " Chop Suey "

7. 鳳尾腰花　feng⁴ wei³ yao¹ hua¹
Fried Kidneys

8. 火爆肚尖　huo³ pao⁴ tu³ chien¹
Fried Pig's Tripe

9. 蜜汁火腿　mi⁴ chih¹ huo² t'ui³
Ham w/Honey Sauce